1979

Christmas
Greetings
AND BEST WISHES
FOR THE
New Year

Dear Dad —

Prop this up on your
desk/reading table and do
read it. It will tell you
where many of my values
come from, and perhaps
why I will always be
grateful that my parents
brought me here.
This is one of the Feingold
[ ] have been working on
during the past few years.

I hope you will enjoy
it. Much love,
Bev

A Singular School

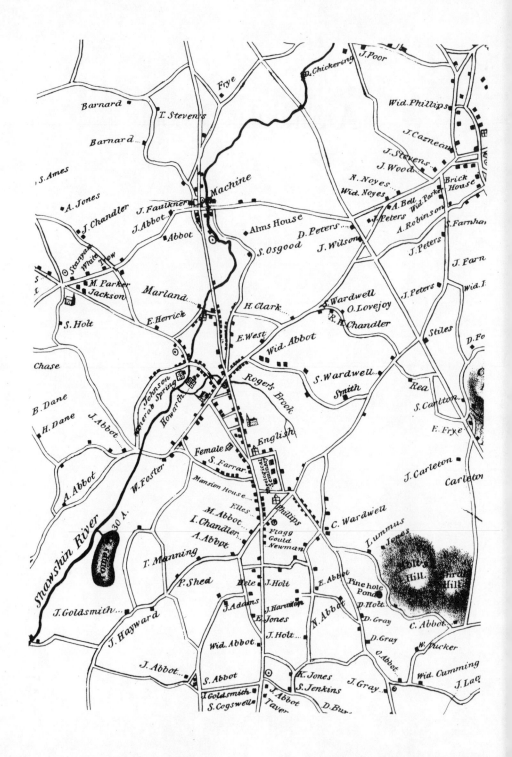

Susan McIntosh Lloyd

A Singular School

Abbot Academy 1828-1973

Published by Phillips Academy, Andover

Distributed by the University Press of New England

Hanover, New Hampshire 1979

Frontispiece: *Andover center and Andover Hill. Detail from a map drawn in 1830 showing the population center of the South parish. Andover Memorial Library.*

Copyright © 1979 by Trustees of Phillips Academy, Andover

All rights reserved

Library of Congress Catalogue Card Number: 78–56167

International Standard Book Number: 0-87451-161-5

Printed in the United States of America

Library of Congress Cataloging in Publication data
will be found on the last printed page of this book.

The University Press of New England

Brandeis University

Clark University

Dartmouth College

University of New Hampshire

University of Rhode Island

University of Vermont

Preface

This is the biography of a school: Abbot Academy of Andover, Massachusetts. One of the first educational institutions in New England to be founded for girls and women alone, Abbot had by far the longest corporate life of any: it opened its doors to seventy students on May 6, 1829, and endured until those same doors and all the material good inside them were entrusted to Phillips Academy on June 28, 1973.

A legal mind must acknowledge Abbot Academy a thing of the past. But schools, being congregations of human beings, are always defying rigid definition. Like a bride from a proud and ancient family, Abbot brought to the new coeducational Phillips Academy a commitment to its own historic purposes and a stubborn loyalty to the character set during its 144 years of life. Thus for earnest, present reasons, Abbot's history commands attention. Earnestness aside, it is a plain good tale— or ought to be—worth the telling for its own sake, and for all it says of American education and of the history of American women. There is no way to do Abbot full justice. The school has encompassed thousands of lives, each with its own particular history; if all these lives were named and accounted for, this would be not a book but an encyclopedia. A book must have characters, but not too many. Hundreds of teachers and trustees who did great work, hundreds of the mediocre ones too, will have to be assumed by the reader. Two appendices list all Abbot trustees since 1828, and all teachers, with their colleges and degrees, since 1936. In the text, however, a few students, teachers, and trustees must stand for the many who created and expressed Abbot's special character in each age.

So many people have helped me with this research that they cannot all be named here. Alumnae recalled their experiences to me at every reunion and Abbot gathering I could attend; conversations on buses and planes often proved as fruitful as formal interviews. A number of Abbot's alumnae and friends wrote helpful letters in response to my requests for recollections, or lent me relevant papers they had written. To these correspondents I am most grateful: Bethiah Crane Accetta, '62; Harriet Murdock Andersson, '17; Dorothy Bigelow Arms, '11; John

and Helen Barss; Louisa Lehmann Birch, '47; Helen Thiel Graven-
gaard, '20; Gale Barton Hartch, '59; Cynthia Lund Heck, '71; Esther
Kilton, '16; Maud Lavin, '72; Lucy Lippard, '54; Julie Owen, '61;
Barbara Moore Pease, '12; Shirley Ritchie; Andrea Ruff, '70; Pamela
Schwartz, Phillips, '75; Katherine Staples, '65; Joan List VanNess, '41;
and Genevieve Young, '48.

Other former students, faculty, trustees and townspeople gave time
for interviews or long conversations; many of them also reviewed the
sections of the manuscript to which they had contributed: Helen Allen
(Henry) Anderson, '32; Carolyn Appen, Phillips '76; Mary Bertucio
Arnold, '42; Germaine Arosa; Jane Baldwin, '22; Marie Baratte; Jean
Bennett; Josephine and Alan Blackmer; John Buckey; Barbara Brown
Hogan, '40; Eleanor Thomson Castle, '96; E. Barton Chapin, Jr.; Mel-
ville Chapin; Constance Parker Chipman, '06; Susan Clark; Sally Cooper,
'73; Mary Crane; Mary Carpenter Dake; William Doherty; James K.
and Katherine Stirling Dow, '55; Arthur Drinkwater, Phillips '96; Susan
Trafton Edmonds, '64; Elizabeth Fauver, '73; Marion Finbury; Louis
Finger; Carolyn Goodwin; Donald Gordon; Jane Hoover, '76; Faith
Howland; Carolyn Johnston; Abby Castle Kemper, '31; Valeria Knapp;
Alexandra Kubler-Merrill, '56; Mildred Bryant Kussmaul, '13; Jennifer
Martin, '71; Rennie McQuilkin; Mary Minard, '55; Ruth Newcomb,
'10; Lia Pascale, Phillips '76; Stephen and Stephanie Perrin; Virginia
Powel; Ruth Pringle, '05; Caroline Rogers; Jean St. Pierre, George and
Frances Flagg Sanborn, '26; Richard Sheahan; Mary Byers Smith, '04;
Nora Sweeney, '12; Alexina Wilkins Talmadge, '22; Elizabeth Marshall
Thomas, '49; Evelyn Neumark; Sandra Urie Thorpe, '70; Eleanor
Tucker; Catherine VonKlemperer, '73; Elaine Boutwell VonWeber, '25;
Beth Chandler Warren, '55; Teresa Wasilewski, '71; and Anne Lise
Witten.

At various times in the past three years eight Phillips Academy students have served skillfully as research assistants for ten weeks or
more: Daniel Aibel, Elizabeth Friese, Mary Jean Hu, Louise Kennedy,
Peter Marvit, Constantine Prentakis, Isabel Schaff, and Judith Sizer.
Charlotte Taylor and Angela Leech, secretaries of the South and West
Parish Churches, found important records and documents for me, and
gave me full use of them. Some special typists have helped with much
more than typing: Rebecca King, Cynthia Stableford and Clare O'Con-
nell Sullivan, '32; these three and Juliet Kellogg, Phillips Academy
Archivist, have brought good cheer as well as expertise to the work.
Arthur M. Gilbert of the Historical Society in Dorset, Vermont,
searched for and found some helpful material on Samuel C. Jackson

and his family. Adeline Wright and several other townspeople have described to me the Andover they have lived and worked in.

The following gave of their time and knowledge in a variety of ways that have been crucial to the research, or to the writing or to both: Grace Baruch, James McIntosh, Kathryn Kish Sklar, and Blair Stambaugh made valuable criticisms of the first six chapters and gave equally valuable encouragement. Theodore Sizer read much of the manuscript, and provided special help on the last chapter. Roger Murray reviewed the chapter on the Depression, while J. K. Dow and Richard Griggs brought their financial expertise to bear on an array of more recent conundrums. Frederick Allis, Robert Lloyd, Millicent and Rustin McIntosh, David Tyack, and Genevieve Young have read the entire manuscript and have contributed greatly to the visions and re-visions which make a book.

Five people have given so much work and thought to the entire enterprise that without them the book would have been a far poorer story. Beverly Brooks Floe collaborated on much of the oral history research, accompanying me on many interviews and conducting several herself, bringing with her the interest and financial support which the Abbot Academy Association has offered from the very beginning, and tirelessly helping me over some high and difficult passes. Frances Connelly Dowd gave weeks of time to confirm virtually every reference, and put uncounted extra hours into compiling the index. Philip Allen, Marguerite Hearsey, and Alice Sweeney talked at length with me about the Abbot they knew, and reviewed every chapter. At some times they contested my interpretations, and at all times they generously granted me the freedom essential to a historian's task.

Finally, I owe thanks to the Trustees of Phillips Academy for faith-fully supporting—and refusing to interfere with—a project consider-ably larger than the one they first bargained for.

For all they have contributed to the book, none of these helpers and friends can in any way be held responsible for its faults. These are the author's special responsibility.

A word about sources: The nineteenth-century Abbot is like a pic-ture puzzle with many pieces missing. So long as the gaps are small, one can recreate the design from the surrounding pieces, but there are great spaces without clues. No one, for example, can be certain what single person was most responsible for Abbot's founding. Rev. Samuel Jackson's diary might tell us—we know from his daughter's recollec-tions that he kept one—but in spite of a far search, it has not been

found. Phebe McKeen's diary is also lost, as is much personal correspondence that might shed light on Abbot Academy. Self-effacing,
perhaps, or simply wishing privacy, women often burn such things, or
order their heirs to lock them up. There are no faculty meeting minutes at all. There are, however, scrapbooks contributed by granddaughters and great nieces, a few journals, student notebooks, and
caches of alumnae letters found in musty closets. One such set of letters was written to Phebe McKeen in 1879 and drawn upon by her
in compiling her and her sister's *Annals of Abbot Academy, 1829–79.*
This volume, with its sequel written by Philena McKeen alone, is "A
story told, not to the great, general public" but to "a dearer family
circle."* Still, these books are eminently useful. There is fiction written
by teachers and alumnae. There is all the more conventional (and invaluable) archival material organized by Jane Brodie Carpenter, keeper
of alumnae and school records from 1910 to 1952, and author of many
historical articles for the *Alumnae Bulletin* as well as of a book about
Abbot and Miss Bailey; Miss Carpenter's contribution to the present
volume cannot be measured. Two other helpful books are Katherine
Kelsey's *Abbot Academy Sketches* (1892–1912), and Alice Sweeney's
Brief Account of the Hearsey Years. I have followed information found
in all of the historical works back to original sources wherever possible. Student publications, Trustees' Minutes from 1828 to 1973, and
Principals' and Treasurers' reports after 1915 have been essential to the
research, even though Trustees' Minutes tend to be short on detail and
devoid of debate and student periodicals were heavily censored for
many decades.

After 1895 live witnesses come in, fleshing out the archival and literary record. Many former faculty, trustees, and alumnae have generously written or talked with me about the Abbot they knew. Each
person's Abbot is unique, a vessel for her or his own concerns, but I
have used recollections of people or events in this history wherever
they can be corroborated by other sources. "Alumnae remember . . ."
generally means that many people volunteered a recollection of some
event of importance to them and to Abbot. "A few alumnae" remembering may be as few as three. Occasionally, a single person's recollection is used (and identified as such) in situations where that one person
is likely to have been the only one who could know of an incident.
Jane Sullivan, Constance Strohecker, and the staff of the Abbot Alum-

*Wesley Churchill, *Sequel to the History of Abbot Academy* (Andover,
Warren Draper, 1897), xi.

nae Office have been enormously helpful in providing student records
and leads toward perceptive alumnae. I have also looked for and found
several alumnae who were disappointed in Abbot, women who have,
for the most part, refused to keep in touch with the school. Their
memories must count too, for they represent a small, significant minority in every era. Altogether, sixty people were formally interviewed.

The last five years of Abbot's existence have been seen through a
personal filter, since I taught history at the school from 1968 to 1973.
This participant-observer stance has had both advantages and drawbacks. My effort in researching the period has been to find observations and opinions supplementary to or contrary to my own, but inevitably, an accounting of events so recent is bound to be more journal-
ism than history. The best one can hope for here is responsible journal-
ism. Especially for the modern period, I have found important material
in confidential files, some lent by trustees or former principals, others
available on a restricted basis from the Abbot and Phillips Academy
Archives. I have drawn directly on none of these sources except where
those involved have given their permission to do so. Within them often
lay confirmation of facts gathered elsewhere, however, or clues as to
where to look for more.

Throughout this research I have been inspired and informed by
books that help to establish the context of Abbot's story. Many of
these are period pieces: nineteenth-century histories of the town of
Andover (doubtless read by teachers and trustees of those times); inspirational tracts; textbooks and novels read by Abbot girls; speeches,
books, and articles written by educators and psychologists from 1826
on. *The American Journal of Education* (1826–30) and *The American
Annals of Education and Instruction* (1830–1839) are relevant if often
verbose. Federal publications issued by the U.S. Bureau of Education
(later, Office of Education) contain important statistics not available
elsewhere, and written debates on a variety of pedagogical issues, especially the U.S. Commissioner of Education *Reports*, and the *Bulletins*,
beginning 1906. Thomas Woody's *History of Women's Education*
(1929) is invaluable because Woody so often prefers long excerpts
from primary sources to short, pithy quotations. I have read several
histories of schools and academies other than Abbot, have talked at
length with retired and current principals of girls' schools, and have
frequently used *Sargent's Handbook of Private Schools* as a reference
work in comparing Abbot to institutions that serve a smilar clientele.
Finally contemporary historians' writings on education, on cultural
and social life, on the history of women, and on individual women

educators have been eminently useful: works by Lawrence Cremin, Barbara Cross, Ann Douglas, Paula Fass, Edith Finch, Eleanor Flexner, Joseph Kett, Theodore Sizer, Kathryn Kish Sklar, and David Tyack are foremost here.

Andover, Massachusetts   *S.M.L.*
July 1978

Contents

Illustrations

Early Days, 1828-1852

Abbot's infancy, healthy and precarious by turns, demands a full description, for the school's character was grounded in its first quarter-century and set in firm relationship to the needs of the age. Granted, some features of this early period could not survive, and others—such as the pedagogical partnership with Phillips Academy—were set aside, not to be revived until the twentieth century; but the essentials were laid down: a double commitment to basic intellectual training and moral guidance, a commitment strengthened by a habit of resistance to passing fashions, and by—above all—a respect for the importance of women in American society.

Of Times, Town, and Founding Fathers

*During a ministry of a quarter of a century, I
have been much tried, and have witnessed the trials of
many pious parents, on account of the levity and folly
of youth generally, from fourteen to twenty-two. That
period of seven or eight years, which seals the destiny
of so many for time and eternity, causes more anxiety
to the pious of my acquaintance than any other period.*
A rural clergyman of 1828

Do females possess minds as capable of improvement as males?
Subject of Philomathean Society debate,
Phillips Academy, 1827

On February 15, 1828, this notice appeared on trees and buildings
throughout the town of Andover:

> Those persons who feel favorably disposed toward the establish-
> ment of a FEMALE HIGH SCHOOL in the South Parish of
> Andover, are requested to meet at Mr. James Locke's, on Tuesday
> evening next, the 19th inst., at 6 o'clock, P.M.

No documents tell us who first decided on the founding of Abbot
Academy. Had a single person been responsible, the story might have
been simpler. We do know that the above announcement was drawn
up by five men: Samuel C. Jackson and Milton Badger, the ministers of
South Andover's two Congregational churches; Amos Abbott and
Mark Newman, two of their deacons; and Samuel Farrar, Esquire, the
Treasurer of Phillips Academy, Andover. Guessing at where their constituency could be found, they posted it in the churches, in the shops,
in the Andover National Bank, and in the classroom building of Andover Theological Seminary, the most imposing structure on Andover
Hill. The response must have pleased them, for "a goodly number of
citizens met upon the evening appointed," as Abbot's first historian

wrote fifty years later.[1] The assembled company voted to establish a school, and set to work.

It would not be easy. More than once, almost everyone lost heart; for a few hours one July day, the project was officially abandoned. Only determined men and women could found a "female high school" in 1828, and only a special community could sustain it. Yet however weak the plant would appear during stressful seasons both early and late, it was firmly rooted. The American republic was finally ready to experiment with education for young women; ideas as to its shape and direction abounded in the late 1820's. The town of Andover, though conservative, was peculiarly hospitable to institutions of learning, and several of its women residents felt it was high time that Andover girls had their own. Finally, the careful, stubborn men who set out the seedling knew their business and their law as they knew their community: the deeply Christian idealism that moved them was lifeless, they realized, without the practical stays by which human works prosper.

The Times

The year 1828 was a dramatic moment in a turbulent time. Andrew Jackson's presidential campaign and election were political expressions of social changes that had been building for decades. The sixty years since the American colonies had begun their drift away from England had been difficult ones, brimming with emergencies and excitement. As early as 1776, Samuel Phillips, Jr., the founder of Phillips Academy, was lamenting "the prevalence of public and private vice, the amazing change in the tempers, dispositions and conduct of people in this country." He diagnosed the trouble as "public ignorance" and deplored the "neglect of sound instruction," a dangerous indifference, given that "the comfort and grief of parents . . . the glory or ruin of the state" depend on youth, in all its vulnerability and volatility. Phillips right then resolved to repair this neglect of education. His Phillips Academy opened in 1778, the United States' first incorporated boarding school and the first of the educational institutions on Andover Hill. What Judge Phillips resolved upon, he accomplished.[2]

In voicing his anxiety, this up-and-coming citizen of Andover town was not just indulging his age-old adult right to mourn the weakness of youth. Twentieth-century scholar Philip Greven documents the fundamental change in family and communal relationships that took place in Andover as in many New England towns after 1750.[3] For a century after the incorporation of the township in 1646, Andover fathers had ruled their families and their lands together, passing on their farms intact to eldest sons. Churches had successfully imposed a single religion; dissenters held their peace or moved away. No more. The Great Awakening, by kindling evangelical enthusiasms, had intensified sectarian divisions throughout Massachusetts. Rural sons no longer waited into their thirties and forties for fathers to turn them from unpaid help to partners or heirs. More often they declared independence from family and village constraints; they went soldiering, and never returned, or found apprenticeships in faraway towns, or (with their young wives) sought land of their own in western Massachusetts or the Ohio Valley.[4] Finally, the ten-year-old economic and political conflict between Massachusetts Bay Colony and England had shaken the larger framework of young people's lives. It was no wonder that Samuel Phillips was worried.

This was the generation that would eventually set itself and its own children on a self-conscious search for new certainties to replace those worn thin, the generation that would carry on the academy movement the Phillips family had fostered, and in Andover would raise many of the founders of Abbot Female Academy. From a twentieth-century vantage point, it looks remarkably resilient. When Revolution washed over the colonies, these local youngsters found it more congenial than most of their parents did; later, as adults with families of their own, they could better tolerate the restive peace that followed, with its political perplexities and its challenges to ancient social forms. In spite of privations, Andover handled the post-Revolutionary stresses with a peculiar unity: "When the state was embarrassed with discontent and intestine commotion" during Shays' Rebellion, "the town preserved order and peace," wrote Abiel Abbot, a contemporary observer and local historian.[5] More impressive, two years later this common commitment to order survived a serious split in Town Meeting over ratification of the Federal Constitution (115 yea, 124 nay). And though the residents (nearly all of them stout Federalists) had some struggle to adjust to the economic pressures created by the decades of boycott and embargo that followed, the ending of the European wars in 1815 brought freedom at last from foreign threats for Andover and the infant republic. Americans could concentrate on nation-building, on making plans for generations of republicans to come.

With what should they build? By the 1820's, conservatives had more to mourn than the patriarchal family and the rigid Calvinism that had disciplined colonial New England. Each individual's world had widened toward confusion as scientific discoveries became public knowledge, population grew, new roads and canals made once self-sufficient towns dependent on each other, cities filled up and became more accessible. Too accessible, thought many sober citizens of Andover. "Seldom visit the capital," Reverend Abiel Abbot warned Phillips Academy seniors on their way to Harvard at the turn of the century. "It is dangerous ground. . . . Town pleasures, like forbidden fruit, are tempting to the senses; but the most innocent of them have a mixture of deadly poison."[6]

Perhaps most disturbing—as well as most promising—the rise of industry was transforming the face and mind of the Northeastern United States. Women's work was affected no less than men's. During the colonial era, leisured women were few. Ann Bradstreet, who with her husband Simon was one of Andover's original settlers, was criticized by her neighbors for writing poetry when she should be plying her needle, though President Rogers of Harvard College wrote that "twice drinking of the nectar of her lines" left him "weltering in delight."[7] When her first Andover house burned to the ground in 1666, a library of 800 books was destroyed. A certain Abigail Foote of the next century was more typical. A glance at a day out of her diary in 1775 shows us how a young woman's basic productive tasks filled her life:

> Fix'd gown for Prude—Mend Mother's Riding-hood—Spun short thread—fix'd two gowns for Welsh's girls—Carded tow—Spun linen—Worked on Cheese basket, Hatchel'd flax with Hannah, we did fifty-one pounds apiece—Milked the cows—Spun linen, did fifty knots—Made a Broom of Guinea-wheat straw—Spun thread to whiten—Set a Red dye—Had two scholars from Mrs. Taylor's— I carded two pounds of wool and felt Nationly—Spun harness twine, scoured the pewter.[8]

Abigail's daughters would spend their days differently. Even before the factories were raised along the Shawsheen and Merrimack rivers, farming communities like Andover were inwardly changing in ways that were to have momentous implications for New England education. Increasingly, the self-sufficient household made itself dependent on the town merchant and his wares, while the merchant's wife or daughter was herself released from the intricate tasks of cloth and soap making, animal husbandry and gardening, until, on the eve of the founding of Abbot Academy, the profound, life-sustaining partnership between husbands, wives, and their older children had broken down.

At the same time, certain work opportunities for women outside their homes were shrinking. Eighteenth-century women with time to spare had found scope for their entrepreneurial and other talents in a colonial economy where talent was always scarce: women merchants, journalists, even physicians were welcome enough.[9] Post-revolutionary maritime strife put home-bound women to work: these earned cash for their families on an unprecedented scale when the overseas textile trade flagged and American housewives at their looms took the place of the mills of Birmingham and Glasgow. Historian Kathryn Sklar believes that women gained during this time a sense of pride and power—and a material influence on family financial outlays—that was crucial to the advent of the female seminary, though none but spinsters and widows could legally keep their earnings for themselves.[10] In the 1820's, however, men were reclaiming all entrepreneurial and professional jobs and hungering for more, especially in long-settled New England, while women did their weaving in the new water-powered mills under men's supervision, or stayed home—often idle if children were grown or not yet born. As Morton Hunt has put it, "The industrial revolution had both relieved [woman] of her labors and robbed her of her functions."[11] A question seldom before asked by Americans began to surface everywhere: what were women to do with themselves?

For decades if not millennia, the problem had generally been posed in a different way: What were men to do with women? They could ignore them, and many tried, including the early Puritan preacher Nathaniel Ward, who advised his readers to think of woman as "the very gizzard of a trifle, the product of the quarter of a cipher, the *epitome of nothing*." Unfortunately this did not prevent a fashionably dressed young lady from disturbing him. "If I see any of them accidently [he wrote] I cannot cleanse my phansie of them for at least a month after."[12] The Puritans, at least, did not fear sex itself; they thought it necessary and good within marriage. But husbands must keep their wives and daughters under strict control, removing every possible occasion for "phansies" like Ward's.

Given the temptations women represented, men could also demand of Eve's daughters that they share in the "fall of man [and] the depravity of human nature." The Westminster Catechism defined it and Andover's South Church endorsed it with a matchless single-mindedness from its founding in 1708 through 1828 and beyond. Thus, though men allowed them little say in the practical affairs of the Parish, women had to support the Church. Women made up the majority of Andover Church members after 1650; it was the women who shook heads at the goings-on in the North Parish after 1820: how could those *dances* which the Reverend Bailey Loring arranged for his young parishioners lead them to be born again when every one knew that boy-girl dancing led straight to perdition? There would be no Unitarian backsliding at the foot of Andover Hill. It was conversion or Hellfire.

Andover men could do more. They could vote unanimous resolutions in their (all male) Town Meeting, commanding women to help the community ride out the economic storms of 1787. Women must

> by their engaging examples . . . devote that power of influence with which nature hath endowed them to the purpose of encouraging every species of economy in living, and particularly that neat plainness and simplicity in dress, which are among the best tokens of a good mind.[13]

All new clothes were to be woven from local wool or flax, and elegant mourning clothes must not be made at all.

In a multitude of ways did men thus define Andover women's lives and work. One might expect that they would have long since provided for their education, but this they had not done, beyond arranging that girls learn just enough of reading to scan the Church's message of salvation. In most Andover families, girls' education had taken second place to boys'. Once Ann Bradstreet's generation of British-educated settlers had died off, literary women were almost unknown in Andover. To the theocracy of Massachusetts Bay colony, higher education had only one purpose: the training of ministers. It would be frivolous to allow young women to participate. John Winthrop, Massachusetts' first governor, wrote with distress in his journal of a lady who went insane "by giving herself largely to reading and writing."[14] During Andover's first hundred years, many women could not even write their names. This ignorance was typical of New England women throughout the eighteenth century, only half of whom were functionally literate.[15] The grammar schools that the ever-optimistic Massachusetts legislature periodically endorsed were maintained in Andover almost exclusively for boys—or not maintained at all, for in Andover, as in many New England towns, citizens counted on their local private academy for an inexpensive secondary education. There was no secondary schooling available to Andover girls until the North Parish Free School (later Franklin Academy) opened a "female department" in 1801, and this was gradually allowed to languish after the first teacher, Mrs. Elizabeth Peabody, left in 1804. Franklin's situation was typical: shaky academies were forever being taken in charge by able and idealistic teachers, then dropped when idealism was spent or local supporters grew complacent. Mrs. Peabody, as it turned out, had another destiny as mother of two brilliant daughters who married Horace Mann and Nathaniel Hawthorne; Andover's bright young women must shift for themselves. "Thus learning in this ancient town" (wrote an Andover rhymester in 1854)

> Did early take its stand;
> The fruits now everywhere abound,
>   Throughout this wide-spread land.
> But while the *males* were thus cared for—
>   The *females* were forgotten;
> The *boys* of yore got all the lore;
>   The *girls* spun all the cotton.[16]

The best the South Parish could do was done, as usual, by Samuel Phillips, Jr. Though it never occurred to Judge Phillips that young women might share in the "higher education" his beloved Academy provided young men, he did bequeath $4,000 in trust to the Phillips Academy Trustees, the income to be used "partly for rendering those females who may be employed as instructors in the several District Schools, within the aforesaid Town of Andover, better qualified for the discharge of their delicate and important trust; and partly for extending the term of their instruction." In purchasing books for this teacher education project, the bequest went on, "all possible care will be taken . . . to guard against the dissemination of the least particle of Infidelity or Modern Philosophy; and also against the dispersion of such theological treatises or speculations, as tend to undermine the fundamental principles of the Gospel plan of salvation, or to reduce the Christian religion to a system of mere morality."[17] To Judge Phillips, education and religion were inseparable. Most of Andover agreed, especially when the Phillips family relieved the taxpayer of funding them. At least until 1810 the town's priorities were often confused: in each of the several previous years $15,000 had been spent on "ardent spirits," sniffed the South Church minister, Justin Edwards—more than twice the entire town budget for schools and other services.[18] Yet in spite of taxpayer footdragging, the public elementary ("common") schools gained ground steadily in the following two decades; by 1828 an Andover boy could count on learning to read, write, and cipher, even though girls were usually relegated to the brief summer session.

All this is not to say that Andover's women were helpless without formal secondary education. Married, they reared and ran large households, or if part of Andover's "great company of old maids," they boarded with relatives, nursed them in illness, sewed and cooked for them or labored in their fields. One doughty spinster cousin of Samuel Phillips, Jr., a Mistress Abbot, was "help" in the family of Judge Phillips' father, and took care of the Phillips farm after the old Squire died. She was "a large, strong woman, as able for out-door work as housework," wrote local historian Sarah Loring Bailey in 1880. She raised a nursery of ten thousand trees, which she "grafted and sold profitably." She lived to be 94. "She was blind before she died, and being unable to give up her out-door exercise, used to walk by a rope."[19] Girls and young women found much informal education in the "literary sewing circles" and the prayer or bible-study groups they arranged for themselves apart from men's plans for them. Furthermore, in the fifty years following the Revolution there arrived in the town a small group of women who had been educated elsewhere. Principal among them was Madam Phebe Phillips, a woman whose influence on education in Andover—though more quietly exercised—was nearly as important as that of her husband, Samuel Phillips, Jr. Abiel Abbot knew her and praised her highly. The youngest daughter of the sophisticated Foxcroft family of Cambridge, she was "a lady formed by the dignity of her person, and the virtues of her mind, to move in the higher walks of life." She had wit, imagination, and "an ardent thirst for knowledge" which she slaked by extensive reading and writing. "She was the ornament and delight of the sentimental circle," writes Abbot, possibly in reference to the women's literary society that she conducted in the Phillips "Mansion House" after her husband's death.[20] One of her contemporaries said that "her style of conversation surpassed that of anyone, male or female, in this country."[21] Kind always to the poor, she also made the first founding gift of $5,000 to Andover Theological Seminary in 1808, contributing $20,000 more before her death in 1812. Among her closest friends was lawyer Samuel Farrar, who was to be a critical figure in the founding of Abbot Academy. Madam Phillips was a special inspiration to the devout wives of those theological professors who moved to Andover from much larger, more various university towns after the Theological Seminary was opened in 1808.

Fine women there were, then, in Andover town, along with men who admired them and girls who looked up to them. It is typical of Andover that once the community began to take notice of these ladies, it claimed them as though by birthright. For Andover was special and Andover knew it. Even in straits, this "ancient and respectable town" maintained its self-respect,[22] so much so that one English visitor scolded his hosts: "One thing I must observe which I think wants rectifying is their pluming pride when adjoin'd to apparent poverty, no uncommon case."[23]

Andover, in fact, may be pardoned for a bit of pride. The town had survived the tumults of political independence and the early industrial revolution with far more confidence than many communities. Overarching the dislocations and difficulties of the last sixty years was every native townsman's sense of a long past reaching back to the twenty-one original proprietors. "Most of the families which first settled in Andover became as deeply rooted to the land and the community as it is possible for families to be."[24] If the resulting stability tended sometimes toward suspicion of all things unfamiliar, including education for young women, it also bore advantages. Once launched, a new school might count on calm waters. The private educational institutions that had taken over Andover Hill must have powerfully contributed to the optimism that apparently prevailed among the citizens who met at Mr. Locke's tavern to found a female high school. By the mid-1820's, Andover had become an intellectual center of New England. The establishment of the Theological Seminary under Phillips Academy's Trustees, so many of whose professors and students would become involved with Abbot Academy, marked Andover Hill as a Zion rising above the contentious multitudes. New England theology was beginning to soften, and Harvard University had long since ceased to teach proper Congregational doctrine: "Truth in Cambridge becomes a lie in Andover, and the same of Andover truth when carried to Cambridge," wrote Amos A. Lawrence from Andover during his forced rustication from Harvard in 1832.[25] Andover, at least, was certain it knew God's Truth.

Andover also knew it had a future. A regular stagecoach from Boston (soon to be replaced by a steam-powered train) now brought urban ideas to the small town, as well as wags who thrust their hands out of the coach windows into the winter air at the Mansion House stop to warm them in the fires of "Brimstone Hill." Despite its conservative orientation, the town was learning to accommodate divergent opinions. Baptists, Methodists, and Episcopalians were busy organizing churches of their own, and although the Unitarians were still safely centered in North Andover, there was more "pulpit exchange" than had been tolerated in the old days. On its way from 3,389 souls in 1820 to 4,530 in 1830, Andover was growing—though not too fast—and the town was filled with young people in a young populace (the median age of all Americans alive in 1830 was 17). Successful manufactories of cotton and woolen goods along the Shawsheen River were being expanded to employ hundreds of operatives, to make modest fortunes for their hardworking owners, and slowly to build the prosperity of the merchants, bankers, and professional people who would, with the

Hill families, become Abbot's first constituency. The year 1828 found the town of Andover better prepared than most to support the education of young women.

Planning

Education, yes, but what kind? In theory, a high school offered Andover parents an admirable answer to the question "What shall we do with our daughters?" Putting theory into practice meant that the founders of a female academy must transcend Andover's cautious stance toward all change, assess well-known schools already serving young women, and find a way through the maze of conflicting educational ideas current in the 1820's.

A small number of female high schools had already proven their worth in other towns and villages; it is likely that these institutions were known to the Andover pioneers. Some of the older finishing schools provided an attractive model for the socially ambitious parents of Andover, though simpler citizens would be skeptical. The famed school founded in 1792 by Miss Pierce in Litchfield, Connecticut, offered "instruction on those rules of delicacy and propriety so important for every young woman." Dabbling in fashionable British textbooks, girls polished their literary skills;[26] they practiced lady-like manners and elegant conversation.[27] The "theatrics" enjoyed by Miss Pierce's students might at first glance shock the pious, but every play acted was adapted from a biblical text. As in most contemporary female academies, the primary task was to refine the Christian sensitivities of wives-and-mothers-to-be. One of the first American education journalists put it well: "Girls should zealously seek to bring the temper and feelings into order and proper subjection, and task themselves to the daily and hourly duty of acting out the beauty and symmetry of the precepts of our Saviour."[28]

Above all, American opinion endorsed Rousseau's dictum that women's education "should always be relative to men." In the bustling, competitive 1820's this meant that women should cease whatever efforts they had made to intrude on men's sphere. Even traditional women's work, such as midwifery, was being aggressively preempted by male obstetricians, who were usually far less experienced and little better trained than the midwives. That many husbands fought their own private battles with the weaker sex is indicated in the popular article on female education quoted above. If only girls could receive "instruction from birth to maturity in the things which belong to [their] peace," it continued, "women might cease to desire to engage in discussions, or influence the decisions of men in affairs foreign to their peculiar departments." Indeed, many a physician insisted that intensive study of such "higher subjects" as philosophy and mathematics would render women infertile, thus unfitting them for their most basic function.

A few dissented. To Benjamin Rush, physician, educator, and statesman, building a nation required a new kind of female education no longer based on British models. "It is high time," he said,

> to awake from this servility—to study our own character—to examine the age of our country—and to adopt manners in everything that shall be accommodated to our state of society, and our form of government. In particular, it is incumbent on us to make ornamental accomplishment yield to principles and knowledge, in the education of our women.[29]

Proceeding from the Society of Friends' central concept of women as men's equals before God, some Quaker educators experimented with an entirely un-British idea: coeducation. Other coeducational or coordinate schools were founded not from principle but from penury. It was cheaper for Bradford Academy near Haverhill (Fd. 1804) to conduct separate male and female departments under one roof than it was to build two different buildings; thirty-three other academies throughout Massachusetts, Maine, and New Hampshire did likewise.

Yet preference was vying with practicality in favor of all-female schools. Bradford would bow to it in 1836. Emma Willard felt that her school, first opened in 1814 in Middlebury, Vermont, for girls alone, had provided an extra measure of encouragement for her pupils, and amply proved the ability of young women to master the higher subjects with nothing but advantage to themselves and their future husbands. She herself had absorbed mathematics and philosophy by assiduously questioning her nephew every evening on his return home from his classes at Middlebury College. She studied his lecture notes and textbooks, and asked him to examine her in each field. Mrs. Willard's commitment to mothering her own small son increased her scorn of the purely "ornamental" skills that had made a name for schools such as Miss Pierce's. "When we consider that the character of the next generation will be formed by the mothers of this, how important does it become that their reason should be strengthened to overcome their insignificant vanities and prejudices!" she wrote.[30] This theme resounded in the minds of many citizens who had begun to realize that "the mothers of republicans" must be well educated if the vulnerable new republic was to survive, and Emma Willard expanded on it often to mollify the conservatives in her constituency. Child of loving, open-minded parents, she serenely avoided superficial obstacles, all the while pursuing her goal of higher education for women. When she moved her school to New York state, she decided to call it a Seminary instead of a College, even though—like Abbot's founders—she fully intended some college subjects to be taught. "That word . . . will not create a jealousy that we mean to intrude upon the province of the men."[31]

Catharine Beecher was not so subtle in her push for serious schooling for young women. Bent on enlarging the successful Hartford Female Seminary she had begun in 1823 with her sister Harriet (later Mrs. Stowe of Andover) as pupil and assistant, she wrote in 1827 a widely read article on "Female Education" in which she unashamedly called on the public to support girls' schools as enthusiastically as boys'. Sorely needed were "suitable apparatus and facilities" for the study of chemistry and natural philosophy; specialist teachers who could concentrate on one field instead of pursuing "twenty-two different branches of learning" at once, along with professional libraries for their reference, ample schoolrooms, charts, maps, research materials, and history books that communicate more than "the bones of history . . . as dry and bare of interest as was the gloomy collection in the valley of vision."[32] Catharine Beecher's articles were close in their evangelical spirit to the sermons of her "zestful and demanding father," Lyman Beecher, whom Catharine intensely loved.[33] "A woman should study, not to *shine* but to *act*," she concluded.[34]

Reactions against such sentiments often burst into print. A correspondent to the *Connecticut Courant* said of Miss Beecher's educational views that he had rather his "daughters would go to school and sit down and do nothing, than to study Philosophy, etc. These branches fill young misses with *vanity*." The girl who undertakes them "will be a dandizette at eighteen, an old maid at thirty."[35] Opposition took concrete form in Boston, where the city-run Girls Latin School had proudly opened in 1826. So alarmed were its detractors by its popularity that they forced its closing in 1828.[36]

Yet some brave schools thrived. By 1828 Hartford Seminary's enrollment had reached 100. The female department of the generously endowed Friends Yearly Meeting Boarding School in Providence attracted students of all faiths, while at Emma Willard's Troy Academy, more than 200 girls took advantage of Miss Willard's innovative teaching methods. Nearer Andover, Joseph Emerson had been talking to the young ladies of Saugus as if they had brains, according to a contemporary observer.[37] Two of Emerson's former pupils, Zilpah Grant and Mary Lyon, had left prosperous Adams Academy in Derry, New Hampshire, protesting its constituents' slide away from strict Calvinism, to found their own female Seminary in Ipswich. Thus Abbot Academy's founders had some solid models to emulate: pious, hard-working schools that embraced intellectual goals similar to those declared by the institutions already standing on Andover Hill. True, they had to thread their way through the tangled controversy over the purposes of female education, but that made an appropriate beginning, for the controversy would reappear in many guises over the 144 years of Abbot's existence. In the 1820's the very liveliness of this national argument must have opened many people's minds to the possibilities of higher education for girls, and pricked Andover citizens to create a superior school of their own. Thus the times favored female education; the town seemed likely to welcome it. Now the founders must bend to their task.

The Founding

There is no record of what happened at the first meeting. We do know that all seven of the men who would serve as Abbot's original Trustees were there, and that at least five of them were accustomed to being listened to. These five had much in common to certify them as belonging to the Andover Establishment. They all served as directors of Andover's only Bank, Samuel Farrar being President and Amos Blanchard, Cashier. None could keep clear of politics, whether as advisers or public officers. Amos Abbott took the prize here, for he served at one time or another as town clerk, treasurer, moderator of Town Meeting, and School Committee member. He was either Andover's State Senator or Representative for much of his adult life, and he served three terms in Congress. The man of slightest build and fewest words was Deacon Mark Newman, but Newman was a Phillips Academy Trustee, having been Phillips Headmaster for fourteen years, and if his colleagues on the Hill-top rarely lamented his departure from the Headmaster's post, the men of Main Street respected him, returning him to the Abbot Board presidency again and again. Businessmen Hobart Clark and Amos Blanchard made money to use for the Lord's service as well as to keep their fine houses. More than once these two would search their own pockets to pay the interest on Abbot's debt. Indeed, all five were church members who had long held expensive center-section pews in South Church. Deacon Abbott's pew had come down to him from his grandfather, who had won the right to buy it because he paid one of the highest tax bills in Andover, and the rich had first choice even in the old days.[38] "Throughout the nineteenth century," writes Joseph Kett, "no group surpassed evangelical Protestants in their intellectual and institutional concern with youth."[39] These leaders and churchmen of Andover were unusual only in their special concern for the education of female youth.

The two young ministers needed no pews, having pulpits. Though they were new to their jobs, their status in the community was crucial, Reverend Milton Badger's most of all because he led the South Parish. But Samuel Jackson, an outsider, was a fresh wind, and we will hear more of him. South Church snobs found it fitting that the upstart West Parish congregation should be supporting a *Vermonter* as its minister. Still up north and always too far away to suit Jackson were several sisters much beloved, a sophisticated, well-schooled mother, and a minister father, all of whom believed in higher education for women. Much evidence suggests that it was Samuel Jackson and his energetic wife Caroline who first determined that Andover should have the female high school its leading citizens had long dreamed of.[40] Strange though it seems at first glance, it is not so surprising that this young newcomer should solidify and lead the inchoate group that had for years supported the idea of young women's education in Andover. For one thing, Jackson was already well-regarded on Andover Hill: he had just graduated first in his class at the Theological Seminary. He also knew the law: before entering Andover Seminary, he had spent four years clerking in a law firm and studying at Yale Law School. He assumed that any dream could be made reality, given need, energy and practical know-how—and though Jackson was slight of build and would often fight off illness in later life, now he had energy to spare.[41] He was already famous among the West Parish youth for being able to vault a five-rail fence, and for doing so when need or impulse arose; less dramatically, he had been working to improve the several elementary schools in his Parish. He enjoyed the respect of both young and old.

Jackson seems to have looked around his infant parish and discerned what many a stodgier New England clergyman would discover too late: women were essential to the Church. Even in Andover, the state-supported Congregational Church must now plead its case rather than take its power for granted. Its disestablishment—to be legally completed in 1833—had long been in progress *de facto* as ever more citizens neglected to pay their church taxes, turning instead to town and state government for the care of local poor, the education of the young, and

1. Samuel C. Jackson, Trustee, 1828–1879. Portrait by William McMaster, 1856, currently hanging in Morton House, Phillips Academy.

the general ordering of community affairs.[42] Merchants, lawyers, and manufacturers no longer granted to their ministers the unquestioned sway that Reverend Phillips had once sustained over Andover residents' lives and fortunes. Although Andover church membership held up remarkably well at a time when most of the traditionalist congregations were shrinking, there were twice as many female communicants as male in the West Parish, a ratio that would obtain throughout the twenty-two years of Jackson's ministry.[43] Men might hold all the offices for this parish of 870 souls, but it was the women who, increasingly, filled the pews for three services a Sunday, taught most of the Sabbath School classes, raised the funds that would send missionaries to the heathen, and knelt to pray at the weekday prayer meetings. A solid, Christian education could only make their church work more effective—yet the daughters of West Andover's farm families lived much too far afield for easy access to Franklin Academy. To Samuel Jackson, a nearby female high school must have seemed an essential stay both for his parish and for his position within it.[44]

Reverend Jackson took seriously the Creator's impartiality as he worked among his male and female parishioners seeking to inspire and save. Since boyhood he had "been repelled by stated, formal, pungent exhortations to live a Christian life";[45] his ministry consisted as much of mediating his parishioners' disputes and helping them write fair wills as it did of preaching the Word.[46] He also believed that churches must join with families and schools to build the goodness and intelligence of all children. A warm-hearted, generous man, he felt more at home than his older colleagues with the egalitarian ethos that prevailed through much of the nation in 1828. Later in his life he would work energetically to improve Andover's public schools and serve for years as Assistant State Librarian, and as Secretary to the Massachusetts Board of Education. He was a Trusteee of Phillips Academy and the Theological Seminary for thirty years, a Trustee of Abbot for fifty. His philosophical approach to any educational issue, his practical skills, and his openness to careful innovation remained invaluable assets to all who would listen, and his Abbot colleagues usually would.

For all Samuel Jackson's enthusiasm, Squire Samuel Farrar was first among equals, if only because he had for so many years been hoping for the advent of a female high school in Andover. Squire Farrar was not a writing man; we have no sermons or essays in which to search his mind. A technical lawyer, an amateur architect, an "incorruptible mathematician"[47] who husbanded every penny as Abbot's financial adviser and as Treasurer of both Phillips Academy and the Theological Seminary, his head was filled with schedules, lists, and practical plans, not fine phrases awaiting an audience. He had, moreover, a genius for risk-taking which went to work on every project he thought worthy of his faith, no matter how difficult of execution. Abbot Academy was not the only survivor of odds. Farrar was also to be chief architect of both building and program for the Andover Teachers' Seminary (later Phillips Academy's English Department) and designer of Phillips Academy's first, cheapest (and ugliest) dormitories.[48] He was also cherished as a friend and counselor by many of the residents of Zion's Hill. Sarah Stuart Robbins remembered him well from her girlhood days.

> Samuel Farrar was not a common man to any of us. With his delicate face, his long gray hair falling back from a rather peculiar forehead, a shy, retiring manner, and a very sweet, grave expres-

sion, even of his hands, he was to us by turns, Moses, David, Isaiah, John whom the Blessed One loved—any and almost every Biblical saint. He was a responsible man, carrying on his shoulders not only all the great pecuniary interests of the Seminary, but also, seemingly, the responsibility for its theology. He listened to every word spoken in the small wooden pulpit as if for one and all he must give account at the last great day.[49]

Most important to Abbot's founding, Farrar had faith in women's intelligence. He had been one of Madam Phillips' ardent admirers, having boarded with the Phillips family during his bachelor days, and had taken her into his own home during her last years of widowhood. He surely absorbed from her some of his enthusiasm for women's education. Late in his life, he told his fellow Trustee Samuel Jackson of the "bargain" Samuel Phillips, Jr., made with his "refined and accomplished" bride to persuade her to move to rustic Andover from a "pleasant mansion" and "the high life at Cambridge": "It was understood between them [said Jackson] that if she would unite with him in building up Phillips Academy, he would afterwards join her in founding an Academy for girls in the North Parish."[50] Phillips died too young to accomplish this, and his wife's death ten years later left Farrar apparently bereft. He was a coffin bearer at her funeral, and was addressed in the funeral sermon "as one of the chief mourners—as if he had been her son."[51] Farrar soon married the granddaughter of the great theologian Jonathan Edwards, herself a woman of remarkable intellectual gifts to whom "theology was . . . like prayer," as Sarah Robbins later wrote.[52] But it was Phebe Phillips who had been Farrar's original "model for womanhood." He was "constitutionally free from romance," Edwards Park assures us, "but he had been electrified by Madam Phillips." For fifteen years after her death, his commitment to young women's education remained strong; it was readily activated in 1828 when his fellow townsmen begain to catch up with him.

Although Farrar and Jackson were prime movers, other Trustees were immediately helpful. Even before the Board had been formally elected, Amos Abbott and Mark Newman each offered an acre of land for the school building site, Abbott's on Main Street and Newman's on School Street, half way up the Hill. Progress so far was smooth. A committee of seven had decided to accept the Main Street site, to raise funds by subscription, and to build a two-story brick building. Ten days later the Trustees met at the home of Deacon Amos Blanchard, their first Treasurer; they appointed Squire Farrar and the two ministers to draft a constitution, and appointed a Building Committee composed of Hobart Clark and Mark Newman, who quickly arranged for the Main Street lot to be fenced in.

These sons of intellectual Andover, with its "certain disinclination to economics,"[53] could produce a constitution more easily than the funds needed to put principles into practice. Still, principles came first. The Trustees were determined that their institution would be a corporate entity, with a legal framework braced against the weaknesses and failures of individuals. Abbot's constitution, though a period piece, was to prove durable. Its detail expresses Samuel Farrar's care for contingencies, its statement of educational purposes the entire group's concern for young women's souls as well as for the workaday needs of their lives in this world.

> The primary objects to be aimed at in this School shall ever be to regulate the tempers, to improve the taste, to discipline and enlarge the minds, and form the morals of the youth who may be members of it. To form the immortal mind to habits suited to an immortal being, and to instill principles of conduct and form the character for an immortal destiny, shall be subordinate to no other care. Solid acquirements shall always have precedence of those which are merely showy, and the useful of those which are merely ornamental.

The curriculum was ambitious indeed:

> There shall be taught in the Seminary Reading, Spelling, Chirography, Arithmetic, Geography, Composition, History, Geometry, Algebra, Natural Philosophy, Astronomy, Sacred Music, and such other Sciences and Arts, and such of the languages, ancient or modern, as opportunity and ability may permit, and as the Trustees shall direct.

The Principal Instructor could be either "male or female." The Trustees must all be "professors of [meaning those who profess belief in] religion of the Congregational or Presbyterian denomination." The Supreme Trustee's support was assumed in the document's closing sentence.

> Trusting to the All-wise and Beneficient Disposer of events to favor this our humble attempt to advance the cause of human happiness, we humbly commit it to his patronage and blessing.

The constitution was unanimously adopted on July 4, 1828, and signed by the seven founding Trustees.

It is not clear what the women supporters of the "female high school" were doing at this point—not even certain that they were present and voting at the initial organizational meeting. Most likely, their major influence was exerted in conversation and argument at the breakfast table. The active wives of ministers, schoolmasters, and theology professors of whom we read in Sarah Robbins' memoir are not apt to have kept silent on the subject of their daughters' education. Legally, however, they were powerless to join in any formal decisions. The status of Massachusetts women as citizens had actually deteriorated since colonial times. They had lost the franchise completely after the colony's earliest decades, when the Old Province Charter formally granted them the right to vote for a few local officers. Even when the right obtained, women could rarely meet property qualifications for suffrage. Under English common law and American practice, only single women and widows might hold and control property, make contracts with other persons, sue and be sued. Married women had no such rights. "The very being or legal existence of the woman is suspended during the marriage," explained Blackstone in his *Commentaries*.[54] Wives were not to gain independent property rights in any state until 1839, and these state-protected rights were to remain minimal throughout the nineteenth century.

The belittlement of women's legal and economic status may be one reason why money for the new female high school was proving so hard to come by. Founders of schools for young men had a far easier time of it. In an Act which underlined the semi-public character of the early academies, the General Court in 1797 had supported with 450,000 acres of land grants the founding of academies throughout Massachusetts and Maine—but only a few of these had female departments, and none was for girls alone. By 1828 Phillips Academy had already accumulated donations of nearly $75,000 in addition to the original gifts of land (141 acres in Andover and another 200 in Jaffrey, New Hampshire). The Theological Seminary's buildings and equipment cost well over $200,000, assets that are worth millions today. Meanwhile, advocates of women's education were exhilarated by Zilpah Grant's success in securing a bequest of $4000 for Adams Academy in 1824. No one found it strange that Miss Grant's next Seminary in Ipswich had to open in a building rented from a group of male investors looking for a profit. Catharine Beecher could not herself persuade the wealthy men of Hartford to give a penny of the $5000 she needed to expand her Hartford Female Seminary. Women were not altogether without resources, however. Miss Beecher finally rallied the ladies who had attended her weekly prayer meetings, and the $5000 materialized after all, the largest donation coming from the father of a student whom Catharine Beecher herself had converted to confession of Christian faith the year before.

Another cause of the Trustees' fund-raising difficulties soon became clear. The women might not vote, but they could exercise an informal veto over the men's plans. Emily Adams Bancroft, Abbot 1829 and daughter of Phillips Academy's Headmaster John Adams, later described what they were up to.

> It was the determination to locate the institution on Main Street. But many of the mothers were dissatisfied, as this was the street most frequented by the "Theologues and Academy boys." My mother and Mrs. Stuart consequently drew up a petition, requesting a change in location. Elizabeth Stuart and I circulated said petition. When we had received a sufficient number of signatures, it was handed to the Trustees.[55]

On the morning of July 24 the Trustees, discouraged by these and other "formidable objections" met in the Banking Room of the new Andover Bank and "voted, That it is not expedient to erect a building for a Female Academy on our present plan, with our present means." All the Trustees were in attendance, "Dea. Newman excepted."

It is almost certain that Samuel Farrar spent one of the next few hours talking earnestly with his client and friend, Madam Sarah Abbot. Though childless herself, Madam Abbot had been a close companion to Madam Phillips and a member of the Phillips literary circle, who had doubtless joined in conversation about young women's education. In her quiet way, she was a charitable soul. For two years she had given a home to Obookiah, the young Hawaiian boy brought to Andover by a Theological Seminarian determined to educate the heathen; Madam Sarah had prayed with him every day, and had seen to his schooling. She was not wealthy—her late husband Nehemiah (a descendant of George Abbot of Rowley) had resigned as first Treasurer of the Phillips Academy Trustees because his colleagues had too grudgingly responded to his request for a stipend—but she was frugal and comfortable. She doubtless felt a certain prim satisfaction at being an Abbot by birth as well as marriage. A direct descendant both of George Abbot, one of Andover's twenty-one original proprietors, and the Reverend George Phillips, Judge Phillips' progenitor, she was surrounded by

*2. Sarah Abbot, supposed to have been painted by T. Buchanan Read,
currently hanging in Abbot Chapel, Andover.*

prestigious relatives—and probably as many who were less prestigious,
for there were over forty Abbot and Abbott families in Andover. In
such a setting a woman need do nothing special to distinguish herself.
Until now Madam Sarah had merely lived an inconspicious life between
her home near the top of Andover Hill and her church at its foot.

In a single afternoon, all this would change. Legend has it that Sarah
Abbot asked Squire Farrar, "What shall I do with my surplus funds?"
and that he, as though he had been waiting years for this very moment, immediately replied "Found an Academy in Andover for the

education of women." This conversation probably took place some-time before July 24, but Madam Sarah was one of the women who quietly opposed the Main Street site, and her gift had not been made.

In any case, a few hours after the first meeting had been so dismally adjourned, a second was called. Deacon Newman was present this time. Squire Farrar announced Madam Abbot's promise of a bequest of $1000, conditional on the building location being moved, as Farrar had undoubtedly told her it could be. Mark Newman again offered his acre on School Street, and both gifts were accepted. Farrar would lend the Trustees the $1,000 immediately needed, with Sarah Abbot's bequest as surety. "The day was saved!" exults Jane Carpenter, Abbot's chief archivist, in her lively account of the school's founding.[56] The Academy building could now be raised.

When the Trustees met to prepare their application to the General Court for an act of incorporation, they readily voted to name the school Abbot Female Academy after its principal donor. As Reverend Raymond Calkins later remarked, "How cheaply some people have bought immortality!"[57] Like most Abbots, Sarah would live long. Her lingering was to keep Abbot in suspenseful debt for twenty-two years; but her final legacy to the Academy amounted to $10,109.04, a crucial sum for the struggling school. The money had not come cheap-ly to Sarah. A latter-day Abbott[58] wrote that to his Jewett grand-mother, "the Abbotts were educated fools, who would put beautiful books and grand pianos into leaky houses. . . . I suppose every one of old George's descendants is highly individualistic and original." But Sarah Abbot was neither educated nor foolish. To give so generously of what she had for women's education was an uncommon if not an original act in her time. She earned the honor that Andover has granted her these many years.

Abiel Abbot, in his *History of Andover*, 1829, rounds off his descrip-tion of the town's most prominent buildings by noting "an elegant brick building for the Andover Female Academy, soon to be com-pleted."[59] It had been swift work. Contractor David Hidden of New-buryport, who was on hand during the summer of 1828 erecting one of the Theological Seminary buildings, was immediately engaged to plan the Academy structure, with ample advice from Squire Farrar and Principal-elect Charles Goddard. Hidden hired three carpenters at the end of August and began the work, paying Mr. Berry $1.16 a day, Mr. Holt $1.49½ a day, and himself as master carpenter $1.50. Hidden's tally book with its minute notation of detail suggests that he and Farrar must have agreed well together.

My Work on the Academy
Female

Began to Work Stately on the Academy Friday August 29, 1828.
Raisd Oct 25th

myself	69¾ & 14¼ days
Mr. Parker	68½ & 4¾ days
Mr. Holt	46½ & 4¼ days
Mr. Berry	66¾ & 6½ days

Mr. Saunders workd on the Colums 13½ Days & on the Bases
8⅓ Days at Cambridge

My Expenses of Jorneys on the Academy

August 30—my Expenses of horse keeping & Dinner to Tyngsbury
to se about Stones 62
Sep 11—Dr to 34 Feet of pine Plank for Bord Timber . . .85
Sep 15—Dr to 15 feet more of Plank 37
*What work my hands on the academy has Done at other places
to be taken out of time I have set Down*
Sep 17—Mr. Berry half a Day helping me make a Coffin
Sep 18—Mr. Amos Holt half a Day making a Box for Mrs.
Hitchings

By November the roof had been raised, and the original donations
were spent. Farrar offered to advance $1000 toward the building's com-
pletion, "the said building to be considered as pledged to him for the
eventual payment of the money with interest,"[60] but the Trustees
chose instead to accept a similarly canny offer from the Phillips Academy Board, on which both Farrar and Newman served, along with
$2000 more lent by Madam Abbot, who apparently found her pocket
deeper as she watched Abbot Academy taking shape, with its grand
portico, its full-story upstairs hall, and its two large classrooms below.
Gratefully, the Trustees authorized finishing off the basement "for
chemical purposes," and granted Sarah Abbot the right to place one
scholar free in her namesake school as long as she lived.[61]

Hidden and his "hands" were able to finish most of the interior by
spring. The Reverends Badger and Jackson wrote a prospectus advertising the "elegant and spacious edifice, seventy feet front, by forty
feet deep," solid proof of the seriousness of the enterprise. Abbot
Academy promised "to meet the high demands, corresponding with
the progress of public sentiment on the subject of female education,
and with its consequent improvements." If the Phillips Academy Philomathean Society could resolve in the affirmative its question as to fe-

males' capacity for intellectual improvement—as it did—perhaps the rest of the world could do so too. At nine o'clock on the morning of May 6, 1829, Abbot Female Academy welcomed seventy girls and young women into its halls.

Pious Pioneers

*Our classes are now all arranged. The vessel is
ready, sails spread, and we are hoping the pro-
pitious breeze of Industry will soon waft us to
the shores of Knowledge.*
Abbot student, Julia Ann Pierce, April 21, 1840

A letter from Samuel C. Jackson to Henrietta Jackson, Dorset, Vermont; written in April 1829:

Dear sister Henrietta,
    You perceive from the foregoing page when the school com-
mences, and also the terms of instruction. I spoke the other
evening to the deacon's folks about your coming here to spend
the summer and attend school with Phebe. The deacon said I
must board you & that your living would make but *little* difference, that he might as well provide for three as for two.[1] You will
of course eat but two meals here a day, & will do your own washing & ironing, & we shall find your house room & bedding, so
that the deacon can afford to board you very cheap. If you be-
have well, *I* shall not charge you much, though I shall expect
to be at considerable trouble to take care of you—you must, *most*
of the time, be carried to, or brought from school, once a day.
I feel anxious to have you finish your education—to pursue your
studies now in the season of acquiring, & feel as though you might
do it with little expense during the ensuing summer. It is very
decidedly my opinion that you had better fix up immediately &
purpose to be here at the opening of the school, or as soon as
possible. . . .
    It will be about a mile & a-half from here to the school, & this
you can & *ought* to walk *once* a day, & in good weather you can
on a pinch do it twice . . . You may think perhaps, that it will
be too much trouble to carry or bring you once a day, but as
Phebe will go too, & as the deacon has a horse & chaise & boys,

& as I have a horse & chaise, we can between us do it with little trouble. Please to write immediately your conclusions about it, & when you shall come, if you come at all.

Having begun with one of his favorite topics—female education—Jackson goes on to his other two: politics and religion. He feels he must explain why he voted for Andrew Jackson, since he was one of a mere handful of Andover citizens to do so.[2]

> Anything but a Unitarian for President. Since Adam's downfall countenances have fallen several degrees below zero. Adams has come off rather *sneaking*; but no more of politics, lest I have Mother in my hair—I'm really sorry, though, that she is so favorable to Unitarians; I *used* to think her sound in the faith . . .
>
> You will see by the last *Recorder* that Mr. Carleton's wife is *dead*. I have heard of no particulars. She has been cut down in the midst of her hopes—in the morning of her glory, & *where* is she, Ah! where? Whether she had hope in her death, I know not. If she had no Saviour, she has wasted life & lost her soul!! No accomplishments, no acquisitions, no worldly prospects can avail her *now*—they could not avert the arrow of death, or prepare her spirit to dwell with Christ. Be admonished, & be wise.
>
> Sam'l C. Jackson

Clearly, the saving of Henrietta's soul was as important to her brother as her education. And politics absorbed him as politics absorbed nearly everyone in those times. Andrew Jackson had been president for only a few weeks, and already Whiggish Andover citizens were pulling long faces; it says worlds of Samuel Jackson's tact and talents that his middle-aged Trustee–colleagues (bank directors all) were willing to accept his Democratic leanings. President Jackson and his immediate successors would be hard pressed to give direction to the "mad, shifting world" of the 1830's and 1840's:[3] business's boom-bust-boom cycle would make families' fortunes less certain than ever, while the democratization of economic and political opportunity gathered speed and intellectuals tried to make sense of it all from their pulpits, university lecture rooms, or science laboratories, or in their shaky, exhilarating utopian communities. Educators, too, contended with one another over the purposes and techniques of their profession on the pages of the new educational journals. Many were experimenting with innovations first observed in Europe, or inventing their own. This first quarter century of Abbot's career was the grand era of the privately founded academy. Abbot both drew strength from the common academic culture and responded in its unique way to the needs of its constituency.

Man's Place

Henrietta Jackson, nineteen years old and capable of responding sensibly to her brother's letter, hurried to make her arrangements in time to arrive in Andover for the opening of Abbot. She would stay at the Academy for only one term. As will be seen, however, Abbot was to figure largely in her own and her children's lives, and to be in many ways a Jackson family affair.

Henrietta came to an Abbot founded for women and run by men. Masculinity did not, however, guarantee stability. Count the number of principals in Abbot's first fifteen years and the school looks like a "mad, shifting world" in itself.

1829–1831   Charles Goddard
1832–1834   Samuel Lamson
1834–1835   Miss Louise Tenney (acting principal)
1835–1838   Samuel Gilman Brown
1838–1839   Rev. Lorenzo Lorraine Langstroth
1839–1842   Timothy Dwight Porter Stone

Special teachers and assistants also changed rapidly, except for the gentle Miss Stone, teacher of the Introductory Class for eight- to twelve-year-olds. The Academy was deep in debt, its entire plant mortgaged to Phillips Academy and to Squire Farrar. Though Madam Sarah Abbot continued to add to her legacy for Abbot's future, she was still very much alive. In this situation, the Trustees were Abbot's ballast, always managing to staff the school and (except for one term during Goddard's tenure) to keep it open. In the leanest years, several of them paid the interest on the mortgage notes out of their own pockets. Students, too, were constant: for every "flitting scholar" who stayed for just a term there was another who attended five years or more. Trustee Amos Abbott sent all seven of his daughters to the school.

Meanwhile, the succession of principals played counterpoint to the institutional *cantus firmus*. All were young, all scholarly gentlemen, and this in itself made Abbot rather unusual. Gentility was not to be taken for granted in a day when many schoolmasters were barely educated boors. Mr. Goddard's "refined and polished manners were a constant surprise to those of us who had formed our ideas of the male teacher by the average master of those times," wrote Mrs. Mary Ann Durant Bullard '37, in a letter to Miss McKeen.[4] Three of the principals were students at Andover Theological Seminary during part or all of their time at Abbot. Samuel Lamson brought sober orthodoxy from the Seminary, "quite in contrast to the wide-awake, almost sportive manner of Mr. Goddard," said Mrs. Bullard. "Of all the teachers I have known, no one knew so well as [Mr. Lamson] how to reach the conscience in matters generally considered too trivial to be referred to it at all."[5] The "vivacious" Timothy Porter Stone, adopted son of Seminary professor Ebenezer Porter, was more appealing. He brought a barrage of new ideas—so many that "he hardly stayed to place one plan steadily on its feet before he dropped it for another," according to Philena McKeen.[6] At least one alumna found him a "delightful teacher," and recalled that he managed to be simultaneously a writer, a father, and a kindly landlord for Abbot boarders as well as a theological student.[7] The special language instructors were often "theologues" too. William G. Schauffler, just arrived from Germany for his ministerial studies, was a master teacher of both French and German at a time when few academies offered German at all. A highly cultured man, he also (writes Miss McKeen) possessed a "weird power" over his flute,[8] and his commitment to missionary work in the Near East was even then an inspiration to a Christian academy.

Goddard and Lamson were capable men, but it is Samuel Gilman Brown, the third of Abbot's six male preceptors who best illustrates the benefits Abbot gained by functioning on the principle articulated by M. Carey Thomas, first woman president of Bryn Mawr college. Said Miss Thomas of her extraordinary faculty: "We get them while they are young, exciting teachers, and they leave to grow old in the universities."[9] Abbot's Brown was not a Woodrow Wilson (a young teacher whom President Thomas never liked), and one can hardly say he later ossified as professor at Dartmouth and President of Hamilton College; he was, said alumnae, "one of the kindest and best of men . . . very decided but not harsh;" "a most refined and scholarly man, a faithful, accurate and enthusiastic teacher."[10] Earlier, Mr. Lamson had begun the Abbot tradition of frequent walks or buggy rides to the ocean or other places of interest (some of these started at 4:30 A.M.); from alumnae recollections we get an image of Samuel Brown patiently lifting one sodden adventurer out of a ditch on a berry-picking expedition to which the whole school had traveled by train. The engineer waited while her clothes were dried at a nearby farmhouse, then covered the seven miles from Wilmington to Andover in only *twelve minutes*, a "wonderful feat" in those days.[11]

The public expected the principal of an academy to attend to each pupil's moral character, to "the improvement of her mind as a *whole*," and to her intellect's connection with "the great purposes of life."[12] Brought up since age seven by his "serene, saintly" mother,[13] Principal Brown seems to have had a special understanding of young girls' needs. He also possessed a determination modeled on his memories of his minister father, "one of the most honorable representatives of a profession which then controlled society," and president of Dartmouth College at the time of his death in 1820.[14] Serious though his purposes might be, he must have had a sense of humor. He required one composition class to "prove there is no such man as Andrew Jackson." This problem had a "Miss Stow" stumped at first, according to a friend, "but she did it at last and a spicy thing it was."[15] Brown was a man of wide sympathies: he loved music as he loved children, with a simple joy that touched his friends. At the same time, "he was familiar with the whole range of English literature, from its crudest, roughest elements in Chaucer and Gower to the . . . most refined and polished numbers."[16] It may have been under Brown that Abbot pupils first attended Shakespeare lectures at the Teachers' Seminary, a daring expedient at a time when most female academies forbade the study or acting of Shakespeare altogether, and Harvard's Shakespeare course was twenty-five years in the future.

Whatever subject Brown taught, "We caught his enthusiasm," wrote an alumna, "and strove to study well so as not to disappoint him, as well as for learning's sake."[17] Brown's successor, the Reverend Lorenzo Langstroth of South Church, was also inspiring; everyone regretted his departure after just two terms to devote full time to his parish. The best indicators of Langstroth's imagination and scientific interests are that he tutored math at Yale before coming to Abbot, and that he later invented the Langstroth movable frame beehive. His design revolutionized beekeeping at the time and has remained basically unchanged ever since.[18] He had no difficulty persuading his students to do their mathematics and botany, even though his mind was often on parish problems. Indeed, Abbot's first six principals, young though they were, seem to have had few problems with discipline.[19] They contrast poignantly with Phillips Academy's "Master Adams, [whose] wand of office was a villainous ferule about a foot long,"[20] of whom his students said, "pretty often we could 'trace the day's disasters in his morning face.' "[21] True, Adams resigned from the Academy in 1832, acknowledging himself old-fashioned, but "Uncle Sam" Taylor, who came soon after and stayed till 1871, was equally fierce—and equally old-fashioned. Caning and humiliation were approved pedagogical techniques in many antebellum boys' schools and colleges; fortunately they were rare in female seminaries.[22]

Asa Farwell, the sixth and last man to serve as principal, was not so commanding or vital as the first five, but he had one great virtue: he stayed. For ten years after coming down to Abbot from the Theological Seminary he stayed, applying his "Vermont grit" to practical and financial problems that had been the despair of his predecessors.[23] Abbot's male principals took on their indigent enterprise at their own risk, serving as their own business managers and reserving for themselves whatever tuition money remained after all expenses were paid, including interest on the debt and a dollar a day for each assistant teacher.[24] After Goddard had resigned in discouragement, the Trustees decided to guarantee each principal $800 a year (the same sum Samuel Jackson received from his parishioners), but the system was apparently allowed to lapse back to the original "no-profit-no-salary" rule whenever the $800 could not be raised through tuitions and fees. Thus the Trustees could not pay a single salary out of the "empty treasury" Farwell found on his arrival in 1842.[25] So often did principals change that it is perhaps a wonder that Abbot's enrollment held up at all. Yet by the time Asa Farwell had been principal for three years, the roster of pupils had grown to 180. As slow to spend as he was quick to get, Farwell acted as the school's gardener and day laborer; students often came upon him with his shirtsleeves rolled, landscaping Abbot's one-acre grounds himself.

Pleased to have many of their maintenance and money cares removed, the Trustees tended to overlook Farwell's faults as an educator. They gave him a good press: it is difficult to see beyond the smooth surface of Abbot's official history and find out all one wishes to know about Principal Farwell. We learn of his single-minded determination from his success late in life as a home missionary who brought a frontier congregation of five souls (or four, since he had one man excommunicated soon after his arrival) to self-supporting prosperity in a year. Yet even Farwell's memorialists (traditionally effusive) acknowledge that "there have been many men of more showy and . . . popular talent than this modest man of God."[26] Is it possible that he stayed at Abbot ten years because he had nowhere else to go?

Farwell's principalship was not quite the "unprecedented success" the McKeens describe.[27] Ten fathers with twenty-seven Abbot daughters between them petitioned the Trustees to fire Farwell in September of 1848. The protesters believed Farwell wholly lacking in "that gentlemanly deportment and refinement of manner which are best calculated to make favorable impressions in the formation of female character." They accused him of managing the seminary "with direct reference" to his own "pecuniary interests" rather than for "the good of the pupils." He was often absent, even during devotions. They felt he made a habit of inflicting disgrace "when the pupil was unconscious of any fault," and found it "an unwarrantable assumption of authority" for Farwell "to pronounce sentence of expulsion upon individuals who voluntarily withdraw from the school."[28]

Strong words, these. Is there confirming evidence? We know something of Farwell's quirks from alumnae recollections. He gave one incorrigible trickster a choice between expulsion and having a note sent home to her father about her misdeeds; then locked her in the classroom during recess. That Farwell looked the other way while she lowered strings out the classroom window so her friends below could tie on snacks for her refreshment, and that he never *did* send the note after all suggests that he was more wishy-washy than tyrant.[29] However, we know from Elizabeth Stuart Phelps's recollections how Farwell taught spelling: the method "was severe, no doubt. We stood in a class of forty, and lost our places for the misfit of a syllable, a letter, a definition, or even a stumble in elocution."[30] We can read in many letters to Phebe McKeen of the collective sigh of relief that greeted the Reverend Joseph Bittinger, "a teacher of rare power"—who took Farwell's place for a single year, and seemed to several correspondents both kinder and more inspiring than any teacher they had ever had before (Farwell included).[31]

Finally, there is proof of Farwell's "pecuniary interests" in the sixteen house lots he managed to amass along School and Abbot streets. One may assume that they were bought with the profits of his Abbot work, since he had no other known source of income, and that he made a pretty penny from the Abbot Trustees when he sold most of them for $400–$600 an acre before moving west to take charge of an Iowa mission church in 1866.[32] Thus we have at least a suggestion of the substance behind the protesters' accusations.

In private the Trustees probably took the anti-Farwell petition seriously. Circumstantial evidence suggests a covert effort behind a public whitewash to make the Principal and his school once more acceptable to the disaffected parents. Trustee Peter Smith may have played a crucial role here, for he was a model of tact, and with seven daughters in or coming to Abbot, he had a large stake in the school's success. Smith was business partner to protester John Dove, and the wealthy Dove had contributed generously to the Theological Seminary; Abbot could ill afford any wholesale defection from the protesters, and their friends. In public, however, the Board's only response was nonresponse. They refused the protesters a formal hearing—and denied everything. In all likelihood they were so grateful to Farwell for running a reasonably full school that they were unwilling to question his day-to-day management; yet the dust-up seems to have wrought some quiet changes, since only four of the daughters left Abbot after the protest had failed. Possibly most important, Farwell's young wife, who had been suffering a painful illness during the year that the protesters were gathering evidence for their case against him, finally died. His anxiety for her life ended, one surmises that he was able to give his Abbot students the attention they needed. In any case the rumbles ceased. When Farwell left Abbot for a trip to Europe a year later, nine of the protesters' daughters left the school too, although the year's acting principal was highly recommended.

Like his part-time predecessors, Farwell never had time to become Catharine Beecher's ideal principal, who, besides being moral leader, determined each student's course of study and could claim some knowledge of the intellectual character and education of *every individual member* of the school."[33] Instead, parents generally chose the course they were buying for their Abbot daughter, true to the laissez-faire spirit of Jacksonian America, while Farwell was left with "keen grief that so large a portion of my time must be employed in duties 'outside' of school and school hours; but it was the *sine qua non* of there being any 'inside' to be cared for."[34] Possibly, Abbot would have thrived still better under a single, powerful woman principal, such as Emma Willard or Zilpah Grant. Yet the school's succession of men, along with its part-time specialists and several gifted woman assistants, may have helped to confirm its students' sense of worth as they tackled traditional men's subjects in a male-dominated society. Thomas Woody comments:

> Abbot Academy was unique in that it was presided over entirely by men in its early years. The course of study was not regularly pursued, nor were diplomas granted until after Miss Hasseltine took charge (1853). But a very liberal series of studies was offered, and the scholarship of Goddard, Schauffler, Lamson, Brown, and others, all college graduates, probably insured more excellent instruction than was available in most girls' academies.[35]

Woman's World

It is students who finally make the school, resisting or embracing the opportunity to learn from their teachers and from each other. Abbot's girls were a special lot—not only the day scholars from "the Hill and the Mill" or from the merchant families of Andover town, but the boarders from the New England states, New York, New Jersey, and Pennsylvania who made up over a third of every school roll through 1852.

They came in all ages and sizes. Henrietta Jackson was older than most of the others "in the season of acquiring" who were Abbot's first students but not the oldest: academies served girls as both high school and college in those days. It was common for young women to alternate teaching in a common (elementary public) school with study at an academy. Throughout the nineteenth century, Abbot's senior class was largely composed of women twenty years old or more, and several in each decade were twenty-three or twenty-four. Small girls came, too, to join the Introductory Class, their parents paying a weekly fee of twenty-five cents for the privilege. Sarah Flagg was one: she, like many of her friends, was less interested in lofty educational purposes than in the fact that her father came along that first day "for protector," and that she and her sister were "wearing little pink gingham calashes, with a bridle attached, to keep them on."[36] Elizabeth Stuart, later Mrs. E. S. Phelps, a prolific and popular writer, was a member of the Introductory Class, while several of her sisters and other precocious girls from the Hill were sorted into First, Second, or Third Year students.

The Stuarts, the five Woods girls, and the Adams and Murdock girls were daughters of warm, intelligent mothers and of scholarly theology professors or schoolmasters. For decades to come these unusual families' lives would intersect with Abbot's progress. Sarah Stuart (Robbins) later recalled that "the Hill, with its great common, its severe buildings, its monastic human figures, made up our whole child world . . . we never went to the circus or to dancing-school; but were always expected to take part in whatever went on of services or celebrations within those studious walls."[37] From infancy the Stuart girls had heard their renowned professor-father reading Hebrew passages aloud behind his study door, or watched him hurrying "like a long-legged colt"[38] from lecture room to Hill printing shop, where for years he set all the Hebrew type for his books himself. And the sense of being something special continued into the second and third generation. Mrs. Phelps's daughter (who took her mother's name when she, too, became a writer) remembered her own friends on the Hill as "especially open-hearted, gentle-minded girls," innocent as only youngsters prayerfully raised in a circumscribed "university town" can be.[39] Andover girls did not waltz or attend Christmas parties. They did leave notes for boys in the cleft of a certain well-known rock, and they knew their way through the forest to the safest meeting places.

The Stuart and Woods girls especially helped to set the intellectual tone of Abbot Academy. Harriet Woods later wrote that "during the year which followed, I woke up wonderfully and enjoyed my studies exceedingly."[40] Harriet would eventually join the company of women writers born on Zion's Hill. So would her sister Margaret, whose writings are of special interest, for she reached out to—and touched—Henrietta Jackson. In her memorial to Henrietta, Margaret remembered how her lifelong friend struggled at Abbot to master her moods, those "heart-sinkings" that would plague her until her marriage.[41] Henrietta had "a deep, earnest, kindling eye, which told of a world of hidden emotions beneath her calm and reserved exterior."[42] The two friends had a future in common, for all but one of the first twenty-one Hill students married ministers. Yet they cannot have taken themselves as seriously as did the Seminary men, "professors and students alike," all of whom "felt themselves anointed kings and priests, with momentous tasks to perform for the world."[43] Orderly though their upbringing was, a schoolmate called the Stuarts and Woodses "the jolliest girls among us."[44] The Sabbath was silence itself, but it ended at sundown, and often enough the Stuart girls could be found gaily shaking off the day's torpors with a clamorous game of ball among the pillars of the Abbot Academy porch.

Unfortunately, Andover's "Mill and Till" girls have left us fewer words about themselves. However, they too had grown up enjoying advantages to match the restrictions with which all girls were then raised. The fathers of the Flagg and Gould girls were engaged in an ambitious printing enterprise, one which they consciously operated to serve the cause of Christ, printing the nation's first temperance newspaper and the first publications of the American Tract Society.[45] The Marland sisters must have had a particularly eventful childhood, since their father ran one of the largest mills on the Shawsheen river. Women might not boss men, but in Marland Mills, as elsewhere, so Sarah Bailey tells us, "it was the custom for the wives and daughters of the managers and owners to work, just as it had been for them to spin or weave or perform domestic service in their homes."[46] Owners' families had not yet put such distance between themselves and the run-of-the-mill as they would later create, and Abbot Academy day scholars seem at this time to have considered themselves the pride of their town, not a cut above it.

During Abbot's early years, the local Andover elite—bankers and wealthy farmers and theological professors—shared a sense of Christian mission, a spirit that verified the potential of the humble even as it reminded them how far they were from being perfect in Christ. The community, wrote Elizabeth Phelps, had "an everlasting scorn of worldliness [and of] that tendency to seek the lower motive . . . to confuse sounds or appearances with values."[47] Surely status distinctions were apparent to the inhabitants of this increasingly heterogeneous community; after 1845 they must have been aware of the "shanty Irish" pouring into Lawrence, swelling the new mill town's population to over 5000 in 1850, larger than South Andover's already and heading for 100,000 by the turn of the century.[48] But there are no sounds of class struggle heard by Andover's local historians.[49] Abbot's and Phillips' formal curricula completely ignore the changes industrialization was bringing to so many New England towns. At mid-century Henry Ward Beecher would explain the silence by weighing the balance of power between the townsmen: the lower and middle classes' "wholesome jealousy of their rights, and a suspicion among the poor that wealth and strength always breed danger to the weak, made the upper class . . . politically weaker than any other."[50] Too weak in Andover to dare raise the subject of class conflict? It is more likely that Andover's industrialists and intellectuals were too self-assured, too immersed in supporting and carrying out their grand educational missions to notice. The community divided on social issues (abolitionism was one) far more readily than it split into economic factions. Town records show that such elected posts as selectman or school committeeman were roughly distributed three ways: to the newly wealthy, to the men of importance in academy or church, and to the descendants of the oldest Andover families. Members of the latter two groups could be rich or penurious; regardless, Andover seems to have acknowledged their right to leadership.

New England's elite might found academies partly to make up for their political weakness, but the early Abbot does not seem to have been a snobbish place. The only suggestion of social division we have is in the protest against Farwell, for all of the protesters were townsmen, while Farwell himself and most of the Trustees were strongly associated with the intellectuals from Andover Hill. A school founded with a mission in mind was bound to welcome any white Protestant girl who could pay the fee. Tuition for a term ($5.00) could be—and occasionally was—earned by a week's work at a cotton loom.[51] Accommodations were meager. One broken stove "heated" the entire recitation hall. The Academy building was nearly bare of library books and teaching equipment, and it was fortunate that the students had the capacity to "supply by their own bright minds and earnest will what was lacking in their surroundings," as Samuel Brown put it.[52] After 1832 families looking for a more select school could send their daughters to Mrs. Bela Edwards' small and expensive seminary on Main Street, dubbed "the Nunnery" by the Phillips students and theologues, and considered more aristocratic than Abbot. (The Stuart family may have found Abbot principal Lamson too severe, for Elizabeth later became one of two day students at the Nunnery.) The wealthier Andover families could easily have afforded the more costly academies like Ipswich Seminary ($25 a term in 1829), or Miss Beecher's Hartford Seminary, where an upper-crust urban constituency fully satisfied her social ambitions. But in Andover both the rich and the far-from-rich seem to have chosen their own town's frugal "self-made school," Abbot Academy.[53]

Early Boarders

Henrietta Jackson had a room at Deacon True's. The first Abbot prospectus promised accommodations for others:

> Arrangements are making to establish in conexion a boarding department, where young ladies may enjoy the advantages of home in an unremitting attention to their habits and deportment, in the parental tenderness and fidelity with which they will be treated, and in the care and exertion which will be used to form and guard the character. Situations for boarding can also be obtained in highly respectable families of the village.

In Abbot's first ten years, formal "arrangements" never finished making, but students nevertheless found space, wrote one alumna, "with private families, some of which were rare homes, indeed, for us young girls, giving us privileges scarcely less than those of the school itself."[54] Samuel Brown's venerated mother took boarders; so did Professor and Mrs. Bela Edwards, who offered house room to some theological students along with a few fortunate Abbot girls. Each boarding-house keeper was made responsible to the Trustees for imposing a bracing routine of early rising, study hours, and prayer, while the boarding students were expected to exercise "Christian courtesy and kindness in heart, speech, and action" within their boarding houses as everywhere else.[55] The "Commons," the Abbot-sponsored boarding house that finally materialized in 1839, was inspired by a season of unsuccessful negotiations with the pioneering educator, Mary Lyon. In 1834 Miss Lyon began seeking offers of help to found her New England Seminary for Teachers, a residential school to be generously endowed from the first, so that young women of limited means might receive excellent training under "missionary" teachers for whom great work required small pay.[56] Mary Lyon was still young at this time, but well on her way to renown as one of "the nursing mothers of higher education and larger work for women," in the words of a latter-day Abbot student.[57] She agreed with Catharine Beecher that the hours outside formal class were inevitably "the hours of access to the heart."[58] "The teachers and pupils will constitute one family, and none will be received to board elsewhere," said the circular addressed "to the Friends of Female Education" which she broadcast throughout New England. The "style of living" was to be "neat, but very plain and simple. Domestic work of the family to be performed by members of the school. Board and tuition to be placed at cost."[59]

Abbot's Trustees received this circular just after Principal Goddard had left. Louise Tenney was running the school successfully, but a permanent principal was not in sight. As the Trustees' idealism warmed them to Miss Lyon's proposal, the Academy's practical difficulties hastened an enthusiastic response. Yes, they wrote back, they would "change the character of this prosperous institution to meet the general views" Mary Lyon had expressed.[60] "We propose to give up to this object, free of charge, the spacious and splendid edifice erected for our school, at the expense of several thousand dollars." They promised to help raise money for "commons" (a dormitory). They expanded on the advantages of locating the new Seminary for Teachers in a "religious and literary" community of "flourishing schools . . . institutions consecrated to the kingdom of Christ," some of which would share such equipment as science apparatus, and all of which would attract students to one another.[61] Abbot's Trustees ended by offering their services as trustees of the new Seminary. Samuel Jackson was appointed chief negotiator.

Mary Lyon politely rejected the Trustees' offer, saying she wished the Seminary's location to be selected "by a committee representative of the public" (not by the Abbot Trustees, apparently) and that "difficulties" would surely attend an Andover site. Perhaps these unspecified difficulties turned on the proximity of two schools for males; or perhaps they were financial: she needed $27,000, and Abbot's cash box was empty. In any case, Miss Lyon moved on to other towns—and for a while, to further discouragements. She attributed her fund-raising failures to "good men's fear of greatness in women."[62] Finally, after years of labor, she found welcome and funds in South Hadley, Massachusetts, a smaller, simpler town whose rural virtues were congenial to a farm-reared educator-pioneer. There Mt. Holyoke Female Seminary opened in 1837, pitching both its charges and its exacting course of study to "the class most likely to be benefited from it and to use it for the good of the world."[63]

The Trustees' subsequent efforts to raise funds for an Abbot boarding house came to little, but the Academy did not forget Mary Lyon's arguments for a residential school. In 1839 the ebullient Timothy Stone opened an Abbot Commons at his own risk in the large house north of the Academy building, later to be known as Davis Hall. By having each boarder bring her own minimum furnishings, and by asking all takers to share in "family" housekeeping, Stone was able to set board charges as low as $1.12½ a week at a time when most landlords charged $2.50 to $5.00.

It worked. They worked. The first two boarders (later nicknamed Sisters Melody and Cheerfulness by their friends) entered a bare, cold shelter on October 26, 1840, and cooked their supper in a single copper pot and a broken tea kettle, using stones for andirons. Soon Sisters Temperance, Mercy, Music, Calmness, and seven others arrived, with Sister Affection as student directress. Smoky bread was baked, half-cooked pies were devoured, and Saturday's washing duly done. The Trustees began to believe in Commons: they sent the little band a table, a bread trough, and a pudding stick, each "hailed with delight," wrote Mercy and Calmness in their account of the first year's adventures.[64] To celebrate, the girls planned a "molasses candy scrape...and we entered heart or rather mouth and hand into it." "Far sweeter" than the most splendid ballroom dance "were our enjoyments," gloated the Commons chroniclers, surely Abbot's first Yearbook editors.

By Spring the place was livable. On Presidential Inauguration Day in March of 1841, "all being Whigs, [we]welcomed the hero of Tippecanoe by ringing all the bells in the house and giving three hearty cheers." Soon after, however, the well failed. "The water [was] so bad that horses would turn from it in disgust...We have heard of emigrants to the west who have lived in this style, but never in the literary and wealthy town of Andover did the like happen." Still, Commons was home. "Never can we forget the happy days spent together... When hill and valley intervene, fond memory will love to linger around these scenes."

After several years, Asa Farwell bought the Commons house for his own residence, married the directress, Miss Hannah Sexton, and kept on the boarders "at cost." The Commons idea, however, was to be revived. And in the meantime, faraway students continued to travel by stage to "the 'Hill of Science' on fair Andover's brow," as Julia Pierce, '41, put it in one of her letters home to Illinois, enjoying alike the benefits of town and Academy.[65]

Abbot Academy as Teachers Seminary

One purpose behind Mary Lyon's scheme was to answer a new demand for women teachers. There was nation-building to do and not enough men to do it, especially in a field where women's willingness to earn low pay had driven schoolmaster's salaries in many villages to "a dollar a week and board round." Emma Willard had early proposed that "female seminaries" could "place the business of teaching children in [the] hands [of unmarried women] now nearly useless to society; and take it from those whose services the state wants in many other ways."[66] Horace Mann endorsed women teachers, since there were never enough capable men willing to do the job—and by 1840 60 percent of Massachusetts' teachers were women. Girls growing to womanhood in small towns and rural areas saw schoolteaching as a respectable way to cut loose from the circumscribed lives their mothers led, an opportunity for travel and personal independence which approximated that available to young men in these footloose times.[67] By mid-century, Henry Ward Beecher in his novel *Norwood* would have old Uncle Ebeneezer saying to the hero, "No, sir, a man should never be a schoolmaster. That's a woman's business."[68]

The West especially needed missionaries of civilization. Catharine Beecher thought every intelligent woman should do her stint of teaching before marriage.

> I can see no other way in which our country can so surely be saved from the inroads of vice, infidelity and error. Let the leading females of this country become refined, pious and active and the salt is scattered through the land to purify and save.[69]

These "leading females" were in for a shock. The tough farm boys who came to winter schools could bully a teacher unmercifully; a young man was beaten so badly in Almanzo Wilder's upstate New York school that he died.[70] Later, Wilder's fiancée, Laura Ingalls, earned twenty-five dollars for her family with two terms of teaching five "children" (two of them older than the fifteen-year-old Laura) in an abandoned claim shack in Minnesota. Snow swirled through its cracks all winter. The tiny school district was twelve miles from the nearest village; Laura had to live in the cabin of the school board chairman, a homesteader whose wife hated him, the prairie, and Laura by turns. Her bed was separated from the others' by a curtain strung across a single dirty room.[71]

Still, the hardships only increased many young women's ardor. Men also responded to the need for trained teachers. Samuel Farrar made sure that Phillips Academy's Trustees would find an extraordinary educator to head the Hill's fledgling Teachers Seminary. By the time of his appointment to the post in 1830, Samuel R. Hall, a self-taught minister, had already organized the first "normal school" in the nation. His student teachers had helped him run a model elementary school in Concord, Vermont, while he edited his influential *Lectures on School Keeping*, published in 1829. Hall's Andover students came to the new Seminary to prepare for work, not for college. They arranged their courses to suit their professional plans, whatever these might be. They learned scientific agriculture by keeping their own garden, surveying and navigation through field experience, and teaching by daily practice in a model school on the Hill. Abbot students might be denied access to the Phillips Classical Department, but they were warmly welcomed at many Teachers Seminary classes.

The enthusiasm for teacher training soon reached Abbot. Samuel Hall's daughter attended the Academy (class of 1835). Hall himself seems to have been a watchful if distant adviser to Abbot's teachers, and Hall's successor as Seminary principal, Reverend Lyman Coleman, joined Abbot's Board of Trustees in 1838. In 1839, Timothy Stone determined that Abbot should systematically prepare young women for teaching. He introduced a three-year Teacher's Course (possibly modeled on the Mt. Holyoke curriculum, for they are almost identical), which he hoped would become the school's primary offering. It included special lectures and practice sessions for teaching candidates, in addition to many subjects to be taken in common with the girls who were committed to two-year "Latin" or "French" Courses of Study. Graduates would thus be qualified for secondary as well as elementary school teaching. Stone's first catalogue advertised the new offerings.

> The habits formed in all the studies here pursued are designed to render Young Ladies qualified to *impart* as well as to *acquire* knowledge; and for those who wish to prepare themselves to instruct in Academies and Higher Schools, all the facilities are

furnished to pursue a course as extensive as their circumstances
require.

Stone himself seems to have been an exacting Principal as well as a
cheerful one, in spite of his many commitments. He supervised six
teachers, and kept *"perfect order . . .* throughout the school," wrote
Julia Ann Pierce, whose appreciation of Abbot only increased during
her second year as the teachers-in-training began to arrive in significant numbers. "Much more intellect is displayed" than previously, she
crowed.[72]

The Abbot "Female Seminary" for teachers, as Stone entitled it, did
not survive his departure in 1842, except as the theologues' and Phillips
boys' pet name for Abbot and the students (the "Fem Sems") who attended there. Possibly Asa Farwell realized that the future of formal
teacher training lay with the new state-operated normal schools, four
of which had opened by 1840. Farrar's and Hall's "educational experiment"[73] on the Hill also closed, becoming Phillips Academy's English
Department, a vigorous school that would thrive separately from the
college preparatory Classics Department until the two were combined
in the 1870's. But Abbot continued to promise "special assistance . . . to
young ladies who design to engage in teaching."[74] While the faddish
monitorial system was never used at Abbot, for years there were a few
student teachers listed under other staff in the catalogue—"girl-teach-
ers" as the youngest pupils called them. The Academy undoubtedly
benefited from the reflection on sensible teaching methods that must
have been stimulated by its own three-year experiment. In addition to
Susan Hall, hundreds of nineteenth-century Abbot students eventually became teachers, some distinguished, many unsung.

What did they think and talk about, these almost-women and girls,
and what did they take from Abbot into their adult lives? It is difficult
to tell. Surely little was said of the joys of chemistry, or pneumatics, or
Latin grammar. Clothes, yes, though not—so far as one can tell from
the few letters and journals we have—with the compulsiveness common
to most of their contemporaries, an obsession to which writers would
cater incessantly a little later in the century when more girls were allowed to read fiction. The two Dodge girls, both boarders in 1833, may
have been unusually apathetic: they found that "the wearisome mono-
tony of school-girl life" yielded only to the "kindly interest" shown
them by the three Marland sisters, whose hospitality they formally acknowledged before returning home.[75] Pleasure in personalities emerges
in the catty comments written next to the names listed in one student's

1840 catalogue: "spoiled by indulgence," she says of one schoolmate; "gay, open-hearted joyousness" is another's tag.

> moral and intellectual beauty
> alas! that falsehood should appear in such a lovely form
> a perfect enigma
> I cannot love that which looks so much like affectation
> The mead of willing sympathy thou gave, and oh!
>   experience only teaches how sweet it is.[76]

An 1835 alumna told Phebe McKeen how she "and companions equally venturesome" had explored the unfinished cellar of the Academy building on their hands and knees and washed off at the pump afterwards. Students' letters home speak of "delightful walks" in the countryside after the close of school at 3:00 o'clock each afternoon, of being too busy to sleep enough, of clothes and money needed.[77]

Perhaps Abbot's greatest contribution to its older students' lives was the protected space in which they might develop their independent powers, free from the pressures for early marriage that alternately excited and harassed so many young women of the time.[78] Henrietta Jackson never forgot her short term of attendance there. Abbot helped prepare her to serve as a common school teacher in Sutton, Massachusetts and as a co-founder of Catskill Female Academy before her marriage in 1838 to the Reverend Cyrus Hamlin. She shared with her husband a profound dedication to Christianity: one month after their wedding, they sailed for Constantinople, where Hamlin would found Bebek Seminary (and later would help found Robert College) to educate Armenian and Turkish Christians in spite of everything the Turkish officials and their Russian overlords could do to discourage him. There Henrietta met up again with several old acquaintances, come from Andover to serve the Lord in heathen lands, among them Solomon Holt, the son of her Andover landlord and companion of her rides in the deacon's chaise to Andover Hill, and William G. Schauffler, her Abbot French teacher. Schauffler headed the Evangelical missionaries' campaign against official opposition; at one point, he went to the Russian Ambassador to protest the capture and deportation to Siberia of Cyrus' and Henrietta's Armenian language tutor, Mesrobe Taliatine. The Ambassador was emphatic. "The Emperor of Russia, who is my master, will never allow Protestantism to set its foot in Turkey," he told his visitor. Schauffler bowed low and replied, "Your Excellency, the kingdom of Christ, who is my Master, will never ask the Emperor of all the Russians where it may set its foot."[79]

The Armenian lessons soon resumed. Henrietta's friends were sure she was the first American woman ever to learn the language. "It is very difficult," she wrote her old Abbot friend Margaret Woods Lawrence in 1839, "and must be learned without the help of grammar or dictionary. Do you think I am discouraged? It is not time yet. I . . . am now reading in short syllables. Such choking sounds you never heard."[80]

Henrietta's mother was certain her daughter had been sent by God to "the place where the great battle would be fought between Michael and his angels, and the dragon . . . where the mighty hosts of Gog and Magog will be slain."[81] But from the Hamlins' viewpoint, the holy war was an endless series of skirmishes to win over an alien people one by one. Plague, fleas, and stubborn officials were antagonists more immediate than Gog and Magog. Only two extraordinarily resourceful people could make a home in such a land. The Sultan having put all Protestants under the ban, none could even find work, much less a Christian education. The local Greek patriarch encouraged the Hamlins' neighbors to drive them away by any means, as they had successfully driven the last missionary from Bebek. Though Henrietta and Cyrus had moved into the Seminary building to protect it and its students, small boys threw stones at Henrietta as she passed through the village on her household errands; stones smashed the tiles on their roof at night. In spite of this, the couple persisted. Not for nothing had Cyrus grown up fatherless on a stony Maine farm. He set up a workshop where students might make stoves, rat traps, and other goods for sale to keep themselves fed and clothed. Henrietta opened their home to all visitors, often providing sick-bed care to invalid missionaries. Curious Armenians, Jews, and Greeks would come to watch Cyrus' "Satanic" machines one week, would shyly play with the Hamlins' merry little daughter, "Henrietta the Second," the next, and often enough attend Bible classes, English language classes or Protestant services the third.

Henrietta became fluent in modern Greek, which she found a "beautiful and cultivated language."[82] Gone was the sense of purposelessness that had dogged her since her term at Abbot. She taught three of Cyrus' youngest students herself, served as chief stewardess and counselor for the entire Seminary of over forty boarding students, and cared for her "fat, rosy-cheeked little girl . . . the daily delight of her mother's heart, and the hourly hindrance to her business."[83] While Cyrus' administrative duties increased, Henrietta quietly won the support of the leading Greek and Turkish families of Bebek. The community came to accept the pioneers, even to rely on them to protect its weaker members from the cruelty and excesses of their own officials.

Four more daughters were born, three of whom would later follow Henrietta the Second to Abbot Academy for their secondary education. Wife and children sustained Hamlin—by their playfulness as much as by their practical help—through the years of complex, often dangerous work until Henrietta's weak health overcame her, and she died of tuberculosis on the island of Rhodes in 1850. But the daughters she had raised with such love continued to keep the family's cheerful home, and to care for their small half-sisters after their father's second wife also died. They grew up to attend Abbot and teach school as their mother had done, to marry missionaries or physicians, and carry on their mother's work.

"A Very Liberal Series of Studies"

A woman should study not to shine, but to act.
Catharine Beecher

The 1830's and 40's were exciting times for educators. No longer was secondary-school teaching merely an extension of the ministry or an "adventure" effort by a lone pedagogue who advertised his or her services weekly for perusers of urban newspapers; it had finally become a distinct, self-conscious profession centered in private or public institutions. Academies had proved to be respectable supplements to parental instruction in a society where the discipline of farm work or craft affected ever fewer young people. Even the financial situation was changing for young women's schools: poverty was only a likelihood now, not a foregone conclusion. Several new institutions such as Wheaton Seminary and Mt. Holyoke Female Seminary opened in the 1830's with endowments of over $20,000 that would support matriculation of poorer students. The new Oberlin Collegiate Institute admitted both black and white students, and allowed women to attend classes in "selected higher departments."[1]

Curriculum offerings in many academies and colleges reflected the democratization of learning. Said Robert H. Bishop, the first president of Ohio's Miami University (proudly advertised as a "Farmer's College"), "Literary and scientific knowledge is no longer to be the exclusive property of a few professional men. It is to become the common property of the mass of the human family."[2] Massachusetts boasted few local grammar schools, but these were beginning to respond to the state "high-school law" of 1827, which required them to add "general history, bookkeeping, algebra, geometry, surveying, rhetoric and logic" to their already mandated courses in classics and English. Though Yale professor James Kingsley and President Jeremiah Day stoutly defended the classical curriculum in their famous Yale Report of 1828, shoring up the arguments of the traditionalists at Phillips Academy for the next half century, Abbot and other academies offered far more than the "Latin, Greek and a bit of Mathematics" that one Charles Phelps Taft received at Phillips in 1859.[3]

Mental Discipline and Motherhood

Abbot's early curriculum is outlined in the school's 1844 catalogue.

I. ENGLISH STUDIES

First Year

Fall Term
- Greenleaf's Arithmetic.
- Murray's Grammar.
- Modern and Ancient Geography.
- Ancient History.

Winter Term
- Arithmetic finished.
- Grammar Continued.
- Watts on the Mind.
- Modern History.

Spring Term
- Mrs. Lincoln's Botany.
- Mineralogy.
- Parsing select passages of Poetry.
- Linear Drawing.

Second Year

Fall Term
- Day's Algebra.
- Lane's Physiology.
- Smellie's Philosophy of Natural History.
- Drawing and Pencil Shading.

Winter Term
- Algebra finished.
- Newman's Rhetoric.
- Analysis of Cowper's Task.
- Euclid.

Spring Term
- Euclid finished.
- Gray's Chemistry.
- Burritt's Geography of the Heavens.
- Hitchcock's Geology.

Third Year

Fall Term
- Olmsted's Philosophy.
- Whately's Rhetoric.
- Upham's Intellectual Philosophy.
- Analysis of Thomson's Seasons.

Winter Term
- Wilkin's Astronomy.
- Marsh's Eccl. History.
- Analysis of Paradise Lost.
- Butler's Analogy.

Spring Term
- Whately's Logic.
- Wayland's Moral Philosophy.
- Paley's Natural Theology.
- Landscape Drawing and Painting.

II. LANGUAGES

Latin—Weld's Latin Lessons; Andrews and Stoddard's Latin Grammar, Andrews' Latin Reader; Krebs' Guide for Writing Latin; Nepos; Cicero de Senectute et Amicitia; Virgil; Sallust.

Greek—Goodrich's Greek Lessons, Kühner's Elementary Greek Grammar; Greek Reader; Xenophon's Memorabilia; Homer's Iliad.

French—Collot's Levizac's French Grammar; Collot's French Reader; French

Introduction; De L'Allemagne par Madame De Staël; Telemachus; Charles XII; Henriade.

Italian—Bachi's Italian Grammar; Graglia's Italian Dictionary; Scella di Prose Italiane Conversazione Italiana.

German—Ollendorf's Grammar; Nöhden's Dictionary; Follen's German Reader; Schiller; DeWette's German Bible.

> Young Ladies are admitted to the privileges of the Institution to pursue the studies as marked out above, so far as their time and circumstances will allow.

The subjects and texts here described differ little from those listed in the earliest catalogues, and match the course Asa Farwell continued through 1852. The catalogue goes on to advertise the lectures in chemistry and geology that all members of the school might attend at the English Department of Phillips Academy, successor to the Teachers' Seminary (although Phillips' Classical Department students were severely discouraged from doing the same). Each language bears a charge of 20 cents a week over the $5.00-per-term regular tuition for those students who undertake this "speediest and surest method of attaining that discipline which is the main object of all study." Vocal music and drawing are each about 20 cents extra too, and the twenty-four piano lessons offered every term cost $10.00.

Most of the required texts were widely used in academies and colleges of the time. Watts' *On the Mind*, Butler's *Analogy of Natural and Revealed Religion*, Almira Lincoln's *Botany*,[4] Paley's *Natural Theology*, and Milton's *Paradise Lost*—all were universal favorites in the better schools. Butler and Paley were staples for upperclassmen at Harvard, Yale, and Dartmouth through 1828. Abbot also experimented with some ambitious texts less often offered. Francis Wayland's *Moral Philosophy* was popular in men's colleges, but rarely used by academies in its 1837 college edition. Smellie's *Philosophy of Natural History* delineated a sequence of the emergence of animal forms that anticiapted Darwin's *Origin of the Species*. Colburn's *Arithmetic*, used throughout Abbot's first decade, abandoned mere memory work to emphasize "the processes by which the answer is obtained, and the reason for it."[5] Harriet Woods had always disliked arithmetic, but at Abbot, she wrote, "I became enamored of mental arithmetic, and carried my Colburn's Sequel back and forth from school, trying to puzzle my father and brothers over the examples I had conquered."[6] Another student (Abbot 1840) said Miss Parker "taught me to love geometry above my natural food."[7]

We don't know whether Miss Parker used conic sections cut from turnips to illustrate solid geometry as did Emma Willard, but she undoubtedly agreed with Mrs. Williard that Mathematics was "of prime importance because it would train women to think for themselves in an orderly way, help them impersonalize their problems and solve them on the basis of abstract truth. Women . . . must learn to reason and face a subject."[8] The "mental discipline" imparted by math—as by language study—is offered in the 1830's and 40's as prime justification for almost any subject that might appear initially irrelevant to almost any student. Even "a severe course of the most persistent gerund-grinding,"[9] such as Phillips headmasters Adams and Taylor served up for sixty years, is supposed to "call into vigorous exercise all faculties of the soul."[10] Botany, writes Mrs. Lincoln in the text read by Abbot girls, teaches use of "the laws of association [and] system," which are essential "not only in the grave and elevated departments of science, but . . . . in the most common concerns and operations of ordinary life." Botany thus "has, without a doubt, a tendency to induce in the mind the habit and love of order."[11] Nor is music to be studied for its own sake, but because its "cultivation . . . has a direct tendency to soften the ferocious passions, meliorate the manners, and socialize the discordant feelings of man."[12] Any exacting subject will teach concentration and strengthen the memory; it will build the power of judgment, without which "no lady can make a custard or a cooky," says John Todd in his widely read book *The Daughter at School*.[13]

The "mental discipline" doctrine was as nice an excuse to teach what you please as was the "transfer theory" of the early twentieth century. There's no doubt, however, that it shored up confidence in the value of difficult subjects for women. Not everyone agreed with it. Many traditionalists continued to feel that "the current apology that whatever is good mental discipline for the male sex, is equally so for the female, assumes false ground," as one critic wrote when the argument was still young.

> A woman's station in life is one of *moral* usefulness . . . The studies, then, which should preponderate in female education are those which affect the disposition rather than the intellect . . . Moral excellence should be the great object of all human education; but this is peculiarly true in that of woman, whose offices in life, and whose influence on society, are those of a purer and gentler being.[14]

After all, this "purer and gentler being" was almost sure to be a mother. Her motherhood must be wisely informed, for "the soul of her infant is uncovered before her. She knows that the images which she enshrines in that unpolluted sanctuary must rise before her at the bar of doom."[15]

But Education for Motherhood could be wonderfully extended also. It embraced the natural sciences, through which a woman could teach her little ones observational skills and appreciation of God's creation; it sanctioned the reading and discussion of fine literature. Said William Russell, Abbot's prestigious Oral Reading teacher for over ten years, in an address to the school in 1843: "to recount orally the topics of a useful book is one of the best preparations for intelligent and useful conversation . . . To the female sex, as destined to furnish the mothers and teachers of the human race in the stage of infancy, the power of communicating appropriately, is of inexpressible value . . . If the mother is silent, the soul of the child by her side lies torpid and helpless."[16] Most important was study of the mind itself through logic and "Intellectual Philosophy," guaranteed to help women analyze their children's changing mental patterns and fit maternal instruction to each phase. Thus Abbot's young women spent much of their time on ethics and philosophy in various guises.

Science for Souls

Christian educators like Mrs. Lincoln and Francis Wayland thought of the mind as an extensor of God's original Creation. According to Mrs. Lincoln:

> The Universe, as composed of *mind* and *matter*, gives rise to various sciences. The SUPREME BEING we believe to be *immaterial*, or *pure mind*. The knowledge of *mind* may be considered under two general heads.
> 1. THEOLOGY, or that science which comprehends our views of the Deity and our duties to Him.
> 2. PHILOSOPHY OF THE HUMAN MIND, or *metaphysics*, analyzes and arranges its faculties. The knowledge of *matter* which is the science that investigates the mind of man, and is included under the general term, *Physics*, may be considered under *three general heads*.
> 1. NATURAL PHILOSOPHY, which considers the effects of bodies acting upon each other by their weight and motion.
> 2. CHEMISTRY, in which the properties and mutual action of the elementary atoms are investigated.

3. NATURAL HISTORY, which considers the external forms and characters of objects, and arranges them in classes.[17]

Clearly the study of both mind and matter was a sacred duty. On the other hand, no one pretended that Abbot students' "knowledge of matter" was deep or specialized. Homemade science demonstration equipment was the rule in all academies except Phillips Exeter; physics labs were rare even in colleges. It was difficult to square the study of physiology with "female delicacy." (Characteristically, Emma Willard did her best: her response to the protests of shocked parents was to paste heavy paper over all the offending illustrations in the physiology text.) No Abbot principal that we know of conducted botanizing walks as enthusiastically as educational reformers were advocating them. But field trips were frequent, and the daily excursions up the Hill to the lectures in botany, geology, or other sciences stimulated high interest among some girls, if one can assume that alumnae recollections are colored as much by the lecturers' dramatic demonstrations as by the presence of *young men* in the hall.[18] Samuel Brown imparted his love of astronomy and meteorology to several students, one of whom wrote Miss McKeen that since her Abbot days, "everything connected with the heavens is always interesting." This alumna had been "terribly afraid of lightning till Mr. Brown gave us a lecture one evening."[19]

Pious Andover had a special problem with science. Scientific study might be an amateur affair in most academies—the scientists themselves were often amateurs—but some scientific findings were seriously threatening religious orthodoxy. Moses Stuart, to whom most scholarly dilemmas were food and drink, finally rejected the tortuous analogies drawn by Butler and many others between the thousand, then million years of geological evolution and each biblical day of Creation. Stuart declared that a man must choose between geology and religion. Mrs. Lincoln had an easier time with botany, for she had no doubt that its study "naturally leads to greater love and reverence for the Deity; [for those] who see in the natural world the workings of His power, can look abroad, and adopting the language of a christian poet, exclaim, 'My Father made them all.' "[20] Similarly, William Paley could with good conscience pack his *Natural Theology* with comparative anatomy, botany, entomology, physics, and astronomy once he had introduced the Deity as First Cause and Supreme Watchmaker of the universe. He concludes that because science can only hint at the character of this "stupendous Being,"[21] we must depend on Revelation to complete our understanding. If only one did not look closely, science and religion might stand side by side, but tough-minded reconciliation of the two was more difficult every year.

Pedagogy in a moral universe

Abbot students benefited daily from the pedagogical revolution of the 1830's and 1840's. Class recitations were no longer *memoriter* reproductions of an entire Latin grammar book. (Little Josiah Quincy, an eighteenth-century Phillips student, was sent back to his seat twenty times to get it word perfect.) William Woodbridge and Abbot's William Russell had traveled abroad to observe the Swiss educator Johann Pestalozzi at work in his model school. Their *Journal of American Education*, begun in 1826, was filled with progressive suggestions for teachers. "Let the obsolete system hitherto followed be entirely abandoned," they implored as early as 1827. "Make instruction interesting." Make it "practical; let its relation to business be constantly pointed out; let it be mingled with business . . . Let the natural progress of the mind be consulted. Let knowledge commence at home, and gradually extend itself abroad."[22] This meant beginning with the concrete, and moving toward the abstract. To Abbot Principal Stone, it meant opening a "store" for his younger pupils, to make mental arithmetic a natural part of playful financial transactions. In composition, it was supposed to eliminate favorite essay topics such as "The Right Improvement of Time," or "Happiness." Composition should not be "practised as a separate art, as a thing that can exist apart from the thoughts it is meant to convey."[23]

By 1836 Abbot students were hand-copying and issuing their own magazine, *The Workbasket*. The November 2nd issue contains a stirring story of Greek revolutionaries. The heroic Lysander's children are torn from their peaceful rural existence (where every evening, seated before their dwelling, Xanthe and her brother Alexis "unite their artless voices in a Greek song") by Turkish marauders, who sell them to slave dealers in retaliation for their father's triumphs as partisan leader. It also announces

The Thimble Robbery

> Beware!! Last Friday one of the members of this school had her "indispensible" broken open by one of her associates and despoiled of its contents. Money to the amount of 37½ ¢ was taken . . . and a silver thimble.

That did come close to home. Woodbridge and Russell would have been pleased.

For all the reformers' labors, Abbot teachers' duty to promote moral character retarded full acceptance of the new methods. Harriet Woods, made by "the pretty Miss LeRow" to write a composition ("On

Charity") thought her "brain must have been black and blue with
[that] painful effort. I'm sure my eyes smarted with the effort to keep
back tears." She finally produced a single sentence: "Charity is a good
thing."[24] "No activity [was] outside the holy purpose of the overarching covenant," writes Richard Sewall of nineteenth-century New England puritanism, and every skill taught Abbot girls had to be accompanied by a moral lesson.[25] Abbot teachers could not bring themselves to throw away their grammar books, as progressives advised.
After *Murray's Abridged English Grammar* had brought the student
through a tortuous passage of twenty-two rules pertaining to the In-
finitive, Indicative, Imperative, and Potential moods, it offered pages
of ill-written sentences to correct, such as these didactic gems:

> To do good to them that hate us, and on no occasion to seek re-
> venge, is the duty of a Christian. [pp. 178–179]

> Each of the sexes should keep within their peculiar bounds, and
> content themselves with the advantages of their particular dis-
> tricts. [p. 131][26]

History especially, must elevate and inspire. It was too bad, said one
early critic, that history books were so often written in "formal, uninteresting style," which tended to "deaden the spirit of patriotism
rather than excite it."[27] William Russell joined the reformers who
railed against historical "abridgements and compends."[28] Unfortunately, to inspire may be to distort. It is hard for the late twentieth-century skeptic to understand what credible inspiration can be drawn from
those "ample" volumes Russell endorses, which present history as "the
great treasury of just sentiment, the grand depository of character, the
moral record of the world."[29]

The rhetoric of history and English books often became so elevated
that it left reality behind. Most texts of the time suffered sadly from
their "lofty diction," which students inevitably absorbed into their own
essays. Said a graduate of Coburn's Classical Institute in Maine: "Every
man became a mortal; a horse, a courser or a steed; a glass, a crystal
vase; the moon, Pale Diana."[30] The chief aim of many an instructor
was to teach his students to write like John Milton.

The new pedagogues insisted that all teaching techniques reflect
sound values. Abbot followed the usual practice of evaluating students'
learning through public, oral examinations. For these, remembers Miss
Theodosia Stockbridge,

> the school was attired in uniform, a unique feature of which was
> small black lace caps trimmed with narrow pink lustring ribbon

... [At the] examinations, both dreaded and enjoyed by the pupils, the upper hall, door-way, vestibule, and stairway were literally thronged with Theological, Latin, and English students [from the Hill], with friends from the village and friends from abroad. One of the most formidable ordeals was the drawing of geometrical designs on the blackboards . . . also piano solos, given from the center of [the] platform, and facing the audience.[31]

The Academy boys kept their own texts open on their knees to check every girl's answer for themselves. Examinations made some educators uneasy: they did not square with the prevailing expectations of women, who, unless they were Quakers or (worse) actresses, should not even wish to speak before an audience. One skeptic charged that all exhibitions "were calculated to foster pride, to raise [the scholars] in their own view to men and women before their time."[32] They encouraged emulation, always a suspect motive in the nineteenth century. Like the intricate report cards used at Boston Girls' Latin school, they fostered "rivalry and ambition," said Zilpah Grant.[33] Nevertheless, Abbot continued to hold them throughout its first quarter century.

Abbot's curriculum was above all flexible. Students might "fail" again and again, yet not be asked to leave. In languages they could go as far as they were able beyond the prescribed texts. There were prerequisites, but no requirements; it must have been a disappointment to Abbot's founders that only four girls on the 1831 school rolls had taken enough Latin to be eligible for Greek. Students could enter for a term, then quit. Eighty-three girls attended Abbot some time in 1839, but the Spring term roll was only sixty-four. All female academies shared the problem of the "flitting scholar." Of 1600 students attending Derry and Ipswich under Zilpah Grant, only 156 received diplomas. Abbot gave no diploma at all until 1853.

Reformers bewailed in prose and verse the shallow exposure to a multitude of subjects encouraged by the average female academy. Many felt the more fashionable schools were fitting out intellectual dolls who would know nothing of women's domestic duties. "Madame Cancan's" seminary was a popular caricature. There, Madame Cancan spent

all her skill in moulding her pets
Into very-genteelly-got-up marionettes.
Yes! Puppet's the word; for there's nothing inside
But a clockwork of vanity, fashion and pride!
Puppets warranted sound, that without any falter
When wound-up will go—just as far as the altar;

> But when once the cap's donned with the matronly border,
> Lo! the quiet machine goes at once out of order.[34]

Because of Abbot's solid course offerings and its generally serious atmosphere, Abbot students largely avoided these pitfalls. In addition, the "system of allowing everyone to do that which was right in her own eyes" was exactly what many girls needed.[35] It was only because Elizabeth Emerson so loved wild flowers that Mr. Farwell reluctantly allowed her to take Botany, but she did well in it, and found it an "unbounded delight." When Elizabeth had at last gained the " 'mental discipline' . . . for that truly advanced study, Greenleaf's Arithmetic, the progress through its every problem was a constant rapture."[36] Still, to several of Abbot's Trustees, flexibility implied weakness. For all Abbot's early successes, they looked forward to the day when their Academy could boast a fixed course of study leading to a diploma.

"To Form the Immortal Mind"

Abbot's constitution made the school responsible for each student's soul. Sunday church was required for boarders, the morning service at Andover's South Church, whose Congregationalism was guaranteed pure, the afternoon service at the Seminary chapel on the Hill, where it was purer still. Though Phillips students sat just behind the Abbot contingent in both churches, all communication was proscribed; older girls must "write the sermon" for the principal afterwards to prove they had listened. ("Our Sabbaths had not the element of *rest*," recalled Julia Ann Griggs, Abbot 1839–41, later on.)[37] Wednesday was "free day," but on Wednesday mornings and evenings, roommates were required to leave each other in solitude for a "half-hour" of meditation. Every student received weekly religious instruction. Each one of Abbot's nineteenth-century preceptors would have agreed with Principal Samuel Brown, who told a Dartmouth Centennial audience in 1869 that

> education, to be truly and in the largest sense beneficent, must
> also be religious; must affect that which is deepest in man; must
> lead him, if it can, to the contemplation of truths most personal,
> central, and essential; must open to him some of those depths where
> the soul swings helplessly in the midst of experiences and powers
> unfathomable and infinite, where the intellect falters and hesitates,
> and finds no solution till it yields to faith.[38]

On Andover Hill in 1829, "yielding to faith" meant the personal conversion that Samuel Jackson was urging on his sister Henrietta: a climactic confession of one's utter depravity and helplessness as Adam's seed, along with realization of one's total dependence on God and His Saviour Son. In a much-thumbed book called *the Pastor's Daughter*, found in an Abbot student's library, a minister tells his child's story. "Reader," warns its introduction, "this small volume conducts *you* to the lowly tomb of Susan Amelia, from which, though dead, she speaketh, and bids *you* PREPARE TO MEET YOUR GOD."[39] Susan's private journal shows how she first resisted "surrender to God" at the age of eighteen: "*March 19, 1842.* Spent an hour this morning in reading a *novel*; of such works I am too fond . . . Of course my Bible for this morning was neglected. . . . Would to God I could keep my resolutions." Susan tries to convert her friend Fanny while she works on herself. "Many and severe are the conflicts I have with the destroyer of souls," she writes Fanny; "oftentimes I am nearly overcome, but my Deliverer appears."

Though ill, Susan resolves to become a missionary. She prays every Monday "for the persecuted Christians of Madagascar," every Tuesday "for the Queen of Madagascar." She admits she is a sinner, and that "life is a vapor." Susan's imminent death rallies her friends to Christ's cause, and they pray for a "holy submission" to match hers. Finally Susan dies happy, called away in "perfect peace" to Jesus.[40]

The evangelical Protestant's concern for "the heart and its motivations" combined with his [or her] sense of each soul's infinite worth could lend strength to precarious lives.[41] Good parents began putting pressure on their children to make their "holy submission" at age seven or eight; but the most reliable conversions took place after puberty, stimulated by the young person's general anxiety over physical-emotional changes and life plans. Conversion thus often served to certify the converted as an adult, and it is not surprising that secondary educators felt it their duty to assist in the process.[42] Mary Lyon personally brought a quarter of all her Mt. Holyoke students to Christ. Phillips Headmaster Adams was a "revival man"; Taylor also "savingly converted" many of his boys.[43] The spring of 1840 was a season of powerful religious enthusiasm at Abbot: with the help of some of the good women of the town, who visited and prayed with the girls on recreation days, about fifty conversions were accomplished. Andover's general enthusiasm for conversion could be overdone. Describing Mrs. Porter's "zeal in good works," Samuel Jackson's daughter Susannah recounts a story told her by one of Headmaster Adams' daughters, an

Abbot student at the time: "As she was passing, Mrs. Porter called her in, took her to an upper room, locked her in, saying that herself and Miss Mary Hasseltine from Bradford would spend the day praying for her, and she must pray too. No wonder the little girl yielded more tears than prayers, and ever after took the opposite side of the street in her trips down town."[44] Yet there was no doubt that to "become a Christian" at Abbot (or Mt. Holyoke, or Hartford, or wherever) was to confirm the institution's worth as well as one's own.

But the conversion experience could not be had for the asking. Catharine Beecher struggled in vain for her own and her fiancé's souls: all her father's and brothers' urgings only brought her to nervous collapse after months of family effort. Finally, she, along with many other Americans, rejected the exacting system that condemned the unconverted to join still-born infants and uncatechized children in Hell.[45] One of Miss Beecher's critics wrote that if St. Paul were on earth, he would "discourage the female sex, however gifted and learned, from mixing themselves in theological and ecclesiastical controversies."[46] Andover professor Leonard Woods argued more respectfully with her in print.[47] To no avail. Ironically, the conversions stimulated by revival movements blurred the doctrinal questions which had been so fervently argued on Andover Hill ever since the Seminary opened.[48] By the mid–1840's, many believed with Miss Beecher that Grace could be won by steady good works even though no dramatic inner submission had occurred. Evidence of one's Christianity was no longer an inward change of heart, but a social style.[49] The local pastor, defender against hellfire, seemed less important now. "Conscience" and "character" began to displace conversion as the dominant religious and educational concern.

These changes must have impressed Abbot girls with a new sense of the Christian woman's opportunities. With the (all-male) ministry's slip in status came a gain for women. Not only did women convert in larger numbers than men; they were considered peculiarly adapted to God's work.[50] As mothers, they would "educate not merely a virtuous member of society, but a Christian, an angel, a servant of the Most High."[51] Samuel Jackson's early intuitions about women's special function were being borne out in new social realities. While men grew ever busier with worldly affairs, women had to prepare to become the mainstays of the church, as well as of a Christian home where children would be kept from "the contagion" of money-making as long as possible.[52] Mothers took over the leading of evening prayers in many families. Increasingly, church work and missionary activity were accepted as ways for women to use their talents outside the home—as legitimate and safely conservative escapes from domesticity. Andover Theological

Seminary opposed women's leadership in parish affairs long after mid-western revivalists began inviting it, yet the theologues gladly accepted the tuition support raised for them by church ladies in their own parishes, and after ordination welcomed women's willingness to carry the main burden of Sunday School teaching.[53] It was an ironic affair, this alliance between the minister and the lady, for together they were expected to function as "champions of sensibility"; yet the lady's involvement undermined the minister's traditional hegemony in subtle ways.[54] Her Sunday Schools continued to draw emphasis away from the conversion process which those like Jackson worked so hard to inspire, for they taught not sudden enlightenment but gradual self-mastery.[55] "These women will be in the pulpit next!" exclaimed a New England critic of the new Sunday Schools;[56] and the Massachusetts Council of Congregationalist Ministers formally warned women against carrying their Christian zeal into reform movements that men should lead: "The power of woman is her dependence, flowing from the consciousness of that weakness which God has given her for her protection."[57] But the clergy could not have it both ways, simultaneously inviting women's help within the church and suppressing the radical messages of Christianity. Women church members became troopers for temperance crusades which ministers like Jackson initiated and led; in the West Parish their children made up a "cold water army" and paraded round the parish of a Saturday under the church ladies' eyes. This was all very well until the confidence that women gained from their parish labors was applied to more controversial public affairs such as abolitionism, an issue that would involve many West Parish women and ultimately split the congregation in two.

The American woman's field for Christian action was steadily widening, then. The metaphysical texts Abbot students read seem to have been chosen to follow Catharine Beecher's view that action should take precedence over erudition. "Forming the immortal mind" meant subjecting conscience and character to intellectual scrutiny. Abbot girls studied Francis Wayland's exhaustive rationale of conscience and its God-given authority, instead of the terrifying sermons of Jonathan Edwards with which the theologues were regaled during their meals. Julia Ann Pierce, studying Wayland with twenty-three classmates under a second-year theologue, thought him "very hard";[58] but at least Wayland found a neat way around the conflict between religion and science which hounded the Orthodox. He believed that the startling progress of contemporary science was only more evidence "that a tendency to universal extension has been impressed upon [each branch of knowledge] by its Creator."[59] Religion remains primary because it "fosters a love of truth," wrote Wayland.[60] To prove how this reasoning works, he deftly blended Biblical sanction with liberal thought in one grand system of "practical ethics," justifying gradual abolition of slavery, enjoyment of sexual intercourse within marriage, liberty of the press, and a multitude of benevolent projects to aid the poor. His twentieth-century editor, Joseph Blau, points to the "arrogance in the way in which Wayland uses God as the cosmic guarantor of whatever Wayland believes."[61] Surely Abbot's teachers sympathized, however. In their less pretentious ways, most of them were doing the same thing.

Abbot reached the 1850's with solid experience on which to build. Despite flitting scholars and flitting principals, its course of study had remained remarkably stable. Compromises with the original high academic ideals were surely made, but Abbot remained, said William Russell with emphasis, an *academy*: it allowed its students the rewards of "uninterrupted mental application" rather than diverting them to study of needlework or other domestic arts. Russell felt proud of Abbot's having avoided the "universal ridicule" that greeted the "encyclopedic" curricula of many girls' schools. He praised Abbot's concern with "actual proficiency" and its scorn of "extensive and perhaps superficial cultivation."[62]

Furthermore, Abbot was clear of debt at last. Upon receipt of Madam Sarah Abbot's legacy in 1850, Samuel Farrar, that "good old, wrinkled, immemorial squire," as Oliver Wendell Holmes called him, resigned from the Board of Trustees.[63] "Our debts are all honorably paid," Farrar wrote his colleagues. He blessed "a kind Providence" for sustaining him through "so many years of anxious solicitude," and allowing him to witness "so happy a result."[64] As one of Abbot's chief creditors, Farrar must have felt even more relief than he expressed. A last-minute drama over the Sarah Abbot legacy bears recounting, for it had put $2000 of the expected $10,000 in jeopardy. Soon after Madam Abbot finally died in 1848, Lucretia Johnson, widow of the short-lived and highly promising Phillips Principal Osgood Johnson, made a $2000 claim on the Abbot estate to compensate her for her care of the old lady during the last three years of her life.[65] Madam Abbot was "intemperate" as well as ill, claimed Mrs. Johnson, and thus could do almost nothing for herself.[66] The widow Johnson lived just across Main and School streets from Mrs. Abbot in what is now called "Samaritan House" in her honor; she had kept her family out of the poor farm by nursing sick students and townspeople for small pay. Good neighbor she had been, but she had to be paid.[67]

Mrs. Johnson never got her $2,000. All Abbot's Trustees rallied to protect the founding donor's reputation and the school's legacy. Mrs. Abbot had told her friends, "I pay Mrs. Johnson as I go along,"—though Mrs. Johnson disputed this. The friends insisted that she had also given Mrs. Johnson clothes, furniture, and household goods; most important, she had paid some or all of the Phillips Academy tuition for one of the Johnson boys after his father's death. It seems that Madam Abbot thought Mrs. Johnson's care of her was done "as a neighborly kindness," and never worried herself about formal payment.[68] Witnesses for the Probate Court insisted, furthermore, that they "never saw Madam Abbot disguised" [in drink] or "intoxicated" although she did use "spirits."[69] If old Sarah Abbot was a little too fond of liquor, we shall never know it for certain.

So Abbot got its $10,109.04 and paid off its debt of twenty-two years, and the documents that revealed more than Abbot's later admirers wanted to know of a good woman's failing years were tucked away in a cupboard. Whatever we may think of the justice of the outcome, the efficiency with which the case was resolved and then covered up testifies to the strength of the Academy's corporate character and of those wily, faithful Trustees who came with it. This was no fly-by-night "adventure" school, but an institution with plans to continue, come what might.[70]

Solid Acquirements, 1852-1892

In the forty years from 1852 to 1892, Abbot Academy passed from uncertain adolescence to adulthood. The local day school with its catch-
as-catch-can arrangements for out-of-town students became a nation-
ally known boarding school. The parade of men principals gave way
to a shorter parade of women; then in 1859 the Misses Philena and
Phebe McKeen arrived. The sisters were to make Abbot their home,
and give it the rest of their lives.

Before the school could fully benefit from the McKeens' committed
leadership, however, there was a period of swift, unexpected transi-
tions: Abbot had to face a local crisis of competition from a new public high school, then the national crisis of Civil War. Meanwhile, the
Trustees met the happier challenge of finding and keeping the McKeen
sisters. The McKeens ushered in a kind of golden age full three decades long during which Abbot prospered as never before, an era to
which, later, more harried generations would look back with both
envy and gratitude.

Mid-Century Transitions

We were told by the historian that
the age of lords has gone out, and
the age of ladies has come in.
J. B. Bittinger, 1879

The 1850's were pivotal years for New England education, as they were for the life of the nation. Like most private academies, Abbot glided easily into them down the way established by the confident (if penurious) forties; but the year 1860 found the school changed, forced by circumstances into a new mold.

Much happened that the Trustees could not have foreseen. They had planned, for example, to replace Asa Farwell with yet another man. "Andover was a masculine place . . . used to eminent men," wrote Elizabeth Stuart Phelps of this time. "At the subject of eminent women, the Hill had not yet arrived."[1] Abbot's male Trustees duly elected to the vacant post Peter Smith Byers, a brilliant assistant teacher at Phillips Academy—the only brilliant one in the thirty-eight years of Taylor's administration, says Claude Fuess.[2] Byers first accepted, then took a closer look. Concluding that Abbot's boarding arrangements were inadequate, he withdrew. The Trustees tried to lure Ipswich Seminary's principal and his wife to Abbot. Politely, the couple refused.

Meanwhile, Abbot was being ably led by two acting principals, first Mrs. Susan Hutchinson, then Miss Abby W. Chapman. Mrs. Hutchinson was a young widow whose major education had been the discipline of misfortune. Early on, her father became "imbued with the then prevailing spirit of speculation in Maine lands"[3] and lost the money he had planned to spend on Susan's schooling. She learned enough to support herself by teaching elementary school, then married. But her husband died of consumption while she was sickening with child-bed fever; her infant died, and she was so much weakened in spite of her "grand and stately" appearance that her health could not stand the rigors of her Abbot work for more than half a year. While she was there, she proved extraordinarily kind, capable, and good-humored. "The crude efforts of her pupils, exciting her mirthfulness, aided her in manifesting the needed patience," wrote her teacher-biographer, who knew that teachers must either laugh or give up.

Mrs. Hutchinson ended Mr. Farwell's military drill, substituting reels, winding-circle dances, and calisthenics performed with "backwands" held between the shoulder blades to encourage perfect posture. Abby Chapman carried on these innovations, proving equally competent if not so colorful. Enrollment stayed high with an average of ninety-five students each term, 150 for the year.

That Abbot's women teachers and students could continue to prosper during this rudderless year of 1852–53 is testimony to the school's basic durability. It is worth pausing to take a look at one indicator of educational vitality at the time: *The Experiment,* a hand-copied school newspaper "published" in the summer of 1853. As the *Andover Advertiser* reported with mock anxiety about this new competitor, "subjects of vital importance from 'Mother Goose's Melodies' to the invasion of Turkey and the probable consequences of a war, were discussed in a manner worthy of diplomatists."[4] "Foreign Intelligence"[5] reporter Hattie Stowe also kept subscribers informed of her parents' activities; the Seminary's newly arrived Professor Calvin Stowe and his wife Harriet Beecher Stowe were touring Europe, keeping tabs on the London publishers of *Uncle Tom's Cabin,* speaking to British anti-slavery societies, "and creating quite a sensation in Scotland."[6]

The Experiment is a bursting trunk of girl thoughts, girl jokes, and young-woman dreams, eighty pages long. Poems, solemn memorials to dead friends, articles on intemperance, and book reviews (on Thackery's latest novel, on a collection of antislavery essays) are interspersed with riddles, mock political news of 1864, a gossip column, playful autobiographies (of a broom, of a piece of sheet music), lists of spurious marriages—

> AT INK FARM, June 16th, by Rev. Mr. Merciful, Mr. Worthy
> Caution to Miss Prudence Heedlessness

and advertisements—

a new Saloon offers four kinds of ice cream: Catnip, Spearmint, Wormwood and Horseradish.

Information wanted
Lost: Dropped out of a second story window, a small child about two years old.

Found: A bundle of disconnected ideas (believed to be those advertised as lost in the last issue). Finder attempted to make use of them but without success.

The hard-pressed editors must have needed some hilarity to keep them at their copy-work. New subscriptions were always wanted, "terms reasonable." The quality of writing is high, the syntax over-elegant but orderly, the spelling impeccable, the penmanship incredible to observers from this typewriter age.

Mrs. Hutchinson's and Miss Chapman's success seems to have given the Trustees the last proof they required of women's ability as educators. After all, Mt. Holyoke had never needed a man. Bradford Academy near Haverhill had been booming for years under Abigail Hasseltine, with over 200 girls enrolled. The proportion of women teachers to men in Massachusetts was on its way from 60 percent in 1850 to 86 percent in 1860.[7] The Trustees knew that action must be taken. It was midsummer, and Abbot must open on August 31, 1853.

Open it did, with two major changes. The Trustees not only installed as Abbot's ninth principal Miss Nancy J. Hasseltine, the energetic niece and protégée of Bradford's Abigail; they also gave up all that was left of Farrar's Yankee scheme for keeping principals on their toes and Trustees off the hook. They offered Miss Hasseltine a firm salary of $500, and took on themselves the full financial risk of the school.[8] Miss Hasseltine arrived fresh from the principalship of a school in Townsend, Massachusetts, bringing with her a crowd of Townsend pupils and "three valuable teachers."[9] With great energy, she set about organizing the school. She found Abbot familiar. Bradford and Abbot had competed for a similar constituency since 1829. Bradford's own new principal, Rebecca Gilman, was an Abbot graduate. Sixty-eight girls had attended both Abbot and Bradford, finding Bradford perhaps a bit more straitlaced under the aging Abigail Hasseltine, but otherwise much the same.

Young Miss Hasseltine worked a quiet revolution in her two-and-a-half year tenure. If men had managed Abbot well, she would manage Abbot better. She strengthened the curriculum, systematizing the English course with the help of her Associate Principal, Miss Mary Blair, and offering English and French "certificates" to Seniors who had fulfilled set course requirements. She was "full of strength and cheerfulness," wrote Miss Blair years later.[10] While supervising her assistants and keeping most of the school's business affairs in order, she taught five or six hours each day. The women in the Bible became heroines in her hands. "An empress!" exclaimed one alumna.[11] But she was an empress with a sense of humor. She jollied into action the girls who turned sullen under her usual firm handling; one alumna remembered "many small kindnesses to unattractive students."[12] She took for her own roommate "one of the most care-requiring children in school."

"Delightfully vigorous and breezy," she had both "a very strong hand" and "that peculiar power of making the right popular."[13] The Trustees' Examining Committee reported in July 1854 that "happiness in well-doing seems to be general." They found the Bible exercise impressive, and praised the Virgil translations. "We regard it as a prominent peculiarity and excellence of this school [they wrote] that the pupils are taught to think for themselves."[14]

As soon as she arrived, Miss Hasseltine told the Trustees what they already knew: Abbot must have its own dormitory. More than a matter of convenience, this had become a matter of survival. In 1850 Benjamin Punchard of Andover had died, leaving $50,000 in his will, with $20,000 more after his wife's death, to found a free high school for the young men and women of his town. Almost immediately after saying "No" to the Abbot principalship, the talented Peter Smith Byers had said "Yes" to the Punchard High School one.[15] A building was being erected within easy walking distance of Abbot, to open in 1856.

Fitting it was that Andover, the "New England Athens,"[16] should undertake to provide free to all what Abbot and Phillips had been offering to the many for a fee—even if a low one. Punchard School was an early prototype of the burgeoning number of public high schools which would gradually bring the age of the academies to an end.[17] Inertia would be fatal to any academy with hopes for a future: Abbot must change its spots if it would continue to be useful. Shortly after Miss Hasseltine came, therefore, the Trustees "*Resolved*, That it is indispensable to the prosperity, and even perpetuity of the Academy, to raise the sum of eight thousand dollars in order to procure suitable accommodations for the boarding of pupils."[18]

Several Trustees went straight to work. Still convinced that "the chief ground of reliance aside from religion" for any community "is the general education of the people," Samuel Jackson had resigned his pulpit in 1850 to pursue his broad educational interests as Assistant State Librarian and Secretary to the Massachusetts Board of Education.[19] He had long foreseen that Abbot must become a boarding school in order to continue its mission, and he could still work heartily for a private school that could supplement public educational opportunities, knowing that thousands of American communities had no high schools. With its low fees, Abbot could remain attractive to students from the many high schools that locked their student clients into the social niches already defined for them by birthplace and parentage.[20] The backing of two newer Trustees—Theological Seminary professor Edwards A. Park and Board President Peter Smith, Esquire—[21] also proved crucial, coming as it did from men of opposite back-

3. Edwards Amasa Park, Trustee and preacher to Andover Hill, 1851–1900. Photograph from Abbot Archives. Originals of all illustrations may be found in Abbot Archives, unless otherwise noted.

4. Deacon Peter Smith, Trustee, and donor, with his brother, of Smith Hall. From Memorial to Peter Smith.

grounds. Both were parents, Park of one Abbot daughter, Smith of nine. Park was the last of the great blue-blood Calvinist theologians, Smith a Scottish immigrant and highly successful member of Andover's rising industrialist class. Park's elaborate education had prepared him for life in a shadow-world of contending ideas. As professor of Hebrew, Sacred Rhetoric, and later Christian Theology at Andover Theological Seminary, 1836–82, he was a "superb scholar," a "royal preacher,"[22] and a devastating opponent in logical argument, for he invariably "tried to arrange things so that he could have the last word."[23] His favorite advice to both theologues and Abbot students: "Whenever you meet a ghost, examine him." Meanwhile, Peter Smith's day was spent seeing to the welfare of the operatives in the prosperous Smith brothers' flax mills, ordering new machinery or hiring new workers from Scotland.[24] "A stranger to pride,"[25] Smith had hesitated to accept election to Abbot's Board because of his "want of literary knowledge," but he finally agreed to serve "in any way that will promote Knowledge, Virtue and Religion."[26]

Each in his own way, Park and Smith confirmed Abbot's character. Edwards Park would be Abbot's link through half a century with the old Calvinist tradition, which measured man's capacity for both piety and sinfulness on a grand scale, and spoke to the soul in a language of awful beauty. Park's fame fed the Academy's pride. Even such a skeptic as Emily Dickinson found herself amazed by his intellectual power the first time she heard him preach in Amherst.[27] For years after he became too old to take an active part in the Trustees' work, he remained the Board President, and every Abbot graduate received her diploma from his hand. Peter Smith, the self-made man, found Abbot, the self-made school, congenial. He knew what struggle was, having worked steadily as farmhand and millhand since the age of eight to support his widowed mother. He accepted the terms on which the canny survive, admiring and enhancing all that was practical in Abbot Academy.

Smith backed with his money the move to transform Abbot from day school to boarding school. When he saw that his initial challenge gift of $1000 challenged practically no one, he and his brother John together first loaned, then gave over $5500 more to meet nearly the whole cost of the dormitory themselves. Like several of their later contributions to the institutions of Andover Hill, the Smith brothers' gift was a tribute to Samuel Jackson, for so many years their pastor at West Parish Church.[28] Though Jackson himself had no money to spare, he was a magnet for others' wealth. Under his persuasion, a few other Trustees and parents finally yielded the rest of the $7033.64 required, but Abbot's tight-fisted constituents could hardly quarrel with the Trustees' name for the new building: Smith Hall.[29]

Smith Hall was a large wooden box divided into about thirty rooms, each twelve feet by twelve feet, with a dining room, kitchen, music room, and matron's apartment on the first floor. At first it was an empty, useless box, for its construction had more than exhausted available funds. Into this vacuum stepped the wives and mothers, led by Caroline True Jackson and Harriet Beecher Stowe. Mrs. Stowe knew how to raise money for the furnishings: "We must have a festival," she reportedly told Mrs. Jackson.[30] At first the idea seemed outlandish—but then, so did many of Mrs. Stowe's ideas. If Professor Park and other high priests of the Hill grumbled that her trips to the Boston theater and her merry, popular levees led to "dissipation for the students" (at one party, a *Christmas tree* was displayed), much of Andover approved her "glowing enthusiasm."[31] To southern critics, *Uncle Tom's Cabin* was a "desecration of woman's nature,"[32] but Mrs. Stowe's friends knew her as "the most unselfish and loving of Mothers."[33] About thirty-five ladies, including representatives from each of Andover's Protestant churches and Mrs. Park, met in the Academy Hall to hear her "telling speech"[34] in favor of Abbot's first Bazaar. Quickly they organized, and on the evening of September 29, 1854, greeted throngs of the curious, the generous, and the eager-to-be-seen at fifty cents admission apiece (about $6.00 in 1978 currency). The Academy Hall was transformed by flowers indoors and Japanese lanterns outside, the last hung by Phillips Academy boys. Richly appointed tea and coffee tables offered free beverages; Mrs. Stowe poured, wearing a gold bracelet in the form of a slave's shackle, commissioned for her by the Duchess of Sutherland.[35] Oysters, ice cream, and endless baked goods were presented for sale. Two thousand dollars was raised in all, enough to buy furniture for every room and equipment for the kitchen and dining room, everything "plain and cheap."[36] Local merchants sold these goods to Abbot at generous discounts, along with materials for curtains and slipcovers, which the ladies sewed themselves in the weeks following the festival.

Miss Hasseltine strove consciously to make her school worthy of all this help. As Annie Sawyer Downs would write years later, "If (Abbot) was born in 1829, it was born again in 1853" when the Hasseltine years began.[37] Smith Hall made it possible to offer board, washing, and pew-rent for $2.50 a week from 1854 to 1862, more than the pittance paid by the Commons-dwellers both at Abbot in the 1840's and at Phillips next door, but still a moderate sum to match the tuition charges of $6.00 or $7.00 a term. (Piano lessons were $10.00 extra, Latin $3.00,

French $5.00, and a "Course of Lessons in Wax Flowers" was $3.00 a term.) Increasingly, girls stayed the full forty-week year, paying about $140.00 for all regular expenses. With the building of Smith Hall, Abbot had become a "school-home" (the term is used again and again after 1854), a self-contained community run by women for women which left much less of students' lives to chance than had the earlier, more casual day school.[38] Head matron Mrs. H. B. Willard was assisted by Mrs. Angelina Kimball, who would herself become head matron in 1860 and stay forty years. Resident teachers helped them manage the large household. Mrs. Kimball was a jolly, efficient woman with whom secrets were always safe—and thus she heard a great many of them. Bridget the cook ruled in the kitchen, regularly sneaking pieces of pie up the back stairs to her favorite girls, no matter what economies the Trustees might order her to make.

The Trustees' description of Smith Hall as a "commodious and costly building"[39] might seem exaggerated to the students who lived in those tiny bare rooms and felt the winter in their bones during those first ten years without a furnace, but "we were happy and content," remembers an early resident.[40] Nor was Smith Hall quite the "still and secluded home" the Trustees imagined.[41] A decade before its construction, there was exactly one piano in all of Andover;[42] Smith Hall soon had two of its own. The girls danced in the music room while waiting for their mail each day, and on summer afternoons aspiring young pianists enjoyed the unseen presence of an appreciative male audience: the Phillips boys boarding in the two houses that flanked Abbot on School Street. Students from ten years of age to twenty-two or three made the dormitory a lively place. It was a new experience for the many hailing from rural and small-town New England to meet such as the four Stowell sisters, who had come from San Francisco for schooling in New England. With the building of Smith Hall, out-of-class experience became central to an Abbot education.

Abbot's enrollment rose to 212 in 1856. It was 185 in the recession year of 1857, while Bradford's roll was dropping alarmingly from 209 in 1855 to 125 in 1857. Bradford did not learn the dormitory lesson until 1868. Abbot's numbers soon leveled off, but the pattern of enrollments changed significantly during Miss Hasseltine's tenure and the decade following her resignation. Punchard High School gradually took Abbot's place as Andover's major secondary school for local girls. In Miss Hasseltine's first year, 94 of her 169 students were Andover or North Andover girls, 56 percent of the total; the number declined only slightly through 1856 when Punchard actually opened after a delay complicated by Peter Smith Byers' untimely death. By the fall of 1858, however, the Punchard Trustees had found an extraordinarily capable principal in William Goldsmith, Harvard A.B. Goldsmith organized the school into four classes. With the help of his assistants, including Abbot alumnae Rebecca Nourse and Sarah Loring Bailey, he taught most of the subjects Abbot offered and some others besides: Butler's *Analogy*, Trigonometry, one year of French, "Uranography" (star mapping), and, to those few students anxious for classics instruction, Xenaphon and Homer as well as Latin through Virgil. During Punchard's first three years, seven or eight Abbot girls left the Academy to attend the High School each year, among them Mary S. Nourse, one of Abbot's most talented students, who used her one year at Abbot to prepare for the classical course at Punchard; but the transfers dwindled as the years went on, undoubtedly because more local students went straight from elementary school to the high school. By 1865, the year Abbot's minimum day scholar tuition jumped from twenty-four dollars to thirty-two dollars and twenty-five cents, the local student enrollment had fallen to 16 percent of the total (27 out of 167).

There are some curious twists to this story. Several students finished their education at Abbot *after* trying Punchard. Youngest daughters of two fathers active in the 1848 protest against Farwell preferred Abbot over Punchard. Ellen Punchard, daughter of the High School's founder, spent five years at Abbot before finishing in 1863—and is not listed on the Punchard rolls at all.[43] As far as can be told from scanty records, none of the Punchard Trustees except Edward Taylor, an Abbot Trustee from 1859 to 1870, had daughters at Abbot, but the venerable Squire Farrar helped draw up organizational plans for the High School shortly before he died. The two schools would remain on speaking terms and better for many years. After Punchard's opening, however, there were to be far fewer efforts to accommodate the Academy to the local clientele and fewer brakes applied to tuition raises. The advent of Andover's first public high school pushed Abbot to take its own more independent course as boarding school.[44]

Principal Hasseltine believed in women. She made her teachers colleagues rather than mere assistants, consulting them often on disciplinary and curricular decisions, a practice Phillips Academy's "Uncle Sam" Taylor eschewed as compromising to his supreme authority. Her teachers seem to have been eminently worthy of this responsibility. Miss Blair was a true scholar, "the first teacher to send me to original sources," wrote a student who went on to Wheaton College.[45] This patient and sensitive woman "taught everything as if that was her favorite study."[46] Samuel Jackson's daughter Susannah, Abbot '51, proved "a remarkable teacher," recalled Marion Park. She was more than smart; she was "kind, public-spirited," and possessed of "a tremendous sense of duty."[47] No men teachers need apply to the Abbot of the fifties. With the exception of an occasional visiting lecturer such as the renowned geography professor Arnold H. Guyot from Harvard, and two part-time music instructors in 1856, Abbot relied on its own women. Miss Hasseltine severed all formal teaching connections with Theological Seminary students and professors, and put a stop to the daily trips up the Hill to lectures on science or literature at the Phillips Academy English Department. After her marriage in 1856, her successors Maria J. B. Browne and the competent Emma Taylor, sister of "Uncle Sam," successfully maintained the distance thus measured out between Abbot and the Hilltop.

Why this change? Miss Hasseltine could have simply been copying Bradford, her old family school, which had been decidedly single-sex for two decades. But there is a subdued militancy in her actions which makes one wonder to what degree the new Abbot women were moved by the push for women's suffrage that characterized the 1840's and 50's. Had any of them heard or read Elizabeth Cady Stanton's speech at the Seneca Falls convention in 1848?

> Woman herself must do this work; for woman alone can understand the height, the depth, the length and the breadth of her degradation.[48]

Occupational opportunities were widening once again. True, pioneers like Elizabeth Blackwell, physician, Maria Mitchell, astronomer, and Jane Swisshelm, newspaper publisher, might be more notorious than they were respected, for the numbers of professional women were still tiny; but their success inspired thousands of young women to reach for the training they would need to do such work themselves. Susannah Jackson recalls Harriet Beecher Stowe's telling girls that "women should do whatever their gifts qualified them to do."[49] Although no woman suffragists had yet appeared in Andover, the antislavery movement made women a political force to be reckoned with. Mrs. Stowe was only its most famous adherent; there were others like Caroline True Jackson, who supported Essex County antislavery societies with far too much verve to suit her colonizationist husband Samuel. Similarly, the temperance movement began educating women citizens long before women voters existed.

Here is a paradox: While a few women were demanding entry into man's world, many Americans shared a new consensus emphasizing the *differences* between men's and women's roles, a view to which Abbot may have been responding.[50] It is ironic but probably not coincidental that the fifties should hold side by side the expansion of women's opportunities and the early-Victorian retreat back into the home. While the first half of the nineteenth century saw an absolute increase in women's political and economic activities outside the home, they lost real power relative to men. This was a time of dramatic expansion of manhood suffrage, and a girl's chance to work in a mill for low wages was small compensation for woman's loss of responsibility for basic production. New England had completed the "transition from mother and daughter power to water and steam power," said Horace Bushnell in 1851.[51] Men wanted—and took—the new supervisory and professional jobs. Many of the stronger sex panicked on hearing the suffragist rhetoric; it was much to their interest to put women back in their places. Too, women themselves often feared the clamor of the marketplace or the hustings as much as men feared their competition within them, especially as the end of the decade added economic panic to wrenching political cleavages. Better (thought many) to accept the power trade-off implied by Horace Bushnell in his popular book *Christian Nurture:*[52] as wife and mother of immortal souls, woman must be supreme in the home while man remains supreme in the world at large. A "cult of true womanhood" had gradually evolved between 1820 and 1860, as historian Barbara Welter asserts. Man, the "busy builder," "occasionally felt some guilt that he had turned this new land, this temple of the chosen people, into one vast counting-house. But he could salve his conscience by reflecting that he had left behind a hostage, not only to fortune, but to all the values which he held so dear and treated so lightly. Woman . . . was the hostage in the home."[53] Within that home, one German visitor observed, "Woman is the center and the lawgiver, and the American man loves it so."[54] According to another, woman's status in society was certified by men's "limitless respect [for] and boundless submission" to "The Ladies!"[55] Thus in the 1820's Catharine Beecher had stood for woman's right to an education equaling that of her brothers, while in the fifties Miss Beecher more often exalted "Woman's Profession" as the manager of family and household. Even more than her sister Harriet—who at least gave lip service to woman suffrage—Miss Beecher had shied from the logic which asserted that women's proven ability to pursue equal education entitled her to equal political rights; instead she urged her contemporaries toward acceptance of a legally subordinate role. Women's self-sacrifice would help to create a new national ethic to balance the rampant self-seeking that characterized men's affairs.[56]

Whatever Miss Hasseltine's views on sexual equality, her successors fell in line with Victorian convention. The 1857 catalogue pledged Abbot "not only to develop and invigorate the *intellectual* growth, but also to refine and soften the *manners*, cultivate the *moral affections*, and mould into symmetrical proportions the entire character." The Commencement speaker of 1858 chose "Women's Rights" as his topic, and warned the Abbot students not to assert them: "Every female of delicacy must revolt at finding herself in contaminating contact with the influences of the polls," lest she "be placed in conflict and on a level with every blackguard."[57] The queenly Maria Browne advised her graduating Seniors to welcome the difference between their own futures and the "active life" open to male graduates of "classic halls." From men's "grand activities divine Wisdom has excluded *you* . . . The miserable contest upon equality of power and place is vain, and idle, and preposterous. God has written the answer to the question with his own finger upon the very constitution of woman." She is not "an independence," but "a co-operating power."[58] For the time being, the cult of true womanhood had won out.

Such sentiments came naturally to Miss Browne, who had been teaching belles lettres[59] to young ladies in Virginia when she was called to Abbot for the 1856–57 school year. Her successor Emma Taylor did nothing to challenge them. "Lovely in character, with the culture that comes from travel, she was the material of which noble, true, forgiving friends are made," wrote Elizabeth Emerson, '56, who had needed forgiving friends as a novice teacher under Miss Taylor. Miss Taylor specialized in women's specialties. She organized the study of art by using photographs she had brought back from Europe; she further enriched the literature offerings. And as she was later to record, just before she left Abbot to return to Adams Academy, "We were blessed with a revival of religion, and quite a number became Christians . . . A citizen remarked of one of the converts that he would know by her walk on the streets that a change had taken place."[60] The revival spirit might be waning among Congregationalists and Presbyterians elsewhere; not so on Andover Hill.

The McKeens Arrive

Abbot Academy was flourishing, but the Trustees were having no better luck holding the female principals of the fifties than they had the male ones of the thirties. By 1859, the Board was determined to find a committed woman who would not marry, like Miss Hasseltine, or leave for a more comfortable position, like the misses Browne and Taylor. To their surprise and satisfaction, they finally found not one such person, but two. Philena and Phebe McKeen came to Abbot as Principal and Assistant Principal from Western Female Seminary in Oxford, Ohio, where they had been teaching together since that institution had been founded "upon the Holyoke Plan" in 1855.[61]

Given their ages—thirty-seven and twenty-eight—one might suppose that Philena and Phebe McKeen had long ago left behind their original home in Bradford, Vermont; both women had been teaching in schools and boarding seminaries from the age of sixteen. But ages deceive. Throughout their lives, the sisters carried within them memories of their home life and powerful images of the ideal family that shaped their work at Abbot. In their hands, the "school-home" became also the "family," an ever-larger company whose values mirrored those instilled in these two, the fourth and the youngest of seven children, by their parents and by the circumstances of the simple farming community in which they grew up. Indeed, Philena had never attended a formal school: her minister father had taught her himself, consciously turning every conversation into a lesson. A benevolent authoritarian, Silas McKeen "never allowed an ungrammatical expression to escape correction."[62] Furthermore, he urged his children always to put their imaginations into words, himself delighting in speaking to trees and stones, each according to its special character, when he took his daughters on long drives around his parish. Any child might be commanded at dinner time to "address a table," or "address a vine."[63] He took personal responsibility for each child's religious conversion; he taught his older daughters to read the New Testament in the original Greek at a time when Greek was considered impossibly difficult for any girl to learn. To Abbot, Philena and Phebe brought the unquestioned assumption that "beyond learning was character, that religion was indeed the chief end and aim of life," and that all students and teachers should rejoice in the opportunity to serve others.[64]

Above all, both sisters learned from their parents to educate themselves. To them, teaching and learning were companion processes. Phebe's three-year tenure as instructor at Mt. Holyoke was especially stimulating to her. Philena liked to say that "Whatever I study I become interested in,"[65] and whatever interested her she taught to others. Each summer vacation from Abbot, Phebe would take up her writing, and Philena would immerse herself in Bible study, or in the history of art, bringing fresh ideas to her students in the fall. Philena was the more serious of the two. "She was a wonderful listener," wrote one of her young colleagues,[66] with a "lucid and logical mind" which brooked

5. *"The binary star"; Philena and Phebe McKeen, 1864.*

no obstacles.[67] As teacher, wrote a pupil and colleague, she "sought not merely facts and dates, but required opinions . . . Before her clear-sighted inspection, mere fluency disappeared."[68] She brought a profusion of visual materials to the classroom to illustrate her lectures, yet she never said or did anything merely for effect. She was a practical person, and deliberate show was wasteful.

Philena McKeen—always "Miss McKeen" to her students—was large-framed, tireless, certain of her authority. Marion Park, who tagged along as a child of eight or nine on carriage rides with her grandmother Park and Miss McKeen, remembered her size, and her frightening way of asking small children questions to which she already knew the answers. "Miss Phebe" was taller, slimmer, with quick black eyes behind spectacles, eyes that missed nothing. She had a brilliant mind, as well as a "mordant wit"[69] ready to turn upon the student with the shoddy answer. A sensitive, lively writer, her published novels and stories reflect her joy in nature—a gift of her father and of long childhood rambles in the mountains near her home—and her complex perceptions of other people.[70] *Theodora, a Home Story* is partly about her girlhood; it is an intricate novel that is constantly overflowing the boundaries of conventional religious fiction. Abbot alumnae absorbed Phebe's holy enthusiasm for the "sparkling snow" and the "mellow, fragrant" summer "because in the excellence of your wisdom you made us go out to look at these things every single day of our lives."[71] They remembered her extraordinary skill in conversation and her teaching of Chaucer and Horace. Through her encouragement, her students came to feel "that they too were worthy to read Milton and Wordsworth."[72] Her greatest power as a teacher seems to have been her open love for and interest in every one of her girls. The older ones were as sisters, the younger as daughters.

Philena McKeen drew for herself on Phebe's love. Clearly they were to each other much of what husband and wife can become; each had also that rich comfortableness in the other's company that only siblings can share. They were often referred to as "the Principals" of Abbot Academy[73] or, as Professor Park called them, Abbot's "binary star."[74]

One of the first things the Trustees said to Miss McKeen was that "she must be content with what she had," recalled Marion Park. "But she was never content for a single moment, and from her discontent rose the Academy itself."[75] Smith Hall might be adequate for now, but the worn Academy building, its walls smoked gray by many whale-oil lamps and nearly bare of pictures or other ornament, the tiny shelf of books that was Abbot's entire library (a pitiful contrast to Bradford's 1500 volumes), the empty equipment closets—all cried out for improvement. Miss McKeen had a bit of the hustler in her: if this was to be her home, she would fix it up in a manner that befitted her station, no matter how low her salary at first. As she wrote much later, "We began to devise, as women will."[76]

The Principal ordered that all waste paper be saved and sold to buy framed pictures for the classrooms. She and her teachers mounted a series of lectures and entertainments, for which admission was charged. One was a cantata, "The Haymakers," the parts sung and acted by Abbot girls and theological students who raked real hay in a performance so near to a stage play that one Seminary professor took his daughter and walked out in disdain. Another was a charades party with both Phillips boys and theologues as guests. (The theologues played crows in one skit, flapping their umbrella wings.)[77] For a good cause, Hilltop males were now welcome at Abbot once more, and thus Miss McKeen found funds for carpets and for classroom whitewashing. When she surveyed the motley drawerful of Smith Hall spoons—a few silver teaspoons left behind by old scholars, plus a ghastly matched set of cheap alloy dessert spoons provided by the Trustees—she invited the Board to tea. The dessert spoons had an annoying tendency to upset the teacups, but Miss McKeen wiped up efficiently and kept the conversation going; shortly afterward, Trustee George Davis sent a set of seven dozen monogrammed silver spoons to Abbot Academy for the use of the Smith Hall family.

In spite of her energy as collector of goods, Miss McKeen probably had no more material pretensions than anyone else in Victorian America. Abbot's setting was in many ways congenial to simple tastes. The sisters' small-town background made them deeply suspicious of city life with its "mad scramble for money and place . . . wretchedness and luxury mocking each other," as Miss Phebe wrote in *Theodora*.[78] "There are no 'servants' in Vermont,"[79]—and though there was abundance of Protestant pride at Abbot, there would also be conscious effort to minimize class snobbishness. To Miss Phebe (or at least to Theodora's favorite uncle), "the most hopeless sort of folks are those regular society people, who are all run in one mould."[80] Much evidence suggests, however, that Miss McKeen took seriously the Puritan equation of wealth and virtue: powered by her desire to match Abbot's physical setting with its educational worth, she would lead the school through an expansion of buildings, grounds, and teaching resources that was to have dramatic consequences for Abbot's own place in the educational world.

Civil War

Within a year of the McKeens' arrival in 1859 Abbot was immersed in the general excitement over the presidential election. Women might not vote, but the whole Abbot community joined in celebrating Lincoln's victory. Andover had passed from Whig loyalty through Know-Nothing insanity in 1854 to solid Republicanism. The theologues purchased 1200 candles to "illuminate" on the night of November 7, and Smith Hall residents answered with candles in each of their windows. Hannibal Hamlin's vice-presidential election meant as much as Lincoln's to Abbot, since Hamlin was the brother of Cyrus and the uncle of all the Abbot Hamlins.

The McKeens' childhood home had been a station on the Underground Railroad. Miss Phebe especially admired the militants' courage and decisiveness. When the Civil War began, Abbot swung enthusiastically behind the Northern cause. Students spent all of Wednesday and Saturday afternoons "working for soldiers."[81] They sewed uniforms for Phillips Academy's Ellsworth Guards, rolled bandages and knitted socks for soldiers, and sent comfort bags to border state hospi-

6. Smith Hall "celebrating the surrender of Jefferson Davis," according to the penciled legend: the students in their gym suits. 1864.

tals accompanied by encouraging notes, to which they signed fictitious names, in obedience to their teachers. "Carrie Felton," probably Caroline Jackson, received thanks from a wounded soldier in Washington, D.C., who finished his letter by writing, "A man must be a good soldier when sustained by smiles and encouraging deeds of fair young ladies whose hands can knit . . . such comforts . . . for the rude rough man of war."[82]

The war seemed to underline the differences between man as activist and woman as the moral power back home. As Abbot's major Semicentennial speaker Richard S. Storrs, D.D., was to say: "It was that conscience in the American woman, sending out half a million of men, its instruments and ministers, to the bloody field, which finally . . . swept from existence that detestable system [of slavery]."[83] Theodora tells one of her soldier-suitors:

> "I want you to feel you are one of the champions of a Government as strong as it is free, which will bless the nation years after these armies are all dead."
> "Perhaps I might [he replies] if I could always kindle my enthusiasm at those beautiful eyes."[84]

But contradictory trends again appear. The war also opened a multitude of chances for women to do "man's work," whether in the hayfields, the offices, or the hospitals. Harriet Beecher Stowe was certain that the end of slavery would allow the nation to turn its attention to women's rights and needs, "to purge out" aristocratic and

"Old World" ideas.[85] Though one can find no talk of women's rights among Abbot students, they gladly put up with shortages and extra work on the upkeep of buildings and grounds. Certainly the Academy shared in the elation of a job well done at the war's end. The whole population of Smith Hall students climbed onto the roof dressed in their gym suits and kicked their heels, through their gymnastic exercises, the closest thing to a dance ever allowed in those days. (They displaced so many tiles that the next rain brought floods into the third-floor rooms.) On April 15, 1865, however, all the teachers arrived at morning prayers in tears. Miss McKeen could not read the news of Lincoln's assassination; Miss Phebe barely managed it. An alumna remembered the collective grief: "Down went one head after another on the desk in front, and the sobbing continued until we were dismissed."[86]

Thus ended the elation for Abbot as for all of Republican Andover; but the long-term effects of the war years remained. The Academy had prospered. In spite of raised yearly charges—now $251.25, partly a response to wartime inflation—the halls were overfull; many an Abbot father was making tuition payments out of the high price of apples,[87] or by supplying the endless requirements of the Grand Army. In 1865 Trustee Davis purchased the Farwell house and land just north of Academy Hall for $4500 and donated it to the school, protesting the name his colleagues gave the new boarding house: "Davis Hall." He then lent the Trustees funds enough to buy "South Hall" next door. The next year, Smith Hall was enlarged and provided with bathrooms. For the first time the Academy was reaping steady profits, most of which were used to enlarge and landscape the grounds. The McKeens had early taken over from the Trustees the receiving and screening of applications. Now an admissions examination was instituted; for a decade afterward, enrollment in the school ranged between 110 and 181 pupils, and boarding applicants were often turned away.

Well might the McKeen sisters be pleased. The students had tried them—both were "studied day by day," one wrote a friend in 1859— and, on the whole, approved them. "We have learned to love our new teachers dearly, but we think some of the new rules *monstrous*." Still, the "universal verdict" was that they "were true, consistent and devoted."[88] Miss McKeen chatted contentedly of her daily concerns in a letter to one of her relatives in 1864: "The school has been full and pleasant this year. We mourn the loss of the senior class . . . Katie Johnson is with us this term and is doing very well. She is a good scholar, and patient & cheerful & beloved. I wish she might become a Christian." Abbot had successfully negotiated its bumpy adolescence, and entered into its Golden Age.

7. *Philena McKeen with her first Senior Class (1860) and the Class of 1861.*

8. *A boarding school. The students' entrance to the Academy building (later Abbot Hall) faced Smith Hall for thirty-five years, ignoring School Street.*

Abbot in the Golden Age

There were giants in those days
Anna L. Dawes, 1921

By the mid 1860's the McKeen sisters were well settled at Abbot. They were strong-willed, yet ideologically moderate; they juggled nicely the often contradictory interests of their expanding constituency. They wove new ties with the prosperous Andover community, and brought Old Scholars (the "Dear Old Girls") back into the Family. Almost immediately they reestablished some of the Hill connections that Miss Hasseltine had broken. Happy in the memory of their minister father and brother, they were more fond than wary of men—the right sort of men. Nor did Philena McKeen scorn town for gown, as Farwell seems to have done. She did all she could to involve Abbot in the churches, clubs, and entertainments of Andover. No flaming reformers, both McKeens believed the world could best be saved "man by man."[1] Abbot's growth during the McKeen era would be woman by woman, gradual but enduring. By the time the McKeen era ended in 1892, the basic pattern the twentieth-century school would follow had been well laid down.

Offerings

Abbot's formal curriculum looks much the same during the McKeens' tenure as it did in the 1850's. A few subjects were added as time went on, but one can find little sign of coherent academic planning. The Course of Studies conformed to teachers' particular interests or skills. Philena McKeen was fascinated by the history of the early Christian Church, so she made it a staple of the Senior year. History of Art entered the Senior curriculum by the same route. Yet Abbot did not entirely give in to the usual Victorian division of labor, whereby men were the serious artists and women studied all their works,[2] for studio art became a favorite course when the exacting Emily Means began coming every Saturday to teach it.

Some themes recurred under new headings: the concerns of Psychology, added to the Senior course in 1876, were little different from those which Abbot women studied in their "Moral and Mental Philosophy" classes of the thirties and forties. Wayland had been dropped, as had many of the early textbooks, but teachers like Elizabeth Storrs Mead continued to ask Wayland's questions: "What is knowing?" "What is seeing?" "How does the infant develop?" "How does the soul know its own states?"[3] English reading lists were conservative. While Emily Dickinson was reading Emerson and Thoreau at her Amherst retreat and expressing her release from the old formalism in her poetry, Abbot girls stayed safe with Milton and Tennyson.[4] One Abbot student of 1861 copied some of Margaret Fuller's *Woman in the Nineteenth Century* into her journal, but there is no evidence that such radical readings were ever assigned by Abbot teachers. The McKeen sisters' History of the English Language,[5] first offered as an alternative to the Senior Trigonometry requirement, was so often chosen that Trigonometry was eventually dropped. All surviving student composition books suggest that standards for writing were high. One alumna, responding to Phebe McKeen's request for alumnae reminiscences, tells us how well the teaching stuck.

> I feel a good many qualms about writing to you, remembering so distinctly as I do all the personal remarks that used to be in my compositions. I don't believe you will have time to correct this and send it back, but if you do I will copy it in my best hand even if it takes me *four hours* . . .
> Yours with ever so much love to both you and your sister,
> Sarah Maria Barrows Dummer, '67
> Her Mark X[6]

Science laboratory facilities were pathetic, however. It took the enthusiasm of Wellesley graduate Isabella French to make physics and chemistry finally worth while in the 1880's, and to prepare for Katherine Kelsey's and Alice Hamlin's wider offerings and more extensive sharing of Phillips Academy science equipment later on.

Abbot's modern language program was one exception to this rather haphazard evolution of curriculum. Though it is doubtful that either of the McKeens spoke French or German themselves, they carefully fostered the study of both languages. They concentrated on improving offerings in these two instead of reviving the showy smatterings of Abbot's earlier years, when Italian and Spanish instruction was advertised along with French, German, Latin, and Greek.[7] They introduced a systematic oral language program that put Abbot's language training on a par with Harvard's elective French and German courses and far outdistanced Phillips Academy, which would offer no modern language at all until the mid 1870's, when a single year of elementary French or German was added to the Classical Department curriculum. This seems surprising until one realizes that Abbot in the early McKeen era served much the same age group as did Harvard (about fifteen to twenty-two), while the Phillips Classics Department was a college preparatory school.[8] Miss McKeen early encouraged Caroline Hamlin, '66, Henrietta Jackson's daughter and a Senior so proficient in French as to be listed with the faculty, to head a French-speaking table in Smith Hall. After 1869 French students lived and ate together in Davis Hall, speaking French for all but two hours of their out-of-class day under the care of the French teacher, who (said Phebe McKeen) gave them "admirable instruction along with that home influence that is more to them than any gift of tongues."[9] Separate diplomas for the English, French, Latin, and German courses were given until 1876, when—because too many students were avoiding it—language study became required of all students, as it had been for several years at Bradford. By that time German had become a fairly popular subject, and a German House in South Hall soon opened. South Hall's Vassar-trained preceptresses first felt obliged to expurgate most of the German texts, but their native German successors were more daring;[10] Frau Natalie Schiefferdecker, the most skillful and interesting of these, would stay a full twenty-one years. Even Miss McKeen's antipathy to theater was softened by educational logic when language students asked permission to put on German and French plays. Both were enthusiastically presented from the early eighties on, often with elaborate costumes and scenery.[11] The audience inevitably included "the elite of this old literary town," said the *Andover Townsman*,[12] as well as crowds of Abbot, Phillips, and Theological Seminary students.

As with many of Miss McKeen's projects, her desire for rigorous language teaching was strengthened by her attentiveness to the fashions of the times. The McKeens knew that fluency in French or German was the mark of a sophisticated lady; this knowledge was motive enough to bring Abbot's language program in line with those in the best schools and colleges for young women. Meanwhile, serious modern language study was considered frippery for busy young men. M. Carey Thomas, bemoaning the provincial character of her native Baltimore long before she left it to become Bryn Mawr's first dean, complained that "French and Germans were only teachers in girls' schools."[13] Not until the twentieth century did boys' schools catch up in this area. Comparisons over time are complex, because nineteenth-

9. German Play in the Chapel, 1892: Die Huldigung der Kunste *(Schiller)*.

century students scanned their French texts clause by clause much as they did their Latin or Greek; thus they could work their way through literature as difficult as that now read in the most advanced (college level) Phillips Academy courses. There seems no doubt, however, that the McKeens' *oral* language program was first rate for its time and would be first rate now.[14]

Throughout the third quarter of the nineteenth century, in fact, the "Fem Sem" down the Hill was offering a richer academic experience than the renowned prep school on the Hilltop. In a sense, it was fortunate that the majority of America still refused to take women's education seriously: Abbot students were free of that thralldom to the ancient college preparatory tradition which Phillips boys suffered under Principals Adams and Taylor. It was only when Phillips graduates found their "Latin, Greek and a smattering of Mathematics"[15] inadequate for entrance to Harvard and other of the more progressive colleges that Uncle Sam Taylor began to open the door for Principal Cecil Bancroft's reform.[16] After Bancroft took over in 1873, Phillips' curriculum swiftly improved. Abbot grew as proud of its neighboring Academy as it was of the Theological Seminary, and the two schools invited each other's students to lectures, concerts, religious services and other special occasions throughout the Bancroft era. In Professor Wesley Churchill's often quoted phrase, this was "the trinity of Andover schools" whose influence on each other—subtle though it was—constituted a fact of life on the Hill.

Increasingly, Abbot became home to a stable corps of teachers, many of whom stayed ten years or longer. Every year they were joined by younger women, often favored recent graduates who would shine for a year or two then marry, or by ambitious career teachers who would soon leave for higher-paid posts. One of these was Mrs. Elizabeth Mead, Abbot 1883–89, and president of Mt. Holyoke College 1889–1900, years that spanned the Seminary's transition to college status. Male professors from the Theological Seminary or from the New England men's colleges would periodically offer a course of lectures in subjects such as astronomy or ethics.

The McKeens' most enduring colleague was Professor Samuel Morse Downs, who came to teach music the year after their arrival and taught up to 71 pupils each year (with an average of about 40) in piano, voice, and theory until 1907. Students were devoted to this small, quick man whose "humor and courtesy" were "his only weapons of discipline."[17] His tenure coincided with the great age of American concertgoing, a time when the New York Festival of Classical Music with its 320 piece orchestra and chorus of 3500 could attract 18,000 listeners two years in a row (1881 and '82). Boston area audiences were smaller but no less discerning. An enthusiastic performer and composer also, Downs divided his time after 1868 between Abbot, Bradford, and Boston's Old South Church, where he served as organist. In 1876, Downs set up an Andover recital series of three concerts a year at his own financial risk—and sometimes loss. Abbot students could hear groups such as the Kniesel String Quartet and the Boston Symphony Woodwind Choir at one third the price they would have paid for tickets to similar programs in Boston. When Downs retired, no one was surprised that two teachers had to be hired to take his place.

Of course, Downs's success soon meant that Abbot must have more pianos. By 1892 there were twelve, including two grand pianos. Historians maintain that the nineteenth-century family changed from a producing unit to a consuming unit, with profound consequences for family relationships. During the McKeen era the Abbot Family became consumer *extraordinaire*. Botany required specimens: Miss McKeen, Collector, encouraged the building of a herbarium, into which teachers packed everything from dried wildflowers to a rare collection of Japanese ferns from Kyoto. By 1880 the zoological cabinet contained (among hundreds of other things) 81 Indian bird skins, and a number of bright-hued African birds sent by a missionary father in lieu of his daughter's tuition. A fine collection of shells bought at bargain price from a young missionary meant that there *must* be a Conchology course. Grandest of all was Abbot's telescope and observatory, a resource almost unique in schools for young women when it was first acquired in 1875, and one fine enough to be used by William M. Reed of the Harvard Observatory for several months of astronomical observations in photometry.

How did Abbot gather all these goods? The telescope was the result of a $1300 drive led by Latin-Astronomy teacher Mary Belcher among the students, and later among the Trustees. (A student-teacher of gymnastics donated her entire $85.00 salary.) But Miss McKeen herself was the most gifted of gift-seekers. An example: she had long yearned to have a life-sized papier-maché model of a woman, with detachable limbs and organs, to supplement the Physiology class's ancient skeleton.[18] She mentioned this wish every time she dared, pointedly reminding the Trustees that *Bradford*'s Board "had lately presented their school with just such a model,"[19] and as a last resort used the fiftieth anniversary *History of Abbot Academy* to declare the need in print. Whether in shame or in amusement—we can't know—the Trustees finally ordered the model from Paris for $600.00.

Professor Park connived with Miss McKeen to gain one of her most triumphant acquisitions. In 1877, she mentioned to him the need for a statue to decorate the teachers' platform in the Academy Hall. Park found a beautiful marble pedestal in Boston, and persuaded Trustee George Ripley to donate it. "A pedestal suggests a statue," observed Miss McKeen,[20] and of course no one could disagree. The McKeens asked Miss Emily Means, Abbot painting teacher on vacation in Paris, to find a statue suitable both as decoration and as illustration for Miss McKeen's ever-expanding Art History course. That year the students sold 50¢ tickets to the Draper Reading exercises, creating as much suspense as they could about the great unveiling. By the time the bronze copy of Michelangelo's Lorenzo of Urbino had been revealed to a packed audience, its whole cost ($240 in gold) had been returned to the school.

Abbot had always promised order, but the McKeen sisters delivered it in spades. They loved schedules. Up at 6:00, breakfast at 6:30, clean your room—and perhaps a teacher's parlor as well. Though four Irish maids also helped out at $1.98 a week, the McKeens considered housework part of education. As Lucy Larcom put it in her *New England Girlhood*, "changes of fortune come so abruptly that the millionaire's daughter of to-day may be glad to earn her living by sewing or sweeping to-morrow."[21] Miss McKeen might ask a girl to help her change guest beds, questioning her the while on Butler's *Analogy*. Between 8:00 and 9:00 A.M. older students often climbed the Hill for a Geology lecture while younger ones did their daily calisthenics, but all must be on hand for the Devotions that formally opened the school day. Before mid-day dinner everyone wore gym suits with pantaloons, and skirts ten inches from the ground. Though bloomers were taboo at Abbot (one critic had termed them "one of the many manifestations of that wild spirit of socialism and agrarian radicalism which is . . . so rife in our land"),[22] the gym suits were a crucial concession to comfort where the afternoon alternative was whalebone corsets and hems below the ankles. "I don't think I shall ever adopt bloomers," wrote an alumna of 1871, "but if anything could bring me to it, it would be the remembrance of how lightfooted and lighthearted I used to feel flitting about mornings in my gymnastic suit. I keep it still, and use it for a bathing dress."[23]

Recitations continued till 3:30, then came Recreation Hours, with time for walking in pairs, studying, mending, croquet, or (after 1886) tennis. Supper followed; the evening was an alternation of study hours, "half-hours" for individual meditation (roommates took these in turns so each girl could be alone once a day), and "quarters" for room-to-room visiting. Evening Devotions might mean anything from a hymn sing to a prayerful scolding. Bed at 10:00.

Like many other schools, Abbot had its Saturday "composition day," dreaded by some as "the hobgoblin that stares us in the face" each week,[24] welcomed by others as a chance to write their minds on subjects like "Castles in the Air," "Kissing," or "Is it Best for a Lady without Superior Musical Talents to Study Music?"[25] Every student came to Hall, heard other students present the week's news or read an inspiring selection, and took notes while a teacher or outside lecturer presented a subject worthy of an hour essay. Tuesday evening one could visit other dormitories. Wednesday was theoretically Recreation Day, free for unsupervised walks and chaperoned trips out of town. It was also, however, a rug-beating, mattress-turning clean-up day. One corridor teacher inspected with such vehemence that students would warn each other of her coming by a special five-fingered signal tap on the door, giving the inmate time to arrange bureau drawers and hide forbidden food.

After 1873 all this was commanded by electric bells, the McKeens' pride and the students' bane. Mary Delight Twichell vented her feelings in a five-verse poem, "The Bells." Verse 4:

10. The first of seven student sketches of life at Abbot, six by Harriet Chapell and one by Kate C. Geer. The one above is Harriet's sketch of herself on clean-up, from her Journal, 25 February 1874. The other five sketches (Nos. 11–15) are between pages 96–108, below.

Hear the sharp stroke of the bell,—
The "*tardy*" bell!
What a hurrying of footsteps does its sound foretell!
What a scamper o'er the floors;
What a banging of the doors;
What a sighing o'er their fate,
By those who are too late!
Oh sudden tardy bell!
Oh cruel tardy bell!
Oh, bell, bell, bell, bell,
bell, bell, bell!
Why so quick with your click, tardy bell?[26]

Many of Abbot's offerings were not strictly scheduled. Periodically, Mr. Downs's students presented their own musicales to the community. A *Townsman* reporter of 1891 described "spirited and noble" renditions of difficult music.[27] Favorites were Schubert symphonies arranged for eight hands, and part songs sung by the choir or (after 1887) the Fidelio Society. Romantic music dominated both student and professional recitals—a professional whistler specialized in Verdi opera arias—but on one occasion, Mr. Downs presented an extraordinary program in the Town Hall called "Precursors of the Piano," including solos and trio sonatas from J. S. Bach through Mozart and Beethoven to Paganini, played by Mr. M. Steinert and others on the Steinert collection: a clavichord, a 1630 spinet, a 1755 harpsichord, a bowed clavier, a hammerclavier, a Vertical Grand piano of 1779, an 1815 pianoforte, and Abbot's contemporary Steinway Concert Grand.

Abbot's most exciting home-grown event was always the Draper Reading, begun in 1868 with a thirty dollar donation by Irene Rowley Draper, '43, a sum that was later increased to $40 each year. It started as an elocution contest similar to the Prize Readings Mr. Warren Draper had initiated at Phillips Academy, but the McKeen sisters and Professor Wesley Churchill, Abbot's part-time elocution teacher, soon decided there should be less competition and more instruction. After this, sixteen or twenty readers were elected by the students for a run-off reading, and half of them were chosen by both students and teachers to receive private teaching from Seminary Professor Churchill in preparation for the final Reading. The Draper Readings usually took place at graduation ("Anniversary") time—grand occasions followed always by a party for the readers and the Seniors in the Churchills' home. Thus a close association with Professor Churchill was the real prize. So widely known was Churchill's skill that Matthew Arnold came to him for coaching before making a speaking tour of the United

11. Chapell Sketch: A Draper Reader with "Miss Phebe and teachers," Miss McKeen and Professor Churchill watching, 27 May 1974.

States. A warm-hearted, urbane man, a lover of language whether in the Bible or elsewhere, he encouraged Abbot students to select from a wide—if safe—variety of readings. (A letter to the *Andover Advertiser* of 23 February 1880 described a course of four lectures Churchill gave in Baltimore, saying that "some Baltimorians seem dazed to find so much fun coming out of staid New England.") In time Churchill became Trustee as well as valued friend of Abbot.

Debates and tableaux also had their places in the occasional entertainments given by student literary societies, or at the Anniversary itself, where in 1875 the Seniors contended over the question whether the sixteenth or the nineteenth century had contributed most to world civilization. Gradually, a carefully rehearsed Exhibition took the place of Abbot's summer oral examinations. After 1883 all serious academic evaluation was done by teachers through written exams, and the Anniversary became Abbot's end-of-year celebration.

Visitors to Abbot or Andover were an important resource for both students and teachers. Students would go to Town Hall "in a body" to hear a comic lecture by John Gough or an exhortation on the "demon of intemperance." (Miss McKeen, a fervent temperance advocate, somehow arranged for the proceeds of this last to be donated to the Abbot Art department.) They climbed to the Seminary for a lecture on the relation of science to the Christian religion, or welcomed Professor William W. Clapp to the Academy Hall for his winter series of Shakespeare lectures, and were impressed by Clapp's "revelation of Shylock in all his malice and cruelty as the natural outgrowth of years of hatred and prejudice on the part of Christians."[28] They were hosts to Professor Charles A. Young of Princeton, who lived at Abbot for a week in 1891 and gave interested girls an intensive course in Astronomy.[29] They enjoyed frequent literary lectures by "Mrs. Professor Downs" (Annie Sawyer Downs) with wondrous stereopticon views of Southern English cathedrals and Lake District cottages; they heard snowy-haired Bronson Alcott, "the venerable conversor of Concord," talk about his daughters.[30] Especially, they were moved by Helen Keller, who came at age 13 with her teacher for the first of several overnight visits. Helen delighted in the vibrations she could feel from the piano music played by her Senior hostesses, and in the shapes of the art room's plaster cast collection, quite large by 1890. Nero seemed "Proud," she observed. "It is *sorrow*," she said, as she passed her hands over Niobe's face. On hearing Helen's thank-you letter to the School, one girl wept; another said, "Think of her being so grateful for what she has, and see what a pig I am."[31]

Wednesday and Saturday afternoons were often used for special trips to Boston's museums, to Concord with Annie Sawyer Downs, who had grown up there with the Alcott children, to the ocean, to Lawrence's Pacific Mills and its Cathedral, where—wrote Harriet Chapell, '76—the confession boxes "looked like small barrooms to our Protestant eyes." Harriet was "stirred way down deep" by a painting in a Boston art gallery.[32] The Cambridge Botanical Gardens made a favorite destination, especially when a Harvard Professor of Botany brought everyone to his house afterward for a talk about his own collection. Several Physiology classes were invited to the lecture room of a professor at the New England Female Medical College, where they examined "preparations and models with the benefit of her instructions."[33] One spring fifteen girls traveled by beachwagon to Danvers to visit the tomb of Rebecca Nourse, hanged witch (also progenitor of two twentieth-century Abbot students), and to meet the poet Whittier in his home.

Ordinarily only the wealthier students could take advantage of a Boston Wagner festival or concert of Bach's Passion music, and theater attendance was proscribed for everyone; but in 1890 Miss McKeen unbent so much as to encourage the whole Senior class to attend *Hamlet*, starring Edwin Booth. Their teacher had conducted an hour-long "Hamlet Match" in Shakespeare class that week, reading first lines of speeches to jog student recitations of the remaining lines, so they were well prepared. It was a perfect day. The Phillips Glee Club sang all the way in on the train; the play was relished as fully as were the ice cream sodas afterward ("chocolate, of course"), and the girls returned to a late tea that had been kept specially for them in Smith Hall.[34]

The town of Andover continued to be Abbot students' most immediate off-campus resource. Teachers urged them to supplement the small Abbot Library with books from the Theological Seminary collection of 37,000 volumes, limited in scope though this was by the strictures of the Calvinist *Index Expurgatorius*. Thus Abbot women probably had access to more books than Princeton undergraduates of the 1860's, whose 14,000 volume library was open exactly one hour each week until 1868.[35] After 1873 the girls went often to the town's Memorial Hall Library (with 7,000 volumes in 1880), to which Abbot's public-spirited Trustee Peter Smith and his business partners had given over $35,000. Andover's November Club for literary ladies met in the Academy Hall, and Abbot students were regularly invited to literary tableaux or charades in private homes and to conventions of the American Missionary Society, the American Temperance Society, and other Andover-based organizations. Far more than the other schools on Andover Hill, wrote Susannah Jackson, Abbot made constant use of the advantages offered by its home town.

The Community of Women

Abbot was no cloister then. It *was* a self-contained community of women in many respects, however, with conscious and unconscious borders which men might cross only upon invitation. The girls had "the freedom of the streets and fields," as the McKeen sisters wrote,[36] but their walks to Sunset Rock and their botanizing or nutting expeditions on Indian Ridge were For Women Only. One can be sure this rule was broken often enough by individuals (Abbot's most famous sleigh ride had a Phillips boy along disguised as a girl).[37] Still, it was formally honored. Twenty-one nut-gatherers all dressed in gym suits fled so fast when they spotted a theologue in the tree above them that they never gathered a single chestnut, and lost their way in a swamp in their rush to get back to Smith Hall.[38]

Abbot might be a Family, but women commanded it, keeping a useful distance between themselves and the male Trustees or visiting teachers. Particularly in New England, where women substantially outnumbered men, the unmarried teacher held an honorable role. Abbot's women and girls could enjoy one another as persons without self-consciousness or shame. One thinks of Victorian women as confined, and so they were. They could not openly initiate friendship with boys or men; they were expected to hide their interest in sex or to subsume it within coquettish formulae, no matter how interested they really were. Partly because of this relative isolation from men, however, loving, lasting friendships between women could quietly thrive, modeled often on the close mother-daughter or sister-sister relationships that existed apart from men's affairs.[39]

Abbot's increasingly varied group of students offered a fair field both for close and for casual friendships. Educational historian Patricia Graham points out that this was an era when girls from upper-middle-income families almost routinely spent a year or more in boarding school.[40] There was more money about for the education of fewer children. The birth rate was falling steadily, especially in cities; by the century's close, it would be 3.5 for each married woman, or just half what it had been in 1800.[41] Even a short stay at Abbot was an important respite from domesticity for those who would marry at twenty-two or twenty-three, the average age for marriage among women during the last half of the century. True, Abbot could no longer draw many students of small means, for tuition-boarding charges kept slowly rising: they were never lowered after wartime inflation subsided; they increased to $300 a year in 1876. Still, they remained lower than Bradford's and Vassar's until 1890.[42] Scholarship endowments (totaling $6,000 in 1880 and $11,500 in 1890) made it possible to welcome a few overseas missionaries' daughters and other desirable candidates for whatever their parents could pay.

Andover was ideally situated between city and village to attract students from both. Each decade more rising city businessmen, nostalgic about their rural childhoods and disturbed by the "overwhelming dislocations of the giant cities"[43] with their "frenzied commercial spirit and . . . dazzling entertainments" sent Abbot their urban-raised daughters as though to free them from this "prime source of corrupting influences for the young."[44] Yet the school did not suffer the fate of the many small-town academies whose local constituencies were weakening or disappearing altogether. Once-proud Adams Academy just fifteen miles to the north was absorbed by the Derry public school system soon after its fiftieth anniversary in 1872, partly because "many of the old families which made Derry society famous had thinned out or passed away."[45] And Adams was only one of hundreds of dying academies. Meanwhile, Abbot's small Western contingent was growing along with its urban one, the girls' parents undoubtedly aware that Boston with its satellites had become unique for its "aristocratic culture" in a nation where "distinction of manners and dress . . . dignity and repose" had been replaced by a "bumptious restlessness, a straining for originality and individuality that exuded in a shoddy and meaningless grotesque."[46] Antoinette Louise Bancroft, '83, of Galesburg, Illinois, wrote to her brother that "nearly half" of the students were from the West. (This could only be accurate if Antoinette included western Massachusetts and New York and Pennsylvania; only fourteen out of 115 girls came from Ohio, Illinois, or further west in 1882–83.) She could "tell a Western girl" almost as soon as she saw her "by her dignity," while Eastern girls were "easy to get acquainted with," and "always kissing each other." This Eastern sanctuary also had its boors, and Antoinette said so in response to her brother's anxious warnings. "Do you think I will be laughed at when there are girls around me who have to be told that one should keep the mouth closed while eating?" she asked her brother. "Now please don't tell me any more nonsense."[47] So much for his advice.

A few Southerners came, too. One of them, Harriet Elizabeth Gibson, wrote in 1879 that "a Southerner feels lonely here in New En-

gland, where she finds no friendly black faces . . . no real plantation
'Ha! ha!' to disturb the busy buzz of New England air; no kind flattering black auntie to attend to all her wants; no merry black uncle
to . . . interpret her dreams, and tell her fortune. Most of all she finds
no time for this dreaming. Everyone is in a hurry, and hurry is contagious."[48] Despite her complaints, Harriet Gibson stayed on, graduated
in 1881, and accompanied her physician husband to Korea, where she
became the first woman missionary to that country. Not a single student of recent immigrant stock can be found in the McKeens' Abbot
Academy, however. One graduate of 1887 felt she must explain to her
classmates that her great-grandfather was "an Irishman but a gentleman."[49] The majority continued to come from New England in spite
of its growing numbers of public schools.[50] "Our public schools give
us little real culture," an Abbot girl complained in 1884.[51] Parents were
looking (one supposes) for smaller classes at a time when the ideal size
of a public school class was considered by the "experts" to be forty-
five or fifty students;[52] they wanted their daughters to have special opportunities to learn a foreign language or a Christian's heritage, or, in
the case of the older students, a chance for a refined "higher education" beyond public high school, with curriculum offerings similar to
those of most women's colleges before the founding of Bryn Mawr.[53]

One of an Abbot historian's most interesting and useful sources is
the journal of Harriet Chapell, '76, written from January 1874, the year
Harriet left her home in New London, Connecticut, through 18 November 1877, six weeks after she married Frederick Newcomb. Spirited,
mischievous daughter of the vice-president of a New London Whaling
and Guano firm, she may have been sent to Abbot because she was
such a handful at home—at least her mother wrote her in April of her
first year a "dear, good letter," saying that "she thinks I have improved
a good deal."[54] Whatever the reasons, we are lucky she came, and
luckier still that she left this 254-page illustrated record of a girl growing up in the community of women. She seldom mentions teachers or
lessons, though she spent much time in the painting studio and was
occasionally "taken by storm" by a visiting lecturer, such as Charles
Kingsley. When teachers do appear in Hattie's first-year record, they
are there to interfere with more important activities. Or they are mercifully absent. "Miss McKeen was in Boston, so we had a jolly time at
our table."[55] When she's home, "Philo" is always on the lookout. One
evening "in half-hour"—that is, during meditation time—"we were all
having a nice lively time in the music room, dancing—squarely—like
mad, when Miss McKeen opened the door and read us one little lecture about the exercise—must be confined to the gym and the day time,

etc. Louie Karr stood behind her as you see and made up all sorts of faces and gestures. I do think she is just as jolly and splendid as she can be, though I know she can be awfully cutting if she chooses. Hattie Aiken too is full of the old cat if she wants to be. She looked for all the world like Mr. Tyler this evening, as she was Helen Bartlett's gent (in the dancing). So we had a grand time all round."[56]

12. Chapell sketch: "Dancing squarely like mad," 7 April 1874.

Again, "Miss Palmer gave us all a little lecture at devotions tonight about whistling . . . perfectly scathing—and you see everybody knew who she meant . . . well, everybody thinks I am a reprobate, so I suppose I am one, but . . . they can think what they like for all I care."[57]

Harriet's day is filled with conversations, walks downtown to buy sweets, and parties to enjoy them (an eternal preoccupation of schoolgirls, in spite of Miss McKeen's injunctions against "eatables" bought in town or sent from home: "the effect is wholly evil"),[58] throwing snowballs, sliding in the trunk room, or sloshing through Andover's famous spring mud—*and* dropping her hymnbook *and* stomping upon it—on the way up the Hill to Professor Park's Sunday sermon.[59]

The Journal's major actors are Hattie's many girl-friends and her few girl-enemies, richly described; the plots center on expeditions, escapades, and quarrels begun or made up. Tilly and Lizzie are her first favorites, especially "dear little Lizzie" Abbott, who comes from Andover but boards at the Academy. It is not in class, so far as Harriet tells us, but with these friends that "lots of conversation on a number of moral and metaphysical points" takes place. Harriet might make a botch of the "topic" she has to give in "Hall," but she and Lizzie "read considerable together," one sewing while the other reads aloud from the *Pickwick Papers*, or Thomas Bailey Aldrich's *Prudence Palfrey*. At supper table they take the parts of fictional characters (Hattie is Prue) or after supper they give "a little musicale among themselves."[60] Harriet begins her Abbot years in South Hall, rooming with Mame Green "who is very lively and keeps us all in a roar most of the time,"[61] but by mid-winter, Hattie is "crazy to get over (to Smith Hall) to live," where the "halls are full of girls and noise." Miss McKeen engineers the change, and she and Lizzie move into one of the 12′ × 12′ rooms together.

Lizzie is Hattie's "Darling girl,"[62] a "motherless little soul . . . short and fat, but not overgrown, with blue eyes and lovely golden hair" which she lets fly every day but Sunday. Like nearly all Abbot boarders, the two girls shared a bed. Even before they roomed together, they arranged with their teachers and with other girls to exchange bedfellows, and "had a right warm, cosy time together."[63] The retiring bells meant practically nothing to friends determined to talk. Often enough, Hattie, Tillie, Lizzie, and Mame spent much of the night at it, on one occasion going back to bed just before breakfast to warm each other up.

Lizzie proved to be "a perfect treasure of a roommate." The two kept together all they could. They played ball, they collected wildflowers and copied epitaphs in the graveyard, they gave each other

13. Chapell sketch: Buying "comfits" downtown, 24 April 1874.

Max + Parkie

The tardy tolls the knell of parting day

By Kate C. Geer —

14. Geer sketch: Bedfellows, 1882, from Kate Geer's copybook.

their journals and letters to read. On a Sunday afternoon when there was no church service, they "spent part of [their] time on the bed, reading and snuggling up close to each other by turns."[64]

The physical closeness these two enjoyed in no way suggests any serious or lasting homosexual interest. They had "endless things to talk about" precisely because each one had "a somebody at home."[65] Harriet often spent a happy Recreation Day walking in the woods with her visiting Fred, then returned to her "cosy bed" and Lizzie at night. When Lizzie did not come back in September, Harriet went through a period of dreariness and longing; but by November she was making new friends, and comforting herself with the thought that she and Lizzie would always love one another, and would visit often in each other's homes after they were married. Occasionally she went to Lizzie's house to enjoy some "real talk" and "real food," and have "a very good time together, such as only girls can have."[66]

The second year, Hattie's Fred, a hometown boy several years older than she, won her secret promise to marry him.[67] Increasingly, her love for Fred absorbed her feelings and "guided all [her] life."[68] She began to long for marriage, even though she felt "a kind of dread and regret at leaving behind my happy girl life." As things turned out, she never did leave behind her pleasure in other girls and women. A few weeks after her marriage, she and Fred visited an old New London friend, and while Fred talked with the husband, the two wives shared old and new interests. When it was time to leave, Hattie wrote, "I could not bear to go away from them, and Alice clung to me—she felt truly that I understood her deep feeling as no one else save a woman could have done."[69] Harriet Chapell's daughter, Ruth Wetmore Newcomb, '10, remembers her as the warmest of mothers and friends, strict enough but "full of fun" to the end of her long life.[70]

Throughout Abbot's first half-century, one finds ample evidence of friendships such as these between the girls who boarded at the Academy. They were part of American life, open to discussion in print as well as in private. A letter to the Yale *Courant* of 1873 reported that "Vassar numbers her smashes by the score. [There are] bouquet-sendings interspersed with tinted notes, mysterious packages of 'Ridley mixed candies,' locks of hair . . ."[71] and M. Carey Thomas' mother wrote her at Howland Institute, a Quaker boarding school, in response to Carey's description of her most intense relationship: "I guess thy feeling is quite natural. I used to have the same romantic love for my friends. It is a *real pleasure*."[72]

Until educators and psychologists began to scrutinize these deep same-sex friendships during the last quarter of the century, inspirational tracts and religious fiction put them on holy ground. "Love is with me a religion," wrote one young woman. Its nature precludes any element that is "not absolutely pure and sacred." But this unfortunate recorded her feelings too late in the century. Quoting her, psychologist Havelock Ellis stated that such sentiments had come "under the ban of society," numbered her "case #29," and wrote darkly of "sexual inversion."[73] The male psychologists' judgments would look like mere Freudian prudery were not women beginning to make them too. A research committee fielded by the Association of Collegiate Alumnae (later the American Association of University Women) concluded that "smashing" led to sleeplessness and emotional exhaustion; it advocated expanded physical education programs to provide for "healthier" discharge of physical and emotional energies.[74] Thus toward the end of the McKeen era there were a few Abbot adults who frowned on friendships like Hattie's and Lizzie's, instead of smiling. Student letters, journals, and the messages scrawled on yearbooks all suggest that the friendships continued anyway. It took years for student realities to catch up with the new adult anxieties.

Harriet Chapell might seldom mention them, but the resident teachers were essential members of this community of women, drawing strength from it as they gave themselves to it. They had not come to Abbot solely to earn money. A few had incomes of their own, if elaborate summer travel is any indicator of wealth. Occasionally one would leave to teach in public school, where salaries were higher, or another would importune the Trustees for a raise, as French teacher Maria Stockbridge Merrill did in 1881: "I have felt this year that I can not come back for the salary I am receiving now—$400—."[75] What Abbot did provide was a *living*, a place of dignity for an unmarried woman in a large, bustling Family.

Under the no-nonsense McKeens, Abbot had its rules to regulate the Family's life—a long list not shortened until late in the McKeen era. Abbot was similar in this respect to the other female institutions of the day, and more liberal than some. Mary Sharp College in Tennessee and Wesleyan Female College in Cincinnati also forbade walking out alone or using nicknames; but Abbot published no injunctions against making purchases without permission as these colleges did, nor did it share Elmira College's prohibitions against "light and trifling conversations," or "meeting in companies in each others' rooms for purposes of festivity."[76] Abbot Academy's aim continued to be "self-regulation," just as it had been in earlier decades. One means toward this goal was "self-reporting," a much-vaunted honor system which asked the penitent at each confession to consider whether her offense was "avoidable or unavoidable?" Supposed to preserve trust between students and teachers, self-reporting actually seems to have created more guilt and teacher-avoidance than anything else. Again and again one reads the Abbot girl's lament: "You can't have any fun here, for if you do, you have to go and report on yourselves."[77] Naturally, a Stowe daughter would be the first to object. "Miss Phebe says it makes us truthful" to give our self-reports every night, wrote one student. "Miss Georgie Stowe expressed her mind quite freely," saying the reports were not much use, "probably because she makes so many of them herself."[78]

"Miss McKeen's lecture this afternoon was on eating, and it made us mad," wrote one girl to her parents. It was terribly hard for some Abbot girls to adjust to "the rigorous ordering of our ways."[79] Surely some never did. American children were known the world over for their overindulged precociousness. "Democratic sucklings!" one Englishman sputtered—"the theory of the equality of man is rampant in the nursery!"[80] Lucy Larcom in her *New England Girlhood* tells how she "clung to the child's inalienable privilege of running half-wild." To her, "the transition from childhood to girlhood . . . is practically the toning down of a mild sort of barbarianism, and is often attended by a painfully awkward self-consciousness."[81] But Abbot teachers' affection eased many girls through girlhood toward womanhood. "The hearty welcome" from the McKeens that each student received in September[82] was always a good beginning. For every cross teacher there seem to have been at least two kind ones. Miss Merrill—who eventually got her raise and stayed on till 1907[83]— bent the ten o'clock curfew night after night. When the moon was full, she would take her girls for walks in the silver dark. She loved to read aloud to them, and they delighted each evening to hear her; they basked in her "gay friendliness" and "loved her devotedly." Often enough, Miss Merrill argued with these same students, "always disagreeing with us as equals" instead of lecturing them to make her point, as one alumna recalled years later.[84] Naturally, many students stole their pleasures where they could find them—but this was often done so blatantly that one can only suppose teachers were looking the other way. Now and then, the bell girl would provide her friends a welcome break from the tyrannous schedule by simply failing to ring the bell; thus Harriet and Lizzie had three quarters of an hour to chat on Lizzie's bed instead of a rushed "quarter." After-hours parties were a subject of special pride to the editors of '87's manuscript yearbook. Eight of the seventeen graduates had participated in twenty-nine "midnight revelries" altogether, with "Emma T.," that "wicked but happy mortal," having attended eight herself.[85] It is interesting that this bold accounting was made public *before* Commencement. In spite of Miss McKeen's warnings that breaking rules was "taking poison,"[86] everyone graduated. The teachers cannot have been such terrible ogres after all. "Last evening at tea," wrote Harriet Chapell after a unique Recreation Day,

> we were joking and laughing, saying we guessed we would lie in bed till noon today, when Miss Palmer astounded us all by telling us we might stay in bed till noon, indeed, we need not have any

rules until dinner time, when we must appear. I suppose she thought we boarding school girls would go through anything rather than lose one meal, but we took her up, and not one of us eight girls was down to breakfast. It was so cosy and warm to cuddle down in bed with Mame, and hear Miss Palmer and Mrs. Watson having their devotions all alone in the music room,—we had hard work to keep from laughing out loud.

Of course they made their own breakfast later from the snack crackers always available in the closet, and jelly, figs, nuts, and chocolate sent from home. "We did just as we pleased all the long morning, entered rooms, had lunch every few minutes and did all manner of outlandish things."[87]

"Philo" herself created special occasions: an hours-long sleigh ride one Washington's Birthday for everyone who was healthy enough to stand the cold, a surprise "Orange Party" in Smith Hall for which she and the teachers arranged into pyramids and patterns the hundreds of oranges sent by a friend from Florida. On the night of October 2, 1875, there was a total eclipse of the moon. Miss McKeen had a student ring the bell fifty times at 2 A.M., and all who wanted to watch it brought pillows down to the back veranda. Harriet and her friends "lay there an hour or so, looking all the time and having an easy time."[88] Then, of course, there was that greatest occasion of Abbot's nineteenth century history, the Semicentennial celebration in June 1879. Phillips Principal Bancroft assisted the McKeens with the preparations, and the Phillips Glee Club gave a concert to raise money for the great day. Invitations went out to every known alumna, to college presidents throughout New England, to the Massachusetts Governor and the United States President (who sent their polite regrets). Students scoured the buildings to prepare for the Old Scholars, then decked them with bunting. Two thousand guests lunched under a great pavillion set up on the lawn near South Church.[89] All of Phillips Academy and the Theological Seminary arrived in time for the speeches, which on paper look endless: fifty years was worth at least three hours' oratory in those days, and after all, no ex-principal (so long as he was male) or parent/college president or university professor could be left out. Not a single woman spoke, but multitudes of young women must have been glad of Trustee Egbert Smyth's final announcement to the youths from the Hilltop:

The stern dame whom all her daughters love as *Alma Mater* has said to me very privately—so that no one else heard the pleasant tune of her voice, or saw the lambent flame in her eye—that, for

15. Chapell sketch: The eclipse, 17 October 1874.

all, *to-day* and *to-morrow* are as TUESDAY *evening*; and, that till the shades of evening fall the second time, all her daughters may be to you as your sisters, and your cousins, and your aunts.

That is, for once no special parent sanction was required for male callers outside the girls' families.

Miss McKeen felt herself particularly responsible for the Smith Hall girls' character and behavior. She was a less formal person in Smith Hall, "her only home," than she was as an academic principal, remembered one alumna. "This strong, serene head of our matriarchy to whom we confessed our sins . . . had a remarkable opportunity to know each one for what she really was. She certainly was very keen to detect subterfuge or untruth, and equally just in commending honesty." While students' individuality was less encouraged than was conformity to "a standardized type . . . we were her family . . . in whom she was constantly striving to awaken and develop Christian woman-liness."[90]

As in the early Abbot, religious conversion was still sometimes the ultimate solution to conflict between an adult and a girl or young woman, or a young woman's struggles with herself. Phebe McKeen's novel of boarding life, *Thornton Hall*,[91] accepted by her contemporaries as a barely disguised description of Abbot in the 1860's and 70's, emphasizes the religious character of all social exchanges. While its plot rambles along like some spinster soap opera, its complex characters with their intricate human tangles suggest Phebe's own powerful sympathy and understanding as a resident teacher in Abbot's community of women. The community is wide and deep: it includes the reserved Miss Atherton, inwardly hurt by the desertion of her "half-ruined brother" and her "stolen sister"[92] (probably Abbot's Tace Wardwell, whom students held in "especial awe"),[93] as well as the open-hearted Miss Lincoln. Behind scenes stand parents, one father virtuous but poor, another amoral and indulgent.

The *Thornton Hall* teachers leave girls alone to work trouble out themselves until a real crisis looms. Virginia Raleigh "loved her few friends with passionate intensity, and she demanded the same in return. No love seemed to her real which was not exclusive." She became jealous of Kate Campbell's other friendships. As for "merry Kate," Virginia was to her "the desire of her eyes!" but "what right had she to try to manage her so? She ought to be satisfied with what she well knew was given her—dearest love."[94]

> For several days, Virginia Raleigh went about with a kind of marble hardness in her face, and passed her late friend, everywhere, without seeming to see her. Even the little acts of common courtesy which Kate offered, she ignored. The girls were asking each other, "What has come over Kate Campbell?" "Had a flare-up with Miss Raleigh—don't speak to each other," was a sufficient answer.

Finally Miss Lincoln called Virginia to her room. "I know your soul sets deep and strong towards the few you love," she tells Virginia, "but . . . you cannot be Christlike while you are utterly indifferent to all but your chosen few." . . .

> Virginia's heart was touched by the blending of love and indignant sorrow in the face of her friend. She threw her arms around her saying, "But He is divine."

CHAPTER V.

SCHOOL-GIRL FRIENDSHIP.

OR several days, Virginia Raleigh went about with a kind of marble hardness in her face, and passed her late friend, everywhere, without seeming to see her. Even the little acts of common courtesy which Kate offered, she ignored. The girls were asking each other, " What has come over Kate Campbell?" "Had a flare-up with Miss Raleigh—don't speak to each other," was a sufficient answer.

After things had been going on in this way for about a week, Miss Lincoln sent for the two girls

(51)

16. "Kate and Virginia" of Thornton Hall, *illustrator unknown. (Edward O. Jenkins, "printer and stereotyper.")*

"Yes, dear, but we are His offspring, and He meant to teach us how to love. It seems to me a dreadful waste, Virginia, for one to carry a great warm heart like yours through life, wrapped up in selfishness and pride." . . .

"But I can't be unselfish," groaned Virginia. "I love papa and mamma, and you and Kate, and one other; and I want you all, all, all, to myself."

"The only way for you, darling, is to give your heart to your heavenly Father," said her friend, very tenderly. "Loving God, you would come to love your brother also."

Virginia lifted her eyes, dewy with tears, kissed the lips that had spoken so plain truth to her, and went silently away to her room.[95]

Finally, Virginia was able to "love the Savior," even though her conversion cost her the suit of a rakish sophomore from the neighboring college for young men.

Phebe McKeen doubtless had her sister in mind when she created Miss Douglass, the principal of *Thornton Hall*. Many a girl's headstrong rebellion against rules or roommate ended in penitent weeping upon Miss Douglass' lap, or in student and principal kneeling together to pray. Abbot letters and diaries suggest that such encounters were common in the real-life Academy. Harriet Chapell's journal describes how first Lizzie, then Harriet herself talks at length with Miss McKeen when each is gathering courage to join the church and "become a Christian."

As Harriet's Abbot years go on, adults gradually join the other people who are helping her toward maturity. First and youngest of her helpers is Lizzie, with her "loveliness that is born of a Christlike spirit," whom she cares for like a little mother during the frequent illnesses that eventually keep Lizzie home from Abbot for good. Lizzie is "such a darling, confiding little thing." She "helps me to be good more than anyone can ever know." Her later friend Jessie Cole is an excellent student, editor of *Courant* and "a jewel right through." Harriet respects her, and tries hard to emulate her. Fred regularly holds long talks with her about religion, and describes to her the Baptist revivals at which he has been speaking back in New London. "I do want to be better," Harriet writes in December of her second year, "more as Lizzie and Fred believe me to be." With the passing of time, we read less and less of Smith Hall shenanigans, more of her absorption in painting and bible reading. Instead of being annoyed by confining weather, a day of rain increases her sense of "myselfness." Sundays are now "quiet and solemn" times. She no longer naps during church sermons, but finds the services beautiful and inspiring.[96]

Harriet's parents become dearer with distance. Deep into her first Abbot spring, she writes, "Now that they miss me so much more than usual, I feel that I ought to do everything I can for them." After her "blessed father's" death over the summer of 1874, she thinks and wonders often about heaven. Her love for Fred increasingly seems to her a holy thing, as does his for her. "Surely there never was a nobler, tenderer lover," she writes after one of his visits to Abbot—prolonged a day in spite of Miss McKeen's displeasure.[97] Abbot does not so much create Harriet's growth as it grudgingly or encouragingly gives it room.

Students had always organized clubs and enjoyed rituals at Abbot. During the stable McKeen years, student organizations and traditions, once seeded, could evolve uninterrupted by administrative upheaval. To be sure, some were short-lived: rival boat clubs (the Nereids and the Undines) did not survive the graduation of their six members in 1874, and the Cecilia Society lasted just two years and several musical soirées. The *Sphinx* had ten years to live up to its name, gained "from the fact that the Sphinx (ancient) was the embodiment of feminine wisdom and strength." The Sphinx was much like Phillips students' Philomathean Society in form. "What do we do? Our program is varied. At times debate arouses us to give more of a reason than the woman's 'because.' "[98] At other times the twenty to thirty members would spend an evening reading aloud from a favorite book and acting out characters and scenes (these activities at times must have verged dangerously close to theater), or would mount their own minstrel shows, or exchange extemporaneous speeches on historical or current political issues.

Most important of organizations was *Courant* and its editorial board. This enduring periodical was begun by students in 1873 and warmly encouraged by the faculty. Alumnae remembered the excitement that filled the school when it was founded, for few female seminaries or colleges had published anything so ambitious. The *Courant* editors were the acknowledged intellectual leaders of the school. Their meetings ranged wide: "Very dire were the discussions as to why a girl's mind was not constructed to endure the strain of competition," wrote Alice Merriam Moore, '74, who served on the first editorial board, and soon after her graduation became co-editor with her husband of a small Michigan newspaper.[99] Early *Courant* writing is particularly lively: a fashion column; "St. Selmo," a take-off of the novel-melodrama *St. Elmo*; travel essays from Rome and Egypt; an essay comparing the French poet Boileau with Horace; editorial "commiseration to the unfortunate Harvard freshman who was seized while attempting to enter our Academy on Hallowe'en" (and later jailed overnight);[100] news of lectures or Draper Readings for alumnae ("the old scholars will be glad to know . . ."); and feisty editorial comments on practically everything. "It has been said that girls can write only nonsense," wrote the first editors (among them Clara Hamlin, Senior Editor for 1873).[101] These editors expose the nonsense around them. They freely criticize other school and college publications. They have a wonderful time with a dead-serious poem called "Willie's Prize," which they have read in the Phillips boys' Philomathean *Mirror*. "It is neither epic nor lyric in its character," they write. "Indeed, it seems to usher in a new era in letters." In the poem Willie describes to "his mamma" his sorrow at losing a prize competition. Finally, he sobs himself to sleep on her lap: "Under the tender lids a flow/of humid grief came stealing." The *Courant's* editors are merciless:

> We appreciate, as never before, the grandeur of that self-command which they [the Phillips students] preserve throughout the trying ordeal of defeat, though their little hearts are swelling well-nigh to bursting. We infer that Willie thought that only a manly soul could endure this tremendous grief, for he asks earnestly,
>   "Do women have ambition?"
> Yes, Willie, they do.[102]

They even take on the Reverend Henry Ward Beecher, who spoke on "Education" in Town Hall. "To those who had listened to him before, he seemed a faint suggestion of the great Beecher, he was so far below his own mark. We hope that all who heard him as a lecturer may hear the preacher; and we know they will wonder that he can put his grand powers to such inferior uses."[103]

Courant had proudly begun as a periodical unread by faculty till after publication, but rather quickly some of this life goes out of it. The right of adult scrutiny was eventually asserted. Indeed, it is amazing that the faculty held off for six years, for censorship was taken for granted in those times. *The Knife* and *The Fork*, rival class newspapers for '71 and '72 had died under the McKeens' critical glare. Bradford Academy's *Lantern* editors would print only one issue in 1887, and even this was never sold because an editor had dared to criticize a lecture given by a Trustee. Around 1879, the year Phebe McKeen resigned as faculty adviser, the *Courant* becomes tame: no more cutting criticism of other school and college periodicals, no ironic comments about Abbot's rules. The essays "are too prim and precise," complained the *Phillipian* in 1883, as if the writers feared "some dreadful punishment" for using less conventional styles.[104] By 1888 Miss McKeen herself is editing the "Driftwood" section—news for the Dear Old Girls. In the June 1889 issue seven of the Driftwood's nine pages describe religious occasions or speakers; one more whole page is devoted to the cute sayings of "Abbot grandchildren." It is hard to tell who is controlling the article content. A pious alumna argues in "Some Dangerous Tendencies" against elective courses, asserting that "the late labor troubles" (probably the Chicago Haymarket riots) show how "unlimited freedom is often abused."[105] The editors of 1889–90 are agog over a *Courant* writing contest for students and alumnae on the subject of "clover."[106] The winner's story begins, "Everything and everybody loved little White Clover." All the poetry suffers from the genteel tradition which, as Santayana pointed out, had long been a disease in New England.

Still, there are some wonderful pieces in *Courant*: the best of student course papers (on "the Ramayana" and "Chaucer's Women," November 1879); a graphic description of an Indian missionary station in Montana run by an alumna and her mother ("The first thing to be done was to give the children citizen's dress . . . It was pitiful to see the old people waiting outside the door to ask for their children's hair.")[107] An indignant *Courant* editor might rail against the degeneration of written English among modern students, but Abbot's best writing was very good indeed. The experience young women gained in organizations like the *Sphinx* and the *Courant* sharpened skills that would undergird lifetimes of involvement in women's clubs, churches, and reform groups. American girls might learn parliamentary procedure almost in fun, but the suffrage, temperance, and settlement house movements would use it in earnest, just as they drew strength from the adult network of woman friends and kin which for most boarding school alumnae was a continuation of the community of women they had known in their student days.

Students' sense of identification with their own classes was much strengthened during the McKeen period. This process was well begun in the 1850's by Miss Hasseltine's precise classing of pupils, but it was enhanced by the increasing tendency of all girls to stay at least one full year instead of coming for a term or two, then leaving.[108] Class parties, class breakfasts at Sunset Rock, class sleigh rides, and class representatives on *Courant* all raised class consciousness. The Seniors were special,

17. A Picnic, 1888.

and knew it. Generally a small group of twelve, more or less, they felt themselves to be women, not girls, and at age twenty to twenty-two they usually were.[109] The Class of '73 prided itself on being the first to wear class pins, the first to "indulge in a class sleighride and form a baseball nine."[110] Every Senior class held special entertainments in Smith Hall. Sometimes they dressed up as classical Greeks (or gypsies or Japanese nobility), decorating their own Senior parlor accordingly, and inviting the school to enjoy a period tableau, a Virginia reel, or a "conversation party" in which the contestants must hold a five-minute discussion on questions such as "Does the incubated chicken love its mother?" At other times, they invited their own special friends: favorite adults, fiancés from home, theologues from the Hilltop. In the fall of 1878 they transformed the Academy Hall into a drawing room and invited 140 guests. On one occasion the Seniors danced ballroom figures in boy-girl couples, but Miss McKeen came in, told everyone what she thought of the new "positions," and responded to the few feeble protests by asking, "How would you feel if the music stopped?"[111]

Graduation ("Anniversary") time was the biggest class party of the year, and the most solemn. It followed a flurry of preparations, during which the old cramming for examinations was little in evidence, and the "dissipations of closing weeks" were uppermost.[112] "Study is highly beneficial and quite interesting, but never less so than during the last week of the term," one student wrote.[113] The "Senior Exhibition" began Anniversary Day with music, a French or German or Latin oration, and essay reading in Hall. Then the whole school repaired to the Grove, the landscaped wood behind Smith Hall, for the reading of a Class History and the planting of the class vine or tree, with appropriate "Oak Song" or this "Pale Ivy" vine song of 1876:

> Symbol of our trust! When sorrow
> Darkens on our shadowy way,
> Be thou sign of bright to-morrow,—
> Climb to where the sunbeams play.
> (verse 1 of five verses)[114]

After the song and the "vine oration" came the presentation of the Class Spade to the president of the Senior Middle class, a change into white dresses, and the "charming procession . . . down the leafy path" to South Church.[15] There the school heard a Commencement address, and President Park of the Trustees would deliver a short sermon and present the diplomas. Traditionally, the Parting Hymn was sung by all assembled,

> Father, I know that all my life
> Is portioned out to me.
> The changes that will surely come
> I do not fear to see.
> I ask thee for a present mind
> Intent on pleasing thee.[116]

and traditionally, everyone wept. Thus were Abbot's graduates sent off with much the same advice that Maria Browne had given in 1857; accept what comes; subdue your own desires; be of service to others.

Class mottoes underline it: 1874's was "Set Free to Serve"; 1880's, "Happy in my Lot."

The noon or evening farewell party was a grand levee, a bewildering display (reported the *Congregationalist*)[117] of "feminine grace, personal intelligence, and social culture." Finally, with a turn of the clock hand, the year's community of women dissolved, its particular human chemistry too intricate to be duplicated.

Progress of a Victorian School

Christ has established the soul-rights of women.
Rev. James Hoppin to Abbot, 1856

Even during its golden age, Abbot was not static. Its students and teachers underwent private evolutions that mirrored the changes taking place in the world beyond; Philena McKeen herself passed through stages of personal crisis and fresh-won assurance during her thirty-three year tenure. Some of Abbot's Victorian values grew stronger than ever: thrift, punctuality, the systemization of daily life, the exaltation of the school "family"—they gradually became Abbot traditions whose venerability was justification enough. Other Victorian ideas contained the seeds of their own destruction: if self-sufficiency, will power, and controlled drive were admirable in men, why might they not be so in women? As Abbot Academy developed its own resources apart from the male-dominated Hilltop, Abbot girls learned to be less submissive. Intersex relationships within the Abbot-Andover community, religious practices, and the Abbot students' evolving self-images reflected simultaneous tendencies to rigidity and change that characterized Victorian America.

Male and Female

The girls Harriet Chapell knew "went for *men*," no matter how "silly and conceited," "like sheep after salt."[1] The McKeen sisters realized this as fully as Harriet did, but took quite a different view of what to do about it. There is no suggestion that they feared or hated men: quite the contrary. "Many a love affair they sped on its way," remembered Anna Dawes, '70.[2] To be wife and mother was woman's sacred calling—but the McKeens felt that far too many girls rushed into marriage.[3] Every young woman must have protection while she carefully prepared and waited for the *right* man. To Phebe, speaking through her novel *Theodora*, a girl's beloved brothers were the best models and guides for her choice of a husband; it is her martyred brother's comrade-in-arms whom Theodora finally marries, after rejecting two ardent suitors. To Philena a minister was the ideal husband for an Abbot graduate, an orthodox parsonage the ideal home.[4] She was backed in this opinion by Professor Park, to whom "the great aim of Andover is to train the minds of women so they will prefer an intelligent preacher to a pretty one."[5]

The McKeens' immediate problem was to shelter the growing girl from her own "ominous sexual awakening," as a twentieth-century historian terms it.[6] The elderly Catharine Beecher described female adolescence more subtly as the "period when the young, especially the highly gifted, find an outbursting of sensibilities that they have not learned to control."[7] This concern with the special stress of puberty and sexual maturation was quite new to a society that had long considered youth fourteen to twenty-one years old capable of adult labor in factory, farm or home, and of active participation in church affairs. Abbot did its bit to help invent the concept of adolescence: the McKeen sisters erected a wall of rules to provide Abbot girls the needed protection, cutting chinks only in those places they themselves approved. Chinks there were: calling hours Wednesdays and Saturdays— any time outside of prayer or study hours—provided callers had first been introduced to the girl's family. This was restrictive enough for girls far from home: "It was very funny that you should write about my behavior in society when I see no society at all," Antoinette Bancroft wrote her oversolicitous brother.[8] Phillips boys' attendance at every Abbot occasion, when not forbidden outright, was ordained beforehand, and chief secret policeman Uncle Sam Taylor did his best to help the McKeens keep control, with the assistance of student spies. Phillips alumnus Nathaniel Niles described how the invisible wall functioned.

> One night there was to be a party at the Fem. Sem. Of course, those boys who, through their sisters or cousins or aunts, were to be guests were the envy of every boy in the school. Two boys "not expected" at the entertainment conceived the idea that perhaps it would be an evidence of gratitude to heave a cat through one of the windows.

They started down the Hill, carrying the cat in their arms. They barely avoided Dr. Taylor, who intercepted them and gave chase, but "when they reached Abbot, they found the grounds so thoroughly patrolled that they had to give up their plan."[9]

*18. Male and female at the boundary, Harriet Chapell's Journal,
10 May 1874.*

19. Behind the barrier between Abbot and Phillips Academy.

Miss McKeen's "methods of government" "were often disagreeable," says a teacher colleague.[10] She suspended one girl and expelled another for "flirting." Harriet Chapell tells how "Philo" gathered the evidence for conviction by commanding every girl in Hall to answer ten questions in writing about her own or others' doings with the Phillipians.[11] Even when legitimate invitations were received from the Hill, (as for a football game in the fall of 1878), a "higher power" might talk the girls out of going.[12] Gone were the days of coeducational boarding houses. Miss McKeen wrote Cecil Bancroft twice in 1885 to insist that one of the Phillips boarding-house keepers *not allow boys to occupy any room upon our side of her house*. It is a constant source of evil to you and to me to have that post of observation occupied."

> The effect of having young men, or *man*, there is pernicious every moment, as it keeps the *idea* of *boys* in the thoughts of the young ladies all the time: indeed, they can neither study, nor dress, nor undress, nor walk, nor play, nor sit still, except under observation, usually of several pairs of eyes.[13]

Strong measures. They chiefly serve to suggest that their purpose was impossible of achievement. Even the valued theologues could not be trusted to escort Abbot girls the shortest way home from an eveing lecture or a professor's levee. Miss McKeen could make a Commencement usher out of a seemingly respectable Phillipian like Headmaster Bancroft's nephew, Alfred E. Stearns (himself Headmaster from 1903 to 1933), but she could not keep him from "raising cain"—as he wrote his sister Mabel—with a lot of girls "in a room back of the stage" while the essays were being read, or spending all afternoon of Anniversary Day in the Grove with "Miss———."[14] Stearns had already taken many a Fem Sem's measure from the back of South Church or the Academy Hall at sermons and public recitals ("they looked too smooth"—Stearns's supreme compliment).[15] Where Phillipians habitually kept

> the town in constant fright
> By prowling round it half the night,[16]

peeking through Smith Hall blinds, or serenading their favorite girls,[17] not even Philena McKeen could stem the tide. "Did you know," Stearns asked his sister,

> that the Fem. Sem. got a terrible blowing up for not coming straight home after the Senior Party? Miss Hinkley got an especially bad one as Miss McKeen told her that she did not expect

such things from her. Miss McKeen further told them that fellows who would do such things would have no respect for them and would make fun of them and talk lightly of them behind their backs. As far as I have been able to learn, though, the thought of such shameful treatment at the hands of the fellows does not disturb the girls much. If Miss McK. had known that I was one of the base mortals concerned, I fear that I would have looked in vain for my invitation to usher.[18]

Abbot students' friendships with the "Lord's Annointed"[19] from the Theological Seminary were often serious business, and numerous marriages resulted. Their relationship to the Phillips Academy students, or "Cads," was usually more of a brother-sister affair, with teasing and bickering to match. Indeed, there still were several actual sister-brother pairs at the two schools each year, even though the number had greatly diminished following the opening of Punchard High School.[20] It was easy for a nineteen- or twenty-year-old Abbot woman to look down upon the "Cad," to answer a *Mirror* barb at *Courant* by noting that "rudeness is easily pardoned in small boys," or to lecture a Cad correspondent from the height of the *Courant* editor's throne: "Yes, modesty is always commendable in the young. But don't be too humble. Remember that in time the little acorn becomes the great oak, and perhaps, if you are a good boy, and mind your book, you will grow to be a theologue, and can call at the Fem. Sem."[21] They quickly shed their hauteur when there was fun to be had, however—a spelling match between Phillips and Abbot, or a school-sanctioned expedition "in full force" and fancy dress[22] to a Philomathean Society declamation, or a Seminary professor's party, or the Andover-Exeter baseball game. It was probably in vain that the McKeens had their girls sing the hymn "Calm me, my God, and Keep me Calm" at evening prayers before one of these co-educational events "to keep them from getting upset by the coming gaiety," a procedure that one alumna, a "staid minister's wife," never forgot.[23] "All of the Fem. Sems." watched one boxing exhibition from the gallery, wrote young Stearns. "When a fellow would get hit a pretty good crack in the face, there would be a sympathetic O–W! rustle the whole length of the gallery, which sounded very funny and in some cases broke up the boxers for a time."[24]

Better still were the surreptitious skating on Pomps Pond or the Cads' makeshift rink and the coasting parties on School Street with snow flying and the boys' cries of "Road!" ringing in the air.[25] "Philo" brought these to a halt each winter, of course, but not until mid-

February in at least two years, 1879 and 1881. One wonders how she could have missed them. Did she simply pretend not to notice? For one way or another, Abbot girls and Hilltop students met and mingled. The chronicler of 1887 added the total number of the seventeen Seniors' Hill acquaintances and got 376: 316 Phillips students and 60 theologues. Of these, only eleven Phillipians and six theologues had formal permission to call at Abbot. And this was the count "*before* the Senior party–*"* the writer exults.

Except for restrictions on his Fem Sem calls, the nineteenth-century Phillips student had a freedom unthinkable a generation later: this was a school where a fellow had to learn on his own to be a man, where boys arranged their own revenges for unfair bullying, their own athletic contests, their own free-time amusements. As soon as chapel ended on a perfect winter day, there was a race for the bobsleds and a tearing down the icy hill past Abbot right to the railroad station. The manliest fellows would rather crash into a tree (and did now and then, with consequent concussions) than refuse a challenge from a pal. This freedom can only have emphasized to Abbot students the restrictions under which they lived. The "American girl" was considered "a very delicate plant."[26] If there was a heavy snowstorm, a day scholar's brother might tramp through it to Abbot to tell his sister she was not to come home for the night, but the girl herself could not venture out, no matter how strong she felt. It was the boys who played heroes at the fire that destroyed the Mansion House early one morning in 1887, while the girls stayed in their beds, listening.

Still, there must also have been some comfort in Andover Hill's regard for woman's delicacy. No Abbot girl had to stand fast before a Samuel Taylor, who believed in "the doctrine of total depravity as applied to boys,"[27] or suffer the persecution of bullies with no hope of a resident teacher's intervention.[28] Further, many girls probably appreciated the protective barriers more than they would admit. Even the sociable Harriet Chapell, crammed into a chair under the pulpit of the Seminary Chapel to hear Professor Park's famous sermon on Peter's denial of Christ, thought it "just horrid to sit perched up in the face of the Phillipians." The jokes and talks she exchanged with boys met by chance (or by secret design) on the street would not be nearly so much fun had they been permitted. Harriet cannot have suffered too much from Abbot's rules. "Anyway," she wrote at the end of her first year, "it's a splendid school."[29]

Off and on, a vague vision of coeducation tempted Abbot's nineteenth-century trustees or teachers; but Dr. Taylor's narrow Phillips Academy seems to have been unappealing to the McKeens, and the

advantages of what Edwards Park approvingly called "proximate education" were too many to forgo lightly.[30] Abbot was far more accessible
to boys and men than schools like Bradford, whose principal, Annie
Johnson, did not allow a single visit from a boys' school till 1888, when
the Phillips glee club gave a concert . In making final arrangements for
this event, Miss Johnson wrote to Bancroft:

> Of course I should not suggest the theol. sem. men's coming. I do
> not know that they are more safe than other men, as a class.[31]

There certainly was no doubt about the feeling of Phillips students for
the Fem Sems. They received Abbot's centennial gift of a hand-sewn
Phillips banner with "a sudden burst, as of thunder out of a clear sky,
of a round of cheers," lasting a full five minutes. "It is very much to be
doubted whether *this* art of speaking be consistent with the constitu-
tional foundations of the Academy . . . The Trustees should look into
it," chuckled the *Congregationalist*.[32]

   The coeducation issue surfaced in Andover after Taylor died in 1871.
The success of several coeducational colleges and public high schools
was intriguing;[33] so were the arguments sprinkled through the educational journals during the last quarter of the century. Henry Barnard
cited the advantages of coeducation in his *American Pedagogy* (1876):
economy of means and forces; convenience to patrons (brothers and
sisters can attend the same school, and "each is safer from the presence
of the other"); "wholesome incitements to study," along with the social
culture that females lend to males; and the opportunity for girls to respond with womanly qualities to manly behavior.[34] Four of the speakers at Abbot's Semicentennial celebration felt called upon to address
the issue: three were for, one against. Much of Miss McKeen's enormous correspondence is lost,[35] and there is no way of knowing whether
this public airing of the coeducation question was preceded by serious
private negotiations between Abbot and Phillips. Philena McKeen was
delighted with Reverend Cecil F. P. Bancroft, who had taken over as
Phillips principal in 1873; she spoke repeatedly of her respect for his
scholarly interests, his kindness, and his concern for Christian character. On December 28, 1878, she wrote him in response to some act or
letter of his now hidden to us:

> My Dear Mr. Bancroft,
>   Your goodness is incomprehensible. I don't know but it would
> be the best thing that could be done, to join Abbott to Phillips
> & put you over all.[36]

That is all she says. If there *was* a genuine interest in merger, it seems to have died. Miss McKeen did propose some joint science facilities, suggesting that "the ideal arrangement" might be for "Phillips, Punchard, and Abbot, to combine in building one detached laboratory for common use, with one lecture-room and separate working-rooms, bringing together their treasures, and committing the most perfect appointments they could secure to the use of one professor, so fitted and endowed as to give the finest possible instruction to all, either collectively or severally or both."[37] But Punchard's Goldsmith was preoccupied with his own constituency, and Bancroft had work enough bringing together Phillips' Classical and English Departments to prepare boys for newly broadened college entrance requirements. Once Bancroft had raised his school's own funds for a new chemistry laboratory (1882) and for Graves Hall (1892), Phillips laboratories were for several years open to Abbot science classes; except for the helpful Professor Graves, however, they were at such times empty of men. Then, gradually, Abbot developed its own simpler labs in the basement of the Academy Hall, and the two schools edged away from academic cooperation.

Why did separate education win out? The arguments for it in Andover and throughout the United States were manifold and contradictory. Some men needed only to repeat the old assertions of women's intellectual inferiority. To others, females were worse than inferior: they were a naked threat to orderly civilization, compelled by their extravagant tastes and their sexual desires or social pretentions to grab always for power over men. The Rumanian-Jewish visitor I. J. Benjamin expressed one version of this harsh view:

> America worships two idols. First is that deaf, dumb, blind
> Mammon before whom the masses humbly bow in this land.
> They kneel before him, setting their honor aside, day and night
> thinking only of amassing wealth, of building palaces. The
> second idol, on the contrary, sees, hears, walks, and talks, and is
> above all full of life; it is the female sex. Both idols live together
> in constant warfare. What one builds, the other tears down; what
> one accumulates, the other scatters; what one makes good, the
> other spoils.[38]

Many girls absorbed men's notions of women's weaknesses. "If a boy is not trained to endure and to bear trouble," wrote an Abbot student in her journal, "he will grow up like a girl; and a boy that is a girl has all a girl's weakness without any of her regal qualities."[39] Or, as a popular lecturer put it, "Woman despises in man everything like herself except a tender heart. It is enough that she is effeminate and weak; she does not want another like herself."[40]

At the other extreme, there were those who thought women so far above men as to be vulnerable to corruption by *their* influence. Phebe McKeen's *Thornton Hall* characters keep all males at arm's length, and speak of girls as intellectually "equal, nay superior to boys."[41] M. Carey Thomas, supplementing graduate school tedium with study-conversation meetings among her women friends, determined to face squarely the role passion and sensuality played in men's lives, otherwise "what can we do against them?" She and her friends studied fifteen of her father's medical books, and were horrified at what they thought they had learned. "Religion, philanthropy, may as well cease; *Sense* remains . . . I am more thankful than ever to be a woman," for "the time a man has to spend in struggling against his lower nature she has to advance in."[42] Miss Thomas' undergraduate career as one of Cornell's first woman students convinced her that only in an all-female institution could women achieve the serenity and sense of freedom necessary for scholarly activity.

Some advocates of coeducation drew support from the widely held assumption that woman's unique susceptibility to religion made her a repository of purity and gave her special responsibility for developing virtue in men. "There is no more powerful preacher of righteousness for a young man from eighteen to twenty-five," wrote Phebe McKeen, "than a lively, winning, warmhearted, right-minded girl, all whose beauty and brightness is sacred to truth and purity."[43] Therefore, as "Marmee" told her Little Women, "let the boys be boys, the longer the better, and let the young men sow their wild oats if they must; but mothers, sisters and friends may help to make the crop a small one."[44] The McKeens thought that love and marriage could elevate both partners. Theodora's "love came upon [her fiancé Vincent Rolf] like a holy annointing, to set him apart to a nobler life."[45] Philena wrote with concern to one alumna about another, noting that Mary Tarbox, '71,

> pleased me better than when I have seen her before for years. As I told her, I have been expecting that the Lord would either let her fall deeply in love, or let some great discipline come upon her. I think the more agreeable method of development has overtaken her, and it is working admirably.[46]

Certainly Harriet Chapell's experience confirmed the sisters' intuitions. She wrote of Fred that she had "advanced years in knowing his heart."[47] Both sisters seem to have felt, however, that these happy results could only come about if the differences between women and men were valued and preserved. *Thornton Hall's* principal implored her girls to treasure their womanly qualities. Philena McKeen proudly published in *Courant* a letter sent her by Dorothea Dix soon after this pioneer reformer had spoken at Abbot: "Tell your girls to be women, not men; to show what a true woman is, and how great a power she has."[48] After a speaker described to all Abbot his theory of women's rights, Harriet Chapell recorded his conviction that "woman has her best rights in her duty . . . of guiding the heart and actions of man. . . . Then he said we must all strive to be angels in our homes."[49] Throngs of female and male celebrants applauded Reverend A. P. Peabody's Abbot Semicentennial speech describing the implications of this view for education. Men and women have different aptitudes, not equal ones, Harvard's Peabody said, thinking, no doubt, of Cambridge's new experiment in "proximate education"—the Harvard Annex (later Radcliffe):

> His is the wider; hers the richer field. His is the strength of reasoning; hers the quicker intuition and clearer insight. His the more easy mastery of abstract sciences; hers the far finer-seeing nature, the keener sense of beauty in art and in literature, and the larger capacity of culture in all that pertains to the beauty, charm, ornament, and joy of home society. I would not have the same culture pursued by both, for I should dread to find always in the parlor a duplicate of the counting-room or office.[50]

In return for the influence her special qualities commanded, Peabody suggested, woman should gladly submit to man's formal, legal authority in the home and the state. Abbot seems to have agreed; certainly there is no evidence that Philena or Phebe gave time to suffragist activities.[51] Yet this was not Maria J. B. Browne's retreat of the 1850's. Abbot women had to prepare themselves for active, useful lives outside their homes in churches, schools, missionary stations, and temperance societies. Their power in this "glorious work"[52] and in their families was sufficient without the vote. A true woman's cup was already full.

By 1892 a respectful distance had been established between Abbot and the two Hill schools. The "medium course"[53] created ambiguities, but none that daunted the Principals. Miss McKeen wrote her friend Bancroft with a request just before the Breakfast that was to honor her at her retirement:

Dear Mr. Bancroft,
    In your "Remarks" at the Breakfast, at the [Hotel] Vendome,

would you throw a morsel to appease two classes of people: the one, those who wonder at our carelessness in regard to the young ladies, that we allow them to take their exercise unattended by a teacher, and the second and larger class, who are constantly scolding because we do not promise the freest intercourse possible between the two schools and invite all of the boys to spend every evening in our parlors: Mrs. Prof. Hains and Mrs. Shirrell are such groaners.

So I thought a word from you, quite incidentally dropped, of course, might be a word in season: that is if you think as I'm sure I do, that P.A. & A.A. have stood in right relations so far as the administration of the schools is concerned.

Warmly yours,
P. McKeen Philena[54]

In the final decade of the McKeen era, then, Abbot determined on a future of its own, laying the groundwork for a resistance to coeducation that would last another seventy-five years.

Religion in the Golden Age

The nearest a woman could come in 1859 to being a Protestant minister was to be principal of a committed Protestant school.[55] Ministering to Abbot was a heady responsibility for Philena McKeen (her father's daughter)—one that both awed and stimulated her. As the Reverend Silas McKeen had met monthly for discussion with his fellow ministers, Miss McKeen consorted with giants in her many meetings and conversations with fellow minister-educators like Park, Churchill, and Bancroft. Her friendship may have been as important to them as was their support for her; it was especially sustaining to Professor Park, who grieved to find one friend after another abandoning him as the years went by. She and her school made up a concern the three men could hold in common, though they were divided on many philosophical issues. The kindly Churchill could not agree with Park that "Immortal souls have been lost in consequence of a wrong definition."[56] Park was a stubborn holdout for the old theology during the Theological Seminary "heresy trial" of 1886 and 87: from his semiretirement he supported the prosecuting Visitors Committee in its effort to remove the five "liberal" professor-editors of the Seminary's *Andover Review*. Meanwhile, Miss McKeen's "precious friend"[57] Churchill and Abbot Trustee Egbert Smyth (Abbot Board 1870–89) were two of the five defendants.[58] It must have needed tolerance and tact to navigate

20. Professor Churchill and his son come to tea with the sisters, Harriet Chapell's Journal, 24 June 1875.

between these poles, especially considering Park's "rather feudal views of women."[59] Miss McKeen had both. She also had, said one of her younger contemporaries, an "intellect of no common sort. It was masculine in its strength and in its acquirements, and she easily held her own in the great dialectic of Andover Hill,"[60] a dialectic which sought a synthesis of "the Theology of the Intellect and the Theology of the Feelings,"[61] even while the younger professors strove to construct a theology of action, the grounds for a crusade against social inequities and urban ills.

Smiling, Philena McKeen stepped into the middle of the fray. Though she was, like Park, an evangelical whose greatest joy was a student brought to Christ, she was too much immersed in the practical challenges of day-to-day soul-shepherding within a varied student flock to be fussy about doctrinal details, too worried about the effects of card-playing and dancing to contemplate the nature of Purgatory.[62]

If her prayers are fair evidence, her God could do most anything. She prayed that the Lord would send new students when Abbot's applications fell off. While raising money for the new main building, she thought of Him as a kind of heavenly Contractor whom she was assisting, and prayed Him "to use every dollar and every brick to His own glory."[63] To Philena McKeen, subjects such as her beloved art history were "the handmaids of religion;"[64] any true scholar or musician or artist was a proof of God's goodness,[65] while Christianity itself was more concerned with service to others than with the intricacies of salvation and afterlife which preoccupied men like Edwards Park.

If Park, Churchill, and Bancroft were Miss McKeen's chief ministerial colleagues and her teaching colleagues were her "vicars in the school,"[66] Trustee Warren Draper was her most important lay communicant, deacon, and keeper of the collection plate. Draper had come to Phillips Academy an almost penniless farmboy in the early 1840's. Working as a janitor at Abbot to pay his expenses, he met Irene ("Patience") Rowley (Abbot, '43), who was a student supervisor of Abbot's short-lived Commons; after his graduation from Amherst, they married. His dream had been the ministry, but ill health intervened. Shortly after entering Andover Theological Seminary, he had to give up his plans, involving as they did a grueling combination of study and work-for-pay. Instead he took over management of Andover Hill's Bookstore and Press. Though he thought of himself as tongue-tied, ineloquent, his new enterprise was the Seminary's propaganda arm: "the catalogue of his books became a catalogue of Homer's ships,"[67] as he sent out to the ends of the earth all manner of religious publications, including the *Andover Review* and *Bibliotheca Sacra*, the latter considered by many "the most learned and important theological review published in this country."[68] His typesetters could work in Hebrew, Greek, and Sanskrit. Much like Abbot's earlier Trustee Peter Smith, the staunch and kindly Draper "linked 'commercial honor' and 'personal virtue,'" becoming part of that responsible aristocracy on which—says historian Sklar—the nineteenth century American's sense of social stability depended.[69] He was "Mechanic, Merchant, Employer, Reader, Editor, Traveller, Patriot,"[70] running the Seminary's business— and after 1866 his own—till profits filled his pockets, and stayed there. He and Irene Draper lived frugally, childless, waiting for worthy causes.

One of his causes was the preservation of Indian Ridge Forest for public use, which he and others finally accomplished by Town Meeting vote in 1897. Another was the temperance movement, which he fought for in Town Meeting in spite of several arson attempts on his office by the opposition. "Don't be surprised that mischief has been done me," he wrote his father. "I am right, and the right will prevail in the end."[71] Here was an enthusiasm he could share with Miss Mc-Keen, who was doing her part by holding WCTU chapter meetings in the Abbot Grove, called "Temperance Woods" during this period. To Draper all good causes were religious causes, and education was above all a religious enterprise. Phillips Academy and Punchard High School he assisted in many ways, but his deepest interest was Abbot Academy. Drawn to the school by his old associations, and probably because he felt more at home a bit removed from the intellectual gymnastics of the Hilltop, he and the McKeens found common ground in their mutual passion for temperance, among many other things.[72] Philena gladly welcomed Draper to the Board as Trustee in 1868, and as Treasurer in 1876. In doing so she welcomed his wife, too, for as Irene Draper was her husband's partner in all his business affairs, she was his chief consultant in all Abbot ones. The Drapers built their "homestead" just opposite the Abbot gates so that there could be as much coming and going as possible with the Abbot family.[73] They invited girls to taffy pulls; they joined the Smith Hall Thanksgiving feasts; they welcomed and cared for ill or homesick students; they made their home a small dormitory when the school was overfull in 1882. Whenever a sum needed for a specific purpose could not be found—as when the first *Courants* required funding—Warren or Irene Draper managed to find it somewhere. Before his death in 1901, Warren Draper was to give a total of $80,000 to Abbot, and his long-lived wife would add still more.

Thus the Drapers joined the Parks, the Churchills, the Bancrofts, and the McKeens in "that matrix of social institutions and web of personal interdependence" which was Victorian America[74] and Victorian Andover, a matrix to which religion was still central. If some of the "exuberance and openness" of the early 1800's was gone, Andover did not miss it.[75] Exuberance in the young could be dangerous, as we have already seen. Englishman Alexander Mackay, observing American girls' tyrannous demands on their parents, had years ago complained that American society was "under the absolute sway of young ladies in their teens."[76] Many Americans (especially men) believed that religious training could efficiently tame women to their proper role. "Religion is exactly what a woman needs, for it gives her that dignity that best suits her dependence," wrote Caleb Atwater in *The Ladies Repository*.[77] Abbot's education for "Christian womanhood" convinced the 1890 *Courant* editors that "to do the daily grind faithfully is the duty of each one toward bringing about the coming of the kingdom."[78] Religious training could fit women for their great tasks as mothers or

21. Warren Fales Draper, a Yankee benefactor. From Memorial *to* W. F. Draper.

teachers of souls; it served alternately as "a kind of tranquilizer for the many undefined longings which swept even the most pious young girl, and about which it was better to pray than to think."[79]

Begin with the Lord's day. Abbot's Sabbath was (said the Catalogue) to "be observed as in any other Christian family. Calls will neither be made nor received on that day. Unless providentially called away, no young lady will be absent from her home here a single Sabbath during the term, as we consider excitement and change of scene opposed to that quiet thoughtfulness which belong to holy time."[80] This was the traditional compulsory New England Sabbath in which, complained a visitor of 1858, "the rest of Sunday is the rest of the tomb."[81] Harriet Chapell heartily agreed at first:

> Such horrid Sundays we have here—fish balls, brown bread, mustard, and doughnuts for breakfast, then half-hours, and three quarters to dress, go to Church, sit perked up in the gallery, home to dinner, off immediately to service, then home to stay with your room-mate till tea time; after that the visiting quarters, half-hours, and solitude with the victimized roommate, then bed ends the long day. Not a bit of home Sunday life, not one minute of being all together for a good earnest talk.[82]

Hardest of all was "reporting the sermon" to Miss McKeen or a teacher every Sunday, sometimes in writing; for Harriet so often slept through sermons.

Eventually, Harriet learned how to survive Sundays. She laid in food supplies each Saturday so that she and her friends could find comfort in secret parties. She and Mame made so much noise during one half-hour that "Miss Palmer comes tripping" to their door: " 'Aren't we getting into a frolic?' Mame said 'Yes'm, thank you Miss Palmer' so humbly that I was about convulsed with laughter." An hour or so later: "We are in perfect agony now, for we have tried to laugh quietly to ourselves and it is such hard work."[83]

Even Christmas was just an extra Sabbath day on Zion's Hill until the mid-1870's. At least the Abbot girls had no classes as Phillips students did, but they probably went to hear Professor Park's hour-long sermon on December 25 of the McKeen's first year, when Phillips student Charles Phelps Taft wrote his father about it. "The chief thing he seemed to be driving at was, that there was no end to eternity. I could not make anything else out of it. This don't seem at all like Christmas."[84]

In addition to half-hours and daily "devotions," time was set aside every Thursday evening for an evening prayer meeting and inspirational talk; and on Saturday afternoon or evening all students gathered to hear a lecture by one of the McKeens, or to receive special preparation by Dr. Bancroft or another minister for Communion Service. There were special meetings for the fervent; a dozen Seniors habitually crowded into the class president's Smith Hall room to pray for one another. Many girls complained, but others thrived (or, like Harriet, complained at first and thrived later). A student of 1861 wrote of walking back to Abbot after an inspiring meeting on the Hill. "In the calm light of the Sabbath sunset, my former indecision returned. Duty and inclination, the one cold and stern, the other fair and winning, alternately presented their claims."[85] Later entries suggest that duty won out for this young woman. A student music teacher from the McKeens' first year recalled to them in 1879 that

> It was while I was at Abbott Academy that I gained the first knowledge of my soul's wants . . . What I felt most and have never forgotten was the ease and power with which you both labored and prayed with the girls under your care for the salvation of their souls.

She wrote with passion, for she felt that her own conversion at age thirty-three and the religious change it impelled in her profligate husband and five children had come only just in time to save her family.[86]

Yet Abbot was no longer obsessed by conversion, as Phillips occasionally was under Taylor and as Mount Holyoke had been for decades to the distress of free spirits like Emily Dickinson. Phebe McKeen expressed in *Theodora* her understanding of the ambiguities the conversion process presented in a world of expanding scientific knowledge.[87] Like many boarding schools of the time, Abbot modeled itself on the Christian home: both McKeens emphasized the school Family's responsibility for orderly Christian nurture.[88] We hear less of the inner storms of conversion as the McKeen era progresses. Apparently this Family was busy responding to the universal desire of middle class Americans to protect their growing daughters "from the howling storm outside."[89]

Abbot approached religion intellectually as well as ritually. Graduates remembered the theological professors who came down the Hill to Abbot, Calvin Stowe to teach Biblical History, Trustee Park to secure Abbot girls against Hellfire by reminding them that "an infinite wrong against an Infinite Being deserves an infinite punishment."[90] Meanwhile, Philena McKeen worked to perfect her course in Butler's Analogy. This rite of passage was the crown (or was it the fetish?)[91] of every Senior's career. Said an 1879 report in the *Congregationalist*, young women are not supposed to excel in "metaphysical studies," but "in Abbot Academy, Andover, Massachusetts, there is no examination in which pupils shine more brilliantly than in that on Butler's *Analogy*." In time she took over the Biblical and ecclesiastical history courses from the men. Draper published her ambitious Church History syllabus (it went from "Noah and the Flood, 2348 B.C." and "Abraham, 2247 B.C." through the mid-nineteenth century), and she filled it with her own lesson plans and marginal scrawls. She notes that "Adam was put in the garden to 'dress and keep it.' Employment, if not labor, was a condition of happiness in paradise." She found it important that an Egyptologist had discovered inscriptions confirming the drought during the "seven lean years," and had dated it at 1900 B.C. She mingled a fuzzy knowledge of Darwin's theories with ancient Congregationalist prejudices in her endorsement of a Michigan University professor, who, she writes, had asserted that "the negro race is older than Adam. His chief argument is derived from the *lack of time* between Adam and Ham for the black race to deteriorate so much, as we see so little change since men began to observe." She drew sounder lessons from chemistry, noting that "64 original elements form all the earth," including the humans who people it. Thus " 'Dust thou art and to dust shalt thou return' is literally true."[92] The course itself alternated dreary sectarian controversies with stirring, detailed stories of Roman emperors or Christian martyrs and extraordinarily clear explanations of competing philosophies. Supplementary reading consisted of scholarly works like Stanley's *History of the Jewish Church* and articles from *Bibliotheca Sacra*.

Miss McKeen's syllabus shows no sign of the interest Elizabeth Cady Stanton had provoked among woman's rights activists in a new biblical scholarship resentful of the almost total dominance of men in biblical history and attentive to women's deserved place in Christian tradition.[93] Perhaps nothing Mrs. Stanton proposed could move Philena McKeen, uncomfortable as she seems to have been with the suffragist creed. She did keep a clipping reporting a meeting where Lady Henry Somerset criticised Protestant Christianity: "So long as the Virgin Mary could not be recognized, so long would women not be recognized."[94]

Abbot students were continually reminded of the larger Christian community connected with their school. Over and over again, missionaries or their Abbot alumna wives came to spend the Sabbath and to speak. William Schauffler visited his old classrooms in 1880. A *Courant* reporter was particularly interested in a talk by Rev. Dr. Crumwell, black missionary in Liberia, who told the girls that "the condition of morals under [American] slavery was far lower than [under] paganism." The whole school went to South Church to hear evening lectures by Professor Stowe, now living in Hartford, and Phillips Brooks, friend of the Seminary's liberals; the older students traveled to nearby towns on several occasions to attend convocations run by the American Board of Foreign Missions. (Miss McKeen once allowed fifty girls to spend the night on the floor of a church in Lowell when teachers and students decided to stay on an extra day. They used pew cushions for mattresses and slept under quilts provided by a local merchant.[95]) Letters were regularly read in

Hall from Old Scholars describing their work "among the lowly" in a city mission, in Hampton Institute, or in Turkey,[96] and requesting Christmas boxes of the linen or clothes that Abbot students often sewed and packed for the needy. This was a more practical Christianity than that traditionally emphasized on the Hilltop, where a professor once scolded a theologue for spending his time helping poor families in the Andover mill district: "That——is wasting his Seminary course in what *he calls doing good*."[97] It was also a Christianity that brought alien places close, involving Abbot students in Bulgarian or Japanese political tangles as in a cosmic battle between the Heathen and the Saved. Seminary professor John Phelps Taylor told the graduating Class of 1891 that each Senior would "take the diploma today as a symbol of your union and communion with a shining host, the living and the dead, graduates and friends of Abbot Academy, who long for a clearer union and a more perfect ministry in the steps of Mary and Mary's son."

With the waning of Abbot's golden age, one senses Philena McKeen tiring of the constant effort needed to pit her beliefs against the "destructive tendency of this age," as one *Courant* writer put it.[98] The scientific mentality was displacing the theological mentality to which she had been raised; Miss McKeen could not hold back the wave alone. For a while, her painful rheumatism and the school's day-to-day problems eroded her optimism and her faith. When her own and Abbot's health improved during the summer of 1888, she wrote to Irene Draper, chiding herself: "I am often obliged to turn upon myself as distrust rises in regard to God's purposes toward the school and to myself, with 'O fool, and slow of heart *to believe!*'" So many girls were now apathetic about Abbot's rigorous Christian routine that Miss McKeen retreated from the concept of an entire "community in Christ," and in 1891 encouraged the really devoted few (thirty or so at first) to organize the "Christian Workers," a precursor of the Abbot Religious Association. In another area, disillusionment had a happier result. The self-reporting system, which had rubbed consciences raw for a generation, seemed now to be creating only cynicism and distrust. It was abandoned by universal consent in 1890, and its originator found herself pleased to see it go.

Miss McKeen, so long tolerant of the Congregationalists' bias against women's formal leadership in the church, gradually lost patience with her own denomination. She wrote the *Congregationalist* in 1879 to express gratitude for the reinstitution of the "day of Prayer" for schools and colleges, but asked why women's institutions could not be explicitly included? "Is it because women are naturally good enough, or because they have no souls?" Her answer is a cynical one: men have always supported all-male schools with financial gifts, therefore they keep watch over the spiritual health of those institutions as though to make certain of the worth of their investment. "Let money find its way to girls' schools, and prayer would naturally follow."[99] Though the McKeens had come East in 1859 as educational missionaries to a threadbare Abbot Acadmy, faith, hope, and love were no longer sufficient for the now "celebrated school."[100] Speaking for the Trustees at Philena McKeen's last Commencement, Seminary professor John Phelps Taylor might compare her thirty-three year "ministry" at Abbot with "the Master's" span of life on earth, but the minister herself had by then lost her original fervor. Toward the end of her life, Miss McKeen often attended services at Andover's Episcopal Church. We cannot know whether she was looking for more of the Virgin Mary or for a new social status, since so many of Andover's business leaders were now Episcopalians.[101] In any case, her discouragement, along with the Theological Seminary's declining national influence and the secular distractions of the late nineteenth century, combined to weaken the confident, unifying Congregationalist orientation which Abbot's founders had built into its constitution.[102] It was the end of an era for this "elder daughter of Christian Academies in New England."[103]

Self Images

Like young people anywhere, any time, Abbot students had their worries and their dreams. Their lives had boundaries ours have not; for them also, life's possibilities extended to places few of us ever visit in our minds.

Death was a near boundary. Though most of women's physical "weakness" was myth, many young people did sicken and die. One tried to prepare for it. Rarely was dying hidden in hospitals; student Julia Downs died in her South Hall room on 6 October 1873. Almost every issue of *Courant* reports the death of at least one student or young alumna.

> Among those of that happy family in Smith Hall during the few years following 1870 is a name spoken always with love . . . a name which is now spoken with tears . . . Dear Minnie Lewis is a saint in heaven. Our hearts are full; but remembering what she was, we can ask no questions. She was the Lord's; is it not lawful for Him to do what He will with His own?

Was it any real comfort for the dying to be "the Lord's"? Martha Bailey, '71, had time to seek that solace, at least, and a death well prepared for was valued. "I long to see my Father in Heaven . . . Oh I never thought it could be so beautiful to die." The horror expressed in *Courant* of a student drowned reflects these young women's fear of sudden death. It is most pronounced in the record of alumna Gertrude Spalding Hayden's murder, though here we can also detect a crude relish in the drama of it all.

> It was the old story, too often told, of a young orphan heiress infatuated by a worthless man, who loved her with a love more cruel than the grave—a wilful, stolen marriage—a gay life for a little while—then years of enduring all the indignities and wrongs that the brutal selfishness of a drinking man can inflict upon a timid young wife.

The husband soon got "in the habit of extorting her property from her . . . with his pistol at her head." Gertie, no longer the "playful, kittenlike creature" she had been at Abbot, finally "took refuge with her sisters" in a Vermont border town, but her husband traveled 200 miles to force his way into her home (wounding her brother-in-law) and shoot her. While she lingered a few hours, her husband sent from prison to ask her forgiveness. She gave it, and died.[104]

Life's boundary crossed, afterlife waited. For many, heaven was real. Alumna Elizabeth Stuart Phelps (Mrs. Ward) found the public much preferred her two "Gates" novels about heaven to her book on the evils of this industrializing world, *The Silent Partner*. *The Gates Ajar* was the most popular of her fifty-two published books. Within these pearly gates, men and women are equal and Christ protects woman against male incursions whenever her worth is questioned. *The Gates Beyond* describes a Heaven much like the decorous Old Andover of Elizabeth's girlhood,—"everything in its place,"—with one improvement: one's Heaven-husband was one's God-intended soulmate, not necessarily one's husband-on-earth. (Mr. Ward had been a great disappointment to Elizabeth Phelps.)[105] For everyone, revered memory could extend individual life. One would expect Phebe McKeen's death at age forty-eight to absorb the whole Abbot community, but what is striking is the sense of her continued presence into the 1890's as a kind of local school saint. In spite of her intense intellectual energy, Phebe had had "consumption" for years. Philena had greatly hoped that a long European holiday would restore her; this the Trustees granted the two sisters in 1875–76, but it did no permanent good. Phebe left before Commencement in 1879 to try to get well. "Be my sister's counselor and comforter while I am gone," she wrote Headmaster Bancroft soon after her leavetaking. For her graduating Seniors she sent a special message.

> I am more sorry than I will try to tell you to desert you so, and not to be there to give you my parting blessing when you go away. But my Heavenly Father lays his hand upon me saying "Be still," and that is the end of it.

She gave them careful instructions for the oral examination.

> I won't let anyone else examine you in Milton, [because] I cannot give you the review you need. Instead, prepare to recite *Lycidas* and *Comus*. Rehearse well under Helen Page. And be sure to read *Paradise Lost* some time within the next three years. I shall love to hear from each of you, dear girls. With heartfelt love,
>
> Phebe McKeen.

Her instructions were followed to the letter, and the Senior Literature course remained "Miss Phebe's class" throughout the next year, though Phebe herself was convalescing with a friend in Baltimore. On the night train back to Andover and the 1880 Commencement, she went to sleep after speaking over the 121st Psalm (I will lift up mine eyes unto the hills . . .) and she never woke up.

Death was no stranger to Philena McKeen. Long before, her mother had been killed in an accident; her father, her only brother, and three of her sisters had died of tuberculosis. But Phebe had been her whole family, her closest friend and colleague, for twenty-four years. "Neither could be understood without the other," wrote Professor Park. Phebe's "habitual gladness"[106] was Philena's daily leaven, her courage in illness Philena's inspiration. After Phebe died, Philena set a portrait of her sister on an easel in her parlor. Emily Means had lovingly painted it from photographs, and had caught Phebe's "kindling eye." Ever afterward it was next to the portrait that Philena knelt for her prayers; it was Phebe's spirit she consulted when a serious decision was to be made. Lonely one night in 1890, she wrote Old Scholar and teacher Mary Belcher:

> I write tonight because I need to speak to someone who has belonged to the same past as me. I have been speaking to Phebe's portrait; she looks as if she heard me and felt with me, but I do not hear her voice.[107]

It was years before Miss McKeen's memory of her sister ceased to interfere with her enjoyment of the charades and games and puns in which Phebe had delighted. But ultimately the tragedy left her stronger. It brought her "still nearer to the unseen world," deepening her own faith, Miss Merrill recalled later.[108] Her gradual acceptance of Phebe's death helped to create in her "a heart at leisure from itself to sympathize with the experience of others," as a friend of her old age put it.[109]

Abbot teachers often conjured up Phebe's image as scholar, goad, and Christian comforter. Students who had never actually known her came to share in her memory. "Miss McKeen often called us by our first names," one remembered, "but one of the new Smith Hall girls was 'Phebe', and our principal could not say *her* name without tears coming to her eyes."[110] Mr. Downs set the 121st Psalm to music, and it was sung for years at Commencement time, a hymn to Abbot's own angelic symbol of the undying soul.

Women still could not vote or fully control their financial affairs or enter many professions. Even Quaker-founded Johns Hopkins University would not accept a woman graduate student unless she agreed to sit behind a screen in the classroom. Yet as Abbot's golden age progressed, most students apparently absorbed a wondrous optimism about the future of women in particular and America in general. For all the disturbing ideas introduced by Darwin, and by the gloomy "Social Darwinists" who wrenched Darwin's theories to fit their economic or political conservatism,[111] for all the "struggle for existence" that seemed actually to be taking place in cities or on the railway workers' picket lines, *Courant* editors wrote repeatedly about "our great Nineteenth Century."[112] Two thousand Abbot students, Old Scholars, and friends listened to Dr. Storrs's Semicentennial address, as he spoke of society coming ever "nearer to God's plans . . . This progress is all the time going forward; and the current is as irresistible, as irreversible, as the current of a mighty river, as the passage of stars across the meridian."[113] The students behaved as though "we, the women of America"[114] would soon have the same political rights men had. They held mock elections of their own in every presidential election from 1876 on; they attended their first political meeting in 1880; they ran their own caucuses and conventions. The Democratic faction of 1888 stuffed the ballot box as if in imitation of the male Democrats of those days. (In spite of this perfidy, the Democrats lost seventy-two to nine.) Even Miss McKeen was interested enough that year to write Irene Draper and ask that "Mr. Edmund's article 'Why I am a Republican'" be sent to her. "I wish to be clear on my political creed," she explained.

According to men's ideal images, "woman as a sex ought not to do the hard work of the world, either social, intellectual, or moral,"[115] and it seemed natural for Maggie of *Thorton Hall* to complain, "There are so few things a girl can do."[116] Actual employment statistics, however, showed an ever-increasing percentage of women in the labor force. Though most were menial workers, more each year were college professors, librarians, lawyers, and doctors—this in spite of protests from such as A.M.A. President Dr. Alfred Stille (1871) that woman is "unfitted by nature to become a physician."[117] Abbot's Trustees were still all male, but women served widely as public school board members. "The world is in need of women, not animated fashion plates," wrote the *Courant* editors of 1874–75.[118] A delightful *Courant* story, "About Us," describes the decision of two imaginary Abbot graduates not to accept "that the whole duty of woman was to teach her Sunday School class and take care of her house if she had one, and if not wait until one (or the owner of one) came along." They become partners in a rollicking grain business, two heroines as different as can be from the vapid "Prue" in Thomas B. Aldrich's *Prudence Palfrey*.[119] (Prue idles at home through the entire book while her two suitors roam the United States in exhausting adventures.)

"We were taught to be intellectual women," wrote Anna Dawes '70, recalling her Abbot days.[120] *Courant* editors of 1878 were excited by reports from Smith College (founded in 1871) that college women could succeed in the advanced studies expected of seniors at Harvard or Yale. They acknowledged the argument that many women were presently too weak for heavy study (Mary Belcher told her gymnastics classes—and anyone else who would listen—that "not one in five [American women] are enjoying good health").[121] They insisted, however, that such "destruction" was due not to "natural weakness," but to "unceasing stuffing with candy," lack of exercise, "improper dress" and other "imprudence." "Girls, why not let us who are now coming into womanhood prove to the world that we can get an education equal to that of boys . . . and still turn out strong, healthy women?"[122] The 1883–84 editors decided Abbot women had improved, even though "we [still] have too much mental and nervous force to match our bodily development . . . One thing we know—that woman of the future will be grander and nobler than the woman of to-day, and to the intellect of the nineteenth century will join the perfect body whose fair mould the Greeks have left us."[123] By the close of the McKeen era, Abbot girls, like girls throughout the country, enjoyed many more active running sports than had been allowed at midcentury. The "perfect body" might not be a delusion after all.

22. Tennis, 1886.

Abbot students often dreamed of travel, whether or not they had the means to undertake it. As "the rich capitalists of Boston look[ed] . . . with a kind of piety on Old England" when the Pulsky brothers observed them in 1852,[124] so the Abbot community revered old world culture. A yen for travel was in the Andover air, asserts Marion Park. "All Andover took the $100 or the $200 that it had saved and started for Europe every summer."[125] One feels that no Abbot woman was considered quite complete until she had made her pilgrimage abroad, seen for herself the great cathedrals and paintings she had studied, and tested her language skills. Students of the sixties told how Henrietta and Susan Hamlin, traveling alone, had talked their way into a German fortress at Verona by dazzling the guards with their fluency in *Deutsch*. An alumna wrote *Courant* of her triumphant passage through Europe, shepherding three non-Abbot friends—two of them college graduates, all speechless in foreign tongues—with her Abbot Academy French. *Courant* is filled with travel accounts by alumnae and teachers. Mrs. Mead's "A Letter from Melrose" needs no further identification: Melrose, Scotland, with its famous abbey, would never be mistaken by the *Courant* audience for Melrose, Massachusetts, not far from Andover. The McKeens were delighted at the prospect of their own pilgrimage. In her letter thanking the Trustees for their generosity, Philena McKeen said that the thought of the coming trip "makes me tingle with joy to the ends of my fingers."[126]

Abbot women went North, South, and West too. A.A.H, '89, wrote of her trip to Alaska; Alice French, '68, explored Arkansas and wrote (as "Octave Thanet") a dialect story for *Courant*; S.F.A., '81, shot the Sault Sainte Marie rapids; E.S., '92, sailed twelve hours in an old schooner to camp out on a California island; A.A., '92, became the first American woman to climb to the Moon Temple above Kobe, Japan. They brought their prejudices along. In a letter from Washington, D.C., M.P.K., '84, described the "amusing" behavior of black families in her mission class and in their own churches: "Some of the negroes are educated and well-off; but our idea of the 'darkey' is a black, jolly person, with thick lips, broad nose, white teeth, and a not very graceful figure, and it is this class who are the most interesting."[127] This was handy confirmation of Miss McKeen's notes on the evolution of the black race. Travel could narrow minds too.

In spite of adventurous dreams and deeds, the surest future for every Abbot girl was still a home and family of her own. She had heard Miss McKeen urging her to "rejoice in her womanhood";[128] her school was praised as one of the "safe-guards and beautifiers and purifiers" of the American home.[129] The "blessed work"[130] of wife and mother constantly beckoned, colliding with newer, broader aspirations. It is interesting that by 1913 only half of all Abbot alumnae had married. The probable reasons for this are complex, and bear discussion in a later chapter; but at the least, one can surmise that the school's lively spinster teachers helped to make the single life an acceptable alternative. Perhaps it is a tribute to the McKeens and their colleagues that Abbot could contain as many dreams as it did, that the school did not insist on a single pattern for adult life. The medals struck during Abbot's golden age were of infinite variety.

Alumnae data show that bold self-images often shaped adult realities. The very security students found within the Abbot Family apparently gave many Abbot graduates the strength to live futures unforeseen by Philena McKeen. This was a confirmation of Victorian educators' hopes: the confusions of modern life were so great that it was better, they reasoned, to isolate young people from temptation than to allow them to test and temper themselves within the adult world of work or marriage. Like all boarding seminaries and colleges for young women, Abbot early provided the carefully controlled environment that would become the ideal for boys' preparatory schools and coeducational public high schools after about 1885.[131] Victorian America "associated puberty with psychological turbulence and moral incapacity," and adults must step in.[132] The McKeens and their teachers prescribed dress, food, exercise, sleeping hours, intellectual labor, and religious practice for an entire community of girls and young women; if all did not go exactly as planned, it was not for lack of adult effort. As Joseph Kett points out, teenaged girls from middle- and upper-income families were the earliest adolescents, the group seen as most vulnerable to the pressures of modern life, most in need of protection against hasty marriage and the precocious assumption of adult status in an uncertain world, as well as the one whose economic services were least needed. Decades had passed since the Marland girls operated the power looms in their father's Andover mill, mingling daily with farmers' daughters. After the Civil War, only immigrants and poor people sent their girls into factory work; the better sort arranged for their daughters a moratorium between childhood and adulthood whose purest expression was the boarding school.[133] One result of this combination of genuine parental concern and push for status was that many American girls were better educated than their brothers. European visitors remarked on the fact, and a society convinced that women had a special talent for religious and cultural pursuits accepted and welcomed it.[134] Not until the 1890's would large numbers of parents demand an equally thorough secondary education for their sons. By that time, rapid industrialization had greatly expanded professional and managerial opportunities for men, while the old apprenticeship routes to vocational competence were being closed off.[135]

Developments in young men's education only confirmed the Abbot adults' confidence in the path their school had chosen before the Civil War. Miss Hasseltine had sketched it, and Miss McKeen traveled it with her colleagues for over three decades. The McKeens created their own cheering section along the route, as their students graduated and sent encouragement back to the Family.[136] Emily Means, '69, remembered Miss Phebe moving always "in advance of her girls," with "a brilliant smile of approval" for those who "climbed the heights" with her, "a scathing scorn if they fell behind." Meanwhile Philena was at the rear "with a steady force pushing [them] on, like the irresistible movement of a glacier. Between two such stimuli, how could one help moving forward?"[137] It was well that Abbot had gathered its strength, for mountains lay ahead.

Forth and Back, 1885-1912

The mid-1880's found Abbot entered upon a period of enthusiastic physical expansion and reluctant educational redefinition, a phase which lasted through the final McKeen years, tried two more principals, and ushered in Bertha Bailey, the first Abbot principal to have prepared for her career in college. Buildings that had seemed luxurious at midcentury looked inadequate by 1880, especially to Miss McKeen, who longed to immortalize her pedagogical ideas in brick and stone. Abbot had also to shift its academic ground just enough to find a secure niche in an educational scene suddenly dominated by the new women's colleges, without losing strengths built into the school during earlier years. For only the strong could negotiate a way through the mounting confusion over women's roles around the turn of the century. Images of women's progress toward equality were fast becoming realities, and the luxury of anticipation had to give way to disciplined, practical efforts to deal with these realities. In spite of perplexity, Abbot would do its best.

Expansion

In his Report for 1876 the U.S. Commissioner of Education listed Abbot Academy among the "institutions for the superior instruction of females," along with Vassar, Bradford, Mt. Holyoke Seminary, and several mid-western colleges. The Commissioner acknowledged that his office was baffled: many "colleges" were providing the barest high school training, while the best "seminaries" matched the true colleges in their curricular offerings and the age range and quality of their students.[1] Though Abbot could not touch Vassar's $400,000 founding endowment or Mt. Holyoke's library collection, its courses almost exactly duplicated those offered by her sister institutions.

Ten years later, although all chartered "seminaries" like Abbot had disappeared from the Commissioner's list, the confusion remained. The U.S. Office could still give no clear answer to the vexing question, "When is a 'college' or seminary truly a college?"[2] By 1889 the Commissioner was lamenting the condition of the typical state-chartered degree-granting female "college" running unendowed "like an engine without a flywheel," owned or leased by a president who "makes out of it what he can."[3] The Commissioner was comfortable with only about fifteen institutions of the 179 on the "college" list, among them Wellesley, Smith, Mt. Holyoke, Vassar, the new co-ordinate colleges, Barnard and Radcliffe, and innovative, self-conscious Bryn Mawr.

Abbot had not changed; the educational world had changed. The Abbot of the 1880's was in fact a thriving enterprise, rich for its time in teaching equipment and well-equipped teachers. But this Abbot was also uneasy, jealous of the new "instant institutions" endowed by millionaires, chafing at the limitations imposed by its frugal Trustees. As early as 1877 the privations of Abbot life had begun to tell on both McKeens. News that Bradford's Annie Johnson had been hired at $3000 stimulated a proud plea from Philena to Trustee Chairman George Ripley: "Are not *we two* worth as much to Abbot Academy?" she asked. (Apparently the answer was "not quite," for the Trustees raised the McKeens' combined salary from $1600 to just $2000.)[4] The same year, indignant *Courant* editors advertised Abbot's departmental and housing needs, and asked why girls' schools should so often want for money. Student writers pointed out that "the current expense of a student for one year at Harvard would pay the current expenses of a four year's course at Wellesley; yet there are many girls who cannot afford this whose brothers are at Harvard."[5] Shortly after the Semi-centennial orators had called for the expansion of Abbot, this "engine of good,"[6] Miss McKeen wrote the Trustees the first of many anxious letters. Improved transportation and the proliferation of new institutions had brought Abbot "into direct and sharp competition with other prominent schools and colleges for girls," she told the Board.[7] The dormitories at Wheaton, Bradford, and Wellesley offered students both bedrooms and parlors at little more cost than the Abbot student paid to share an attic room in South Hall. Abbot salaries could not obtain "a teacher who seems absolutely essential to the prosperity of the school," one who might want to come but could not make the $200 sacrifice below her present salary; $150,000 would provide a new dormitory, a small endowment to tide the school over business panics, and the teaching space needed to house the abundant equipment then packed in boxes.[8] Abbot's richly endowed "sister schools," Vassar and Wellesley, most excited Miss McKeen's envy. But at a minimum, "Shall not Abbot keep up with Bradford in its opportunities for study, though it cannot in its buildings?"[9]

No response—at least none that we know of. For the next few years the problem simmered in faculty sitting rooms and in gatherings of the growing Alumnae Association. All Abbot watched the physical changes being made on top of Andover Hill, where Dr. Bancroft's Centennial drive had pulled Phillips Academy from penury to a condition that allowed significant dormitory construction, even (eventually) the construction of bathrooms. Miss McKeen gradually became convinced that physical improvements were the key to Abbot's future: no legal application for college status such as Mt. Holyoke Seminary was soon to make seemed called for when most Abbot students and teachers—even those few teachers who were college graduates—were so content with the original format, and she herself was so suspicious of credentialism.

In private she worried about inferior lighting systems and double beds. College administrators were anxious about the effects of "smashing"; Victorian New England had finally confessed itself stung by criticisms like those of French visitor Moreau de Saint-Mery.

> I am about to say something almost incredible. [America's young women are not] strangers to the taste for the pleasures

of a misguided imagination in a person of the same sex . . .
In the space of eight or ten years a girl may share her bed with
fifty or sixty different creatures, of whom no more may be
known than their names, who may be . . . infected with com-
municable diseases and with habits fatal to a young person.[10]

Harriet Chapell would have laughed at such fulminations; another
alumna of the seventies could recall her bedfellow with amusement
("I love her dearly, but I always said and I always will say that she
took three quarters of the bed").[11] Yet Miss McKeen could not afford
to ignore the prevailing anxiety. The technology was at hand to alter
the custom that had kept so many bedfellows warm, happy, and
cramped for so long. None of the new colleges had double beds or
kerosene lamps; neither would Abbot Academy.

In public Miss McKeen pressed the Trustees to raise the needed
funds. By 1884 she was insistent: *"Better accommodation"* is what we
need, she wrote the Trustees in January 1884. "You do not know the
deep feeling of Old Scholars in regard to this matter." Alumnae Association members had recently pledged $2000 to begin a building
drive. "I should be unwilling to attend another meeting of that Association, unless I could report the sympathy and efficient cooperation
of the Trustees." She reminded them that she would not be Principal
much longer, and that her "long experience would be of practical
worth" in helping plan new buildings.[12]

Perhaps it was her postscript that set them thinking: "P.S. It cannot
have escaped your notice that our numbers have fallen off during the
last two years; there is every reason to fear that this decrease will go
on, unless we can compete with neighboring schools in the accommodations we offer for the same, or more, money." The decline had
been small, but the threat was palpable. In June she again asked for
action, and this time the men of the Board took the bait. Upon the
Drapers' dining room table one evening that fall, a grand plan emerged,
the sum of faculty suggestions, McKeen ambitions, and architects' con-
sultations with the Trustees' planning and building committees including Professor Churchill, George Ripley, Mortimer Mason, and Warren
Draper. The architects' sketches envisioned an entirely new campus of
four large buildings, including an enormous "Administration Building"
with rooms for English course students, two language halls, and a new
Academy building, each built in "eleventh century Romanesque," a
style that all agreed would greatly surpass the outmoded simplicities
of Smith Hall and the original Academy building.

The company was delighted with the covered walkways and the

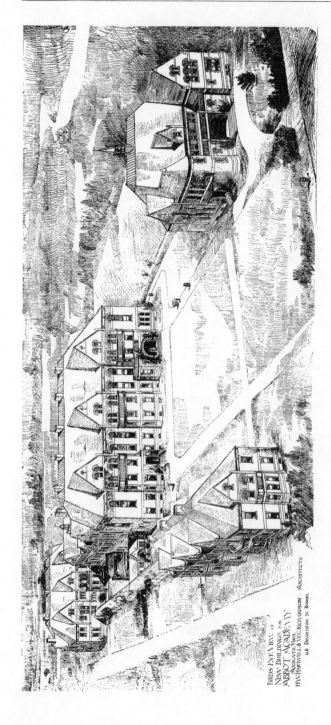

BIRDS EYE VIEW OF
NEW BUILDINGS FOR
ABBOT ACADEMY
ANDOVER, 1886
HW.HARTWELL & W.C.RICHARDSON · ARCHITECTS
68 Devonshire St. Boston.

23. *"Plan for Erecting a Group of New Buildings," 1886. Architect's sketch drawn for fund-raising pamphlet.*

plans for minimizing stair climbing, features designed to maintain the delicate health of young women.[13] They made plans to publicize the school's absolute commitment to central heating and to single beds, whether in single rooms or two-room suites. Full of optimism and of what was later to seem to Miss McKeen an "almost pathetic" courage,[14] they set about organizing themselves to raise $150,000 from a constituency that had never given more than $7,000 for any one project, from alumnae who had repeatedly pleaded "reduced circumstances" or "father is bankrupt" during the Semicentennial drive five years earlier.[15]

The Trustees expressed their "earnest desire" that Philena McKeen should actively aid in the fund-raising, and promised to cover her expenses.[16] Miss McKeen had not expected this; always before, the men had raised the building funds. Fearful of horses, terrified of traveling by night,[17] she was at first "overwhelmed" by the idea of herself conducting "a campaign of begging," but she agreed in spite of her fears to take the major responsibility—"I shall do it if it kills me," she said— so long as the Board did not insist that she approach strangers who knew nothing of Abbot.[18] Here was a stipulation that Miss McKeen could make with some confidence, for Abbot Academy had by now a small but loyal Alumnae Association, begun by Phebe McKeen and Susanna Jackson in 1871 and strengthened through the efforts of many —most notably the Corresponding Secretaries, trustee daughters Charlotte Swift and Agnes Park, both Class of 1858. A $5.00 life membership fee soon created funds sufficient to invest, the interest to be used for needed gifts to the school—maps, books, microscopes for the botany class, and more books. Most important, the 350 Association members could be counted on to help with the new drive, as could others of the more than 1000 alumnae who were not yet members but had shown their interest by returning for the Old Scholars Day at the Semicentennial Celebration or by coming back at Commencement time.[19] With much help from the records that had been gathered for the Semicentennial Celebration, Miss McKeen and a special secretary mapped her routes and planned the central meetings of Abbot alumnae and friends. All contributions were to be made conditional upon $100,000 being subscribed on or before July 1st, 1886. She went first to the Trustees, to the Alumnae Association and to Abbot's Hill and Town neighbors; armed with their pledges, totaling about $34,000, she and a companion set forth in January 1886 on her tour of prospective donors in five northeastern states.

It was a bold departure for an elderly lady. The two braved New York snowstorms and New England floods, hoping for, and almost receiving, a welcome at each city or town in an alumna or parent home. They set forth every day on calls to nearby alumnae, and wrote pledge cards by night for people off her route. There were "days and *days*," Miss McKeen wrote later.[20] At one house in Pottsville, Pennsylvania, she was given $600, in all of Springfield, Massachusetts, only $70, in New York City, $5010.

She hated it; she loved it. "I dreaded the last call I made as much as I had dreaded the first." Worst of all was her "unpleasant duty" to "seek gentlemen in their place of business." But her reward was the welcome her Dear Old Girls gave her in their own homes, which she found "centres of refinement and intelligence and usefulness."[21] Gradually as she visited ever more alumnae, "the new buildings, which had so long filled my vision, sank to less importance, and *the school* rose, a beautiful temple, of which our (daughters) were as cornerstones, polished after the similitude of a palace."[22] Wrenching metaphor this, but typically earnest sentiment.

The Trustees helped her mount receptions in Lowell, Boston, and New York. At the Boston gathering, Rev. Phillips Brooks, distant cousin of Sarah Abbot and "beloved friend" of her namesake school, spoke movingly of Abbot's capacity for combining the old and the new; Edwin Reed, Abbot husband, asserted that women's education should be first to receive support, not last, for "Great men always have great mothers." Reverend Cyrus Hamlin, now over eighty years old and returned from Turkey, sent a message saying "Abbot has no superior . . . It cannot be spared." Hamlin also came to Lowell to rejoice that his wife Henrietta and six of his daughters had been educated at Abbot. In April, Philena McKeen came home with about $55,000 in total pledges, exhausted but hopeful. Even the Smith Hall cook and laundry girls handed back to her part of their wages that spring. She felt that the remainder of the $100,000 might yet come in.

It did not. July approached, with the goal only half attained. The Trustees wrote all those who had promised to give, asking that they allow the school more time to reach its minimum goal. Most respondents agreed, but some withdrew their pledges. It was a discouraging time. The Trustees went ahead with more modest building plans: at the least, they could break ground for the large central building. Regretfully, they suppressed their Victorian-Romanesque vision, and resigned themselves to keeping Academy Hall, which could be moved onto a new one-story foundation and thus provide barely adequate teaching space. In spite of this initiative, donations slowed to a trickle.

Miss McKeen took it hardest. Well over sixty now, rheumatic, and simply tired, she brooded. The fund drive seemed "hopelessly rutted."[23] Why could Abbot's friends not give more? While she was begging for a dollar, ten dollars, the Bryn Mawr day school in Baltimore had been launched by a single heir of the B. & O. Railroad fortune with gifts which would amount to over half a million dollars by 1890. Abbot Academy had grown up in circles where an "everlasting scorn of worldliness"[24] made great wealth suspect. Was her school now to run on soul alone? Finally, regretfully, in June of 1888, she wrote the Trustees a letter of resignation, promising to continue helping Abbot wherever she could do so "without seeming officiousness." This was too much for Abbot's old friend Warren Draper. On July 3 he declared to the Trustees that he would add $22,000 to his pledge of $3000, payable upon the receipts of $60,000 cash from all other old pledges and new donations.

Everyone took heart. The Trustees had already asked Miss McKeen to withdraw her resignation. She now did so. The Board then voted to name the new building Draper Hall in honor of its most generous and most determined donor. They asked Miss McKeen to go fundraising once more to meet Draper's condition, and she set out with new energy, her rheumatism much diminished, again to delight in the hospitality and piety of the many alumnae "who are honoring the Master and the school which He founded in Andover."[25] Though cash receipts were still only $54,500 by the following June, construction had gone ahead, with Draper himself supervising the works. The Academy building was jacked onto great rollers and drawn by oxen to its present site, an operation accomplished so smoothly that a vase accidentally left on its bracket was found whole and in place after the move. Smith Hall had already been moved back toward the Grove; now it was South Hall's turn. Patrick the custodian waved from his South Hall window to Miss McKeen in her Smith Hall apartment as the old house glided majestically by toward the Abbot Street site. Finally the circular driveway could be staked out, and the shape of the modern Abbot quadrangle discerned. With joy, Miss McKeen dug out the first spadeful of earth for the Draper Hall excavation.

Ceremony over, chaos reigned for months: pits yawned, piles of debris rose everywhere. To one visiting alumna, "it looked as if a very orderly earthquake had visited the old place."[26] A new student thought she had reached "the land of modern mound-builders."[27] Miss McKeen wrote that "Our friends dreaded to enter the grounds; and horses were frightened by new complications; Miss Merrill and her French family at Davis Hall and we at Smith Hall were absolutely separated after nightfall. Telegrams were coming from fathers to daughters: 'Unless nuisances are immediately abated come home.' "[28] The nuisances remained, but so did the daughters. When Draper Hall was finished in 1890, one great problem was still to be solved: the furnishing of over one hundred student rooms, teacher apartments, music rooms, and dining and receiving rooms. Many nights, Philena McKeen lay sleepless, "room after room pass[ing] in melancholy procession before me."[29]

At last she committed the problem to the Lord, "–and He solved it."[30] One faithful Abbot friend after another came forth with furnishings at $100 a student room—and well over $1000 for the profusely decorated Mason Drawing Room, named for its Trustee benefactor. Trustee wives Mrs. George Smith and Mrs. John Phelps Taylor (Antoinette Hall Taylor) provided for the guest rooms, one with "dainty white furniture," the other in deep mahogany, "with portieres and lace draperies, with rich toilet fancies."[31] The November Club furnished the main library, and many new books were given to fill empty shelves in the Jackson Memorial Reading Room, the most exciting donation being a copy of *Uncle Tom's Cabin* sent by Mrs. Stowe and autographed especially for Miss McKeen. Professor and Mrs. Downs donated two pianos for the music rooms. Harriet Chapell Newcomb discovered that the guest entrance was bare and immediately joined with her former art teacher, Emily Means, to design and oversee the installation of wall friezes and coverings and to buy the furnishings needed. The Phillips Academy teachers and students asked if they might donate an English hall-clock to complete the furniture for the entrance; a lecture on the Oberammergau Passion Play was given by an old friend to raise funds for the carpeting. Miss McKeen's rooms on the first floor front were done up with papering and wood carving "in a quiet phase of the Byzantine Romanesque."[32]

Abbot moved into Draper Hall in September 1890, but Miss McKeen dreamed on, this time of a great housewarming. She mailed 1,000 invitations, then asked Mr. Draper, would he kindly pay for the party? Mr. Draper demurred. The building had cost $90,000, $11,000 more than the sum raised. Was a celebration in order when Abbot was still in debt for construction? Later the same day he changed his mind (probably pushed by his wife to consider the advantage of thanking donors and publicizing Abbot) and promised all the ice cream, fruit juices, and fancy cakes that the celebrants could eat. Thus on January 21 a throng from Hill and Town and out-of-town gathered in gratitude and jubilation. Trustee George Davis, the donor of the first and

24. *The "McKeen Rooms" with Phebe's portrait, decorated "in a quiet phase of the Byzantine Romanesque." The Mason Drawing Room can be seen through the door.*

largest contribution before Mr. Draper's, gazed at the scene through tears of joy, grieving not at all for the imminent retirement of his earlier gift, Davis Hall, whose twenty-five student French family would live one-to-a-room in Smith Hall while the English course students and the "Teutonic population" took over sumptuous Draper Hall. For while Abbot Academy was not the half-million dollar "Renaissance Palace" the B. & O. fortune had built for the new Bryn Mawr School in Baltimore,[33] it now resembled nothing so much as a vast Victorian honeycomb, with only the Georgian Academy building (now renamed Abbot Hall) to compromise its effusive elegance.

More buildings would be added, but none would surpass in their bulk or in the drama of their construction this symbol of Abbot's claim on a new and wealthier constituency—Draper Hall. Gone were the days of "crushing economy" which had for so long been "one of the conditions of life on Andover Hill."[34] Miss McKeen and the Trustees had convinced each other that many of those upper-class girls who had been choosing Smith and Vassar would really prefer Abbot once its accommodations were improved. An electric lighting system, a heating plant that had cost $10,000 to install, then more to

25. The Abbot campus, 1890–1897. Davis Hall or "French Hall" is at the right.

improve, better food at Miss McKeen's insistence (for she saw the school "suffering from the bad reputation of its table")[35]—all were to add further expense. The Board voted in 1890 to cover new costs by raising tuition from $300 to $400 for the following year ($75.00 for day scholars), a sum that was higher than Bradford's and Wellesley's charges and double the $200 fee for Mt. Holyoke College and Seminary. It was a daring move, and it set parents' boarding-tuition bill at a level *three times* that of the year of the McKeen's arrival in 1859.

Now where were the applicants? Even before the raise, it had taken all of Miss McKeen's leverage with her Lord to produce a near-full school for the construction year of 1888-89. In midsummer she had written Mrs. Draper that

> to fill the three halls attics and all, we need *twenty-seven more* pupils than have applied. *I think it would not be wise to speak of this*, as there is nothing worse for a school than to have the impression get abroad that it is running down. But I am constantly praying, earnestly, that the Father above will turn the hearts of parents toward us, and give us wisdom and grace to take care of their daughters: . . . I try to do it in faith and with a single eye of His glory, although it is difficult to keep our own honor, and that of the school out of mind in praying. Do help me *pray for pupils* and such as may bring and receive a blessing.

The Father undoubtedly did His best, but enrollments had slipped

by 1890 to sixty-nine pupils. Great must have been the relief when they began rising again the following year, and held their own at 126–144 after Miss McKeen's retirement in 1892 through the serious depression of 1893–97. After all, the rich still had money, some more than ever after the dog days ended. Day-scholar enrollment increased dramatically from 17 percent in 1891 to 44 percent in 1897; the Merrimack Valley was evidently impressed with Abbot's new quarters, and perhaps more important, heartened by the welcome given its daughters under a new regime.

Philena McKeen had been "mother, sister, friend"[36] to nearly two thousand young women during her thirty-three years at Abbot Academy. The Alumnae Association and Trustees gave her a magnificent send-off at a reception and noon-hour "Breakfast" in Boston's Hotel Vendome. Abbot's closest friends were there—350 in all—or sent messages. Former Trustee Egbert Smyth's greeting from the Theological Seminary was perhaps the most poignant, considering his painful experience at the hands of Board President Park (sitting right there on the platform in spite of his age and frailty) and other theological conservatives at the time of the heresy trial. "*All* the brethren salute thee," he said to Miss McKeen with emphasis. Sisters and daughters from everywhere in Abbot's enormous Family did the same. Philena McKeen retired to old South Hall—redecorated by the Trustees for her use as a private home and renamed "Sunset Cottage" at her request in honor of her declining years.

Briefly, a Heroine

Laura S. Watson, Abbot's next Principal, lasted only six years. She was a woman of fine looks, "commanding intelligence" and "especial delight in art."[37] One feels she should have stayed for decades. Nobody alive knows exactly why she left; but one can suspect she earned her rest, for she "took the helm under circumstances demanding peculiar tact and self-restraint"[38] and she accomplished what Miss McKeen and many of her teachers had been resisting: without compromising Abbot's traditional strengths, she created a solid college preparatory course for those young women who saw beyond Abbot to further education.

There were Abbot students who had seen beyond Abbot for years. Two went together to Oberlin in 1856. Soon afterward the tiny library in the back of the Hall ended the Abbot career of another girl, who read every book there; when she came to the English translation of Plato's *Phaedo* (surely bowdlerized for young ladies' use), she decided she must leave for college, where she could learn Greek. Against much opposition, some state colleges and universities were admitting women. The Vassar "family" had 353 students the spring after its opening in 1865, and while Vassar's admissions standards did not yet match those of the best men's colleges, Smith's founders promised to correct this. Rejoicing in these new departures, the 1875 *Courant* editors wrote:

> We want to congratulate our sisters that their opportunities for making themselves really highly educated women are so greatly improved . . . Shall we be willing to give up eight or ten years of our life to hard study? Statistics from the higher class of boarding-schools show that not more than one half, often not one third, of those who enter remain until they graduate . . . Ought we, now that schools of a superior order are open to us, to be content with this surface cultivation? Shall we be willing to be mental pigmies all our lives?[39]

They urged their peers to use Abbot's excellent education to prepare for college. Yet only twenty-six alumnae—.009 percent of the total—had graduated from four-year colleges before Miss Watson came.[40] It was much more common for both graduates and nongraduates to take a year or two of further study in music, art, teaching, or nursing. Abbot prepared students directly for such specific training; four graduates went straight from Abbot to medical school and became physicians. With strong support from the Trustees, Miss Watson changed

26. *Laura S. Watson, Principal, 1892–1898. Artist unknown. Portrait currently hanging in Abbot Chapel.*

all this, resurfacing the roadbed the McKeen sisters had laid without altering the route which Abbot had traveled since 1853.

The Abbot Trustees brought Laura Watson to Andover at a salary of $1200 from her position as preceptress at the school where she had begun her education, St. Johnsbury Academy in Vermont.[41] She herself had no undergraduate college degree. She had gone from Mt. Holyoke Seminary to teach at Lawrence Academy in Groton, Massachusetts, then became principal of Albert Lea College for women in Minnesota. While she was teaching in the Midwest, she studied for and received the Ph.B. and M.A. degrees from Wesleyan University in Bloomington, Illinois. Contemporaries describe her as "a lady of power."[42] She would need it. She began her Abbot work at a time of general soul-searching on the part of secondary-school educators. The college admissions standards for graduating high-school students had become badly confused, some colleges requiring broad scientific and liberal arts preparation, others still satisfied by the old classics-and-minimal-mathematics combination in which Phillips Academy had specialized before 1871. Proliferating public high schools compounded the problem while trying to solve it. The American public had begun to demand clarity. The older female seminaries, which had always offered both secondary and college level subjects, must define themselves or go under.

Essentially, the opening of the century's final decade presented Abbot's Trustees and Principal with four choices:

1. To follow Miss Watson's own alma mater, Mt. Holyoke, and become a four-year college, keeping a small preparatory department.

2. To become a "fitting school" and concentrate all resources on college preparation.

3. To cling to the status quo and hope, counting on the strengths and challenges of the traditional course—so much of which overlapped with the usual college work—to attract good students.

4. To create a college preparatory course within the traditional school so that all who wished to elect college preparation could do so.

The first choice was tempting, but it would be terribly difficult to undertake. Long since, Abbot had tried and failed to endow a "Phebe McKeen Professorship of Literature and Belle Lettres." Wellesley was paying its professors (all of them women) liberally and providing superior research facilities; Vassar offered full professors $2500 plus board, and built for renowned astronomer Maria Mitchell an observatory that far surpassed Abbot's once-unique telescopic equipment. Even Mt. Holyoke Seminary had boasted endowed teaching chairs and ample scholarships long before its formal conversion to college status.[43] Abbot's latest fund-raising experience did not suggest ready success for this course of action.

The second choice—a college preparatory school—would be most economical, and prestigious to boot. Children of the newly rich were flocking to new Northeastern preparatory schools for the polish that Smith and Bryn Mawr required of their applicants.[44] A college degree was valuable coin for young women aspiring to be teachers or other professionals (30 percent of female high school teachers now had Bachelor's degrees). Was it not time to bow to the inevitable? But the inevitable alone was seldom persuasive at proud Abbot Academy. To settle for the simple college preparatory alternative would be to fly in the face of Abbot tradition, early articulated by alumna Anna Dawes, '70, who saw American society "hurrying on both blindly and too fast" to make college and "the higher branches compulsory" for girls. "I protest," said Miss Dawes. "Excellent" young women have been educated in the seminaries of New England, schools "now fast pushed out of sight by the rage for a collegiate education, or passed over in the search for fashionable polish."[45] Abbot as a mere college preparatory school would quickly lose its character as a school for life.

The third choice, both the Trustees and the new Principal were convinced, was merely wishful thinking. Bradford might indulge itself thus (and did through the turn of the century); Abbot would not.[46]

The Trustees, Miss Watson, and most of Abbot's teachers therefore committed themselves to the fourth choice. The Trustees promised in the 1892–93 catalogue to make Abbot "no less famous a fitting school that it has been and will continue to be as a finishing school." Immediately upon her arrival, the new Principal began plans to institute a College Preparatory ("C.P.") course, adding the instruction in Greek, modern literature, science, and mathematics that would be necessary for college entrance. Fifteen students signed up for the C.P. course in its very first year. During Miss Watson's six-year tenure, forty-five students went on to colleges, and twenty of these received Bachelors degrees; in the last six years of Miss McKeen's tenure when college opportunities for women had been equally plentiful, the numbers of college entrants were nineteen, of college graduates, seven. In Miss Watson's two final years, twenty of the sixty-eight Seniors were taking the C.P. course, while those in the traditional Academic course could select from three other groups of studies, one emphasizing science and art, a second emphasizing modern languages and literature, a third concentrating in classics, with three years of Latin and Greek. Every student was required to study Bible, English composition, and elocution.

Throughout Miss Watson's tenure, Abbot seems to have drawn both inspiration and support from the work of a group of highly influential educators who were studying the articulation of curriculum between school and college. Philena McKeen and Abbot alumna Anna Dawes were not the only people who found many college admissions requirements "tyrannical" and "petty," as Columbia professor Nicholas Murray Butler put it in 1892.[47] In 1890 Harvard's President Charles W. Eliot had complained before the National Education Association (N.E.A.) that hasty Massachusetts legislators had created "a large number of low-grade high schools without really expecting them to effect any junction with colleges."[48] The N.E.A. quickly determined that the chaos in college admissions was a national problem, and appointed a national "Committee of Ten" headed by President Eliot to clear the tangle. Five other college presidents joined Eliot, as did the brilliant U.S. Commissioner of Education, William T. Harris, and three secondary school principals. All were men; all were hopeful that their recommendations might set new standards for high school curricula throughout the country.

Private educators eagerly read the Committee's interim reports, which suggested a bias away from practical courses and toward the traditional curriculum most of them had boasted for decades. As it was, privately operated schools were preparing two thirds of the nation's college entrants for college-level work.[49] They hoped to hold on to this role in spite of the dramatic increase in public high school enrollment then under way. Eliot's final report of 1893—distributed free by the U.S. Department of Interior to 30,000 principals, superintendents, and school board members—did indeed stress that "mental discipline" that had been a pedagogical watchword since the 1820's, but it gave its blessing equally to the traditional classic subjects and to the "moderns" (English, modern languages, social sciences, and natural sciences). Not surprisingly, given the make-up of the Committee, the report recommended that the high school curriculum be constituted in such a way that college entrance would be available to every student, even though only a fraction would actually go; thus it offered support to Laura Watson if she wished to take it, and provided clear guidelines for the reconstruction of the Abbot curriculum.

It is impossible to tell whether Miss Watson or the Faculty and Trustees actually read the Committee of Ten *Report*. Abbot's four new courses of study roughly matched the four alternatives recommended by the Committee; its classics and literature texts were in line with those proposed by the subject area "conferences" which the Committee organized to inform its deliberations.[50] Advanced offerings in mathematics at Abbot were slimmer than those the Committee had suggested, however, and one may wonder how Latin fared after Phebe McKeen's death, given that at least one Punchard High School graduate of 1898 remembers choosing the public school over Abbot because its Latin instruction was so far superior.[51] The Abbot science and history courses suggest that the Academy paid scant attention to the Committee's injunction that each subject be taught for long enough "to win from it the kind of mental training it is fitted to supply."[52] Students took but half a year of physics and chemistry; Seniors got one bite apiece of astronomy (fall), political science or American history (winter), and geology (spring).

Miss Watson eventually took care of Abbot's own college admissions problem by persuading most of the Northeastern women's colleges to accept her graduates on certificate of recommendation from the faculty and by including in the C.P. course all preparation required for entrance examinations to Bryn Mawr, Radcliffe and the state universities. The most important effect of the Committee of Ten was on Abbot's potential constituency. Well before the Committee had completed its study, Abbot was responding to the problems that had stimulated the Committee's formation, and was making ready to enrich its traditional offerings with courses similar to those the Committee was to recommend for all students. Rising applications soon testified to the Trustees' foresight, while the overwhelming success of graduates in winning college admission for the next two decades suggested that Abbot's new College Preparatory course served its purpose well.

None of these curricular gymnastics guaranteed good teaching, of course. Alumnae of the Watson years later recalled the enthusiasm of the several new college graduate teachers Miss Watson hired, but Eleanor Thomson Castle, '96, found her classes dull. She best remembers (1) her friends (female) and (2) their friends (male, Phillips Academy).[53] Abbot teaching did not need to be very strong to be better than the ordinary, for the standard pedagogy of the day still depended on the memorization and recitation of textbook pages, in spite of criticism leveled at this practice by leading educators.[54] It was satisfying that Abbot could now boast a 5,000-volume library with a growing collection of periodicals and primary sources; a highly capable part-time librarian; and teachers like Mabel Bacon, Miss Merrill, and Fraulein Schiefferdecker, who welcomed give-and-take within relatively small classes. Miss Watson's own lively mind provided still more. We have evidence of it in a *Courant* editor's account of her "as toastmaster" for her first Abbot Thanksgiving.[55] She "never allowed the fun to flag, and her opening address, delivered with all the gravity of a judge and the inscrutable calmness of a sphinx, was condensed merriment throughout. Allusion was made to the patriotic sentiments of a certain history class who rejoiced that Columbus landed at Plymouth Rock and that Jason came over in the Mayflower."

Abbot's daily schedule and its social traditions Miss Watson left intact.[56] The parties and the trips were held as always, but the limits remained clear. Dr. Bancroft received from her a stiff note protesting the behavior of Phillips boys in a nearby house, who made a habit of using their shaving mirrors to beam sunlight into the eyes of the Seniors reciting psychology with her on the top floors of Abbot Hall. The officially sanctioned visiting of the "Cads" went on, as did the semi-

legal evening serenades and, above all, the celebrations following football victories over Exeter Academy, when hundreds of pajama-clad
boys shot off Roman candles and yelled their "well known yells" as
they followed their teams around the Abbot Circle.[57] The Circle always emptied on cue when the Hilltop bonfire was ready for lighting;
the Draper windows closed and the girls went back to their studying
or prayers. All this provided a sense of continuity for the alumnae and
the older teachers. Meanwhile, with no weakening of such traditional
courses as art history and church history, the academic program was
enriched. Abbot's Principal encouraged clearer departmental division,
much as Phillips' Principal was doing on the Hilltop. A two-year
course in music theory, practice, and history provided one point for
college entrance. Miss Nellie Mason, teacher from 1892 to 1932, who
had studied science at both Wellesley and Radcliffe, used wisely the
funds provided by the Trustees to modernize physics and chemistry
equipment and make possible the "training in scientific method" which
Miss Watson valued so much.[58] Laboratory science requirements were
increased for C.P. and "General" students, while girls from other
courses benefited from being able to elect the strengthened science
courses. Similarly, a three-year course in Greek was a costly addition,
but it, too, widened the choices open to Academic Course students.
Abbot had far more electives than most high schools until the turn of
the century, when public high schools began to copy Harvard's touted
elective system. Applications for both Academic and C.P. courses increased. A thirty-year-old married woman already equipped with
undergraduate college training spent a year as a day scholar filling gaps
in her preparation for Radcliffe Graduate School. The "brilliant" Miss
Ingalls, class of '82, added Anglo-Saxon and Italian Renaissance literature to the Literature sequence in order to accommodate such advanced students.

Miss Watson did not neglect the non-college Academic students.
Abbot's challenging Senior course had been its pride for decades. Miss
Watson put *Butler's Analogy* away at last, and replaced it with William James's equally difficult but less stupefying *Psychology*.[59] Here
was a basic change in the Abbot ethos. At the outset of his book James
warns that "Psychology is to be treated as a natural science." "Mental
facts cannot be properly studied apart from the physical environment
of which they take cognizance."[60] He then plunges into detailed discussion of the occipital lobes, epithelial cells, afferent nerves, and
motor and sensory aphasia. He reports on the experimental removal of
parts of the pigeon's brain, and its effect upon sexual function.

Nevertheless, Wayland's and Butler's concerns whisper at the door.

James describes a hierarchy of "selfs," the bodily (material) self, the social self, and finally the "supremely precious" spiritual self.[61] He admits in his conclusion that his discipline is a science "peculiarly fragile, into which the waters of metaphysical criticism leak at every joint."[62] Abbot students alternately gloried in and moaned over their work in psychology. There was plenty of contrary emotion vented in this Class Book poem by the Seniors of 1901.

Ah when we were Senior Middlers
We were frisky and fresh as you,
But one day last September
We all turned prussian blue.

They dragged us into a classroom,
They set us round in a row.
They opened those grim brown covers,
And said, "How much do you know?"

They hauled us through those pages,
(The process was very slow)
Til we wished that the cerebellum
Would put on its hat and go.

They steeped us in Sensation,
Habit, Attention, Will.
Of Memorable Emotion
Each victim had her fill.

They smiled at our hopeless confusion,
They choked us with horrible names,
And whenever we pleaded, reproachful,
They said, "You must blame Mr. James."

Enrollment during the Watson years averaged 133 students each year in spite of the depression of the 1890's, which played havoc with many private schools.[63] Abbot's friends and alumnae remained loyal—giving, pledging, or bequeathing $65,000 in new funds (including $40,000 from the Drapers) for scholarships, lectureships, the beginning of a new building fund, and improvements for Abbot Hall. The Trustees and Miss Watson together struggled to make Draper Hall a workable building. The frugality with which it was first constructed had left it short on radiators and electric fixtures, and its fire protection and hot water systems were entirely inadequate.[64] To help the Principal salvage Draper Hall, Warren Draper himself came back from retirement as Trustee Building Superintendent in 1897, after a series of inept professionals had been tried and dismissed.[65] From her first year at the Academy, Miss Watson gently pushed the Trustees for a new classroom building equipped to accommodate modern teaching methods,[66] and her students began raising money for the new structure. These spirited young women also became secretly proud of Abbot Hall's age and simple dignity; they helped teachers feature it in a prize-winning exhibit at the 1893 World's Fair and Exposition in Chicago. Meantime a gradual stabilizing of the ratio between boarders and day scholars allowed the Trustees finally to close Smith Hall in 1897, eliminating the now shabby, unfashionable dormitory without loss of income for the school.[67]

Still, there could be no smooth sailing through such a changeful period. Almost everyone assures us that Philena McKeen retired with perfect humility to Sunset Lodge. Certainly much of her energy went into old and new Andover friendships and expanded civic work for the November Club and the Andover Village Improvement Society. Esther Parker Lovett, '08, one of the few living graduates who knew Miss McKeen, remembers, for instance, how serene the old lady seemed, under her beautiful white curls, when she stayed with the Parker family. She ate her morning oatmeal Scottish fashion, dipping her spoon alternately into a bowl of porridge and a bowl of cream, and laughed when one of Esther's brothers sang her a slightly ribald railroad song popular in the mid-nineties.[68] She continued to fear, however, that her Academy would "sink to the level of a [college] preparatory school," and to believe that Abbot's own Academic Course should have "the place of honor"; she said so often and in public.[69] She was always near at hand, substituting for a convalescent teacher of church history through the winter of 1896, being invited to lecture on Saturday afternoons. Laura Watson's "task was made no easier by Miss McKeen's presence at Sunset Lodge," said former teacher Mabel Bacon Ripley from the safe distance of the year 1941.[70] Nor could veteran teachers like Katherine Kelsey hide their nostalgia for the time when girls read "Livy and Horace . . . because they wished to do it, and not because the reading was prescribed by any college for admission to its doors," as Miss Kelsey put it in later years.[71] In her search for college-trained teachers, Miss Watson broke Miss McKeen's tradition of hiring the standout graduates of almost every Senior class; even the presence of teacher-alumna Henrietta Learoyd Sperry on the Board of Trustees did not assuage all alumna grumbling.[72] Both older teachers and alumnae may well have complained with education journalist Frank Kasson that President Eliot's male-dominated study-pressure group was trying to "capture" the American high school "and recon-

struct it in the interest of the university."[73] Abbot's freedom from the
rigidity and pretentiousness that characterized many institutions was a
precious commodity; Laura Watson was a singularly independent soul
herself, but she had to modernize Abbot's curriculum amid punishing
cross-pressures from her strong-minded constituency.

For all Miss Watson's courage, she was shy with most students and
difficult to know. Those who knew her well loved her well, but the
countless others who were more distant realized the importance of her
quiet, transforming work for Abbot Academy too late to reassure her
when she most needed support. Miss Watson "gave it up," supposedly
for reasons of health, in June 1898. Almost immediately she left for
Europe and a period of extended study. Perhaps it had all been just
too much. Or possibly she had resigned for the good of the school,
realizing that someone new could more easily consolidate the curricular innovations she had wrought. If so, the Trustees' choice of a new
principal was ironic, for they elected Emily A. Means, an Abbot graduate of 1869 from a respected Abbot-Andover family, who had been
part of school life for much of the McKeen era, having left only when
Miss McKeen retired. Following years of art study in Boston and
Paris, Miss Means had taken charge of the Abbot Art Department
for fifteen years—a part-time job, to be sure, but one which involved
her increasingly in the life of the school as she took over some
of Miss McKeen's teaching and dormitory duties during those last
busy years. The Class of '87, having had her as teacher in both art history and painting, unanimously voted art "their favorite study."[74] She
was the active President of the Abbot Academy Alumnae Association
from 1890 to 1898, serving six of those years from her brother's home
in Summit, New Jersey, where she painted, wrote, and gave art lessons. Those who knew her best were most surprised when she accepted
the principalship, for she was trading the freedom of a creative, leisured artist for the merciless demands sure to be made upon the chief
administrator of a boarding academy. They guessed that her love of
Abbot had moved her, along with the Trustees' assurance of Miss Mc-
Keen's continued presence and advice.

Then, unexpectedly, Philena McKeen died. It was May of 1898 and
Emily Means had not yet arrived in Andover. Bereft, but far too
proud to back down now, Miss Means came on to make all she could
of the new-old school Miss Watson had left her, stiffening herself
against the winds that were already ushering in the twentieth century.

Futures

The disquiet of women . . . is part of the general disturbance.
Edward Sandford Martin, 1912

You, alumnae . . . by you Abbot is judged.
Bertha Bailey, 1912

The girls and women living through change within Abbot Academy could see much greater changes without, were they willing to look—transformations that affected their Abbot careers and shaped all graduates' futures. As Henry Steele Commager has written of the 1890's, "The new America came in as on a floodtide."[1] A national population once overwhelmingly rural was now 40 percent urban. Per capita wealth had nearly doubled in the last two decades of the century—and the gap between rich and poor was astonishing. At a time when the disappearance of free or cheap western lands was narrowing economic opportunity, Darwin's theories lent these disparities a new seriousness: for the wealthy and "fit," they brought self-justification, for the poor and their sympathizers, an erosion of Victorian optimism. "The survival of the fittest" at first buttressed the missionary enthusiasm that had been central to Abbot's values. A *Courant* writer cheered the Protestant missionaries' conversion of the "ignorant and degraded" Hawaiians;[2] she failed to record that the sons of these same missionaries quietly took over the best of the Hawaiians' land for pineapple and sugar plantations. As religious concerns waned, semi-secular enthusiasms filled the vacuum. Americans were wild with excitement at the triumph in Cuba of their freedom fighters over the cruel Catholic Spaniards in 1898. Abbot's Emily Means wrote a friend that her mind was so absorbed by the "Cuba affair" that she could think of nothing else.[3] A United States just staggering out from a frightening period of depression, rural despair and labor strife had needed that swift proof of its fitness and virtue. Few of the patriots knew or cared that the Spanish-American War ended three years later in a remote Pacific archipelago after the slaughter of 300,000 Philippino "pagans" and "rebels" by American soldiers.

By 1900 the "New American" Progressives, both male and female, had pushed messy overseas crusades aside and were organizing to attack domestic disparities of wealth and power. A growing coalition pushed for wider suffrage, for better jobs and working conditions, for improved schooling. On the women's rights front, the pioneers fought on, but there have always been pioneers. More impressive is the number of women who now accepted once-radical rhetoric or who were goaded to join an antisuffrage opposition just as loud, active, and unladylike. The question Abbot's founders had asked in the 1820's was now more insistent than ever: For what futures should young women prepare?

The founders' answers had been provoking enough when it was still assumed by many that study of mathematics and Greek would shrivel up the generative organs, and grade-school teaching was the only non-manual occupation widely open to women "of the better sort."[4] Now work opportunities had mushroomed. Although the actual number of women in the nonteaching professions was small (they made 6 percent of all physicians in 1910), 20 percent of all women were bringing money home, or keeping it and living with a new sense of independence from men.[5] Their husbands' increasing income did its part too, freeing large numbers of middle and upper class women to immerse themselves in volunteer social service, club activities, or suffrage campaigns. "What chiefly makes the disturbance" women feel, Edward Martin pontificated, "is enlargement of opportunity."[6] By 1909 the word "obey" had disappeared from civil marriage vows. In vain did the influential *Ladies Home Journal* remind its readers that "what men liked most in women was milk."[7]

Within Abbot and without, faith in education as a means to national progress had never been stronger: as Lawrence Cremin has written of this new reformist generation, "the Progressive mind was ultimately an educator's mind."[8] And for wealthier women, at least, equal educational opportunities were at last a reality. Bryn Mawr College had let the world know it would accept only students who could qualify for the best men's colleges, and would award its diploma only to those who had met graduate-school admissions standards. All-female governing boards in a few new private schools proved that women could found and run educational institutions without men's help. The Trustees of the new and excellent Johns Hopkins Medical School had reluctantly accepted their largest founding donation from a group of women who made their gift conditional on the school's accepting qualified women students on the same basis as men.[9]

Not everyone cheered. Truth seemed to be catching up with the predictions of Cassandras that independence for women would lead to decline of the Anglo-Saxon race. Americans were alarmed to find in 1910 that only half of all women college graduates (and little more than one quarter of Bryn Mawr graduates of 1890) were married. The national birth rate was falling fast, and that for educated women even faster. The average number of children for each woman of child-bearing age went from 5.2 in 1860 to 3.4 in 1910; for Abbot alumnae it was 0.9. The Commissioner of Education himself worried about the problem, quoting male observers who bemoaned the "calamity" of educated women's refusal to marry. College was an "artificial world," insisted one of them, a theater stage with "its Bengal lights and its self-centered interests." No wonder marriage looked dim; it suggested "narrowness and social limitation" to the pampered college girl.[10] Even women's dress was changing. Abbot students of the 90's were amused and almost convinced by an alumna lecture on bloomers and other liberating clothes. The college girl's mother might have worn her corset only under protest, but many a college girl refused to wear it at all.

The reaction of women to these developments was often as confused as that of men. By about 1900, for example, the original unity of the suffrage movement had disappeared. It was easy enough to go to war on the principle that women should vote, but when opportunities for specific battles presented themselves, strategists flew in all directions. Should the suffragists go all out for a federal amendment, work state by state, or make common cause with the usually moderate WCTU to get a foot in the door through local liquor-license referenda? Should women insist on full occupational equality, or support the "special legislation" now being pushed by Progressive politicians, which promised better working conditions for women and children? The stances taken by individual women—including the women of Abbot Academy—usually depended on their ambition to join the world that men had made.

To educators and to many of their pupils, M. Carey Thomas, first dean and first woman president of Bryn Mawr College, was perhaps the most striking model for those seeking full and immediate equality in a man's world. From her girlhood as oldest child in a large Quaker family, she had determined on it for herself. When she was fourteen, she heard a lecturer draw disparaging conclusions from the "fact" that women's brains weigh less than men. She decided then that "by the time I die *my* brain shall weigh as much as any man's, if study and learning can make it so." Loving furious physical activity, she raged in her diary against the confinement of girls to quiet play and housework: "Oh my how terrible how *fearfully* unjust. A girl can certainly do what she chooses as well as a boy. When I grow up—we'll see what will happen."[11] What happened was that she became a member of Cornell University's first coeducational class, having "spurned Vassar as an advanced female seminary";[12] sampled but refused to tolerate the restrictions set on women graduate students at Johns Hopkins; and pursued graduate study in Germany in spite of the shock expressed by her parents' Quaker friends, who either spoke to her mother as though Carey had become a Fallen Woman or refused even to mention her name. She won her Doctorate in Philology *summa cum laude* from the University of Zurich, an accomplishment rare for men and unprecedented for women. At age thirty-six she was elected President of Bryn Mawr, temporarily satisfying what she called her "troublesome desire to get to the bottom and the top of everything,"[13] though years later she would sigh regretfully to a friend over her frustration that she should be "*only* the President of Bryn Mawr College."[14]

But Carey Thomas' ambition created more than an ornamental model of women's scholarly and administrative competence; indeed she had her full share of human quirks, all played out in large scale. She aimed to make her college and all the women's political and educational organizations which she also led engines of sexual equality, truly useful to everyone from the upper-class women who flocked to Bryn Mawr College and Graduate School to the women factory hands and union organizers who studied at the Bryn Mawr Summer School for Women Workers. She was as much a publicist for women's equality as she was an educator. Just as the trainees from the Summer School fanned out all over the country, speaking several times to appreciative Abbot audiences to raise money for their School, Carey Thomas wrote and spoke everywhere. She railed against fashionable male physicians such as Dr. Edward Clarke, who had insisted that women were too delicate for college study, and had scolded secondary schools for expecting sustained intellectual effort of girls every day of the month, thus "ignor(ing) the periodical tide," and forcing their bodies to "divert blood from the reproductive apparatus to the head."[15] She contested the august judgments of such as Harvard's President Eliot, who in 1899 declared at Wellesley that women's colleges should not shape themselves by the old scholarly traditions: after all, said Eliot, women had had no part in creating these traditions, and furthermore their bodies were so different from men's that their intellects must be also. It was national news when President Thomas rebuked Eliot for having "sun spots" on his brain.[16] Thus it was not only the Titans who squared off. This new debate over the purposes of women's education echoed at Abbot Academy's dining tables, in its faculty room, on the pages of *Courant*, and, doubtless, around many an Abbot alumna's sewing circle as well.

President Eliot might be a tempting target for women seeking unquestioned equality with men, but many women, at Abbot and elsewhere, found they agreed with him. They wondered why Carey Thomas and her ilk should be "fighting to get an education just as bad as the boys'," as Diana Trilling has put it. Had not *Godey's Lady's Book* long ago scolded Vassar for trying to copy the "semi-obselete" curricula of Harvard and Yale?[17] These careful skeptics saw the leeway that had been so beneficial to schools like Abbot disappearing as America began to take women scholars seriously, and to demand that they and their schools prove themselves against male competition.

Well might graduating seniors and their parents ask, "After College, What?" as a popular pamphlet put it. Many of these young women were "all dressed up with no place to go."[18] In spite of new opportunities, the professions could not or would not absorb the majority of new graduates looking for work that matched their educational status. Had all that tuition money bought nothing but frustration? A Baccalaureate speaker (male, as always) provided an easy answer for the Abbot Seniors of 1905: "do well the little things next door instead of longing for a career."[19] In Andover's upper-income circles alumna Eleanor Thomson Castle (Abbot, '92–'96) remembers from her childhood that to take a job was to insult your father or husband and to deprive a poorer woman of her rightful work. She herself knew no woman who had a job, except the family servants. (It should be said that several of Mrs. Castle's Abbot contemporaries vehemently expressed their disagreement in *Courant* editorials.)[20] It was easy to be flattered when male anti-suffragists asserted that woman

> has not incorporated in her nature those qualities as mystical and holy as the life which she transmits to the world; she has not become . . . the very savior of our life, in order that she may turn traitor to herself and her ideal for a paltry bit of paper, and boast that, from being man's superior, she has now become his equal.[21]

Many young women sincerely believed with "Mrs. George of Brookline," who came twice to speak to Abbot students under Miss Means, that women could accomplish more to improve society if they refused the vote, for the disenfranchised "are not hindered by political scruples and can act unbiased by party opinions."[22] The audience liked it. Mary Byers Smith, '04, remembers few feminists in Miss Means' Abbot.[23]

Curiously, the mass of traditionalists found themselves on the same side of the suffrage issue as angry social critics like Emma Goldman, who rejected the whole corrupt political system, along with capitalism and traditional, male-dominated marriage. These radicals saw little worth voting about in American society. They found it ridiculous that colleges like Bryn Mawr should set faculty hiring standards which very few women could meet. They added an alluring, man-threatening voice to the debate over women's roles—and Abbot students' futures.

The Dear Old Girls

For Abbot alumnae, the future was here. The alumnae group was now so large, and so many Old Scholars kept in touch with their school, that their lives and doings became for the students of the Watson-Means era a part of Abbot education. Though alumnae statistics usually tell less about a school than they do about the families who sent their daughters there and the opportunities open to women, they do say something about a private school's attractive powers, its general ethos, and its capacity for skill training. This last may be discounted by the alumnae themselves, especially those thousands who achieve no great eminence in later life. One early Abbot graduate, Ellen Bartlett Hodgdon, '69, put it frankly in her message to the Semicentennial, a letter which (to Abbot's credit) was read aloud at the Old Scholars celebration: "My prevailing feeling is dissatisfaction that I labored so hard to learn many things that after all I have not particularly needed." But Mrs. Hodgdon went on to show how a school—especially a boarding school—may impart its values and its human spirit, for better or worse. "The education was being with women like Miss McKeen, Miss Phebe and all the teachers," she finished. These influences are difficult for scholars to quantify.

Most Abbot alumnae before 1900, married and unmarried, stayed close to home with their 0.9 children (married alumnae had an average of two), their church work, their painting or music, and, toward the end of the century, their social service and women's club work. Numbers of these taught briefly before marriage, joining the 10 percent of all Abbot graduates who made education a career. On the roster of the earliest Abbot alumnae there is a principal of Mt. Holyoke Seminary, another principal of Bradford, one of an urban girls' high school (fourteen years), of a city grammar school (thirty years), of a Massachusetts coeducational academy, and a founder-principal of a small Boston school (ten years). After 1840, however, Abbot was not especially known for training teachers, as were Ipswich and Mt. Holyoke.[24] Of the fraction who had careers outside of teaching, several were musicians, artists, authors, accountants, or nurses; twenty-four were foreign missionaries, and as many more worked full time in home missions to the Indians, the freed blacks, or city slum-dwellers. In the nineteenth century secretaries, accountants, and librarians were usually men, as were physicians, but Abbot gave the world a few such anyway, including Caroline Jackson, '51, who ably assisted her father, Samuel, in his job as Massachusetts' Assistant Secretary of Education. Mary Graves, '58, became an ordained Unitarian minister, active and successful in her work.

Alumnae of the years before Philena McKeen retired, whether married or not, were much less likely to have a full-time job during their lives (about 16 percent) than were alumnae of the Watson-Means era (about 25 percent, with 30 percent for the final decade of this period).[25] Married alumnae of the later period chose handsomely, nearly all of them marrying college-educated men of the business-professional class (two thirds of whom were graduates of prominent Ivy League level Northeastern colleges), with about 40 percent marrying businessmen or bankers, 30 percent professionals such as lawyers, professors, or physicians, and 15 percent marrying ministers. The last figure is interesting in the light of earlier statistics, for a quarter of all wedded alumnae before 1870 married ministers or missionaries, and the *Congregationalist* reported of Abbot alumnae: "Some have said that they make the best wives in the whole country for ministers."[26] Only a few alumnae of the Watson-Means era were happy (or unhappy) with farmers, musician-composers, news reporters, and baggage-masters.

The working alumnae chose some intriguing jobs. Mary R. Kimball, '43, traveled south to Roanoke, N.C., as soon as the Union troups had pacified the island, and taught the "freed people, very earnest to learn" for ten years.[27] Rebecca Bacon, '37, helped to launch Hampton Institute; in fact she had entire charge of the school during two of its early years, though, typically, the titular head was a man. Elizabeth Richardson, '99, trained to become a nurse for the Grenfell mission in Labrador. Cora Brown Campbell, '91, was a builder-contractor, Annie Edwards, '55, the first postmistress in the nation. Mary C. Wheeler, '66, skilled artist and teacher, became so dissatisfied with the schools she taught in after Abbot that she founded one of her own, the still-existing Wheeler School in Providence, Rhode Island. Sarah Jenness, '64, went to the Boston University School of Medicine soon after it was opened to women in the 1880's and became a physician to the poor—first in Boston, then in rural New Hampshire. Abbie Hamlin, '66, Henrietta's youngest daughter, and her half-sister, Clara Hamlin,

'73, taught at Vassar and at Skutari, Turkey, respectively, before marrying missionaries and taking up their parents' work. Helen Bartlett, '74, B.A. and Ph.D. Bryn Mawr, and Alice Hamlin, '87, Ph.D. Cornell, became college professors, though Alice Hamlin Hinman gave up paid teaching while her children needed her care, and devoted much of her time to organizing midwestern church support for the Turkish missions.

Emily Skilton, '84, entered "Woman Rescue Work"[28] as a Florence Crittenton League volunteer, became a city missionary and prominent figure in the Lowell, Massachusetts, police court as advocate and friend of wayward girls, then enrolled in the Boston School for Social Work, qualifying to become probation officer and, finally, Lowell's first policewoman. She lived happily with other single women at the Lowell YWCA, an organization powerfully supported by Abbot's alumnae, especially those of the several years during the Watson-Means era when the "Abbot Christian Workers" functioned as a YWCA club. Unusual as policewomen were at the time, Emily Skilton's career followed a common pattern for ambitious Abbot graduates and women professionals generally: they began by doing volunteer work that had become accepted as "woman's work" with children or church, took professional training, then became fully paid career workers in fields that had once been dominated by men. Jane Greeley, '84, Abbot teacher 1886–93, M.D. '97, then practitioner, did exactly this; so did her medical colleague Sarah Jenness, '64. Others began and ended with the world of children. Mrs. Kate Douglas Wiggin, an early *Courant* editor, was known in her time as much for her organization of kindergartens in the poorer districts of San Francisco as for her best-selling children's books.[29]

Only the thinnest of lines could be drawn between the alumna career-woman and the unmarried alumna volunteer, who subsisted on an independent income and made an unpaid career of social service in city slum or windswept prairie mission. Clearly there was great work to be done for which the market would not pay; since so many men exhausted themselves in their search for riches, women must do that higher work. Jane Addams, Lillian Wald, and other women of means had become heroines among some Abbot students; all heard many lectures each year from lesser but equally devoted figures in the settlement house or Consumer's League Movement. Like many spinsters, Caroline Jackson, '51, was alternately teacher, secretary, and community volunteer. With Philena McKeen she organized Andover's local WCTU, then led the victorious no-license campaign of 1905. Mrs. Charlotte Emerson Brown, '51, married but childless, drew on her early experience in teaching and administration eventually to found several women's organizations and to carry out her demanding duties as first president of the General Federation of Women's Clubs, founded in 1890, with a membership of 185 clubs in twenty-nine states.[30] Married alumnae often became full-time volunteers once their children were grown. However, Emily Reed, '67, didn't let twelve children prevent her from working indefatigably for suffrage. She and Agnes Park went to the State House repeatedly to push for the 1895 suffrage referendum. "These two women stood alone in conservative Andover for the progress of women," a League of Women Voters bulletin reported in 1931.

Many Abbot alumnae married late, as did most graduates of the newer women's colleges, after a season of paid work;[31] their experience as newspaper reporters or school administrators was invaluable to the women's literary clubs or service organizations they soon joined. If they had had a job *or* been to college, their daughters were very likely to become college graduates.[32] One minister's wife (Sarah Rockwell Leete, '81) had three daughters, all college graduates, and three sons, two of them distinguished businessmen and the third a missionary to China. Alice Purington Holt, '95, marvelously exemplified Abbot's nineteenth-century ideal. She needed no further education to teach history, literature, and music at Gould Academy, Maine, for six years, nor to find a "solid citizen" and highly respected businessman from one of Andover's oldest families as husband in 1901.[33] Her two children were born several years apart, and the mother had ample time to be president of the November Club, to lead the Women's Missionary Committee at South Church, and to work for the Abbot Alumnae Association. She eventually became a chief organizer and president of the Massachusetts Congregationalist Women's Association Conference and of the Inter-Church Missionary Rally. With her powerful energy and executive ability, she could easily have commanded a salary somewhere, but she worked for love—and, doubtless, for the excitement and prestige of it all.

Numbers of alumnae became writers. Two of those most widely read by Abbot students—and by the public—were Anna Fuller, '72, and Octave Thanet (Alice French, '68);[34] the lives and writings of these two presented images of outside-Abbot realities as contradictory as the world itself appeared from inside Abbot's walls. Nearly all Anna Fuller's heroines are fresh young things of sixteen to twenty-three, lovely to look at, inventive and high-spirited, but ultrafeminine. They never go to college, though they may be at art school. They come either from fashionable families or from poor-but-virtuous families whom they by their luck and pluck manage to elevate into the rich-but-virtuous category. In "Blythe Halliday's Voyage," the heroine is crossing the Atlantic with her "Mumsey" and a select group of fellow first-class passengers, including a handsome (safely married) poet and an old Italian count. By chance she discovers a pale Italian waif in steerage whose fine eyes betray her aristocratic ancestry and who is reunited with her long lost grandfather (the Italian count, of course) by the compassionate detective work of Blythe and her platonic poet-friend. "Oh Mumsey!" she concludes, "How beautiful the world is with you and me right in the very middle of it!"[35]

Meanwhile, Octave Thanet continued her frenetic explorations of places and ideas, flitting through Andover for some "delicious repartee" with Abbot students,[36] settling down only in summertime at the deserted Cape Cod mill which she rented at $3.00 a summer for her writing and photography work. Born in 1850 in the Double Brick house on Andover Hill, she had gone West as a small child when her father determined that Davenport, Iowa, offered him a scope for his financial ambitions that old Andover could never provide. Alice found as much to learn from the polyglot Mississippi River town as from its public high school, but when it was time to complete her education, only Vassar would do for this oldest, only girl of the French family. Yet once she got there, Vassar seemed to her narrowly snobbish, a place where the pretentious daughters of the Civil War rich certified their new status, and she left after a term, entering Abbot Academy in 1867 for her Senior year. There on Andover Hill, the meld of intellectual elitism and protestant virtue was so firmly ensconced that it required no proofs. Alice French reveled in a rich mix of friends, and in the thorough training in writing and English literature given the Smith Hall contingent. Her biographer writes that "the school's reflection of a stable and ordered society shaped her virtues and heightened her delusions."[37] When she graduated, she was not at all sure she was ready for her future. As she wrote her classmate Anna Dawes,

> I'm sorry and I'm glad and I'm a little frightened. The world is so large and a woman's future is so uncertain. Life is getting to look remarkably queer and earnest.[38]

In spite of uncertainty, Alice French–Octave Thanet remained independent of men. She was a saleswoman for her own books (one of the first woman writers to do this), an avid supporter of striking workers in her youth, later a foe of woman suffrage and a friend of Teddy Roosevelt. She specialized in dialect studies of families from Quebec or the bottom lands of Arkansas, but she admired Tolstoi, and one of her most urgent concerns was the plight of the sharecropper and the urban factory worker. For a while her thinking assumed a Marxist cast. She gave up fellow alumna Elizabeth Stuart Phelps' hope for "justice" in the mills "based on understanding and Christian kindliness."[39] A reviewer of one of her early articles, "The English Workingmen and Commercial Crises" praised "Mr. Thanet's" insight into the history of labor struggles and their relationship to technological change.[40] Thanet predicted in this article the beginning of a "class contest"; she elaborated on the capital-labor conflict in The Lion's Share; than finally, in her voluminous novel The Man of the Hour (1905), she found a synthesis between her youthful enthusiasm for European socialist thought and her admiration of the American entrepreneur. It takes her 465 pages to bring John Ivan Winslow from lisping boyhood in a Missouri river town, through impetuous socialist youth (during which he travels to Russia to visit the new grave of his beautiful Nihilist-aristocrat mother), to manhood as a benevolent capitalist of "stainless life," a manhood well schooled by his earlier strivings as an anonymous trade-union organizer through the great and futile Pullman Strike. One is impatient with the length and complexity of the tale until one suddenly realizes that this is a Russian novel written in English! And sure enough, on page 323 John-Ivan's difficulty and promise are at once made clear: "He had a Puritan conscience and a Russian imagination." The same might be said for Octave Thanet. Together, hero and author recognize that the tyranny of labor can be as ruinous as the tyranny of capital, and praise the tenacity of the Anglo-Saxon spirit, which "always demands the works without which faith is dead."[41] It is a brave if undisciplined book; one doubts it would ever have found a place in the Abbot library next to the works of Longfellow and Stevenson had Octave Thanet–Alice French not been one of Abbot's own.

Again, Anna Fuller and Alice French, along with many other alumnae, testify to the variety of fledglings that Abbot could hatch. Unlike Bryn Mawr students, Abbot students do not seem to have been graduated with the insistence they do something Grand, nor were they easy prey to the guilt that later attaches to unrealized aspirations. Life in the ordinary muddled world was challenge enough for many: if most alumnae added little to the public record of these turn-of-the century years, each one must cope in her own way with their confusion and their promise, drawing for help on whatever resources Abbot Academy had provided them.

"A New England Aristocrat"

Earth's noblest thing—a woman perfected
James Russell Lowell

Emily Means, '69, appeared unintimidated by the catches and changes of life within Abbot and beyond. Short in stature but as straight as those lines she made her beginning art pupils endlessly draw, she was "a lady of the old school"[1] in every sense of the word. She dressed much as she had done in the McKeen years, with a high-boned collar and a rich satin train that swished slowly as she walked.[2] In her photographs she has a dignified beauty, but her contemporaries say no, she was not beautiful; she was impressive, rather—erect and severe with a set mouth, a person of few words and powerful opinions.

One of her opinions was that college was not necessary to a lady's future. Indeed, Miss Means seems to have felt that there was some social taint attached to college attendance, ironic in view of the fact that most of the students in women's colleges clearly came from upper income (if not upper class) groups, and Abbot's own College Preparatory scholars "felt contemptuous of the finishing school idea" as embodied in the Academic Course.[3] Emily Means herself had not required college training to become a sophisticated artist and linguist. She had traveled extensively and was literate in three foreign languages; her library shelves were heavy with French, Italian, and German works. Her intellectual mother and minister father had prepared her so well for Abbot that she taught French instead of studying it when she first entered the school in 1867. A profoundly independent person, she saw no reason for most young women to continue to depend upon formal institutions or the credentials they conferred: Abbot Academy should be sufficient.[4]

But Miss Means was dutiful as well. If the Trustees had ordained a C.P. Program, she would continue it, adjusting it here to the needs of Abbot's C.P. students, there to the standards of the new College Entrance Examination Board, well enough organized by 1901 to supply uniform entrance exams for most colleges in the Middle Atlantic states.[5] Some colleges could be trusted more than others. Had not

27. Emily A. Means, Principal, 1898–1912. The picture was taken when she was an art instructor at Abbot.

Smith been founded for the young woman "to preserve her woman-liness," in the words of Clark Seelye, Smith's first President and Abbot's friend?[6] Though Bryn Mawr and Radcliffe continued to insist on their own entrance exams, Abbot had by this time obtained "certificate privileges" at Smith, Vassar, Simmons, Mt. Holyoke, and Wellesley, the colleges attended by most of Abbot's C.P. students since 1892. The numbers of C.P. students would decline under Miss Means to fewer than half those of Laura Watson's final years (there were two C.P. Seniors in 1903), but Abbot's academic standing would remain high. Miss Means did not actively discourage even the Academic Course graduates from going on to further training and a few gained advanced standing in four-year colleges on the basis of the Abbot Academic diploma.[7] Bowing to student and parent complaints, she hid her opinion that graduating C.P. Seniors "were leaving before they were done,"[8] and acceded to the Trustees' injunction that they be allowed to receive diplomas and to march to Commencement behind the Academic Seniors near the head of the line, no longer behind the Prep class at its very tail.[9] She asked the Trustees to strengthen science and history courses to meet the colleges' standards. To her credit, some of those who most admired Miss Means' independence and learning were C.P. students.[10]

There was much else to admire—and much to criticize. "Her great quality, inspiring to some, to others rather terrifying, was her power to discern the best in people; and to tolerate nothing less," wrote Mabel Bacon Ripley, who had known Miss Means as one of her vulnerable beginning teachers.[11] "The best" had some prerequisites. Miss Means believed in aristocracies, both natural and established. In seeking both teachers and students, she looked for long family lines. "Blood tells, blood counts, doesn't it?" she rhetorically asked Trustee Burton Flagg in discussing a would-be teacher.[12] Without formal entrance examinations (they had been dropped when applications fell during the final McKeen decade), Abbot got some blooded students who found languages or mathematics almost impossible; it seems to still-living alumnae that a few wealthy parents simply dumped their daughters there, and were disappointed when they failed to graduate. For the faculty did not shrink from denying diplomas. After all, Abbot's academic standards remained uppermost: the Academy was not considered a "social school" like Farmington. Genuine academic effort was rewarded, even for the feeble, says Constance Parker Chipman, '06: "I think they were quite compassionate, that is, when they knew it was hopeless." But the indolent were dropped.

Abbot students heard Saturday lectures about Jewish immigrants and the Irish communities in Boston, but neither Jew nor Catholic was allowed anywhere near the Academy itself. This was not unusual at the time: the wealthiest Jewish families could no more get their daughters into the typical girls' private school than they could join the suburban country clubs or take the waters at Saratoga Springs.[13] Yet most colleges were becoming nonsectarian, and the pioneering Bryn Mawr School had long admitted girls of any race or religion who would be "suitable companions" to those already in the school,[14] thereby attracting a wealthy and daring Jewish clientele. Miss Means's social adventurousness took another direction. Years before, she had demonstrated it in her free evening school for twenty working men and boys, who came every Tuesday night for two years to study drawing and design in the Andover Town Hall. Uninterested in the commonplace, she cared deeply about the unpromising girl who showed some small streak of talent or worth. She accepted one little farm girl from Maine, "an absolute aborigine," remembers a friend of Emily Means, who eventually graduated and brought a wealth of intellectual and artistic interests from Abbot to enrich the life of her home town. This search for pearls had its drawbacks, however. Students sometimes felt that Miss Means had far less concern for the average girl than for the unruly one: "she liked the naughty girls who weren't afraid of her," and she spent much time and kindness upon them,[15] while an ordinary student in trouble would be harshly scolded, often enough reduced to tears, and then dismissed from her mind—sometimes from the school itself.

To Miss Means decorum and civilization were synonymous. She was not amused when day scholars Eleanor Thomson and her sister came to Chapel with black armbands, mourning the death of their beloved dog. With the Principal's encouragement, the elocution and posture teacher barked at the students in her classes ("Lift your torso!") and at the practice "tea parties" in the library ("Straighten up" or "Don't make a meal of your tea!").[16] Though the food was delicious, especially following the tuition raise in 1903, dining-room decorum made it hard to enjoy one's meal, and still harder for mediocre language students, who had to eat in French or German.[17] Neither gossip nor shop talk about academies was allowed in any language at any table; at Miss Means's table one dared not even ask for a second helping. Young Mabel Bacon loved to laugh with her students and tell jokes; despite the supposed formality, her entire table was "in roars of laughter" at many a meal, says Mary Byers Smith, '04. Too many. Miss Means arranged for this "youngish, gay individual" to eat at the table right next to hers. The punchline one night was an imitation of a parrot that had learned to say "TO HELL WITH YALE." The Principal stopped what she was saying in midsentence and glared over at Miss Bacon with such force that the raconteur fainted.[18]

A few students became bitter about Miss Means's behavior toward both teachers and students. They suspected she *enjoyed* making girls cry. An outsider remarked, "She carries herself as if you were a bad odor," while one of her oldest Andover friends, Alice Buck, '57, shook her head and said, "I don't know *why* Emily acts the way she does since she came back."[19] Neither do we who look backward in time; yet one can surmise. Miss Means, essentially a private person, had a passion for order. She bore heavily her responsibility for keeping a various community in close array when the world outside offered so many unfamiliar alternatives to the old-Abbot and old-Andover traditions within which she had grown to womanhood. Someone had to stand strong for the right, someone who still knew what right was. When she relaxed her guard, as at her summer island in Maine, or even at Abbot—when she encountered a bright, hardworking student like Mary Byers Smith who "would walk right up to the lion" and say her piece for the other day scholars or C.P. students[20]—she showed her sympathetic side and her marvelous, dry sense of humor. To a few of her students she became a lifelong friend, with whom she shared her wit, her literary interests, and her island in Maine.[21] Even those who did not like her found her "always interesting." They were stimulated not only by her reverent teaching of Henry James, but by the "strain in the air": the three-way tension between Miss Means's almost fanatic defense of traditional behavior against "modernistic" incursions, their own modern aspirations, and the example their Principal presented of a resourceful individual who had created her own life plan.[22]

A school, of course, is much more than its principal. Miss Means's Abbot had inherited some fine teachers from Miss Watson, and she chose new teachers with scrupulous care. Foremost, perhaps, was Rebekah Chickering, one of Miss Watson's last gifts to Abbot. Fresh from Bryn Mawr College, where she had excelled in literature, history, and basketball, she never staled during the entire thirty-nine years of her stay. She had come to teach the College English and Church History sections, but she was passionately interested in current events. This passion generated student extracurricular debates, then a current events elective; it stimulated discussion of complex foreign policy questions in the Modern European History course. A suffragist, she also chaired the Social Science Department of the November Club. She delighted in some of the modern novels that found no place on College Preparatory reading lists. Throughout her life, her Bryn Mawr classmates and her Abbot students came to her for advice on what to read. Though seemingly shy at first, she was warm-hearted, quick with a joke, and marvelously absent-minded. Students loved to come upon her talking to herself in the library; at table they watched spellbound while she served meat from the platter, passed filled plates to the right, then received the plates from the left and unloaded the meat once more onto the platter, talking graciously all the time. For Miss Chickering herself, her dream world seems to have been an always ready source of self-renewal. She coached the basketball players as ably as the actors in Shakespeare plays. Miss Means had returned to Abbot ambitious to bring its history and French offerings up to the best of the McKeen years, for she felt Miss Watson, with her too-many-irons-in-the-fire, had let them slide. Miss Chickering would be the inspiration of a parade of younger history teachers for decades to come. In her hands even the dreaded senior Church History became an experience to treasure; her keen scholarship and her B.A. degree made her a special model for the C.P. students.[23]

Miss Chickering was only one of several young college-trained teachers, women who had often overcome family objections and local suspicion to win their education. They brought a sense of fun along with their skills. Barbara Moore Pease, '11, initially found Latin alien and difficult. Latin teacher Olive Runner won her devotion first to teacher and then to subject by inviting her to read poetry aloud with her on rainy afternoons, and by "borrowing" tin trays from the dining room so the two could zoom screaming down the hill behind Abbot Hall when the snowcrust was right and the moon was full. Apparently, older teachers warmly welcomed the new: Nellie Mason was outwardly severe in her inevitable black dress, but she was grateful for the younger teachers' help in radically improving the laboratory science program; round-faced Frau Schiefferdecker was as jolly and friendly outside of German class as she was firm within it (*her* favorite tray-sliding place was the orchard hill). "Kit" Kelsey might strike some as a feeble mathematics teacher, but she was kindness itself to new teachers, and they admired her energetic organization of geology field trips and other school events.[24] Complex and reluctant though it sometimes was, the process by which Abbot incorporated the new with the old had by now become fairly well systematized. The number of years teachers stayed at the school indicates growing academic continuity.

Table 1.

Number of Years Tenure	Number of Teachers Arriving during Abbot's First Forty Years, (1829–69)	Number of Teachers Arriving during the Second Forty Years (1869–1909)
1–2	113	63 teachers
3–10	25	36 teachers
10–20	2*	8 teachers
20+	3*	9 teachers

*The five long-tenured teachers of the early period all arrived during the first McKeen decade, 1859–69, and included both McKeen sisters and Mr. Downs, a part-time teacher.

The alumnae had also become a powerful force for institutional stability and growth. They had been contributing toward lecture or concert series and scholarships for years; now they endowed them. As soon as they had finished helping to build and furnish Draper Hall, they began a new building fund. After Miss McKeen's death, this became seed money for McKeen Memorial Hall to which they would add generously before its erection in 1904. The active Boston and New York Abbot clubs (founded in 1892 and 1898) supplemented the organizational efforts of the Alumnae Association, ably run from Andover by secretary-treasurer Agnes Park. This "tall and plain" daughter of Professor Park was "vigorously intellectual and staunch in devotion to people and causes."[25] She had long since declared her independence from all that was fossilized on Andover Hill, and she was "the mainspring" of Abbot's Alumnae Association for forty-two years. After 1909 she had much help from Jane Carpenter, '92, B.A. Mt. Holyoke, M.A. Teachers College, Columbia, and Record Keeper Extraordinary. For Jane Carpenter, alumnae history was paid vocation and heartwhole avocation in one. It was Abbot's next door neighbor and new Trustee, Burton Flagg, who had the foresight to urge creation of the salaried alumnae post. Trustees and alumnae knew by now that they needed one another.

By chance the first decade of the new century brought in an almost wholly new Board. Professors Park and Churchill both died in 1900, having served forty and twenty-one years respectively. Of twelve Trustees, only three of the older men spanned the new decade, among them the Reverend Professor John Phelps Taylor, D.D., Abbot's final link with the Theological Seminary, famous among alumnae for his profuse and garbled rhetoric (at one Commencement he prayed fervently that "these young girls would become streams of living water on their hearth fires").[26] Mrs. John Harlow, one of the first two woman Trustees, and the aging Draper and Ripley stayed a few years into the century; but once they had departed, the group was fresh, attuned to modern business principles, aware of the great progress being made by the private educational institutions that were Abbot's contemporaries and competitors. Colonel George Ripley had already laid away Draper's almost undecipherable account books and improved the Treasurer's bookkeeping and reporting system. The Trustees voted to move the securities from the secret compartment Draper had built into his chimney to a safety deposit box in Andover or Boston.[27] Reverend Daniel Merriman, Board President from 1900 to 1912, encouraged Burton Flagg, then a young insurance executive, to polish Ripley's accounting method to a sheen that would last throughout Flagg's fifty-nine-year term as Treasurer. Finally, Mary Donald Churchill, '63, Professor Churchill's widow, took to her Trustee duties (they were to last three decades) with an energy and a forward look which belied her years. Together, Trustees, alumnae, and Principal set out to complete the buildings Abbot seemed to need for its ideal enrollment, about 110 by Miss Means's reckoning.

Bricks

Planning for a new classroom building had already begun. In the spring of her first year, Miss Watson had received $200 from the students for such a hall, and Seniors had been given permission to appeal for more funds to the Boston Abbot Club. Throughout the Watson years, students and alumnae worked at the project, holding benefits and festivals. After Miss McKeen's death in 1898, an active memorial campaign completed the raising of $24,000 to start the building; this included the proceeds of three Senior plays and a dramatic entertainment jointly presented by faculty members from Abbot, Phillips, the Theological Seminary, and several Phillips alumnae. Warren Draper offered $7,500 more on condition the building be completed by Abbot's seventy-fifth anniversary,[28] and Miss Means herself lent $10,000 so that construction could be started in time to meet Draper's stipulations. Shortly after the ground breaking, George G. Davis donated a further $10,000 in honor of his Trustee father to build on an assembly hall–gymnasium. The Abbot faculty produced a play to raise money for a stage curtain. Still more donors gave furniture; to their earlier gifts of plaster casts, Reverend and Mrs. Merriman added a cast of the Parthenon frieze fully as fine as the one at the Bryn Mawr School, which seems to have begun this fashion.

McKeen Hall was ready for use in the fall of 1904, and the attached "Davis Hall" was finished in time for a December lecture by Booker T. Washington. All Andover was invited, and most of Andover came, Miss Kelsey reports. Abbot stretched its limbs and moved equipment from the old academy building; shortly afterward, alumnae gifts and bequests made it possible to refurbish Abbot Hall's first two floors for expanded science laboratories, with advice on design from Trustee-chemist John Alden.

In the Abbot Hall renovations, as in other building projects, Miss Means's alumnae connections were proving invaluable. With a $40,000 bequest from Esther Smith Byers, '56, an entire are gallery was built against the east wall of Abbot Hall to house the collection that John and Esther Byers had gathered in their New York home. Miss Means had given practical counsel in the design of all the new construction, but this project especially intrigued her. The fireproof second floor invited other art donations, and the workrooms and sculpture exhibition hall on the first floor added valuable space for the art program, which used the new John-Esther gallery constantly. The public was invited in every Saturday.

Harvard's President Eliot spoke at the dedication of the John-Esther Gallery, addressing his audience on the "higher education" of girls and young women with more humility than he had displayed in the Wellesley speech that had so annoyed M. Carey Thomas. He confessed that he was "singularly uninformed about the education of girls"; although he described the woman's body and "the woman's heart" as having "larger elements of delicacy, tenderness, and deftness" than the man's, he went on to defend training in self-control, courage, and intellectual and aesthetic excellence as appropriate both to young men and young women. "The home which [woman] creates, illumines and blesses" benefits as much from this education as does the work of the world which men must do.[29] It was a welcome concession, however timid, from the nation's chief spokesman for liberal education, and Abbot was grateful.

Across from Abbot Hall on School Street, the old Judge Morton House also came into Abbot's hands, bought by gifts from Mrs. Draper and four others. Doubtless its acquisition was a relief to the Abbot administration, which had long bridled at Phillips student-boarders who trained their binoculars on Smith or Draper Hall, and later, at the number of boys the large Morton family contained. John Phelps Taylor contributed $5000 to outbid "the menace" on another house adjacent to Abbot: the competitor was threatening to convert it to apartments. "Miss Means is aghast at the prospect," he wrote Mrs. Draper, from whom he subtly requested a contribution:

> Instead of a home for a quiet family . . . we should have the blotch of a more extended tenement-district with the battering ram of its head fronting the fairest temple of knowledge in Andover. Now in this peril is an opportunity . . .[30]

Finally, Smith Hall, empty of students since 1897, was demolished, too outdated by Draper Hall's superior heating and lighting arrangements for anyone but alumnae to mourn its loss. Abbot was above such primitive accommodations now; a clientele paying $500 per daughter cared not at all for those gas lamps and those 12' × 12' rooms which had seemed splendid to so many pairs of girls in simpler times. The empty site stood waiting for an infirmary to replace the makeshift arrangements in Draper Hall—a few rooms on the top floor separated from the rest by a sheet soaked in carbolic acid. So confident were the Trustees that donors for an infirmary would materialize that they had begun weaving plans in their heads well before Miss Means's retirement. For there was money about, especially in that upper fifth of the turn-of-the-century population that owned most of the nation's wealth. The building of Draper Hall had inspired a confidence in Abbot's future—a confidence mere people do not generate—and it was soon vindicated by the major building additions and renovations of the Means era. Given this enormous outlay for real estate, it is surprising to read enrollment and budget figures for the first five years of Miss

Means's tenure. Enrollment dropped steadily after Miss Watson left, to a low of seventy-seven in 1903–04, the year McKeen Hall was constructed, before leveling off at about 100 after 1907. Neither the diminished student roster nor the "shortages" of $5,000 to $7,000 each year apparently shook the faith of Principal or Trustees.[31] People might come and go; those bulky brick sentinels with their fashionably appointed insides assured the world that Abbot Academy would endure.

Beyond Bricks

Meanwhile, within and around the buildings, student life continued. Almost imperceptibly, it had grown more Abbot-centered since Miss McKeen's retirement. Many students still came as much for Andover as for Abbot—an Andover "lovely in trees, fine architecture and old homes and gardens," remembers Ruth Newcomb. Members of the Abbot Christian Association might still go to a Theological Seminary lecture now and then; forty or fifty students would enjoy the annual May Day Breakfast at Town Hall; but the sharing grew less each year. The Theological Seminary's extraordinary power over regional—and national—cultural life was now much dimmed by secular forces. The number of theologues had dwindled by two thirds since the heresy trial—to the point where there were more professors than Seniors.[32] Abbot day-student enrollment dropped again under Miss Means. Not since the McKeens arrived had this "school-home" equipped for boarders paid much attention to day scholars (and if behavior follows the dollar, perhaps this is no wonder, since they paid only one fifth of the boarders' total fee). Now they were "the scum of the earth," says a day scholar who graduated in 1904. Even the brightest and most active rarely led school organizations, belonged to many clubs, or took part in informal recreation-day activities. It was not until Mary Byers Smith reminded Miss Means that the day scholars had to complete their bag lunches by wiping their hands on their slips that towels appeared in the day scholars' basement dressing room.

This was a chicken-egg affair. Students needed less of "down-town" because their Academy created more diversion. Partly as a result of student pressure, organized sports played an ever greater role in school life. Girls expected to be more active than their mothers had been. Running sports were now popular in women's colleges; tennis and bicycling had killed no one at Abbot. Despite the insistence of many male physicians that menstruating girls were weak and vulnerable to disease (the eminent Dr. John Thornton said that "they should adjust

28. A Grecian phase, circa 1900: "Night and the Fates."

themselves to the law of nature and lie fallow about a quarter of the time"),[33] "women's delicacy" was gradually going out of date. On two afternoons a week in 1898–99 most of Abbot cheered at the baseball contests between three rotating teams. The same year, four basketball teams were organized under Rebekah Chickering's enthusiastic direction. Horrified when she came to find the contenders tripping over their long skirts, she won them the right to wear black stockings and bloomers (to be sure, the bloomers were made with yards and yards of cloth). Academic Seniors competed heartily with the Senior-Mid (eleventh grade) teams that spring at Abbot's first Field Day, which was much enlivened by a group of Phillips boys who crept into the Grove and formed a waiting block just beyond the finish tape: the Abbot racers who broke the tape flung themselves willy-nilly into many open arms. Young faculty brought field hockey from the colleges by 1902, and soon Abbot was playing Bradford in both hockey and baseball. Miss Means's anticollege bias extended to the athletic field: the C.P. baseball nine was never allowed to play in outside games or on Field Day. Fortunately, Field Day was more than baseball. Within a few years it had become an all-school festival, with the two upper classes striving to outdo each other in their costumes, songs, and antics in an atmosphere of general jubilation that gave a special shine to the games, the track and field contests, and the tennis matches on the new dirt courts. The growing emphasis on athletics at Abbot reflected a general trend toward secondary and college students' absorption in school as a community-in-itself. Discouraged by labor unions and social pressures from taking jobs, youth made the extracurriculum "a substitute for attendance at comparable activities in the world outside."[34] Sports helped make Abbot more of a school-world than the school-home it had been since 1854.

No one was obliged to be sporty, however; even Phillips up the Hill had no required athletics until 1906. There were also walking and croquet clubs, mandolin and glee clubs. There was *Odeon*, a literary society where students could read aloud and discuss the contemporary plays or novels that were excluded from English classes—and even from library shelves—in favor of Tennyson and Longfellow. Finally, there were those clubbiest of clubs, the three sororities. Miss Means had given official blessing to these once secret societies when she arrived, feeling they would contribute more to Abbot as recognized groups, however exclusive (there were eight to ten members in each sorority, usually the "big wheels" of the school). In turn, each sorority made her an honorary member. The sisters also sponsored certain receptions or fund-raising events during the year, and enjoyed looking

29. The Senior Nine, 1902.

down their noses at the thirty or forty Seniors and Senior-Mids who were not members.

The Abbot sorority girls were not alone: such groups were characteristic of secondary schools and colleges of the time, in spite of the opposition of the National Education Association, which had judged them "Undemocratic . . . and subversive of discipline."[35] Phillips Academy's example in this area—as in organized sports—was stimulating, sometimes pleasantly intrusive. The captain of the track team, in love with a certain "Becca" (and she with him), ordered one of his fraternity's new initiates to send her some flowers. The youngster thought it would be funnier to send her a funeral wreath. It arrived in Miss Means's rooms, stiff with lacquer and reeking of embalming fluid, and Becca, summoned, arrived soon afterward. Miss Means stood nose uplifted, asking "*What* does this mean?" The girl didn't know, but promising to discuss it later, she staggered up to her room with it and (naturally) hung it out the window so the fast-gathering Phillipians could see it. The corridor teacher, alarmed, came in and threw a sheet over it, which made it all the easier to spot from the Hill. Enough was enough. Principal ordered girl and wreath back to her room, and told her to throw it in the fire. The lacquered flowers exploded into flames when they hit the coals, setting fire to the chimney so that the fire department had to come and put it out. By the time the fire engine was well into its work, long lines of Phillips boys were snake dancing on the Circle, jumping hoses and singing, and every girl at Abbot was hanging out the Draper Hall windows.[36.]

The sororities added to the cliquishness typical of all girls' schools. New girls like Mildred Bryant Kussmaul, '13, longed to join, but the sorority women refused to come to her creamed-chicken room supper. C.P. and day scholars were rarely invited in. The C.P. girls were used to this, of course; if they were allowed in the Senior Shakespeare play at all, it was usually as servants or outlaws.[37] "To be a College Senior, was to be almost a worm," remarked one of them much later.[38] Part of this snubbery was a function of age. Most C.P.'s were one to two years younger than the Academic Seniors, who were now twenty years old, on the average, at graduation; this was one reason why Miss Watson had established separate courses for C.P. students. They had their own class officers, their own class flower, their own Senior banquet. Apparently they were thought essential to the *Courant* Board, however. *Courant* applauded the first awarding of diplomas to C.P. Seniors in 1904, noting that "they also have worked earnestly for their standing."[39] The editors invited alumna college freshmen to describe Bryn Mawr or Mt. Holyoke for present students in letters-to-the-editors. The magazine generally served as C.P. advocate so far as possible, given the Means era publication code, which seems to have ruled out all serious criticism of the school itself and reduced the editors to preaching at their peers for their overdone hair styles, their raucous laughs, their floppy ribbons, or their flabby handshakes.

No difference between day scholar and boarder could be discerned in students' dress, which was uniformly ridiculous, as Mary Byers Smith recalled in a speech to alumnae on Abbot's Centennial:

> Our skirts trailed on the ground. Our boned collars dug into our necks. The wearer of a Ferris waist was too conspicuous. Anyone's pompadour might have concealed a pair of stockings, and a really stylish pair of gloves besides, and an orange. Can't some of you old ladies feel your hair tugging at its roots as you remember tacking across the street in a gale of wind, with an immense picture hat pinned on the back of your head?

Many of the entertainments of this time were equally sumptuous. Abbot boarders continued to enjoy the traditional festive occasions, and added a few new ones. At "corridor parties" one corridor hosted the whole school costumed according to its chosen theme—Mother Goose characters, or cupids (for Valentine's Day), or babies. Hallowe'en was now a huge costume dinner party. Thanksgiving for all Abbot and Phillips boarders left behind was a jolly, informal reception at the house of Phillips' new Principal, Alfred E. Stearns, who had assumed his position after Bancroft's untimely death in 1901 with a serious-ness one would hardly have thought could belong to the waggish Com-mencement usher of 1890. Frau Schiefferdecker made two young Ger-man teachers from Phillips her frequent guests at the German table, and even arranged a few joint German entertainments for audiences from both schools. The Phillips Senior prom was now an annual event. Abbot held its first prom soon after Davis Hall was opened. One could now go (chaperoned) on a legal Phillips-Abbot hay ride, or (unchaperoned) with an Abbot friend to Boston, perhaps to take one's turn with the two symphony tickets Miss Means used to reserve.

Phillips-Abbot cooperation had its somber side. Those who attended the memorial service for Warren Draper in 1905 remember the singing of the joint Abbot–Phillips–Theological Seminary Choir as the most poignant moment in the ceremony.[40] The chapel services up and down the Hill occasionally sounded common themes. When Helen Abbott and her roommate discovered the joys of dropping light bulbs onto the Draper Hall driveway from their third floor window, both Miss Means *and* the Phillips minister on the Hilltop prayed for them the following Sunday, Miss Means begging God's forgiveness for Helen's "temporary aberration of the mind."[41]

As of old, what adults had not arranged was often most memorable. Day scholars were a marvelous resource here: Miss Means trusted the Thomson family on Central Street, and it was a safe place to go to meet a Phillips boy. Officially "we weren't allowed to see the boys," Miss Smith remembers, "but we knew them." They managed to find each other in spite of limits carefully set for girls' walks or for social-izing time following Mr. Stearns's new Sunday Vesper services or the occasional Phillips–Abbot choral service. One Phillips student asked his girl to go canoeing on the Shawsheen; unfortunately they passed under the railroad bridge just as Miss Means was returning from Boston on the 5:14. The girl was given a blistering lecture that very evening. A Phillips boy was dismissed for riding to Lawrence with an Abbot Senior, another for walking with his girl during church time.[42] Miss Means expelled an Abbot girl just about to graduate for meeting a theologue behind one of the Hilltop buildings.[43] Yet for each tryst

confounded, hundreds were held in peace down by the old Andover-
Wilmington railroad bed, or out in the country when you had been
"punging"—hitching a secret ride on the back runners of a delivery
sleigh, traveling sometimes for miles in the hope that you could beg
a ride back, but not too soon. The students were marched to church in
pairs, a teacher walking watchful at the end of the line, but no one
could stop the younger Cads from taunting them on their way:

> There she goes
> There she goes
> All dressed up in Sunday clothes!
>
> Who knows
> Who knows
> What she's got on for underclothes?[44]

Nor were all of the "corridor stunts" approved by the school. The
Class of 1900 described in Abbot's first published Yearbook the early
months of its organization as a class:

> '99 soon found that her younger sister was not to be imposed
> upon, and began to respect the spirit which resented our being
> tied into our rooms, considering herself fortunate to escape the
> pitcher of water which [unluckily] fell upon one higher in
> authority.

The higher authority did not record her reaction to the water.

One of the C.P. students, Marion Brown, '11, kept a scrapbook record of her five years at Abbot which shows how much fun—legal and
illegal—the Academy could afford a lively girl.[45] Her father's darling,
Marion seems to have thought she could do no wrong.[46] "She's a great
favorite with Emily Means," her friends jibed, recounting the number
of "summons" she received each month. Miss Means had her hands full
persuading Marion's indulgent family (altogether too close in Lawrence) to keep her from going to the vaudeville theatre every Wednesday—and if she *must* go, to provide proper chaperonage for their
boarder-daughter.[47] The parents did comply, but Marion felt free to
speak her mind about it afterward:

> "Don't go to the theatre without a chap'ne" Did we? well I
> should say not. She looks as though she were playing hookey
> from a grave yard and she sings as though her feet hurt her.[48]

Marion was a fair scholar at first, a fine one by graduation. She must
have done some studying, for she has left us her Senior-Mid schedule.

Table 2.

Schedule of a Senior-Mid Student

NAME Marion Brown   COURSE College Prep 1910

Hour	Monday		Tuesday		Thursday		Friday		Saturday	
	Subject	Room	Subject	Room	Subject	Room	Subject	Room	Subject	Room
9:00	Practice	3	Practice	3	Practice	3	Practice	3	Greek	7
9:45	Study	72	Study	72	Study	72	Study	72	Study	72
10:30	"	"	"	"	"	"	"	"	Coll. Eng.	9
11:15	Latin III	8	Latin III	8	Latin III	8	Latin III	8	Study	72
12:45	Study	72	Study	72	Study	72	Study	72	Elocution	
1:15	"	"	"	"	"	"	"	"	Latin III	
2:00	Greek III	9	Greek III	9	Greek III	9	Greek III	9	Drawing studies	
2:45	Coll. Eng.	3	Study	72	Coll. Eng.	3	Study	72	Hall Exercises	

Much of her energy, however, went into extracurricular enthusiasms. She kept letters from her boy and men friends (her older brother Needham apparently introduced her to this one of many, a military academy student);

> I know how it is to feel like raising H——, for we feel that way often here. [5 October 1906]

> Darling, as I sat here all alone trying to study . . . [undated]

> I can even now see your hair glittering in the gas light . . . [21 January 1907]

From her girl friends:

> How I missed you tonight at dinner! . . . Would that you and I could always sit by each other. Yes dear I care a lot for you, tell me dear that you care just a little for me? Dearest my eyes were so blinded with tears [at dinner time] that I did not hear Miss Means speak to me, dearest I cannot stand many such things—she looked at me and in the coldest way asked if I would have more meat. . . .

(On the envelope M.B. has written "Put on your rubbers. You will need them to go through this slush.")[49]

Even from her kid brother (and the family dog). [15 January 1907]

> My Dear Sister How are you getting along up to school Have you good manners up to school . . . Do you know My Mother has bought an Automobile . . . Do the boys have Double Runners up to school? Good Bye Write
> > I send Buster's Dog Kisses X X X X
> > From your Dear Brother Joseph C. Brown

The daily goofiness of younger Abbot students produced a document we can only hope Miss Means never saw:

> We therefore agree to a bet that if Marion keeps on the underclothing she has on this day, November twelfth nineteen hundred and six until the first day of May nineteen hundred and seven, I will owe her a bag of Campions potato chips which will be bought at the price of ten cents.
> > > > Signed
> > > > Helen Chaffee
>
> I swear to keep this bet
> > > > Marion Brown

Marion yawned at some of the entertainment Abbot provided. About the Faculty Reception of 1906 for Andover townspeople, she wrote, "No one under forty invited. Nobody under sixty came." But Phillips events were next to vaudeville among her pleasures. She enjoyed P.A. intramural games, P.A.–Exeter games, P.A. football heroes— and simply P.A. Though a rendezvous took some forethought, Marion and one J. Wallace Scott arranged them with ease through the underground mail:[50]

> Miss Marion Brown [from J. Wallace Scott, 21 January 1907]
>   Kindness of Miss Cole
> My friend Mr. Tree would like to know if it will be convenient for you and your delightful friend to meet us on Wednesday afternoon say about 3:30. Will you kindly answer and state the place as I do not know where it would be safe.

> Miss Marion Brown [from JWS]
>   Kindness of Miss Lee
> My dear Marion.
> That letter of yours was pretty strong for the first one. I had to hold Tree in a chair . . . Do you really want to meet us? We do. We have been thinking it over and we think that down by the railroad bridge would be the safest. There is nothing like being too safe when Miss Means is in existence . . . Did you get Doc's note for Gladys that other crazy acting girl?
>   Yours forever lovingly, JWS

So did "Peaches and Pinkie," whoever they may have been:

> Come on down to the Grove.
> What do you care if EM is looking?

The task of bringing up such as Marion Brown to polite society and scholarly accomplishment seems almost beyond possibility, but this task Abbot struggled with anyway, year after year. And Marion herself went on to Wellesley, later earning her Master's degree at Boston University and studying at the University of Toulouse, Columbia, and Harvard. Despite her early loves, she never married. Instead she taught French and Latin nearly all her life in both college and secondary school, serving briefly as Preceptress of Montpelier Seminary in Vermont and for many years as Dean of Girls and head of the Language Department at Lawrence High School next door to Andover. Miss Means would have been happy to know that Dean Brown shared her talent for dealing with the mischevious and the difficult. One Lawrence graduate remembers her well: "Very nice she was—a stern hand with plenty of humor and kindness."[51]

By the spring of 1909, Emily Means felt she must have rest. The Trustees hoped a year away with half-salary would restore her. Leaving Abbot in Miss Kelsey's care, she went first to her Maine retreat, then to her old haunts in Europe. She did return to Abbot for the year 1910–11, but resigned permanently after that, saying that there were many activities of her own she wished to undertake. When she wrote back to her Abbot friends of the thrill of camping under the stars on the Libyan desert and told them her intricate plans for a new house on her island, they knew she had done the right thing.

Katherine Kelsey was a competent interim head. True, she so often met student initiatives with the calm rejoinder, "it never has been done" and their protests with "it always has been done" that girls found themselves nostalgic for Miss Means' brusk reasons. But Miss Kelsey eventually proved responsive. Rules had multiplied once again under Miss Means: Do not be seen buttoning your gloves while leaving your room; stay in your room after 8:00 whether studying or not; cover your elbows at dinner time. If you weren't wearing a long-sleeved dress, you were handed a pair of elbow cuffs to wear in the dining room. "We were treated like children, and we acted accordingly," writes Barbara Moore Pease, '11, recalling the guilty fun she and her roommate enjoyed filling their corridor teacher's water pitcher with June bugs or bullheads, depending on the season. With her teaching colleagues, Miss Kelsey instituted a Student Council of elected representatives, whose purpose, said the *Courant* editors, was "to prevent . . . any injury to the reputation of the school, and at the same time to make a closer sympathy and unity between the faculty and the girls."[52] An echo of the enthusiasm for student government in many women's colleges, this was nothing like the Bryn Mawr Executive Committee, which was directly responsible to the trustees for all student behavior and whose recommendations for dismissal were "equivalent to a sentence."[53] But it was a beginning.

The Trustees went about the search for a new principal with great deliberation. They were seeking a Lady, for Emily Means was a powerful after-image in their minds, but they also wanted a person of recognized academic experience who would strengthen the College Preparatory course, for it had not thrived under Miss Means's half-hearted guidance. Seemingly, the Lady came first. Miriam Titcomb, a highly gifted teacher and administrator who knew Abbot well (she taught mathematics there from 1906 to 1908) seems not to have measured up to the selection committee's standards for dress and bearing, yet went on to become principal of the prestigious Bancroft School in Worcester and to found the Hillsdale School in Cincinnati. The Trustees heard about a Bertha Bailey, B.S. Wellesley, who was coprincipal and co-owner of the new Taconic School in Connecticut. This position—not unlike Asa Farwell's at the early Abbot—demanded business sense as well as academic leadership, and Taconic was doing well. Here was a woman of "good inheritance and fine breeding"[54] who had— so it seemed—taught almost everything (science, mathematics, and history from the Greeks to the present) almost everywhere in the Northeast. She had done voluntary social work among Bohemian immigrants in Cleveland and the West Side poor in New York City. What was she like as a person? Trustee Markham Stackpole asked her present and former colleagues. "Daughter of a Presbyterian clergyman," "a lady of ideas and ideals," they answered.[55] "A woman of remarkable ability and of beautiful character," wrote the wife of her first employer.[56] "Vigorous," wrote Taconic again when questioned more closely (could Stackpole have been worried about the implications for Miss Bailey's health of her size and weight?), "exceedingly efficient" in administration and discipline, "something of a martinette . . . she is *very* firm." She was hired.

Miss Bailey visited Abbot and was pleased to find herself in agreement with the "progressive spirit" of the Trustees. She accepted the offered salary of $2000, "for the present. Should my value to the school increase, as I trust it may, I am sure the Trustees would recognize the fact."[57] A business sense indeed!

It was Bertha Bailey's suggestion that an inauguration be held. On 19 October 1912 the whole school gathered together with neighbors and faraway friends, former faculty and Trustees, and a procession of Old Scholars from 1845 on. A greeting was read from Miss Mary Cornelius, '36, who had entered Abbot on its opening day in 1829. Bands of yellow ribbon distinguished the present students whose mothers, aunts, grandmothers, great-aunts or great-grandmothers had been Abbot girls before them. It was a grand occasion. It was, in fact, the first grand Abbot occasion on which women made major speeches: Wellesley's President Pendleton and Bradford's Principal Knott eloquently greeted their new colleague. The tone of Miss Bailey's own speech made clear to the skeptics that the gathering was a celebration of Abbot Academy far more than of Bertha Bailey. Again, the leader of a new era set herself firmly and deliberately upon an old foundation.

Against the Tide, 1912-1954

During the Means years, Abbot had walked backward into the future. With the change in administration, it was time to take stock, a task for which Bertha Bailey, outsider, was well qualified.

Times had changed; they kept on changing. High school enrollment throughout the country had multiplied: nearly 60 percent of all young people 14 to 17 years of age were in school by 1912, compared with 8 percent in 1890. Increasingly a high school diploma or bachelor's degree was the prerequisite for skilled or professional occupations. The new Progressive educators were making powerful efforts to expand the schools beyond "mental discipline" in ways that truly met the vocational and personal needs of youth in an industrializing society, now that the educative influences of the old agrarian community had been so much weakened. As a contemporary social theorist put it, "The modern community is not real enough, not sufficiently organized to provide the old time social integrations as a matter of course."[1] The Church, the Grange, the informal apprenticeships under one's farmer or farm-wife mother or under a local master craftsman—these were either unavailable or unappealing. John Dewey proposed that educators reject the "blatantly aristocratic" view of culture too common in college preparatory high schools, and instead create "embryonic communities" which would foster social responsibility and experienced personal competence within a protective, democratic setting.[2] The junior college movement was raising an infant cry for attention, its proponents hoping to persuade a larger proportion of eighteen-year-olds to stay in secondary school or come to college for two years of advanced or vocational training.

Abbot Academy had to ask again the question often before asked and answered: what special benefits could Abbot offer to young women in this changing educational world? The Academy was now competing against the public high schools of the whole country instead of little Punchard High of Andover, to say nothing of the women's colleges, which were still the measure of the older students' Academic Course. Board and tuition together were $600; they would gradually rise to $1400 by 1926, an escalation that would outpace the cost of living by 33 percent.[3]

On the other hand, Abbot had its advantages. The school had nearly a century of experience in an academic program similar to that which President Eliot still advocated for all high schools, though with ever less success. College entrants found that their English, history, and language work at Abbot had given them superior training for college, even though the same could not be said for mathematics or science. A few Academic Course graduates who changed their minds about college gained admission to the second or third year in reputable universities. More important, the whole nation was now experiencing the "unrest of women," those social growing pains that had so perturbed Miss Means. Public high school teachers "complain[ed] of the distractions of parties, theatres, bazaars, and amusements generally, which exhaust the strength of the girls in particular," a visiting British schoolmistress observed.[4] Especially after the War, worried adults thought they saw the automobile, the radio, and the moving pictures destroying traditional definitions and limitations in favor of a plastic world within which youth wandered, posing and strutting to hide its confusion.[5] An orderly, close-knit boarding school was one solution.

Finally, with rapid growth, a public secondary school bureaucracy (largely male) was enforcing arbitrary departmental divisions, and weakening what authority teachers had had over their large classes by demanding entire submissiveness to system-wide curricula. What influence teachers had left was often exercised in desperate attempts to maintain appearances ("How can you learn anything with your knees and toes out of order?!" barked one teacher to a cowed pupil),[6] while Abbot teachers specialized in authority as of old, yet continued to offer electives to almost any group larger than two which asked for them. Faced with an eager clutch of advanced French students, for example, two teachers might assign Le Chanson de Roland to coincide with a study of fourteenth-century art through museum trips and studio work.[7] The student-teacher ratio was about 10:1 when Bertha Bailey arrived, better even than Phillips Academy's at 17 to 1.

Abbot also had snob appeal. To be sure the Academy was more likely to interest the intellectual elite than the purely "social" families, but day scholar alumna Eleanor Thomson Castle, '98, remembers how much more "classy" Abbot seemed to her "set" than the perfectly good Andover public high school. The Hill intellectuals and all who admired them "were entirely separate from the man who owned the grocery store."[8] Along with the still-dignified town of Andover, Abbot offered an escape from "the great mass of people," rich and poor, with their "identical mental life," and from the typical American's "disdain of delicacy," his love of "enormities, giganticism, excess."[9] The more young Americans attended public high school, the more distinctive an Abbot education became.

Abbot was resolved upon distinction, then. There would be no compromises with a society that seemed increasingly bent on self-indulgence, increasingly obsessed with a mass youth "culture" born in the colleges and popularized by the advertisers of all material goods designed to sustain it. Though students might chafe at Victorian restrictions, enough parents applauded Abbot's stance to keep the school filled throughout the decade of the twenties. The early thirties were another matter. The tide that then threatened to engulf Abbot Academy brought wave after wave of financial disaster. It would take more than moral certainty to keep from going under.

The Ladies Stand Fast

You are Abbot ...
letter from a parent to Bertha Bailey, 1914

Everything about the young ... threatened the traditionalist
Paula S. Fass, 1977

The Trustees hoped Bertha Bailey would carry forward the best of
Abbot's traditions, adding her own strengths to those of the school. As
if to underline the Board's commitment, the school's loving neighbor
Irene Rowley Draper, now in her eighties, welcomed Miss Bailey as
warmly as she had Miss Watson and Miss Means, with a present for
the McKeen Rooms of a grandfather clock and a promise of close
friendship.[1] This promise was soon fulfilled, as were many others in
the Bailey era. Indeed, Miss Bailey during her 23 years at Abbot combined in her own way the high social standards of Emily Means, the
devotion to college preparation of Laura Watson and the missionary
zeal of Philena McKeen. Her Abbot was in many respects the old
Abbot, only more so.

Bertha Bailey herself was more so in several ways. Her ample figure
soon made her Big Bertha to almost everyone out of earshot. It was a
nickname used as much in affection as in fun: no alumna whom she
ever either disciplined or embraced forgot her bosom, which shook
with anger at blatant offenders as impressively as it offered comfort to
the distressed or welcome to returning alumnae. She had left her co-
principalship at Taconic School partly because Taconic was, as she put
it, "not big enough for two."[2] She wanted, needed, a larger stage on
which to exercise her capacity for usefulness. Schooled by her father's
example, she was a "splendid speaker,"[3] but she spoke and preached as
a true missionary: to uplift her audience, not herself. Far from being
self-aggrandizing,[4] she was rather shy, especially with men, who often
took her grim formality for disdain. Her warmth and generosity only
emerged with friends she knew well, or with students she could trust.

It was not easy for the students who most admired Miss Means to
accept her successor. Mary Byers Smith remembers that Miss Bailey

seemed "pillowy, soft" by comparison when she first met her, and thought it "quite a comedown" that her books (all in English, some unread) filled only a third of the shelves Miss Means had required. Though Miss Bailey later extended the school's hospitality whenever Miss Smith returned to visit or help, the distance remained. One correspondent wrote Trustee Stackpole that Bertha Bailey stood "for high and noble things," but, in fairness, added a short list of her "failings": "she is apt to be better in handling a group of girls than in dealing with one alone."[5] She could hardly have been called "soft" with individual students who had transgressed. Mildred Bryant Kussmaul, '13, remembers—and still resents—being summoned to her office, set down under a strong light, and interrogated. "Bertha B., she shined that light on me. She was watching my face all the time, trying to look inside my conscience." Early students thought she had an "all-seeing eye,"[6] which was good or distressing, depending on how you were behaving. Indeed, Miss Bailey herself underlined this impression with a well-remembered Chapel talk on the text "As he thinketh in his heart, so is he" (Proverbs 23:7).

> The most secret and private thoughts of each one of us work
> out day by day to the light. They show in our faces, they speak
> in our words . . . we *are* what they have made us. . . . What is
> in your mind when you are alone? Do you think it does not
> matter?[7]

Though she relaxed a bit with time, "growing in her job," as Mabel Bacon Ripley put it, Abbot never knew a more thorough enforcer of its many rules than Bertha Bailey.[8]

Miss Bailey had attended Wellesley in its first decade, when college students were pioneers and Wellesley in particular impressed such searching critics as M. Carey Thomas with its all-female faculty and its efficient use of small means.[9] Thoroughly committed to college education for women, Bertha Bailey nevertheless respected Trustee and alumna support of the Academic Course. Her first catalogue (1913) described it with pardonable pride (and perhaps some exaggeration) as the equivalent of the first two years of college.

In 1921, the Trustees charged a faculty committee to study the desirability of Abbot's concentrating its resources on one course of study instead of two. The group decided "after considerable discussion" that it was "distinctly advantageous" to keep both the Academic and the College Preparatory departments. "Each contributes directly to the success of the other," they concluded, the Academic Course offering a greater variety of subjects and the C.P. course keeping

30. Bertha Bailey, photograph from 1913 Class Book.

scholastic standards high.[10] There was no danger of teachers' energies being spread too thin; students shared most classes anyway in the first three years, and there were so many candidates for the final two years' classes that the sections would never be too small for efficient teaching. Until the early thirties, the C.P. and Academic group were quite evenly balanced in numbers if not in academic ability. (Although there were a few very able Academic students, nearly all of the 50 highest scorers on the 1921 IQ tests were C.P. students.)[11] Alumnae from each still insist that theirs was the superior course of study. There is no doubt that Academic students immeasurably enriched the culture of the school with their varied interests and talents. And just as Miss Watson had predicted, the College course attracted new families to Abbot, once Abbot's principal was championing it again. Enrollment climbed steadily from the 95 a year average of the Means era; once the postwar depression had passed, it reached and exceeded the level of the Watson years, peaking at 189 in 1927. Money-conscious Trustees might have shared a bit of Bertha Bailey's gratitude to her minister father, who taught her, she said, "to see, to think, to help myself, and never to say 'I can't.' "[12]

War Time

Not two years after Miss Bailey's arrival, war broke out in Europe. Her leadership during the next five years set the tone for her whole administration. In a sense, the western world's tragedy was Andover Hill's tonic: the missionary spirit that had sustained all three Hill institutions during the nineteenth century was reborn as Christian patriotism at both Abbot and Phillips academies.

To Bertha Bailey teaching at any time was "an expression of love of country, of desire to serve humanity."[13] From the Davis Hall pulpit at Christmas Vespers, 1914, she saw in this "colossal struggle . . . this agony and suffering and woe" the failure of Christians everywhere to live the teachings of Christ. Americans were not exempt from the "disintegrating forces."

> We have shut Him out of our politics . . . our society . . . Even *we women who should have kept our vision clear* and our hearts true, have been caught in a whirl of fashion and luxury, of extravagance and social competition . . . Against the background of a Cross of light . . . is thrown up a black iron cross, dripping with blood . . . It is hate thrown up against Love; greed against self-sacrifice; destruction against redemption. Which cross is yours?

"The war is tearing the scales from our eyes," she went on; now we can see that "the world is one. The roar of artillery in Belgium means suffering women and children in Lawrence [and] persecutions in Turkey." All Americans, all Abbot girls must "take up our cross," and "share to the point of suffering" to recreate "the brotherhood of man."[14]

Many a school and youth organization resounded with a similar "drum-and-trumpet Christianity,"[15] but the Abbot version did beat all for earnestness. Miss Bailey gave her Christmas sermon two and a half years before the United States' entry into the War, years during which Abbot prepared for the Lord's "great work waiting to be done."[16] Rebekah Chickering had a Saturday afternoon lecture on Balkan problems ready when war first broke out; she followed it up with a map talk the next fall on "Fundamental Causes of the European War." She and other teachers offered a new Current Events elective and voluntary out-of-hours classes in Principles of Democracy and Civic Problems. In the Fall of 1917 students of French staged a "Thé Chantant" complete with cafe tables and singing "peasant" waitresses, for the benefit of the wounded French soldiers; soon 40 French orphans were "adopted" by students and faculty together. That same term the Student Government Association held an all-school meeting to found the Patriotic League. Nearly all students and faculty signed its Constitution, pledging themselves to

(1) personal efficiency, including attention to hygiene, posture thrift, alertness; and

(2) service, including, in addition to excellence in studies, sports, voluntary training classes, and military drill, self-denying contributions of time, work, and money for extra needs caused by the war.[17]

They promised further "to stand for the sincerity, honor and purity of American girlhood, and in our friendship with boys to uplift and not lower their ideals of womanhood."[18] Looking back on her wartime Abbot days, one student expressed the students' sense of these two fervent years as a "glorious height, where stood the hope of a world ruled by practical Christianity." "Our lives would be productive, efficient for the good of others," said another. "We were the hope of the world."[19] Working with the Student Council, Miss Bailey divided the school into groups of ten, both students and faculty; they made 4,500 surgical dressings, knit soldiers' socks, and worked in the war vegetable garden or on the grounds. Two rival companies of the "Abbot Battalion" (150 students and faculty in all) carried on military drill for two years under the Phillips military instructor. Even the slackers must go without butter and sugar when the majority did the same. American students are "*begging* for training," Miss Bailey exulted in a 1918 speech to the New England Association of Colleges and Secondary Schools. "They recognize that they are destined to take a hand in framing a new world."

Meanwhile, the larger Abbot family was hard at work, one alumna directing thirty regional Red Cross Workshops in the Middle West, another nursing tubercular patients and organizing ambulance service during the Paris bombardment, a third taking over medical work for physicians called abroad, thousands of others doing their part. As

many as 2,500 alumnae later reported war-time service of one kind or
another. Some were promoted to the jobs men left behind. Sara Patrick, '98, after the War an instructor in Industrial Arts at Teachers
College, Columbia, would write that the First World War challenged
her "to reconstruct my experience, to recognize my colossal ignorance
on many important questions and . . . to think for myself regardless of
what my group believed. Out of that ordeal, I came . . . to a sense of
belonging to a world society with responsibility for its welfare."[20]
Countless American women had similar experiences. Bertha Bailey expressed their new seriousness in her speech "War and the Schools,"
saying that "the biggest job on earth at this moment is not fighting
Germany, but making the women of the world equal to the task of
saving humanity."[21] Make girls "good mothers," she implored fellow
educators, "and they will be good workers and good citizens." "Apply
motherhood to civic problems . . . to regulation of child labor and
other conditions of industrial activity . . . now soon perhaps to state-
craft . . . that human values in every problem [may] be considered."[22]
Back in Davis Hall, she urged all Abbot girls to prove themselves "as
truly women" as their "boy friends" are "proving themselves men."

> If you do not draw the line where you should, in speech, in
> laughter, in easy intimacy, they know, and in their hearts con-
> demn you. You have lowered an ideal . . . Strengthen their ideals
> . . . hold up to them something worth suffering and dying for . . .
> That is your part of service now and always."[23]

Abbot Academy did not intend to share in the "collapse of noble
womanhood" which vitiated a society retreating step by step from
Victorian norms.[24]

For a while after the War's end, the task of "framing a new world"
according to a "new vision of God"[25] absorbed Abbot. Students had
already earned thousands of dollars for Y.M.C.A. and Red Cross work
at the Front: now students and faculty raised $3,000 more for refugee
relief, bringing the total of war-related contributions to about $10,000.
For several more years, the Principal proposed, and students voted to
hold, "Hoover Dinners" or "Golden Rule Dinners"—simple food by
the light of a single candle which saved $60.00 on each occasion, to be
spent for some worthy cause.[26] *Odeon* short stories continued to de-
pict the heroics of soldiers and the heart-rendings of their women left
at home. Miss Bailey's sermons described how the ideal young woman
must build on her traditional role to create a new society on the Progressive model. "She looketh well to the ways of her household," said
Miss Bailey, quoting her biblical text as always. "But how can she look

well to the ways of her household unless she inspects the bakeries, and cleans the canneries, and watches the stockyards, and guards the factories, and sweeps the streets . . . and elects the President?"[27]

Yet the wartime pace could not be sustained forever, and the missionary fervor gradually died. The Patriotic League was disbanded. A crisis that would once have been close to Abbot's heart—the Turkish slaughter of the Armenian Christians while U.S. officials and even some missionaries merely looked on, hoping not to offend a new ally—passed unnoticed in *Courant* and in school lecture programs, with only individuals like Alice Hamlin Hinman, '87, working sadly for survivor relief.

Abbot's relaxation was minimal, however, compared with America's general exhaustion. Women war workers were disillusioned to find that their proven competence went unrecognized by the returning men, who took to the streets if necessary to win back their jobs. With the national surge back to normalcy, pay scales returned to their discriminatory prewar levels; even in federal government work, women were either paid less for doing the same jobs as men or, in some departments, were not hired at all. Two thirds of the civil service examinations for professional posts were closed to women. Woman suffrage, so long fought for and finally achieved in 1920, proved not to be "a biscuit thrown to a whale,"[28] as male detractors had feared: most women demanded no further rights, being perfectly content to vote as their husbands voted (or not to vote at all) and to watch the broad women's rights coalition—two million strong in 1919—disintegrate into small, often futile successor organizations. Prohibition, pride of the "conservative Progressives" and considered by many to be women's supreme political accomplishment, was no panacea after all, only a messy failure. It was a time of "surging . . . disillusion," more discouraging to such as Vida Scudder, reformer and Wellesley professor, than any other time of her life. Another observer wrote, "Feminism has become a term of opprobrium."[29] Back in Andover, an era seemed to have ended when Agnes Park died in 1922; a special brand of toughness, generosity, and humor had gone out of the world. "She was unique in her generation," wrote the Abbot Trustees. "How much more did she stand out against the stereotyped society of the present day."[30]

Ironically, many of the "new" women convinced themselves that their liberation was complete. They smoked and drank at "petting" parties, they danced cheek to cheek with men, they reveled in the freedom to enjoy the "vamp" movies and the novels of James Joyce (censored, but widely available). The divorce rate soared.[31] Illegal birth control devices could be found, given money enough. Psycho-analysts had put their blessing on women's sexual pleasure. A careful study conducted after the twenties had run their course revealed that while 74 percent of middle-income women born between 1890 and 1900 had remained virgins before marriage, only 32 percent born after 1910 made the same claim.[32] As early as 1915, socialite-intellectual Mabel Dodge Luhan had emerged from her own psychoanalysis to intone: "The sex act is the cornerstone of any life, and its chief reality." What more could an independent woman want?[33] Though this rebellious pleasure-seeking was not nearly so widespread as the conventional picture of the twenties suggests, it permeated the college student culture that beckoned to young people nearing graduation from secondary school and thus presented a palpable threat to Miss Bailey's Abbot Academy.[34] With the vocal support of older faculty like Miss Kelsey and Miss Mason and the passive assent of the rest, the Principal set out to provide against the assault on Abbot ways.

Building the Walls

Walls of various kinds had protected Abbot from its earliest years, but Bertha Bailey was one of the school's more resourceful engineers. As soon as she arrived, she made clear how high and how detailed were her expectations. She intercepted all food packages at the mailroom, then either confiscated them or commanded each recipient to share the entire contents with corridor or tablemates.[35] To warn girls to "dress simply" allowed of too many interpretations. Miss Bailey made clear in the 1913 catalogue that "elaborate lingerie waists, decolleté gowns, trains and expensive jewelry" would not be tolerated. Then as later, the Principal proved to her school that her warnings were no mere empty words. In order to make certain that the older students would heed them at prom time, Miss Bailey deputized Katherine Kelsey to stand on a chair (boy-height) while the girls paraded by, offering their necklines for inspection and their bosoms—if too evident—for censure.[36] Walking shoes were the daily wear, and high button shoes were required after November 1st, "one of the theories being that if we did not wear them our ankles would become large and our hus-bands would not love us" as a *Courant* cynic of after years quipped.[37] Time passed, and injunctions against sleeveless dresses, flapper skirts, and three kinds of heels had to be added. After 1917 only Stearns of Boston carried the black lisle stockings Abbot required. In 1918 silk ones were finally allowed for ordinary wear, but black or blue cotton remained the rule with gym bloomers. Alumnae parents asked Constance Chipman, '06, Trustee and Alumnae Field Secretary in the early thirties, to persuade Miss Bailey to abandon black cotton, but in vain. "Constance," the Principal replied, "I don't like legs."[38]

Even the Abbot Seal embarrassed Miss Bailey. "Truth" with her burning torch had been designed by Emily Means in the 1880's for a school taught to reverence classical sculpture. Miss Watson had had her drapery expanded to cover the bared breast. Miss Bailey put up with Truth's shoulder and elbows until 1929, when she finally asked the Trustees to find another design. Just in time for the Centennial Issue of *Courant*, the Abbot family coat of arms was adopted, and "Truth" became history.

Miss Bailey moved fast to block the routes out into the countryside or down the road to the Orchard Street ice cream parlor (where one could always find Phillips boys in Miss Means' day) by mapping first fifteen, then twenty-three "approved walks," the shorter ones to be taken with a companion dictated by the master schedule, those longer than four or five miles to be chaperoned. Mr. Stackpole, who loved solitary hiking and had understood when he and his fellow Trustees hired her that Miss Bailey also enjoyed it, was horrified by the "walking squads," but kept his counsel.[39] Andover tea rooms were off bounds each year as soon as townsfolk reported unladylike deportment, once after girls piled all their dishes in a pyramid before leaving. "Not easy," an alumna of 1916 remembers, "and far too hilarious."[40] The two Boston Symphony tickets became three, one for a chaperone paid by the two student ticket holders, when an alert Andover neighbor reported the two Abbot seats empty one afternoon. Questioning back in the Principal's office revealed that once in Boston, the two miscreants had decided a vaudeville show would be more fun.[41] Seldom after this were girls allowed to go unchaperoned on shopping or concert expeditions to Boston.

These restrictions were not the Principal's whims. Miss Bailey had read her William James *Psychology*; she truly believed that right action becomes habitual, and that useful habits free the individual to use her "consciousness," her "higher" mental powers. "Truth" said James in *Pragmatism*, "is *made* true by events."[42] Increasingly, Bertha Bailey preached "habit" and "manners" from the chapel pulpit. Each September she took three or four Saturday afternoon and Sunday evening hours to speak on Rules, on "The forming of a Christ-like life," on Personality, before letting other speakers have their say. As the twenties progressed and she watched the "exceptional fathers and mothers and teachers . . . struggle against the rising tide," she invoked all her gods

31. (a) from Courant, *1886   (b) From* Courant, *1896   (c) From* Courant, *Centennial Number 1929.*

against young people's tendency to "go the limit." Good manners both create and express "fineness of spirit, beauty of soul," and, most important, "social power," that combination of self-restraint and generosity that is essential to "good breeding."[43]

Aware of James or not, students seemed not to mind too much. Says Frances Flagg Sanborn, "We never thought of rebelling." Jane Baldwin, '22, remembers that she "had received much discipline at home, and expected the same at school." Most girls' schools were nearly as strict as Abbot, and, indeed, Abbot's rules coincided with the standards enforced by many parents at this time. Mildred Bryant Kussmaul's father told his daughter exactly where he stood in a letter of 1913:

> Your letter received, and now *forget it* as concerns the theatre. When boys ask your mother for permission to take you to the theatre with a chaperone it is time enough to talk it over.
>
> Girls who are not "chumps" don't buy tickets to take boys to the theatre.
>
> No! is the answer . . . It's a cheap crowd at night and not suitable for you or your young ladies.
>
> Love from Pa

"We never minded the lisle stockings," says another alumna. Or (writes a fourth), "we moaned and complained, thinking it was utter nonsense to ban silk stockings . . . but if it hadn't been about silk stockings it might well have been about something more fundamental."[44] What caprice could not be expressed in fashionable clothes was lavishly expended in hair styles: a "hair bobbing epidemic" in April 1920, a hair-growing one at the end of the decade, with every imaginable hot-wave and curlicue in between. Not even Miss Bailey could detect every midnight "spread," with "all the gooey things that could be assembled."[45] Saturday lectures by such moralizers as Mrs. Augustus Trowbridge on "evils of modern dancing," "the reasons for chaperoning," and so forth[46] were just talk to the older or more self-sufficient students; they did no harm, they made the teachers feel better, and they probably protected a few of the weaker girls.

The Hilltop presented special problems, for Bertha Bailey appears to have shared with many of her contemporaries a "frantic fear of sexual promiscuity" which colored her every action.[47] Before she made up her mind to come to Abbot, Miss Bailey had asked the Trustees, "to what extent would the life of the household be complicated by the proximity of Phillips Academy?"[48] Her answer after her arrival seemed to be a hopeful "not a bit, provided all Abbot ignores all Phillips except on rare special occasions and heavily chaperoned Friday calling hours." Alumnae remember almost no other legal communication with Phillips Academy. Even telephone calls were chaperoned. Miss Bailey made sure that Stearns' joint Vesper services were never resumed after he returned from Sabbatical leave in 1913. Faculty receptions ended on both sides; so did the lightly chaperoned sleighrides and picnics that Helen Abbott Allen remembered from earlier days.

Was Miss Bailey responsible for the change? "Yes, indeed, that was Big Bertha, whom I adored," says Helen Abbott's daughter, Helen Allen Henry, '32. As a day scholar, she could not speak with her own brothers because they were Phillips boarding students.[49] If a young Phillips teacher wished to visit a sister or sister-in-law at Abbot, Big Bertha provided a chaperone to supervise.[50] To sit with your sister or your girl at a football game was out of the question. Two girls came home from a midnight walk with their Phillips' beaux to find Miss Bailey waiting for them in their suite. They were dismissed the following morning. "There is ordinarily no communication between the students of the two schools," wrote Bertha Bailey with conviction.[51]

All this might have been understandable to students in the mid-nineteenth century or even to the younger bodies in the early Bailey era, when the average age of menarche was 14 years;[52] it became less so to Abbot's older students during the 1920's when college women of the same age (with the conspicuous exception of Wellesley, Miss Bailey's alma mater) often had no restrictions beyond a 10:00 P.M. sign-in. Rather suddenly, Abbot's social rules assumed an antediluvian cast.

Yet there was more to Abbot's defensiveness than Abbot: Phillips Academy was in its own way widening the chasm between the two schools. As Phillips prospered under Alfred E. Stearns, as it gave heroes and martyrs to the War for Democracy, it became ever more self-consciously masculine. Athletic contests now replicated those battles only a few Phillips students had actually had a chance to fight. Girls could never experience "the hour of glorious conflict, when the blood leaps, and the muscles rally for mastery, the decent manly pride in taking one's punishment . . . as long as one can stand and see," as J. Adams Puffer put it in *The Boy and His Gang*,[53] but the Hilltop boys could do just this on Brothers football field. Teacher-housemasters actually enforced dormitory rules. They backed Stearns in his decision to suspend the winter prom for two successive years when "the extravagances" and "dangers involved" in modern dancing appeared unmanageable.[54] It took an aggressive faculty to dispel the image of teaching as a "feminized" profession; many of them doubtless agreed with F. E. Chadwick, who told the world in 1914 that the "woman peril" in the public schools was producing "a feminized manhood, emotional, illogical, non-combative against public evils."[55] On the playing fields, in the rough-and-tumble dormitory life, the masters did all they could to wean boys away from their overprotective mothers.[56] In the meantime, a Hilltop building boom underlined the material power behind male aspirations, most dramatically in the construction of the War Memorial bell tower and the Cochran Chapel with its soaring steeple. If Freud had known, he would have smiled.

Alfred Stearns grew to be as wary as Miss Bailey of "the softening influences of modern social life," of unrestrained auto rides and unchaperoned dances, and called in his *Challenge of Youth* for family, church, and school to renew the "eternal fight for virile and self-controlled manhood and womanhood" (sic), that Christian civilization might be saved.[57] In Stearns's view as in Miss Bailey's, this was best accomplished in single sex schools. Although Stearns had nothing but scorn for the "self expression and self realization" advocated by modern psychology ("they all spell *self*ishness" he wrote),[58] he agreed with G. Stanley Hall, the child-study guru, that coeducation could be disastrous for adolescent boys. Convinced that females were made for mature men to cherish, not for boys to play with, impatient with "woman" and her "shouts for 'rights,' " Stearns thought it best to keep Abbot at a distance.[59]

Besides, he did not care for Bertha Bailey. He advised an inquiring friend, President Ernest Hopkins of Dartmouth, to send his daughter elsewhere. "When it comes to scholarship, etc., I feel pretty safe in saying that the school ranks very high," but Miss Bailey is "terribly austere and reserved," her regime "overstrict" and "a bit old fashioned."[60] Even the more open-minded of Phillips instructors "thought the Abbot rules were so absurd that nothing else about Abbot could be any good at all," Alan Blackmer remembered in 1975. Blackmer and his friends, most of them graduates of boys' schools and men's colleges, found girls' schools in general "simply irrelevant," and felt "only condescension" toward Abbot in particular. As Blackmer was glad to admit 45 years later, "This was male chauvinism in its purest form."

In spite of everything, Phillips-Abbot connections could not be wholly severed. Friday night meant "fish, ice cream and callers" at Abbot; dedicated couples made the best of calling hours, the boys lining up sometimes for an hour ahead of time to secure seats as far from the chaperone-on-duty as possible.[61] Two "married couples" once linked arms on a bet and skipped around the Circle, running smack into Miss Bailey next to Draper Hall. (In her surprise, she laughed!)[62] Numbers of Abbot alumnae had married Phillips teachers, including

Bessie Goodhue, wife of Claude Fuess, who would soon be Phillips' Headmaster. Abbot's Fidelio Society occasionally sang with the Phillips Glee Club; a Phillips band played music for the Maypole dance one bright spring; Abbot girls and their chaperones attended many a football game; and, best of all, a victory over Exeter brought swarms of cheering Phillips students to the Circle, waving their torches and shouting "Bertha! Bertha! Bertha!" until Miss Bailey appeared to wave at them.

Still the walls remained. In the Principal's anxious mind, those 500 males on the Hill threatened chaos at the least, if not rapine, and the near-nightmare came true just often enough to perpetuate her fearful images. One May morning long after Miss Bailey had forbidden all Abbot to go near the town's annual May Breakfast, a gang of rowdy Cads celebrated that festive occasion by hurling buns at each other and being bounced out of the Town Hall. They jumped on the traffic light triggers till they broke, streamed into the snarled streets gathering reinforcements as they ran, and headed for the Abbot gates, hundreds strong and roaring. Miss Bailey's indignant scoldings from her apartment window accomplished absolutely nothing. The girls were thrilled. Al Stearns chugged through the gate in his coupé just in time to save Abbot from who knows what fate—but by the time he and Bertha Bailey met at the Draper Doors, there was not a boy to be seen, and every bush and hedge was quivering, every tree trunk alive with suppressed laughter.[63]

It is interesting that the only structures other than the Taylor infirmary that were built under Miss Bailey were gates that could be closed at sundown and all day Sunday: the Merrill Gate in honor of Maria Stockbridge Merrill and the George G. Davis entranceway. The gates completed the privet hedge wall that soon concealed much of Abbot from the view of passersby.

Behind the Walls

It was not a nunnery. It was just that the world outside had to be held off, its stimulations and confusions filtered through the privet hedge. Even the ancient town held who knows what dangers, now that Lawrence pulsed and smoked to the north, now that automobiles could go anywhere. True to Elizabeth Stuart Phelps's prediction, "the Andover of New England theology—the Andover of a peculiar people, the Andover that held herself apart from the world and all that was therein—" had become "an interesting wraith."[64] The town still had its special beauties, but Abbot could no longer count on its perfect discretion.

Abbot's student body was, if anything, more homogenous now than in Miss Means's day, even though the geographical spread was greater than ever before.[65] "We were more or less all alike, I think," says an alumna of the mid-1920's. "The girls from Duluth hadn't had our advantages, we knew, but we didn't look down on them. They were darlings." Abby Castle Kemper, '31, on the other hand, feels that she and the other Midwesterners had had as many advantages as the others. Mrs. Kemper does remember the practical problems that the twelve to fifteen scholarship girls and missionary daughters confronted—finding time to do one's own laundry, for example, or amassing money enough to join the expeditions down town—but "Abbot was far from fashionable, far from wealthy." There was none of the social exclusion so often found in girls' boarding schools.[66]

Miss Bailey did not take chances on "aborigines" from Maine, and new entrance requirements kept out the interesting academic cripples. To be sure, Abbot still felt responsible to the constituency it regularly attracted in simpler days, and the Principal pitched her scholarship appeals accordingly:

> How many ministers and missionaries and farmers and professors can afford to pay a thousand dollars a year to educate their daughters at Abbot Academy? Yet these are the girls who most value the opportunity here, and who work hardest to use it to advantage . . . the girls we particularly desire. [1919]

Bertha Bailey brought in a handful of Chinese and Japanese girls. One of them, Tsing Lien Li, '16, a brilliant scholar, paid her tuition from the U.S. indemnity funds negotiated at the time of the Boxer Rebellion—and returned to Abbot as a young physician to be married in the Chapel. Miss Bailey constructed the traditional bridal arch herself, and gave the bride away. A Greek student and a Serbian refugee were also exotic companions; a few more day scholars of Irish descent followed the four Sweeney sisters, and the Trustees added ten small competitive scholarships to the twenty-three existing in 1927. But Abbot was a bit bland considering that New York City's population in the early 1920's was about equally divided between Catholics, Jews, and Protestants, and in nearby Lawrence, 80 percent of the population were either immigrants or the children of immigrants.[67] A Southern student, Class of 1922, found that she and another deep South girl were the only two Democrats in the school. There was not a single Jew at Abbot until 1930, though stereotypes abounded.[68] One alumna social worker wrote of her astonished delight at finding bearded Jews reading Tolstoi in their tenements, as though she had assumed that this strange race could not possibly be literate. "You learn," she said, "that the chief interest of the Jewish father is not money, but his family."[69] Did she not learn such things at Abbot?

Still, the school's talent for fostering the various in its chosen students remained undiminished. By encouraging Academic and C.P. students to combine in most out-of-class activities, Miss Bailey contributed much to each group's social experience; the faculty also welcomed an ever-increasing group of one-year special C.P. students, who brought a piece of the world in with them.[70] In her first winter at Abbot, Miss Bailey invited all the Seniors on an after-exams winter sports expedition to Intervale, New Hampshire. By the time she and the students had snowshoed, coasted, and cooked hot dogs together for three days, the girls felt more like Seniors than C.P.'s or A.C.'s, and all felt a new warmth for their awesome Principal, whose keen sense of humor and love of nature blossomed in that relaxed setting. The trip was so much fun that Miss Bailey repeated it every year. In 1914 the Seniors voted to have one set of class officers; all other classes followed their example. Most class plays were still dominated by Academic students, but then, C.P.'s held as many offices as Academic students; alumnae remember many close friendships that crossed the C.P.-Academic line.[71] Day scholars too were well represented. Field Day events were open to all. It helped that a few Academic students proved to be top scholars: Louise M. Greenough and Constance Ling won third-year status at the University of Michigan following their graduation in 1920. It is interesting to contrast Abbot's way of responding to differences in student interest and abilities with Bradford's design. Bradford Academy tried to add junior college work to a secondary-level preparatory department, but the older students tipped the balance: tension over differences in rules along with other problems upset the combination. Bradford finally was rechartered as a junior college in 1932. Abbot was, as always, more pragmatic, even if no more successful, than its sister school, and most everyone seems to have benefited.

The faculty helped immeasurably to sustain both variety and community. The old hands had their niches; Miss Chickering—or "Mother Chick," since she gave students so much extra help—remained for many "the best teacher I ever had";[72] but young Ruth Baker with her passion for German was also "best" for some, and the fortunate few who took English with Alice Sweeney, '14, shortly after she graduated from Vassar found her classes unforgettable. Miss Sweeney would return near the close of the Bailey years and become a key figure in Abbot's future. The Academy created both refuge and opportunity for women who had won their independence through scholarly success, but who scorned, feared—or simply had no interest in—the uses many college women made of their freedom. For much of what passed for opportunity in the twenties actually channeled young women into constricted roles. The new emphasis on women's sexual enjoyment might liberate and deepen one's emotions, but ordinarily one had to depend on a man to express them. It was exciting to read Proust and Stein, but as the cry for self-fulfillment drowned out the voices of those still passionately committed to social reform, women were ever less likely to consider political or social service their special mission. Few men were willing to have their wives continue careers: only 12 percent of professional women were married in 1920. Thus society's expectations of women stagnated even though legal barriers to their progress had diminished. Graduate school attendance leveled off. Except in clerical work, occupational opportunities ceased to expand.

Women teaching in public high schools found that men were awarded nearly all the department chairmanships and administrative posts. At least Abbot faculty members could run their own show. This took both resourcefulness and the courage to defy still-dominant concepts of woman's place, now enshrined in scientific terms by such as G. Stanley Hall in his influential *Adolescence*. Woman "works by intuition and feeling," Hall told his large and eager audience. "Her sympathetic and ganglionic system is relatively to the cerebro-spinal more dominant." "If she abandons her natural naiveté and takes up the burden of guiding and accounting for her life by consciousness, she is likely to lose more than she gains." "Woman's body and soul are made for maternity, and she can never find repose for either without it." A "bachelor woman," especially one given to intensive intellectual pursuits, first loses mammary function, then becomes sterile. "The apotheothis of selfishness," she "has overdrawn her account with heredity." So much for the single teacher.[73]

Abbot's long if muted tradition of respect for women's competence armored its faculty against such nonsensical expressions of old prejudices, while the closed community created a sphere within which unmarried women could do self-respecting, useful work. If "Abbot was Victorian in those days,"[74] so be it. The righteous work for worthy causes in which the Victorians specialized was as much needed as ever, and the Victorian spirit continued to energize the Abbot faculty, many of whom felt with Miss Bailey that they were teaching "to serve humanity."[75] Safe behind the walls, they carried on their generous and intricate art, selecting from the array of Progressive ideas whatever seemed best to suit them and their school.

In spite of his forays into pseudo-science, G. Stanley Hall had contributed to the field of education his powerful conviction that the understanding of adolescent development could be strengthened by scientific investigation. His students, Arnold Gesell and Lewis Terman, more cautious than their mentor, set out to develop further the tests for mental development that Binet had pioneered in France. Phillips English teacher Claude Fuess came down to Abbot in 1920 to administer the first so-called intelligence tests, which teachers found helpful—though never in themselves decisive—for placing students in appropriate classes.[76] The seeming success of the "mental ability" and "achievement" testing movement along with work of E. L. Thorndike and other learning psychologists helped convince educators that theirs was a true profession with its own body of technique, as well as an art and a moral commitment. By the twenties professional associations had been founded for almost every teaching field, and Abbot teachers took advantage of many of their gatherings to gain fresh ideas. Dorothy Hopkins, Abbot's first professional librarian, and the enduring Mary Carpenter, first full-time director of physical education, participated in or led a professional conference every year;[77] other teachers joined the Modern Language Association, the Classical Association, or the School and College Conference on English. Several studied for advanced degrees in Education at Harvard or Cornell. Some of the faculty's professional training was directly sponsored by the Academy. In 1929–30 the Trustees expressed their admiration of History teacher Helen Bean (Abbot 1920–39; "very strict but very good" says Abby Castle Kemper) by supporting her during a year of study at Oxford. Principal and teachers together organized a six-year series of in-house faculty discussions to explore various phases of educational theory and practice: "the Adolescent Girl," "the Library as Laboratory," and "Science and Modern Life" were a few of the many topics covered. The Trustees also supplied tuition and board to two or three teachers a year for summer study after 1934. Miss Bailey joined the Progressive Education Association upon its founding in 1919, was the hard-working Treasurer of the Headmistresses Association, a member of the National Association of School Principals, and an Alumna Trustee of Wellesley. She urged teachers to visit innovative schools, and invited known (but safe) Progressive principals like Katherine Lord of Winsor to speak to the faculty. Implicit in many of her speeches and Chapel talks is the Progressive ed-

32. Homemaking laboratory in the basement of Abbot Hall, circa 1917.

ucator's central question, which casts aside traditional emphases on what should be taught and asks instead: how does the inner person change?[78] Thus did Abbot stay current with the new while it treasured the old.

In addition to this pride of profession, attention to the sciences and arts was central to the Progressive spirit. John Dewey himself had wanted to bring the work of the world into the school in forms manageable and comprehensible to the young person, and the "Domestic Science" course was Abbot's response. It was instituted, according to the 1913–14 catalogue, "to help girls realize the importance of the home as a unit of national life and the influence of a scientifically conducted house on the welfare of the state." This was small but serious business. Only Academic Senior-Mids or Seniors who had taken (or were taking) chemistry were allowed into the laboratory kitchen in the basement of Abbot Hall. The student cooks contributed pickles and cakes to the main dining room, sometimes using materials from the school's vegetable garden. The prerequisites themselves seem to have been less exciting: seemingly after 1894, Abbot rarely did more than meet colleges' minimum demands in the laboratory sciences. The school added a short business course in 1934, and throughout the Bailey era brought in speakers to describe the vocations most hospitable to young women—medicine, nursing, social work, library and clerical work, education, psychology, and homemaking. One business-like lecturer, Dr. Mary W. Calkins of Wellesley, who had written the psychology text which Abbot Seniors used after 1918 in place of James's *Shorter Psychology*, spoke on "Efficiency in the Management of Ourselves." As a *Courant* reviewer dutifully repeated, this efficiency was similar to the efficiency needed in business management. "Because of her limited time, Dr. Calkins gave her talk in outline form."[79] Indeed, Abbot's attention to all the sciences was somewhat abbreviated. Nellie Mason, the Department Chairman, acquired little new laboratory equipment after the Watson-Means years. Though the

Senior Class president spoke at Miss Mason's retirement in 1932 of "the clear flame of her intellect" and her "great power of personality";[80] though she was deeply kind to unhappy students; many alumnae remember Miss Mason as "dry, quiet, and unstimulating" in the classroom. One compares Abbot physics to "taking castor oil."[81] Mathematics also continued to be unevenly taught, in spite of Miss Bailey's deliberate attempts to strengthen C.P. Algebra.[82]

The arts were a longer, richer story. Abbot met the post-Deweyite surge in favor of the arts with its own traditional commitment to music and the visual arts, and with its students' irrepressible love of drama, now no longer repressed. Mr. and Mrs. Ashton had taken over capably enough from Mr. Downs, but Walter Howe (1922–48) and his fulltime resident assistant and successor-to-be, Kate Friskin (1922–61), were overflowing with energy and inventiveness. Like Downs, Mr. Howe was both composer and organist. Though he also gave only part of his time to Abbot, he loved to play his organ compositions ("Dedicace" was written to christen the enlarged Davis Hall organ) and to conduct any group willing to perform his piano concerto, "Youth" (which was, the *Townsman* reported, "a very interesting musical interpretation of the delirious abandon of youth"),[83] or his cantata, "Ode to Youth" (the text was written by Bertha Bailey and the Chatauqua Choir gave the world premiere). Howe persuaded the faculty to require Chorus Singing of every student, every year; he woke up Fidelio in such a manner that it never again was so inert as it was under Mr. Ashton.[84] He was "an enthusiast with temperament," an alumna recalls; a "wonderful musician," says another, who never gave up on any would-be singer no matter how tone deaf.[85] A third traces to his teaching her own "deep joy in music."[86] Once a performer in the Baltimore String Quartet, Howe encouraged the exhilarating and difficult art of ensemble playing, adding a cello teacher to the department and (with Miss Friskin) coaching ensembles, including such unlikely combinations as the new Aeolian Honor Society, founded in 1927 with a cellist, a violinist, a guitarist, several pianists, and a trumpet player. Miss Friskin, a professional concert pianist who had studied with the great musicologist Donald Tovey, was British, brusque, and demanding. "*Nobody* ever said no to Kate Friskin," remembers William Schneider of Phillips' Music Department. This force from down the Hill proved irresistible at times: you cannot sing a Bach cantata with girls or boys alone, and ambitious musicians do not rest short of Bach cantatas. Bach's *Deck Thyself My Soul with Gladness* was the centerpiece of a 1935 Phillips-Abbot program that began and ended with Howe's organ compositions. Often after supper Miss

Friskin played generously and beautifully to all who wished to hear; faculty and student recitals abounded. Every time Kate Friskin and her brother James gave a two-piano concert in Jordan Hall, they would repeat it for Abbot audiences soon after. The Downs concert series continued (one year Ratan Devi played Hindu music on a sitar), and an average of 73 students studied music each year during the twenties.

Painting, sculpture, and art history went on much as they had before. To "experience the joy of creating" was more the point of it all during the twenties than were the disciplined seeing or the profuse cultural learnings of the McKeen era, but this was consistent with general cultural enthusiasms.[87] Stripped of its social vision, the child-centered pedagogical Progressivism of the twenties worshiped self-expression,[88] and occasional Abbot art teachers participated in this craze. However, a staff member of the Boston Fine Arts Museum came once a week after 1928 to give a course in "design" that brought back some of the old values. Thus, though no longer central to the curriculum as in Miss McKeen's day, art continued to thrive.

Dramatics boomed. There were class plays, day scholar plays, corridor skits, charity benefits, language plays, Dramatic Society plays, plays written and acted by the Academic Seniors, even faculty skits and plays, prepared in secret and uproariously received. Draper Readings became Draper Dramatics in 1924, and Bertha Morgan Gray directed both with equal enthusiasm from 1917 to 1948. "Balmy Martha Melissa Howey" supervised the writing and production of the Seniors' one-act plays. "She was an enormously interesting woman," Elaine Von Weber remembers. "She was literally passionate about [teaching playwriting], and if we disappointed her she burst into tears." Rarely did they disappoint her.

No sooner had the Davis Hall stage been cleared of one set than another was constructed. Elaborate stage effects often accompanied them: Esther Kilton remembers a thunderstorm so successfully mounted from backstage that no one heard her lines, shouted through the din. One of the community heroes was Michael Scannell, School Engineer for thirty years, who read each play before rehearsals began, designed the scenery with pride and care, procured props from everywhere (Mr. Flagg's birdbath made a perfect fountain), and supervised Mr. Hammer, the carpenter, in the set construction. He had a stake in almost every production. When a rehearsal-watcher gushed, "That is the best scenery Abbot ever had!" Mr. Scannell quickly replied, "Then the play ought to be the best work Abbot ever did."[89] Miss Bailey also did her part, always remembering to come backstage after a play

33. Senior Class play, 1913: "Twig of Thorn."

34. "Masque of the Flowers," 1914.

to congratulate the players and their faculty director. The girls brought off men's parts with panache. Petrucio in *The Taming of the Shrew* and the Irish villagers of Lady Gregory's *Spreading the News* surprised new audiences; the pleasure taken in this skill can still be seen in commemorative photographs.

Abbot seems to have stayed clear of the avant garde: cubism in art, Dadaism in drama and poetry, anything other than Howe in contemporary music—these never appear in studio, on stage, or on class reading lists. Bits of blank verse creep into *Courant* toward the late twenties, emblems of easing resistance to the modern in the English curriculum. Through about 1930 however, the British classics dominated reading lists. Abbot students had to learn to write a sonnet:

> Sometimes on winter days the ghost of spring
> Returns again to haunt us for a space,
> And with her spirit fingers seems to fling
> Upon the earth à semblance of the grace
> And loveliness with which she used to rule.
> Snows vanish at her phantom touch; the grass
> Puts on its faded green as if to fool
> Itself; and all the drowsy, frozen mass
> That is the world stirs in its sleep and dreams
> Of summer time; and what few birds remain
> Feel in their breasts a strange new joy that seems
> To burst forth from their throats, a glad refrain.
>> But man smiles wistfully and shakes his head,
>> For he alone remembers Spring is dead.
>>> [Harriet P. Wright, "The Ghost of Spring," in *Courant*,
>>> February 1932, 20]

before trying a contemporary idiom:

> Savagely I love
> The sight of fleet, grey rain,
> The rip of snagged thunder,
> The snarl of frustrate wind,
> The sudden hissing silence
> Of beaten waves.
>> [Dorothy Rockwell, "Poem," ibid., 36]

English teacher Josephine Hammond, with her advanced degrees and her experience in college teaching, was a poet herself: she held several readings before the school. Lady Gregory came twice to eat Saturday luncheon and lecture afterward. The English V playwrights produced some marvelous pieces amid much dross. The Flapper girl in "Flapper Rule" written by Paulina Miller, '20, and set in the early war years, appears interested only in flirting—but gentle reader, look again! This coy facade is a cover-up for her plan to join the Italian Women's Battalion, a purpose revealed by mistake and reviled by her college fop of a brother, but, it turns out, much admired by her handsome suitor (the brother's archaeology professor), who has secretly resolved to join the Foreign Legion. Now and then a bit of Freudianism erupts in student writing: one student's Emily Dickinson "had formed habits of repression; and all her life, she renounced resolutely the things she unconsciously longed for."[90] Most Abbot writers kept such fancies under strict control.

Though the Academic Course students could adventure in classic American novels, College English was essentially a history of English literature from Chaucer through Stevenson. Yet college requirements were not completely static, nor was the English program. By 1928 Miss Chickering was asking her students both to analyze a Shakespeare sonnet and to "quote part of some modern poem that you like and explain why you like it";[91] and when Alice Sweeney rejoined the faculty in 1935, she helped further to modernize the English offerings: Hardy, Rolvaag, Ibsen, Shaw, Aeschylus, and Virginia Woolf had found their way to Abbot by the end of the Bailey era. Although this was a bit late, one is impressed by the richness and variety of the older English curriculum within its self-imposed limitations. After all, a lot happened in literature before 1900. Considering how wholeheartedly many secondary schools embraced the "life-adjustment" curriculum during the twenties and considering the number of educators "in full flight from the ideal of intellectual education"[92] which had powered Abbot for decades, it now seems fortunate that Bertha Bailey and her colleagues were so stubborn, so very old-fashioned.

Finally, Abbot made giant strides to deal with an aspect of schooling dear to educators of the whole child—physical education. Backed by the Trustees, Miss Bailey made this more than a matter of hockey, basketball, and daily exercise. There were the four to six required "hygiene" lectures given by Mary Carpenter, physical education director, and by a visiting woman doctor in which sex was mentioned more than once. While the *Courant* editors' enthusiasm for these lectures appears to be contrived to please their faculty advisers,[93] there is no doubt of Mary Carpenter's kindness, or of the familiarity with every Abbot student she gained through her single-handed leadership of the physical education program. She was an accesible confidante for many students with physical problems—or any problem—and her inventive enthusiasm persuaded even the reluctant to exercise. For those who hated gymnastics, there were folk and rhythmic dancing classes, while the gymnasts climbed ropes, leaped "horses," and tumbled in Davis Hall to their hearts' content. Field Day was potato races, horseback riding games, and a tug-of-war as well as a track-tennis-team sport meet. For Saturdays Miss Carpenter organized canoe trips or "picnic walks" to the more remote woods and farmlands of Andover, and on rainy Wednesday afternoons half the school flocked to Mc-Keen Hall to enjoy the intrigue of a game of "Beckons Wanted" or "Sardines." Best of all was the construction of a winter sports ground just west of the school—a toboggan slide, a small ski hill, and a skating pond for informal sports. Mary Carpenter made sure that every girl in the school had a pair of skis to use.[94] A sign on the bulletin board, "Skating today" meant fun—and no excuse to sneak off skating with the Phillips boys (who were by now too busy sweating in the gym to go along anyway). One winter there was a full fifty days of skating weather. The little pond was always the center of Abbot's annual Winter Carnival, a day-long, mid-winter frolic; in the late spring it filled up with as many as seventy swimmers (or splashers), all female.

Progressive critics would have approved this emphasis on self-development and healthy recreation. They would have had less enthusiasm for the coercion involved (*everyone* must exercise at least one hour a day, and prove it each week by her exercise card) or for the competition generated by the new team and "point" system, which replaced the class contests of earlier years. With Mary Carpenter's help, the Senior athletic captains divided the school into the "Gargoyles" and the "Griffins." "Points" recorded every physical activity or accomplishment: approved walks, posture improvement, hours spent riding or playing golf, and winning scores for tennis matches, hockey games, and Field Day events.[95] After Field Day, the team with the most points won for the year, and celebrated at the athletic award assembly. There was a Posture Honor Roll (with but eighteen members in 1923–24), an "A" Society for students with 200 points, and as if that wasn't enough, an "Honor A" Society for three or four citizen-scholar-athletes with flawless disciplinary records and 300 points. Student Council members immensely enjoyed their role in nominating the "Honor A's" to the faculty each year: thus was school-girl cattiness legitimized by hallowed purpose. Competition might be suspect in female academies of the mid-nineteenth century and even more so in Greenwich Village of the twenties; not so at Miss Bailey's Abbot Academy.[96] The *Courant* editors may have sounded overwrought even to contemporary ears when badgering their peers to pull in their torsos and act like "real, live, wide-awake, enthusiastic girls, full of 'pep and go.' "[97] Abbot alumnae, however, remember the Bailey era physical education program with pleasure, perhaps in part because the few who were truly lazy managed to do no more each day than walk down to Lowe's Drug Store for a soda—and got away with a glowing falsification on their Exercise Cards—while gung-ho students could enter the fray of point-competition, and others could simply enjoy the fun of exercise in multiple forms.

There was no doubt of Bertha Bailey's devotion to competition. The social striving fostered by the sororities repelled her, and she closed them down in 1914, but she soon instituted a Scholastic Honor Roll whose much-publicized roster excluded all but 5 to 10 percent of the students, since a scholastic average of 88 or above and a good citizenship record were the requisite qualifications. After 1925 the name of every student who received an A grade was read aloud in Chapel. The girls who presented the day's news most eloquently at dinnertime were voted members of the newsgivers' Honor Roll. Odeon ceased to be an open literary club and became an Honor Society limited to twelve members; Science, Art, and Music Honor societies joined Odeon in the twenties. The first Cum Laude chapter ever founded in a girls' school was Abbot's pride after 1926.[98] These societies and the Athletic and Student Government leaders had many members in common; one wonders how the left-outs felt about the interlocking directorate. Did they ever complain, as an Abbot student of the late sixties did, that "At this school the same people always get chosen for *everything?*"[99] Few alumnae admit to having minded; it was called "keeping standards high." Moreover, there were so many different honors at Abbot that almost any girl was bound to win at least one of them. Seemingly there was always some Abbot adult or older student ready to encourage and approve even the weakest, so long as the weakest kept on trying.[100] This combination of clear standards and warm encouragement would be a continuing source of strength for the twentieth-century school—never mind that it satisfied neither Progressive ideologue nor traditionalist pedagogue. For most students it seemed to work.

Bertha Bailey

A good principal takes ultimate responsibility, and Miss Bailey was ready. She must have known before she came, for example, how an Abbot principal must become pastor to the school if religion is to con-

35. The Abbot Chapel.

tinue to have meaning and power. Alumnae speak of her as a person who "lived her religion" with utter sincerity.[101] Her pulpit eloquence never seemed like self-display, for it always started from Scripture and reached toward each individual in the audience, striving to inspire and help. "Stir up the gift that is in thee," one sermon began, "for God gave us not a spirit of fearfulness, but of power and love and discipline" (Paul's letters to Timothy II, I:6, 7). After elucidating the quotation with further biblical references, Miss Bailey explained that she had chosen it for her 1934 New Year's message "because I think you need to be reminded, even as Timothy did, of the gift that is in you. Perhaps you have been unaware that you had any gift . . ." The rest is a paean to faith in oneself and in the ultimate good of God's purposes. Even unbelievers believed at such time—in Bertha Bailey's goodness if not in God's—and felt that "power and love and discipline" might someday be within their grasp. Like Miss McKeen, Miss Bailey was happiest when students voluntarily joined the Church while at Abbot ("The universe is ours but *we have to take it*")[102] or came of their own will to her special Lenten services; but she also felt keenly her responsibility to each member of that captive Chapel congregation, and everyone knew it. To Dorothy Rockwell, '32, Bertha Bailey was

a "faith-lifted personality," to Miriam Sweeney, '23, "the most inspiring person I have ever known."[103]

Seniors after 1925 had special attention from Miss Bailey in the
ethics and theism courses. Growing in confidence as Abbot's unordained minister, she took these over after the highly capable Rev.
Charles Oliphant died, and gave them her all. Each year's syllabus
was freshly thought out with the purpose of "removing *obstructions*
to faith" for the particular Seniors involved.[104] The class began with
different forms of unbelief ("I don't believe in the God of the Bible")
and dealt with these one by one. (Given modern theories of evolution,
the Bible indeed reveals itself as "a childish explanation of nature,"
but study and see how the Creation God of Genesis evolves by the
time of the Prophets: *"which God are you talking about?"*). Each
week students handed her an account of their reading from a list dealing with "the Cause," the "personality of God," "creative evolution,"
the Trinity. They mulled over the relationship of the spiritual and the
material by discussing the query "How much time would it take to
throw away a million silver dollars?" ("5 ¾ days," answered one girl,
"Hardly worth becoming a nervous wreck.")[105] Few cynics could
altogether reject her efforts.

For some girls Miss Bailey was "a ship in full sail," a person of such
awesome power and authority that you avoided her whenever she
hove into sight.[106] To these few her moral outrage could be overwhelming: one remembers two girls expelled for spending the night
with two Phillips boys, and a morning-after diatribe in Chapel so
withering that the offenders' sin paled beside their judge's anger. Others loved Abbot in spite of her. "The beauty and wholesomeness of
the whole two and a half years were so great I hardly felt Miss Bailey's
unkindness to me," wrote one graduate of 1933. "I could even sympathize with Miss Bailey. She liked people with some life to them,
and I was a rag of a creature, too busy taking everything in to give
anything." Until Commencement day itself the Principal threatened
every week to withhold this "creature's" diploma.[107]

But most students felt free to come to Miss Bailey in time of trouble,
whether the trouble began with the school or with themselves. She was
"kind and calm and strong," remembers Alice Sweeney, '14 "ready
equally to listen to a problem or a joke."[108] Yes, she was a harsh disciplinarian—but almost everyone agrees she was entirely fair. "We
were all afraid of her, but we all admired and loved her," says one
alumna.[109] She tried hard to work with representatives of the Student
Government. If they sometimes failed her by too much respecting
the injunction "See no evil, speak no evil, hear no evil,"[110] she usually

managed to identify the more responsible student councils that could handle all minor and some major infractions; thus girls saw that she was consulting with their respected peers, and rarely felt abused.[111] The haggling over school constitutions and lists of demerit offenses ("visiting other students in negligee: one demerit") was often petty and self-righteous; "Stu G" nevertheless gave many girls experience in running affairs, and opened privileged access to Miss Bailey for a few ("Miss Bailey is just wonderful . . . Always tell her *everything*," the outgoing Council president of 1923 advised her successor).[112] Everyone knew that she had given up her apartment to a girl who was critically ill with double pneumonia before the Infirmary was available and conducted prayers for the same girl in Chapel, that she would spend hours with a student who was struggling to cope with some agonizing family situation,[113] that she herself had nursed her dearest friend through her final illness,[114] and had suffered the death of a beloved niece. Big Bertha would understand. Much she did in secret. Perhaps a handful of people realized how little her public stance toward sex matched her private support and comfort of one student who had become pregnant.[115] Rarely did she confuse Abbot's real business with its reputation.

Now and then Miss Bailey relaxed. The first woman in all Andover to own a car, she loved to motor into the country or to visit friends. Her professional travels were also a release, for they brought her occasionally out of reach of Abbot's reputation. A younger colleague from Bradford still remembers her astonishment at Miss Bailey's behavior inside a New York City taxicab en route to a meeting of the Headmistresses Association. She put up the jump seat in front of her, set her feet upon it, leaned back and lit a *cigarette*. And she joked and laughed in a manner which the *Courant* editors would not have found at all "decently and sweetly feminine."[116] This too was Bertha Bailey, but few ever knew it. More of her associates were aware of her love for her great-nephew and niece, whose visits to her at Abbot were among her greatest joys.

Except for the Senior Bible and Theism classes, Miss Bailey left most of the teaching to the teachers, considering herself not so much an intellectual leader as a court of appeal for others' initiatives.[117] Her first inclination when presented with a new idea was always to say "No," but she was willing to reconsider if a staff member presented a clear counterargument.[118] She encouraged her teachers to run their own departments, taking onto herself the endless housekeeping chores that make a boarding school work. Her correspondence files are filled with letters to carpet dealers, invitations to speakers, and letters to thank the same speakers. Miss Means had done all this ably, too—but Miss Means's Abbot had nothing like the thirty-eight nonteaching household staff members whom Miss Bailey accumulated, or the paperwork involved in arranging a testing session or a prom. It is little wonder that Miss Bailey had time to build nothing but the Antoinette Hall Taylor Infirmary, planned by the Trustees before she arrived and soon provided for by Phillips benefactor Melville Day and other donors, most of whom made their contributions at the behest of Emily Means.[119] Though she carried through some renovations in the older buildings and helped outfit Sunset Lodge, Draper Homestead, and Sherman Cottage for student dormitories, more brick structures were not needed at this time. Bertha Bailey was busy building the school within the walls.

High and Low

Burton S. Flagg? Well, I should say I do.
He's the biggest man we've got . . .
Andover filling station attendant
quoted in *Worcester Academy Bulletin*

Abbot had seen crises before, crises that tested the school's strength
and adaptability, but the Great Depression put the survival of all independent schools in question. For a while, private enterprise itself was
at the barricades. Who could be sure at the time that the crisis would
pass? Not the corporation lawyers who bought subsistence farms in
the Berkshires and waited for Armageddon; certainly not the adults
who steered Abbot through the rising flood. Behind the calm face the
Academy presented to the world, its Principal and Trustees struggled
to hold off disaster. Their success came just in time, for new challenges
were to follow hard upon those presented by the Depression: the
sudden death of Bertha Bailey in 1935 and the installation of a dynamic
new principal amid the gathering clouds of war.

Celebration

It was ironic that the stock market crash of 1929 should break into
Abbot's Centennial year, but there was good fortune as well as irony
in that conjunction. The major celebration was months behind when
the Crash came, and if Abbot's constituency became quite suddenly
unable to fulfill Abbot's dreams for the future, much of the hard work
that was to ensure its passage intact through the Depression had already been done in preparation for the grand birthday.

Abbot's alumnae were the wheelhorses, while Principal Bailey and
Treasurer Flagg cajoled from behind or canvassed the financial country ahead, organizing supply bases for the expedition and preparing to
put its findings and accumulations to the best possible use. An active
minority of alumnae had begun planning just after the end of the
First World War to make the Centennial worthy of the Academy.

They were pleased with Bertha Bailey; they wanted to revive the long-range plan for Abbot's future that she and Mr. Flagg had set before the Trustees in 1915, when $100,000 was needed to fuel the expanding school. The War had intervened but the school expanded anyway, and was now too full to admit all who would enter. These graduates were readying proposals of their own for a Centennial fund in the fall of 1919 when Miss Bailey sent around to all alumnae a letter describing Abbot's need for funds. Running expenses had almost doubled since 1915; tuition would go up yet another notch, wrote Miss Bailey, and still Abbot must have outside help to maintain the community in the style to which it had become accustomed in the Means years, to offer salaries that matched the dignity and importance of the teacher's job, and scholarships to those daughters of clergymen, teachers, and social workers who had for so long been central to the school's mission.

In the months following, a conference of alumnae, faculty, and Trustees sorted out the tasks: the alumnae took on the actual job of raising a ten-year endowment fund; Miss Bailey would travel and speak, encourage and inspire; the Trustees would provide Jane Carpenter to help organize the work, and would take care of all office expenses so that every dollar given could go into the fund itself. The Loyalty Endowment Fund was born.

A few alumnae were soon off on their own tack planning a new Library in memory of Emily Means, who died in 1922, an appropriate memorial indeed for a lady who "was always reading, reading," as one donor put it.[1] Mary Byers Smith's Committee was as determined and independent as the lady it wished to honor; it was not until 1924 that its members made their own fund, standing then at $7,000, a subdivision of the Loyalty Fund. The Means Library Committee found strong support for its efforts from Abbot's Librarian, Dorothy Hopkins, who would manage in the first decade of her tenure to double both the collection (8000 volumes in 1930 compared with 2400 for the average private secondary school)[2] and its yearly circulation (2100 for books alone). With its browsing section, its system for guidance of student research, and its active periodical circulation, Abbot's library was already a model for schools throughout the Northeast.[3] It asked only for better housing, and this Miss Smith was bound she would provide.

Other alumnae were interested in ensuring smaller classes, still others in establishing a Laura Watson Art Fund or an Agnes Park Chair of History, in raising the level of all teachers' salaries, or in increasing scholarships. Thus many concerns were funneled into the single fund; appeal after appeal went out and was answered; every cord of sentiment was pulled to commit alumnae to repaying their debt of honor to the old school. Large lump-sum gifts were encouraged, but the alumnae leaders' zeal was most of all to reconnect each Dear Old Girl to Abbot with annual gifts, for "the family tie seems a little closer if one sends a special remembrance to the Mother regularly."[4]

Alumnae activities of all kinds increased. Connecticut graduates started another Abbot club in 1923 as the fund reached $40,000. The Alumnae *Bulletin*, begun in 1923 and edited by Jane Carpenter for all alumnae, publicized the D.O.G.s' activities and their school's needs much more effectively than could the student-run *Courant* with its limited circulation. There was more interest than ever in the Alumnae Advisory Committee, a rotating group of "visitors" founded by Anna Dawes and Miss Bailey soon after the latter's arrival and chaired for years by Agnes Park. (True, they did more visiting than advising, for Abbot never absorbed criticism easily, but the Committee brought many old girls back in touch with their school.) Alumnae were asked to recruit new students: "Send us some more," urged Miss Bailey in the *Bulletin*, "the best you can find . . ."[5] Reunions were enthusiastically arranged and attended. Every living member of the Fifty Year class returned in 1926, several traveling thousands of miles to do so. Alice C. Twitchell, '86, the Volunteer Fund Director, held many gatherings at Abbot, and traveled from one Abbot Club to another, asking always for money and more money. Faculty and students at the school raised contributions in the time-honored ways: the Bazaar of Six Nations, held in May 1925, and a faculty recital the same weekend brought a total of $1,100 to the Fund. The *Bulletin* wove together the many strands of this alumnae effort, kept people informed of school and alumnae news, and as the Centennial itself drew near, excited ever-increasing interest in the coming celebration.

A grand celebration it was.[6] Just four days wide, including the two Commencement days of June 1929, the birthday box came packed with 600 alumnae, as many parents and friends, students, townspeople, and luminaries from the world of education—about 2,000 folk in all. Baccalaureate and Commencement came first, the graduation address on Loyalty given by President William Allan Neilson of Smith College, but all the students stayed on for the further festivities. The third day there was an all-class parade led by Sarah Abbott Martin, class of 1856, with several classes marching around the circle in costume—painter's smocks and palettes for 1904 in honor of Emily Means, huge red hats and boas in memory of 1907's fashions. In the evening a movie of contemporary school life flickered through several showings in the big tent, while students and faculty mounted an historical tableau in

36. The Dear Old Girls: Class of 1886 at their Fiftieth Reunion.

37. Back When.

Davis Hall, all its characters costumed with impeccable accuracy, from
Squire Farrar and Harriet Beecher Stowe through croquet-playing
students of the 1870's to the barelegged rhythmic dancers of 1929.

On the final day, the whole crowd filled the Circle to hear a historical address by President Mary E. Woolley of Mt. Holyoke, one of the
most prominent woman educators of the time, and shorter speeches by
Vassar's President, Bradford's Principal, a parent (Governor Charles
W. Tobey of New Hampshire), and Rev. Markham Stackpole for the
Trustees. No one had been invited to speak for Phillips Academy, al-
though Alfred Stearns sat among the 19 "Delegates from the Schools."[7]
Perhaps there was some female chauvinism in the enthusiasm with
which the 180 Abbot girls sang out Holst's anthem, "Lord Who Hast
Made Us for Thine Own," thrilling their audience.[8]

At this great gathering, the hard workers were publicly thanked,
including the editors of the various Centennial publications—though
Editor Chickering of *A Cycle of Abbot Verse* could not immediately
be found. "I think she has misplaced herself," said Chairman Constance
Chipman to roars of laughter.[9] Finally Alice Twitchell presented to
the Treasurer a scroll of parchment which announced the completed
Centennial Loyalty Fund: $160,000. True, the total was less than all
had hoped for. When large endowment gifts failed to come in, the
Fund's name had been quietly changed to remove the word "Endowment"[10] and free the school to use the money for immediate needs as
well as long-range ones. Some $47,000 of gifts specifically donated as
endowment funds were announced separately so that the extraordinary
alumnae effort could stand for all to see. Ninety-eight percent of Abbot's graduates had given to the Loyalty Fund;[11] the final sum had been
built out of hundreds of small gifts. Abbot had no millionaires, but it
had many, many friends.

Luncheon over, Abbot and friends looked to the future. Miss Bailey
had arranged a symposium to be chaired by Trustee Ellen Fitz Pendleton, President of Wellesley, and entitled "Art and Life." Four well
known representatives of the arts, including conductor and composer
Alfred Soessel of New York University, spoke briefly and eloquently
about the ways that art might shape life, and Abbot's own alumna
Mira Wilson, '10, principal-elect of Northfield Seminary, spoke for
scholarship.

The Abbot family could well go home content from its birthday
party. The dignity of the celebration had been balanced by joyful
meetings, by the much-remarked welcome that the students gave to
the D.O.G.'s,[12] and by tearful leavetakings. The Academy was more
prosperous than at any time in its history, with its $850,000 of assets,[13]

its respected Principal and Trustees, its body of teachers, students and alumnae with their varying but usually genuine devotion to the school. "It's a *grand* school!" enthused Marion Brooks in nearly the same words Harriet Chapell had used 55 years before.[14]

Crash

"And it came to pass!" wrote one participant. 'The Centennial was in the distant future, it was near—it was here—it was over and gone."[15] And indeed, the class banners were no sooner hung in their places in Davis Hall the next October than warning rumbles were heard from Wall Street. The warning was late; the collapse was swift. Businessmen and all who depended on them were bewildered: for the first time on record, a quorum could not be found for the late fall Trustees Meeting of 1929. The meeting "has been adjourned indefinitely," reads the ominous record.[16] In fact, Abbot was very much a going concern. On March 6, 1930, the Trustees picked themselves up and met as usual, watchful but apparently recovered from the first shock and prepared to make some decisions.

In the first months following the Crash, no one could be sure how deep the disturbance would go. On reflection, some anomalies of the last two years began to fall into place: Principal payments on Abbot's Chicago City Railway bonds had been in default since 1927; five boarders had withdrawn for financial reasons during the summer of 1928; enrollments had been lagging in all girls' schools. Treasurer Flagg went through the winter of 1930 cautiously worrying. Did the depressed market signal fundamental weakness, or was it just a drawn-out slump?[17] Should Abbot go ahead with another fund-raising campaign? While Trustees pondered, signs of trouble abounded. The executor of a California estate left to Abbot could not settle it because no market had appeared for real estate appraised at $20,000. The Hoover Conference reestablished confidence (wrote Flagg to the Trustees) and demonstrated that business was "fundamentally on a sound basis," but "the recent holocaust in the securities market" could not be ignored. Anything might happen.[18]

All through the fall and early winter of 1929–30 the Trustees went ahead with their plans for a professional fund-raising campaign to complete the work that the amateur alumnae had so bravely begun. Impelled by a sense that there must be big money for Abbot somewhere and that men would know how to get it out of men if the women could not find it or give it, they moved through the uncertain months following the Crash, testing the water. Inquiries of parent intentions for 1930–31 promised only a small drop in enrollment; the school seemed calm. Abby Kemper remembers just one girl in 1929–30 whose father was in big business and vulnerable; the daughter was fearful that her coming-out party would be canceled. (It was.) *Courant* never mentioned the Crash. The Trustees voted to increase Miss Bailey's salary from $6000 to $6600; they voted a leave of absence with full salary for Kate Friskin; they thanked Treasurer Flagg for his gift of land to enlarge the skating pond, and authorized him to construct a dam "when the finances of the school make it advisable."[19] Abbot business as usual. But the long future was less sure, and "in view of the fact that the present conditions do not afford favorable prospects for the raising of money,"[20] the Trustees voted to suspend negotiations with Tamblyn and Brown, the fund-raising firm they had counted on to find that hidden gold. The Means library project was soon to be dropped also: the building estimates "were so overpowering" that the consulting architects were sent away until more money could be raised.[21] Regret and mild anxiety pervade these records of the early Depression. Still, the school had work to do. The big campaign and the library could wait six months, a year if necessary.

Depression, and "Abbot's Staunchest Friend"[22]

Four years later, Abbot Academy was in fear of closing its doors. According to Flagg's account of the first five years of Depression,[23] the school lost an average of $60,000 a year from its $850,000 net worth in tuition income and in the market value of its securities. This does not even count the drop in value of all the school's real estate—assets whose market worth was never tested in the grim years. 1932 and 1933 were the worst: income alone dropped $60,000 from $216,000 in June 1932 to $156,000 a year later. The worth of securities fell drastically:

	Bonds	Stocks
1931	$140,800	$141,200
1932	$ 78,300	$ 51,500[24]

After 1932, the Treasurer simply ceased printing market values in his Report. Why should he dwell on Abbot's agony? We hear of neither bond nor stock again until the 1935 Report, when they had recovered to $136,300 and $79,600 respectively. Enrollments looked as bad—or worse, for students make a school. They slipped from 181

(135 boarders) in 1929–30 to 110 (71 boarders) in 1933–34, a drop that more than halved tuition income because tuition had by then been lowered to $1200 to reflect falling prices. Furthermore, 45 of the 110 girls attended on scholarship. Most of the $26,000 set aside to support them was income foregone: Abbot's endowed scholarships could provide less than $4000 a year.

How did Abbot Academy manage to keep going? Many private schools ceased to exist during the Depression. Others closed for two or three years and reopened after the worst was over, often much changed.[25] Abbot endured. Deep in its bones was something close to a preference for adversity, for situations in which the missionary could show her stuff to a soft world. The school had survived the 1850's when so many New England academies had shut down for good; it had adjusted to turn-of-the-century challenges that finished less resilient institutions. In crucial ways, Abbot emerged from the decade of Depression stronger than it was on the eve of the Crash.

Treasurer Burton Sanderson Flagg was the hero of those first five years. A scholarship student and Greek major at Brown University, Flagg took up the insurance business in Fitchburg, Massachusetts, after graduation but was drawn to Andover in 1901 by Cecil Bancroft's invitation to teach at Phillips. Once arrived, he decided instead to go into business in the town. Not long afterward insurance assistant Flagg was partner Flagg of the Smart and Flagg insurance agency, and president of Merrimack Mutual Fire Insurance Company, founded in 1828 and by 1948 to become one of the largest mutual insurance concerns in the United States. Abbot's early fortunes had turned on the school's local connections, but Academy and town had grown apart in the twenties. Now that Abbot needed all the allies it could find, this Treasurer's status as exemplar of Andover's Yankee aristocracy and his experience as top dog in innumerable enterprises were central to Abbot's strength.

On the eve of the Crash, Burton Flagg probably wielded more power in Andover than had any single individual since Samuel Phillips, Jr., died in 1802. Simultaneously an insurance agent and company president, Flagg was a (perfectly legal) one-man interlocking directorate—and director of several other New England insurance companies as well. The Andover Press continued to print all of Abbot's publications, and Flagg was on its board. He was as much in demand as Abbot's founder, Squire Farrar, for he had Farrar's social conscience, his eye for detail and his talent for organization. "He was ambitious, but not desiring," says a friend who knew him well. He became director, then president of two Andover banks, positions of important responsibility which earned him only a token salary. Was a new building and better site needed for the Savings Bank? Flagg would make sure they were obtained in a way that respected the townspeople's interests while it advanced those of the Bank,[26] for to Flagg, the businessman who put private capital to constructive uses was the cornerstone of American society.[27] A good man also owed his time and talent to public and charitable institutions. Flagg was a pillar of South Church and clerk of the South Parish (until 1931 a separate corporation with membership restricted to male churchgoers). He served for years on the town Finance Committee, on the Board of Memorial Hall Library and on the School Committee. "He *ruled the town*," one former day scholar remembers; to a Hilltop friend he was "the Squire of Andover." If envious townsmen occasionally felt that he controlled more than his share of local affairs, most were nevertheless grateful for his uses of power.[28]

For all this, Abbot Academy was Flagg's dearest concern, "his daughter." A father who loved to see every curl and button in place, Flagg had the same stern, doting pride in Abbot that his great friend Warren Draper had held; the Drapers had in fact introduced him to Abbot when the young Flagg first lived in Andover, years when (according to Frances Flagg Sanborn, '26) "he was like a son to them." Like Draper also, and like his more distant predecessor Samuel C. Jackson, Flagg saw himself as a champion of education, who believed that the school's mission was complementary to that of the Church. Since the Church reached ever fewer young people, the school must do more. Flagg was invited to be a Trustee of Andover Newton Theological Seminary, an honor Draper would have prized, but he declined on the ground that he was too busy with a more urgent concern: the schooling of young women.[29]

Burton Flagg and his wife Anne[30] had three daughters of their own who came with them to live in Taylor Homestead, the house next door to John-Esther Gallery; all three attended Abbot. Responsive to Rev. John Phelps Taylor's wishes for the disposition of his family home, the Trustees in 1924 granted Taylor's friends, the Flaggs, a minimal rent for the brick house; then later,[31] recognizing that this "Treasurer" was singly a business manager, securities broker, grounds superintendent, and educational planner, all at a minimal salary ($500 at first, then raised by degrees to $2,500 in 1922), they gave him free use of the house during his lifetime.[32] Flagg seemed always to be out and around the campus, his tall, stately figure making Jane Carpenter, his loyal consultant on all alumnae matters, look like a quick, inquisitive bird, making scurrying puppies of the students scrambling about his hockey field or his skating pond (for he had supervised the build-

38. Jane B. Carpenter and Burton S. Flagg: A partnership. Photograph taken in 1937 by Dorothy Jarvis.

ing or rebuilding of every outdoor sports facility at Abbot by 1941).
When alumnae or parents or potential donors came to visit, Flagg
was on hand to walk them around. He was a somber, remote man to
those who knew him only casually outside the Abbot gates, but Abbot
brought out all that was kind in his character. The school was always
on his mind: the Chapin boys, Barton Jr. and Melville, rarely heard
him talk of anything else to their father, who was first clerk, then
president of the Abbot Board from 1920 to 1952.[33] Recalling his kindness, Beverly Brooks Floe, '41 says that "we students had this feeling
of being cherished, like his family, like his own."

Flagg admired and loved Miss Bailey with a depth of feeling he
never summoned for any other Abbot principal after her death, and
she in turn consulted him on everything from rug purchases to salary
changes. Though she was not good at delegating tasks to her female
teachers, preferring to attend to them herself,[34] she could leave almost
anything to her Treasurer.[35] Mr. Flagg noted "a certain masculinity in
Miss Bailey's mental processes,"[36] high praise from a man clearly conscious of his own role as chief male in this female institution. Flagg
made a point of inviting the Abbot fathers for a round of golf at the
country club during the Commencement dither, and corresponding at
length with some of them about matters educational and financial. He
persuaded the Andover Sportsman's Club to stock Abbot's pond with
1,000 trout, which were to be fed with 40,000 fresh-water shrimp and
gratefully caught by Abbot fathers and Andover sportsmen upon maturity.[37] Each summer he verified his place in the Andover male establishment with his week-long house party at Kennebunkport, Maine,
for a "group of friends who direct the affairs of Andover,"[38] as one of
Flagg's former schoolmates put it, including several bankers, real estate
men, Phillips Academy masters, the Andover School Superintendent,
and the Postmaster.

Indeed, Flagg epitomized the Protestant Yankee spirit in which Abbot had been founded, infused as he was with its frugality, its seriousness, even at times its missionary righteousness. William Doherty,
whose large Catholic family had sought its own piece of political and
financial power in Andover since the first Doherty arrived after the
Civil war, claims that Flagg and his friends arranged almost everything
to exclude newcomers, whether from the insurance business or the
local educational establishment. "He ran the show," Doherty says. "He
was an aristocratic gentleman who could do no wrong." If "the Irish
had everything sewed up in Lawrence," Flagg was "the Mayor Daley
of the old Yankee crowd in Andover." During the Depression, Doherty
recalls, the jobless turned to Flagg for jobs. Would-be teachers learned

by the grapevine that they'd have a better chance if they joined South Church and bought their insurance at Smart and Flagg, though no demonstrable threat was ever made to those who refused such advice. Here was a man of power in whose name, inevitably, some things must have been said or done which he did not approve.[39] A small insurance agent who tried to open accounts for his new clients with the big stock companies received refusals and apologies—and later discovered that these insurers had quite naturally been protecting their own profitable relationship with the Merrimack Mutual. Other banks might fail, but Flagg and his fellow Andover Savings directors had friends in the Nathaniel and J. P. Stevens textile family who would help keep their bank sound. "All legal," Doherty acknowledges. "Any businessman would do the same if he could." It was, again, perfectly legal at this time, if not commendable, for the Savings Bank loan officers to suggest to applicants for mortgages that they have their houses insured against fire loss with a reliable outfit like Smart and Flagg—but frustrating for the outsider trying to forge for himself the connections that allow a business to survive hard times.[40] While the Depression deepened and the Dohertys fumed, Flagg continued to build on his advantages, certain that what was best in Andover could be preserved —including both Abbot Academy and the Merrimack Mutual. His local influence and regional connections lent Abbot Academy a legitimacy within the still-conservative town similar to that created by Farrar's and Draper's involvement during the nineteenth century. Doubters, take note! This is a solid enterprise! As time went on, and Flagg's Trusteeship entered its fortieth, then fiftieth year, one can wonder if this very confidence did not protect the school overlong from realizing the need to adjust to mid-twentieth-century conditions.

Within Abbot, Treasurer Flagg had been building his power for good throughout a full quarter century. He made himself indispensable soon after his appointment to the Board in 1906. It was to him that many aspiring parents applied during the last years of the Means era, when it was difficult for outsiders to know whether Miss Means was at Abbot or on leave; it was he who decided for Miss Means how many boarders the school could take, for Miss Bailey what special comforts old Mrs. Draper needed during her last "days of waiting,"[41] and what compensation a teacher should receive while recovering from a thyroid condition.[42] As the Bailey era progressed, he became a member or *ex officio* participant of every Trustee Standing Committee, and chairman of the Committees on Alumnae Relations, on Investments, and on Business Policy. By 1947 he was such a fixture that a fellow Trustee wrote him after one of the handful of meetings he missed in all his 59 years as Treasurer, "I wasn't at all sure that [the meeting] was even official."[43] He often presided at Commencement. He took to incorporating brief sermons about educational goals into his Treasurer's Reports. Melville Chapin thinks that Mr. Flagg and Miss Bailey often decided ahead of time what these should include, which explains the Principal's enthusiastic efforts to follow up on the Treasurer's suggestions.[44]

Everything about Abbot interested Flagg. He knew each bush and tree on the grounds by heart. When the Cedar Apple Rust appeared on Abbot's apples he made sure future cedar seedlings were planted the necessary 1000 feet away from the orchard. He instructed the Trustees on the tendency of the aphis insect to exude from two tiny tubes on its back a honeydew which in dry weather formed an ideal culture for black-leaf mildew, and reported that he had brought the situation fully under control by ordering applications of the proper amount of oils and Black Leaf 40 to the affected trees.[45] He warned the Trustees of the hazards presented by curling irons in dormitories.[46] He supervised the installation of sprinkler systems to bring all buildings in line with the fire code. Wishing the students to learn modern business methods, he set up an internal "bank" that helped Abbot girls balance their own checkbooks until the school changed to a simple $2.00 allowance system after Miss Bailey died.

Reared to understand the intricacies of farmwork by his father, Flagg had profound respect for the man who knew trees, or lawns, or buildings, or dam construction. He was even known to change his mind when Michael Scannell questioned one of his practical decisions. His personal concern for each man on the grounds staff was reciprocated by a loyalty so great as to obscure certain perennial problems, such as low wages and the complete lack of a staff pension plan.[47] Paternalistic to the last, Flagg wished to be utterly fair, to consult all interested parties in every decision, but he always preferred to take care of specific needs as they arose rather than setting up a mechanistic system; thus, while annual grants were made to a few retirees like the Misses Kelsey and Mason, he long resisted formal retirement provisions for the faculty too, preferring to pay endless nursing home and insurance bills for ancient ladies rather than grant them a steady sum to use or abuse as they would.

Flagg was always looking for ways to provide Abbot the special treats with which any father loves to surprise his child. Because he watched every penny, there was usually some small reserve available from school funds. Was a diving platform needed for the Abbot pond? Too frivolous for a school budget, perhaps, but Flagg would have it constructed himself. In 1933 he gave over to the school the lounge and kitchenette above his garage where his daughters had entertained their friends. Teachers could smoke there (and nowhere else, ruled Miss Bailey); Seniors were allowed to use it on Saturdays; fathers compared cigars and daughters there at Commencement time. He thought of everything: an extra draft of expense money for Constance Chipman when she was delayed in Cleveland, a carnation for each teacher at the annual Christmas dinner, two tons each of bone meal and sheep manure to give newly planted saplings exactly the boost needed for their first summer at Abbot,[48] a school advertising policy based on precise reports of magazine readership, and so on and so on.

It was Flagg who had opened Abbot's drive for a permanent endowment in 1910 with a special appeal to alumnae. Painstakingly he built Abbot's assets from the $61,400 of securities and deposits in the vault when he arrived to the $400,000 portfolio of conservative investments with which Abbot greeted the Depression.[49] He watched the market, bought and sold, always building capital. Trustee John Alden (1900–16) confided to his wife that his young colleague was "the best man I know with whom to advise on matters of investment."[50] Flagg took it on himself to buy $10,000 worth of bonds from the Phillips Trustees as "an act of friendship and cooperation" during the building of Bishop Hall, and like so many similar acts, this one paid a faithful 4 percent.[51] He set up a bequest program that brought $90,000 from the Antoinette Hall Taylor estate in 1925. He and the Trustees offered annuities to alumnae, and Mary Byers Smith advertised them with characteristic directness in the *Bulletin*, asking, "Why not have the fun of giving before you are dead?"[52] His name was caution (what else would you do with $20,000 of new contributions to an Abbot fund drive but deposit them in sixteen different savings banks?),[53] and those cautious D.O.G.'s who wished their surplus funds to go far for education would entrust them to such a Treasurer. Throughout the twenties, Flagg reminded Trustees and alumnae of the tax benefits that would accrue to donors who traded large donations for annuities or gave Abbot high value stocks to sell. Thus when the Crash descended, Abbot was in a far stronger financial condition than many private schools.

Abbot Pulls Through

The Depression made for tough going, but most of Abbot's investments continued to pay dividends amounting to over $4,000 annually throughout the lean years. A few concerns postponed principal payments on their bonds,[54] yet even these finally did deliver after the worst was over.[55] Abbot's rental income, the hedge that Flagg built, proved more precarious than its endowment income. Flagg's prudent program to purchase all the houses on the Abbot Street border of the campus backfired when tenants began vacating them for cheaper housing during the Depression. Taxes must be paid whether or not the houses were full; worst of all, the "cottages," emptied of students when enrollments dropped, became taxable rental property for which tenants could not be found. Then, as the securities market flattened out and Roosevelt took over the Presidency, Flagg deposited ever more of the school's assets in local and nearby savings banks ($147,000 in 1932 and $185,300 in 1933). Andover Savings Bank and the Charlestown Five might yet escape the reach of That Man in the White House.[56]

All this time, buildings must be heated, students must be fed, taught, and nursed when sick, and faculty must either be paid or dismissed. These were the days when men waited at dawn near the post office for the WPA recruiter to hire them, and if he refused them, waited all day on the curb for the wagons to rumble in from the countryside with a cabbage for each destitute family. Flagg cut costs wherever he could. Unlike many schools whose teachers worked gratefully for room and board, however, Abbot resisted going backward on salary payments as long as possible. Much progress had been made toward adequate teacher compensation during the twenties: prodded by Miss Bailey, the Trustees had brought the average salary, $2412 plus room and board in 1928, to well above both the median for girls' schools and the $2378 average (1928 figures) for public high school teachers in large towns and cities,[57] a real accomplishment in spite of anomalies that turned on the world's calculation of what women will put up with (Mr. Howe got $4000 and an Abbot-owned house for part-time work, for example). As prices fell, teachers were willing to accept a 10 percent salary cut in 1932 and another in 1933, but no teacher was dismissed without clear cause. Though the grounds crew was reduced and all but emergency maintenance jobs were suspended for two years, Flagg made sure to look for the very workers he had had to lay off whenever there were special tasks requiring extra labor.

Flagg felt Abbot would do best to take care of its own rather than accepting government help. When federal unemployment and social security programs appeared, Flagg concluded that they were no more than "rackets" which the lazy exploited at the expense of the industrious[58] and which only impeded Abbot's efforts to make a fair income.

To his credit, however, he dispassionately informed the Trustees of every state or federal government action that might affect their school, cooperated with the NRA, and put to work two archivists assigned to Abbot by the Work Progress Administration (one of them an unemployed minister). Thus duty overcame his recorded distaste for the American body politic's "insatiable desire to settle all economic ills by legislation."[59] He also did his best to warn the Trustees of impending changes in tax exemption clauses so that they could lean on friends in the State House or the Town Hall to forestall still further government encroachment on Abbot's independence.[60] Throughout its history, the pinchpenny school had relied on none but itself and its own closest friends. Hard times were no excuse for giving in now.

The Trustees' strategy for survival was to eschew extreme solutions and rely on Abbot's proven worth to attract students. "We believe," wrote Flagg in December 1933,[61] "that our budgetary plan for this year tends to preserve the essential elements of the school intact." Far from keeping girls at any cost, Miss Bailey and her faculty continued to dismiss unruly or lazy students just as though their tuition payments did not matter. She knew the school would be several short of full enrollment for 1930–31, but this inhibited her not a bit when two girls left for P.A. one May night after tucking dummies into their beds, and another, a Student Council member, spent the night in New Haven with a Yale man. Five more were ousted the following spring for "persistent disobedience," and six underclassmen were invited to leave after Commencement for failing to prepare their classes properly.[62] Trustees and Principal flatly refused to "buy" enrollees, as so many schools were doing, by offering the shopping applicant a year's education for $100 less than whatever the tuition quoted her at school Y or school Z. "We will not bargain," said Flagg.[63] The $1200 tuition was to remain the target figure for all applicants. Scholarships based on need the Trustees would continue to offer, but never would they participate in the manic, unethical undercutting that now made chaos of the once orderly private-school market.

Yet for all his sang-froid, Flagg insisted that "an unusual and well-organized effort must be made to prevent the school from closing."[64] The Trustees stepped up advertising. They engaged first the capable Mildred Winship, then Trustee Constance Chipman, as their "field representative" to organize alumna meetings all over the Northeast. They hired a professional field recruiter to tap promising veins in the Midwest and to be paid per capita for every student who matriculated by her agency. Most important, they enlisted alumnae help in finding new students for Abbot. All the lines cast out in preparation for the Centennial were baited again with appeals to alumnae energy: their banks might have failed, but their daughters or their friends' daughters could still come to Abbot on large scholarships.[65] Miss Bailey set up "visiting days," when any alumna or prospective parent might inspect the school. Constance Chipman cajoled Abbot Club members and the guests at "Abbot teas" to recruit students—almost any student. Of all the three measures taken, this alumnae work proved most effective. The vaunted professional recruiter plied the coffee circuit around Chicago for two years and came up with exactly one applicant; advertisements brought a handful more; all the rest enrolled because friends, relatives, or grade school teachers had recommended Abbot.

Just enough students came to keep Abbot going—but only if they paid their bills. Near-full schools were foundering because the tuition checks never arrived: many Abbot parents delayed their payments for months or years. Treasurer Flagg wrote to each one, gently prodding. He was especially patient with the parents of returning students or with old Abbot families to whom he and the school felt committed, and they usually responded with equal good will, in a few cases setting up a payment schedule that eventually reimbursed Abbot for the scholarships the Trustees had granted their daughters as well as for tuition defaulted. The character of Abbot's clientele was a crucial factor in the school's successful journey through the Depression. The majority of fathers were salaried professionals, local businessmen whose custom was not wiped out by ticker tape transactions in New York or Chicago, or physicians or lawyers with a localized practice.[66] Abbot's fund-raisers might wish this were otherwise in better times, but in the Depression years a stable clientele of relatively modest means proved to be the school's salvation. Of the forty-three schools whose situation seemed most comparable to Abbot's, only five reached 1933 with a lower percentage of enrollment change than Abbot could boast.[67] That was the year when hundreds of private schools simply closed down.[68]

Within, the school was as it had always been in times of crisis: braced and bracing, reassured by the confluence of its own sober ideals and the world's necessities. Miss Bailey followed her over-full days of making ends meet with night correspondence for the Headmistresses Association Emergency Teachers Unemployment Committee, which she chaired. Teachers took on extra work without complaint; students again cleaned corridors and bathrooms where maids had once waited upon young ladies' wishes. Because the Abbot Family had shrunk, there

39. Cooking outdoors in the Grove, 1933. Egan Photo Service.

was an intimacy that had been lacking in the twenties: no snobbery, few cliques, recalls Abby Castle Kemper, '31—the school was simply too small to tolerate serious divisions. Off-campus excursions were few; the clutch of Boston-Symphony-goers diminished from seven to five to three a week; the horseback riding contingent shrank by two thirds. Only twenty-eight of forty-six Seniors could afford to go to Intervale in 1933, that "year of limitations."[69] Since you could not escape, you made your fun at the school—and you used its opportunities to advance newly serious purposes of your own. Hemlines dropped again, curling irons were put away. Almost every older student planned on further education: the proud advocates of the Academic Course could not turn back the enthusiasm for precollege training that had swept through middle-class America on a wave of anxiety about employment, for college entrance was becoming increasingly competitive.[70] Academic Course students were now "the dumbbells," Abby Kemper remembers, though she was happy enough to be one of them. It seemed an age since Ruth Newcomb and several of her contemporaries had come to Abbot in 1908 for a leisurely two years after graduation from excellent high schools. Late in 1932 the Trustees planned a modernized catalogue offering a new two-year "graduate course," but so few students enrolled in it that ten months later Miss Bailey asked the Trustees to consider dropping the Academic Course altogether. The following autumn only eight Academic Seniors enrolled out of a class of fifty-six students.

"The life of the school is free and happy," promised the catalogue after 1933. Yet over and over, Principal's Reports and alumnae recollections mention the seriousness and determination that predominated among Depression-era students. In their yearbook photographs the Seniors looked forty years old. "The relations between students and teachers are sympathetic and understanding," the new catalogue went on. With fewer students there could be more individual attention than ever. Indeed, one of Abbot's attractions was its low pupil-teacher ratio at a time when public high-school enrollments had quite suddenly soared (17 percent between 1930 and 1932), and the average teacher taught more than thirty-five students in each class—for here, too, education was preferable to unemployment.[71] It cannot be said that the real Abbot fully matched the catalogue description, however. Most of the teachers were aging along with their Principal. "Nearly all octogenarians," Mrs. Kemper exclaims with mild exaggeration. Except for Mary Carpenter—"she had a heart," says Jane Sullivan, '31, "and in my day there weren't many who had a heart"—there were few to overcome the formality that seems to have prevailed between the young and the elderly at this time.[72] The Principal set the tone by requiring every boarder personally to give her "Good morning" at breakfast time. "It was very rigid," Abby Kemper recalls; she was scolded by a Senior for saying "hello" to Miss Bailey instead of "good afternoon." Even teachers such as Katherine Kelsey, whose kindness and pedagogical skill only increased with her long experience, were ladies first, friends long afterward.

Mrs. Chipman brought back messages from loyal alumnae who were sure their recruiting would be more successful if only Abbot were not so old-fashioned. A few changes were made. The traditional full page of directions for student dress disappeared in the 1933–34 catalogue, to be replaced after 1934 by two short sentences beginning "students dress simply . . ." Precisely because the girls—and American society at large—had left behind the madness of the twenties, Miss Bailey was willing to lower Abbot's walls here and there, allowing boy-girl dancing in the Recreation Room during the calling hour, and other small freedoms. She eased the ancient Sunday regimen a bit by ordering the gates to the campus opened, and permitting inter-room visiting, outdoor walks, frivolous reading, occasional visits from parents, even studying, in the afternoon. She granted the Student Council's request for Seniors to be allowed to go on Wednesdays in pairs to Boston once more, as they had in Miss Means's day. But chaperones made sure no dancing couple indulged in torso contact; the Senior privileges were soon abused (said Miss Bailey) and rescinded;[73] and Sundays were still largely consumed by solemn occasions.

In the larger educational world, this was a time of daring experiment—Black Mountain College and coeducational Putney School were founded the very year that Miss Bailey was tightening the Senior rules again—and Abbot appeared staid indeed. Midwestern alumnae "wish we would meet the competition by presenting new subjects in the advanced Academic course," reported Mrs. Chipman.[74] Both Principal and Treasurer exerted genuine leadership to move Abbot off academic dead center. Miss Bailey urged teachers to try some of the new teaching methods she had learned about at meetings of the Progressive Education Association. Flagg proposed applying business principles to help teachers "broaden their educational horizons" through intensive discussion within faculty meetings, through visits to other schools "which may help to dislodge any one particular . . . educational line of thinking" among the faculty, and through systematic connections between extracurricular activities and class work, an educational technique "thoroughly practised in business."[75]

There is no sign that these efforts changed minds already made up about education. Yet good things continued, for neither Ruth Baker's nor "Mother Chick's" teaching respected clichés about youth and age; Dorothy Hopkins substituted imagination for library acquisition; and others took advantage of small classes to move faster or more sensitively through academic work. Helen Bean's history students wrote papers on "The Child Labor Amendment," or "The Work of the C.C.C." in the fall of 1933. Miss Bailey's Ethics class asked how women could improve working conditions and prisons, and outlined the roles they might effectively play in politics and industry. In 1934 Miss Bailey and a Trustee instituted a business course which immediately became a popular elective. Alice Sweeney's efforts in the fall of 1935 to update the English curriculum matched the energy brought earlier to the Mathematics Department by young Esther Comegys, M.A. Miss Bailey engaged Miss Comegys for the new position of Academic Dean in 1932, plucking her from her doctoral studies at Radcliffe and her teaching job at Simmons College to take over much of the work Miss Mason and Miss Kelsey had together done until their retirement in 1932. Thus the majority of the faculty might be set in their ways, but wrinkles appeared now and then on the smoothest surfaces, providing a measure of traction for venturesome young minds.

A Sober Recovery

We think of the year 1930 as the norm for Abbot, Flagg told the Trustees in the gloom of winter 1934, when it looked as though another year like 1933–34 would finish Abbot off. Yet "our charts indicate that it has been one hundred years since 1930."[76] But at the very same Trustees' meeting, Mrs. Chipman reported more interest in Abbot than she had encountered for years. That spring applications began to rise again at last. One hundred and thirty-five students registered for 1934–35, including forty two day scholars, the largest number since 1915. The business index no sooner began to climb than Flagg and Bailey began plotting new building projects—or, rather, replotting the ones left in limbo in 1930. One of the two salary cuts was restored for 1934–35, and restoration of the second was planned for 1935–36. Abbot had a future.

Yet that future would be shaped for years to come by the worst period of the Depression. It was more than a test of Abbot's survival value; like the World War era, it was a time of rededication to old ideals. The mood of Miss Bailey's Easter address of 1932 echoed that of her 1918 speeches, though she fashioned her lesson from contemporary materials:

> The responsibility of world reconstruction lies on our
> generation. As the Crucifixion showed us the way, so will the
> kidnapping of the Lindbergh baby bring us to our senses.[77]

A 1932 graduate today looks back approvingly at the fit between Abbot's ways and the demands of a tough world. "Part of the plan," she writes, "was to accustom us to the fact that life requires one to recognize and accept discipline if one is to survive."[78] Abbot's traditional style suited the times.

There was also a new recognition that Abbot would have to deserve whatever future it earned, and a healthy sense of uncertainty. The school's determination to enlarge its constituency did not disappear with the passing of the crisis; ("Minneapolis and Duluth were new territory," reported Mrs. Chipman in December of 1935, "and very promising.")[79] Miss Bailey herself articulated a courageous realism about things to come in a speech to the Wellesley alumnae. She was now a trustee of her old college, but she declined the privilege of omniscience. "All that we know of the world our students are to meet is that we know nothing of it," she said. "The only thing they have to expect is the unexpected." Given this, she went on, a young woman required more than ever a deep sense of social responsibility, excellent health, intellectual readiness, and, interestingly, a capacity for "ease, dignity and freedom in her contact with young men."[80] Abbot Academy would never again take itself for granted.

None of Bertha Bailey's faculty and students realized how quickly the unexpected would storm the school. On November 16, 1935, Miss Bailey died of pneumonia while visiting relatives in New York State. Abbot was stunned. "She had been so well–" remembers an alumna. She was only sixty-nine years old! One feels that the Abbot Family had expected this mother to go on forever. She had been so long at Abbot that large numbers of "her" alumnae were sending their daughters to be "her" students, and Phillips alumni who had felt her judgmental glare during her first few years as guardian of the virgin gates came to her quaking with anxious memories when presenting their daughters for admission.[81] Only a few people knew that she had had diabetes for some time, or realized how heavily the four lean years had taxed her. Miss Bailey herself had known she must rest a while. Secretly, she arranged with the Trustees for a seven-month leave with full salary, to begin in mid-fall of 1935 after school was under way, and end before Commencement. She dared not stay away longer–dared not even tell most of Abbot she was leaving–for fear of setting back the Academy's precarious recovery. The farewell party seemed barely over when the bad news came. "A tremendous shock, an overpowering sorrow, has come to Abbot Academy that will be felt round the world." The November *Bulletin* stopped press to insert this announcement of her death. Tributes to her deluged the *Courant* editors. A Senior remembered how "freely and joyously" she lived under Miss Bailey's guidance because of her Principal's faith in "the goodness of life."[82] Madame Marie Craig, French teacher, wrote that "the very center of our lives" was gone,[83] and a seventy-year old alumna turned her thoughts to poetry:

> Dear heart–suddenly still–
> Your book of life was beautifully written.
> Stinging the tears which fill
> Our eyes,
> Against our will they flow
> Soon, all too soon, the story's ended,
> Just in life's afternoon.
> Reverently the pages we retrace.[84]

There was only one thing to be thankful for: the Trustees and Miss Bailey had provided for her absence. Dean Comegys had already agreed to serve as Acting Principal for the year. Registrar Fanny Jencks, who had been Miss Bailey's assistant and secretary for years, was ready to supervise dormitory life and other nonacademic activities. Seasoned by past emergencies, Abbot set itself to get on without Bertha Bailey.

It would be difficult at times, but on the whole, the rest of the year went smoothly. The faculty decided to present the play they had been rehearsing when Miss Bailey died; the Christmas service, the Intervale trip, the "corridor stunts," the class picnics, the weekly lectures and daily classes—all were carried on as before. "Miss Bailey planned the calendar very carefully before she left," wrote Esther Comegys to the Trustees. "The older girls have felt the loss very keenly," she went on; the Senior leaders are still finding their feet, and "the school as a whole seems young and noisy,"[85] but it survives.

The sudden change impelled the Trustees to take stock. What kind of school should Abbot become? Where should they look for a new principal? By March both questions had become urgent. The retirement for health or personal reasons of three elderly teachers and the firm forced resignation of a fourth made it seem as though Miss Bailey's Abbot was quietly folding up. Esther Comegys was not a serious candidate for Miss Bailey's successor. She was functioning more as a superconscientious Dean than as a Principal-proper—and in any case, she was to leave Abbot in June for an instructorship at Bryn Mawr, where she would continue work on her doctorate. No other obvious Abbot-connected candidates came to mind. Of the several outside-Abbot women whom Constance Chipman was sent to interview, only the principal of an Illinois college seemed just right, but she found the offered salary too low and, worse, found Abbot's history uninteresting—an unforgivable sin in Mrs. Chipman's eyes. The well seemed dry.

Then, from the least expected direction, word reached north to the Trustees of a young English professor and Dean at Hollins College, Virginia, who might possibly be interested in a New England school. Marguerite Hearsey had talked to the Abbot family about the advantages of Hollins in the winter of 1933 when her college was hungering for applicants. Even then both sides were impressed, and since that first visit the grapevine had brought other news of her. Abby Castle Kemper, '31, had gone from Abbot to Hollins, and found Miss Hearsey a wonderfully stimulating teacher as well as a "manager" who had ideas for every occasion—with one left over to create the next occasion. "She was just born to run a place," Mrs. Kemper remembers. When the Hollins presidency fell vacant and the college Trustees chose an older woman, not a few students and faculty there wished Marguerite Hearsey had been named instead.[86] She was a true scholar, with a Radcliffe M.A., a Yale Ph.D., and a soon-to-be-published thesis on Thomas Sackville's *Complaint of Henry Duke of Buckingham*. She had studied abroad and had taught at Wellesley and Bryn Mawr. She knew both the Northeast and the Upper South and might thus realize Abbot's aspirations as a national school. The Trustees sent Constance Chipman to meet her, instructing her to discern how Miss Hearsey would appear to the faculty, to the alumnae, and to the townspeople of Andover.[87] (Did the students' opinion not count?) Mrs. Chipman, entirely satisfied, telegraphed Board President Chapin that the candidate should be invited to visit Abbot forthwith. At a special Trustees meeting on April 8, 1936, Marguerite Hearsey was appointed by unanimous vote Abbot's fourteenth principal, and a new age began.

Singular Women

. . . Above all, intelligence.
—Marguerite Hearsey to opening meeting of
Student Council, September 1941 and 1942

Marguerite Hearsey was a scholar. She came to Abbot, she says, because the years between fourteen and eighteen are critical and exciting in a young woman's intellectual and personal development.[1] She could easily have stayed on at Hollins College; she had already turned down a department chairmanship at another woman's college. In spite of the press of able academics seeking jobs in 1936, she could almost surely have returned to Bryn Mawr or Wellesley, for her superiors in both colleges had hated to lose her when she moved on from her instructorships, first to her doctoral studies, then to her full professorship at Hollins. But this academic was also an adventurer, who had loved equally the detail work of her deanship and the rich contact with students afforded by administrative work in a small college, and she knew that at age forty-three she was ready to "run a place," ready to pour all her energies and feelings into a single institution. No one could fail to notice this emotional vitality, or her big-bone physical health, or her warm capacity for taking others as seriously as she took herself.[2]

Her particular scholarly interests also impelled her toward Abbot. She had a passion for history, and Abbot had plenty of it. She was especially happy to meet Burton Flagg, who had lived through so much of Abbot's history himself; her first request of Abbot after she was hired in the spring of 1936 was addressed to him: would he send her any and all historical material that could be safely mailed to Virginia? Delighted, he replied. Making her maiden address to alumnae in June 1936, she invoked first Philena McKeen and Bertha Bailey, then Christopher Marlowe of the English Renaissance; behind this speech and many later ones is a woman who has consciously stepped in to advance a unique cultural tradition. Finally, she was, like all of Abbot's founders, a Christian who sought the meaning of her own work in the larger social mission of Christianity. Abbot was congenial

40. Miss Hearsey greeting dancers at the Senior Prom, 1941.

to such a "consecrated soul," as the Treasurer would term the Principal at her retirement in 1955. Jesus was to her above all a human being of surpassing courage whose historical reality could speak worlds to young people, given a scholarly interpreter and an articulate voice.[3]

She seemed almost too good to be true. When they learned of Miss Hearsey's appointment, older alumnae who had despaired at Miss Bailey's death—including the entire Fiftieth Reunion class—happily predicted a return to the intellectual vitality of the McKeen period.[4] Another alumna saw promising analogies between Miss Hearsey and Miss Means. The graduates who had been pushing their school to join the twentieth century were thrilled to hear of Miss Hearsey's varied experience, her "wise enthusiasms," and her broad interest in contemporary affairs.[5] If a few of Abbot's own faculty, still grieving over Bertha Bailey, could not bring themselves to wish success for Miss Bailey's successor,[6] most expectations for the new Principal were incredibly high.

Moving to the school in July of 1936, Miss Hearsey set herself at once to fulfill them. She began carefully. She was, it seems, the only person around Abbot who understood her limitations. Knowing perhaps her own tendency to be swept into the emotional tangles of a small academic community, knowing certainly that all good administrators require some minimum of distance from their charges, she had specially requested that the Trustees arrange for her to live in an apartment or house of her own outside Draper Hall, where Abbot principals since 1890 had lived surrounded by students. Trustee Mira Wilson, Principal of Northfield School, gave her experienced support to this plan, and the Board agreed to fix up Sunset Cottage for Miss Hearsey's use. Before school began in September, she was welcoming teachers into her new home with a gentle hospitality absorbed from her nine years at Hollins; students and alumnae would soon follow. New England visibly melted when it crossed Virginia's threshold. Marguerite Hearsey understood also that one woman cannot do everything. Far more readily than Miss Bailey had done, she delegated tasks to others, holding the college admissions and household supervisory work just long enough to understand it and then pointedly handing it on.[7]

Almost immediately, Alice Sweeney became Miss Hearsey's indispensable colleague, to whom she would soon assign college admissions responsibility, the Senior English courses, and, in addition, the crucial post of Director of Studies. The two women were about the same age, but while Miss Hearsey was always somewhat of an outsider to Andover town,[8] Alice Sweeney had lived in the Lawrence-Andover-

Methuen community for most of her life, and had been watching Abbot women's interchanges with outside-Abbot realities for twenty-five years as student, townswoman, occasional teacher, and alumna. Her roots went deep in the Merrimack valley: her grandfather had helped to build the great dam that would turn thousands of spindles, power the cotton looms, and create a city. He also made the family fortune. His bosses delayed giving him his wages for a full year, and after living in squalid poverty beside his fellow Irish laborers, he suddenly had money enough to buy land on the North bank of the Merrimack River, which no one then seemed to want. The next generation of Sweeneys were local public school teachers and newspaper publishers and politicians; John P. Sweeney, father of Alice, Nora, Mary, Louise, and Arthur Sweeney, was a lawyer—and a Protestant, for the Sweeneys left Catholicism without abandoning their Catholic friends, or their catholic sympathies, or their interest in all who struggle upward. Alice Sweeney had gone happily enough to the Methuen high school before following her sisters to Abbot. Secure in her local "place," content to have lived most of her life with her beloved sisters, Alice combined a comfortable, almost aristocratic sense of family importance with an entire lack of pretentiousness.[9] It was a steady vantage point.

And her sight grew keener with years: Miss Sweeney accumulated an extraordinary sense of the relatedness of things, a capacity for absorbing the unexpected while respecting the givens of any situation. This was in character with Abbot Academy at its historic best. Not so much in character was a sense of humor with which she could as readily make sport of herself as of the world in general. A superb teacher, she must have known how good she was, for she never needed to intrude herself on her students' aspirations, nor did she spare them from their failures in search of gratitude. To Miss Sweeney, it could not be kind to be less than honest. Parents were doubtless surprised the first time they learned from one of her Dean's letters that "——— has less than the average equipment for the grade in which she is placed," or that "———tends to substitute efficiency for thought."[10] She was just as direct with students in class. When one of them did well, a "Well done" from Miss Sweeney struck home. Admiring, many Abbot colleagues absorbed these high and frank academic expectations much as Miss Sweeney had nourished herself on the qualities Rebekah Chickering so abundantly possessed. As a practical matter, Alice Sweeney's skill in taking care of the home front was invaluable during Miss Hearsey's many duties away from the school, for the Principal's reputation and experience were soon in demand at meetings and working committees of the Headmistresses Association; the newer

41. Miss Sweeney greeting dancers at the Senior Prom, 1941.

NAPSG (National Association of Principals of Schools for Girls), which she served as both director and President; boards of trustees throughout New England; even as judge at Phillips Exeter Academy Public Speaking Contests.[11] Both Town and Hill were reassured by Miss Sweeney's pervasive presence.[12] The two women's collaboration proved as successful for Abbot as that of the McKeen sisters, for this generous and competent woman made an ideal temperamental complement for her Principal. Supported by Alice Sweeney's capacity for objectivity, Miss Hearsey's ardent identification of self with school could almost always be a source of energy for Abbot rather than a weakness.[13] Miss Hearsey's own estimate of Alice Sweeney? "A great person. I don't know what I would have done without her."

Miss Sweeney, Burton Flagg, Trustee President Barton Chapin, and several other powers from the Andover community were immediately helpful in arranging a reception, so that 800 alumnae, townspeople, and Phillips Academy faculty could meet the new Principal. The party confirmed Abbot's symbiosis with the town, as expected, but it was especially symbolic of Miss Hearsey's openness and cordiality toward the men—if not the boys—of the Hilltop. Before long, Alan Blackmer and his wife had dined at Sunset. Blackmer was already Chairman of the Phillips English Department and would soon be Dean of the Faculty; this initiative opened a social interchange that each faculty found welcome, and Blackmer began to feel something more than the "condescension towards the school at the foot of the Hill"[14] which had been most Phillips teachers' stance in Miss Bailey's day. Never again would an Abbot principal dig such chasms between Abbot and Phillips as did Bertha Bailey. With many other Phillips faculty, the Blackmers sent their daughter to Abbot. After the War, Headmaster John M. Kemper did likewise, and called Miss Hearsey "Peggy." For her part, Marguerite Hearsey openly enjoyed men's colleagueship, and she approached Stearns, Fuess, and Kemper as friends, inviting them to speak at Sunday night Vespers in successive years. In fact, during nineteen years of Sunday nights, women would come from the outside to speak on only six occasions; not once would a woman give the Commencement Address. Thus men confirmed the value of this female institution from a distance, much as they had in the McKeen years. For his part, Fuess renewed Stearns's invitation—rejected by Abbot from 1912 on— to attend Sunday services in the Phillips Chapel, and Miss Hearsey took him up on it for a few Sundays each year.

Of all her male co-workers, the closest was the Board President, Barton Chapin, who greatly admired her and strove to bring her many plans to fruition. Flagg remained official "adviser-in-chief."[15] Miss

Hearsey drew gratefully on his experience, and before acting on any idea that cost money, made certain that he was sympathetic to it.[16] She found that his sense of humor resonated happily with her own, and the two became good friends. However, she listened less to his day-to-day advice as he grew older and gave ever more of it: an administrative colleague remembers often seeing her holding the telephone with one hand and writing parent letters with the other, while the Treasurer went on and on.[17] She did accept the Flagg tradition that the parent who pays the bills is a school's formal client; for fifteen years all Miss Hearsey's and Miss Sweeney's student report letters were written to the fathers. This practice ended only after mothers protested ("This is the second time you have sent a letter to me which is not addressed to me except on the envelope," wrote one divorced mother in 1949, returning the letter). Occasionally after 1950—for fun and for the fathers' sakes—a letter like this from Miss Hearsey arrived home:

My dear Mr. and Mrs. ———

I rather wish that we could send you———'s mid-year grades in the form of a stock market report because it would sound so spectacular to be able to say—"History up, 18 points . . ."[18]

At the same time, Miss Hearsey encouraged women's help, including that of the female Trustees. Miss Bailey's penchant for stocking the Board with Wellesley presidents and deans would be a congenial tradition to Miss Hearsey, and the various alumna Trustees of the period were workhorses whose energy matched the Principal's. Marguerite Hearsey unabashedly asked for a formal vote in all Board deliberations and a place on three major committees, and got them. Already, a few of the older faculty were finding her overassertive once she had decided on a given course of action—for this neophyte Principal was concerned with the details of departmental organization and teaching as Miss Bailey had never been—but Trustees expect to be pushed while decisions are still making, and the Board welcomed its Principal's drive.[19]

Trustees and teachers waited eagerly to see how this educator so knowledgeable about college study would assess the Abbot curriculum. It was reassuring to learn that she found it good. "She would not engage in fads," her endorsers from Radcliffe had written, and while she carefully kept both the faculty and the Board in touch with developments in the larger world of education, her chief faith was in teachers, not in programs. Within her first two years, she had chosen eleven new ones, including Isabel Hancock, a Hollins alumna who had an M.A. from the University of Virginia, and Eleanor Tucker with a B.A. and M.A. from Smith college and two years' experience as an instructor of chemistry there, to strengthen Abbot mathematics and chemistry. The basic College Preparatory requirements stood pat, dictated largely by the Northeastern private colleges:

3 years of English
5 years of languages, (including 2 or 3 of Latin)
2 or 3 years of Mathematics
1 year of Science
1 year of History

College Preparatory students must take at least four courses a term, including electives, and must also take

Physical Education (3 to 4 afternoons a week)
All-school Choral class (2 hours a week)
Bible (one hour a week)

The Trustees added the course in business principles that Miss Bailey and Mr. Flagg had long wanted. Since about a quarter of Abbot students appeared to be weak in reading, Miss Hearsey brought back Jane Sullivan, '31, to teach remedial reading, and later to serve as Alumnae Secretary as well. That Miss Sullivan was Abbot's first Catholic teacher was happily unremarkable, given the Principal's and Board President's endorsement of her.[20] The only traditional subject that Miss Hearsey consciously sought to redefine was Bible study. While Miss Bailey taught theism, Bible had languished. To the new Principal "form(ing) the immortal *mind*" was a scholarly exercise worthy of every student's attention, whatever her faith or lack of it. In time she would draw for support on the position of the American Council on Education, which deplored the retreat of public schools from constitutionally permissible study of the American religious tradition, and urged that all schools teach "the role of religion in our history, its relation to other phases of the culture, and the ways in which the religious life of the American community is expressed."[21] Students were almost immediately to notice that the intellectual exploration of the Bible was taken seriously once more (had they known it, as seriously as in the McKeen-Watson days), while faith was now left to Chapel. A typical alumna remembers Dr. Hans Sidon as "a wonderful man" whose Bible teaching thrilled her "all the time that my religious beliefs were gradually slipping away."[22]

One programmatic decision was required. Once more the under-enrolled Academic Course must be voted up or down.[23] Characteristically, Marguerite Hearsey chose in favor of tradition, and of keeping curricular alternatives that met a variety of student interests. Moreover, the school was not yet full, nor would it be until the following year;[24] this was the wrong time to abandon a program that still attracted applicants. The Principal did propose a more demanding domestic science course. She also admired Abbot's offerings in music, art, and speech; hoping to emphasize these and to reverse the steady decline in music enrollments (from ninety-one in 1926 to twenty-six a decade later), she suggested giving the Academic Course a title more appropriate to its contemporary purposes. Thus "Fine and Practical Arts" students whose major interests were musical, artistic, or domestic rather than bookish continued to enrich the school long after applications began again to outnumber openings, reminding the community that there was more to Abbot than college preparation. The F.P.A. requirements:

> 4 or 5 years of English
> 3 years of Modern language, (or 2 of modern language,
>   2 of Latin)
> 2 years of History
> One year of Science
> One year of Mathematics
> 2 years of Art, Music, home making or business principles
> Physical Education   same as for
> Chorus and hymn singing   C.P. students
> Bible (2 years)
> Senior Bible (ethics)

Courses or activities open to both C.P. and F.P.A. students, in addition to the requirements for each, which could be taken as electives by the other:

> Fourth year French and Latin   Fidelio and Choir
> Review or remedial years in   Elements of Psychology
>   English and Latin   and Ethics
> Astronomy   Problems of Democracy
> Geology   Third year Math (Completion
> Ancient, Medieval and Modern   of algebra and plane
>   and English History   geometry; Trigonometry)
>   Speech and Dramatics

Consistent with Miss Hearsey's interest in world affairs, Problems of Democracy gave a full year's credit, where Current Events had always been more casual. The gradual updating of Literature texts continued, creeping almost always about twenty years behind the present. Fortunately, Ibsen and Robert Frost are always modern. It is interesting to note that the French and German texts Abbot students read under Bertha Bailey were still in use in 1945—and none was as advanced as those given to the McKeen-era Seniors.[25] Oral language training had also deteriorated after the French and German residences were given up at the turn of the century; it would take years for Miss Hearsey and her successor to reverse the trend.

"All is well," said Miss Hearsey to the Trustees both at the end of her first year and in the middle of her second.[26] Yet for all the Principal's knowledge and experience, Abbot found those first two years difficult. Some vocal alumnae expected miracles; students thought new social freedoms would surely follow a change in administrators. "See if you can get back some of the privileges Miss Bailey took away," the Student Council President for 1934–35 had written the President for 1935–36, and some student leaders would press Miss Hearsey still harder for more downtown leaves, for lipstick, for every freedom left behind in home-town high schools. With Big Bertha no longer on the watch, many girls made their own rules, with no one's leave. A blizzard of demerits from on high—for the student proctors were more and more reluctant to give them—seemed useless to cool this petty rebellion, and the heroic efforts of the 1936–38 Student Council presidents to help their Principal accomplished little more.[27] For Marguerite Hearsey it was an unprecedented situation: there had been no young adolescents at Hollins or Bryn Mawr to contest her "methods and procedures . . . of a scholar"[28] with little-girl gripes and surreptitious trips up the Hill, with smoking, or even drinking. Near-frantic faculty efforts to clear the mess only seemed to make it worse. In an informal memorandum proposing smaller dormitories, Flagg expressed his concern to the Trustees about the "confusion" that resulted from "regimentation" of the Draper Hall residents. "It was struggle, struggle, struggle," remembers one teacher, and for a person of Marguerite Hearsey's temperament and training it was bound to be terribly frustrating. As a teacher-scholar, you can have a gem of a class; you can write a gem of a monograph. But there is no such thing—for more than five minutes at a time—as a gem of a school: the whole is too complex. The administrator who carries final responsibility for the whole must grin and bear it.

Finally she did. And though she tended to take student or faculty discontent personally and could not but feel hurt by students' restiveness, she would not give in to it in any fundamental way. Principal and teachers were quite willing to relinquish the age-old black stockings and the ban against Sabbath Day hair-washing, but they added late-afternoon and Saturday Study Halls. They found it convenient to change the free day from Wednesday to Saturday so that students could visit home for one full weekend and two overnight weekends a year—especially since Wednesday was now Phillips' free day, and fraught with the danger of chance meetings between boy and girl—but the basic Abbot routine remained intact. The adults believed in it, whatever the students might think.

Early upsets were compounded by Rebekah Chickering's sudden death while on summer vacation in Europe in 1937, and by a sharp drop in the business index early in 1938 which seemed to portend new trouble for all private schools. The economy bounced back, but nature disregarded men's little successes: three days before the school was to open in September 1938, the worst hurricane Andover could remember ripped through the township, uprooting seventy-one huge red oaks (as old, on the average, as Abbot Academy) from the ancient Grove and scouring the campus of some of its most beautiful recent plantings. "Mr. Flagg was out in the wildness of the storm, seeing the pride of his heart laid low," wrote Jane Carpenter in the *Bulletin*.[29] Though actual damage to buildings was relatively slight, the school's opening had to be put off a week until power returned and the worst mess was cleared. For the old students who finally arrived on campus, the landscape was changed.

Strangely, this meteorological disaster seems to have marked a turning point for Abbot. By mid-fall of 1938 it was clear that things were different in more ways than one.[30] The new Principal had taken hold. The faculty (nearly half of them hired by her) was behind her. The students seemed to have accepted her. Miss Hearsey thought this might have been partly the result of the late opening: told they could not come back to school, most of the reluctant suddenly wanted to.[31] In any case, events were conspiring to help create those subtle chemical changes that make each school year different from the last. Early in the fall Miss Hearsey proposed and the students had tried out a fresh disciplinary "honor system" which was intended to substitute for the mathematical demerit system a set of positive rewards: a "citation" or "rating" of "Alpha" with extra privileges to match for the few most outstanding girls, "Beta" for the majority who deserved the ordinary privileges of the school, and "Gamma" for the shaky sinner until she had redeemed herself—which she well might do, for a student-faculty committee decided ratings several times each year. An offender could be apprehended by other students for wearing loafers, say, or for flirting with bus drivers, then brought before the Student Council and warned of an impending Gamma rating without the faculty being aware of her misdeeds. The Council continued to recommend punishments, including dismissal. Student leaders had helped keep order ever since the early Bailey years, but this felt like a real change.

On the whole, the girls found it an improvement. Whether rating was done at Miss Hearsey's home or (later) in separate student-faculty sessions, it was exhilarating for Council members to have adults listening to their judgments of other girls; most of them sincerely tried to deserve Miss Hearsey's trust, and struggled not to revel in those cattier rating discussions which they could hardly help enjoying.[32] Honor systems were the thing at smaller colleges now; the McKeens' "self-reporting" tradition was still remembered at Abbot. The new system had a chance of working. Inevitably, there were difficulties, for what government satisfies everyone? The Student Council President bore the double burden of persuading her Council to accept and defend Abbot's Victorian rules[33] and trying for her constituency's sake to get the faculty to ease up a bit. Presidents' speeches and the traditional "Presidents' letters" to their successors are filled with warnings and laments:

> You have a tough job ahead . . . [Pres., 1935–37]

> Try to *deeply* impress upon (the Council members) the seriousness of their positions, and that nothing, absolutely nothing, must be carried beyond the meeting. Somewhere there is a leak in the Council and it is very bad. [Pres., 1936–37]

> I strongly advise your having *no gripe meetings*. [Pres., 1937–38]

> It's the worst thing to keep order in Chapel, on the streets in fact everywhere. [Pres., 1936–37]

> Our class has . . . split. We've got to stop Parties after lights and changing of roommates for a night and things like that which can seem so trivial on the surface but which underneath can cause a great deal of damage and ruin. [Pres., 1939–40, in Senior–Senior-mid meeting]

> The Rec Room needs a *very* firm hand. For this and wherever you appoint people, get them from every group . . . so that never does one crowd "take the lead." [Pres., 1938–39]

> I guess you remember that last year was *not* (by far) one of Abbot's best years. [Pres., 1943–44]

No swearing if possible in Council meetings . . . Don't say too much about "spirit" and "attitude." [Pres., 1941–42]

It will undoubtedly be your hardest year, but your fullest and most appreciated as well. [Pres., 1941–42]

Though it sat well with many girls to be adults' allies in enforcing rules, the faculty always had the last word, and some years the gap between adolescent aspirations and adult standards was enormous. Ultimately, few were fooled by the show of student-faculty unity which the opening school meeting always assumed. Now as in years past, a few individuals each year openly revolted against the honor system's expectation that girls turn in their scofflaw peers, though no one ran away from school to avoid cooperating in an investigation of some cigarette-smoking friends, as had happened once under Miss Bailey.[34] As one frustrated Student Council secretary put it after Miss Hearsey's rejection of the Council's Honor A nominees:

May 22, 1946:
One hellish meeting (catty?!) was called for Honor A.
Miss Hearsey came in half way through (no longer catty).
We have to re-consider girls for Honor A; she doesn't
think we did them correctly, although we did them as she is
telling us. (This shows how important Stu G is if the faculty
are not in agreement. We fight, but against stone walls.)
. . . The meeting was adjourned and I have a headache.
                                        Respectfully? submitted

Yet "Stu G" ratings continued. Successive Student Councils tinkered with the system under Miss Hearsey's patient eye, adding a "High Beta" category whose members were free to sleep through Sunday breakfast now and then and to study in their rooms instead of study hall, adding this, adding that; but the essentials remained intact for fifteen years.

A Room of One's Own

One could live with such an arrangement. "Submit yourself gladly to the discipline of mind and character which Abbot—like a wise and kindly parent—will require of you," Miss Hearsey advised her charges,[35] and by 1938, most students seemed willing to take the advice. Overall, the decade following September 1938 had the flavor of a little golden age, similar to the middle McKeen and Bailey periods

42. *The Abbot Faculty, October, 1938: Under the Old Oak.* Top Row, *left to right: Gertrud Rath, Assistant to Principal;* *Lucile Tuttle, English; Margaret Snow, Librarian; Laura Pettingell, Latin; Walter Howe, Music; Ruth Baker, Languages; Louise Robinson, Assistant Secretary; Alice Sweeney, English; Miss Hearsey, Principal; Helen Robinson, Latin;* *Hilda Baynes, French;* *Laura Smith, History.* Middle Row: *Virginia Rogers, Speech; Mrs. Hannah Richmond Duncan, Nurse; Hope Baynes, Financial Secretary; Kate Friskin, Piano;* *Marjorie Hill, History;* *Rowena Rhodes, Physical Education; Mary Dodge, Household Sciences;* *Dorothy Baker, English; Mrs. Roberta Gilmore Poland, Physics; Octavia Mathews, Spanish.* Front Row: *Hope Coolidge, Dietitian; Eleanor Tucker, Chemistry and Mathematics; Mary Carpenter, Physical Education; Mrs. Eunice Murray Campbell, Business; Mrs. Jeanne Vical Miller, French; Isabel Hancock, Mathematics; Barbara Humes, Secretary to Principal. Part-time members of the faculty not shown in this picture: Bertha Morgan Gray, Elocution; Rev. Winthrop Richardson, Bible; Mr. Francis Merritt, Art; Gertrude Tingley, Singing. (Asterisks indicate new teachers.)*

in students' general acceptance of the school's requirements and their enthusiasm for its special offerings. *Courant* editors had begun to write of "the new Abbot" as soon as Miss Hearsey was hired. Now the "new Abbot" seemed to be taking shape; if student government changes were just a different set of clothes on an old body, the girls themselves approached their school with a fresh spirit.

It helped that the few disgruntled Bailey partisans had left or been eased out,[36] and that Miss Hearsey had added a strong group of teachers to those committed veterans who still remained from the Bailey years. Many were young; young and old were willing to involve themselves in all phases of school life. The Spanish teacher taught skiing ("Advance not so much the nose, advance more the *k-nees!*"

she could be heard imploring her beginners). The chemistry teacher loved field hockey. A young British teacher found that ninth and tenth graders could put on a Shakespeare play with nearly as much success as the Seniors. The whole school was show-struck again. Now that money came a little easier, three or four adult drama enthusiasts took 100 students at a time to a Boston Shakespeare production with Maurice Evans or Helen Hayes. And Shakespeare wasn't all, for (almost) anything went on the active Abbot stage. A Yearbook account of *Curse You Jack Dalton* (or *The Villain Still Pursues Her*) described it as "always encouraging when the main character makes his grand entrance and all the decorations fall dramatically on his head."[37] Miss Hearsey chose Francis Merritt as art teacher even though he was a handsome twenty-six years old (something Miss Bailey would never have done), and Merritt began a revival of studio art that later would be skillfully advanced by Maud Morgan, already in the 1940's a painter-teacher of extraordinary talent and now in the 1970's an artist of national renown. By 1943–44 ninety students a year were taking studio art.

The older women who kept their distance were nevertheless richly *present* to students: Kate Friskin's tenth graders in Homestead seldom brought her their problems, but she surrounded them with her music, practicing for hours each day, demanding so much of herself that it was difficult to resist the demands she made on them. "Miss Friskin was the first teacher I ever encountered who took me seriously," says one of her students. "Do you know that from the very first day of chorus, she expected real music from us? This was not what you ask of children! We were to create something beautiful that anyone would delight to hear."[38] Others still conjure up the awesome beauty of the Christmas music, and the yearly ritual the choir itself carried on of walking through the dark corridors carrying candles, singing carols to waken the whole school before dawn of the day Christmas vacation began. Alumnae of this period remember Walter Howe as rather subdued and passive, but Miss Friskin was teaching a full load and performing more than ever in Andover, Boston, and New York. The Principal herself taught the Senior English students one day a week; several recall being moved to a love of poetry for the first time by her sensitive discussion of it.[39] *Courant* flourished with Alice Sweeney as adviser. The editors who served during the 1940 diphtheria quarantine were undaunted by the requirement that every page of proof be baked in an oven before being sent to the printer. ("The *Courant* has been roasted, but never before has it been baked!" laughed Miss Sweeney).[40]

One active *Courant* Board member for that year, Joan List Van Ness, remembers living "most of our lives at a positive boiling point of excitement." "We cared passionately about everything," she goes on, surmising that rich intellectual fare and "a higher standard of teaching than I have ever encountered since" had much to do with this.[41] "You weren't pushed into it but you always found yourself trying things you hadn't dared try before," says Beverly Brooks Floe, '41, who became Editor-in-Chief of *Courant* the following year. Beverly Brooks had failed both mathematics and Latin during a year of illness and came to Abbot convinced of her inadequacy, but Miss Hancock and Miss Harriet McKee simply assumed that she could do them and do them beautifully. She did. She sang in Fidelio for love of Abbot music (and of the Exeter dances which followed joint concerts); she learned fencing first "out of sheer romanticism" from French teacher Jeanne Vical, an Olympic fencer, but kept at it out of appreciation for the discipline and precision the sport demanded. There was never enough time for her or most of her classmates to do all they wanted to do.[42] No individual seems to have felt constricted by established programs. Though the majority were able scholars and knew it ("the rest went to Briarcliff," sniffs one), nothing was static: a C.P. graduate of 1940 went from Katherine Gibbs to real estate management, a Fine and Practical Arts graduate of 1941 eventually went on to teaching and doctoral studies in home economics.

Miss Hearsey tried to know every student. Her effort went way beyond her personal good night to each girl after Vespers, and the Sunday night suppers at Sunset—though these were important too, as were many of the older rituals, including the yearly Christmas dinner, the Ring ceremonies and Tree Songs that had touched adolescent hearts since the McKeen days. True, the old forms of competition still goaded everyone: it took 20 athletic points and a High Beta rating to win membership in the A Society now, 450 points to earn an Abbot Blazer. The names of all Alpha and High Beta girls were read at Chapel. The anonymous student Posture Markers still lurked, watchful for slumped shoulders. But most important for alumnae of these years was the general sense that standards were high, that anyone good enough to be at Abbot in the first place could meet them, and that to do so one would get all the help one deserved. No one was ever sent to a psychiatrist: one dropped out first (or at most went discreetly for summer vacation therapy).[43] The adulthood that the Abbot faculty represented was comprehensible and on the whole admirable at this time. Adolescents were hurtling toward such an adulthood—or toward another future not far afield—and there was serious work to be done! Miss Hearsey's rhyme read in honor of Burton Flagg could have applied to Abbot Academy itself:

> Whether you've taught better that work is play,
> Or play is work, it's hard to say.[44]

The old Puritan equation held.

Beverly Brooks somehow made sure she had Miss Sweeney for an English teacher two years in a row, and Miss Sweeney made sure that no Abbot girl left the school without having read Virginia Woolf's *A Room of One's Own*. This guide to an unencumbered imagination combines ruthless historical analysis of the logic of oppression with a celebration of women's possibilities—given 500 pounds a year and a room of her own. Woolf described the obstacles women writers and scholars face: "The world said (to woman) with a guffaw, Write? What's the good of your writing?"[45] Equally it asked her, why found women's colleges (or academies)? and taunted her: try if you can to match our grand grey halls of learning, monuments to masculine creativity built on the wealth we have wrested from peoples less manly, more ignorant than we, and rightly kept from our women's free use. Woolf's book was an eloquent reminder to Abbot students of all that young women and their schools contend with on the way to a full humanity that is free of self-centeredness and self-pity. At the same time, Abbot Academy seems to have been for many a young woman a room of her own, where her present, personal strivings could find support in a consciousness that generations of women had there striven and succeeded before her. Woolf considered this consciousness of successful forebearers crucial to men's creative accomplishments. Abbot kept it alive through the Principal's welcome in Opening Chapel ("over 5000 girls have climbed these Chapel stairs . . . have sung the hymns we love") and in a host of rituals and traditions that the students of these Hearsey years appeared to love as much as their Abbot grandmothers had. Most simply and pervasively, "Abbot's not good because it's old, it's old because it's good," Marguerite Hearsey would say,[46] and most of her students believed her. It is no accident that of the five woman Trustees now serving the co-educational Phillips Academy, four attended the school during this brief golden age.[47]

No educational ideology seemed necessary to Abbot; history was sufficient. Miss Hearsey gave up Miss Bailey's membership in the Progressive Education Association. True, she did describe to the Trustees in 1941 the outcome of the Eight-Year Study, organized by the P.E.A. to compare the college records of students from relatively unconventional secondary school programs with a comparable group from those traditional high schools that still followed the college preparatory course laid out by the Committee of Ten. The progressive school graduates did as well or better in college. College admissions officers concluded that they might make course-unit requirements more flexible; Miss Hearsey, unimpressed, concluded that her faculty could

43. Christmas Vespers, 1949.

continue offering a curriculum built around teachers' talents and Abbot's traditional leanings toward the arts.[48] Especially after 1944, when the F.P.A. course was abandoned, she felt she must urge faculty against "priming the pump" for college admissions tests.[49] The key to education was teachers who knew their subjects, she said, not cram courses or pedagogues trained in normal schools. Marguerite Hearsey's tenure coincided with the acme of the professional educationist brand of progressivism and with the P.E.A.'s divorce from lay interests and concerns.[50] The Eight-Year Study was the only one of the Association's works she thought worthy of mention. She hired not a single classroom teacher with a college or graduate degree in education. In part this represented a self-perpetuating upper-middle class loyalty to upper-middle class private liberal arts college training—but not entirely, for Miss Hearsey eventually added several language and arts teachers whose formal education was unconventional, incomplete or both. Abbot teachers would visit Putney School and other progressive shops to learn what they had to offer; they would create an interlocking history-English-music-art core course for tenth graders and draw on a variety of specific progressive ideas; but "it's primarily the quality of the teachers" that counts, wrote Miss Hearsey,[51] and which of those chosen high-quality Abbot teachers would disagree? Miss Bailey's faculty seminars had ended; faculty asked for little discussion of educational issues. "We didn't much question what we were doing or why, and neither did the students of those days," says Alice Sweeney. Once Miss Hearsey and Miss Sweeney were satisfied that all was going well with a new teacher, they might offer help but they never imposed it. Thus each teacher also had a room of her own, for better or worse, and would have till Abbot's corporate life was over.

Master Builders

By the fall of 1937 Miss Hearsey was well enough established to join the Trustees in their plans to add to Abbot's material goods. The Depression's worst dangers past, Tamblyn and Brown were rehired to launch the Second Century Fund at last, with $250,000 as its five-year goal. These consultants were already helping six other schools and colleges raise from $500,000–$4,000,000; their analysis of Abbot's constituency convinced them Abbot could find its half-million with a decade or so of effort. The Trustees had recently retained Mr. Jens Frederick Larson of Dartmouth College, a distinguished and ambitious institutional architect, to advise them on expansion of library, living, and dining space. Though Draper Hall was only forty-five years old, its original pinch-penny construction was already beginning to tell. The foundation under the dining-room staircase had begun to sag in mid-Depression; the supports buckled and the staircase leaned dangerously. Flagg solved this problem with a new concrete foundation and steel bracing, but no amount of tinkering could restore fourth-floor dormitory space lost to fire regulations, for the Fire Department did not approve of an escape system which depended on individual "fire ropes," employed largely for fun or for night escapades once students had been instructed in their use, seldom during Abbot's frequent fire drills.[52] The ceremonious prediction that the memory of Warren Draper's "benefactions will outlast the Hall that bears his name"[53] seemed likely to be borne out all too soon. On the other hand, Larson looked at tough old Abbot Hall and waxed lyrical. He thought it must have been designed according to some standard Bulfinch plan if not by Charles Bulfinch himself,[54] and he immediately proposed that all new construction be of similar design. Excited and hopeful, the Trustees and Miss Hearsey put all their dreams into an appeal to Edward S. Harkness, who had given a $7,000,000 gift to Phillips Exeter Academy six years before.

The appeal is important as an expression of Abbot's values during the Hearsey period, even though Harkness refused to respond. "During its long and honorable history," it began, "Abbot has educated many young women who have won distinction themselves and many who have become the mothers of distinguished sons. The ideal of Abbot has never been a 'feminist' one. Thorough and solid in its instruction, from the first it has aimed constantly at the cultivation of womanly qualities. It places much emphasis on art and music and offers good training in 'Home-making.' "[55] The appeal quoted Abbot's Constitution and described the school's fund-raising effort, then criticized the present accommodations for one hundred girls in Draper and twenty-five in the cottages. No official document had ever expressed such discontent with Abbot's traditional living arrangements: "This division is not only undesirable from a practical point of view, but it is illogical and unsound from an educational point of view. It allows for no reasonable grouping of the girls, nor for any natural and close relationship between teachers and girls." As little as $12,500 of Harkness money added to Second Century funds would allow demolition of the long southern wing of that aging elephant, Draper Hall, and an entire remodeling of the rest that would lower the roof and redesign the facade in accordance with Bulfinch-Larson specifications. This new "Draper Hall" could accommodate a kitchen-dining room, a library, and forty Seniors. Would Harkness also pay for two or three small dormitories of about twenty-seven girls each and endow salaries for three additional "Dons or Counselors" so that Abbot, like Exeter, could foster "constant and natural association" between youth and adult "during these most impressionable adolescent years?" "We conceive of education as a process involving the entire life of a young person"; would not Harkness make this possible "for girls as well as for boys" by giving Abbot $282,500?[56]

No, Harkness would not. Not for Abbot, not for girls anywhere.[57] The Trustees began a retreat to less ambitious goals, determining that at least the top two stories of Draper be amputated, that a new roof and exterior be constructed in the Bulfinch style of Abbot Hall, and that two new wings in the same architectural tradition be added. But the fund was limping, short of $50,000 in spite of prodigious campaign efforts and expensive efforts by Tamblyn and Brown. All Miss Hearsey's trips and speeches, all *Bulletin* pulls on alumnae heart strings,[58] and the "tactful cultivation" of the sixty-one "large gifts" prospects[59] could not change the fact that the 1938 recession had halved stock market values once again. An alumna's letter in December 1938 apologized for the size of her contribution, asserting that it would have been more, "if the author of our 'fireside chats' were not so uncertain a quantity, and the future . . . less dark."[60] Another added, a year later, "Of course if things continue on the inclined plane, we shall probably all end our lives at the county farm."[61]

Fortunately, one Abbot friend was just rich enough and just eccentric enough[62] to give $50,000 for a dormitory on three conditions: that it be built immediately, that it be named for her, and that she be given an 8 percent life annuity on the contribution.[63] Gratefully, Abbot accepted this gift from Emily Abbey Gill, and work on Abbey House, a dormitory for twenty-six students, started in the spring of 1939. Just two years later construction began on the two new Draper wings, in spite of ominous sounds of war in Europe and the Trustees' fear of strikes, inflation, and short supplies, soon to be borne out. The buildings rose, even while the total fund seemed stuck at $130,000 and Flagg grumbled about $5.00 contributors who owned yachts or the costliness of Tamblyn and Brown's advice.[64] Ten thousand dollars of contributions were memorials to Bertha Bailey, $7,500 to Miss Chickering, and $24,000 to Miss Means; dining room, reading room, and library were built and equipped with these funds. Unfortunately, roof reconstruction had to be abandoned after the builder discovered that Draper's west foundation was weakly made of "field boulders poorly laid with large voids" and must be rebuilt;[65] as it was, the total cost

came to $71,000 more than total contributions. For the first time since
1890, Abbot went in debt to finish the job. Flagg procured a 1.5
percent loan of $20,000 from the Andover National Bank, where he
still served as director, and borrowed the rest from the endowment.[66]

A world out of joint favored such bold action. Robert Hutchins
went so far as to ask "What good are endowments?" in an article
which Miss Hearsey reported to the Trustees a year before Pearl
Harbor; he answered his own question by invoking the futility of
"conserv[ing] assets for an unpredictable future, the conditions of
which we cannot ever guess."[67] Still, it seemed a drastic risk for the
traditionally frugal Abbot Trustees to take, and one senses from accounts of Trustee deliberations that lacking Miss Hearsey's optimism
and Barton Chapin's responsiveness to her constant pushing, it would
never have been taken at all. Yet it paid. Increased enrollments during
the War were to bring in a surplus of at least $20,000 every year, and
more than restore the endowment to full strength. Sitting on its refurbished physical plant at War's end, sitting on an endowment of
$514,800 in 1946, a far larger total than that of any other school for
girls (even if endowment interest was now only half of the 5 percent
of pre-Depression days), Abbot Academy could be extraordinarily
pleased with itself. As in the late McKeen era, dreams that outstripped
Abbot's capabilities had produced real gains, despite the odds.[68]

Again War

Rumbles in Europe had long sounded faintly at Abbot Academy. A
speaker compared Hitler, Stalin, Mussolini, and Roosevelt in 1934,
and QED held a debate the same spring on the subject "Resolved,
that Nazi Control in Austria will endanger the Peace of Europe." If
most students were at first oblivious to foreign affairs,[69] the many
Abbot teachers who had studied or vacationed in Europe kept in
touch with European friends, and worried. A British countess spoke in
1937 on the dark mood of English youth. Miss Hearsey asked (and
received) the Trustee's permission to hire a Jewish refugee "on a maintenance basis" in December 1938, as Shady Hill School in Cambridge
was doing.[70] With the invasion of Poland, *Courant* writers and Saturday lecturers came alive to the impending danger. Just as had happened during World War I, war began for Abbot Academy well before most of the nation had any interest in war at all.[71]

For Marguerite Hearsey, as for Miss Bailey, the danger without gave
point to the educator's mission. At Opening Chapel in 1939, she told

all Abbot that "we must be willing to go into a sort of voluntary training for service to a world so needing our help." In the spring of 1940 she urged alumnae to come to Commencement to be "reconfirmed in your faith that a school like Abbot is an influence of incalculable value in our modern social order."[72] Her antennae were especially sensitive to the drawing in of Great Britain. She had done several years of YWCA war work in World War I; her academic field was Elizabethan England, and her heart was with the British as they began to buckle before the juggernaut. "In the face of such suffering and heroism, we all feel, I am sure, that there is no place for self indulgence, for littleness or laziness or softness," said the Principal in 1940, in her opening speech to the school. Students made plans to devote the year's Bazaar to British war relief, while the Trustees agreed to provide full scholarships for British Refugee children. The Principal had hired Dorothy Baker, her first British teacher in 1939, and Miss Baker soon offered to seek out six English girls who could make good use of Abbot. The youngsters were chosen, packed, and ready to sail (one had been "so proud of my white dress," which had taken "some scheming" and many ration coupons to acquire)[73] when an evacuee transport was bombed and sunk, drowning hundreds of children, and the British government decided to allow no more to leave that year. It was a great disappointment, for Abbot had wanted desperately to help.

Another chance came early in 1941. Ten eastern private schools cooperated to fund a British ambulance unit, and they invited Abbot to join them. Miss Hearsey jumped at the idea. She brought in a British friend fresh from the London nursing stations to join her in speaking to the school through a two-hour special meeting about the project, hoping to convince both girls and teachers that Abbot Academy should support an ambulance unit all on its own. If the entire student body would contribute all the cash they had or could raise, if the faculty would sacrifice a portion of their salaries, and, most of all, if parents would make contributions according to their means, a $10,000 Abbot ambulance could roll. Yes, yes, said everyone. "Overwhelmed with exhortation . . . we dazedly voted away our allowances and every other little amenity of our somewhat option-lacking lives," writes one alumna.

"A few hours later, sobered up" from the afternoon's "revival meeting," she goes on, some of the older girls had time to decide that they "had been railroaded." "Taxation without representation!" exclaimed one, and the slogan started around the school.[74] These students knew how much work it had taken to earn just $1,000 for worthy causes at the last two Bazaars. Earlier in the year, QED had seriously asked in one of the student-run Chapel services, "Is Hitler's defeat essential for the United States?" All who took Bible had heard Reverend Richardson argue for pacifism and neutrality.[75] Students were no more sure than were their parents that the nation, much less Abbot, should commit itself heart and soul to Great Britain's cause. Though they wanted very much to join the ten-school ambulance project, they balked at footing the whole bill. Had advanced Anglophilia possessed both their Principal and all their teachers, they wondered? Or was this simply an assemblage of strong women distressed by their helplessness to fight a man's war?[76] Spontaneously, the group made Beverly Brooks, '41, their spokesman; all of the *Courant* board, most of Fidelio, then the school itself quickly followed. Beverly went to Miss Hearsey and described the students' mood. They would gladly raise all they could through rummage sales and canteens, and they were planning an all-out Bazaar, she said, but they could not see soliciting parents or forcing a sacrifice of $1.25 weekly allowances for what should be an inside-Abbot volunteer effort.

Now it was Miss Hearsey's turn to be incredulous. She could not believe her students would protest this generous, heart-felt proposal—and indeed, she seems to several alumnae to have felt sure they were rejecting her, not just her idea. Sadly, she retreated from the $10,000 project. Yet a visitor on campus would not have guessed that anyone was rejecting anything. The Seniors' canteen was supplying snacks as good as the downtown fare, and it had become a mark of patriotism to forego luxurious food in Andover or new Easter clothes at home. Miss Hearsey would not agree to let the most enthusiastic skip Sunday night suppers, but the school ate one spartan meal each week, and donated the savings to the cause. "We worked terribly hard," say two of the leaders. Another still holds shreds of resentment against the administration for throwing bureaucratic roadblocks in the way of some of the most promising projects merely (she thinks) "because we had opposed Miss Hearsey's original fund-raising ideas and had mounted our own drive for the ten-school ambulance." Rumor convinced many Seniors that the faculty had considered withholding the diploma from at least one student leader for stirring up the younger girls, and that they might well have done so had not Alice Sweeney and a few others turned the tide. When the Student Council unanimously recommended this same girl for an Honor A, the faculty rejected the recommendation. Whatever the cause, there was tension to spare between many Abbot students and adults that spring, as well as a "wretched inner turmoil" for individual students who greatly admired their Principal and her idealism but felt out of phase with her expectations.[77]

Eventually, things quieted down. The faculty allowed the endangered student leader to graduate cum laude with her class, and wished her Godspeed; the students sent nearly $2,000 for the ambulance and British War Relief. In a sense it was nothing but one of those spring tempests in a boarding school teapot, yet it plunged half the two upper classes into a soul-search that several still remember as one milestone on the way to womanhood: respected adults could go overboard.[78]

On December 7, 1941, Abbot's only Oriental girls, a Chinese and a Japanese, walked off together down the Maple Walk, both equally upset. The formal entry of the United States into war cleared all ambiguities and divisions for the rest of the school, however. "We shall try to avoid emotionalism . . . Our orders are to carry on," Miss Hearsey told the students the next day, before instructing them in air raid procedures against Japanese fighter-bombers. Flagg arranged $1,000,000 worth of war damage insurance with Merrimack Mutual and passed the purchasing lessons of his World War I experience on to Hope Coolidge, Abbot's unflappable household superintendent. Teachers helped townspeople with plane spotting, students again took defense courses (Home Nursing, Motor Mechanics, World Events), ate "golden rule" dinners, rolled bandages, and waited on tables to replace the maids who had left for defense plants seeking more than the eleven dollars a week they got from Abbot Academy. Odeon, ADS, and the other societies were suspended for the duration. "Study, Save, Strive for Strength" was the wartime Abbot slogan, and for the most part everyone measured up. "This is no time for 'education as usual,' for anything as usual," wrote the Principal. "The War will not wait. Total war must be totally waged."[79]

Stimulated by the national discussion of training priorities, the faculty considered changing the emphasis of the curriculum from liberal arts to applied sciences, mathematics, modern languages, and other immediately useful skills.[80] Phillips Academy ran a summer school to offer such training to young men hurrying toward enlistment; should not Abbot do its part? On second thought, however, Abbot decided with many other girls' schools that a liberal arts education was the best defense of those civilized values the Axis sought to destroy. As in past wars, American men would fight, and the traditional American culture would "have to be sustained largely by women."[81] John Dewey and other philosophers of the original Progressive movement had urged schools to deemphasize this "cumulative experience of the race," to cultivate instead the young person's immediate sense of purpose and his capacity to solve those problems he himself identifies.[82] But Abbot Academy was already simmering with purpose within an "embryonic community" such as those Dewey advocated for all schools.[83] "Our School is a little democracy," Miss Hearsey often said in Chapel; if one could discount the process by which the elite gathered at Abbot in the first place, the statement was credible now that wartime fervor had overcome student preoccupations with style and status—the way to set off one's string of pearls against one's Shetland sweater, for example, or the place to buy exactly the right "reversible" raincoat (which one never reversed).[84] Petty divisions vanished before the great national task.

As in the Depression years, travel was limited (spring vacations were canceled to avoid it) and one must make the best of Andover Hill. "The sense of community was stronger during the war than it would ever be again," remembers Eleanor Tucker. Fancy entertainments and casual Boston trips were out, but each teacher's tea set served her colleagues in turn, while students roller-skated around the Sacred Circle. Homegrown shows were mobbed. Music, drama, and dance faculty jostled each other for stage space in Davis Hall (and music usually won—"You had to try to hold your own against Kate Friskin," says Miss Tucker); about sixty piano and voice students each year gave recitals; with the help of her husband, Phillips Art Instructor Patrick Morgan, Maud Morgan arranged Phillips-Abbot art competitions; Phillips and Abbot students mounted Gilbert and Sullivan operettas together for four successive springs, the first joint productions since Miss McKeen had allowed the *Haymakers* Chapel space in the 1860's. The stiff "calling hour" was abandoned for informal Friday night dancing in the recreation room. One girl broke her leg jitterbugging, but the dancing went on. An alumna has written that the "warm and sheltered life within the gates" contrasted strangely, sometimes disturbingly, with the "savage forces outside" as girls tried to put their fears aside and concentrate on school responsibilities. For some who had taken on serious summer jobs, Abbot's rules suddenly seemed insulting; for others, the school was a haven.[85] It is interesting that Miss Hearsey herself found time in the middle of the war to write a poem for the *Christian Science Monitor*.

> So still the woods that dappled light and shade
> Lie gentlier, and ants moving in moss

> Seem noisy in their immemorial trade.
> Soundless, the pines with slow rhythm toss . . .[86]

No one need worry overmuch about the liberal arts at Abbot.

Unlike most secondary schools, Abbot kept nearly all its teachers, adding only a few refugee or other European teachers to its staff.[87] For ten years after Pearl Harbor, fully one third of Abbot's twenty teaching faculty were European born, European educated, or both. Abbot had drunk of European culture since the Civil war; now the cup was filled every day by teachers who had seen the Spanish Civil war or the French Resistance first hand.

Applications soared. The trend had begun in 1939 as college entrance competition intensified, but the war hastened it so much that the school had filled its 130–143 boarding places with promising applicants or returning students by March of almost every year; and many had to be turned away.[88] Boarding tuition had already returned to $1,400 in 1937; it mounted to $1,500 in 1945 and $1,700 in 1948, to meet a 50 percent war and postwar rise in wholesale prices. Still, it was lower than almost all other eastern girls' boarding schools,[89] and parents newly affluent with wartime wealth could pay it.[90] If IQ tests measure anything, applicants' academic ability was also higher; 14 percent in 1938–39 had IQ's in the 80–98 range, (15 percent were over 120) while in 1941 only 3.4 percent fell in the 94–100 range. By 1949 the average IQ for Abbot's 190 students would be 118; the Seniors who had made it all the way through averaged 125.[91] Abbot was not unique. "All of the good preparatory schools are overflowing this year," said Miss Hearsey in the fall of 1944.[92] In part the competition for college admissions was responsible, for by that year the major women's colleges could accept only one in four or five applicants; but the disruptions in families where parents were undertaking defense work or serving abroad must also be accounted. Yet Abbot applications would keep on growing during these postwar years when many schools went hungry for students, as though parents were continuing to seek some still, orderly place for their daughters in a troubled world.

One World

V-E Day found Abbot thankful, and already preparing for worldwide peace and brotherhood. Miss Hearsey prayed with deep emotion for the millions of young heroes who "in their courage and devotion to the cause of righteousness, followed the way the Master went." The Choir was ready with several suitable anthems of thanksgiving. For over two years, Abbot had kept in close touch with "World Peace Plans" as one of the monthly wartime discussion groups was entitled. Beginning in the fall of 1943, Abbot mounted a series of lectures on Postwar Problems, including experts on Russia, on China, and on plans for international organization and cooperation. Miss Hearsey joined Alan and Josephine Blackmer to speak on the Dumbarton Oaks proposals at the Andover Public Library; she regularly brought news of the ambitious discussions of "World Citizenship" from meetings of the Headmistresses Association and the NAPSG. The students raised $2,000 for the World Student Service Fund in 1946, more than any school in the country.[93] Briefly, Andover was considered as an alternative to New York City for the permanent site of the United Nations.[94] Abbot students participated in World Youth Forums, in World Government weeks, and in model international free-trade councils; they gave Bazaar proceeds to the World Student Service Fund; a small group of World Federalists campaigned vigorously inside the school.[95] One World was coming, if not here already, and Marguerite Hearsey's Abbot was determined to be part of it. It would be a far more complex world community than the Utopia which the nineteenth-century Abbot had envisioned—where all humanity were to become evangelical Protestants—but it would be as surely One.

Practical postwar problems at Abbot required attention: Should students continue to wait on table in spite of the sacrifice of dignity that went with the rush and clatter of well-intentioned amateurs?[96] (After a trial of the old system it was decided that the maids were too slow and too unreliable, so student crews returned—including "dawn patrol" for the breakfast waitresses.) How should Abbot handle the crowds of visitors and parents that arrived almost every week now that cars were available again, bringing fresh applicants or requests for special week-end leaves for their daughters? Miss Hearsey eventually appointed Isabel Hancock as Admissions Director and hostess, and set up a yearly Parents' Weekend to alleviate part of the problem.[97] Yet none of these deterred the Principal from the challenges her idealism had posed her. "Noblesse oblige," she would tell her students, and not with a snicker.[98] She had been working for years to sharpen her professional colleagues' interest in private schools' responsibilities within a world soon to be done with tyranny. From 1943 on, all those Anglo-Saxon lady-principals sat together worrying the problem at their New York meetings, sincerely concerned with eliminating their students' sense of Anglo-Saxon superiority, though most of their schools had thrived on a clientele that sent its daughters to them partly to enjoy that supposed superiority.[99] A 1944 exchange of letters between the Rogers Hall Headmistress and the Phillips Headmaster suggests the ladies' courage in even considering Negro admissions. Miss McGay had asked Fuess to keep his one black Glee Club singer home from a joint concert-dance at Rogers Hall.

> Dear Mr. Fuess:
> Quite frankly I still feel like a *worm* to have refused our hospitality to any one of your students. However, I believe that our girls are not old enough to handle such a situation tactfully [We have several from the South who] would be in a state should any one of them draw him for a dancing partner.
> Miss Katherine W. McGay, [November 30, 1944]

Fuess's reply is understanding:

> . . . the situation is different with girls than it is with boys, as I know only too well. Personally I have, I think, no prejudice whatever against Negroes, but I should not like to have them attend our P.A. tea dances, and so far as I am aware, they have not done so . . .

This was a slight improvement over a letter Fuess wrote that same year to an alumnus, in which he stated that the two Negroes attending Phillips were enough; more might cause "excitement and trouble."[100]

Few girls' schools served Jews, much less black students. Abbot, at least, welcomed occasional Jews, brought in black musicians, poets, and lecturers on interracial problems, and sponsored student-faculty forums on minority groups in American life. Oriental students had been to Abbot for decades, including a Japanese girl who had come from Tokyo just before the War to stay through 1942, and the first of the three Young girls who came by way of the Philippines after their father had been murdered by the Japanese.[101] Most of these had loved the school; a few had been top scholars. Abbot was to Genevieve Young, '48, a haven of "order and stability" with its invariant schedule, its polished tea silver, even its constriction of choices. She loved English history with Anna Roth, whose passion for her subject "was so great that your knees knocked and you felt totally wrung out after one of her classes,"[102] and her teachers say she developed brilliantly as a student. Abbot was also accustomed to giving scholarships. The Young sisters had full tuition-board grants; so did two sisters from India and four daughters of Oxford professors; so did Minola Hapsburg, daughter of a deposed Rumanian Princess, who spent several of the war years at Abbot.[103] Most scholarships were small ones spread thin, however, and the percentage of tuition income added each year to the endowed scholarships had fallen from a Depression year high of 11 to a steady 5. Miss Hearsey had been hoping since 1943 to increase and systematize them through a group-scholarship system similar to that of the Seven Sisters Women's colleges.[104] After 1946 a chock-full school could afford to invite three or four girls each year from families without resources, as well as ten to twenty for half tuition.

Abbot knew, if most Americans did not, that thousands of black families could now afford half or even full tuition for private school. Alice Sweeney had been especially cheered to watch the accretion of Jewish, Italian, and Syrian names appearing on the roster, and now she wondered aloud why Abbot should have no Negro students. A Jewish alumna[105] wrote her soon after the War to pose the same question. Students talking with a black social worker in Miss Hearsey's living room after yet another lecture on interracial understanding asked what Abbot was *doing* about it.[106] Together, Miss Sweeney and Miss Hearsey decided Abbot was ready.

Miss Hearsey's first step was to write a respected Abbot father in Rome, Georgia, for his opinion. In his reply he expressed his fears for an interracial Abbot's future. The school would risk the withdrawal of any Southern girl who had to attend a social occasion where male Negro callers were present, and he promised he would withdraw his own daughter if Negro girls were admitted; so would most of his fellow Southerners. After "many years thought," he had concluded that

> The Negro, with many fine qualities, has other qualities which are very undesirable, and are apparently not affected by education or circumstances. Accordingly, I believe that social intermingling should be avoided, since I think it will lead to intermarriage . . . [107]

This was a blow, for Miss Hearsey had been actively and successfully recruiting Southern students; but she persisted. She wrote the Principal of Emma Willard to ask how her one Negro girl was faring. (Fine, was the answer, though the girl has tactfully kept potential black boy friends away.)[108] Miss Hearsey warned the Trustees that Negro girls might soon apply to Abbot on their own, and told them Abbot should make ready either to welcome or to refuse them.[109] She continued to educate them against racial stereotypes, speaking (one feels, with admiration) as much to her own biases as to theirs, for she had a Virginian's pocketful of pickaninny stories which she had used quite often in speeches before 1944.[110] Though most of the Board waxed receptive to her repeated reminders, the kindly Irving Southworth resisted. "It just wouldn't work," he would say.[111] His wife was a Southerner; he had been a Trustee since 1923 and Clerk since 1934, and at Abbot the enduring held much influence.

For three years no black student applied. Then one applied and was rejected: her academic record suggested failure at Abbot. Finally Irving Southworth died. Miss Hearsey called a Southern friend who knew a few of Atlanta's distinguished black families. In the late spring of 1953 the Principal was informing all Abbot parents that Beth Chandler from Atlanta and Sheryl Wormley from Washington had been accepted for admission, and by midsummer three families had withdrawn their daughters. This news did not daunt the Chandlers: Beth's father had been one of a handful of blacks at Middlebury College and had done well; her older brother was at Middlebury now, and her grandfather lived in Andover. Still, Professor and Mrs. Chandler wanted to make certain Beth knew what she was in for. Was she sure she still wanted to go to Abbot? they asked her. "I don't see anything wrong with me," Beth Chandler Warren recalls saying. "Therefore it's their problem, not mine." Thus she entered her Senior-Mid year as an almost-fifteen-year-old, hungry for the academic challenges her local high school could not give her and looking forward to everything Abbot, Andover, and Boston had to offer. She had decided she wouldn't care whether she made friends or not.

Few Abbot girls, if any, had ever known a black person who was not a servant or a porter; one wondered where Beth's stocking cap was, another why her hair wasn't greasy. Beth told them. They learned to laugh at their ignorance, and she got on fine. There was a near crisis when Beth and her closest friend, a white girl, decided to room together for Senior year, and the girl's parents refused to allow it. Miss Hearsey asked the two girls if she could help. Shortly after this a tactful letter from the Principal arrived at the home of Beth's friend, describing the advanced degrees Beth's parents held. It was irresistible: the white parents changed their minds.

Many minds changed in those years at Abbot Academy. "The stereotypes were just shot to pot," says Beth. Beth's stately grandfather came to visit, his British accent still crisp from his young manhood in Jamaica. Her brother came calling from Middlebury, but no more Southern girls withdrew. The faculty waxed nervous at Commencement time: youngsters were one thing but what would the white parents think? "Are we welcome?" Sheryl's parents asked Alice Sweeney as they drove into the gates. "Indeed yes," replied Miss Sweeney, but she had no way of being sure this was true. As it happened, not a ripple of resentment showed. No one could know how close was Supreme Court-ordered integration when two lone blacks entered Abbot; just a few predicted the social revolution that would be under way by the time Beth Chandler graduated with many honors in 1955. And while Abbot had joined up late to claim any medals, the school grew proud of its own small part in that revolution, for however few and however harassed at times, each of its black students was transformed in the minds of her white peers from token to highly valued friend or associate.

Marguerite Hearsey would also leave Abbot with honor in 1955. Several trying years were to precede and follow her retirement, however, years of dissonance between Abbot's standards and the changing aspirations of its students. Dissonance does not preclude individual growth; on the contrary, it often engenders it. But Abbot and its faculty were unaccustomed to serious contradiction, and it would be tough going at times. Fortunate it was that Miss Hearsey had built well during her first dozen years, for some of the best things about Abbot in its final decades were continuations of her initiatives.

The More Things Change,
1945-1963

. . . The more they remained the same at Abbot Academy. Abbot moved, of course; but the world was speeding by so much faster that what strikes one is the amazing inertia of the place, a conservatism partly deliberate and useful, partly perplexed. Although Marguerite Hearsey would retire in 1955, her successor would do all she could for at least eight years to hold Abbot steady amid the tide of change, keeping to the course that had been set in the years following the War. Such changes as Mary Crane did wish to make were resisted by forceful faculty perennials loyal to the Abbot they had known under Miss Hearsey. Those that succeeded were dictated by external pressures more than by internal purposes.

If a school's success can be measured in applications and enrollments, then Abbot was wise to resist rapid change, for while demographers predicted doom for private school enrollments through the early fifties and the President of Harvard did his best to persuade good citizens to send their children to comprehensive public high schools, Abbot's applications steadily increased. Those good citizens wanted their children to get into colleges like Harvard and Radcliffe, or they wished sanctuary for their daughters from worldly confusion, or husbands for their daughters from Phillips Academy or a share for them in a family Abbot tradition—and in ever greater numbers they had the money to buy these things, for family income rose as rapidly as family aspirations for a first-rate education. By 1960 Abbot Academy was riding the crest of the postwar baby boom. Only the tensions of the sixties would prove powerful enough to dislodge the school from old complacencies and set it on a conscious search for a new future.

Teachers and Students
and How They Grew

*Even the most dedicated twentieth century
adherents of Victorianism suffer from a
progressive decrease in certainty.*
Stanley Coben, 1975

The young are insatiable.
Marguerite Hearsey to the Trustees, 1950

Teachers

Through the ten years following the War, Abbot melded new and old with its usual confidence. The half-dozen teachers who joined Abbot immediately after the War found themselves part of a vital community of women, proud of their profession and backed by long tradition. Perhaps the most colorful novice was Germaine Arosa. More students than ever wanted French, and the techniques of language teaching that had been developed during the War were turning teachers back to the oral-aural emphasis in which Abbot had specialized before Miss Bailey came on the scene, and away from the exclusive study of College Board grammar that had become all too common on Andover Hill.[1] Since she was a professional *diseuse*, Mlle. Arosa was a French speaker par excellence. She arrived at Abbot in the fall of 1945 after a decade of touring the nation and delighting audiences by her costumed re-citals of eighteenth-century French songs, monologues, and dances. Travel was exciting, but at age forty-three she wanted a home, and Miss Hearsey, certain that this artist could also teach, offered one.

"She took a chance on me," says Germaine Arosa, who had never taught French to American girls in her life. She was entirely free of American pedagogical tradition, a law unto herself. It was bound to be difficult at first. Mlle. Arosa was aware of great expectations for Abbot teachers but found it hard not simply to fall back on her own school-girl experience in an authoritarian *gymnasium*. The youngest girls were terrified; Miss Hearsey gently reassigned her to French II and III classes. Other colleagues helped too. Alice Sweeney's good-humored response to the new teacher's woes could transform a classroom disaster into an experience to build on; Anna Roth helped her to pick herself up and go on when she thought she had failed as a teacher. She found a fellow artist and warm friend in Kate Friskin, who shared supervision of the Homestead girls with her and whose transatlantic experience spoke to her pride in the cultured Parisian society of her girlhood. Miss Hearsey had already encouraged her to go to Middlebury for a summer's training, and the Trustees would later make a five hundred dollar grant to help her study eighteenth-century poetry at the Sorbonne so that she might add a fifth-year French course.

Above all, she relied on Miss Hearsey. "Marguerite was a queen," says Mlle. Arosa now. The Principal's trust in each of her appointees' capabilities became self-trust in the new teacher, and it was not long before Mlle. Arosa was acting queenly herself. Some younger teachers and timid students found her energy, her physical beauty, and her self-confidence—verging, say a few, on arrogance—overwhelming. But if "arrogance is a common quality in the French," as one of Mlle. Arosa's American colleagues insists, the Mademoiselle was an education all by herself. Among Abbot Academy's greatest strengths was its refusal to stamp teachers in a single mold: within its gates she could be "a woman of extremes" whose very presence was always interesting.[2] Abbot gave Germaine Arosa a fair field for her own growth—her "blossoming" as she calls it—and plenty of strong students and fellow teachers who delighted in her humor and refused to be intimidated by her.

Another character off a stage was Emily Hale, the British-trained teacher of drama who came dropping names of renowned friends and associates, casting herself as she would ingeniously cast her students in the roles that allowed most scope for their abilities. For many years a college teacher of drama and literature, she had the reputation at Smith of being "an affected snob." T. S. Matthews, a more recent critic, terms her "arrogant," but also "intelligent, elegant, immensely discriminating,"[3] a Boston Brahmin who conversed, acted and taught so supremely well that her poses reflected the realities of her talents. Matthews gives her a full chapter in his biography of T. S. Eliot, for Emily Hale was Eliot's lifelong friend. She was in love with him when he was an undergraduate at Harvard; she expected to marry him; and her friendship with him ran so deep that she was able to forgive his "impossible" marriage to another—"a temporary lapse"—and remain his closest woman friend and confidante for forty years, still hoping eventually to be his wife, say her friends in both Andover and England.[4] After Eliot left his wife in 1932, he turned to her for solace and companionship. It was she who took him to see Burnt Norton for the first time during one of her English holidays. She read many of his poems in typescript, apparently gave him valuable criticism of a few, and shared her enthusiasm for them with favorite Abbot students.[5] He visited her often; he wrote her over a thousand letters—which we may not see till the year 2020—but he never encroached too far on her spirited independence, though he was the one person for whom she would willingly have relinquished it. On three occasions during his visits to Abbot, he talked about his poetry with the Seniors or with students who were rehearsing *Murder in the Cathedral*, after instructing Miss Hearsey not, under any circumstances, to advertise his presence, so that he could stay on good terms with his agent.

Emily Hale made Abbot her home for the final ten years of her working life, leaving only after Marguerite Hearsey retired.[6] She found friends capable of high repartee all up and down Andover Hill, and fellow Abbot teachers found in her a wonderfully stimulating colleague. "A good person was Emily Hale, intelligent, sensitive, a really fine teacher," Alan Blackmer remembered. Though college entrance competition waxed ever fiercer during her years at Abbot, students clamored to act in her demanding productions just as though term papers did not matter. Eliot made his most enduring tribute to her in his *Family Reunion*: she is Aunt Agatha, says Matthews, "the strongest character in the play and the only one who from the first is aware of what is really happening."[7] To her Abbot students she was much more than a stage presence. Says one, "She found and woke in me an imagination that no one else at Abbot had touched upon."[8]

Others who would stay long arrived by 1948: Dorothy Judd and Shirley Ritchie for athletics, Carolyn Goodwin for mathematics, and Mlle. Marie Baratte, fresh from years of privation during the French Resistance, who found Abbot's New England simplicities luxurious by comparison. Several older teachers combined with Miss Hearsey's earliest appointees and two of the Britishers to become a kind of "court" for the Principal,[9] a group of friends who went with her to her family's summer home in Jaffrey for several days each summer, who entertained her and themselves with a ritual of Canasta parties and country drives during the academic year. So generous with herself and so often sensitive to criticism, the Principal seemed especially to need the uncritical affection of others, and this group gladly provided it, somehow staying free of "that everlasting touching of the nerve" which so often characterizes the faculty groups within "the small room" of a women's school or college.[10] "We all worked, we worked terribly hard," say two survivors, but when they played, they played. "Abbot was a ready-made social life for an unmarried woman"—"a family," our "whole adult life," these two remember.[11]

Miss Hearsey included all the faculty in dinners and receptions for speakers, for the mayoress of Andover, England, when she visited on the town's three-hundredth anniversary, or for the Trustees. Marie Baratte was not one of the in-group, but Miss Hearsey watched over her like "a wonderful mother," warmly encouraging this shy newcomer to give her best.[12] Interestingly, Miss Hearsey also managed special appreciation for the few who preferred independence to membership in the "court." Carolyn Goodwin would not play Canasta on order, or wear the required decorative hat downtown if the weather suggested a woolen scarf to her instead. Other teachers were shocked when she and Alice Sweeney changed places in Chapel, upsetting the seniority seating so that Miss Sweeney, who had become quite deaf by 1948, could hear better; but Miss Hearsey didn't care. She watched Miss Goodwin and Miss Sweeney go their ways and seemed to know, as subsequent principals would also know, that she needed the special perspective they brought from their distance.

Once the War-related vacancies were filled, most teachers settled in with the veterans to stay. The faculty lost only one long-time colleague in these years: Walter Howe committed suicide. For years Howe's ebullience had tended to change without warning to mild depression;[13] more recently his sight had been failing. He tried to hide this by hours-long practice for each Sunday hymn or organ-prelude, but it got harder and harder.[14] Shortly after the Christmas service of 1948, he turned on the gas in his kitchen and lay down to die. For Abbot, it was one of those personal tragedies which hurt a close community so deeply—or hold so many embarrassing overtones—that they are seldom made known outside. It says much of Miss Hearsey that she did not hush it up but sent a brief letter to every student describing what had happened, preferring the truth to schoolgirl fantasies. Howe was strictly an outsider to the community of women, of course, but at his best he had been a fine teacher, and he was long missed by faculty friends.

Students

Given Abbot's capacity to nourish a variety of excellent teachers, it is disconcerting to learn how many alumnae of this period found the place difficult or deadening for students. Elizabeth Marshall Thomas, '49, once sent Abbot a dime.[15] And though twenty years later she sent Abbot her daughter, her single year at the school left her hating the place. Elizabeth's one-year status made her an atypical student, for she never had the time most had to adjust—if not to resign themselves—to Abbot restrictions, and she came from an unusually liberal family who had granted her the independence her extraordinary intelligence seemed to command. Any girls' boarding school would have been alien; her perspective was that of the disaffected minority which all schools harbor. Still, in a small community like Abbot, the disaffected affect everyone, and their perceptions describe certain aspects of reality. Elizabeth spent most of the free time she had with a "large, solid clique" of friends, most of whom had had "zero choice" about coming to Abbot, as she remembers.[16] Some were enrolled by their Abbot mothers, some shipped from South America for a proper New England education; others, like Elizabeth, were there on the recommendation of some college admissions official who felt the candidate needed a year of growing up before entering college. By Commencement time she had won entrance to Smith, and "Miss Hearsey was ready with a post-ceremony pitch to my father," who agreed, with a $250 contribution, that Abbot had made it all possible. ("He had to: she was bigger than he was," laughs Elizabeth.)

Now a writer and a college English instructor, Elizabeth remembers Abbot teaching as the best she has ever had. "College was easier than Abbot" says she—say scores of other alumnae. Biology under young Louise Coffin was "marvelously done," Miss Roth was a "magnificent, fiery teacher," Miss Sweeney was "nice, strict," a kind of missionary for her own "wonderful standards" of taste and workmanship. Ever since, sitting stubbornly through bad movies to the end, Elizabeth has remembered Miss Sweeney's advice to walk out. ("You lose more by staying than by leaving," she had said; "She's right," says Elizabeth.) Drama with Miss Hale was stimulating; the French teacher was sweet and kind in class.

But out of class? To Elizabeth and her circle of friends, there were no out-of-class relationships with teachers. Adults seemed miles away in their own world unless they were enforcing the rules—watching for lipstick and improper footwear, or on patrol through the Phillips campus; "chaperoning" telephone calls[17] and checking mail for Andover postmarks and return addresses to make certain Phillips boys and Abbot girls stayed *incommunicado* except on occasions arranged from above. Since Abbot began, Abbot students had more or less accepted the space between teacher and girl. "When at school I looked up to my dear teachers as occupying a station wholly above me," an 1865 graduate wrote to Miss McKeen, "and when you spoke to me so tenderly I would scarcely ever keep back the tears."[18] None of the students Elizabeth Marshall knew wept tears of happiness over teachers' attentions. Fewer each year accepted the adult-student gulf: in the decades following World War II, it became a problem to be solved.

Among other things, Elizabeth Marshall Thomas has taught writing at the Massachusetts Correctional Institute in Walpole. There, she has observed, wardens and prisoners are purposely kept from making friends; now Abbot seems to her to have been a kind of prison which unconsciously used the same means of social control. To most alumnae the analogy would be extreme, but to the few it was apt. When one Senior who really liked the school was caught smoking for the first time and suspended, her friends felt they had no one to whom they could appeal to reverse the ruling, though undoubtedly there were willing ears on the faculty.[19] They only despaired—and returned to the studied rule-breaking which made out-of-class life bearable for them, checking off their sins in the rule book one by one. "We had never known such a loss of freedom," Elizabeth remembers; "the very dullness of it all" made you *like* academic work, she says, and numbers of graduates through the mid 1960's echo her lament.[20] Student Government officers were the "trusties" who turned in offenders who refused to honor the honor system and turn in themselves. According to a 1954 alumna, the free-spirited developed "a whole system of deception" to get messages to Phillips boys—delivering notes through day students or dropping them under designated bushes. The same girl, though "an atheist then and now," took Confirmation classes downtown and actually got herself confirmed, "just to get out of the walls on Wednesday afternoons."[21] Elizabeth Thomas admits that she smokes precisely because Abbot so vehemently forbade it; others remember the elaborate exhaust-piping system which one Draper Hall crowd ran from their "smoking closet" to an open window, and the drinking parties that climaxed the spring term of Senior year. Drinking was the worst thing you could do: temperance was an ancient cause at Abbot; Andover still tended to frown on any educator who bought a cocktail in public. It was in 1950 that the preps in Sherman House bloodied their fingers carving a secret compartment into the floor of Room E, a safe place for cigarettes, beer, a favorite onion extract that was 80 percent alcohol ("tastes God awful," wrote a 1957-58 resident), and—eventually—for twenty years' worth of secret letters to the next year's inmates written by tradition the night before Commencement.

The letters instruct new girls how to hold a secret midnight party for town boys on the roof, and advise that "You can do almost anything here . . . Mrs.——is so lazy . . . but watch out for Mrs. B., the maid. She prys around your room and tells Hatchet about everything." "Butter up to Hatchet, D & B, and you'll go places. I know cause I didn't."[22]

For her part, Miss Hearsey blamed the rebels' restiveness on their families, who had provided their daughters with "little education at home in accepting any limitation in freedom."[23] But Elizabeth Marshall's questioning went beyond prohibitions against drinking (which she understood) to the core of Abbot's values. "Why was the faculty so intent on having the school go on in that crazy old fashioned way?" she wondered then and wonders still. "Abbot was the only place I'd heard of in 1949 where 1849 was still preserved." Though "Miss Hearsey always listened" when students dared ask her such questions,[24] she could not give to such as Elizabeth a satisfactory answer.

What grated most upon this alienated minority was being expected to admire and cheer the school when you were angry at it. "It was like East Germany," says a 1955 graduate. "You were just constantly being rounded up to do stupid things that nobody in their right minds would want to do, and having to sing songs about what a good time you were having." This woman's memories of forced daily worship in Chapel bear no resemblance to the "simple and reverent" services of the Means years.[25] Year after year, Student Council minutes describe the futility of "Stu G" efforts to control hymn-book slamming, gum-chewing, reading, whispering, and note passing. No longer was the Abbot constituency almost uniformly Protestant Christian and church-going. Some of the Catholic families—along with unchurched girls—chafed against the Bible requirement, and one girl left in 1948 because the school refused to release her from Bible study in order to spend more time in the art studio.[26] A few Seniors even refused to sing the "Parting Hymn," protesting that their lives and futures were entirely their own, not "portioned out to me" by God above.[27] Of the prayers Miss Hearsey led at Vesper Services which some students found so beautiful, Elizabeth Thomas says simply, "They were lost on me. I didn't let them in."

Yet even those to whom teachers were "the enemy," found solace in friends and fellow sufferers.[28] Miss Hearsey's efforts to attract interesting applicants brought a brighter, more various group to the school than ever. The children of Latin American diplomats and businessmen took the place of the missionaries' daughters. Alumnae of certain classes[29] mention the intellectual stimulation of their peers before any of Abbot's more formal offerings. The rising national divorce rate

meant that for a number of girls, Abbot friends became a kind of sur-
rogate family;[30] these counted themselves lucky to have landed in a
school where a tradition of care for fellow students had been passed
from one student generation to another for more than a century. The
secret Sherman House letters contain as many offers of comfort and
help to new preps as enticements to rule-breaking. "No matter how
you feel about Abbot," says one, "it's so terrific to be able to make
friends like we have." "I learned . . . how to love" in this school and
this room, says another.[31]

Students of almost all backgrounds enjoyed exclusive friendships
and crushes that were much like those rich relationships of Harriet
Chapell's day. "It was entirely accepted for tenth grade girls to fall
in love with Seniors," one alumna of the early fifties remembers.
Her own "powerful alliance" with a younger girl proved a source of
strength to both, and grew into a friendship far more durable than the
dozen red roses which the younger delivered to the elder—along with
a "passionate letter"—once each week in the spring before graduation.
These two did not feel the freedom Harriet and her friends had enjoyed to express this quasi-physical affection, but they poured into it
their inmost selves, and each found in the other a confirmation of her
worth as a person. "All my friends had tenth graders too," says this
woman, who now combines a career as teacher and therapist with
equal responsibilities as wife and mother. Though relatively few students were sophisticated enough to cope with the barriers Abbot
threw up against natural and easy friendships with boys, these girl-to-
girl affairs absorbed much psychic energy. Teachers seemed to understand their importance to the girls, and did not interfere; a few, like
Emily Hale, encouraged them in a friendly low-key way by inviting
"pairs" to tea.

There was other comfort. Through most of the 1950's Abbot teachers shared their students' confinement to a large degree; many sympathized, and provided what parties and treats they could to make
things jollier.[32] The adults had to wear hats and stockings downtown
too. They also wondered (with amusement) whether they should be
eating their potato chips with their forks, if their dining tables were in
sight of the one over which Latin teacher Marion DeGavre presided,
though most agreed with the student who later wrote "Mrs. D" of her
admiration for "a person who knew what table manners were."[33]
Though they could skip the required Saturday evening "entertainments," they had to be on their corridors with their doors open two
weekends out of three and every weekday after 4:30. They could not
have private telephones, or smoke in their rooms, or skip Tiffin or

Chapel or lunch any more than students could. Germaine Arosa felt she "had had [her] life," and did not mind, but she knew how hard it was on younger teachers. Some teachers shared students' pet hates as well. Perhaps the most distasteful of the Abbot adults to such as Elizabeth Marshall was the secretary who guarded the entrance to Draper Hall like a local FBI agent, assiduously listening for boys' voices on the extension phone, checking male callers in with suspicion and out with relief; but some of the faculty also suffered from her zeal. Every time she spoke to you, remembers one teacher, "she would get something out of you that you didn't want to tell her," and report it all to Miss Hearsey, whether Miss Hearsey wanted to hear it or not; she recalls her initial pleasure at being invited downtown for tea by this woman, and then her surprise when the occasion proved to be a quiz session about her department chairman. Similarly, many younger faculty no more enjoyed downtown or dormitory patrols than the girls enjoyed being constantly watched.

A few students admitted they'd brought it on themselves. Spy work among the girls seemed more and more necessary as the student leaders became ever less willing to push one another toward righteousness or judge peers who had gone astray.[34] The "Honor A" was given up in 1951 after several years of irreconcilable faculty-student dispute over the nominees,[35] and fewer students were willing to report themselves for offenses like listening to the last presidential election returns, as Carol Hardin Kimball dutifully did in 1952. Little concessions such as being allowed to wear make-up to the Exeter-Andover football game no longer thrilled the girls[36] but merely whetted appetites for more.[37] The "Citation" or rating system failed badly in 1946–47 under a weak Student Council,[38] and was abandoned altogether in the early fifties in favor of a shifting, uneasy combination of "honor rules" and general rules enforced largely by the faculty. It was small comfort for Alice Sweeney to reflect on how natural it was for girls who had taken unusual responsibilities in wartime to wish more freedom in peacetime,[39] or for Marguerite Hearsey to learn that other headmistresses were experiencing many of the same problems.

Yet in spite of all, many students thrived at Abbot through the postwar decade. They say they didn't expect to be closer to faculty than worlds apart, or that they found a satisfying foothold in classroom interchange. If one rather shy 1955 graduate dreaded the way Mlle. Baratte "humiliated" her in class no matter how hard she worked, most girls loved her as she loved them.[40] As might be expected from a girl afraid of the gentle Mlle. Baratte, this alumna has extreme memories of Mlle. Arosa's treatment of weaker students—"she'd stomp on

their fingers as they were clinging to the cliff." A Phillips teacher recalls both her extraordinary knowledge of French drama and her way
of embarrassing her clumsier actresses to tears in front of the Phillips
actors during rehearsals of the Phillips-Abbot French plays ("she was
terribly difficult to get along with, but she certainly knew her
stuff");[41] and Germaine Arosa herself acknowledges that some students found her "a terror." Yet there are many others who loved her
volatility, who thrived on her determination to face her students with
their faults and show them how often success follows only on struggle
and near failure.[42] Beth Warren had had no oral French in her Atlanta
high school: "at first I was petrified" of Mlle. Arosa, she says, but "the
terror" brought her along with loving firmness. The French "stars"
were the Mademoiselle's special pets. "She owned us, and she said so,"
says one, who also recalls Mlle. Arosa's special gift to her: "She taught
me to laugh at myself."[43] Ambitious French scholars often preferred
her to the kinder, softer American teachers of which Abbot had its
share. More than one alumna recalls Mlle. Arosa's after-hours kindnesses: a full evening spent listening to one girl whose worry over her
parents' troubled marriage had made concentration on French verbs
impossible, for example. Dorothea Wilkinson found her British-bred
standards of excellence exactly consistent with Abbot's rigorous expectations, and for years she passed them on to her English students.
A few who knew Miss Hancock in her earlier days as a corridor
teacher remember her as "The Virginia Creeper" whose crepe-soled
shoes allowed for a swift approach to unsuspecting rule-breakers,[44] but
many, many more are grateful for her enthusiasm for astronomy, the
quiet skill with which she took a trouble-maker aside and talked her
into a constructive act such as helping her to clean the telescope, her
hospitality and warmth as Admissions Officer after 1957, or the extraordinary effectiveness with which both she and her younger colleague,
Carolyn Goodwin, taught mathematics. Miss Tingley brought color
with her voice teaching, say her students, and Miss Judd carried the
spice of friendly sarcasm to the athletic field and later to her Spanish
classes.[45] Many Student Council members who had tangled with teachers over school-government issues agreed that "the faculty are really
pretty fair; they just need reasons."[46] Beth Chandler Warren says that
the trick was to "pick out the best of what was there." There was true
Christian kindliness if one spoke her need to others, as well as the
institutional altruism expressed in the annual Christmas party for indigent Andover children and every season's contributions to the Hind-
man school or other good cause.[47] There was "the joy of an Andover
spring, the mischief that was permitted at Intervale."[48] There was

above all "the wonderful tranquility of the place," says one of the women who spent some of her adolescence smoking in the Draper Hall closet. Through its varied faculty, Abbot offered students "a whole spectrum of approaches to womanhood." By its strict ordering of community life, its very determination to take some decisions out of adolescent hands (Shall I drink or not? How much time shall I spend with this or that boy?), the school cleared time and space for that "peaceful collection of self" which is the young person's most important task. "How safe we were!" marvels another grateful alumna.[49] Once they had got over what one Southern alumna calls "the shock of confinement," all who more or less accepted the rules found much the same support for growth and accomplishment throughout the earlier fifties that prewar students had enjoyed, and dissolved as readily into tears over the singing of "Abbot Beautiful" at Commencement.[50] And finally, almost every alumna speaks of Marguerite Hearsey with either awe or affection. Elizabeth Thomas says, "I remember being very touched by her—I still am. She was honest, tough, very intelligent. I liked her . . . she was doing very strong things: to be so out of touch with modern times required a lot of character."[51]

New Faces

Miss Hearsey was still several years younger than Abbot's retirement age when she decided it was time for her to leave. At 207 students, the school was larger and more in demand in September 1954 than it had ever been.[52] The endowment Flagg and his colleagues had built was worth $1,000,000. The 125th Anniversary drive was nearly complete; the alumnae looked strong and willing, if not very affluent; new traditions—an all-school picnic at Crane's Beach, the Principal reading Winnie-the-Pooh aloud at Intervale, and many others—had established themselves among the old; above all, the faculty seemed stable and competent. Miss Hearsey was secure enough not to feel indispensable; except for some student government problems, the school had got along well under Miss Sweeney during her year's leave in 1946–47. Early retirement seemed only sensible for a woman who had further plans of her own in mind: to try some new teaching projects while she had ample energy, and to set up housekeeping with her great friend Ella Keats Whiting, with whom she had lived for some years before taking her job at Hollins, and who was dean of Wellesley College at this time. Miss Hearsey also had, she says, a sense that some of the parents whose daughters she took in charge needed an empathy

44. Miss Hancock with a student in the Abbot observatory.
45. Christmas dolls dressed by Abbot students as gifts to the children of the Hinman School in Kentucky, 1949. Andover Art Studio photo.

46. To South Church for Easter Services. Look Photo Service.

she could no longer give them: she and they stood now a full generation apart, and that, she thought, was too much. She felt herself losing
rapport with some of the bright, aggressive girls she had once thoroughly enjoyed, the ones who always, always wanted still more freedom than she had just newly granted them.[53] She had reflected on the
causes of this constant push at a talk to the Boston Abbot Club in 1949:

> It is an interesting phenomenon that while the average school-
> leaving age in the United States, and therefore the age of de-
> pendence, has been extended, there has accompanied this change
> a contradictory process, a steady lowering of what might be
> called the age of protection. Freedom of choice, freedom of
> action, removal of adult supervision begins earlier and earlier in
> our social life.[54]

By 1950 parents, too, were urging Abbot to loosen up in places;[55] yet
boarding schools were expected to be just as responsible as ever for
"dependent" adolescents, and Miss Hearsey felt that Abbot had eased
up on rules to a point where they had reached a bare minimum. If
girls insisted that "some of those rules were *made* to be broken," as
one alumna concludes in retrospect,[56] well, better for rebellion to
spend itself on forbidden eye shadow or fleeting, proscribed rendezvous with Phillips boys than on boundless experiments in dissolution.
Liberty was not a right but an achievement, a status one could amply
earn through Abbot-imposed "discipline and work," as one alumna
gratefully wrote her;[57] or, as Marguerite Hearsey herself said in 1949,

> The only truly free and released individual is the one who has
> voluntarily bound himself to something greater than himself.[58]

Perhaps most pervasive was Miss Hearsey's well-schooled knowledge
that history always moves on, or, as Alice Sweeney terms it, "an in-
stinctive sense that it was time for a change, that someone with a different point of view could now direct more successfully the future
development of the school."[59] She would miss everything, from Sunday morning parent conferences and Student Council meetings to the
planning sessions for each year's bazaar or prom, and those clumsy,
touching notes from Hilltop swains like the tenth grader who wrote
her his regrets just before the big dance: "Due to a case of mumps I
regret my kind acceptance of your invitation." But she would not
wait, complacent, for bitter ends.

The most hardened advocates of a more self-centered freedom were
moved by Miss Hearsey's announcement of her retirement. "It was as
though doom had hit the school," says Beth Warren, '55, who recalls

the tears wept at the unexpected news. Suddenly, no principal could be better. The ceremonial leave-takings were rich with the poetry of reminiscences, with presents given and received, with letters of appreciation.[60] There was just one reassurance: Mrs. Mary Hinckley Crane, Miss Hearsey's successor, was already working at the school, a teacher of English and history of art much admired and liked by all who had come to know her in her one year at Abbot.[61]

The Trustees had long searched for a new head at a time when experienced women administrator-scholars were almost impossible to find.[62] A large group of the faculty expected Eleanor Tucker to become Principal, but "Tuck" herself felt that she was not ready.[63] The last generation of pioneering spinsters—whom even Elizabeth Thomas admired—was nearing retirement age, and relatively few college graduates of the twenties and thirties had committed themselves to administrative careers with the enthusiasm of Miss Hearsey's or Miss Bailey's contemporaries. At last Abbot's old friend Marion Park had suggested that the Trustees look in their own backyard, for one of Bryn Mawr's most promising graduates was right there. True, Mary Crane had never taken anything like the administrative responsibility that Abbot would require—she had been absorbed in taking care of her family—but she was a warm-hearted, intelligent and skillful teacher as well as a practicing archaeologist with considerable field experience.[64] She was also a mother with four young daughters of her own. A widow, she needed a home and a good education for her girls, but more important, thought the Trustees, these restless mid-twentieth-century students might find a family woman more accessible, more sympathetic to their own aspirations than they would another unmarried principal.[65] "Here is just the breath of fresh air Abbot needs," thought Helen Allen Henry as school opened in the fall of 1955.[66]

It certainly was a change. There were little children in the Abbot dining room for the first time ever: curly-haired Juju, just four years old; Lucy, a little older, who seemed to one maiden teacher "always to be crying"; the two eldest, junior high school age, doing their best to help their busy mother field her students' questions and oversee Juju's food intake at the same time. There were also men on the academic faculty. Paul Werner, a rather elderly part-time mathematics teacher, who came with his abrasive and energetic English-teacher wife to live in Ripley House, felt conspicuous and self-conscious at first;[67] but John Iverson, Abbot's first full-time male teacher, soon moved into Cutler House next door, where his wife added ten Abbot boarders to the two small Iversons already in her charge.

Almost immediately, Mrs. Crane put her stamp upon a new Abbot catalogue. Photographs of smiling, busy girls crowded out the somber buildings that had graced catalogues of the Hearsey years. Sunday was still described as "a day of quiet," but the school was no longer labeled "definitely Christian," and special mention was given to the Abbot girl's opportunities to meet the boys from the Hilltop. The fall "mixer" was Mrs. Crane's first social innovation. It seemed to be a great success: certainly it attempted to fulfill the promise many prospective parents had seen in Abbot's position half way up Andover Hill, a promise—Miss Hearsey herself acknowledged—that brought many candidates to Abbot in the first place. Mrs. Crane agreed with her predecessor on the value of a self-sufficient single-sex school, but her emphasis was slightly different. To Marguerite Hearsey the very closeness of the two schools had meant that Abbot must guard its girls all the more strictly.[68] Under Mary Crane, the censoring of telephone calls and the confiscation of Phillips-Abbot mail would gradually disappear; in time girls could actually sit with boys during the second half of a football game and walk with their callers in the Grove at specified hours Saturday afternoon. Similarly, Mrs. Crane agreed with her predecessor that "children are less and less disciplined at home" but she was willing to entertain the possibility "that we really do have too many rules."[69] Mrs. Crane encouraged the "town meetings" which brought together all interested students and faculty once a term or so for an open discussion of school problems. Lights-out time for older girls crept later and later from the original 9:30 curfew, till Seniors might stay up till midnight with special permission. Throughout her eleven-year tenure, Mary Crane would search always for the reasonable response to the students' "annual crusade for change,"[70] instead of taking refuge in tradition, as a few older faculty wished she would do.

At Abbot, however, tradition was so powerful that substantive change was never made if stylistic change would do. Off-campus leaves were a little more plentiful by the early 1960's, but Abbot still dictated its girls' dress and demeanor on trains and planes and whenever they were in Boston, Andover, or nearby towns. No proliferation of chaperoned occasions could disguise the prohibition against meeting any boy outside of "the supervision of the school,"[71] or talking with male passersby for more than two (later five) minutes. (Teachers were obliged to time such encounters whenever they noticed them.) The silver napkin rings and linen napkins were still standard equipment brought from home. Mrs. Crane's deep religious faith, as well as her constant effort to act it in her daily dealings with students and faculty and to communicate it in Chapel, helped to continue Abbot's Christian tradition against mounting odds.[72] Though there were a few new fourth- and fifth-level language and mathematics courses and more girls took five courses in response to college demands, the number of course choices remained about the same through 1960. Except in studio art and in one English course, the content changed little. The English and Latin teachers continued to defend the value of Latin as a major course, much as Miss Hearsey had done in an elaborate argument-by-memo with Phillips Headmaster Fuess just after the War;[73] Ann Werner taught a section of Latin I as well as Advanced Placement English because she was certain that English grammar could best be understood by those steeped in Latin grammar.[74] A 1957 graduate says that Mrs. Crane's own once-a-week Senior English class "was the *only* time during my stay at Abbot that I was taught anything about current trends or thought in the U.S.A. We knews lots about ancient Rome, but almost nothing about modern times."[75]

The biggest difference between the Hearsey and Crane administration came in the two women's styles of leadership, for Mrs. Crane was neither mover nor shaker by nature: rather than dominate events she would steer them along their natural course. If faculty or Trustees rebuffed one of her proposals, such as her fervent request for a regular psychiatric consultant to help the occasional girl in serious trouble, she backed off and did not pursue the issue. "Plus ça change, plus c'est la même chose," Mary Crane wrote the alumnae in the fall of 1964;[76] by the time she resigned in 1966 there seemed no doubt that she had done all she could do to accomplish what the Trustees seemed to expect of her when they hired her: keep this fine school going much as it is.[77]

Teachers Again

"Mary Crane's great contributions were her warmth as a person and her interest in getting good faculty to continue," says Eleanor Tucker. Mrs. Crane learned immediately that mere interest in competent teachers was no longer enough. The old definition of the Abbot teacher's responsibilities was one tradition she felt should not be left to "the momentum" of the Hearsey years which otherwise sustained the school through most of the Crane era.[78] During her last few years at Abbot, Marguerite Hearsey had found it ever more difficult to recruit live-in teachers who would supervise dormitory corridors, take their turns at weekend chaperonage and bell duty, and so forth.[79] Emily Hale agreed to return in 1948 only if she could move to an apartment.[80] A few

47. Mary H. Crane, Principal, 1955-1966.

teachers already lived outside the student corridors on the fourth floor
of Draper; now they, too, moved off the campus. Miss Hearsey set up
a weekend refuge for off-duty faculty in one of the Abbot-owned
houses on Morton Street; she puzzled over how to make "a more adult
form of living" possible in an age when students flocked to the corridor teacher's room to listen to her radio or play their records far
more often than they came for quiet counsel.[81] In 1944 she had begun
to organize Teacher Work-Load Study Committees; new ones were
formed every five or six years. Yet one wonders if her heart would
accept any drastic change. Either the committees decided that teachers' corridor duties could not be sacrificed without great loss to
teacher-student relationships,[82] or teachers found they could not bring
themselves to press their complaints with a Principal who worked so
tirelessly herself and held so much trust in her faculty's capacity to
do likewise.[83]

Mary Crane poured no less energy into her job, but she understood
from personal experience how much adults need some privacy. She

herself had required a separate house as a condition of her hiring, and it would be a constant struggle for her to keep students from using her home as a drop-in social center, a struggle she generously gave up as her own daughters became Abbot students and sought a place to entertain their friends, both male and female.[84] Besides, she was now the one who had to find new teachers, full sixteen of them in her first two years, half of these corridor teachers. It looked like high time to implement the recommendations made by Miss Hearsey's last Teacher Work-Load Study Committee. The group had divided on the question whether to substitute house mothers for corridor teachers, but they made many suggestions for getting the academic teacher out from under the blizzard of trivial duties she had been expected to undertake.

Progress would be slow. Mrs. Crane surveyed the field from her position as chairman of the Teacher Recruitment Committee of the NAPSG, and kept in touch with the efforts of her colleagues in other schools. Her wish to create a more natural community by inviting men to teach would remain hollow, for few men teachers would work for the pay Abbot could offer as long as they were in high demand in boys' private schools or in the public schools: John Iverson stayed just one year before seeking a greener pay envelope. The new Yale and Harvard Master of Arts in Teaching programs, which by their concentration on scholarly disciplines promised to overcome the dis-parities between private-school recruiting standards and those of public schools, availed Abbot little where public high schools tempted the M.A.T.'s with salaries Abbot could not match and a democratic rhetoric to which many idealists responded. Mrs. Crane did hire several new college graduates who did not want state certification.[85] Though she was not an aggressive recruiter,[86] some able women came her way looking for a first job. She also persuaded the Trustees to create po-sitions for several excellent part-time teachers, some of them highly educated Phillips Academy wives who preferred jobs of their own to dispensing tea and sympathy on the Hilltop.

Finally, beginning in 1960, she allowed the corridor teachers to move out of the dormitories one by one, replacing them with house mothers. Only a handful—Marie Baratte was one—preferred to stay. Now new candidates found Abbot more attractive. The old guard had got what they had earned—and they moved thankfully into the apart-ments Abbot opened up for them in Sunset or other houses. In time, most realized that something had been lost—though never regretfully enough to return to corridor duty. Kate Friskin was now only a music teacher, not a counselor who would leave piano practicing to comfort a miserable Junior in her special charge. Those few like Eleanor

Tucker who could be simultaneously a jolly friend and a competent teacher[87] were no longer so accessible as before. Distant though faculty had seemed to students under the old system, they were more so now. "We were a family," says Germaine Arosa, "and then quite suddenly, it was finished. There was no more family: there was a teacher and girls."

For some of the older teachers this sense of loss was sharpened by Marguerite Hearsey's absence. "She was the head and we were part of the school through her," Mlle. Arosa remembers. A few of the "court" became the core of a new in-group, which took Mary Crane in hand, advised and helped her from day to day (or, in one young teacher's view, "told her what to wear or what to do"). But it wasn't the same. Mary Crane was terribly busy with students and daughters. The Friday night Canasta-and-talk sessions at Sunset were no more; rare now were those parties for speakers or Trustees from which Miss Hearsey's teachers had regularly drawn a sense of the larger significance of their work.[88] Though many outside the old Hearsey "court" found Mary Crane extraordinarily accessible and kind, or admired her scholarly mind and enjoyed the enthusiasm with which she spoke to the receptive (including students) about "the things she loved" in classical art or architecture,[89] she could not spare emotional energy for many close collegial friendships.[90] And because "we were not included," as one teacher put it, some felt less obligated toward the school.[91] Thus an inevitable result of the residential change was that the Principal herself must take on still more of the students' complex problems, this at a time when the school was larger and more unwieldly than it had ever been before. Mrs. Crane talked endlessly with unhappy girls or anxious parents, so much, say a few, that some routine parent communications were neglected. A girl in trouble came first, or a grandmother who found herself suddenly responsible for her Abbot granddaughter—her daughter caught in the double bind of a mental breakdown and a messy divorce—and needed help right away, lots of it.[92] Routine must stand aside while Mary Crane listened and with compassion counseled the whole family.

While some left dorms, others left the school. Gone now were the secretaries and administrative assistants like Barbara Humes, Mrs. Ruth Reeves, and Gerda Kaatz who had been willing to work nights and weekends as Miss Hearsey's "stalwart lieutenants."[93] Some of their chaperonage and extra office duties fell again on younger teachers, though Mrs. Crane repeatedly suggested that the Trustees hire enough staff to release teachers for teaching.[94] The more Phillips-Abbot social occasions there were, the more chaperones seemed needed. Dorothy

Judd guarded the Abbot gate on mixer nights, and watched the hedge and Circle, others were sent on "bush patrol" during every tea dance and prom weekend. Mrs. Crane felt each teacher who drove a car must take her turn checking the routes of "approved walks" to prevent unapproved rendezvous; and well might the faculty worry, for students say that the mixers and tea dances bred more of these than ever. Resident faculty could still smoke only in Baronial—must still, if they wished to go out for a drink, find a place to do it where they could be sure neither Abbot parent nor Trustee would see them.[95]

Given all this, given the availability of jobs elsewhere, it is not surprising that teachers went and came with increasing rapidity. The average length of tenure fell from nine years in 1954 to 6½ in 1964— or 4½ if one discounts the six veterans remaining from the early Hearsey years. Abbot was not alone. Mary Crane brought numerous reports from professional meetings that other private and public schools were finding it difficult to hire, and keep, good teachers.[96] A few came fresh to Abbot from college and left in two or three years to marry, but both found and gave much strength while they were there. Blair Danzoll, who later became Headmistress of the Bryn Mawr School, was one of these. Students recall her superb classics teaching—and she thinks of Mary Crane's confidence in her as a crucial ingredient of her willingness to dare large tasks. Hilary Andrade-Thompson served as English Department Chairman just two years before returning to her native England, but she is remembered as an extraordinary teacher and colleague. A few others remained long: Pamela Tinker, a skillful science teacher, came from England under Miss Hearsey to stay a single year—and stayed for ten under Mrs. Crane. Twelve of the Crane appointees taught until the merger of Abbot and Phillips in 1973; eight of these stayed on at the new coeducational school.[97]

The new teachers brought fresh life to traditional courses. Students who took studio art with Virginia Powel wanted to spend so much time painting that Mrs. Crane agreed the course should receive full credit and expanded the studio on the fourth floor of Draper. English teachers Jean St. Pierre and Barbara Sisson worked with the History Department to coordinate literature and history in the tenth and twelfth grades; history teacher Lise Witten, fluent in three languages and expert in European art, could teach interdisciplinary courses all alone, but she joined with others to enrich both their teaching and her own. French and Spanish teachers set up a small, excellent language laboratory, a project for which Dorothy Judd took prime responsibility.

Not wishing to stir a fuss over her retirement after nearly forty years of teaching, Kate Friskin quietly left "on sabbatical" in 1959, but Margot Warner and a series of excellent piano teachers carried on Abbot's music tradition. Mary Crane had long wanted to add Asian history to the curriculum; in Caroline Rees she found an enthusiast to teach it. Eleanor Tucker took over from Alice Sweeney as Director of Studies and college adviser after Miss Sweeney's retirement in 1957; from this position she did much to bind the senior and junior faculty together. Considering the handicaps under which Abbot and most other girls' schools labored to get and keep good faculty, it is a tribute to Mary Crane that Abbot teaching was carried on for the most part at standards as high as ever.

Thus did Abbot's academic success overlay communal tensions and a conscious refusal to bend to increasingly insistent changes in the larger society. Such conservatism had proven wise in the past; it seemed the most comfortable stance for an old school to fall back on now.

History in the Making

History in the making is often uncomfortable.
Mary H. Crane,
Principal's Report, 30 November 1959

Grand Issues, Cautious Responses

Private schools were not left alone to adjust in their own quiet ways
to problems of teacher recruitment and the push-pull of contemporary
mores. During the years that Abbot was searching for a *modus vivendi*
with its bright, restive students, critics in high places were insisting
that these very youngsters would be better off in public high schools,
where they could both add intellectual vitality to student bodies
grown flabby on misdirected progressivism and gain in democratic
sensibilities from the public school mix of social classes, creeds, and
ethnic groups. In June 1952 Miss Hearsey quoted to the Trustees the
speech given by President James Conant of Harvard to the American
Association of School Administrators proposing an end to the nation's
"dual system of education" and urging that "all the youth of the community attend the same school, irrespective of family or cultural background."[1]

Private school educators were aghast; they had not forgotten the
influence commanded by Charles W. Eliot, the last Harvard President
who had mounted the rostrum for public education. Conant's attack
climaxed a season of anxiety for all independent and parochial schools.
They were already uneasy about the decline in applications that
marked the Depression babies' arrival at secondary school age, for this
generation was all too small. Unlike more than half of New England's
girls' schools, Abbot remained full during 1948–50, the leanest years,[2]
but Miss Hearsey wrote anxiously to the Trustees of her fears for
future enrollments,[3] and worried about the ill feeling against nonpublic schools that was bound to emerge from the controversy over
the Congress' first substantial effort to aid secondary schools.[4] During
that effort parochial schoolmen had lobbied hard for funds, made

many enemies for the nonpublic school, and retreated in bitterness after having largely failed. Independent school people found only crumbs of comfort in the more moderate position Conant took the following year, when he insisted that at the least all who love democracy should beat back the efforts of nonpublic school advocates— principally "powerful church leaders"—to gain a share in public funds.[5]

The debate over the role of private schools in national life was many-sided and complex. Conant championed the comprehensive public high school at a time when Cold War rhetoric had thrown all public schools on the defensive and provided Abbot Academy with some embarrassing allies. Looking fearfully at totalitarian Russia, the communization of the Catholic East European nations, and the "fall" of China, many Americans deplored "Godless statism"; extreme critics characterized public schools as centers for propagating a revolutionary new social order.[6] More analytical critics like Arthur Bestor and Albert Lynd made powerful thrusts at the self-perpetuating educationist cartel that had persuaded most state governments to adopt the teacher certification systems that kept them in work, and nourished a wasteful, clumsy state education bureaucracy larger in New York State than in all of England.[7] Conant had his answer ready: granted the public schools have problems—let all citizens pitch in to improve them, and teach their children democracy by practicing it. "It may well be that the ideological struggle with Communism in the next fifty years will be won on the playing fields of the public high schools of the United States," he wrote, in all seriousness.[8]

It is difficult now to imagine how grave the ideological struggle seemed at the time—so grave that rational citizens and their public representatives were willing to tolerate blatant attacks on the civil liberties of individuals and on the integrity of educational institutions. Senator Joseph McCarthy is often blamed, but it was this demagogue's massive, approving audience which made McCarthyism possible. With other private schools, Abbot Academy offered mild but steady resistance to the general hysteria. Marguerite Hearsey had done her share of worrying over "the ideologies of Communism and fascism being spread or practised right here in our own country,"[9] but she and most of her independent school colleagues were determined not to overreact. They looked for the special contributions they might make within a society that had become polarized over issues of ideology and academic freedom. Private schools are uniquely positioned to resist national fetishes, and the Headmistresses Association gladly defined "the Responsibility of the Schools in a Democracy Challenged by Communism" as the obligation to "put great emphasis on civil rights," to "act when they are attacked," to support the United Nations, to keep in mind "our own national shortcomings" while continuing to teach "the great values of the American tradition."[10] In spite of the noises heard from the many states wishing to tighten up private school accreditation requirements, the NAPSG determined to resist all state efforts to sacrifice teachers' independence or their own high hiring standards."[11] Miss Hearsey kept the Trustees informed of various state efforts to eliminate school and college books written by or about Communist or Socialist sympathizers, and of Massachusetts legislators' proposal that all schools rename the English language "the American language."[12] The Trustees agreed with her that students should have full access to material about Communism, even though Abbot should never knowingly hire a Communist.[13] It was not an idle possibility. All private educators knew about the bitter teachers' strike of 1949 at Putney School. Putney, so long accused of harboring Communists, actually found it had a radical labor organizer in its midst, a young man who persuaded fellow teachers to organize under the CIO and demand higher pay, tenure provisions, and faculty representation on an independent board of trustees.[14]

Inside Abbot, teachers met this national ferment with a general effort to do better what they were already doing. One group of critics had excoriated American schools for failing to teach basic academic skills, and for neglecting those gifted students who should be preparing to lead the race against Communism. Abbot faculty tightened the school's testing and placement procedures, wondered if its long tradition of heterogeneous class sections was wise after all,[15] and set up a noncredit seminar in Greek for twenty-five especially able students, who met with Phillips classics scholar Allston Chase once a week. President Conant had taken educators to task for the ill fit between school and college which pinched the most able students. The educators of Andover Hill could accept this charge: for years some Phillips and Abbot graduates—like highly capable students everywhere—had found freshman courses dull and dulling. Pushed by Dean Alan Blackmer, Phillips Academy designed and the Ford Foundation funded a study to discover whether advanced placement in college might not be possible for such young people. Miss Hearsey read every report coming out of "The Andover Study," kept in touch with the few Abbot graduates who had entered college a year early, and sent questionnaires to other college-going alumnae to try to find out—among other things—whether Abbot's education had been proof against the alarmingly high dropout rate for college women.[16] Skeptical of a full-blown Advanced Placement program, the school moved cautiously. The fac-

ulty instituted fourth-year French and mathematics well before Miss
Hearsey's retirement, but Miss Hearsey, Alice Sweeney, and Mary
Crane knew far too much of the complexity of talent to go along with
the fifties fad for exclusive "A-T" (Academically Talented) tracks.
When Marguerite Hearsey was asked in 1959 to address the NAPSG
on the subject "gifted youth," she ignored the expected topics and
presented instead an inspired and scholarly account of John Keats's
education and upbringing. The institution of a fifth-year French class
in 1956 had more to do with Mrs. Crane's and Miss Sweeney's feeling
that Germaine Arosa and her Seniors should be rewarded for moving
swiftly through fourth-level French than it did with keeping up with
the Joneses or the Phillipses in both Exeter and Andover.[17] Like Miss
Hearsey, Mary Crane gave special attention to the academic placement of applicants with unusual records or home problems, ably assisted by Eleanor Tucker, Director of Studies and college adviser from
1956 to 1966. Their careful counseling of students and parents, much
of it incredibly time-consuming, could not be conveyed in catalogues
or proud articles in professional periodicals; it was taken for granted
as part of a private school's responsibility to its clientele.[18]

After 1956 Mary Crane and the Trustees would draw on the work
of the Sputnik-inspired Physical Science Study Committee and similar
groups to revise Abbot's science curriculum. The National Science
Foundation would eventually spend a billion dollars to develop the
new courses, and Abbot would hire a series of teachers trained in
NSA-sponsored institutes to bring the new physics and chemistry to
its students. The New England Association of Colleges and Secondary Schools (NEACSS) accreditation committee came in 1958 to
praise the school's general program—and to recommend more select
A.P. sections. Abbot responded to the nudge by establishing fourth-
year Spanish and sixth-year French courses; Principal and Trustees
created special Advanced Placement English sections, bringing in Ann
Werner—"one of those interesting, difficult Abbot characters," says
Virginia Powel—from her chairmanship of Wheeler School's English
department and her work on Advanced Placement testing for the
CEEB. They continued, however, to insist on a well balanced general
education, rather than countenance the early "majors" that were the
rage in some high schools, or push students beyond sense to build
grade-point averages that would impress the colleges. "Abandon fear,"
Miss Hearsey had told Abbot students in 1944. "Do not work for
grades but for mastery of the subject." Mary Crane rang her own
changes on this theme again and again. Nor would Abbot stretch
teaching resources to accommodate a handful of Advanced Place-

ment candidates in subjects other than English.[19] A joint Phillips-Abbot A.P. program would have been a simple solution to the latter problem, but no one seems to have mentioned it in public.

Abbot must have been doing something right, for applications increased faster than ever throughout the fifties. There was more to it than War babies,[20] than general prosperity, or the Eisenhower administration's benign attitude toward private institutions. The critics of public schools had created a fresh constituency for private schools. Conant's insistence that far too many parents and private schools pushed inept scholars into college did nothing to dampen enthusiasm for college preparatory programs that guaranteed both higher education and higher social status.[21] In spite of Supreme Court integration rulings, in spite of heroic efforts to create the democratic high schools of Conant's dream, the ethnically and economically diverse communities that could support them were becoming ever fewer. Some of the best high schools emerged from one-class suburbs whose homogeneity made the Abbot community seem positively polyglot. Small schools like Abbot looked inviting beside most of those enormous new comprehensive schools which President Conant had inspired, with their two or three thousand students and their often-mechanical organization of academics and activities.[22] Again and again parents and alumnae mention how flexible and sympathetic Abbot was when confronted with students behind in Latin, say, and ahead in mathematics or some other subject.[23] Finally, there was the private school's basic appeal: exclusiveness. Local Andover parents who fretted over their status as the "right" people sometimes sent a daughter to Abbot to confirm it.[24] President Conant could not prevent a pair of Illinois parents—both transplanted Easterners—from noticing with horror their daughter's midwestern accent and shipping her to Abbot for a proper New England education,[25] nor could he keep hundreds of Abbot alumnae from urging Abbot on relatives and friends.[26]

Shoring Up an Island

Generally speaking, new candidates and their families were attracted to Abbot itself, rather than to Andover town and Abbot together, as in years past. The self-contained town of prewar days, with narrow roads leading out from the Abbot campus to woods or farmlands, was no more. Long country walks were rare now, and even the skating pond that Abbot once shared with a few neighbors had been abandoned for a flooded rink on the tennis courts, where the girls could skate on a smoother surface under watchful eyes. Movies and radio, then television, had all but eliminated townspeople's attendance at Abbot's Saturday lectures and student recitals; most of the town's newer residents had no interest in Abbot Academy. Subdivisions were laid over the hay meadows to make more room for the engineers who worked in the new Raytheon missile plant or staffed the electronics industries on Route 128, now that superhighway construction had brought Boston closer than ever. New families came to take advantage of Andover's public schools, not of "in-grown" Abbot Academy.[27] The new population soon outnumbered the old. Those town connections that Abbot had sustained through its Treasurer had lapsed one by one as the ageing Flagg resigned from the various Town Meeting and South Church committees where he and his friends had once held sway, while the newcomers gradually won a loud voice in town affairs. More than ever before, Abbot was on its own.

Though none of the Trustees proposed major changes at this time, the Board took several steps to strengthen the school and adjust its administrative routines to new conditions. It was a strong group and getting stronger, which was well, for several of its members would eventually make decisions for Abbot more momentous than those made by any Abbot Board since the mid-nineteenth century. Philip K. Allen, P.A. '29, a distinguished local resident, came on the Board in 1948, to stay, with a two-year hiatus, until 1973, and to carry through the merger of Abbot and Phillips Academies. Allen had briefly taught both at Phillips and at the progressive Cambridge School, and was Andover's state senator and leading Republican at the time of his election to the Board. Through the years his experience as director of several other schools and of the Boston Symphony was to prove invaluable. Two alumnae would serve long and vigorously: Helen Allen Henry, '32, later Helen Anderson (1945–73), and Jane B. Baldwin, '22, investment banker and trust officer (1948–1970). In 1964 Alice Sweeney would join them. Caroline Stevens Rogers, from North Andover's public-spirited Stevens Mill family was not an alumna herself because her mother, an Abbot day scholar, had found Miss McKeen's Abbot "so terribly old-fashioned," but she was fascinated with education and "thrilled to help."[28] J. Radford Abbot, P.A. 1910, the resourceful architect of the pre-war Draper Hall additions; Mrs. Frances Jordan, of Cambridge; the Reverend Sidney Lovett, Chaplain of Yale and alumna husband; and Margaret Clapp, President of Wellesley—all brought fresh ideas from outside Abbot and were glad to work under Chairman Robert Hunneman, although Barton Chapin was sorely missed after his retirement. All were to become powerful contributors to future plans.[29] And although Flagg had given over many of his duties to a Trustee Investment Committee and a salaried Assistant Treasurer after bringing Abbot through two financially chaotic postwar years, he remained the Board's essential link with Abbot's traditional strengths, speaking up always for continued independence from government encroachment, never forgetting the small helps that meant so much to Abbot teachers. ("I want you to take this letter of credit with you, just in case of emergency," he said to a protesting but grateful Marguerite Hearsey as she embarked for her European trip in 1946.) George Ezra Abbot had joined the Board in 1937 and accepted the chairmanship in 1952—"to keep Flagg from running Abbot pipes down under my backyard," he said, not entirely in jest, for he respected Flagg's ability to accomplish anything Abbot needed done. Though he died shortly afterward, his effectiveness was long remembered.

The War's end, the school's continued popularity, and fast-rising costs impelled Abbot toward long-term planning.[30] Yet again Miss Hearsey was agitating for a financial campaign, this one leading toward Abbot's 125th Anniversary in 1954. The Board sought rational answers to the problem of Abbot's optimum size—and found none but the seating capacity of the Chapel (225), the fit between classroom space and the school's maximum class size of fifteen, and the Principal's hunch that a relatively small school works best. With no more than 200 girls in her charge, Marguerite Hearsey could think of each as an individual, and often handle special problems herself. Principal's files bulge with long letters to students and their parents—for example, to a Senior just expelled following the Student Council's decision that she had not quite met the terms of probation; to the Senior's conservative mother ("Although you are deeply disappointed about this I hope you realize that ——— herself is also suffering because of it, and I hope that you may be able to forgive her . . . We must have faith in her and help her turn this hard experience into good"), to two other schools' heads describing the girl's disciplinary troubles ("she is at an important turning point") and recommending her as a vigorous person of much promise; then finally, in April, to the college where this young woman had applied. In a small school parents could readily be counseled about their daughter's academic placement, or congratulated at her election to an important student office. At any rate, the Abbot buildings could hold only so many. The Chapel seemed to be the ultimate limitation, for in a crucial sense the Chapel *was* Abbot, having held since 1829 those recitations, those Draper Readings, and all those prayers of women old and young seeking after knowledge, goodness, and courage.

Though she was uninterested in expansion, Miss Hearsey hoped for one more dormitory to replace the homelike but inefficient cottages. The Trustees demurred. For several reasons, funds free to fuel expansion of plant were in short supply. Emergency repair costs betrayed the too frugal maintenance schedules of past years. As Flagg gradually gave up his formal responsibilities to Gardner Sutton, the capable Assistant Treasurer, Abbot lost the secretarial help that Flagg and his Merrimack Mutual office staff had been donating for decades. Replacements must be hired, enough of them to handle the mounting paper work attendant on new state regulations, federal school lunch aid, and so forth. Thus nonacademic expenses climbed, and income had to rise to meet them.

Teacher's salaries continued as a major concern.[31] Although Abbot fared extraordinarily well through the immediate postwar shortage of teachers, the mid-fifties found the school unprepared to meet the salary demands of either young or older teachers. At last the Trustees began to feel that they could no longer impose on the loyalty of old-timers. Teacher applicants knew they were in a buyer's market;[32] furthermore, the War had raised women's pay from the half of men's wages which women had received for the same work in 1937 to about two thirds a decade later. By 1955 senior teachers in Andover's public schools were receiving $4,200-4,400 a year; Abbot with its $3,400 average for long-tenured teachers, was losing its position just above the median for girls private schools.[33] Staff members also felt restive. Responding to a polite but forceful protest from the grounds staff, Flagg had raised the nine men's wartime pay 20 percent from the $26-$43 a week they were receiving in 1941, but by 1950 the men were comparing their wages with those of the Phillips staff, and grumbling.[34] The problem was how to raise all salaries without at the same time raising the tuition ($1,800 a year in the early fifties) well beyond the rate that was giving Abbot an edge in the competition against comparable schools. No one seriously considered more drastic measures, such as halving the service staff (fifty-seven strong by 1961) and setting young ladies to grounds and kitchen work in order to bring Abbot's nonacademic costs down to those of schools like Northfield or several of the Quaker academies. Even at its simplest, gracious living cost money.

Pensions were another perennial. Despite Flagg's reservations, a formal faculty retirement plan had been set up with the Teachers Insurance and Annuity Association in 1946, and was made mandatory "except in special cases" by 1949.[35] Abbot was still coping case by case with such older retirees as Mme. Craig, who refused to live in the Andover Nursing Home even though Miss Hearsey or one of the teachers visited her there every week; she had to be gently moved to Salem by Flagg and her other Abbot friends.[36] Alumnae of both the Hearsey and Crane years remember with pity a few weary or ill teachers who should perhaps have retired long before, and might have done so had pensions been really adequate. The students finally told Miss Hearsey about one old woman who would drop off to sleep during class; she was tactfully let go within the week.[37] There was no pension plan at all for staff, though Miss Hearsey urged that the Trustees adopt one.[38] The Trustees would continue through the 1970's to assess each retiring teacher's independent income and pay her yearly supplement to TIAA and Social Security accordingly.[39] Though these were practices guaranteed to appall any unionized public school teacher, they were so deep in the tradition of the girl's boarding school that no one could dislodge them. True, the same tradition provided some compensations: long-time staff retainers had their yearly Christmas presents from the faculty; the most respected teachers could take their turn with the $500 a year the Trustees set aside for summer study, or even win an occasional leave of absence with part or full salary; but none of these benefits quite made up for the financial disparity between working for Abbot Academy and selling similar skills to business, industry, or public schools.

Perhaps the Trustees could not be blamed, for Abbot had little or no financial leeway. Flagg's last detailed financial review before he handed most of the books to the Assistant Treasurer asked the rhetorical question: "What causes the operating deficit?" ($7500 in 1947, $10,000 in 1948). To the Treasurer the answer was obvious: Even though pensions seemed entirely inadequate to some, the total spent for this fixed cost had jumped from $632 in 1939 to over $14,000 in 1947. The jump was the more striking in that operating expenses had risen just 10 percent faster than total income.[40] Thus Flagg was not being merely petulant or old-fashioned: he resisted standardized pensions and a more generous, more systematic salary scale largely because he felt Abbot could not afford them.

Given this hallowed nonsystem, it is perhaps most surprising that Abbot continued to evoke the loyalty it did from teachers and staff. McKeen Custodian David Robb brought his wife to every concert and play that took place in the assembly hall which he himself kept so scrupulously clean, and left Abbot $10,000 at his death in 1973. Mr. and Mrs. Jes Bonde, whom Miss Hearsey brought in to direct the kitchen and the household staff, were so warm-hearted and capable that bakers, dishwashers, and maids were willing to overlook the level of their pay and the entire absence of Abbot pensions to stay for years at the school. The length of teachers' tenure through 1960 also seems remarkable. For many adults, Abbot was still home.

Finally, the Trustees sought to regain the momentum of the fund drive that had been interrupted by the War. None seemed willing to act as fast as Marguerite Hearsey wished. Much as Miss McKeen had done, she reminded them repeatedly of the need for a new campaign, and their response was similar to that of the nineteenth-century Trustees. Too early for the next anniversary, they said. A bad time for a capital campaign, they said.[41] True, the Investment Committee was a little cell of persuasion, taking up Flagg's gentle cudgel for an expanded endowment, and an alumnae-parent fund waxed more successful every year, but these were small things, for endowment interest and donations combined amounted to less than $30,000 a year. One of Abbot's latter-day development officers suspects that the male majority on the Board simply did not take seriously this female institution's need for larger science laboratories and better athletic facilities. From 1945 on, the Trustees went through convincing motions, appointing and retiring committees on School Needs and Development, allowing Miss Hearsey to mount her own campaign among 175 Abbot fathers in 1951 after she and Flagg had become convinced from parents' financial references that the income of the average father had substantially increased since the War. She wanted money for higher salaries, a much larger scholarship fund, a gymnasium, and, simply, for a hedge against the small but persistent yearly deficit.[42] She didn't get much from the fathers, and this convinced her that it was past time to begin the major 125th Anniversary campaign. In the very month that President Conant opened his guns on the United States' dual school system, Miss Hearsey told the Trustees that the time had come. She had been enormously encouraged by the new Alumnae Council's interest in Abbot and its problems, and she was sure the alumnae as a whole were "ready to work for some challenging cause."[43]

At last the Board agreed. Their latest Development Committee had decided that a gymnasium should head the list of building needs: this would free Davis Hall for its many competing uses, as well as for the movies and other "secular programs" now accommodated in the Chapel—most inappropriately, Miss Hearsey felt. The Physical Education program was a full one: four or five hours each week of hockey, basketball, and tennis in the fall; skiing, skating, and gymnastics in winter; softball, track, archery, lacrosse, tennis, and horseback riding in the spring; and modern or folk dancing throughout the year—all led now by two athletics teachers and their faculty amateur assistants rather than by Mary Carpenter and a few enthusiastic Seniors; but it burst at the seams when the weather was poor, especially on those dank February days when nearly every student in the school was either hauled out protesting to ski or confined to Davis Hall. In every age since 1852, Abbot had striven to create a self-sufficiency appropriate to the times; now a gymnasium was a patent necessity.

The Trustees went to work to find large donors, while Helen Allen Henry, '32, and Mary Howard Nutting, '40, took chief responsibility for fund-raising among the alumnae. The campaigners received a heartening boost in the form of a $50,000 gift from the Nathaniel and Elizabeth Stevens Foundation; then fate gave them a rationale to create a special memorial to Board Chairman George Ezra Abbot after his untimely death in 1953. The campaign was entirely Abbot's work: no outside fund-raisers were called in to help—or to interfere with—this grand project of the school's extended family. Alumnae who had loved Abbot sports rallied to lend a hand. One feels that many of the married volunteers warmly welcomed work that was uniquely theirs as women, as individuals with selves rooted in a past their husbands and children, however beloved, had not shared. Surely among 3,400 alumnae a large share of the remaining $250,000 needed to build and maintain the gymnasium could be found.

Miss Hearsey used the school's grand 125th Anniversary dinner to appeal for funds in spring of 1954. The Senior Class of 1953 gave its class gift to the fund, and two years of birthday Bazaars earned $2000 more. John Mason Kemper, Phillips' postwar Headmaster, brought with his own contribution a ringing endorsement of the school his mother had enjoyed in Miss Means's day. Other long memories were awakened by the chosen site on the orchard hill, for that very land had been Andover Theological Seminary's last gift to Abbot before its move to Cambridge in 1908. Helen Henry and Marguerite Hearsey visited other schools to assess their athletic facilities and sat with architect-Trustee Radford Abbot again and again for planning sessions.

By the spring of 1955 $200,000 was in hand.[44] Parents had donated about $50,000, friends and Trustees $125,000; $32,000 had been given by over a thousand alumnae, most of it in small donations, and hundreds of alumnae came to the celebration of the building's completion in February 1956. It was nothing like the Dear Old Girls' accomplishment for the Centennial, but then, no one had expected so much, for they knew that the alumnae as a group had less to give than in 1929. Throughout the twentieth century an ever larger proportion of Abbot graduates had married and given up their jobs or their plans for them;[45] in vain did Flagg remind women who had little income of their own that new tax laws would benefit those who donated up to

3 percent of it to private schools and colleges.[46] Still, the gymnasium campaign showed clearly that Abbot could in two years' time draw major resources from a constituency that believed in private institutions, whatever the critics might think. The simple, handsome two-story building with its 90 × 45 foot main gymnasium was cause both for pride and for an immediate expansion of the sports program. It would prove of central importance to the community of girls and women over Abbot's last two decades.

Thus Mary Crane received from Miss Hearsey and all of Abbot's friends a campus that provided ample space for learning, and room for more students as well. The pressure of increased applications seemed irresistible: by 1959 there were 231 Abbot students, including forty-two day students from a community still keenly interested in education. With a sigh from the older teachers, the school moved to Davis Hall for daily Chapel in 1964, but the crowd meant more tuition income and a richer program, so it was acceptable. Students took more courses in all subjects except in art history and music, and they were demonstrably brighter. Abbot scores on College Entrance Exams and IQ tests show that early sixties girls were the most able as a group that Abbot had enrolled since testing began: while the Seniors' median IQ in 1951 had been about the same as the median for all independent schools (118), the median in 1961 (134) was much higher.[47] More girls took mathematics (77 percent), and nearly twice as many as in 1951 took science (40 percent). Though neither Mrs. Crane nor the Trustees opened new fund drives, the alumnae-parent annual giving effort drew in more each year, until it stood in 1962 at $34,700, with over 40 percent of the alumnae contributing; endowment the same year was $1,542,000. With the recession of the late fifties out of the way, all private schools grew fat. As if to confirm Abbot's treasured independence and its defiance of James Conant's assumptions, the Trustees voted in 1961 a resolution stating their opposition to any federal aid to nonpublic schools, and passed it on to the National Council for Independent Schools. If Abbot salaries were never high enough, if pensions were inadequate and teaching loads were heavy (twenty hours a week, on the average, with three preparations), the school as a whole, nevertheless, appeared to be a healthy old lady, pleasingly plump.

Undercurrents

No matter how prosperous Abbot seemed, no matter how hard the Trustees and Mrs. Crane worked, the fifties and early sixties presented the school with difficulties it had not known before. For generations Abbot had projected a clear design for women's lives. Artist-writers like Phebe McKeen and Emily Means, scholars like Laura Watson and Marguerite Hearsey, powerful personalities like Philena McKeen and Bertha Bailey, female teachers of many disciplines and talents—all had represented in their very persons a life of responsible, fruitful independence. None denied the richness of marriage and family life; indeed most warmly endorsed it,[48] and many had cared gladly for parents, sisters, and other dependent relatives or close woman friends whenever they were needed.[49] The great majority of alumnae now married, but married or single, almost all of Abbot's graduates before 1950 had seen their school as a confirmation of women's need and right to lives of their own. Yet suddenly, postwar America seemed to have a different message for growing girls: by far the most worthy role for a woman is that of wife and mother, seed-bed and support of others' lives. No one can know why this message appeared so convincing at the time. Had it something to do with the mass marketing of teen magazines like *Seventeen*—which Abbot girls devoured—and their pink-fluff visions of romance in a split-level home? Did family life seem a safe utopia to individuals scattered by the War? Did it provide a sanctuary from fearsome international problems that many found overwhelmingly complicated and depressing? Whatever the cause, the marriage and birth rate ballooned to the point where the single woman seemed vaguely incompetent if not perverted to many Americans, the childless woman fatally unfulfilled. Sociologist Betty Friedan blames advertisers among others for creating the "feminine mystique" which glorified mothers and housewives and their sparkling homes stocked with products A-Z; but surely the sincere wish to bring up children conscientiously and well was part of it too. That very wish was creating an unprecedented demand for an Abbot education which peaked at a 4:1 applicant-acceptance ratio in 1960.

Americans had been obsessed with the "momism" issue ever since a gaggle of self-important psychiatrists had told the world that most of the 2,400,000 "psychoneurotics" rejected by Army recruiters or discharged to civilian life during World War II were "the victims of clinging and domineering mothers,"[50] a delicious exaggeration that was only heightened when other psychiatrists found the same cause for the Korean War prisoners' vulnerability to brainwashing. Supposedly, daughters suffered as much as sons: countless urban girls "will be emotionally and morally ruined if some way cannot be found to separate them from their mothers," wrote one enthusiast.[51] Hidden in this foolishness was the truth that a society rushing back to peacetime routines had indeed pushed women out of their defense jobs and into the home, while learned psychoanalysts loaded them with a sense of awesome responsibility for their children's personalities. The women most aware of this responsibility tended to be the college graduates who had the highest aspirations for careers outside the kitchen, and Abbot girls grown to adolescence under the care of such mothers could not but be perplexed about their own futures.

Families newly interested in private schools seemed to care not at all about one of Abbot's original functions: to give young women a respite between girlhood and domesticity. A good secondary and college education was no longer proof against hasty marriage—often quite the contrary. To Patricia Graham the obsession with marriage in colleges of the fifties and early sixties was largely a demographic matter, the result of the vast increase in the number of young women aspiring toward, or attending, college. The less exclusive the group was, says Graham, the more it was trapped in majority mores—and since colonial times, America had basically believed that woman's "great vocation is motherhood."[52] By the late fifties the proportion of women doctoral candidates was lower than it had been for fifty years, and the most common age for a girl to marry was eighteen. Among the Seniors at Smith in 1959, "no one had any real plans," Friedan found. "I don't want to be interested in a career I'll have to give up," a college Junior told her.[53] Similarly, the 135 Abbot Seniors of 1961 and 62 who wrote autobiographies for English class or college counseling responded to teachers' questions about their own futures outside of marriage with only the vaguest thoughts. It is not surprising. Only 18 percent mentioned their mothers' work at all, and of the mothers who did work, just four had paid jobs. Asked what they remember of talk about the future, most Abbot alumnae of this time have echoed a 1955 graduate's recollections: "I don't remember that anybody had great career plans. I think it was mostly agonizing 'will I ever get married?' I agonized as much as everybody else . . . if you weren't engaged by age nineteen or twenty you'd had it."[54] One does not have to assume that these Abbot Seniors of the fifties and early sixties were "terrified of becoming like their mothers" and thus "afraid to grow up"—Friedan's too facile explanation for the general sense of purposelessness among young women; into the 1961–62 Seniors' memoirs of family life—for the most part close and happy—one cannot read such subconscious fears.[55] One *can* wonder whether a growing minority's obsession with "the college of their choice," as Mary Crane described a worrying early-sixties phenomenon, may be related to the pressures that parents put on their daughters to prove to the world by their top grades, their success with boys, and their entrance into prestige colleges how wonderfully brought up they were.[56] On the whole, however, boarding school worked against child-smothering "Momism." The independence that parents granted in sending their daughters to Abbot (an independence cherished by most of the daughters) suggests a healthy respect for their children's need to live lives of their own, while Abbot's conscious building of its students' self-respect very often carried forward parents' deepest hopes for their children.

Nevertheless, inside Abbot the "feminine mystique" had subtle effects. Though many openly scorned its more mindless implications, its pervasive spirit tended to undermine ancient assurances and to cloud visions that had once been sharp and useful. The school's difficulty recruiting committed teachers was one symptom; once teachers arrived, students' attitudes toward them became a central factor in the equation. The quality and character of teachers may have been as high as ever—the point is hard to judge—but where a community of unmarried women seemed "perfectly natural" and on the whole admirable to Elizabeth Marshall in 1949, later students perceived many of the single teachers as lonely and frustrated. As though to exempt herself from these stereotypes, one widow talked constantly to her students about her late husband (a businessman whom she called "Mr. Wallstreet"), her more recent lover, and the fact that she would in no wise be teaching if she had any alternative, but her husband's suicide after the Crash of 1929 had sealed her fate. This was a bit fantastic. More persuasive, especially as housemothers entered the scene, was the number of younger teachers who appeared to their students to be marking time until marriage, and the number of never-married women who seemed "somehow ashamed of themselves," as a disenchanted 1964 graduate put it. Obviously, many Abbot adults felt no such thing, but any who did had chosen a discouraging setting for their careers, for they were surrounded by fresh, nubile teenagers with all of life and sex before them. "They were jealous of us," the 1964 graduate insists. "To all of us a teacher was somebody who couldn't get a husband," says one ten years older. All these views must be taken as they evolved in individual adolescent minds, for inevitably, each girl's Abbot was a mirror of her own problems, hopes, and fears. Inevitably, too, they became part of her particular Abbot education.

A handful of women appeared to their students and to some of the younger teachers to be substituting complex in-school relationships for tangled family ones. "———was the most seductive and manipulative person I've ever known," a fifties alumna reports; "she was constantly using power plays to get students' affections, picking up kids and dropping them when they displeased her." And "she was only one of several" adds '64. These students and young teachers felt much less antipathy toward "Mrs. Wallstreet," the loquacious, openly domineering Latin teacher who frankly made enemies among her colleagues by her refusal to give up smoking or inch-long red fingernails. Alumnae of the sixties actively enjoyed a colorful, capable pair whom to a woman they suspect of having been lesbians. "At least they felt good about themselves," says alienated '64. Abbot had moved a long way from the all-female community which for a full century had confidently offered to single women both a respectable role and a life-long home.

The school itself seemed actually to encourage the idea that one had either a job or a baby. When one young teacher got pregnant, Abbot hired someone to replace her without even asking whether she hoped to return. She did not discover what had happened until she called the school in August to order some books for her English class. To be sure, Mrs. Crane had children in plenty, but "she was a noble widow—she had to work, so it was all right," says this teacher now. Mrs. Crane judges that she brought John Iverson and his wife to Abbot before most teachers were prepared to accept a man and wife with small children, for Abbot's first "house parents" did not feel welcome. Did some of the old hands snub them because they feared to lose the exclusive claim that single women had for so long held on teaching jobs at Abbot? If so, their fears soon came true as another married teacher or two arrived each year. It was not until the sixties that most of the faculty (like all of the students) were ready to appreciate a new crop of part-time married teachers with children, and the teacher who had left to have her first baby happily returned, rejoining the English department in 1969 when the youngest of her four children was two years old. Her eventual return to Abbot was partly inspired by Barbara Sisson, herself a mother of three young children who committed herself heart and soul throughout the 1960's to imaginative leadership of Abbot's English department by day and to her own family by evening and weekend. "She was a really important role model for me," says the mother of four, echoing the feelings of many alumnae. Though formal faculty meetings were consumed with petty argument over stockings downtown and dates up the Hill,[57] Barbara Sisson and numbers of other new teachers both married and single spent much time in these first years of the sixties puzzling out together the problem of how to bring Abbot into step with the new decade.

Some teachers and more students had thought that the trouble lay in all those restrictive rules.Well then, thought the faculty, let them visit each other's rooms and have stereos, and whistle or drink cokes in the hallways. Let them have more legal occasions to meet boys, and they won't be so naughty. But as the rules eased a bit, the girls found ways to be still naughtier. The controls on boy-girl friendships loomed larger as Phillips contacts multiplied and required more and more surveillance. It was one of the ironies of these years when girls were thinking ever more of marriage that Abbot Academy continued to be "terrified of sex," as Elizabeth Thomas expresses it, speaking for many. Actually, news from the colleges suggested that there really was something to worry about now. The accuracy of the Kinsey Report was being demonstrated by student pregnancy and abortion rates and statistics both sensational and reliable on premarital intercourse.[58] At a Columbia University Teachers' Conference a psychiatrist told thirty-four secondary educators that anything in sex "that promotes successful interpersonal relations is moral."[59] Thus the requests of Abbot girls and Phillips boys for closer contacts up and down the Hill were made to anxious ears. The response of Abbot's faculty was more of the same: more chaperoned dances, more calling and dating, more "cattle-market mixers" (as a once boy-shy alumna terms these compulsory parties). After 1960 Mrs. Crane did allow older students to attend regular coeducational drama and singing groups with both Phillips and Brooks School boys, Brooks being favored (as always) because of its safe distance from Abbot, a whole township away.[60] These activities provided really welcome chances to get to know boys outside of the usual, loaded "dating" context, but few younger students were allowed to participate, and the new contacts only whetted older students' appetites for more. Abbot would go no further. No one suggested putting Abbot and Phillips on the same weekly schedule so that joint activities could be easily arranged. There was no serious, frank attempt at sex education beyond a regular biology unit which some took and some did not; a visiting lecturer now and then;[61] and occasional forays made by the bold: Ann Werner, had her 1964 Seniors read and write a critical essay on that contemporary shocker, *Sex and the College Girl*, and Mrs. DeGavre brought Dido and Aeneas to life for her Latin students with explicit descriptions of sexual love and reflections on the responsibilities of a mature relationship.[62] A young married teacher shared the confusions of her first pregnancy and the joy of her first baby with her history students.[63] These were exceptions, however. On the whole the Abbot faculty refused to deal with the sex issue. As they did in response to so many out-of-class problems, they fell back on inherited traditions too long unexamined.

It is true that hundreds and hundreds of students went through Abbot hungry for its opportunities and taking rich advantage of them during these strangely troubled years. They sought and found teachers, friends, and a Principal who met their deepest needs. But there seemed to be a growing minority who found Abbot's dissonance with the world outside more stifling than stimulating, or who constantly created cacophony themselves; and if the brass are out of tune, the loveliness of the string section cannot be heard. The Trustees listened to the orchestra with an ear for portents of Abbot's future, an ear newly sensitive to the possibilities of change now that the conformist fifties were giving way to the more open, restless sixties. They heard only the brass, in spite of the conductor's efforts to bring the ensemble into balance. It was time, they decided, to act.

The Final Decade, 1963-1973

No school is an island: before 1960, every chapter of Abbot's story had been bound in some degree to the realities and dreams of the larger society. Yet insofar as any school could do, the old Abbot had made itself a place apart, especially after the McKeen sisters came, and it did its best to remain so through the early 1960's. During the final decade, the outside world beat upon Abbot's doors with such insistence that they must either be opened up or broken down. The Trustees opened them and the world rushed in like a clumsy repairman, knocking over tables and trampling valuable heirlooms, but also bringing fresh air into musty places, and piling on the floor a heap of lumber and tools with which to build anew.

This was the way of the sixties. They began conventionally enough: a presidential election followed by ringing rhetoric, promises of equal rights at home and a rational foreign policy abroad. But America had heard these before. What was new was the far-off rumble of cracking conformity: the California poets, tousle-haired and vulgar, putting words to their longing for selfhood outside the System;[1] radical educator-writers like Paul Goodman who had finally found a public willing to consider that young Americans were "Growing up Absurd"; above all, black leaders and their people, who had decided they could count on no one but themselves, and had taken the American dream into the streets, the lunch counters, and the schools, insisting that promises would no longer do. New also was the power of the reaction already gathering against all that seemed faddish, treasonous, and dangerous at the extremes of this new activism.

At Abbot, at first, these foreshocks were barely felt. A Senior named Cathlyn Wilkerson wrote an editorial for the March 1962 issue of *Cynosure*, the new school newspaper, describing a chain of East Coast peace marches against nuclear testing and the arms race, a demonstration in which eight Abbot students had taken part. Mary Crane had let them go, but Abbot had been too comfortable to show more than passing curiosity about the burning ideas they brought back with them. Cathy wrote, "The eight of us who participated are also guilty of inaction, of passively letting these ideas smoulder within us." A gentle sensitive girl, she could plead for her cause and not be reviled. Mrs. Crane and a few young teachers listened with interest, but most of Abbot was busy preparing for the Winter prom.

Eight years later the girl had joined the Weathermen; her cause was a desperate revolution against a state so corrupted—she felt—by the misuse of force in Vietnam and the ghetto that only violence could right it; and the ideas had become home-made bombs stored in a Manhattan brownstone. Deep one night before it could ever be used for the cause, the arsenal exploded. Cathy Wilkerson left the ruins and the bodies of three friends and went into hiding from a world that would not forgive. Thus were individual lives wrenched out of shape by the pain and the apocalyptic dreams of the sixties, if they were not lost altogether on the paddy fields, or in a Wisconsin physics laboratory blown up by the Weathermen, or in the cellars of brownstones. Though Cathy Wilkerson has apparently held to her original ideals as she continues in hiding, the force of those years swept away all semblance of normal after-Abbot life for this young woman.

It was force enough to change a school, many schools. The character of change depended on how a given institution responded to the shocks dealt out by events that defied comprehension. Fortunately there was more to the sixties than assassination and urban riot, more than napalm and Nixon: there was also new music, cleansing political satire, black pride, red pride, participatory democracy in suburbs, schools, environmental protection groups, and garbagemen's unions. There was exhilaration and release. There was a revival of the women's liberation movement as radical as any of its nineteenth-century incarnations, as sweeping and influential as the final Woman Suffrage campaign before 1920. Finally, there was a romantic revolution in education which drew together the strands of individualism, of Freudian radicalism and reformist enthusiasm, finding expression in thousands of new private schools. Most of these clung to the lunatic fringes only briefly before dropping into bankruptcy or oblivion, but others survived. The best of them inspired older schools to think anew about their own goals and methods, whether in fear for their futures or in hope.

At Abbot Academy, then, change was inevitable. Yet it would be much more than a helpless giving away to external pressures: an activist Board of Trustees proved eager and able to help lead the school throughout its final decade, meeting the turmoil outside with initiatives of its own. In general, Abbot's response to the sixties and early seventies was to stand on the most durable of its ancient virtues—its small size, its care for individuals and attentiveness to all aspects of their lives, its ideals of academic and artistic excellence—and like a carpenter on a very firm stepladder, to reconstruct both its internal program and its entire relationship to Phillips Academy. As in all revolutions, good people suffered and much was lost, including, at last, the school's corporate identity. The main business of schools is students, however. While the original Abbot Academy was working itself out of a job, more girls attended Abbot than in any decade in its history, and many if not most of them thrived on the school's continual plan-making, its conscious weighing of alternatives, its struggle to sort out the traditional, the fashionable and the truly innovative, all of which mirrored those private, dialectical processes by which an adolescent grows toward independence. The last chapters of Abbot's history are concerned as much with beginnings as with endings.

The Trustees Decide

With great difficulty I begin to write about myself,
because I am changing all the time.
Autobiographical essay by an Abbot Senior, 1961

As Abbot Academy opened the 1962–63 school year, an outsider would have wondered what there was to worry about. According to the numbers and graphs, the school was doing well. The applicant-acceptance ratio had stabilized at about three to one; Abbot's "average student" ranked above the median in independent school testing programs.[1] There were some brilliant scholars and some not so brilliant, but the school's age-old commitment to fostering a variety of talents made it hospitable to both groups. Just five years earlier, an evaluation committee of the New England Association of Schools and Colleges had praised Abbot as "exceptionally well administered," made a few suggestions for Advanced Placement courses, and recommended re-accreditation.[2] Income had more than kept pace with rising expenses; endowments and investments had increased 65 percent in five years. For some students Abbot continued to be "exactly what I needed: protection from the world; an extremely simple place to grow up in at a very complicated time," a community drawn together by morning Chapel ("a special, cherished occasion"), by Phillips-Abbot mixers ("scary but fun") and, above all, by teachers who took time with girls who needed time.[3]

Yet those discontented voices would not be stilled. One alumna who loved the school says that nearly all her "most interesting friends chafed tremendously under the insular, limited character of the place."[4] Years vary, and 1961–62 seems to have been a tough one. To some students and younger faculty, the school seemed stagnant: nothing happened, no issues, no discussion. "We just went along as a good girls' school," two teachers recall. They remember Mary Crane wearying herself trying to nudge it forward, and an active Senior class simply taking over leadership as she grew discouraged.[5] It was the year a Phillips faculty wife and friend remembers her asking, "I'm running, running all the time; why is it that it's so hard to get anywhere?"[6]

College admissions statistics were heartening, and the variety of colleges chosen was on the increase (interestingly, only a third of '62 Seniors went on to the traditional women's colleges, compared with 75 percent in 1935), but the anxious push toward college made Abbot "a place to get through" for numbers of girls and took some of the shine and simple fun out of daily, present school life.[7]

Beginning in 1960, a new school newspaper gave voice to the disheartened as well as to the vibrant students who had long smiled on the pages of the *Alumnae Bulletin*. The winter of 1961 was "confusing and tense," at least for the *Cynosure* editor who wrote about it;[8] attendance at games had fallen and athletes were discouraged; too often the whispering and fooling in Chapel by the many destroyed devotions for the few. Of course students wrote sparkling accounts of dances and plays too, and made genuine attempts to air issues that had long gone unconsidered: the dearth of science courses for younger students (twice as many students now took science as in 1951—40 percent of the school—and more were asking for it); forced attendance at lectures and concerts; the rigid, picayune rules (how can we boast of an honor system centered on chewing gum and nylon stockings? asked one reporter);[9] and grades (why were Abbot's so low when colleges wanted high ones?). One parent insists that "those Latin teachers actually *enjoyed* flunking people."[10] First letter writers, then editors asked why Phillips and Abbot could not combine courses in Physics and German.[11] *Cynosure* described students groping for some comprehensible relationship between their little school world and events outside. A speaker from the Friends Service Committee "was barraged with questions concerning work camps, integration and other aspects of social work."[12] The captive Saturday night audience was startled awake by a Dr. Albert Burke, who quoted Mao Tse-Tung, and described American education as out of touch with modern reality, utterly "irrelevant" to young people's lives.[13] The editors kept all Abbot apprised of the efforts Principal and faculty were making to bring Russian and Far Eastern studies into the curriculum, and to revive the emphasis of the Hearsey years on internationalism.

All this was healthy. None of it could dispel the sense of several Trustees that Abbot was becoming dated—inching forward while the world leapt ahead. Why had Abbot's applications stagnated following the sharp rise in 1957, while applications to most competing girls' schools had gained steadily? *Sargent's Handbook of Private Schools* assured the school-shopper that Abbot had "maintained for more than a century the even tenor of its traditions, undiverted by passing fashions,"[14] but was this *raison d'être* in the sixties? Principal and Trustees had been discussing a new major fund-raising campaign—but Philip Allen, Helen Henry, and others were asking themselves how they could persuade donors to provide for the future of an institution whose present was almost unexamined. The Trustees' unanimous agreement on the need for new funds gave this restless minority the opening they were looking for. They asked for and got a commitment from the Board for a long range plan which would bring Abbot out of limbo.[15]

Philip Allen was the Trustee who least cared for limbo, and now Allen was emerging as the force behind reform. "It was time to take this nineteenth century school with its crinoline and old lace, and pump it up into the twentieth century," Allen has said. Highly experienced in politics of all kinds, from Andover Town Hall where he served as Chairman of the Board of Selectmen, to Washington, D.C., Allen was accustomed to aiming high and getting there; if he didn't make it the first time, he had the confidence to try again. But here was no self-seeking manipulator: Allen is the perfect politican, because he really loves people. He seeks to understand and respond to their interests and needs, even while he refines and pursues his own goals. Long ago in his life he had taught English for two years at the progressive, coeducational Cambridge School. It was a wonderful experience which he kept tucked away in his mind. As he went on to teach at Phillips for two more years and to send his daughters briefly to Abbot, he wondered why these two admirable Andover schools could not shed their hauteur and open themselves to fresh ideas as Cambridge had done with such zest in the 1930's. In his wildest dreams he asked why they couldn't simply combine into one coeducational school? No one who knew Allen laughed. His wildest dreams had a way of coming true.

A special Trustees' meeting in April of 1963 took large first steps; Robert Hunneman, Board Chairman, proposed two Trustee "Visiting Committees," one to meet with the Principal and department heads to consider curriculum and student affairs, the other to examine Abbot's scholarship and salary policy.[16] At the June meeting the Trustees voted to engage a firm of New York educational consultants, Cresap, McCormick and Paget, to conduct a complete review of the organization and administration of the Academy, and to make suggestions for improvements.

Plans

Cresap and Company went to work with a will, interviewing all Trustees and most of the faculty and staff at length, searching books, asking and getting administrative analyses of costs and tasks. By January 1964 its confidential report was ready for the Trustees, all 100 pages of it. It began conservatively enough with a description of Abbot's sound financial position and a recommendation for clearer accounting practices; but the second section, *Organization for Top Management*, must have awakened the most somnolent Trustee reader, for it indicated a substantial discrepancy between Abbot's present structure and its need for clear, tight overall administration, as well as for a system to ensure future planning in tune with mid-twentieth century business and educational practices.

Much of the Report boils down to simple home truths for Trustees: decide policy and long-range goals, delegate power to the Principal to implement them, and evaluate the Principal's success in achieving them. But the implications were more specific, potentially more upsetting—and more helpful to those who wanted real change. If Abbot was to commit itself to college preparation, for example, its academic programs and college advising would have to be based on a thorough knowledge of colleges and their requirements, (considerably more thorough, is the suggestion, than that obtaining). The implication: time for the Board to make sure it happened. The Trustees must finally settle the question of Abbot's optimum size, and plan accordingly. If they were not happy with Abbot's salary scale, they should say so and do something about it. The Board itself required overhauling. Most revolutionary, given Burton Flagg's more than half a century as working Treasurer, Trustee terms should be limited to six years, to be renewed only twice. (After a year's time, an ex-Trustee could be elected again.) No Trustee should serve after age seventy-five. The Treasurer and Assistant Treasurer should "cease to be regarded as members of the administration"; they should provide counsel and guidance, but leave day-to-day financial administration to a staff headed by a full time business manager well versed in modern budgeting and cost-accounting procedures.[17]

In anticipation of this published recommendation, Robert Hunneman had already gone with Phil Allen to visit Mr. Flagg and tell him, gently, that he must retire. "It was one of the hardest things I've ever had to do," says Allen now; it could not but be a terrible blow to the ninety-year-old Flagg, who had apparently assumed that he and Abbot would go on together, while he became ever weaker and more deaf, until he died.[18] The various trustee-treasurers' endurance had been Abbot's strength for 130 years, but by the early sixties, no individual's life-time commitment could itself perpetuate an institution resilient enough to meet the challenges facing independent schools. New blood must be guaranteed by new by-laws.

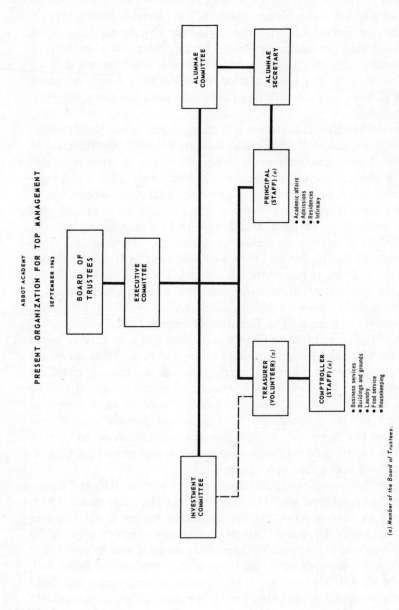

ABBOT ACADEMY

PRESENT ORGANIZATION FOR TOP MANAGEMENT

SEPTEMBER 1963

ALUMNAE COMMITTEE

ALUMNAE SECRETARY

PRINCIPAL (STAFF) (a)
• Academic affairs
• Admissions
• Residences
• Infirmary

BOARD OF TRUSTEES

EXECUTIVE COMMITTEE

TREASURER (VOLUNTEER) (a)

COMPTROLLER (STAFF) (a)
• Business services
• Buildings and grounds
• Laundry
• Food service
• Housekeeping

INVESTMENT COMMITTEE

(a) Member of the Board of Trustees.

48. Lines of Authority: 1964.

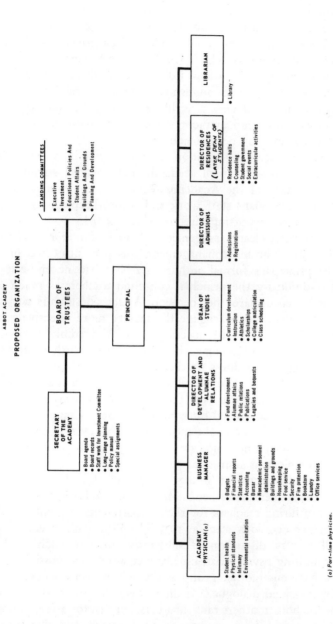

ABBOT ACADEMY

PROPOSED ORGANIZATION

STANDING COMMITTEES
- Executive
- Investment
- Educational Policies And Student Affairs
- Buildings And Grounds
- Planning And Development

BOARD OF TRUSTEES

SECRETARY OF THE ACADEMY
- Board agenda
- Board records
- Staff work for Investment Committee
- Long-range planning
- Policy manual
- Special assignments

PRINCIPAL

ACADEMY PHYSICIAN (a)
- Student health
- Physical standards
- Infirmary
- Environmental sanitation

BUSINESS MANAGER
- Budgets
- Financial reports
- Statistics
- Accounting
- Bursar
- Nonacademic personnel administration
- Buildings and grounds
- Housekeeping
- Food Service
- Security
- Fire protection
- Bookstore
- Laundry
- Office services

DIRECTOR OF DEVELOPMENT AND ALUMNAE RELATIONS
- Fund development
- Alumnae affairs
- Public relations
- Publications
- Legacies and bequests

DEAN OF STUDIES
- Curriculum development
- Instruction
- Athletics
- Scholarships
- College matriculation
- Class scheduling

DIRECTOR OF ADMISSIONS
- Admissions
- Registration

DIRECTOR OF RESIDENCES (LATER DEAN OF STUDENTS)
- Residence halls
- Counseling
- Student government
- Social events
- Extracurricular activities

LIBRARIAN
- Library

(a) Part-time physician.

49. Lines of Authority: proposed.

The Cresap Report proposed other conduits for fresh air: non-trustees to serve on Board committees, and a procedure for setting up ad hoc Trustee committees (these could and eventually would include teachers and students) which would dissolve once their work was done. Members of the Trustees' Educational Policies and Student Affairs Committee must oversee admissions policies, curriculum, scholarships, teaching loads and class size, library standards, "quality and methods of instruction," and extracurricular affairs, with the view to revising policy and judging performance.[19]

Finally, Abbot's overall organization should be simplified, with the principal made responsible for all academic and financial administration, while a Secretary of the Academy would lead long-range planning efforts, organize Board staff work and record-keeping, and take on special assignments, reporting directly to the Board.

Except for the new, clean arrangements of Board functions and the professionalization of business management, this plan projected little change in the principal's formal authority. Abbot had never been a democracy: traditionally the principal consulted teachers as much as she wished, and then declared her decision. As the consultants saw it, Mary Crane's problem was to engage the faculty more effectively in school affairs. Most full faculty meetings were "incredibly boring," teachers of 1962 and 1963 remember, because there was little to decide beyond chaperonage procedures or the question of how one was to tell from a distance—now that seamless stockings were in—whether girls were wearing stockings or not. The resolution of many dilemmas over rules was often determined by who got to Mary Crane first outside of faculty meetings, and spoke most insistently—even to the point of getting her to change her mind on a decision already announced,[20] while most academic and admissions matters were decided in private by Miss Tucker as Director of Studies, the Principal, and, occasionally, individual department chairmen. (Mrs. Crane rarely consulted the chairmen before hiring teachers for their departments, a point which rankled when her decisions went awry.) The Principal's attempts to stimulate full faculty discussion of substantive matters, such as the need for a consulting psychiatrist, usually met stony ears, possibly because the teacher-housemother group as a whole was not accustomed to difficult, many-sided dialogue.[21] It didn't help that some of the old pros thought the housemothers rank amateurs, nor that for a few young teachers, Abbot was only a way-station to marriage, and that more committed women had only scorn for their opinions or their complaints. Cresap and Company pondered the muddle of the day-to-day difficulties their investigations had uncovered and made a series of proposals to clarify faculty and staff responsibilities and to open up communication and reporting within the school.

Their report suggested that the teachers' voice in school decisions be more systematically evoked through an elected faculty "senate," or cabinet. They proposed that the director of studies preside over all curriculum development, athletics, and scholarships as well as college advising and daily instruction, and that a new director of residence take responsibility for students' nonacademic life, leaving the principal free to oversee the whole. They wanted cost accounting for each course (cost per student, cost per class), an equitable rearrangement of teacher workloads, a merit salary scale, and more efficient use of the nonacademic staff, which now amounted to 101 full-time people, including an aging grounds crew, half of whom were over sixty-five (lacking pensions, one puts off retirement).

Consultants' recommendations often go straight to the wastebasket, once Trustees' consciences have been appeased by the appearance of their report. The Cresap Report was important to Abbot Academy because nearly every one of its proposals was implemented during Abbot's final decade. As old-Abbot people accustomed to the more informal arrangements retired or were shifted to other tasks within the school, job descriptions were tightened up, contracts were written, and staff people who had done five or six different jobs concentrated on one or two. These rational schemes generated some irrationalities: Faculty contracts listed a series of specific tasks but always ended with that ominous phrase "and whatever further duties the school shall require of you." Evelyn Neumark, a versatile "secretary" who served for fifteen years as receptionist, as chief assistant to Alice Sweeney and then to Eleanor Tucker, as informal counselor for troubled students, as editor of the Parents' Newsletter, and as organizer of Parents Day and a steadily increasing Alumnae-Parent Annual Giving Fund, began feeling under-used the year after a Director of Development and Secretary of the Academy was finally hired in 1969 at two and a half times her salary, and so left. There would be expensive lags and overlaps: the savings Cresap and Company promised from streamlined deployment of staff could not materialize when able (male) administrators came so high, at least not until Abbot's enrollment expanded in the early seventies to justify their ministrations. Still, the Trustees kept invoking the Cresap Report's principles as they moved into leadership of Abbot. For Philip Allen, who became Board President in 1965 and immediately assumed a more active role than had any Trustee since Samuel C. Jackson in his early heyday, the Report provided outside confirmation of his own long-time worries about Abbot's viability in an age of change, as well as backing for his ideas about modern management practices. The Trustees held two special Board meetings in the spring of 1964 to get the new systems under way; the three subcommittees immediately began functioning, and the Executive Committee met every single month from 1964 to 1973 to carry out the responsibilities the Board had set for itself.[22] One by one over the next eight years, the Trustees' votes turned the Cresap proposals into realities.

Action

Mary Crane happily tackled the new tasks established for her. Though her responsibilities being made more clear were made more awesome, the changes were designed to support her best efforts, and in many respects they did. The Trustees' new Administrative Policy Committee chaired by Frances Jordan, worked most closely with her. The first decision made by the Committee was its most crucial: it recommended that Eleanor Tucker become Vice-Principal in charge of the academic program, giving her authority to direct curricular affairs as well as to advise Mrs. Crane on the hiring of teachers and on all nonacademic matters. The experience Miss Tucker thus gained was shortly to prove invaluable to Abbot. This done, Committee and Principal turned to pensions and salaries, two areas to which Mary Crane could bring much wisdom, thanks to her NAIS and NAPSG Committee work on both subjects. Beginning September 1, 1964, Abbot's share of TIAA contributions was expanded from 50 percent to 75 percent, with each teacher contributing only 2.5 percent of her salary. The Committee backed Mrs. Crane's arguments for higher salaries and merit raises.[23] Some salaries bordered on the ridiculous—$3,400 for a librarian expected to teach library use and reference work, and $4,800 for one long-tenured department head. In five years, teachers' (and librarians') salaries would increase about 40 percent; by 1967, $5,000 was the lowest salary, $5,600 the median, and $8,000 the highest.[24] In the last years of Mary Crane's tenure, the Administrative Policies Committee actually helped the Principal make decisions on individual salary awards. Trustees cannot get much more involved than this.

Backed by the Committee, Mary Crane also initiated a large increase in scholarship aid, to come both from Abbot's own scholarship funds (which doubled to $30,000 by 1967) and from new federal and foundation scholarship programs for underprivileged students, most of them urban blacks.[25] A few years before, Mrs. Crane had brought two Greek students to Abbot on full scholarship, and had welcomed Muthoni Githungo, a Kenyan girl willing to leave her beloved village to prepare for medical or dental training under the J.F. Kennedy Scholarship program. Muthoni described in poetry the sorrows and hopes with which she bade farewell to her grandmother and came to America:

> Tear upon tear falls then,
> Constantly flowing;
> On her wrinkled face
> And she holds me tightly
> And says, "Muthoni dear
> Don't go to America,
> Stay here in Africa
> And take care of me."
>
> Thus she said, and I
> Told her, "Oh Cucu,
> Can't you understand?
> To America I must go;
> The land of freedom,
> Of cowboys and of education.
> There I will be educated
> And I will return as a great doctor."
>
> After I said that,
> She took my hand
> And kissed it.
> She then placed it near her breast
> And blessed me.

Abbot students had raised nearly $2,000 to help match the government grant; thus Muthoni was able to spend two years at Abbot preparing for college, eventually to return to Kenya as an expert dentist.[26] Anxious to increase Abbot's minority enrollment to the four girls a year the outside programs allowed, the Trustees entirely left behind their own resolutions and Flagg's scruples about federal involvement in private enterprise. All over the country, youngsters were seeking quality education; it seemed an age since 1944 when Miss Hearsey and her faculty committee looked for "especially able girls who needed help" and were unable to find any.[27] Now the Trustees' new Planning and Development Committee put the acquisition of scholarship monies high on its list of long range needs, along with increased salaries, and took the first steps toward a major fund drive by again retaining Tamblyn and Brown, fund-raising consultants.

Finally, Cresap and Company had described several of Abbot's older buildings as in "fair" to "poor" shape, and pointed out that only the newest were "excellent." It was not much of a distinction for Draper Hall to boast the oldest hot water heating system in New England.[28] The consultants confirmed Philip Allen's long-held opinion that the whole plant was suffering from a maintenance policy too frugal to do the job; Mrs. Rogers' Buildings and Grounds Committee got right to work on this problem, and began assessing future building needs.

The Cresap report—and the Trustees—had proposed that the Principal consult regularly with elected faculty on matters of school-wide importance. The resulting faculty "Cabinet" represented both young teachers and old,[29] and talked of much more than seamless stockings: student workload, improved counseling, a fairer class ranking system, the question of mixed-class dormitories, the low morale of resident faculty, and the need for better new faculty orientation. (Clothes did intrude when students complained that young faculty wore jeans while they could not.) Mary Crane had worried about such problems for years—"We have no plan for in-service training of teachers, although I cheerfully engage in-experienced ones," she had told the Trustees—[30] but with the Cabinet's help, she would do something about it. The Cabinet helped set the agenda for full faculty meetings, which were now less frequent but more serious.[31] Department heads met together to make long-range academic plans, and arranged for teachers to present particularly worthy teaching innovations to the academic faculty as a whole. To keep track of day-to-day matters, the Directors of Studies, Residence, and Admissions met with Mary Crane as a Faculty Council. All these mechanisms materially strengthened both the Principal's perceptions of faculty needs and opinion, and the teachers' sense of responsibility for Abbot Academy as a complex whole.

The various consultative groups helped Mrs. Crane with one of the most difficult areas of school management: the split between the teaching faculty and the housemothers. Part of this was sheer snobbery by a few teachers, part was their age (the average housemother of the mid-sixties was 64 years old), but part was that a few housemothers were at Abbot earning low salaries because they were untrained for other work.[32] "A really good housemother was harder to find than a good teacher," remembers Mary Crane.[33] Students had no mercy on the weak: "They're just sentimental old bags," wrote a Sherman House correspondent. A housemother was all but helpless when her charges stuffed their beds with dummies and joined each other in a remote bedroom for a midnight beer party, or when the whole of Abbey House embellished a winter night by screaming out their windows from exactly 10:47 to 10:48 P.M.[34] Turnover was swift. " 'Mummsie' ruined parts of our year this year," wrote Sherman House in the early sixties, "but Mummsie is leaving, thanks to the whole dorm." A '62 graduate whose parents worked abroad looked through four years for attention and guidance from Abbot's housemothers, and could not find it. "The gap was enormous," she says now. Some housemothers were successful in spite of the odds. "Mrs. ———— [Mummsie's successor] is a wonderful, wonderful person. You may not appreciate her fully at first, but the more the year goes on . . ."[35] So was Isabelle Trenbath, who also arranged and oversaw student social functions for years; so, apparently, were several others whom alumnae remember with great affection. The majority were simply neutral presences; they could rarely influence, or interfere with, girls already anxious for (and often deserving of) independence. "———— isn't all there," but she tries to be nice, and "it's the thought," wrote one youth who doubtless imagined that she herself would never age.[36]

Few blamed the housemothers for the rules that grated on them. It was the faculty who ordered the main power switch turned off every night at lights-out time, the faculty who forbade earrings for all but Seniors. (If you had had your ears pierced before coming to Abbot, you had nothing but the holes for decoration.) A 1965 alumna sees her three years at Abbot as a fascinating immersion in a superior academic experience and, out of class, in a "dying tradition that taught me a lot—a terrifying amount—" about the constraints most women took for granted just before the women's liberation movement took hold.[37] It was an old story at Abbot, this uneasy combination of rigorous teaching and a social context "overwhelmingly genteel," as Lise Witten has put it. Increasingly, Mrs. Witten and other new teachers questioned the arrangement. In the spring of 1965, the Trustees joined them, hypothesizing that Abbot's antique rule structure might after all be related to stagnating applications, and appointed a three-woman committee (Helen Henry and Abby Kemper from the Trustees and Carolyn Goodwin from the faculty) to propose changes. It was a studied choice of personnel. Abby Castle Kemper, '31, had come back to Andover from her deanship at St. Catherine's School in Virginia to marry John Kemper, Phillips headmaster, and was familiar both with the special traditions of all-girl schools, and with the pressure for more normal access to Abbot that Phillips's student leaders were bringing on her husband, who tried always to respond to their more reasonable requests. Carolyn Goodwin was highly respected by both faculty and students for her tough good sense and her saving wit; Helen Henry had similar qualities, along with the trust of the alumnae. This group listened as attentively to students as they did to faculty, taking on willy-nilly an investigative role which they found discomfiting but necessary to the job.

The Committee proposed no drastic changes. "We cleared out a lot, but there had been so many rules before, you'd hardly notice," says Carolyn Goodwin. All three women agreed with Mary Crane that clear, predictable rules were the more necessary to adolescent growth when the world outside was wobbling toward the unknown, abandoning "long-held beliefs" on its way.[38] They found it reassuring that Miss Porter's School and Emma Willard also required tie shoes. They did, however, plow up the weed-garden of little regulations and recommend that a student-faculty Honor Board free the Student Council from its disciplinary role to concentrate instead on representing and organizing its student constituency. *Cynosure* came alive with printed exchanges on rules and educational philosophy. The Committee's fresh look at the rules inspired gratitude and hope in both students and teachers, who saw now that Abbot could be moved.

Comings and Goings

Perhaps the most pointed criticism the consultants had made was of Mary Crane's teacher-recruiting procedures; she "has relied too heavily upon casual opportunities, as contrasted to establishing objectives for the academic program and then searching for the best available talent to fulfill it."[39] In one of her characteristically self-critical *Reports* to the Trustees, Mrs. Crane had summed up her part of the problem:

> I must confess that it is difficult to assess the value of a teacher who applies for a position involving dormitory duty. Some who seemed very promising, with experience in working closely with girls, have proved not very capable of the leadership, guidance and discipline which the work calls for. This is not entirely any teacher's fault; I am sure there is some lack of conviction on my part, as well, and probably not enough administrative control and encouragement.[40]

One new resident teacher arrived at Abbot in time for the first faculty meeting, assessed her duties, and promptly left. Mrs. Crane replaced her almost immediately—with a person who proved nearly as poor a choice.[41] At the same time, the consultants welcomed the Principal's forceful and well documented assertion that Abbot's salaries were still so low as to make it nearly impossible to find experienced resident teachers.[42] They praised Abbot's success—which was really Mary Crane's success—in retaining "stimulating" nonresident teachers whose outside-Abbot interests had much enriched their relationships with students.

The problem was widespread; it seemed that very few American teachers of the early sixties wanted to live in any dormitory in any boarding school,[43] but that did not solve Abbot's need. One of the Principal's most difficult tasks was to find a director of residence who could take on broad nonacademic responsibilities as the consultants had recommended. Old soldiers like Mildred Hatch ("Hatchet" of the Sherman House documents), who both taught Latin and oversaw Abbot's dormitory life with gruff good humor, simply could not be found.[44] Anyone who cared to enforce every jot and tittle of Abbot's out-of-class rules tended to have little energy left for the job's more friendly responsibilities, such as arranging social occasions and counseling students. Mrs. Crane's nominee for Director of Residence made herself so unpopular by her passion for propriety that girls avoided her. If she saw you wearing a suspiciously short skirt, you had to kneel on the floor in front of her to prove it would touch the carpet. Students taunted her by following the letter of the Sunday dress rules with scorn for their spirit: hats, yes, but the dowdiest or most outlandish you could find; stocking with runs in them ("But they're the only pair I have!")—all these passed inspection but infuriated the inspector.[45] Finally, the Trustees received so many parent complaints about this unbending lady that she was dropped in the middle of the fall term of 1965, and was replaced by Christine Von Erpecom, a personable and effective dramatics teacher who was given the new title Dean of Students.

Mrs. Crane carried her search for teachers farther afield each year after the Cresap Report. True, three of the six full-time women brought in for 1965–66 graduated from Vassar, but MIT gave Abbot a math teacher that year, and Reed College had trained Carolyn Kellogg (later Mrs. Salon), an inventive and demanding biology instructor. Still, the problem would not go away. Though salaries crept upward, Mrs. Crane told the Trustees in 1966 how difficult it was to attract diverse faculty: all of Abbot's teachers were female, and nearly all were either in their twenties or over fifty, a combination that seemed to portend internal division and future instability. No one could know at the time that several of the youngsters would not teach a few years and move on, as so many of Abbot's young teachers had recently done, but would stay to build the school: Jean St. Pierre in English, Faith Howland Kaiser in classics, Jean Bennett in mathematics, and Mary Minard, '55, who became at age twenty-five one of the best organized chairmen the History Department had ever boasted, as well as Carolyn Kellogg Salon and others already mentioned.

Abbot had special cause for discouragement in 1964, when Isabel Hancock, the last of Miss Hearsey's Virginian friends, died tragically of cancer. Still vigorous and comely in her fifties, Miss Hancock had welcomed hundreds of applicants and new girls from her admissions office, given old girls her time as a friend and quiet adviser, and taught many of them mathematics or astronomy. "A beautiful person" says one young teacher, who only came to know her courage and cheerfulness as it shone through illness. Her strength waxed and waned through an agonizing series of treatments, and most of Abbot clung to each shred of hope till all was hopeless. "It was a heartbreaking time," a parent remembers, and when it was over, "a light had gone out." Students and faculty together organized a special memorial service and a fund drive for a mathematics prize to be given in Isabel Hancock's honor. She would not be forgotten, and her absence only underscored the rarity of those devoted, single teachers on which Abbot had so long depended.[46]

Now the key position of admissions director had to be filled. The consultants had urged that Abbot find an admissions expert who could recruit as well as graciously receive, a tall order given the $6,500 salary projected for the position. Mrs. Crane thought she had what Abbot needed in a rather elderly woman who had worked in girls' schools admissions through the 1950's; she hired her without consulting the Board, as was her privilege. The new Director was conscientious, and (say, several teachers and parents) fatally aristocratic. Invariably, she dwelt on Abbot's Brahmin connections when candidates came to visit. Her notes on interviews stressed each girl's clothes, her "poise," and the gentility (or lack thereof) of the parents who had brought the candidate. In a year when several poised but mediocre students were accepted, she turned down a brilliant applicant whose face and accent were apparently all wrong (as a Bryn Mawr student, the same girl urged her sister to apply to a new Abbot Admissions Office, and the sister was accepted). A high point of her year was the first faculty meeting in September, when she briefly described each new student to the faculty ("from a fine old New York family," or "father with Continental Can").[47] Instead of floating on the tide of private school applications through 1967, Abbot's applications slowly declined until they stood at 2:1 (two applicants for each place).[48] No one person can possibly be blamed for this problem—after 1967, all private school applications began to sink—but the Trustees were enough concerned about admissions to ask Mrs. Crane's appointee to retire a year early, and to replace the old admissions operation with an entirely different team for the last four years. Competence and long experience in the world of traditional girl's schools were not enough to meet the challenges of the sixties.[49]

Finally, the woman who had hired and fired and overseen all for eleven years was herself replaced by this determined, activist Board of Trustees. Again, Philip Allen led the change-makers. "I think the position of Chairman is just exactly what you make of it," says Allen now. "You don't want to interfere, but sometimes you have to." Beginning with his election to the Chair in the fall of 1965, Allen "interfered" until an entirely new administration took over in 1968. Not that he was alone: nearly all of the Board supported him with experienced sympathy both for the Principal and the long-term needs of the Academy. Most of the Trustees seem privately to have agreed that Mary Crane should have about two years to work within the new administrative guidelines, but if she could not move fast enough, they were prepared to ask for her resignation. They admired their Principal as a "superb teacher,"[50] a humane and hardworking person—in fact, their very fondness for her and their gratitude for her effort caused them to put off for a year the final resolution of her tenure.[51] Who could fail to be touched by a Principal whose central charge to herself and her faculty was that "we . . . be able to love: our work, our subjects, our students, our colleagues and even ourselves"?[52] Nevertheless, they had begun to feel that the rush and pressure of events now required more energetic, more focused leadership if Abbot was to do more than drift. These days, to drift might be to drown; and this Principal was functioning rather like a skillful dean who fields day-to-day problems, but never really digs into the task of planning for the long future.[53] "It was a holding operation," says one teacher. For all her successes in helping troubled individuals, recent alumnae as a whole were not behind her. Money talks, and so do money-raisers: Tamblyn and Brown, Abbot's fund-raising consultants who came once more in 1966 to survey the field for a major campaign, found that over half of the 45 alumnae they questioned felt the current administration was weak. "She didn't seem happy in her job by the time we left," a 1964 alumna remembers. A 1962 graduate has said for many: "Mary Crane was a wonderful person, but she should never have been a principal."

Perhaps more accurately, the sixties were not the right time for the kind of principal Mary Crane could be. In voice, in demeanor—in all her virtues as well—she was "Old New England, Old School,"[54] while

Abbot was groping toward new modes of thought and action. She herself knew that "in the great stirring of energy and imagination within the field of education, now there is no possibility of remaining static."[55] As one of the first Directors of the National Association of Independent Schools (two years) and a member of the NEACSS Executive Board, she had long been in on the exchange of ideas which these organizations fostered.[56] Now the NAIS spread news of innovative courses and teaching methods in every one of its conferences and publications, and numbers of the Trustees read the NAIS *Bulletin*.[57] Activities on the Hilltop supplied another goad to Abbot. Phil Allen was Trustee for Phillips Academy as well as for Abbot, while Grenville Benedict was simultaneously Abbot Trustee and Phillips Dean of Students. Phillips had just finished a $6,000,000 building program, had expanded the scholarship program to open Phillips to any qualified boy, no matter what his family's income, had raised faculty salaries to match the top secondary schools in the country, and was embarking on a detailed examination of curriculum, admissions, school governance, and residential life through a faculty-administration steering committee that was fully prepared to propose radical changes, if necessary, to bring Phillips in line with the soundest of reformist ideas.

Ironically, Mary Crane's own ideal of a dynamic, responsive school also inspired her Board to ask whether Abbot could not more quickly become such a school with a fresh principal. Mrs. Crane identified the basic problem in spring of 1963:

> The trouble—and the fearful responsibility—is to guess what kind of training we must give girls who are growing up in a world that seems totally different from the one in which we found our experience.[58]

No adult grown to womanhood in that "totally different" world could have tried harder to bridge the distance to her students' lives. Through difficult times she had maintained Abbot's strength even if she could not increase it; thanks to her efforts and those of her most energetic teachers, the old Academy was poised for forward movement at a time when a few other girls' schools seemed hopelessly stuck. When two Trustees spoke to her informally in the winter of 1966 and told her she must resign following her sabbatical leave in 1966–67, she was neither surprised nor angry. She knew her limitations as an administrator, and she soon found herself longing to do more of what she had done supremely well: teaching, and leading students on archeological tours of the ancient world. The last thing in her mind was to dig in her heels and shout for grievance procedures, as did a late fifties principal of the Masters School, who with her assistant simply refused to budge until she was fired. One of Mary Crane's most valuable qualities as an educator had been a conviction born of the changes in her own life that personal growth never stopped, that one "should be continuously aware of the tension between knowledge gained and knowledge yet to be won."[59] In the spring of 1966 Pierce College in Athens invited Mrs. Crane to serve as Interim Principal for the High School division. By summer she had thrown all her energy into planning for this new work, and by November the Trustees had received her letter of resignation and accepted it "with regret."[60] The following year she would begin a second career of art and history teaching at the Winsor School in Boston, where her talents have been much in demand for ten years. From Boston and from Athens she has generously cheered Abbot on, returning for her youngest daughter's graduation and for other grand occasions, and enjoying those special alumnae friends to whom she was—and still is—Principal.

16

"Make No Little Plans"

Everything that once certified culture and
civilization is in doubt.
... The school manager of the old style is a lost man.
Peter Schrag, quoted by Donald Gordon

An explosion is an explosion, and an explosion is
never done little by little.
Germaine Arosa, interview

Resignation became Mary Crane's choice because she wished the best
for Abbot, and she realized that new directions must be steered by a
fresh hand.[1] For much the same reason, Eleanor Tucker took herself
out of the running for Principal[2]—although she agreed in 1966 to serve
as Acting Principal while the Trustees began their two-year search for
the leader Abbot seemed to need.

Eleanor Tucker did much more than wait to be replaced. She had
been chemistry teacher, corridor teacher, Director of Studies, college
counselor, and Vice Principal. Abbot had been her life for thirty
years, and she felt ready to lead the school.[3] "Tuck" was—and is—a
person utterly without pretensions, a tireless, selfless worker who for
years had symbolized the no-nonsense side of Abbot's personality. Her
training was in science, her talents were with methods rather than with
words. The words she did find useful were not metaphors but labels:
factual labels which inspired truthful exchange, free of emotional en-
tanglements. A student in trouble who, relishing some exquisite personal problem, presented it as rationale for aberrant behavior got a
hearing, a brusque, cheerful warning, and a girl-scout handshake. No
brooding allowed in the Principal's office. Verbal embellishments were
as foreign to Miss Tucker as a Dior dress: her inevitable hand-tooled
western belt was all the decoration she required.

In addition to her personal strengths, she had one great political
advantage: "Everyone in the school really liked Tucker," as one
teacher has said. "She was so real and warm and generous. You could
tell her anything." And when she disagreed, she accepted your view

as a reality to be dealt with, not a balloon to be pricked or a threat to her pride. Her friendships crossed barriers of age, of temperament, of intellectual acuity—even of altitude on Andover Hill, for she had won the respect of all the Hilltop teachers who knew her work as the first dean of girls in the Phillips Academy Summer School. There were tensions enough in the outside world; Abbot needed a familiar hand to consolidate the institutional changes already initiated by the Trustees. No one expected an acting principal endlessly to attend professional meetings, as Mary Crane had done, or to build images of self and Abbot among affluent alumnae as the next permanent principal must do. "Tuck" stayed home and tended to business, continuing as college counselor and (through 1966–67) as Director of Studies on top of her Principal's duties.

There was plenty of business. Encouraged by the Trustees, Miss Tucker supported one new initiative after another, including several that were quite out of her ken. "A great innovator," says Virginia Powel, describing Miss Tucker's receptivity to an expanded art program and its unconventional and imaginative new teachers, Audrey Bensley for ceramics and Wendy Snyder for photography. Neither cared two cents for ancient girls' schools as such; they simply saw Abbot as a place where work could be done, and it wasn't long before they and their students were building their own kilns and darkrooms.[4] Girls chafing for "real" work met both its joys and frustrations at the potter's wheel or in dawn-lit photo-taking sessions ("the shadows are good then," Wendy told them), and spoke their own lives as they searched out others' in North End pizzerias—for documentary photography was Wendy Snyder's special art. Several who had teetered on the edge of the drug scene teetered back again, needing clarity to practice craft.[5]

Similarly, Miss Tucker and the Trustees finally made up Abbot's mind to hire a consulting psychiatrist, and to help teachers get expert training in counseling. And when Jean Bennett realized that the new student generation's seeming sophistication about sex almost always disguised deep ignorance, Miss Tucker rearranged Jean's mathematics teaching schedule to allow her to create a sex education course. If Tuck got more than she bargained for, she never blanched. The first full year's course was a series of films and lectures by gynecologists to which many teachers came, bringing questions that Abbot girls had never heard adults ask before. "There was a world of fear-of-sex embodied in the old Abbot," says Carolyn Goodwin. The "effort to open up hidden subjects" was both "strenuous and immensely rewarding" in that it freed discussion throughout the Abbot community. "Is masturbation harmful?" asked one worried girl of the physician-of-the-week. "No, it isn't, if you aren't feeling guilty about it," was the answer, "and a lot of people do it at one time or another. Don't be surprised if you're not the only one on your floor to try it." Whereupon Germaine Arosa put on her gloves and walked out. But the next day's French classes bubbled with conversation (in French) about the lecture, and Mlle. Arosa was reassured by Miss Tucker, who told her she was sure the doctor wasn't actually *advocating* masturbation. Jean Bennett was immensely relieved when Mlle. Arosa returned to the lectures, and joined again in the discussions.[6]

That year it may have been just as well that the Phillips faculty refused to allow boys to attend the Abbot sex education course. Grenville Benedict, Phillips Dean of Students and Abbot Trustee, thought Phillips should have welcomed this near-first in modern Abbot-Phillips history, where Abbot moved into new territory and invited Phillips along. Now it was the Phillips administrators who balked before the unknown, anxious over the restiveness of their own students as they had not been since the Abolitionist cause came to Andover Hill; for the Phillips boy-men were beginning to share in that anguish over Vietnam and the draft which were to shape young people's views toward adult authority for years to come.

Phillips and Abbot students did join one another in community service groups, tutoring school children in Lawrence and organizing a "Contemporary Social Issues" conference on racism. The Phillips Asian Society became co-ed. Abbot flocked up the Hill to see the boys and hear such speakers as Professor John K. Fairbank of Harvard, as well as singers like Judy Collins. Abbot girls were not only welcome at Cochran Chapel every Sunday; Abbot allowed them to attend. An Abbot-Phillips daily mail service flourished, legally now. There were at least a dozen Abbot-Phillips dances and concerts each semester. The Phillips Drama Lab launched more Abbot actresses every month. An awe-inspiring *King Lear* was played on Phillips' main stage, and Goneril, Regan, and Cordelia were Abbot boarders, not Phillips faculty wives. In the Phillips-Abbot Madrigal Society, now five years old, males and females sang instead of flirting, because there was work to do together and plenty of chance to flirt elsewhere.

It would have taken heroic effort to run a dull school in these two years, 1966–68. The blue-clad Seniors with their red roses and bagpipes had marched down School Street as always for the 1966 Commencement, but Norman Thomas, the head of the American Socialist Party, was there awaiting them with a powerful Commencement speech, which he delivered out of his husk of a body in a voice that filled the church, and still sounds in the minds of those who were there that day.[7] *Cynosure* published article upon article of aching, introspective argument over black power and white guilt. For the first time since Miss Bailey had arrived, the value of Abbot's numerical grades and publicized honor roll was questioned by teachers as well as students. "NEW EMPHASIS ON LEARNING," announced *Cynosure*[8] as all numerical grades were eliminated. For the first time, too, there were scattered instances of drug use, along with utter bewilderment among the faculty as to how to respond. Then there were the Abbot perennials: Student Councils pushing for yet one more dining-out day for Seniors, for a few more hours when telephone calls might be made and received, for sandals on Saturdays, and all the little freedoms which meant so much and were still doled out so niggardly. By administrative decree, Phillips-Abbot couples still paced the Circle in front of Draper Hall of a spring day like tigers in a cage, instead of making free of either campus as they had often asked to do. And in spite of (or was it because of?) the new contacts with Phillips boys, alumnae remember a pervasive sense of anxiety which had never occurred to the Abbot girls of Miss Means's and Miss Bailey's day: how well, really, did Abbot measure up beside Phillips? Some Phillips intellectuals delighted in perpetuating the stereotypes that seem to have dogged the two schools ever since the late forties. As Mary Crane puts it, "You should have heard some of those P.A. Seniors telling the Abbot girls that they knew nothing, but nothing, especially in the field of American history." Even close-hand reality could not shake the stereotypes. Where Miss Bailey's students had disdained the typical Phillips boy as richly as he disdained the typical Abbot girl, a '59 alumna "felt that the boys up on the Hill were far superior—except the ones [she] knew." "They seemed so much more grown-up than we were," adds Kathy Dow, '55, "Why, they were reading Hemingway and Faulkner, and we were reading Thomas Hardy and Joseph Conrad!" The sheer numbers of Hilltop students—three times the Abbot enrollment—and the grandeur of the campus weighted many comparisons irrationally in Phillips' favor. The inferiority theme appears over and over in the recollections of recent alumnae.[9] Contrary views also tended to be stereotypical. "How much do you see of the Phillips boys?" a visiting Abbot applicant asked her student guide. The answer: "We see about as much of them as we can stand."[10]

Unknown to most students of these two years, forces both seen and unseen were gathering to push Abbot and Phillips closer together. As early as 1957, Abbot faculty had talked coordinate education among themselves while gearing up for the NEACSS Evaluation Committee.[11]

A decade later, the Phillips faculty was beginning to respond. By the fall of 1967 a Phillips-Abbot committee had been formed to plan a wide range of shared activities. And there was more. The Trustees' search for a permanent principal meant a host of decisions as to the kind of school the New Abbot Academy should be. Philip Allen had made at least one decision of his own years before, when he determined that somehow, some day, Phillips and Abbot should become one institution. Though none breathed a word of this hidden agenda *ex camera*—Allen spoke in public of the great advantages of coordination without merger—he and his Search Committee colleagues were looking for someone who could carry it out if ever the opportunity arose.[12]

Given the size and nature of the challenge, it seemed to the Search Committee a man's job. This was not a put-down of women but an assessment of political realities: it appeared fairly certain that a man could cope more successfully with the "rather Roman Senate environment" of the Hilltop, if not with the "extreme degree of chauvinism" that characterized some Phillips alumni.[13] Men also had a better reputation as fund-raisers, deserved or not. Just as the original Abbot Female Academy seemed to need male leadership to confer legitimacy on its birth and infancy before 1852, so American society in the mid-sixties, suspicious of spinsters and career women, thought it felt safer to have males running schools. Besides, high-powered women administrators were still as few as they had been in the fifties; several girls' schools had recently chosen male principals, and even the exhaustive search that Bryn Mawr was making for a new president at this time would not turn up a woman.[14]

The question seemed settled by the fact that no women from outside the conservative boarding school world were willing to apply for the job. Nor, at first, were any outstanding men. Sixty candidates came and went. It was a full year before the Search Committee learned through Phil Allen's son-in-law of a man named Donald Gordon who headed the Barstow School, a flourishing day school in Kansas City. In his two years at Barstow, Gordon had helped bring boys into the upper elementary division and black students into the entire school. The upper school was still all girls; Donald Gordon had been a missionary for coeducation, but a politic one, who had shown himself an able leader for both male and female in a day-school setting. Philip Allen opened a correspondence with him—and it warmed with each exchange. Gordon immediately responded to Allen's enthusiasm for change with his own large optimism; Allen was impressed. After all, the Trustees were asking for an experienced innovator, a person with no commitments to the old Abbot, eager to design a new school.[15]

Gordon was only 33 years old, but he had taught in private schools all over the country since receiving his Master's degree in American history from the University of Pennsylvania. Such restlessness did not seem strange in the convulsive sixties: youth felt almost obliged to seek, reject, and seek again, always looking for the elbow room a change-maker requires. This innovator had the biggest elbows that had ever pushed Abbot anachronisms out of the way, and a pair of shoulders that looked ready for any burden. The Trustees marveled at their find when Gordon flew east in August to meet the full Board. Standing 6'7", the candidate's frame matched his larger-than-life visions of Abbot's future. At the same time, his sympathies were both ready and generous: "An ideal head for a girls' school," said Trustee Rogers, who never veered from that opinion no matter how strong the crosswinds of the next five years.

The Search Committee had done the preliminary work with such care that it took only two weeks for the Board to decide on Donald Gordon, and less time for Gordon to accept. Barstow was sorry to see him leave—except for one trustee, who had labeled him "a spendthrift," the single qualification to the high praise Abbot had heard of him.[16]

It is impossible to know for certain what Donald Gordon had in mind by giving up the security of his Barstow position and accepting the Abbot job, but some educated guesses are possible. As with Miss Hearsey, history counted: "Abbot had always been a solid academic institution. It didn't attract fluffy heads," Gordon says. And in spite of his wanderings westward, New England itself had a powerful hold on this Massachusetts-born graduate of Phillips Academy and Yale, a person much moved by seasons and daily weather, whose inner thoughts are shaped by the age of the houses and trees along the street where he lives or by the character of the nearest mountain range. New England meant stability, an anchor to a continental imagination. Andover Hill in particular invited the closing of a circle uncomfortably open for a man who was now ready to come to terms with his own adolescence. Gordon had felt uneasy at Phillips. "Odd man out," he says: too tall, too serious, too hungry for dream time ever to be comfortable in the bustling round of Hilltop life—though many boys respected him, and his Greek teacher set aside low grades to marvel at his "fine poetic sense and appreciation of the moral sublimity of Homer," predicting that he would "do surprisingly well as he matures."[17] Don Gordon had had his share of discomfort over a mediocre academic record (he disliked science and mathematics) and a sense of isolation from peers less sensitive than he. To show what he could do to lead Abbot handsomely would be to win a recognition that Andover Hill had largely denied him before. "We'll show 'em!" said Gordon again and again in his five years at Abbot. It was a goad Abbot would use well, on the whole, just as any good teacher tends to learn more from his difficulties than from his successes. His slow-growing but exhilarating mastery of American literature and history at Yale had taught him how nearsighted is the school that types any youngster too soon. He wanted to bring the best of his Phillips Academy experience to Abbot, but he also wanted deeply to create a school where any adolescent willing to do her—or his—part could grow and thrive.

Several people close to Gordon think he must have held in the back of his mind the possibility that he might eventually head the single coeducational school of which Philip Allen dreamed. What man of ambition would not have done? they want to know. Gordon insists this is not the case. Allen had told him at the outset "that he had only one task, and this was to bring Abbot up to the point where it could be part of Phillips Academy. 'You're going to merge yourself right out of a job,'" Allen remembers saying to Gordon, as they talked calmly about all the animosities that were bound to surface in any effort to combine two schools. The idea was easy enough to accept at the time, says Gordon. He assumed Abbot would be going strong for eight or ten years at the least, and to a young man, ten years is an age. There is, however, a poignant tone to all his outside-Abbot writings on the role of a principal.[18] Invariably, in his third-person accounts of his own experience, he refers not to "the principal," but to "the headmaster." His traditional boarding school head had to become both a "new man" and a "super-teacher"[19] in order to remain "headmaster." The word itself implies both power and confirmation of masculinity. Though he would never be called headmaster on Andover Hill, he would strive always to become the ideal man whom the title evoked for him.

Whatever Gordon's private thoughts about the years to come, there was no doubt that Abbot had once again engaged an extraordinarily interesting and complex person for its principal. He visited Andover in November 1967 to meet Abbot students and discuss coordination of social activities with Phillips' Dean of Students John Richards, II. Abbot was fascinated. "The purpose of education is to make a person civilized and brave," he told eager ears. "School must be a dialogue among students and faculty," rather than a closed system imposed by adults. More men teachers were needed he said, (Abbot had one full-time male in the fall of 1967) for a more natural learning environment.[20] "How do we get there tomorrow?" student reporters wanted to know. Gordon, cautious, stuck with generalizations for the time being. As it was, the promise of good things to come was enough to lift from its fall-term doldrums a student body grown tired of waiting. Smelling freedom in the wind, the Class of '68 "fought for changes" in an effort that left *Cynosure* writers exulting, "It's truly getting better all the time."[21] Eleanor Tucker, who had poured into her triple-tiered job "all my time and energy, and what wisdom and compassion I have,"[22] prepared to resume her role as Director of Studies, surrounded by a gratitude almost powerful enough to overcome her weariness and her misgivings about Abbot's future under a man barely known. Amid the encomiums, a headline in the last *Cynosure* of the year told what students were thinking of the year to come:

YOU AIN'T SEEN NOTHING YET.[23]

"Beginnings are wonderful for their freshness."[24]

The first two years of the Gordon administration were a dizzying ride up heights of aspiration and success and down into confusion and near despair. Only the Principal rode the whole track: others would get out and walk for a while after a particularly exciting section of the ride and miss the plunges, and a few left the roller-coaster altogether. Teachers and staff members hired by Miss Hearsey, Mrs. Crane, and Miss Tucker kept time-honored Abbot routines going while Gordon surged ahead, designing the new track to be thrown up before him as he rode. And students. As had happened before in times of turmoil, most students went through Abbot picking and choosing what worked for them from an ever richer jumble of offerings, and found the school a good place for growing. They learned useful lessons about adult fallibility which no one intended to teach. Perhaps most important, Donald Gordon made them conscious as never before of their responsibility for their own education. The malcontents stopped blaming Abbot when things went awry and sought or created more successful alternatives. There are older alumnae and faculty who see these two years as "a catastrophe" (as three have put it) but very few students will agree. Whether Abbot unwittingly did these few real damage is a haunting question, impossible to answer. The outside-Abbot world was damaging lives every day, and one feels that, on the whole, Abbot girls were better off inside.

A new principal is supposed to go slow, and at the very beginning, Gordon did. The trappings of the old Abbot remained intact through much of Year One: students rose to greet their classroom teacher every day; maids pushed tea carts to the faculty room at Tiffin time; traditional dress was the rule. (One new teacher remembers appearing on campus wearing sandals on her first hot-weather working day, and being told by a veteran that stockings and closed-toed shoes were required.) All the pomp and circumstance the school could muster went into a grand Installation for Donald Gordon, organized to a T by Dorothy Judd, Convocation Chairman. Town and Hill gathered to welcome Gordon; South Church rang with Bertha Bailey's (and Vaughan Williams') "Hymn of Praise," Trustee Emeritus Sidney Lovett of Yale prayed everyone in, and Reverend Graham Baldwin of Phillips—retired but much loved by the generations of Abbot girls who had taken his Bible course—pronounced the Benediction. In between, Richard Sewall, one of Don Gordon's favorite English teachers at Yale and the major speaker, grappled with the present dilemmas of young people. They are buffeted between champions of feeling and champions of the intellect, Sewall said, between radicals who see society as hopelessly corrupt and an Educational Establishment struggling to hold the same society together. "Make no little plans, Don, this is a boiling and seething age," Sewall advised his one-time student. Gordon answered in his own address that he planned to do no less than bring Abbot in line "possibly for the first time" with "the proud rhetoric" of its current catalogue and its original charter. The independent schools' struggle for survival in an era of declining applications obliged Abbot to be daring. Each adult and student in the Abbot community must become "sensitive enough to realize what is worth saving and tough enough to manage its implementation." The crowd loved it.

On campus, it was honeymoon time. The year's Crane's Beach picnic was a coeducational festival of sand-castle building, soccer games, and touch football earnestly joined by the Principal, who outreached all the boys as well as the girl players. Don's wife Josie and their small son Jamie were there too, winning hearts. Phillips-Abbot social activities continued to proliferate just as they would likely have done had Miss Tucker still been head; coeducational political and artistic activities boomed, all of them duly reported by an extraordinarily able and enthusiastic *Cynosure* board—and much of the credit naturally fell on Donald Gordon. He would always have a good press at Abbot and beyond, no matter what happened. The Principal helped students initiate two "Creative Days" at the beginning of winter term, when each student and teacher followed whatever craft or art she had been longing to try. According to *Cynosure*, it was Abbot's "trivial traditions" that "inhibited creative change," not its Principal, and *Cynosure* campaigned to topple every one of them."[25] "I was working to build a per-

sonal base with the student body," says Gordon now. "I wasn't thinking in terms of confrontation with the faculty, but I did want the
students' good will in whatever I did and I wanted it quickly." He was
getting it, too. The *Cynosure* Editor-in-Chief talked both with Gordon
and with his student admirers and marveled at his "way of making

50. Donald Gordon on Prize Day.

everyone feel special." Important as he was, he wanted most of all to be "a human being," she wrote. He already was "a teacher, an adviser, a friend and a father."[26] Almost immediately, friendship had been conclusively demonstrated by declaring that students might leave campus almost any weekend. The new Abbot would be open: let the restless stretch their souls outside the walls if they wished.[27] "Our headmaster has an extraordinarily humane understanding of today's youth," the reporters intoned as the fall went on.[28]

Of course other faculty had agreed to the move toward open weekends, just as they had planned for months the modified modular class schedule that went into effect in September, but the new administration got the cheers. That was perfectly all right with those teachers who welcomed the changes. The Abbot faculty had never pretended it participated in a democracy. Like several of his predecessors, Gordon carefully informed the faculty that first year, and consulted them on curricular matters, but rarely asked them to decide anything of school-wide importance. Later on, as Gordon became more rushed and harried, he would employ the more arbitrary features of Abbot's hierarchical tradition and sow anger as well as assent, but for now, the faculty were delighted to be discussing the tough, fascinating educational issues he brought before them or assigned to various faculty committees, instead of debating whether girls should be allowed to sit on their newly made beds in the morning.[29] If a few of the older faculty gathered in a knot of discontent at Tiffin time to talk away their annoyance at the power students seemed to have gained over the Principal, most teachers quietly backed his initiatives.

Their support was not blind loyalty. Whether or not they agreed with all of Gordon's ideas, most were convinced that institutions must somehow respond to the yearnings and fears of this generation of students. Abbot girls would never be quite the same after the political assassinations and urban riots of spring, 1968, or the mayhem in Chicago at the Democratic convention that summer: the school must speak to their needs. Besides, teaching was simply more fun than it had been in recent years. Gordon had been concerned about Abbot's casual student-counseling system, but what Faith Howland Kaiser noticed now was that girls were filled with "a sense of hope, excitement and change," and that the little Latin problems that had been an excuse for asking her special attention in the afternoons had vanished. Several teachers had thought the required mixers "TERRIBLE";[30] now they quietly became optional. The five-minute limit on boy-girl sidewalk conversation lapsed into oblivion. "It was such a relief!" says one teacher of the many small changes that allowed her to concentrate on teaching instead of defending faded rules. Don Gordon showed his respect for teaching by joining the two United States history teachers and doing some teaching himself in a series of topical seminars which the three set up together and conducted simultaneously all winter.

This was his last as well as his first teaching at Abbot. As resistance hardened among the few old-Abbot hold-outs and hiring decisions for the following year had to be made, Gordon left more and more of the daily chores to Miss Tucker and retreated into his office to plan for the next year. The endangered Admissions Director tried to plead with him for one more year's contract, but somehow she could never find an appointment time that was convenient for him. "He just couldn't face her," one teacher recalls.[31] Another Crane appointee—in Miss Tucker's words, an "honorable, vigorous, imaginative teacher"—began experiencing trouble with her classes, but she could not get his attention, so absorbing and difficult were his other problems, and she left, embittered. Others resigned of their own accord. Germaine Arosa and Donald Gordon had met each other's match. She had never liked Gordon, she says, and the feeling seems to have been mutual. She thought he was "wrecking the place," yet she felt that all constructive channels by which she might help were being closed to her. Philip Allen had urged Gordon to hear out his critics with a third person in the room, but this was complicated to arrange; the result was that he rarely met with the critics at all. Already beyond retirement age, Mademoiselle Arosa decided early on that this would be her last year, and she knew she was powerless.[32] This seemed the more clear after she and another teacher had taken their complaints about a third faculty member over the Principal's head to the Trustees and reaped nothing but the whirlwind of Gordon's anger.[33] It disturbed her deeply that Gordon seemed too busy to appreciate some of her closest faculty friends, or to further their plans and suggestions, such as those Margot Warner made for the Music Department. In the end, Mlle. Arosa and Miss Warner both resigned; after them would go the modern Abbot's most enduring teacher, Eleanor Tucker.

Miss Tucker's resignation in mid-spring of 1969 was a terrific blow to the Abbot community, even to those Trustees who had seen it coming. Gordon could not help being saddened by his differences with a person so much beloved by others, but he was philosophical. "By the time I got to Abbot I had long since concluded that all educational problems are problems of culture, not problems of personality," he says.

> I found myself measuring this person who had been acting head and was now my employee in terms of our cultural compatibility.

I think the important question is this: You have to ask what are the perceptions of development of young people that this person holds. As a team, an administrative group must conform to the overall objectives, although individuals can differ. I was the one responsible. The first fall and winter there were endless outcroppings of difference about how to approach problems of dealing with adolescent girls. We did agree that we needed a college counseling person, so I offered her this college counseling job and decided to get a new director of studies. This was an effort to find a place where Tuck would be comfortable. Then she herself decided to leave and I was greatly relieved. I confess that I saw people like Tuck as cultural artifacts in themselves.

It is heartening that several of the "cultural artifacts" found important work to do almost immediately, Mlle. Arosa as a French instructor at the University of Massachusetts and at the Boston University Music School, and Eleanor Tucker as Principal of Winchester-Thurston, a thriving girls' day school (kindergarten through twelfth grade) in Pittsburgh. Abbot had nurtured their talents through these long years as richly as it had those of so many students: they too were prepared for lives beyond the walls.

Don Gordon had prescribed for himself in his Installation address: The independent school must "be conservative when dealing with people, but fearlessly revolutionary when dealing with systems and methods." Yet Abbot's systems could not be changed without the radical sacrifice of people—"No matter what Don had done with Mlle. Arosa, it would have been wrong," says one teacher—and some of the new people whom Gordon was courting to replace the old for 1969–70 would swing the systems so far left by the force of their own lust for change that Gordon himself would wonder if the two can ever be separated, except in speeches. Nevertheless, administrators must never stop struggling, for systems and people—and money—are all they have. Principal and Trustees sat down together in the spring and summer of 1969 to create what new systems they could to make realities out of their visions.

Their most far-reaching decision was to launch at last the New Abbot Fund to increase radically both salaries and scholarships and to build a center for the arts near the Abbot-Phillips border, a facility long dreamed of at Abbot which could serve both schools.[34] Abbot had planned and delayed major endowment fund drives since 1930; now the need for more endowment was clear to everyone. It was not just the palpable sense that Abbot's competitors were catching up with, and surpassing, the old Academy with their own endowment drives (though they were);[35] Abbot must have insurance for any future, whether with Phillips or alone.

None could now fault the Trustees for holding back on fund raising,[36] but the grand plan had its critics. Tamblyn and Brown found the $3,000,000 goal overambitious, given Abbot's consituency. Others felt the strategy too luxurious: with these bold development plans came a new public relations staff and a Director of Development, Richard Sheahan, whom Don Gordon knew from his teaching days in California. There was no way of knowing that Sheahan's office would amply pay for itself in the years to come, and that Sheahan himself would prove an indispensable balance wheel as Abbot's forward engines built up to full steam. Jane Baldwin, always cautious, asked whether it was not far too soon to commit funds to a building before programmatic questions of coordination had been decided. She and others questioned the wisdom of opening the New Abbot drive before most of Abbot had any idea what the new Abbot would be; they were not content with the daring answers they received from Allen and Gordon, who had been mapping the future together for months. Already alumnae seemed to be hesitating: after years of increase, donations to the Annual Fund had dipped $1,000 in 1968–69.[37] But most of the Trustees felt it was time to move. "We must have something special to offer Phillips," they said, "if our own bid for coordination on equal terms is not to be laughed out of court." When Miss Baldwin had heard rationales for such speedy action once too often, she would resign.

Donald Gordon also hired the full-time professional business manager which Cresap had urged upon the Abbot Board six years earlier. Now that Gardner Sutton was close to retirement, a fresh hand was needed. Richard Griggs provided it—and well that he did, for the budgeting and accounting procedures that had served in more stable times had burst at the seams in Gordon's first year. The Board had planned a $7,000 operating deficit for 1968–69; that first year Gordon authorized special projects as they came up, and Abbot finished the year $117,468 in the red. The Trustees were surprised but (with a few exceptions) unruffled by the bill Gordon was running up; most of the special expenditures seemed necessary and commendable. They had wanted an innovator, and they were prepared to support him. "You do not sit on your hands if you have been brought in to save a school," says Carolyn Goodwin;[38] nor do you stint to raise faculty-staff salaries if you are, like Gordon, a person of generous impulses, anxious to right past wrongs. Writing a budget for the following year proved more complicated. Abbot's expenses had traditionally changed so little from one year to the next that the budget had never been drawn up before late spring. Under this system it was as difficult for Assistant Treasurer Gardner Sutton as it was for Donald Gordon to know what extra monies could be committed for 1969–70, yet most of the Trustees agreed with Gordon that Abbot needed a college counselor, a business manager, an associate admissions director, and supporting staff. To get them, they had no choice but to run a deficit even larger than the one for 1968–69. The physical plant also presented both problems and opportunities. Barton Chapin's sons were offering the Trustees the family house. Once renovated, it would make an ideal small dormitory; the proposal seemed far too generous to turn down given the eventual economies implicit in a higher enrollment. $115,500 of other renovations had been proposed to increase dormitory spaces, to provide better dining and study space for the burgeoning crowd of day students, and to make Draper Hall more pleasant and workable.

To several Trustees it seemed insane to contemplate these expenditures; even Allen's optimism began to flag. The full Board met in special session at the Abbot Library on June 26, 1969, the year's bad news before them on balance sheets and budget projections. The mood was gloomy; the rational response seemed obvious: scale down, cut back, forget the new Abbot.

True, there was good news to be considered too, but no hard figures supported it except for a thin, hopeful column of applications statistics for 1969–70. Nearly everyone in the room had a sense of the many seeds sown in the year just past, a year in which accomplishment and promise loomed even larger than pain—though there had been pain in plenty too. The Board questioned Gordon: How could Abbot possibly manage such deficits? Could the school attract candidates enough to enlarge and prosper and thus eliminate them? The most optimistic answers could not dispel the uncertainties yawning before the Board. Only faith could overcome them, and what grounds were there for faith?

It was Alice Sweeney who turned the tide. She rarely spoke, but when she did, everyone listened. "Let's finish the job!" she said. "Either we build a school that meets modern needs or we won't have any school at all."[39] "I've been blamed for everything that happened to Abbot since that day," laughs Miss Sweeney now. Heartened, the Board voted the entire renovations budget, agreed to increase the salary budget to $490,000 (nearly double the figure for 1964–65, including over twice the amount for administrative salaries than had been needed in 1967–68),[40] and decided to ask the Phillips Trustees to join them in an effort finally to decide what the long-term relations between the two schools would be. The Principal had already discussed with the Business Manager-elect the mechanisms by which long-range educational goals could be systematically geared to financial capabilities; with James K. Dow, the Treasurer-elect, Griggs proposed that Abbot adopt the flexible budgetary procedures that had been developed by the NAIS. The Trustees felt confident that they and Griggs could help Gordon control Abbot's purse strings even in an age of rapid change, and this assurance played a crucial part in their willingness to move ahead. Gordon welcomed the help: he knew he would need all he could get. There would be no turning back now.

Blitz

A mid-fall afternoon, 1969. A mother and alumna, Class of '51, drives through the Gates to see her Abbot daughter for the first time. To be sure, they had visited the campus the year before when the daughter came for her interview; then, the mother had been reassured to find Abbot looking much as it did in her own time, with only a handsomely tailored male Principal and some unfamiliar teachers whom Mrs. Crane or Miss Tucker had hired to break the illusion of changelessness. But now! Touch football players romped on the sacred Circle. Not a saddle shoe was to be seen; indeed, one boy and two girls played with no shoes at all, in spite of November. Two pairs of faded blue jeans wandered by, one belted in macrame and filled by a man of bristling beard; he was discussing English papers with the other. Afternoon Study Hall should be beginning just about now—but no one was heading for McKeen. Where had Abbot gone? Perhaps the alumna would find out at supper time: everyone coming freshly dressed to her assigned seat at table, the Grace sung to usher in a dignified meal, the News given. Or at daily Chapel the next morning—surely, Abbot would be there.

It was not. There was no Chapel. There had been no study hall, no Grace, no News, no dignified dinner. The mob ate in its touch football clothes or its pottery-making clothes or whatever clothes it wished. Though several adults and two cheerful babies joined it for dinner, there was no assigned seating. The Phillips boys lay in wait in the social rooms, "calling hours" having been extended to most of the afternoon and evening. It would have been appalling—except that the

Abbot daughter was enjoying it immensely, and seemed to be learning something to boot. Maybe one could get used to it after all. Since
the daughter was to stay, one would try.[41]

In the second of the Gordon years, the space inside the privet hedge
seemed if anything to amplify the revolutionary changes taking place
in the world at large. New teachers and houseparents brought that
world in; many veterans complemented them by virtue of their efforts
to respond (as Abbot had always tried to respond) to students' needs.
The first and most sweeping innovation of the year was the advent of
a town meeting form of government to decide all out-of-classroom
issues touching students' lives. The fall before, the old student government system had come apart when the Student Council president
found herself unable to uphold the "honor system" and turn friends
in. That was nothing new; in the early sixties, five of the six Seniors
on one year's Student Council were among the worst rule-breakers in
the school.[42] The novelty was in this president's refusal to hide her
feelings from Mr. Gordon or anyone else. "Follow Abbot's rules or
resign," said the Principal, and she resigned. Predictably, the remaining
Council members called two old-style town meetings, closed to faculty
and traditionally devoted to subjects such as the design of class rings,
to discuss the situation; unpredictably the girls decided to rewrite the
student government constitution. Warmly backed by the Principal,
they asked Mary Minard to act as their faculty adviser, and set to
work.

What they came up with was nothing new in a larger world that included progressive schools and "free schools,"[43] but it was entirely
new to Abbot. The town meeting would meet regularly, its agenda
organized and published in advance by its officers. These last, one faculty and two student secretaries and one student moderator, were
elected for two terms by the entire community, one woman (or man)
—one vote and never mind seniority. Faculty, houseparents, and students also voted on equal terms at the meetings themselves, which
were run by Robert's Rules. Anyone could propose new business once
the old was disposed of; thus, theoretically at least, anything was dis-
cussable—*anything*. No vote could be taken except on an issue announced beforehand, but once voted, a decision could only be reviewed and vetoed by the Principal. Lacking a veto (Gordon used it
just four times in four years), the majority vote became school policy
a week after it had been taken. To the chagrin of some older faculty
who knew how much Abbot traditions had meant to the girls of years
gone by, the new school government banished all ghostly presences,
all mystical loyalty to the historical Abbot, and defined "Abbot" as no

more than the sum of its present parts: the students and adults who inhabited the campus at any given moment. It seemed an age since 1968, when all Abbot girls had recited for the last time the traditional pledge at the student government induction ceremony—"banded together in our loyalty to Abbot . . ."—and had sung "Abbot Beautiful" to seal it.

To Donald Gordon, pledges and school hymns were relics of an irrelevant past: young people need plain, unvarnished responsibility to grow on. "Students are partners in the educational enterprise," Gordon wrote that fall. "The human spirit needs encouragement and trust," and the key to faculty-student trust is "scrupulous honesty in working with students on school affairs."[44] Town meeting symbolized, and generally carried forward, this central principle throughout Abbot's final four years.

Truly, the new system was an open one. It exposed everyone, ready or not, occasionally laying bare as many reasons for distrust as for trust. For openers, town meeting abolished the old dress code, substituting "neat and clean"[45] (a few teachers later wondered whether "underwear required" should not have been added), and determined that girls be allowed to skip Sunday church and attend instead a Sunday evening gathering organized by the Abbot Religious Association (ARA), whose name had been changed to make Jewish students welcome. Daily Chapel went next. It had already been eliminated at Phillips on the initiative of a new chaplain, who could not see how one could "justify compulsion at any level of worship";[46] and Donald Gordon, a searching agnostic, could not bring himself to wear the pastor's mantle in the McKeen-Bailey tradition. Town meetings established a faculty-student committee to discuss the abolition of grades.[47] At first it looked like revolution. For suspicious teachers, however, a few surprises lay in store. The grades committee investigated other schools' grading systems and organized school-wide discussions on the subject. Seeking to avoid a Principal's veto, the secretaries made sure the final committee report to town meeting culminated in a town meeting "resolution to the faculty" rather than a decisive vote for or against letter grades. This was no runaway democracy. Faculty found that students actually listened when they asked town meeting to consider larger issues such as the meaning and purpose of academic evaluation; as the novelty wore off and the uncommitted students stayed away, adults' voices counted more.[48] Still, it was an enormous change, and for all their frustration with the clumsiness of such an open system, students knew it offered them both a forum for grievances and access to real power. "TOWN MEETING STRIKES AGAIN" cheered *Cynosure*, announcing that Abbot had voted to invite Phillips boys down after dinner, and that the administration would bring the proposal up the Hill.[49]

Most faculty put up cheerfully enough with these unfamiliar forms and enjoyed the discussions they engendered. Some of the old hands found that town meeting, by involving students in school-wide decisions, engaged teachers and housemothers more fully as well. Teachers who recall that they "came, did what they had to and went away again" during the Crane-Tucker years now stayed at school all day and into the evenings.[50] "More freedom for the students always means more work for the adults," Gordon kept telling the faculty. It was true, but to most of the adults, it seemed work worth doing. From the first, Gordon had "wanted a school where people would crack open any subject and talk about it."[51] Rather suddenly, students found it easier to take their grievances or their problems to a teacher. Faculty-room conversation spilled out into student-filled corridors; several new history and English and mathematics courses were hatched and fledged on the strength of student interest or teacher inspiration, or both.

In a certain sense, however, a new common culture was being imposed on Abbot girls. If Chapel was no longer required, "humanities" was. "Watch out! I may be teaching your daughter," Stephen Perrin warned in the new Abbot Forum, which rose live and kicking that fall from the ashes of the staid Bulletin. This bearded, gentle man posed every tenth grader his question: What does it mean to be human? and if he acknowledged that every person has her own answer, he was determined it should be well informed. Robert Ardrey on vertebrate social behavior, Freud, Fromm, Bruner, Erikson, novels and biographies about artists or scientists—these readings demanded effort of a new kind, for Perrin offered them as stimuli to introspection, not artifacts to analyze. Who am I? What do I learn from James Agee about myself? students were encouraged to ask. Write it down, write anything, it's you, it's O.K. The same in Sue Hosmer's philosophy classes, which were explorations of self and universe together. No texts at all were required in Peter Stapleton's and Paul Dyer's English classes. Dyer had put aside the medieval poetry that had stirred him in college. "Students themselves are the content of the course," he told the Forum. "All assignments are optional for all of us in one way or another," said Stapleton; "what is exciting is making the choices."[52] Dyer had students write their own "teacher comments" at the end of each term.

A few parents and alumnae really were appalled. It was Donald Gordon who quoted Eric Hoffer in his Installation speech to warn against excessive freedom:

> A fateful process is set in motion when the individual is released
> to the freedom of his own impotence and left to justify his
> existence by his own efforts.[53]

A year later it seemed to a small minority that Gordon was fostering
the "fateful process" he had deplored. Nevertheless, experimentation
bubbled on. "If you're going to show students that no one should fear
to inquire," says Gordon, "teachers have to be secure enough to do it."
Perrin still recalls that security with gratitude. "Don Gordon hired us
as change-agents, and then left us to ourselves, defending us to the
Trustees when he had to," he says. "It was a wonderful freedom; I
had never felt so creative or worked so hard, or, I think, taught
so well."

Students ran the gamut in their opinions of these new courses. "My
favorite," says one girl of Perrin's humanities class. She was a searching, deliberate reader, who gained "great insight into people" from the
difficult texts. On the other hand—"I found him a hypocrite," who
"couldn't stand to have me to disagree with him," writes another
alumna, herself a sharp, contentious character; "While upholding freedom, he was an absolute authoritarian in class." Stapleton's course had
one Catholic girl amused and angry and distressed to tears all at once.
Knowing she needed stays, her family had sent her to Abbot for a
conservative academic education the year before, and her father was
infuriated by the changes made without warning to parents in the fall
of '69. "If Stapleton is going to be the student and you the teacher,"
he told her, "he should give over his salary to you."[54]

In Hall House lived Phyllis and David Maynard, the first of the
series of young houseparents whom Gordon hired at salaries equivalent to those of the teaching faculty in his effort to revamp dormitory
supervision. They were operating on much the same principle as did
the most radical new teachers: this is your home; you are nearly adult.
Let's work out together the common house rules which meet our
common needs, and stick with them. From his position as the new
Director of Studies, John Buckey, former teacher and admissions officer at Quaker schools, former urban community organizer, listened
as carefully for the personal concerns behind each student's academic
plans as he did to each teacher who came in with a course proposal or
a kid problem. To him, all educational decisions edged learner and
teacher toward social commitments. Sterile talk of college requirements and rank in class obscured the complex processes by which an
individual makes her own unique sense of the larger culture and pre-

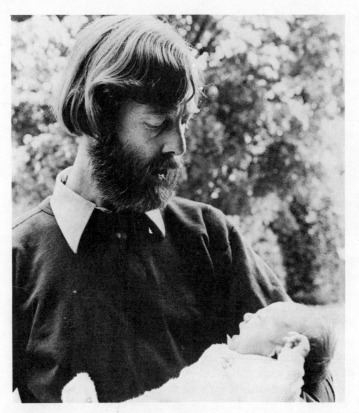

51. Stephen Perrin with Jesse.

52. Coed football on the Sacred Circle.

53. Ceramics.

pares to take on adult responsibility within it. True, Alice Sweeney and Eleanor Tucker also had known how much more there is to academic counseling than meets the eye, but Buckey had just arrived at Abbot from the bruising world outside, and this made him exciting; his own commitment to the civil rights and antiwar movement sensitized him to young people's anger and uncertainty. At first it seemed as though Buckey's warm-hearted activism would wonderfully flesh out Gordon's more abstract sense of the need for "an enlightened radicalism of method" by which a school could join in the best aspects of "the revolt of our times."[55]

Across the hall, Marion Finbury gave full time to college counseling. To Gordon this was no luxury: where Seniors once had asked, "Can I make one of the Seven Sisters?" now they wondered openly, "What do I do with my life?"[56] It could take hours and weeks of talk to break the question into its component parts and deal with each. His faith in high gear, Gordon had found a person with no formal training for this crucial job, a bright Jewish woman ready for work of her own. "Hired off the wall," she says. "I could have been a disaster. It was disaster year." But her qualifications were excellent: for years she had worked to improve public education in her own community; she had been an Abbot parent, and a friendly critic of Abbot's college admissions process; she was ready to learn whatever needed learning; and she and her teen-aged children were still speaking to each other.[57] A fresh eye might make sense of the confusing new patterns of college admissions which were emerging as the colleges pried themselves open to women, minority applicants, and others who had once been beyond the pale. When she arrived in June 1969 to get going, Marion Finbury found that Gordon had locked the old college files; he sent her instead to a Harvard Admissions Institute and on a trip to West Coast colleges ("I hadn't been on a trip without my husband in fifteen *years*") and generally helped her begin that process by which Abbot teachers defined both their work and themselves. In September she "opened for business, shaking from top to toe." She began by talking with each Senior. She called up Radcliffe and told the Director of Admissions, "I want to come see you." "Whatever for?" asked the Director, who knew that in the past two decades only a handful of Abbot girls had applied for and entered Radcliffe.[58] Marion Finbury would badger Radcliffe and Berkeley and every college in between with such good humor and such intricate knowledge of her charges that she was hard to resist. She *knew* one candidate's 450 S.A.T. scores said little of her, and she persuaded New College to take her on probation. In four years the young woman had simultane-

ously finished college and served a term in the New Hampshire legislature; then she scored over 700 in the Law School Aptitude test and
entered Law School. As her predecessors had done, Mrs. Finbury encouraged students to consider an ever wider range of colleges. Four
of seven applicants made Radcliffe that first year; many other graduates were equally well placed in newly coeducational colleges or universities never available to Abbot girls before. Like Gordon, however,
Finbury felt that the process of college counseling was as important
to a student's total education as the result. Again, Miss Sweeney and
Miss Tucker would no doubt have agreed—but Marion Finbury was
the first to be given the time to act on the conviction.

The old birds were by no means sitting still while the new ones
tried their wings: Abbot's swift movement in the first two Gordon
years can only be understood in the light of veteran teachers' readiness
for change and their willingness often to advance it, given the Principal's encouragement. The students who loved Abbot in 1969–70 are
the ones who enjoyed the rigors of Carolyn Goodwin's calculus class
as much as the heady confusions of Paul Dyer's "English" encounter
group. "It didn't matter to me that Stapleton didn't make us read
because suddenly I found I wanted to read all the optional history
stuff, and I wrote about *that* in my English journal," says one such.
Sandra Urie Thorpe, '70, found some changes disturbing, but she was
absorbed in her urban education course field work and in special
Spanish study with Dorothy Judd, work so advanced that she would
be taking senior-level courses at Smith the following year. Georges
Krivobok and Susan Clark were new birds, but their language classes
were as demanding as any that Mlle. Arosa or Mrs. DeGavre had
taught. For spring term the three United States history teachers offered three different approaches to twentieth-century studies, and each
Senior chose her poison. In the Revolution at Home and Abroad
course, a tie-dyed girl fed up with intricate foreign-policy readings
and Black Panther community-organization plans exclaimed, "But the
Revolution is here! All we have to do is *love* each other!" "And read
fifty pages a night," quipped a black girl, to whom knowledge was
strength for the struggle. Still more options appeared as Phillips Academy courses in advanced studio art, religion, Asian history, German,
and Italian were opened to Abbot students, with boys enrolling in
similarly specialized Abbot courses such as Sex Education, Ceramics
and Advanced Placement Spanish. All this was consistent with Donald
Gordon's conviction that the key to growth is the opportunity to
choose among a variety of endeavors. In his view the instilling of
"correct" ambitions only ossifies the soul. He traces his own feeling

back to his childhood and his father's tendency to identify great achievement with narrow, self-denying labor: " 'Work, by God, work your ass off!' "—this was the father's message to the son, as the son conveys it. But the freedom and the responsibility to choose one's work gives the young person "the chance to see that achievement can be pleasurable. . . . I had enormous faith in the subliminal effect on students of a happy, diverse, vibrant community," says Gordon now.[59] Abbot "seeks to be a house of many rooms," Gordon told his public in 1971.[60] Indeed, the greatest strengths of the Gordon years lay in the extraordinary variety of academic and other choices that Abbot offered to any student ready to make them. Strong characters did beautifully from the start, and many others grew strong on this rich fare.[61]

Break-Up

All of Donald Gordon's first three years coincided with an era of student revolution at home and awful foreign policy failures abroad, but for Abbot, 1969–70 was the most tumultuous of all. Universities and secondary schools both public and private had seen their students march and rally and roar their protests over policies out of the White House and dictates from principals' offices. Every month, it seemed, another college president resigned. "We students are in revolt," wrote the *Choate News* early in 1969. "We are part of a worldwide rebellion of the young. We want a say . . . We will not be suppressed."[62] America had seen youth subcultures before: the last three decades had had their Beats and their Young Socialists, who dressed to prove their empathy with the downtrodden, railed against the grey-flannel values of academia, and labored with migrant workers in the summertime; but the scale and the hostility of this new protest were unprecedented. It was the clamor of a generation that saw history itself careening out of control, a generation "by no means sure that it has a future," as George Wald has said.[63] Defensive adults saw only the repulsive hair styles, the obscene dress, and the frightening upsurge in teen-age drug use; the students demanded the right to decide their appearance and devise their own escapes from the realities adults had prepared for them.

Abbot was not doing badly, considering. There was a knot of druggies in one or two dormitories, and there were several boarding school counterparts of the ubiquitous teen-age runaway, but teachers kindly and firmly picked up the familiar hitch-hikers and brought them weeping back again; a few of them were running no further than John

Buckey's house in West Andover anyway. The Maynards advised one troubled girl to clear out on her own for a while; another teacher who could find neither parents nor Principal to grant an abrupt permission took responsibility on herself for a girl who had secretly had an abortion and needed the comfort of her twin sister in Lowell. Gordon was furious when he found out (he could not know about the abortion)— but was this better or worse than in years past when (insist alumnae) at least two students ran away to parts unknown for days at a time, counting on friends to sign them in each night and in other ways assure gullible housemothers of their continued presence on campus?

Principal and faculty did all they could to encourage constructive social action. Given minimal guidance, girls ran YWCA and "Wide Horizons" programs for underprivileged children all year long. With teachers and parents as drivers, over a hundred Abbot and Phillips students tutored immigrant children one to three afternoons a week during the spring at a special Title I school in the middle of the most decrepit neighborhood in Lawrence. The New Abbot had its own "Golden Rule" dinners: Gordon worked with the Bondes, their kitchen staff, and a group of students to arrange a safe Fast for World Hunger and send proceeds to American Friends Service Committee hospitals in Vietnam. He joined teachers and students to launch first an Indochina "teach-in," then an Earth Day, during which classes were moved aside to make room for school-wide assemblies and small group discussions on these urgent world problems. Abbot girls joined with Andover High School students on several antiwar projects and conferences. Longing to shed the elitism that had characterized Andover Hill for over a century, they sought solidarity with those of their own generation everywhere. April 15, Income Tax day, was a milestone: teachers drove Abbot and Phillips and High School students to an early morning protest at the Northeast Internal Revenue Service center in west Andover; John Buckey delighted the protestors by filming on his home movie camera the FBI agents who stood on the roof of the IRS center filming the crowd below. (As he walked toward them, his camera grinding, they folded up their cameras and retreated.) That afternoon two busloads of Abbot and Phillips students and faculty joined 75,000 other citizens in a massive Boston Common rally against the War and the Black Panther trials.

It was wearing for everyone, especially for the man at the helm who was having troubles enough fielding the distress of parents and alumnae and reconciling some of his new appointees with Abbot's long-run needs and plans. Yet Donald Gordon felt more in tune with the upsurge than did Colonel Kemper up on the Hilltop. The sixties had allowed Gordon to "go public," as he puts it, after years of lonely worry over "the degradation of the environment and the stifling of political discussion" in the fifties. Abbot's relatively small size was a large advantage. Phillips Academy "has sometimes been guilty of treating boys impersonally," reported the Phillips Steering Committee.[64] "Pessimism plagues P.A.," wrote *Cynosure* reporters.[65] "Even the best are bad," one "Thomas Doland" told a *Look Magazine* reporter who came hunting revolutionaries on Andover Hill that year.[66] Doland's Andover was an "active tool" of the government warmakers (he said), but the boy himself expressed most of his rebellion in the Phillips medium: eighty-one class cuts a year, jimmied in the records to look like nine, marijuana joints by the gross, and lots of good sex in the Sanctuary with Abbot girls for pleasure and defiance combined.[67] At least, said Doland, there was the new Phillips Art Center, where creative work with other "alienated and artistic intellectuals" earned reluctant academic credit from the anti-art Establishment—and it was too bad about those Abbot girls, "really good chicks," basically, who "don't have the ability . . . to be particularly creative themselves." Because of this, and because so few Abbot girls are "into drugs and other liberating things (Doland continued, relishing his chance to play Norman Mailer), most of them have a very large sexual need which they transfer to the Andover student who is creative."[68] Chauvinist hogwash, but startling nonetheless. Jane Baldwin wrote to Phil Allen when the *Look* article appeared and told him Donald Gordon should be released from his post. "Give the boy a little longer," said Allen.[69] To fire a principal so recently hired would destroy whatever credibility Abbot still possessed.[70] The article was peppered with proven inaccuracies and therefore suspect; and after all, it was about Phillips, not Abbot. Like many teachers, Allen had noticed again and again that year how much happier and more sensible most Abbot students had seemed than the Hilltop students. Being female helped: girls did not have to be drafted, or to kill or die in Vietnam.[71] But Abbot as institution was also working hard to channel rebellion, to counsel girls with sexual and other needs both large and small, and to provide creative outlets everywhere, even if "Doland" couldn't see them.

It wasn't till the crisis in May that Gordon let on how battle-weary he was. On April 30 Nixon ordered American troops to invade Cambodia. On May 4 four innocent college students were shot and killed by panicky National Guardsmen while watching an antiwar demonstration at Kent State University. In Andover all hell broke loose. It was O.K. for Abbot girls to set up a congressman-writing station in Draper Hall; but it was not O.K. for them to strike their classes in order to gather signatures on antiwar petitions (not yet, at least), and it was not at all O.K. for Paul Dyer to defy the Principal and take off for the Washington demonstrations with two Abbot students immediately after Gordon, fearful for their safety, had denied the girls permission to go. Principal gathered faculty for a special meeting, intending a rational discussion of Abbot's response to the crisis. Instead, an exhausted Donald Gordon picked up on a critical comment John Buckey made, talked himself into a rage on the subject of loyalty to him and to the school, and stomped out, leaving the faculty puzzled, stunned. Most felt they had gone out on many a limb for and with the Principal, and that any criticisms they'd made were meant to help. While Gordon drove to Plum Island to walk off his anger, Peter Stapleton led the group through the completion of a plan whereby "striking" students could pick up their assignments and leave for hometown antiwar work, or could join the seminars and action groups already organized at Phillips—for those Hilltop warmongers had laid extraordinarily clear-headed plans for "Strike Week."[72] Gordon returned home that evening to find a bunch of red roses waiting for him, a peace-offering from two concerned teachers.

As it turned out, most students took to these opportunities peacefully and responsibly, and only a few actually went home on strike. A brief town panic over "Communists" from Abbot and Phillips infiltrating the public schools died down when the agitators proved to be two peacable history teachers who were helping the Junior High Principal and some students set up a panel on American business interests in Indochina. (The Junior High group was eventually allowed to attend a packed meeting at the Abbot Chapel in which Philip Allen debated the subject with a gentle socialist-anarchist from Lawrence, the socialist-anarchist read some of his poems, and everyone agreed that both had won.) A massive drug bust on the Hill cleared out several of "Doland's" friends just before Abbot Commencement, though two would spring forth in each one's place the following year.

Finally, painfully, Donald Gordon resolved some of his "loyalty" problems by releasing the teachers who had—in his view—taken his injunction to experiment and run away with it. Of the twelve new faculty members he had hired, half were released from their positions at the end of the 1969–70 school year, including the new Dean of Students and the new Director of Studies. The Maynards and Paul Dyer had been "in tune with the times, close to the kids," remembers Carolyn Johnston; by May they seemed too much so on both counts to Donald Gordon, who, with Johnston, had heard from one too many parents about the liberation of the Maynards' dormitory from legal constraints against marijuana. Such a slaughter had never happened before at Abbot, and it was a wrenching time, as much for Gordon as for all those colleagues who counted them friends. The parting of the ways with John Buckey was the most dramatic. Gordon acknowledged that many of their problems lay in their personal incompatibility rather than in Buckey's professional deficiencies; indeed, Don Gordon and Phil Allen together backed Buckey as he sought and found another excellent job. Through his warm interest in both students and colleagues, and his driving, often stubborn idealism, Buckey had expanded the influence that the Director of Studies traditionally commanded far beyond the boundaries Gordon envisioned for the position, and finally collided so often with the Principal that he knew before his boss fired him that he could not remain. Two alumnae remember Mr. Gordon advising them to do one thing and sending them to check out the details with Mr. Buckey, only to be told to do something quite different. Buckey was endlessly patient with students in trouble; Gordon wanted some of these same girls to go on to Abbot's official psychiatrist for expert counseling. At the juncture between disturbed individual and institution loom all the terrors that no institution can fathom, and those responsible become terribly anxious: a girl who had attempted suicide refused to return to Abbot's psychiatrist, and Buckey and Gordon argued over alternative psychiatrists till they were shouting at each other. Gordon thought Buckey wanted to sacrifice the variety of teachers Abbot enjoyed in order to fill the place with flower children and political radicals. Buckey insists this is not true, but can understand the impasse: a principal needs real authority as well as pride.

And Donald Gordon was nothing if not proud. His pride energized some of the new Abbot's most successful programs, but it also made him terribly vulnerable as a person and a leader. One way to cope with criticisms or human complications was to drown them in talk: a teacher or student who went to Gordon with a curricular proposal or a personal dilemma might get a marvelously responsive hearing— or she might do all the hearing herself while Gordon talked through most of the hour of his own problems and visions.[73] Gordon's loquaciousness certified the distance he had traveled from that "quiet," "extremely shy" youngster whom his Phillips housemasters knew in 1952.[74] Daring much, the Principal needed the reassurance of sympathetic listeners at every turn in his adventurous path.

Some teachers and students found it hard to see Gordon at all, for he was away raising money and attending professional meetings more than any of his predecessors had been.[75] When at Abbot, it was natural for him to spend most of his time with the colleagues who approved his ideas. His favorite conversor was Peter Stapleton, the lively and articulate young English teacher as short as his boss was tall, whom the Principal had named "administrative intern." Gordon had asked him to conduct a study of the headmaster's role in educational change as part of Stapleton's graduate work at Harvard, and had invited him to collaborate on a short book about it. As Phil Allen puts it, "Don needed to have somebody to throw his wild ideas at." The two spent hour upon hour assessing Abbot's progress and talking out plans; it was a process immensely helpful to Gordon, but it left many teachers feeling excluded—especially older ones accustomed to a voice in Abbot affairs: why was the Principal consulting this natty, witty young outsider and not consulting *them?* Gordon had hired him at full salary "to needle my faculty in a constructive way";[76] Stapleton was only an intern observing when he visited their classes or talked with their students, but might not the hilarity they could hear behind the Principal's office door be a joke at their expense?

Occasionally the answer may have been "yes." Drawing a self-conscious circle around himself and his privy councillor as they drafted their account of the principal's job, Gordon enlarged on the lonely eminence a "headmaster" occupies, even the "new" headmaster who refuses to clothe himself in myth or "big Lie."[77] The modern leader "must *truly* be better than average human beings," honest, natural, responsive to students and (most difficult) to his faculty, who, "being teachers, full of educational philosophy, often absolutist . . . know everything. And you are a grubby administrator."[78] When "brute fatigue" or the "endemic bitchiness" of the boarding school overwhelms and unanswered mail piles up (it takes *time* to write a book with your administrative intern) and parents rant on the sidelines, demanding Utopia for their children, what is there left to do but laugh?[79]

Every principal has such problems and such protective egocentricities to some degree. What was surprising (and often deeply appealing) about Donald Gordon was his way of wearing them all on his sleeve—at least within Abbot's boundaries. (Out on the hustings, the image of serenity and control held up pretty well.) This openness was not just a personal need; it was also part of a conscious, candid effort to develop educational policy. An example: many male principals of all-girl or coeducational schools would hesitate to reveal the complex sources of their desire to understand and work with women and girls. Gordon says he was influenced most of all by his strong-minded and sensitive British mother, to whom "a gentleman was a *gentle man*." Her—and his—ideal man embodied "the whole world of sensitivities and sensibility that is excluded from the American archetype."[80] Gordon is certain that such a vision, if openly lived and articulated, can cross sexist boundaries, and inspire young women as well as young men. One highly successful Abbot principal had been equally candid about this issue a century earlier: the Reverend Joseph Bittinger, who took Abbot on for the year 1848–49, when Asa Farwell went to Europe. By his own account, Bittinger personified the alliance between the nineteenth century woman and the male minister:

> I cannot help thinking that (in the years when Abbot was run by clergymen) ministers partook of the nature of both man and woman. I was too much of a woman to be a man, and not fair and gentle enough to be a woman. I was surprised at being called to the head of this school . . . but I am not ashamed that I was accounted worthy to keep a woman's school in Massachusetts. Whatever I taught others, I learned much during that year. . . . Every man and woman must make himself or herself; the working power is not in the institution. The schoolmaster . . . hews a living stone which has an influence on himself.[81]

Bittinger was mildly apologetic, but by the 1970's no apologies were needed. Like Bittinger, Gordon daily demonstrated the range of creative possibilities open to all who refuse to be limited by cultural stereotypes of male and female.

Some of Gordon's difficulties lay in the size of the job he had taken on, and the competing demands of his family. He had taken the Abbot principalship at an age when most married men have seen their children through the years of highest demand on parents; but Gordon had married in his late twenties, and his son and daughter were still babies. Pulled one way by his responsibilities as Principal, another by his equally serious responsibilities as father, he found it terribly hard to live up to Trustees' and parents' images of the serene "family man" and model for young people, managing everything beautifully, every day.

Three Good Years

Gordon certainly did try, however, and in a great many ways he succeeded, especially as he took to heart the lessons of his first two years and settled down to see Abbot through its final three. "If the third year isn't better, I'll hang it up," Gordon remembers thinking; but it *was* better, partly because he made it so. "We came gently down from what was actually a period of excess," says Gordon now. Having dominated the scene, he retreated a bit. Having distrusted many teachers, he began delegating his authority to some of them; if he still considered "dreaming"—the establishment of "sustaining goals"—the headmaster's province, he no longer disdained plans already made as "garbage" to "be handed over to a subordinate" while he went on with his "creative wishing." These tongue-in-cheek terms with which he and Stapleton filled their book would become anachronisms as he brought closer together in his mind the stuff of dreams and the everyday life of the school. At his best he functioned as a coordinator rather than the heroic leader he seems at first to have tried to be, and in doing so, he fostered the communal enterprise he had wanted so much all along. In the first two years Gordon had possessed the place; during most of the last three, Abbot belonged to itself.

First came appointments of new people to fill the places of those who were leaving. Gordon was determined not to be so trusting of appearances—Paul Dyer had come to his Abbot interviews in a Brooks Brothers herringbone suit, which he never wore again—and instead to look for experience. The best place to find this was among the old hands inside Abbot. Carolyn Goodwin already knew academic scheduling and student placement from her work as chairman of the Mathematics Department. She had been twenty-three years at Abbot, a topnotch corridor teacher in the old days and member of dozens of committees in the new days. Whether or not she agreed with them, students admired her as "disciplined, intelligent" and infallibly honest, stern when she must be where Gordon was "too soft."[82] With some difficulty, Gordon persuaded her to become Director of Studies for a one-year trial. A few Trustees were surprised at the choice. "Goodie" was so quiet that they had hardly known her. They were more familiar with Carolyn Johnston as a former Associate Dean, an experienced counselor and a firm but compassionate trouble-shooter who had picked up the pieces for years when a dormitory crisis or a miserable student had proved too complex for one lone Dean of Students to handle. Now Mrs. Johnston became Dean in her own right, and immediately set to work devising a system of weekly guidance for houseparents and resident advisers, and an advisory Dorm Council to keep student representatives in touch with school-wide problems. The two women were to prove themselves equal to almost any challenge their boss was to hand them; perhaps more important still, they patiently took care of the day-to-day details which, from his altitude, he could not even know existed. In time, students who spoke of "the administration," (whether in anger or approval) as often meant Goodwin-Johnston as they meant Gordon, for Gordon "trusted us, let us

54. The deans: Carolyn Johnston and Carolyn Goodwin.

help," "supported us when we did need support, and left us complete-ly alone," as Carolyn Johnston says. "Don was not a good adminis-trator," says one Trustee, summing up the views of several people who worked closely with Gordon, "but he was wise enough finally to find people who were."

The two Carolyns completed Abbot's administrative team, joining Dick Griggs, Dick Sheahan, and Faith Howland Kaiser, Admissions Director, all of whom had made it through 1969–70 more or less un-scathed. Four of the five were middle-aged and tough. Sheahan was thoroughly Republican to boot, with a talent for turning every ideo-logical argument into a friendly discussion, an invaluable gift in this age of acrimony. Faith, just twenty-six years old, had thrown herself with the ardor of the young into the Gordon camp when distressed faculty took sides in the Buckey-Gordon battle the year before, but she and her still younger assistant, Priscilla Peterson, were so able and so excited by the success they were having in recruiting new applicants that they made time to talk comfortably (and endlessly) with Gordon and work hard too. From her special perspective, Faith added her keen sense of student morale, and an enthusiasm for Abbot's future that kindled warmth within the entire adminstrative team.

It helped that the battering political events outside gradually receded over Abbot's last years; once the Vietnam War was hopeless, once Nixon had been proven immoral if not criminal, there was less to fight about everywhere. If there was just as much as ever to do in the cause of social justice, well, Abbot had its long tradition of charitable deeds to back the organizational techniques that students and teachers developed together during that best and worst of years, 1969–70,[83] and the work went on, strongly supported by the administration. By June of 1972 a series of panty raids (three by Phillips boys, one by Abbot girls) was the best Andover Hill could produce in the way of rebellion. Donald Gordon and his faculty could concentrate on extending the most promising reforms and on keeping Abbot's house in order.

This last task was challenge enough by itself. By the time Carolyn Johnston had run two dorm searches for drugs and liquor, had spent half one night tracking down a girl who had run naked from a Phillips dorm, and taken care of several unhappy students at her home for a few days, she began "to wish we still had tie shoes for them to rebel against. It was a lot simpler, a lot simpler!" For every ten alumnae who now rejoice that 1970 saw the last of the "distorted social life" and the "Capezzio shoes stereotype" of the "old Abbot" girl, there is at least one who feels that she "wasn't ready for all the responsibility." "We wanted all that freedom, but once we had it we didn't know what to do with it," writes a '71 alumna.[84]

Even noble impulses sowed trouble. One girl who went to work at a half-way house for mental patients forgot that she was never to give patients her last name or her address; a large, pathetic man known to have beaten up several girl friends told her he must have both so he could reach her when he felt like slashing his wrists—and was shortly prowling around her Abbot dormitory looking for her. The same year a housemother became ill and had to leave. The students on her corridor brought a self-proctoring proposal to Carolyn Johnston, and after much discussion and refinement of the plan, she and Gordon decided they could trust one Senior to be acting counselor for the corridor. The Senior kept all in order: she knew exactly in which Phillips dormitory each vagrant girl could be found if she must be reached by telephone. The girls signaled an end to the experiment themselves when one took off on a terrifying LSD trip and the rest brought her down to Carolyn Johnston for help. Because of such incidents, Mrs. Johnston tightened up on dormitory supervision a little more each year. It meant "a lot of rule-making in the summer, when town meeting wasn't around," says a '73 graduate with resentment. *Cynosure* complained, but the rules stood. Most students accepted them, administered as they were by the generous and responsible young houseparents (six couples in all) and other resident advisers whom Don Gordon managed to find. So long as all went well enough, girls tended to focus affection on them and on special faculty friends, and thought of Mrs. Johnston as School Disciplinarian until they needed her badly. "Then you went to her," writes one former student leader, "and you could never lie to her." Another alumna who habitually went from caper to agonizing problem and back again writes of her, "I still to this day believe that Mrs. Johnston had eyes on the back of her head!"[85] It was just as well, given the job a boarding school must do in the sixties and seventies. The outward decorum girls maintained in Miss Bailey's and Miss Hearsey's day evaporated as both adolescent and adult dug down to find the springs of authority and found them dispersed under and over the land. They were there—in adult experience and capacity to help, in perceived communal needs—but they had lost their magical qualities; they could no longer be taken for granted. Teachers would occasionally wonder whether boarding schools could be made viable in these difficult times.

Yet boarding schools have enormous advantages, and Abbot's administrative team was determined to make the best of them through imaginative scheduling, through expansion of those offerings in the creative and dramatic arts which can blossom in ample evening and weekend time, and through the conscious assembling of an ever more varied community. Abbot drew an average of 10 percent more applicants each year from 1969 on, many of them girls who said they wouldn't have dreamed of applying to Abbot in the old days.[86] Elizabeth Marshall Thomas brought her daughter Stephanie to visit, and Stephanie happily enrolled in 1971 for a four-year stay. Expanded class coordination with Phillips was a major attraction, of course: each year Abbot could offer more academic variety as the two schools' arts and modern language departments opened all courses to students from either one, and upper level electives in science, theatre, music, English, and history drew students from up and down the Hill. Enrollment had expanded by 1972–73 to 330 to take full advantage of Abbot's plant and people, "Antoinette Hall House," the old Infirmary, having been opened for boarders in 1969 and Chapin House in 1970. The roster eventually included 88 day students, who seem to have felt more welcome than at any time since the McKeen sisters arrived to create a "school-home" at Abbot.[87] Boarders hosted them in the dormitories, and the school completed the process (well begun in the Crane-Tucker years) of opening all meals and evening activities to them. "The crumby little room across from the library" (as a '55 graduate describes it) was still headquarters, but it no longer "felt like second

55. *All-girls' soccer, Shirley Ritchie presiding.*

56. *Deborah and Richard Witte, houseparents.*

steerage on the Titanic," because there were so many other places to
go. Perhaps most important, Treasurer J. K. Dow and Richard Griggs
sprung loose twice as much money for scholarships as Abbot had
made available in the years before 1968: $80–95,000 each year after
1969, to support 13 percent of the student body. Eight black students
were on full scholarship. Teachers' salaries, too, were raised until they
stood once again above the median for girls' schools by 1970–71—
though this was not enough for a new breed of young teacher (generally male) who refused to speak softly on the subject, and successfully pushed the administration if not to higher salaries then to a more
rational set of criteria by which to award them.

All this money had to come from somewhere. Griggs and Dow
were ready by early 1970 with a plan to borrow enough from the
endowment to cover the $311,000 deficit that had accumulated from
1966 to 1969, and to use New Abbot Fund monies to finance future
capital improvements, especially those which would generate larger
tuition income. The plan seemed all the more necessary as the 1969–70
deficit approached $362,000.[88] Burton Flagg would have been horri-
fied, but that good old man was dying in a nursing home. At first
Gardner Sutton objected. "I'm from Boston," he said, "and here we
don't believe in spending money we don't have." "Well, I'm from
Virginia," answered Trustee Guerin Todd, a Washington lawyer, "and
down there we spend money we don't have all the time." "Keynesian
economics," Todd dubbed Abbot's system of planned deficits.[89] The
idea seemed reasonable. The fund drive was starting out strong under
Todd's and Sheahan's leadership; it looked as though alumnae would
endorse the New Abbot after all. For this, enormous credit was due
Jane Sullivan, '31, Alumnae Secretary, who had spent nearly half her
life at Abbot and was thus able to dispel much alumnae panic over
passing crises during the Gordon Years. "SRW," '28, wrote to Forum
Editor Sheahan, "to share with you my tremendous excitement and
enthusiasm over what I learned about Abbot through the Forum";
"EBS," '66, said, "All I can say is 'wow!!' "[90] As time went on, the
Trustees grew more discouraged. "So many of the older alumnae saw
the Gordon era as the end of Abbot Academy" and simply refused to
give, says Caroline Rogers. "I found this hard to understand, because I
was enthusiastic about everything Abbot was doing." In the end, Mrs.
Rogers' enthusiasm proved crucial: over half of the $1,175,000 that
Abbot finally raised came from her family or from foundations she
knew well or helped to manage. Important operational funds were
donated by two foundations whose directors liked the looks of the
New Abbot; $75,000 for faculty support from the Mellon Foundation

over three years, and $87,500 for scholarships through 1976 from the Independence Foundation.

Meanwhile, Abbot's budgeteers were sharpening their pencils. Prodded by Jane Baldwin, they helped the Investment Committee find new management for investment funds, and endowment income crept up. They went after unpaid tuition bills to bring in thousands extra each year. They scrutinized the Principal's salary budget, and ran quiet checks on teacher-workload to make certain new positions were needed. Their intent was not to push Abbot teachers back to the twenty-five class-hours-per-week that had been common in earlier days, but to discover—as they did in the spring of '72—that one teacher had just five hours of scheduled teaching each week, and to tighten up on job descriptions. Through higher enrollments and tuition (raised to $4,100 for the 1971–72 school year, which brought Abbot just above the median relative to its major competitors), by careful planning, and by cheerful resistance to Gordon's more expensive inspirations, the Trustees and administration pulled Abbot's annual deficit down toward zero.[91] It was just $6,800 in the last year, 1972–73.

The managers also took a look at outdated assets, and cast sentiment aside to realize as much money as possible for the current operation. No Organ Fund was needed now that Abbot's mechanical organ had been retired. Nor did the Trustees think that those hopeful donors who had put the first and last $7,000 toward a Chair of Literature in memory of Phebe McKeen would turn in their graves if the $103,236 that had accumulated in the savings bank were used to endow salary raises for living teachers. The most valuable anachronism was the John-Esther Gallery collection, which no one seemed to want to exhibit any more even if there had been time to do so between the lively exhibitions of student, faculty, and professional work set up each month or so by curator Stephanie Perrin. Stephanie herself brought to the Trustees a proposal to sell the paintings rather than allow them to deteriorate in the attic of Draper Hall. J. K. Dow and Richard Sheahan knew the paintings must be worth more than the $20,000 that a dealer was willing to offer for the collection as a whole; several auctions by Parke-Bernet realized $98,000 and proved them right. George Innes' "A June Day" brought $39,000 of the sum alone. The rest of the Trustees were as pleased as Dow and Sheahan. The little bonanza was a symbol of the Board's success in working with Abbot's faculty to put money to work prudently for present needs.

"Our job as administrators was to clear away the tactical rubbish so that teachers could get on with teaching," says Donald Gordon. The teaching staff from 1970–73 was as various as the student body. Gordon continued to seek teachers from outside the prep-school-Ivy League nexus—young people, for the most part, who could both accept Abbot's salary scale and further the new Abbot's values. He did not have far to look. In contrast to the Crane years, eager young teachers were a glut on the market: 348 teachers applied for ten openings in 1970–71, at least a third of these serious, competent candidates. Whereas twenty-eight of thirty-three teachers had received their training in women's colleges or abroad in 1960, only fifteen of the forty 1972–73 faculty had done so. A dozen of the latter had completed undergraduate or graduate work at state universities, compared with two in 1960. One third were men, and though the average age of the group as a whole dropped from forty-four to twenty-eight in the five Gordon years, there were teachers scattered in every age bracket. Carolyn Goodwin encouraged every student to try out a range of teachers. After 1970 ninth graders took one trimester of English with each of two old hands as well as one with Peter Stapleton. Upperclasswomen could choose as required courses Black Literature, The Comic Vision, Epic Poetry, and The American Dream, or several English electives, such as Humanities III, Irish Studies, Southern Gothic: Novelists of the Grotesque, or The Expatriates: Paris of the 20's, as well as a host of specialized English courses at Phillips Academy. They had their choice of four different year-long United States history courses, including a full-blown American studies course with as many novels to read and paintings to study as political tracts to analyze. A new mathematics teacher set up an individualized contract-learning course which he described in faculty meeting in detail so that others might adapt its most successful features to their own work. The Mathematics Department hooked into a Cambridge computer and offered one term of computer study for fourth-level mathematics students. But Abbot's laboratory science courses remained limited to one year each of chemistry, physics, and biology. "I found when I got to college that I'd had lady-like science; other students in the pre-med courses were much better trained," says one alumna; another now in nursing agrees. Yet others feel their basic preparation was excellent. In biology, "It depended on what teacher you had," explains one, who says that she was crazy about her teacher, "even though I knew more biology than he did," because he taught her all about white-water canoeing. There was no doubt that quality was more uneven than it had been in the past; there was so much going on that class preparation sometimes went by the board. A Crane appointee puts it in extreme terms: "Hardly anyone had any real commitment to the school as an academic institution." She says, "Tradition was a dirty word." One of the most able eleventh graders on Andover Hill (class of '73) drew four teachers out of five who were simply dull. History was worst. "The teacher was bored. We were bored. We were all bored. We were very bored. Oh dear." Asked why she didn't leave, she describes all the rest of Abbot with warmth: student and faculty friends, basketball Abbot style ("very relaxed, super fun"), helping to organize a Thanksgiving Vespers that could encompass every faith and every agnostic yearning, gathering greens by the Shawsheen River to deck Davis Hall for Christmas Vespers, and working very hard on stage crew for mainstage productions at Phillips. It was an interesting switch from Elizabeth Marshall's day when it was Abbot's academic work that kept the blood moving even if nothing else did. As a Senior, this '73 graduate took four of her five courses on the top of the Hill, including a superb Advanced Placement Biology course.

"We lost some of our professionalism," says one long-time teacher—who also admits to having enjoyed her rest from the pressure of academic work she had felt in the Crane-Tucker years. "It's a shame," says another. "We didn't need to hire any of those friendly incompetents to change the school. Luckily most students knew what they needed, and flocked to the more demanding teachers wherever there was a choice—and usually there was." Pressure or no pressure, many teachers worked terribly hard: they created for another bright, questing girl an experience wholly different from the one Abbot gave to her '73 friend above. "Jean St. Pierre was the best writing teacher I've ever had," says this '72 alumna, speaking for many, "an emotive, perceptive, demanding teacher, really excited about her subject." She also "learned tremendously" from her history class. She cut her teeth on the Abbot computer and then climbed the Hill to join the Phillips computer "club," even though she was denied access to most Phillips mathematics courses. "Academically, it was an incredible treat for me. I came from a high school where one did not discuss ideas or reading, [and] I was beginning to abandon intellectual interests." "Almost forgot Mr. Gordon," her letter goes on. "I liked and respected him. He was very accessible. Three of us went to his house once a week one winter to listen to him talk about economics—unstructured, but fascinating." Her friend of '73 did forget Mr. Gordon, because "he was hardly ever around." "He was busy raising money; he didn't know my name. I kept having to check out plans with him because he was head, but in terms of running the school, he didn't seem to have any say whatsoever," a judgment little different from that of several teachers, one of whom liked Gordon very much but says, simply, that "the faculty was pulling on its own." The '73 student goes on: "My last spring there was this shakedown in Hall House which, in terms of civil liberties, seemed a little appalling. The morning after, Mr. Gordon was to speak in assembly so I had a pen and pad out, ready to write down how he justified it, or whatever. But as usual, he talked and talked—for an hour and ten minutes—and didn't say anything." There is no such thing as a moderate student opinion of Abbot's last Principal. Still, it was a sign of Abbot's good health that students could joke about the one characteristic on which everyone agreed: his overdone eloquence.

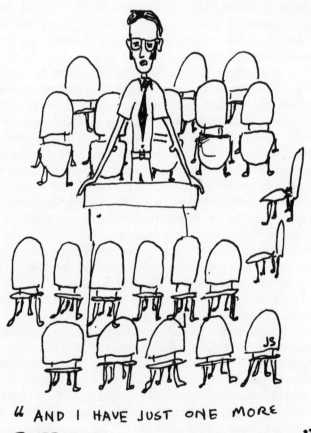

" AND I HAVE JUST ONE MORE BRIEF POINT I'D LIKE TO MAKE... "

57. Talk and Laughter, Cynosure, *15 October 1971.*

The few who really got to know Donald Gordon most appreciated him. A great deal of his attention went to the girls who participated in the two-year Indian exchange program, an experience that profoundly affected them and opened a shutter on the outside-Abbot world for many more. Abbot principals from Miss McKeen through Miss Hearsey had looked toward Europe; Gordon, fascinated with the American West, faced the old Academy toward its own continent. He joined efforts that several Eastern schools were making to include native Americans and Indian studies in their schools and curricula through an Intercultural Exchange Program, which sent six Abbot girls to the Rosebud Reservation in South Dakota during March and brought Dakota (Sioux) Indian girls (as well as one "white" girl living on the Reservation) to the Eastern schools for three weeks in April.[92] Abbot and Concord academies were the first schools to arrange the month at Rosebud. The Abbot pioneers prepared for their adventure through a week-long seminar with Gordon on Dakota culture, and flew west at the begnning of March, where they were met, introduced to the principals of the mission high school and public school to which they would go, and brought to the Reservation families who had agreed to take them on.

"One more won't matter," Mr. and Mrs. Black Spotted Horse had said to the Rosebud coordinator when he asked for host families; they had fifteen children already, in a house about the size of three Draper Hall student rooms. "Sam" Howland shared a bed with five of the children, learned to breakfast on potato-and-meat soup, and to enjoy the Sunday family feasts and the endless driving around in cars which many Dakota considered the only worthwhile winter entertainment. No two girls had the same experience; one lived on a farm with a white family, and two others spent week nights in a barracks dormitory with fifty Dakota girls from the poorest part of the Reservation. Some found high school deadening (one was seated by her teacher and made to write "I will not be late for school" two hundred times), while others found teachers extraordinarily friendly, willing to include and help them. Romantic stereotypes of Plains Indian life disintegrated before the whisky bottles in the grass, the listlessness of unemployed men, and the almost universal preference for indoor life ("It was hard to go on a walk because everyone started worrying that you were upset," said one girl), but every Abbot girl brought back some powerful images: the slower pace of life, the sere beauty of the rolling winter plains, the wind, their dear, close host-families, and, most of all, the sense of having managed well within an unfamiliar American subculture.[93]

Abbot was not entirely prepared for the Dakota girls who came East. It was not just that Don Gordon was leaving most of the details to a few and failing to consult others[94] (the Admissions officers were never brought in at all, though they knew best where space for beds and a friendly reception could be found). It was also that the Rosebud schools had given their girls no clear sense of what to expect or how they should keep up with courses at home. The Dakota girls came to Abbot classes expecting to be as bored as they were by many classes back at Rosebud, and therefore, with a few exceptions, they were. They had never done any serious homework, so they quickly fell behind; several simply stopped going to class at all. Even those who did attend, especially the full-blooded Indian girls who rarely spoke or smiled, baffled students and teachers. Here they were in the land of let-it-all-hang-out; the intense reserve by which these girls hid their homesickness and protected their dignity was entirely unfamiliar to Abbot in the seventies. After a week, Carolyn Goodwin gathered them and their student hosts together, and with them sketched out a plan for their stay which combined modified class schedules with trips to the ocean, to Lexington and Boston, to a conference of Indians staying at Northfield and Concord academies. Nothing worked perfectly, but by the time the girls had to leave, they all wanted to come back again, and several Abbot teachers and students wished they could.[95]

There were ten black students now, most of whom had prepared (or been ill prepared) in ghetto junior high schools and nearly all of whom were highly conscious of the revolutionary responsibilities of black youth. The Dakota visitors were startled by the vehemence with which several of these girls took them aside into special caucus and pleaded solidarity with Third World causes. It was not the only such instance. A few of the more bitter black students felt no blacks could survive unless all stood together against the school; two issued threats to the rest: join us or get beaten up. Abbot gave them space for an Afro-American center, Mrs. Johnston allowed them special late sign-ins when they attended Afro-American dances at other schools, a very few got away with some serious rulebreaking—"if a white girl did that she'd be kicked out," says a white alumna—but the angriest stayed that way. A part-time adviser, a black graduate student from Tufts, only exacerbated the situation, adding her own threats to those others had made, insisting that Abbot and all white America was hopelessly racist, and advising the black girls finally to walk out after Thanksgiving of 1972 and not come back. At that point Gordon called on Beth Chandler Warren, '55, whose husband Ted had joined the Abbot History Department that September. She brought the girls together and told

58. Growing up black at Abbot, 1970.

them, "Yes, Abbot's racist, American society is racist, so what else is new? . . . You think you're being ripped off? Well, then, *you* get in there and rip off all the academic power you can get from this school. Learn everything you can and get yourselves ready to change things."[96] Throughout the Gordon years there had been at least one or two extraordinarily serene and able black students at Abbot each year; almost imperceptibly, leadership of the 1972–73 group of blacks passed over to them, and things rocked back into their usual uneasy balance between the black girls' loyalty to each other and their will to prosper as individuals within a multicolored society.

"No risks, no progress," says one of the veteran Abbot teachers. Abbot's struggle to come to grips with the realities of the sixties and seventies was bound to include failures and awful mistakes, as well as successes even beyond Donald Gordon's dreams. The overwhelming majority of alumnae from these years say they would never have traded their Abbot experience—take it all in all—for anything more sane, more dull. Once the roller-coaster had been taken aside for repairs in 1970, it never came close to being derailed. In fact, by 1972, when Phillips Academy took one last look at Abbot and found the bride worthy, she was riding along smooth track well out of Fun City, going places on her own.

Endings and Beginnings

*The union of Abbot and Phillips Academy
has been achieved, and in a fashion
that will not impoverish either school
but enrich both.*
Abbot Trustees' Minutes, September 20, 1972

Phillips Academy ATE Abbot
Abbot alumna to Phillips student, Class of '78

There remains the merger story to tell. Given Abbot's long life, it is a brief tale, but an intense one, with some surprising turns. Much of it was hidden from students at the time, some of it from faculty as well. "You couldn't let on what you were doing till you were pretty sure it would work out," explains Phil Allen. The school had work of its own to do that must not be weakened by hopes or fears concerning the rest of Andover Hill.

"To the Fem Sems of Andover; so near and yet so far!"

Thus did Phillips' finest toast their Abbot sisters whenever longing coincided with a celebratory mood. The salute rang out on the Phillips Seniors' class sleigh ride of 1883;[1] it encapsulates a paradox not finally resolved until 1973, when Abbot and Phillips became one school under the name of Phillips Academy. The merger was prefigured by historical ties between the two academies, and powered by present urgencies in which both Abbot and Phillips saw far more opportunity than danger.

Long had Abbot considered its mission complementary to that of Phillips. "What the Trustees of Phillips Academy would provide for *young men*, we would provide for *young ladies*," the Abbot Trustees wrote to Mary Lyon in 1834.[2] Though the disparity between the two academies in numbers and economic power would only increase, the idea of their complementarity persisted. Abbot's and Phillips' institutional lives overlapped throughout the nineteenth century: their ancestry in the Sarah Abbot – Samuel Phillips family connection, their board membership, their formal social life, their visiting lecturers and part-time teachers, their constituencies, and their supporters within the town of Andover—all were shared to a greater or lesser extent. Though Abbot let the early experiments in regular academic cooperation lapse and went the way of other post-bellum boarding schools in creating a thoroughly single-sex community, social interchange flourished, as we have seen. The Phillips Class of 1872 held a reunion feast in the Smith Hall dining room, to the delight of Harriet Chapell and her friends.[3] Phillips came down to cheer the Abbot baseball games with such enthusiasm that Miss McKeen wondered whether she had been wise to allow her young ladies to play baseball at all.[4] One institution, the Ladies Benevolent Society of Phillips Academy, aptly foreshadowed the Phillips-Abbot merger: under a charter drawn with the help of several Phillips Trustees, Abbot's real interests were continually advanced. The Society was founded in 1831 by Academy and Theological Seminary wives and daughters, but most of them were also Abbot parents, students, or alumnae. It met regularly in the Abbot Chapel throughout its first few decades. By the 1970's the Society would stand as the oldest woman's club in the United States, yet another Abbot-Phillips connection so ancient that it was simply taken for granted.

The twentieth century witnessed a cooling of the friendship on an official level. In 1912 Abbot students advocated closer ties: Phillips' Charles Forbes had brought greetings from "Abbot's big brother" to Bertha Bailey at her Inaugural, and the *Courant* Editors were slightly miffed; "Let us suggest that, in the future, something be done to make the family get together," they wrote.[5] But 1912 also marked the year Miss Bailey began cutting what lines there were up and down Andover Hill. Merger seemed so far from reality by 1949 that Marguerite Hearsey felt free to joke about a coeducational utopia when she introduced Headmaster John Kemper to the Boston Abbot Club. "There's an idea for us, Mr. Kemper. Think of all the problems it would solve! Well, who knows?"

> When Abbot's last rules have been lifted
>   And no freedom is longer denied:
> When the older critics have left us
>   And the wildest new theories been tried . . .
> We shall learn and the answer seems simple
>   That altho' we have always been two
> We'd better henceforth combine forces
>   And be one without further ado.[6]

Joking aside, the idea of coeducation would not go away. We have seen how extracurricular contacts between the schools gradually widened and deepened through the next two decades, how the privet hedge lost its symbolic loading, how the bushes that had long held illicit notes or sheltered illicit lovers became just bushes again. Students engineered many of the changes themselves, a not surprising development when one considers that in the late 1960's 94 percent of students in northeastern single-sex secondary schools wished for coeducation.[7] A Social Union in the basement of Cochran Chapel near the Abbot-Phillips border, a co-ed Senior ski weekend, coeducation of the Phillips Summer Session, Abbot participation in the Andover-Exeter Washington Intern Program and School Year Abroad—all were responses to students' initiatives or applicants' desire for coeducational programs. Separate corporate identities still kept the two schools "so near and yet so far," but by the end of the sixties the "far" distance had radically diminished, and many on Andover Hill had begun to wonder whether it need exist at all.

"It's a coed world"[8]

Just as the times favored women's education in the 1820's when Abbot began, so now they favored coeducation as never before. Single-sex fortresses were falling fast: In 1968 alone 53 colleges and universities (35 of them women's colleges) either became coeducational or began coordinate instruction. With only 33 men enrolled in its first year of coeducation, Bennington's applications rose 56 percent. Ivy League colleges gearing up for coeducation saw their applications bottom out and begin to rise, while the number applying to all-male Princeton continued to dwindle. (Princeton soon changed its plans.) Popular articles spoke of "cracking the cloister"[9] and likened the remaining hold-outs to prisons.[10] Educators wrote that the young no longer needed a moratorium from worldly concerns. Professors discovered that females could think after all, and deans rang new changes on the nineteenth-century theme of women's civilizing influence on young men. In the ten years from 1962 to 1972, half of all women's colleges became coordinate or coeducational institutions, and those remaining found that they garnered far fewer of the talented students who had flocked to them in their heyday.

"The secondary schools, like the colleges, are yielding to the demands of the times," wrote the *Saturday Review* in 1969.[11] But they yielded cautiously, with many a backward look. The late-Victorian adolescent resurfaced in the *National Review* soon after Exeter admitted girls, "unsure, preoccupied with [his] intense, chaotic sexuality." The slower maturing boy watched girls outshine him in grade point averages and verbal skills, and his rebelliousness flared; meanwhile, because of his need for authoritative controls, his more tractable female classmates suffered a disciplinary system inappropriate to their needs.[12] NAPSG members exchanged poignant accounts of the demonstrated advantages of all-girls' schools as they watched their single-sex membership shrink. In such schools, says Valeria Knapp of Winsor, "there was never any question of girls taking second place. If they've really run things as teenagers, why should they stop running things as adults?"[13]

New research seemed to back Knapp's experienced convictions. Psychologists were fascinated with Matina Horner's evidence that bright women in coeducational colleges were often hampered in competitive situations by an anxiety uncommon in males: a fear of the social and personal consequences of success, such as loss of femininity or rejection by friends. The researchers took Horner's projective tests to coeducational and all-girls' high schools and discovered a far higher proportion of girls possessed of this anxiety in the coeducational schools than in comparable single sex schools.[14] Other scholars did some counting and found that women who had attended all-female high schools or colleges were much more likely to have won doctorates, to have proven their competence as college teachers or administrators, or even to have made "Who's Who in America." They noticed with interest the disproportionate number of women scientists and physicians who had graduated from Mt. Holyoke and Bryn Mawr.[15] The studies confirmed what all feminists and some psychologists had believed for decades: social institutions must consciously take the path of most resistance if women are to become other than "a reflection of a feminine image which men carry about in their heads."[16] Or, as Margaret Mead has put it, "The trouble with American women is too much coeducation."[17]

Finally, the women's liberation movement, born again in the late 1960's, evoked young women's special need for strong female friendships and worthy female models in a society that sold heterosexual love like candy and refused to credit women's need to ground themselves in self-respecting independence from men. A few feminist heroines such as M. Carey Thomas had long ago argued that true coeducation was the ideal school for a world in which "men and women are to live and work together as comrades and dear friends and married friends and lovers." Unfortunately America considered women inferior; thus Thomas felt that true coeducation was impossible, and all-female schools and colleges must be sustained.[18]

Yet there was hope as well as cynicism in President Thomas' view, and many secondary educators seized on the hope as the sixties closed: might not America finally be ready for true coeducation? If so, then all the earlier bets were off—those bets based on the college success of graduates of all-girls' schools, on Ph.D. statistics, and on the sheer fun and personal satisfaction tens of thousands of young women had experienced in single-sex schools. Dean Simeon Hyde of Phillips Academy stated this position in 1970: "As the roles of men and women become less differentiated, differentiated education loses its validity . . . The separation of the sexes in secondary boarding schools is a kind of hiatus in the normal process of growth . . . at odds with the experience of all but a tiny minority of the American population, a status no longer supported by the concept of a special mode of education for a special class."[19]

Both Phillips and Abbot Academies had been founded and maintained as separate institutions in response to particular cultural and economic circumstances. Now, if it was not yet entirely "a coed world," that new world was close enough so that a coed school might help to make it a reality.

On the Hilltop

Phillips Academy held the cards. The Abbot Trustees had effectively committed Abbot to some form of coeducation when they hired Donald Gordon in 1967. The Phillips Trustees balked at any such rash moves, but later the same year the Hilltop faculty followed the recommendation of its Steering Committee and voted to encourage shared social activities and "joint instruction" "with one or more neighboring girls' schools."[20] Though a few were dead set against further sex-mixing, and their voices would become louder as time went on, the traffic up and down Andover Hill warmed the hearts of Phillipians like Frederick Peterson, first dean of the coed Summer School; Simeon Hyde, Dean of the Faculty; and Alan Blackmer, Hyde's predecessor and Phillips' free-spirited elder statesman, who had been talking of coeducation for thirty years. A further, crasser impetus came from the Phillips' Admissions Office: Applications followed the general decline, with no sign of a reversal to match that which Abbot began to record after Gordon's arrival. The decline would become more alarming as St. Paul's, Taft, Northfield—Mt. Hermon, and Exeter became coeducational and an increasing number of boys turned down an Andover admission to accept one from Exeter. Mere resolves would no longer do; Phillips Andover girded itself to catch up with the times. Its faculty set to work with Abbot the spring of 1969 to plan the first experiments in "joint instruction."

The planners already knew from the "coordinate education week" of inter-school class visiting in early 1969 that schedules frustrate the best intentions. School schedules are sacred things: Phillips and Abbot had purposely kept theirs distinct in order to separate male and female. Now Abbot teachers much preferred their flexible modular schedule to Phillips' fifty-three minute time-slots, and were loath to give it up. Though they soon sacrificed it for the cause, early coordination from 1969-71 would remain minimal and largely one way—up the Hill. The experiment would expose the traps of the piecemeal approach: teaching overloads for Phillips Visual Studies teachers, keen disappointment on the part of those Phillips students who found themselves scheduled out of a long-anticipated Senior elective in favor of an Abbot Senior, the anxiety of the single female in a class full of males and vice versa, and the deepest trap of all—serious pedagogical disagreement between Abbot and Phillips departments over how to teach French, say, or whether to combine any classes at all.[21]

Still, these first two years of joint instruction raised some pioneers. The Art departments of the two schools moved first: they planned a group of complementary courses and opened them to Phillips and Abbot students alike. The Music and Modern Language departments followed suit. Early coordination proved that boys and girls could sit together in the same classroom and refrain from flirting—that they could even take Sex Education classes in stride, enjoying their raw humor along with their abundant factual information. (Jean Bennett does recall that the Hilltop administration drew the line at the boys being invited to a special lecture given by a homosexual, a respected physicist and college teacher. She says she did not endear herself to the Phillips brass by putting up announcements throughout the Phillips campus the night before the lecture was to take place.)[22] Altogether, fifty-six major courses and eighteen minors were open to both sexes in 1969-70.

Given this taste of coeducation, most students wanted much more. Yet official negotiations dragged. Early in 1970 some of Phillips showed itself unwilling to wait longer. A faculty-student committee of the "Cooperative," Phillips' school government forum, recommended to the Coop "that P.A. not only press vigorously the development of co-ordination with Abbot Academy, but at the same time the Academy

It's a real turkey. I saw it in our sex ed class!

59. Sex Education, Illustrated. (Cartoon from a 1972 Sex Education Course Exam.)

accept in principle the enrollment of girls as diploma candidates." The Coop then drew up a faculty-student referendum on coordination the enrollment of girls in P.A. Student opinion was strongly in favor of both routes to coeducation. Faculty opinion was divided, but twice as many favored coordination as favored separate moves to coeducation. After a restless month, the Phillips faculty voted to ask their Trustees "to investigate the question of coeducation and coordinate education."[23] In response, the Trustees issued the vaguest resolution conceivable: Phillips Academy might "after study, perhaps contribute to the education of young women." To the Abbot Trustees, already committed to educating young men, this looked timid indeed; but the Phillips Board followed up its vote with a directive to its Educational Policy Committee to "undertake a complete in-depth study of the needs and possibilities and future course, whether positive or negative, of either coordinate education or coeducation at Phillips Academy." The investigation was to be made "in collaboration with an appropriate committee of Abbot Academy," and would draw on such faculty and students as the Headmaster wished to designate.[24] By design, the Phillips Alumni Council was meeting the very same weekend; John

Kemper told the alumni of the Trustees' resolution, and invited Donald Gordon to present his own vision of the two schools under a single administration and board of trustees. Shortly afterward, a summer study committee was organized, including administrators from both schools. So began a full sixteen months of earnest study and planning—a period of hope, of imaginative moves toward the future—and at its close, of bitter disappointment for the advocates of merger. In spite of brave beginnings, no smooth path to coeducation was to be found where small groups of traditionalists and principled advocates of swift solutions held the two extremes, while the large number of Hilltop teachers in between shifted from one coalition to another. Vested interests swept some toward coeducation, others away; fears of disorder vied with the recognition that Phillips Academy's very survival might depend upon its willingness to change. Though all wanted the best for their schools, over two years would pass before Andover Hill could agree on what the best would be.

Leaps of faith: 1970–1971

The key administrators from both schools met throughout July to decide how to move forward, and determined after long discussion that an early commitment to merger by both boards of Trustees was needed to undergird the enormous effort the two faculties must make to plan for a new school. They also set up three complementary Phillips-Abbot committees to start the work: A Curriculum Committee, a committee to study school governance and community organization, and a committee on social life, later to be called the Boy-Girl Relations Committee. In time others would be added, including a committee on Coordination of Athletic Programs. Early on, Simeon Hyde took intellectual leadership of the planning for Phillips, leaving John Kemper to ponder the political problems of how he might persuade a faculty of assertive individuals to come along. For years, a few Abbot Trustees had felt Kemper was stalling on coeducation. He was too much tied to the traditional Abbot, they thought, too imbued by his military past with the idea of women as—above all—wives or daughters whom men must protect, and quite unable to think of women as colleagues.[25] But now Kemper quietly moved onto center stage in the plan-making. His long-time Abbot connections became crucial, and his caution gave essential reassurance to those Phillips faculty who still defended Phillips as a male bastion now and forever more. He had grown up on legends of his grandmother Mason, who refused to be left behind when her army doctor husband set out with his company on campaigns of Indian pacification; she bore her first child on one expedition. His mother (an Abbot graduate) and a favorite maiden aunt were equally powerful people. Some years after his first wife's death, Kemper married another special woman with a long career as teacher and dean behind her: Abby Castle, Abbot '31. His three daughters, one an Abbot alumna, had brought close the problems and joys of female education. Yet the decorous distance between Phillips and Abbot had been comfortable for him; a friend and Phillips alumnus says he dreaded coeducation at first. "He told me so. He was suffering from some relative of the same syndrome as Miss Bailey."[26] In time, however, he moved. Kemper's style was to talk over a dilemma with anyone who would listen; to slowly, deliberately settle his own mind as to the wisdom of a given course of action; then, quietly and informally, to speak his case to others. Friends think he decided for an Abbot-Phillips merger during the 1970 summer conclave; from that time on, he worked to make it happen.[27]

Simeon Hyde, on the other hand, was a master of the position paper. His "Case for Coeducation," October 1970, was an intellectual's argument based on historical and sociological analysis, but it also affirmed the validity of young people's dream of community in a time of social disintegration, a kind of "extended family, founded upon principles of love and respect for individual diversity."[28] He sensitively described how "used" and disillusioned the new Yale and Princeton women had felt as their position of "token females" became clear to them. By joining with Abbot, Phillips Academy could avoid pitfalls such as these.

> A merger, though full of difficulties, seems practical, ethical, and educationally sound. A true merger would bring to either partner the insight, experience, and resources of the other; and with no alteration of numbers, the combined school would have a better start toward an acceptable ratio of boys and girls and of men and women than would be possible at the beginning of any one school's solitary effort . . . If Abbot and Phillips could together commit themselves to the development of a school in which boys and girls and men and women shared equally, they would be far ahead of other institutions striving to escape from the limitations of sexually segregated education.[29]

Hyde's "Case" hit the faculty mailboxes just after the Abbot and Phillips Trustee Subcommittees on Coeducation met jointly and agreed to recommend to their respective Boards that the two schools become one. Nearly everyone on Andover Hill expected that the Phillips Trustees would vote for merger during their fall meeting in 1970.

Yet the majority of the Phillips Board refused merger. This was the first of three votes rejecting an Abbot-Phillips union. Old Phillips grads all, and Ivied over in college, they treasured their biases; but bias was not the whole story. They were legitimately fearful of the financial consequences of merger—the more so given Abbot's enormous deficit for '69–70; they simply would not consider it without further study. They did commit themselves at last to Abbot Academy, voting "that Phillips Academy should be involved in the education of women, and [that it] should not do so independently but in close association with Abbot Academy."[30] Abbot's Trustees made a similar commitment to Phillips in their own fall meeting. So, somehow, Abbot and Phillips were to join forces. The question was, how?

It seemed both fitting and practical for Philip Allen to be made Coordinator of the study and planning of coeducation since he was Trustee for both academies; fitting also for him to set up headquarters in Phillips' Graham House next door to where Sarah Abbot had once lived. He had his work cut out for him. The Abbot and Phillips Admission Officers had never even met: Allen introduced them and many others, too. Plenty of Abbot-Phillips faculty threw themselves into their planning tasks however. The Abbot and Phillips Curriculum Committees first convened in November while the student-faculty committees on School/Community Organization started work in January of 1971. In spite of the Phillips Trustees' hesitations, these and their subgroups still talked in terms of merger. Each committee held frequent, open meetings to keep in touch with teachers and students in both schools as they progressed. The Curriculum Committee, asking "What is the purpose of secondary education?" found itself engaged in an effort to define and prescribe for the future of American society. Its members exchanged extensive readings in the theory and practice of education; they solicited position papers from academic departments and exchanged memoranda until their notebooks bulged with ideas both intricate and grand. Meanwhile, the Abbot School/Community Organization group and the corresponding Phillips Committee almost immediately decided that their concerns were the same, and a tall order they were:

Living arrangements
Decision making
Student organization

Adult roles
Social-cultural activities
Rules
Individual rights
Campus life
Administrative structure
Guidance, Counseling, Religion
Off-Campus learning centers

The Boy-Girl Relations Committee was building no utopias. It talked over details of room visiting, the counseling of boys and girls who became "dangerously involved with one another," the make-up of disciplinary committees, the need for more women teachers, and all the specifics of an environment that recognizes adolescents as sexual beings, yet also supports same-sex privacy where necessary and "discourages sexual license."[31] Academic departments in both schools also got into the act, charged by their administration to define the material and curricular issues at stake in a joint instructional program. A single new language lab, replied the Phillips Modern Language chairman; joint borrowing privileges in both libraries, replied the librarians. It was an exciting time, not least because key members of both faculties were discovering each other as persons and enjoying the process. Little by little, they replaced visions with plans for a new school in Andover Hill.

Deep Waters

By Springtime, however, it was clear that nothing would be easy. The more progress was made by the busy planners, the more resistance coalesced among those men of the Hilltop who realized that the planners were actually serious. A poll of the Phillips teachers taken in March 1971 showed many of them backing away from Abbot: only 5 percent now hoped for full academic coordination. True, there was a sizable group (almost 40 percent) seeking a coeducational school, but asked how coeducation should be achieved, 63 percent preferred that Phillips take in its own girls rather than merge with Abbot. The results testified to the complications that lay ahead for those who had not seen them coming in the stereotypes that were multiplying up and down the Hill. Abbot students had been "dumber," and "more emotional," for years, but a host of new Hilltop characterizations now fed on the few real excesses of the 1969–70 school year. Today's Abbot girls were "spoiled" as well. All decent standards of dress and deportment having been abandoned, they had become "slobs"; they sang siren songs to the weaker, freakier Phillips boys, who fled to the Draper Hall corridors to escape the rigors of Hilltop life. Abbot teachers coddled math cripples; they accepted late papers and atrocious spelling; they sprawled on classroom floors and grooved with their students instead of teaching them; they solved communications problems in "group-grope" sensitivity training sessions rather than submit with dignity to Roberts Rules; the older, more experienced women teachers were fast being outnumbered by pot-smoking, draft-dodging young men.[32] Abbot faculty returned the insults by grumbling in the shelter of their faculty room, and Abbot girls protested, occasionally in print. *Cynosure's* "Bertha B" advice column was the ideal medium:

> Dear Bertha B.,
> I have a problem . . .
> He's all I ever wanted in a guy . . . The basic problem is that he's more interested in my body than my brains. He takes classes at my school because he thinks they're easier than those at his own school. But when I take classes at his school all he does is laugh . . . He thinks I'm stupid but I always end up doing his homework . . . Please help.,
>
> Desperate.[33]

They and their teachers easily latched onto their own stereotypes of Phillips Academy. Phillips was business-like, cold, ruthlessly competitive, insensitive to student needs. The ideal Phillips boy was a hard-muscled automaton, who traveled between classroom and athletic field, head stuffed with outlines of Supreme Court cases. Much of Abbot believed the story about the Phillips math teacher who (it was said) so hated girls that he got a stomachache whenever one appeared in his Summer School classroom, and students attached similar attributes to the Phillips faculty as a whole.

Myths aside, there were real differences between the two schools, some of them hardened over a century of separation; further, there were special stresses on the Hilltop peculiar to the 1970–71 school year which complicated the existing confusions about coeducation. Phillips was three times the size of Abbot. It could not help being less personal, more bureaucratized, more prone to "institutional inertia."[34] Its central Discipline Committee brought formal procedures in cases similar to those which Abbot's house parents and dorm representatives resolved themselves. Faculty moguls sat for years on the Phillips Committee dealing out swift chastisement and often recommending dismissal for first-time offenders, while Abbot's elected student Honor Board would agonize for hours searching for appropriate individual punishments before advising probation. Time and again the Honor Board gave a second or third probation in hope that a girl could pull herself together after all—and often enough she did, with massive help from friends and faculty.[35] A determined girl could win an exception to the rules for almost any reasonable request, or could choose a dorm known for its laissez-faire atmosphere, like Cutler House, where for at least a year, none of the residents even realized that those Phillips boys in and out of the Common Room all day weren't supposed to be there. (To be fair, a few dorms up the Hill were much the same.)[36] Or she could sit back and take a Sherman House letter-writer's advice: "Just take it easy. . . . If you're smart, you will find that most everything is permitted."[37]

Abbot had all but given up trying to prohibit smoking; Phillips boys smoked often but illegally. Phillips had late afternoon and Saturday classes, while Abbot weekends began at 3:30 on Friday afternoon. There were genuine differences in the two schools' approaches to teaching and departmental organization, all of which would have to be resolved, even if the Trustees stopped short of merger and settled for joint instruction. The same was true of dorm life, which was supervised by teacher-housemasters on the Hilltop and by the full-time resident advisers at Abbot. "Abbot took House-counseling far more seriously than Phillips does," says one woman who has run a dormitory in both schools. On the other hand athletics were central to Hilltop life. Down the Hill, now that ballet was no longer required for ninth graders, sports and dance periods were half the length and twice the fun for most. "You could play basketball because you liked it," says one alumna, "the average height of the team was 5'6". We lost every single game."[38] A few Abbot students roundly protested any competitive sports program for girls, insisting that life was now so rich on Andover Hill that such outlets were no longer needed.[39] One other stereotype was largely accurate: many Phillips boys did escape to Abbot as they were accused of doing. But it was not just to breathe in the smoke from the Abbot Seniors' cigarettes. "What makes Abbot so much better than the conventional girls' boarding school?" a Phillips swain queried. "One of the extended attractions for P.A. people is that those down here are human and enjoy it."[40]

A "human" community was desperately wanted by many of the Hilltop residents. Historian Frederick Allis testifies that the years 1971 and early 1972 were the most difficult in the history of Phillips Academy. Student frustration over the war, the draft, and the pace of

60. The butt room.

change on Andover Hill reached a peak; two years of protests and
Memorial Day fracases seemed to have accomplished nothing, and a
large minority were now embittered, ready to back rebellious student
leaders, ready, even, to participate in senseless, capricious acts of van-
dalism that appalled the adults.[41] There was a species of hope in some
teachers' growing sympathy for the antiwar cause, but this solidarity
bred complications too, for it intensified already serious splits within
the Phillips faculty.[42] A pro-Abbot faction developed out of those
who admired Abbot's response to the confusions of the age and to
student desire for authentic communication with adults, and an anti-
Abbot faction sprang up to oppose it. A large middle group cast about
for new directions. The Phillips Seniors would put a seal on their own
discontent in June 1971, when nearly two thirds of the class signed a
statement expressing their "lack of confidence in the administration
and faculty of Phillips Academy." Many faculty were at a loss how to
cope with the impasse.

They were all the more anxious because John Kemper had become
seriously ill with lung cancer. When the one person who could talk
with everyone dropped out for an operation and convalescence, a few
Phillips teachers simply stopped speaking to one another. It was the
worst possible time to arrive at conclusions about the complex issues
raised by the prospect of coeducation. Yet discussions were held, some
of them involving every Abbot and Phillips teacher and 150 Abbot–

Phillips students as well. The Community Organization group made one of the most attractive proposals: that Phillips' experimental system of self-governing residential "clusters"—about 180 students and twenty-five faculty each—be extended to the new 1200–student school that would result from merger, in order to give all students the kind of home base that Abbot students valued so much. The Abbot-Phillips Curriculum Committees were searching the literature of learning theory and discovering how difficult it was to find any solid rationale for the course requirements that had been traditional to Andover Hill. They were preparing a bombshell: the recommendation that students be allowed to design their own course of study according to their own interests and college plans. All the planners began to assume eventual merger as they made their way through the tangle of basic educational questions. Dean John Richards II found himself telling West-coast alumni forums that coeducation was the least difficult of all the decisions facing Phillips Academy. The ferment only heightened anxiety on the Hilltop, however, for most of Phillips was stunned by events, rudderless in spite of Simeon Hyde's able leadership as Acting Headmaster during Kemper's absence. Hyde's open commitment to merger with Abbot set the hold-outs against him as they had never stood against Kemper. It seemed impossible to move ahead, easier far to do nothing.

Just before he went to the hospital, Kemper had invited the anti-coeducation minority to speak their case. They did, and forcefully, through Mathematics Chairman Richard Pieters, who argued in March that girls would seriously distract boys from Phillips' heavy academic demands. The decline in applications may be a result of "concessions we have already made" to prevailing fads, wrote Pieters. The sexual "immorality" and "precocity" in the larger society only confirmed the wisdom of single-sex education: "the stormy emotions of adolescence need restraint, not stimulation." If anything, Andover should be working to retard the erosion of "the natural distinctions between men and women." Pieters' last plaintive question suggests a conviction that sexual distinctions included intellectual ones: Even if Phillips were to put Abbot aside and create an independent, coeducational Phillips Academy, "Where are we to find the 300 or 400 qualified girls for a coed school of the quality we want?"[43]

The division within the Phillips faculty was just what the antimerger members of the Phillips Board needed. Considering merger for the second time at their spring meeting, they looked at Abbot's continuing (though diminishing) deficit and at the Phillips 1970–71 deficit of $165,000; at the financial consequences of stretching the Phillips en-

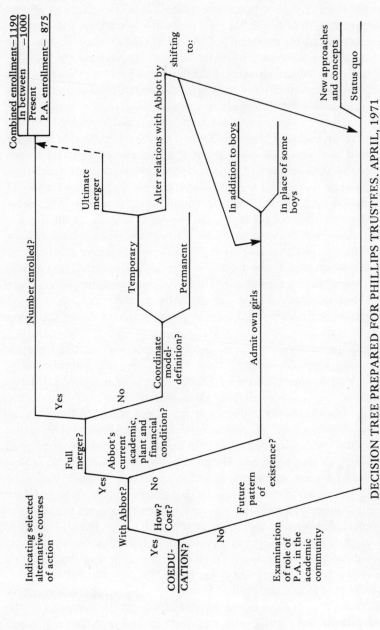

DECISION TREE PREPARED FOR PHILLIPS TRUSTEES. APRIL, 1971

61. Coeducation: A decision tree.

dowment over 1200 students (it would mean raising Phillips tuition at least $600); and at the "decision tree," which their financial consultants had provided. Even this simplified "tree" made Phillips Academy's problem clear: like most rich white males of the time, Phillips had too many options. Choice seemed impossible: this great boys' preparatory school was Absalom, suspended in mid-air from its decision tree. The Trustees voted to stay suspended, determining that "financial considerations make a merger with Abbot impractical at this time."[44]

Issues Joined and Unjoined: Summer, 1971

Once more a summer group of administrators convened at both Boards' behest: for Abbot, Gordon, Goodwin, Johnston, and Sheahan; for Phillips, Kemper, Hyde, Richards, and Frederick Stott. They were to meet under the chairmanship of Philip Allen, "double agent,"[45] to clarify all the issues and devise a workable scheme for long-term coordination. Allen had tried to persuade his fellow Phillips Trustees of what his fellow Abbot Trustees had already accepted: that merger offered both schools the best chance of survival in a new age. However, he strove as hard as anyone that summer to design a coordinated academic program that would overcome the two schools' philosophical differences and would avoid duplications and inequities. The latter seemed almost inevitable, given the disparities in size and economic power. The budgets in hand for the 1971–72 school year made these disparities all too clear.

The summer group decided it couldn't be done: coordination was neither a practical nor a desirable arrangement for the long future. You could have a single dean, you could even (God help you) try to combine Abbot and Phillips academic departments and equalize teaching loads, but the wide differences in teachers' salaries and in resources available for male and female students would remain, grating all the more as teachers' responsibilities approached parity. And who would hire whom? How would the two schools calibrate the relationship between students' out-of-class lives and their academic work? Was it fair to hold all students to common academic standards when they entered through two different admissions offices?

Now that Abbot had abandoned its age-old policy of charging minimal tuition (to balance its budget, Abbot's tuition had to be $4100, or half the income of the average American family), the disparities between the tuition bills issued to the males and the females of Andover Hill looked grossly discriminatory. Finally, there was the num-

Table 1.
Budgets and Resources, Abbot and Phillips Academies, 1971–1972

	Abbot Academy, 316 Students		Phillips Academy, 904 Students	
	Per Student	Total	Per Student	Total
Tuition income	$4,100 ($2,400 day)	$1,230,000	$2,700 ($2,100 day)	$ 2,490,000
Endowment income		60,000		2,221,000
Gifts		100,000		514,000
Other		75,000		129,000
Total income and expense		1,465,000		5,354,000
Operating Deficit		108,000		0
Market value of Endowment				
June 1971		1,772,784		54,746,060
June 1972*		2,360,922		64,673,311
Median teacher salary	$8,100.00		$11,600	
Housing				
(1) for dormitory faculty	provided		provided	
(2) for nondormitory faculty	not provided (though apartments were made available at a reasonable rent)		provided	
Size of campus, plus other acreage owned	45 acres		600 acres	
Market value of campus acreage, plus all buildings	$1,100,000– $1,900,000 (est.)		unavailable	
(Abbot only) Total value, plant and equipment (6/72 figures for replacement value)	$4,000,000			
(Phillips only) Total value of plant (6/72, estimate of replacement value. No equipment figures available)				$100,000,000

*Phillips endowment had risen 18 percent in value between June 1971 and June 1972, while Abbot's rose 33 percent.

bers problem. The conservative members of the Phillips Board found coordination attractive because it preserved 825 Hilltop beds for boys, yet the Abbot-Phillips planning committees were convinced that an equal number of boys and girls was a precondition for a natural community. How could two coordinate schools move toward such equality?

Ultimately, the group decided, the only arguments for coordination were economic ones that favored Phillips Academy: the closer the two schools drew under a coordinate arrangement, the more Phillips' raw power would be felt by the smaller one. Abbot would be dismantled, piece by piece, and would lose its chance to deal from its unique strengths in helping create a new totality.[46] As a weary Kemper wrote his Trustees, the choice for Phillips was now clear: a commitment to merge with Abbot as soon as financial and legal difficulties could be resolved, or a determination to pull away from Abbot altogether, remaining a boys' school or becoming coeducational on its own.[47]

In September 1971 the Phillips faculty were asked to make a choice between these alternatives. Now Richard Pieters, acknowledging that some form of coeducation was inevitable, took leadership of the anti-merger group and introduced his own motion on September 28 for gradual, independent coeducation within Phillips Academy. Given the majority that had favored independent coeducation the spring before, the resolution seemed likely to pass.

John Kemper was ill the night Pieters' motion was scheduled for faculty action, so the discussion was deferred. A few days later, realizing that his health was broken, Kemper submitted his resignation. But he had one last thing to say to the faculty at his final meeting with them on October 12: reject the Pieters motion and go through with the Abbot-Phillips merger. All feasible alternatives denied the two schools' historical ties and obligations to each other. Abbot's plant and equipment were valuable, he argued; its experience in educating girls was priceless. At the least, the new headmaster, whoever he is, must have a say in the matter. The faculty voted to table the Pieters resolution, and Pieters withdrew his motion.

Two weeks later, the Phillips Trustees met in gloom and uncertainty to make their final decision for or against merger. Kemper's plea haunted them, but who now would lead the school to carry it out? Philip Allen spoke for merger, but he was the double agent. The three Alumni Trustees finally persuaded the assembly not to adjourn before it had listened to their arguments for merger, but they could not vote. Allen left the meeting to fling away his own frustrations and to free up discussion. The Trustees couldn't say yes to Abbot, but they couldn't bring themselves to say no either. The alternative was limbo.

The Phillips Board "voted that a merger at this time or in the foresee-
able future would not be in the best interests of Phillips Academy";
they resolved to go on with coordination, and to enter limbo.[48]

Coordination

"That was the year we put the whole merger thing in mothballs," says
Carolyn Goodwin. But teachers and students returning to Abbot in
September 1971 found so much novelty and promise in the Abbot-
Phillips academic program that ultimate questions of the two academies' future receded before present urgencies. There was much to do.
One hundred courses invited cross-enrollment, forty at Abbot, sixty at
Phillips. The Phillips-Abbot Art departments, experienced in coordination, offered a richer program than ever before. The Music and Modern Language departments had combined forces in planning all their
courses, and the hard-working Summer Coordinating Committee had
put on the finishing touches. Now Abbot girls might take Italian as
they had done in the 1830's. Abbot's Modern Language Chairman,
Georges Krivobok could teach French, German, and Russian with
equal ease; Phillips was glad to have his skills and those of others to
enrich its own program. The students voted for joint classes with their
feet: 193 girls enrolled in 302 courses at Phillips, and 327 boys entered
376 courses down the Hill.

"Carolyn Goodwin was the effective implementor of coordination
at Abbot," says Simeon Hyde.[49] Imperturbable, she led teachers through
the intricate mechanics of academic coordination: report forms and
deadlines, a number-grading system from 0 to 6 which Phillips had
initiated two years before, and a trimester system, new to both schools,
which made possible a blizzard of ten-week electives.

Abbot had to give up its penchant for dropping everything now
and then and devoting a whole school day to some urgent public issue
or school government need. Both schools did some adjusting, planning
complementary offerings and adapting work schedules to allow for
joint department meetings. Members of the three fully coordinated departments proved that friction and distrust between the two faculties
could be overcome—and also demonstrated the imbalances built into
every joint planning effort. Abbot teachers were not merely outnumbered. Departmental organization had never been a formal affair
at the smaller school. "When does the English Department meet?" a
novice teacher remembers asking Alice Sweeney. "Oh, whenever you
and I happen to see each other in the book closet," was the reply.

Outside the pioneer departments, most coordinate courses were open only at the 11th and 12th grade level. They included, however, a wealth of Advanced Placement courses and Senior electives, especially in science.

It was a heady beginning. Abbot student pioneers probably exaggerated the stares and sneers they got from Hilltop skeptics, but there was no doubt that coordinating a course sometimes took guts. What a relief to come back to dormmates and Draper corridors and describe one's trials and triumphs to understanding friends! *Cynosure* offered space for gripes and counsel. About a Phillips teacher:

> Don't let him *get* you like that, please! He doesn't really want to humiliate you. He just has never had to *deal* with women before.

"Chins up, Ladies!" the reporter finished, "P.A. teachers may even *like* you, once they no longer have to dislike you on principle."[50]

The two schools' 1971–73 course catalogues reveal by their omissions where problems lay. Phillips students were allowed to take exactly one ten-week Abbot mathematics course, and only three Senior math courses out of all of Phillips' rich offerings were open to Abbot girls. "What would I do with a girl in my A.P. Calculus class?" an old-timer is said to have asked a Phillips Trustee. "Teach her, I suppose," was the answer. He need not have worried, because Abbot students, with two exceptions, were effectively excluded from Advanced Placement Calculus by an intricate web of prerequisites. One Senior who did take it was refused admission to an advanced Computer Course, so she did the problems on her own, and helped the boys with their computer programs. Nor were boys encouraged to leave the sacred precincts of Pearson Hall even though Abbot's classics courses were officially open to Phillips boys. Weren't Cicero and Horace taught in *translation* down there? (They weren't.) Great was the consternation, says Mrs. Susan Clark, when it was discovered that two of Phillips' top students had made their way into Abbot's Latin IV course, were delighted with it, and were urging friends to join them. The bluster from the Hilltop over issues like these came perilously close to comedy—and perhaps, after all, that is what it was meant to be. But Abbot teachers never knew quite how to take it. When one of the Abbot classics teachers showed up at a pre-merger Classics Department party and asked for Bourbon instead of sherry, the reaction from the Grand Old Man of the Phillips department was instantaneous: "Saeva Femina!" (Savage Woman!) he growled, and handed her the drink.

Another place where no female might enter was History 40, that *rite de passage* which for decades had made men of mewling boys. Phillips had softened a bit of late and allowed 11th grade students who wished to do so to fulfill the history requirement by combining a less-demanding U.S. History course with a second year-long course in Senior year. It was O.K., the chairman decided, for Phillips students to take U.S. History at Abbot—but take care not to overdo it! So many boys signed up for the American Studies Course described in the last chapter that Phillips decided something was wrong. Sherry Gershon, the teacher, was too attractive, she made the course "too easy," (or was it "too much fun"?) and failed to come to grips with tariffs and treaties as she should do. "Sherry was a wonderful, imaginative teacher," Mary Minard counters. But Phillips held the latch strings to her course, and boys were discouraged from enrolling.[51] They were flatly forbidden to take another Abbot history course because the readings looked "too difficult" for 11th graders, as Phillips' Acting Chairman told its teacher. Perhaps he was just being tactful. Abbot threw up no such barriers before girls who wished to take Phillips courses. Phillips seemed to know all about the more mediocre teachers at Abbot, yet there was barely a whisper about the few incompetent or impossibly rigid teachers up the Hill—not even in the Abbot faculty room. Though coordination allowed many friendships between individual teachers to blossom on Andover Hill, it tended to push the Abbot faculty on the defensive.

During the first year there was no way of knowing that coordination was serving as an essential bridge to merger, and from time to time Abbot wondered whether it was worth the trouble. For about a month in the early spring of 1971, Gordon and his chief financial aides seriously considered the idea that Abbot should sell its buildings and land and relocate far from Andover, where it could enter a new phase as a coeducational country boarding school, free to realize the promise of its best new ideas. Gordon and Stapleton made a day's visit to Harrisville, New Hampshire, eight miles north of Mt. Monadnock. Most of the town was being offered for sale to a charitable corporation for about half a million dollars: why not Abbot? But the Trustees, committed to Andover and Phillips Academy, showed no interest, and the idea died.[52]

The Board was cool to alternatives partly because coordinate education was proving so successful for Abbot's students. In many ways the girls had the best of both worlds: a secure, relatively small residential community and a host of academic opportunities. *Cynosure*, the Abbot drama course, the soccer and lacrosse teams, and Abbot town meeting were all-female institutions where young women could

62. Coordination: "The Gates Ajar," 1972–1973.

play their parts and try their skills with no males to intrude. Meanwhile, Phillips classes stood open for the bold. If faculty were battling in the background, they concealed it from students pretty well. There were disjunctions and annoyances: no reserve books could leave the Hilltop Library until 9:00 P.M.; Phillips stage crew and art studio work went on until 10:00 P.M.; yet Abbot girls must sign in at 8:00. (Conscienceless, Abbot intellectuals and artists walked down the Hill at 8:00 to sign in, and turned right around to climb up again the back way.) But there were also some wonderful successes for Abbot. By winter of 1971, faculty discovered what Phillips students had long known: coordination, like the Army, lives on its stomach. The Bondes dished up such delicious food in the Abbot dining room (and at only 75 percent the food cost of Hilltop fare) that boys hungered to enroll in the noon and late afternoon Abbot classes which entitled them to eat down the Hill. For this reason among others, Phillips enrollment in Abbot courses continued to rise until Abbot teachers were teaching an entirely disproportionate share of the cross-enrolled students. In 1972–73 more Phillips courses were added to the mix to alleviate the problem; that second year of coordination, Abbot girls had 240 different courses to choose from. Although the two years of coordination were difficult and inefficient, they opened up an extraordinarily varied academic program to students of both schools. No Abbot girls were heard to complain. "I felt *very fortunate* to be living in the loose, happy, responsive Abbot environment and to take classes at both places," writes one. "I enjoyed the freedom and the double standard that worked in my favor."[53]

"The time is now"

Abbot students returned to Andover for the 1972–73 school year expecting more of the same. What was their surprise when Donald Gordon called the school together to announce that Abbot and Phillips Academy would become one school in June 1973. All Abbot buzzed with speculation. Why would the Phillips Board deny merger three times, then suddenly accept it?

Most of Andover's advocates of coeducation had left with relief in June, the Phillips and Abbot Boards having agreed that summer working parties could accomplish nothing more. But one thing was new: The Phillips Trustees were full of hope and pride in their Headmaster-elect, Theodore R. Sizer, scholar of educational history and former dean of the Harvard Graduate School of Education, who would shortly move to Andover with his wife Nancy Faust Sizer and their four children. Here was an experienced, articulate leader who might break the impasse, since it was now clear that neither Phillips faculty nor Trustees could do so. As Sizer has described his Trustees' conflicting desires:

> We want coeducation.
> We'd like to do it with Abbot.
> We can't afford to expand the school.
> We don't want to cut the number of male students.
> But we want coeducation.

The longer the Phillips Trustees lived with coordination, the more keenly they saw the effects of their indecisiveness on their school. The Phillips Admissions Office reported that prospective parents were put off by the Academy's apparent inability to make up its mind on coeducation. The Phillips faculty was—as Sizer puts it—"a proud, wounded bear, uncertain how to heal," tired of its divisions and longing to close them. Time had also wrought good things. One was a deeper trust of the Abbot Board. Melville Chapin, one of that group's newer members and a Phillips alumnus, became a crucial link between Abbot Academy and the warier Phillips Trustees. A first-rate lawyer with a high reputation for caution and skill, he stood in their eyes for the Old Andover virtues at the same time that he sensitively, quietly persuaded them to look toward the future of both academies.

The Phillips Trustees knew Sizer's commitment to full coeducation—they had hired him partly because of that commitment—and now all but a handful of them were ready to welcome a leader who would show them how to settle this issue so they could go on to other challenges. "Meet with Gordon and bring us a plan," they told Sizer. For the first time, the Phillips Headmaster was empowered to work for coeducation as decisively as the Abbot Principal had been for years.

It was Don Gordon who initiated the conversation in mid-June, shortly after Sizer settled in. "Let's talk," Gordon suggested. Something has to give.

> Our position has been and continues to be that the schools should merge, and that until we do, we waste ourselves and our staffs disproportionately on day-to-day mechanics . . . On balance I guess we've accomplished much, but "much" is a relative term. JMK was a superb staff man and administrator who basically didn't see why boys and girls needed to mix it up in schools. We at least are anxious for some clear resolution of basic structures and future intentions.[54]

"So am I," Sizer replied, gratified by Gordon's initiative and uninterested for the moment in arguing the intricacies of J. M. Kemper's role in preparing Phillips Academy for change. The status quo looked as unstable to him as it did to Gordon—unfair to Phillips and impossible, in the long run, for Abbot. "Coordination is real," Gordon wrote. "It's also a drag, as long as department heads rule the process. I would favor across-the-board coordination of all departments" as soon as we can manage it. "As it is now, faculty coordination and non-coordination bears a vague resemblance to a civil conflict in the banana republic of your choice. . . . If the two of us take a fresh look at all the accumulated data," Gordon finished, it may "be possible to move together, sharing the flak."[55]

To Sizer, a bit of flak was all in a day's work. He had visited Abbot in the spring, had liked most of what he saw, and wasn't afraid to say so. Abbot's long academic tradition appealed to the historian in him as much as its present bumptious optimism resounded with his own. Annealed in the fires of the sixties—and Cambridge had been a hot spot indeed—he was as impatient with complacencies as he was with "self-indulgent, self-proclaimed extremist(s)";[56] he believed that the truly liberating environment combined rigorous academic training with a challenging, variegated social milieu. On the whole, he admired Abbot's responses to the genuine needs of adolescents in the seventies, and as husband, parent, and educator he had thought deeply about one of Abbot's major concerns: the rights and responsibilities of women. Conversations with Hilltop teachers and their wives had convinced him that Phillips' "male chauvinism" was in reality "tissue thin," a poor disguise for honest confusion about sex roles, behind which his new colleagues—like himself—were groping for new definitions.[57] The same conversations revealed how much good will Abbot enjoyed among the Phillips faculty, however perplexed they felt about coeducation. Sizer agreed with Gordon that swift action on merger was needed to keep Abbot from being "nibbled to death."[58] He had watched Harvard and Radcliffe trying for years to pretend that they could negotiate merger as equals, and was "horrified by the charade. It was corrupting to both institutions," no matter how worthy the goal.[59] Finally, he welcomed the evidence that the two schools had already learned something from each other, for it suggested the potential of full merger. Coed athletics programs were still small, but expanding. Phillips' experimental cluster system already was demonstrating that a supportive residential community could prosper on the Hilltop much as it did at Abbot's lower altitude. Though the Phillips faculty would not accept the Phillips-

Abbot Curriculum Committee's devastation of the traditional course requirements, Phillips' new curriculum, like Abbot's, had greatly expanded students' academic choices. As his Board Chairman, Donald McLean, had also done, Sizer had taken the trouble to inspect the "stupid Abbot girl" stereotype. True enough, Abbot's students scored lower than Phillips' on some achievement tests and on the few Advanced Placement exams they took, but their grades in coordinated courses, their aptitude scores, and Abbot graduates' success in college convinced both men that all but a small minority were fully as able as Phillips boys.[60] In spite of surface differences, Sizer concluded, "an outsider . . . finds . . . the two schools more similar than not."[61]

Sizer would report his conclusions to Phillips Academy in September, but he had tentatively drawn them by the time he and Donald Gordon sat down together in July to talk, and those summer conversations with a man who had thought deeply about coeducation would make them firm. For his part, Gordon was determined to lead from Abbot's strengths. The school's hard-won financial equilibrium was promising, especially in that halcyon summer of rising stock-market values and general prosperity among Abbot's newly enlarged constituency (winter would embrace Andover Hill all too soon). Richard Griggs judges that Abbot was in a stronger financial position than for many years, its plant refurbished and considerably expanded, its investments doing well under new consultant management, its endowment more than replenished, after a decade of depletion, by the largest fund-raising operation in Abbot's history, its services in high demand, as evidenced by a 22 percent increase in applications for 1972–73. All this is accurate, agrees Treasurer Dow. "We had brought Abbot to the point where we could truthfully say 'this is not a bankruptcy sale.' " Dow was more pessimistic about Abbot's future. According to him and his colleague, Melville Chapin, Abbot had only reached a "safe, short-term plateau." Much overdue maintenance was in the works, but the original wings of Draper Hall were deteriorating still faster. Abbot had had to delay its much needed Arts building, that "showpiece of the New Abbot Fund,"[62] $40,000 worth of plans and models having been regretfully scrapped once it was clear that the fund's goals had indeed been overambitious.[63] Furthermore, it was clear that at least a portion of Abbot's success was owed to coordination with Phillips. What would happen to Abbot if Phillips pulled back and began recruiting its own girls? Abby Kemper thought she knew: Abbot would gradually die out. An ominous sign of applicants' preference for more thorough coeducation appeared in the acceptance-of-admission figures for spring

1972: just 53 percent of those admitted decided to come to Abbot, instead of the usual 80 percent.[64] Some superior prospects chose St. Paul's and Exeter and their bargain tuitions, tokenism be damned.

Gordon and Sizer agreed that merger would o'erleap tokenism, bringing three hundred girls to a new school, benignly forcing the two faculties to share responsibility for a single group of students, and, in one dramatic move, releasing the energy and the generosity that had been spent for two years on intricate half-way accommodations. The same result could be accomplished by the legal absorption of Abbot by Phillips Academy—and this was the form of merger Sizer proposed. Phillips' lawyers had stated in 1970 that only thus could the Phillips Trustees be reasonably sure that their ancient charter and their $70,000,000 worth of assets would remain intact after merger proceedings in the state legislature.[65] Here was a tough problem for Donald Gordon, and for all those to whom symbols shape realities: Abbot would lose its name. "Phillips-Abbot Academy" was already anathema to a few Abbot alumnae; Abbot's corporate disappearance might be absolutely unacceptable to the many. Gordon and Sizer spent several of their hours of talk upon the problem of guaranteeing some kind of significant continuation of Abbot's corporate identity within Phillips Academy. The lawyers had already advised this as a practical way of assuring that the Abbot endowment could be transferred to a coeducational Phillips Academy. A residential cluster might be "Abbot Cluster," a new student center might be "Abbot Hall." Still, thought Gordon miserably, the symbol would be all but lost. Could not the Phillips Board be persuaded to bend?

Symbols aside, the two men worked their way toward a plan to combine the two academies, happy that they could agree on so many of the essentials of a good education. Sizer began preparing a proposal for the Phillips Board, basing it on the specifications he and Gordon had drawn together. The new "Andover" would open on September 1, 1973, with all Abbot students in attendance as well as newly admitted girls (the Admissions Offices would be combined in the fall of 1972); about 300 girls altogether and 900 boys, only slightly fewer than both schools had enrolled for 1972–73. The total number could be brought down toward 980 within four years and the male-female ratio lowered to 2:1; meanwhile the new school would continue Phillips' traditional low-tuition-high-scholarship policy for both boys and girls, covering deficits as effectively as possible through the sale of unneeded property and by borrowing from the bank. Two new residential clusters would be established; all or most clusters would be coeducational. Sizer's proposal outlined staffing policies, questions of law, and, finally,

63. The last board of Trustees, 1972–1973. Top Row: *Leonard Kent,
Melville Chapin, Donald Gordon, Philip Allen, Benjamin Redfield,
Grenville Benedict, Guerin Todd.* Second Row: *Elizabeth Eaton, Abby
Kemper, Anne Russell Long, James K. Dow, Jr.* Front Row: *Mary Howard
Nutting, Sidney Lovett, Caroline Rogers, J. Radford Abbot, Beverly Floe,
Aagot Hinrichsen Stambaugh, Mary Dooley Bragg.*

all those problems of governance, job definition, and school organization that would have to be solved in the year to come if both Boards
agreed that the schools should be joined.

The chances were fair. Subgroups of the two Boards had agreed
fervently on merger for two years; with Sizer's appearance, they took
heart once again and made plans for one more push. Abbot Trustees
might balk at the idea of legal incorporation into Phillips, but the
group was skilled at resolving internal conflict and fearless of tough
decisions. "I've never been on a board that worked so well together, so
given to good, straight talk by strong people, both men and women,"
says Leonard Kent, a new Abbot Trustee in 1972. On the other
hand, the Phillips Board was still bruised by the conflicts of recent
years. A cabal of anti-Abbot Trustees had boycotted the joint dinner
party Board Presidents McLean and Allen arranged on the Phillips
campus in January 1972; the cabal invited all red-blooded Phillips
Trustees to join them for dinner at the Andover Inn instead. The same
men walked out of another joint gathering as soon as the Abbot Trustees arrived. Fending off their anger with one hand, and fielding the
anxieties of Abbot faculty and alumnae with the other, Phil Allen felt
by winter 1972 (he says) like some tall partition between the two
schools, a handball court on the Phillips' side, a wailing wall on the
Abbot one. Few of the Phillips Trustees had even set foot on the Abbot campus since their own school days on Andover Hill. In spite of

the progress toward amity made that spring and summer, it was hard to imagine the two Boards being able to settle anything together.

During the last week of July 1972 Gordon's and Sizer's "Specifications for a Possible Andover-Abbot agreement" made the rounds of the Abbot Trustees. Baldly they began: "P.A. would absorb Abbot, i.e., Abbot as a corporate entity would cease to exist and its assets would be transferred to P.A." Though Abbot's name could be perpetuated in some way within the new school, that school would be named "Phillips Academy." This was almost too much for the faithful alumnae Trustees, whose letters to each other and to Gordon and Allen crisscrossed the country for a month. But by mid-September, when the Abbot Trustees met to consider Sizer's more detailed plan for coeducation, nearly all had become convinced, with Mary Howard Nutting, that "the time is now."[66] "This is the time and the only time [wrote Beverly Floe] in which Abbot will have the leverage" to accomplish Gordon's and Sizer's resolve "that Abbot's interest and strength [in] educating capable young women . . . be fully reflected in the enterprise."[67]

The Principal himself felt "torn between the great substantive possibility" of Abbot's being part of a new school[68] and irritation over the "implacability" and "smallness" of the Phillips Trustees' stand on the school name.[69] In his most discouraged mood, Gordon felt that he and his Board were "being stampeded." We are dealing "with fiduciary minds"—he told the Abbot Trustees—with men stuck in "middle American cultural values." All our "work to rejuvenate Abbot" is about to be "annulled by a less imaginative, fat institution."[70] Treasurer J. K. Dow tried to cheer him by reminding him what Phillips wealth could mean to Abbot girls. To him, as to several other Trustees, the loss of Abbot's name seemed unimportant beside the opportunity that "incorporation" promised 300 girls and young women, who would draw on the vast scholarship and teaching resources that a new Phillips Academy could offer.[71] Thus debate proceeded in that suspenseful period before and during the early fall meetings of both Boards.

Ultimately the Board would accept the loss of Abbot's name because Phillips was fifteen times richer than Abbot. This was no Northfield-Mount-Hermon, nourished by the same endowment, or Choate-Rosemary Hall, which combined far smaller and far less disparate resources. Given that American women as a whole contributed but $1.00 to their schools for every $25.00 men gave to theirs, the ratio of Abbot's to Phillips' wealth was not likely to change very fast.[72] The Board would accept it because Abbot's five-year financial projections showed that the smaller school had only two alternatives: an ever-increasing deficit or an ever-increasing tuition—and several Trustees felt that Abbot's tuition had already brought Abbot too far from the spirit of its founders, whose original Abbot was inexpensive enough for almost any frugal Yankee family.[73] If Abbot refused the Phillips terms and the larger school backed away from coordination to take in its own girls, the future looked grimmer still. Finally, the Board accepted the loss of Abbot's name and corporate identity because of their faith in Theodore Sizer. "In his deep and penetrating questioning of P.A.'s style . . . he is a friend, an educational comrade," wrote Gordon.[74] "He was the key," Allen confirms. They accepted the terms in a spirit of courage and hope because, as Gordon had foreseen, such acceptance proved to be the only way "of achieving the outcome, educationally, that we've sought all along: a new coed school in which the role of capable women would be equal to that of men in framing the institution."[75]

On September 15, 1972, the Phillips Trustees met and made clear their willingness to turn Sizer's "Speculations on Coeducation" into policy if Abbot would agree; the same day, the Abbot Board voted

> That the goal for Abbot Academy of coeducation can be best be accomplished by a combination of this school with Phillips Academy. That in any such combination the spirit and dignity of the current educational scene at Abbot, of the history and tradition of the school, of its students, faculty and alumnae be preserved to the fullest extent possible.

The Board sent back by Phil Allen their willingness to negotiate, and made the first of a series of proposals to ensure that Abbot's basic purposes would be built into the new school. The Phillips Trustees responded immediately to the most concrete of Abbot's suggestions by voting to close their "exclusive men's club":[76] three Abbot Trustees, two of them women, would be invited to join the Phillips Board with the same rights and duties as Phillips Alumni Trustees, and the first of several female Charter Trustees would be elected in the near future. As a further earnest of their intentions, they agreed to Sizer's resolution that Carolyn Goodwin be elected Dean of the new Phillips Academy, and they ratified one by one the major proposals on which Gordon and Sizer had agreed in July.

A week later, the Abbot Trustees were ready. With one abstention, they voted

> To approve and endorse in principle a combination of Abbot Academy and Phillips Academy upon the basis of the resolutions

adopted by the Trustees of Phillips Academy at their meeting of
September 16, 1972, and, therefore, the Trustees of Abbot
Academy propose such a combination.[77]

The Phillips Trustees' response to Philip Allen's presentation of the
fateful resolution made clear what was to happen:

Voted, that this Board welcomes and accepts the proposal of the
Board of Trustees of Abbot Academy . . . to transfer to Phillips
Academy the educational undertakings and assets of Abbot,
and instructs the President and Headmaster to accomplish this
incorporation effective 1 September, 1973.[78]

So, after all, the "combination" was to be an incorporation, not a
merger of equals. "Merger it was not," Jane Baldwin has written,
"rather a complete take-over, lock stock and barrel."[79] Legally and financially, this is exactly what the Phillips Trustees had in mind. Now
that the commitment was made, however, legal strictures—even the
"care and feeding of the merger imagery"[80]—receded before the
broad, human challenge of planning and staffing the coeducational
Phillips Academy for the long future. As Gordon would say to the
Phillips Trustees when both Boards met together for the first time in
history: "The leap of faith we're making, by extinguishing our school's
life, can be made precisely because we believe that with us lodged
firmly within your corpus, you will be incapable of remaining the
same."[81]

Plots and Plans

The Principal called the Abbot faculty together to describe these
momentous events to them in detail. "Any questions?" he wanted to
know. "Yes," said Steve Perrin from the back of the room. "Do I
plant my garden for next summer?" "You do," answered Gordon, re-
assuringly. The two Boards' agreements promised that "Andover and
Abbot personnel will be treated equally" in hiring faculty and staff
for 1973–74, and that all decisions would "be made in close consultation
with Mr. Gordon and Miss Goodwin."[82] A "working party" on Faculty
Appointment Policy began meeting before September was out, including five members of the Phillips faculty (one of them the younger of
Phillips' two female teachers), and Richard Griggs, Jean St. Pierre
and Anne Bugbee from Abbot, all under the chairmanship of Simeon
Hyde. The group sifted a mountain of advice from teachers and
students up and down the Hill advocating or attacking Phillips' "triple-

threat" system, which had the men of the Hilltop moving between classroom, athletic field and dormitory, with their wives (unpaid) picking up the pieces. On October 25, the Abbot town meeting held schoolwide group discussions in order to ask both faculty and students what should be expected of teachers in the new school. Already, students were getting anxious. "If they keep the old P.A. system, my houseparents will have to go," said one.[83] Phillips teachers lived and breathed Andover Hill, while ever since Mary Crane had adapted Abbot workloads to women's needs, many Abbot teachers had lived miles away and pursued their own out-of-Abbot responsibilities—enjoyed also the chance to invite students to their homes and introduce them to Cambridge or Boston. Phillips must have housemasters (or "house counselors," as they now began to be called), but the new Phillips badly needed women teachers too. The working party devised an extraordinarily flexible policy that allowed a large minority of teachers to work as "double-threats," or even, simply, as classroom teachers, if that was where their strongest interest lay.

But people, not policies, choose teachers, and a few Abbot teachers were fighting for their jobs. Though polite, the battle was messy. Neither school had a systematic faculty evaluation policy. Theoretically, every Phillips and Abbot teacher was under scrutiny, but actually, Phillips' policy of granting three and five year appointments to experienced teachers meant that only a minority of Hilltop teachers were due to have their contracts reviewed for 1973–74. Abbot had no formal tenure system: everyone was up for grabs. Equally important, many of Abbot's teachers were at early stages in their careers. Donald Gordon and Carolyn Goodwin had already advised several to get further graduate training; had not merger plans posed the possibility of work at Phillips, these might well have left of their own accord—but their relative lack of experience made them anxious for a chance to get more of it in a Hilltop job even while it made them vulnerable in the hiring process. Phillips department heads, accustomed to power, visited Abbot teachers' classes, but no Abbot chairman climbed the Hill to evaluate Phillips teachers, though the original plan had called for close consultation between each pair of department heads. One Abbot chairman, already invited to teach at Phillips, found herself "suffering acute Phillipsphobia" after a deadening Abbot-Phillips discussion of interdisciplinary courses during which the men introduced "rudimentary ideas" "as though they were revolutionary break-throughs," and her own wide if brief experience was ignored "as if there was nothing much to be learned from other schools. Provincialism, backwardness, naiveté, smugness, male chauvinism, rudeness—all these . . . come to mind as I continue to think of this meeting," she wrote. "Was it a microcosm of next year's Phillips Academy? If so, I want no part of it personally and professionally."[84] Faith Howland Kaiser had been eager to combine Abbot-Phillips admissions operations, but it seemed to her now that Phillips was calling the shots, and that the special needs of female applicants and their families might be getting lost.[85] Eventually, Faith would opt out; so would several others who could not accept the conditions of working for Phillips Academy. Three years before, Rennie McQuilkin had come down from the Hilltop to teach English at Abbot after a particularly distressing decision by the central Discipline Committee concerning one of his dormitory boys; he had gladly accepted Abbot's lower salary in exchange for the challenge and fun of working there. Now Phillips wanted him to return to "house counseling," and he would not. A few other young teachers made the same response, and still others were not invited to return. The deans and heads of the two schools labored long over the hiring task; department chairmen also struggled to be as fair and attentive to individual aspirations as possible. "There was agony both up and down the Hill," says Sizer. In the end just a handful of Phillips teachers were let go that year, while fifteen Abbot teachers were denied jobs in the new Phillips Academy.[86] Nine others decided not to apply for positions, or refused those offered them. Over the next few years, several other Phillips teachers were scrutinized as their contracts came up for renewal, and were released as part of the effort to reduce the combined Abbot-Phillips faculty in the new coeducational school. There was justice here, but Abbot teachers hoping to stay on at Phillips in 1973 could not know it would be done.

It hurt. Steve Perrin did plant his garden, but that was because his wife was asked to stay. There was no room for his special brand of Humanities course at Phillips Academy, or for a man who wanted to stay out of a dormitory until his baby son was older. Now he and others unchosen could only feel depressed as they withdrew from the fray and watched their thirty-four favored friends attending Phillips faculty meetings and planning courses with their Phillips colleagues, working out rules for next year's school, or extending and refining Phillips' new residential cluster system—for the promise that Abbot and Phillips would create the new school together was truly being met in most respects. Abbot Seniors also felt detached, sometimes cynical. *They* wouldn't be going up the Hill next year. Senior Mids watched organizations they had hoped to lead either being dissolved or choosing male presidents and editors-in-chief. The finest achievements of Abbot town meeting, including the schoolwide work program that

town meeting and its committees had planned and instituted for 1972–
73, seemed destined to be short-circuited, and school government reduced to haggling over parietal rules.

At first it looked like a miserable contrast with the past, when Abbot had coped with clashes in student-faculty values so openly and, on
the whole, so well: typically, the original arguments over intersex
room visiting had been accompanied by publication of opinion polls
in *Cynosure* and lively debates on the appropriate roles of sex and
privacy in a boarding school. The students had failed to get the open
visiting policy they wanted, but at least they had known exactly why.
Where else but in a Draper Hall art class could a teacher (Virginia
Powel, of course) walk in for the fourth time on an Abbot-Phillips
couple locked in embrace and deal with the problem by saying, "Hey,
you're not being fair! Have you thought about how the rest of us
feel? *We're* not being kissed." (To be sure, the young rake henceforth
celebrated his entrance to class with a kiss for Mrs. Powel, then one
for each girl!) By mid-winter of 1973, town meeting had little to do
but react to proposals from the Hilltop. Students wondered what
would become of school government at Phillips, where—according to
one Hilltop observer—"the outcome of all debate is predetermined by
a higher authority";[87] they complained in *Cynosure* that already rules
were "being imposed on them by an insecure administration" just to
impress Phillips Academy. "Girls don't require all this surveillance," an
editor insisted. "We do not feel the need to prove our maturity in the
same ways that boys do."[88]

Nevertheless, they were proving themselves in other ways, and there
was hard work done. Like many other Abbot institutions, town meeting handled what business it had with a determination to show Phillips
Academy how responsibly students (and girls) could conduct their
affairs. One Senior got tired of watching her friends moon around.
She hauled them up the Hill to the Phillips woodworking shop, and
together they designed and built an enormous geodesic dome as a
shelter and exhibition for that spring's Bradley Arts Festival. Several
Abbot teachers decided it was now or never for academic projects
that could thrive only in Abbot's flexible work schedule. The last
Spanish students headed for Costa Rica under Dorothy Judd's exchange program. Two U.S. History classes spent eight weeks conducting research and field study on federal and state compensatory education programs in the Greater Lawrence area, and writing a sixty-page
report on their work for the Fifth District Congressman and the
House Education and Labor Committee on which he served. The
year's Phillips-Abbot musical was a smashing success. And Donald

Gordon, who carried a burden of sorrow far greater than he had ever expected to feel over Abbot's demise, spent hours helping jobless teachers find places in other schools for the year to come. The quality of the positions that most of these rejects gained testified both to their worth and to Gordon's effort. Gordon also worked with Phillips and Abbot staff to plan a responsive counseling system for the new school.[89] Two teachers became engaged to each other, to the joy of all Abbot. The more these two saw of Phillips, the more they decided it was not for them; they would kick off the dust of Andover Hill together. Other teachers saw signs that the new coeducational school, large and unfamiliar though it appeared, would be carrying forward the best of the old Abbot's academic traditions and picking up much of the new Abbot's sensitivity to human needs, and they threw their energies into making it happen. As Richard Pieters said for almost everyone after the question of merger had been finally settled: "Now let's make this the best damn coed school in the country!"

Last Things

The "Articles and Agreement of Association," ratified in January 1973 by the two Academies, reflected the Abbot Trustees' labor to build into the contract the assurance that their school's historic mission would not be abandoned:

> The Trustees of both Abbot Academy and Phillips Academy are desirous of accomplishing an Association of the two schools for the education of young persons, both female and male. . . . The said Trustees of Abbot Academy and of Phillips Academy are mindful of the distinguished history of education at Abbot Academy . . . and wish to further the educational purpose and tradition built up over many years at Abbot Academy.

The document continued: "Abbot and its counsel will promptly prepare and file with the Supreme Judicial Court of Massachusetts a petition for the dissolution of Abbot." Abbot would give Phillips all its assets and properties for the sum of $1.00, and Phillips Academy would assume all of Abbot's obligations and responsibilities. How could Phillips and Abbot together ensure that these responsibilities were faithfully met? Here was a crucial test for the "merger"—as it began again to be called, with a fine disregard for the legal terminology.

Once the hiring and firing of next year's teachers was done, it was easier to see how hard most Phillips men were working to live up to the spirit of the Agreement. Administrators from both schools occupied high ground in their negotiations concerning pensions and non-teaching staff, determining to meet moral obligations even when no legal ones existed. Early on, it had been assumed that pensions promised would be sustained; now, with the Phillips Trustees' approval, Abbot doubled some of the lowest ones to provide a dignified living for long-tenured retirees. Cooks and maids and groundsmen were transferred to the Phillips payroll; in the process they joined an annuity plan similar to the one for which a few Abbot Trustees had been lobbying since the mid-sixties, and Abbot made the initial payments into it from its own funds. Long-tenured secretaries and administrative assistants were also guaranteed jobs, although Abbot's pay scale had improved so much and so many jobs had been upgraded in the last decade that several would have to work for lower wages on the Hilltop,[90] in contrast to the teaching faculty, whose salaries went up.

Abbot also had special obligations to its students, who had come expecting to meet Abbot's requirements and gain an Abbot diploma. Gordon and Sizer had agreed during the summer that Abbot girls transferring to Phillips could continue to work for an Abbot diploma if they chose. Now Carolyn Goodwin worked out the process in detail, and sixty-three underclasswomen declared themselves Abbot diploma candidates. Some of them could not have met the Phillips academic standards, but a large minority were strong students who had thrived on Abbot's opportunities for independent work and vigorous extracurricular involvement, and would take Mathematics 30 because they wanted to, not because Phillips demanded it.

The last Abbot girls would graduate in 1976, but the Abbot Trustees had been searching all fall for some tangible means of assuring the welfare of females over the long future of Phillips Academy. In their turn, the Phillips Trustees had promised that the Abbot name would somewhere be embedded within the new Phillips Academy, and in the Agreement the major device for accomplishing both these purposes was unveiled. The planned Abbot Academy Association was much more than a symbol.[91] It was an internal foundation whose directors would control a million dollar endowment for the purposes of advancing within the new school those causes Abbot had made its own for many years: skillful counseling, careful experimentation with pedagogical innovation, and attention to the special needs of female students and to the task to which Abbot's founders had pledged themselves of "enlarg[ing] the minds and form[ing] the morals of the

youth" under the school's care.[92] Like Samuel Phillips, the Abbot consti-
tution-makers had not distinguished between male and female "youth."
The Abbot Academy Association was designed to benefit both.

The student-faculty Residential Planning group drew the boundaries
of the projected new Abbot Cluster around the Abbot campus and
made ready to settle Carroll Bailey, Dean-elect of the Cluster, and his
wife Elaine in Abbot's "French House" up School Street, soon to be
named Bertha Bailey House. Meanwhile the Baileys themselves were
deciding how to take maximum advantage of the Abbot Cluster's own
library, dining room, and recreational facilities.[93] But no one knew
what would eventually become of Abbot's land and buildings. There
was a special poignancy to that last lovely spring as leaf buds opened
on the Maple Walk and on the copper beech and the linden tree
which had been planted by Miss McKeen's and Miss Means's graduating Seniors so long ago. Flowering shrubs bloomed everywhere,

*64. An Abbot birthday party, Jes Bonde presiding: the 100th Anniversary
of the Alumnae Association, 1971.*

ignorant of sadness. Alumnae arrived to help arrange the last all-Abbot reunion—for the Abbot and Phillips Alumnae Association were to combine the next year—and found themselves mourning more than a school. It seemed to them that some priceless piece of the New England conscience and character had fallen away.[94] Perhaps, after the sixties, it could be found nowhere anyway—but this only made Abbot's demise the more devastating. Abbot girls also began to understand what they were about to lose. Friends walked hand in hand, as they could comfortably do within the gates, and wondered about the new Phillips Academy girls who were now visiting Andover Hill to decide whether to accept admission. Boy-hungry they seemed, overambitious, foreign.[95] Each traditional event was a final celebration of Abbot's excellence: the year's Bazaar, the last Spanish Club Yom-Yom, the last Abbot Gilbert and Sullivan performance, with Richard Sheahan as the Mikado. Nevertheless, when it was time to choose dormitories and clusters for 1973–74, every single Abbot underclass student chose the Hilltop. Three all-Abbot teams joined the Hilltop stickball league and ·reveled in their several near-wins. Sadly, interest in the Gargoyles and Griffins was falling off,[96] but Phillips had invited Abbot to participate in several formal Hilltop sports as well as its "Search and Rescue" groups, and nearly a hundred girls got a heady taste of Hilltop sports, while Miss Ritchie worked with the Phillips athletics department to plan still more. Female swimmers, oarswomen, and cross-country skiers and runners left behind the "big pick-up scene"[97] and found real friends among their fellow athletes at Phillips. If Abbot was to be Phillips Academy, the girls would plunge in and make it their own.

"So long as Abbot's future coincided with mine, I could work my heart out for the place," says one teacher who was not re-hired. Now the community was about to break; lives diverged as never before.[98] The divisions made Abbot strange. "Abbot was home. The whole school was closer than most dormitories are up here," a '76 graduate would say after two years on the Hilltop.[99] Along with Abbot's last Senior Class, thirty-five teachers and key staff members were to leave Andover Hill for good.[100] Donald Gordon's "private rage" at Phillips had abated once the name battle was finally lost and the agonies of hiring and firing were over,[101] but he decided not to pursue the possibility of a position at Phillips Academy, wishing to take the salaried leave the two Boards had offered him and start fresh elsewhere. Regrets nagged him: if Abbot was good enough for Phillips Academy, mightn't it have been good enough to go it alone? And as if his own sorrows were insufficient, some alumnae were excoriating him as "the destroyer of Abbot Academy," little recognizing that the Trustees were at least as deeply implicated as he. "Some of the lightning he brought on himself," says Philip Allen, "but most of it he took because we asked him to take it."[102] To this day Gordon will not accept the role of "tragic figure" in which some colleagues have cast him;[103] nor will two former Abbot Trustees, who still feel that "his vision and his persistence." were largely responsible for the success of the merger. Yet, says Gordon, it was terribly difficult to have been asked first "to lead Abbot forward towards a new identity as a vital, modern school, and then suddenly, to take a 90° turn toward Phillips . . . I discovered that Abbot meant almost too much to me." It was harrowing for him to realize that in the moment of agreement with Ted Sizer, July 1972, his power to sustain his particular Abbot Academy had vanished.[104] Nevertheless, in their sadness, Gordon and the others who would leave were not alone. As one of its groundsmen has said of Abbot, "This place had a great heart."[105] Whether or not they had been kept on by Phillips, custodians and switchboard operators and teachers alike recognized the disintegration of a community that had brought them together as friends.[106] Next year, boys would live in Draper and only the Art and History departments would be teaching down the Hill. For those who collected and sorted long-valued Abbot goods—including Abbot's magnificent art history equipment (kept), its shell collection (moved to the Phillips science building) and all the portraits and antiques which had adorned Draper Hall and other treasured spaces—dismemberment was a tangible, material affair. Through their own votes for merger, even the Trustees would be severed from Abbot. Though Philip Allen, the "architect of merger," belonged to the new school as a Phillips Trustee, he felt these many partings as deeply as anyone. "Don Gordon was just like a son to me," he says; "not wayward, but interesting and mercurial . . . It was a marvelous relationship."[107] Some means to comfort—if not to heal—had to be found.

Depressed though he was, Perrin set the faculty looking, and the faculty found it. A winter night's party became the first of at least four dozen gatherings devoted to writing and rehearsing a Faculty Follies more grand, more ridiculous, and more marvelous than any Andover Hill had ever seen. "My Fair Lady" provided the music, but the theme—the marriage of two historic schools—burst the bonds of the original plot. Staid department heads turned out to be smashing actors; rusty dancers kicked heels that hadn't left the ground for years. Everyone helped, all in secret. By the time the curtain opened on May

27 to a packed Davis Hall, the students were breathless with curiosity and the Phillips faculty members as eager as they were wary—for every man of the Hilltop who was to be made sport of that night had been specially invited. The show's title provided a hint:

Pedagogical Philanderings
or
Woman-Child on the Promised Hill
A salacious satire in two acts

Professor Malaprop Chipps (Marion Finbury) appeared in academic gown and sneakers with spectacles askew, and introduced mayhem: Samuel Phillips and Sarah Abbot rising from their graves on being disturbed by a necking Phillips-Abbot couple, and vowing in operatic tones to get uncouth youth back in the classroom where they belonged even if they had to join hands in marriage to do it. There followed a Phillips faculty meeting—grey flannel suits, shining briefcases, discussion pursued with military precision; then the Abbot "faculty womb," filled with flower children; then ribald scenes of the triumphant invasion of Hilltop classrooms, gymnasiums, and dormitories by FEMALES.

> I have often been in this dorm before,
> But I always came through a window on the second floor;
>> Now I find my way
>> By the light of day
> Through the halls of this dorm on the hill,
> And oh, the towering feeling,
> Just to know I'm finally here;
> That overpowering feeling,
> Of being part of Teddy Sizer's New Frontier . . .
> People stop and stare; they don't bother me,
> 'Cause there's nowhere else on earth that I would rather be . . .

The audience roared, stamping its glee with such abandon that sections of the ceiling fell down in two of the basement classrooms below. "Teddy" Sizer asked to have the whole thing repeated in George Washington Hall the following weekend.[108]

"I guess they did it to make us feel better about coming to P.A.," says a 1976 alumna.[109] She was half right. They did it for themselves and for one another as well, much as founder Samuel Jackson had vaulted rail fences. It was Abbot at its funniest and most energetic and best. And the solemn Commencement that soon followed was Abbot for the last time. James Rae Whyte—Abbot father, Abbot faculty spouse, and Phillips Chaplain—prayed the school out with a hope and reverence not unlike that with which it had first opened in 1829.

> Almighty God, unto us a child was given
>> and we called her name Laura or Lucinda,
>> Robin or Julia,
>> Kristin or Jane.
> We called her name Claudia or Barbara,
>> Virginia, Ellen or Anne.
> We called her name Elizabeth or Dorothy or Diana.
> We called her name "Daughter."
> We called her name "Love."
> We thanked Thee in time past for Thy unfailing mercy,
>> grateful for her days,
>> and for her years.
> Now the harvest of our hearts are grown,
>> we ask that Thou will consecrate these lives,
>> their strength, their knowledge,
>> their vision, their sense of justice,
>> their regard for the worth of other people.
> Those of us who have labored in this growth,
>> parents, teachers, friends rejoice, O God,
>> and give praise for this school,
>> this place, this time,
>> these persons.
>
>>>>>>>> Amen.

"I loved Abbot so much as it was; I didn't see how it could possibly change so much. But it did—and so did Phillips," says Marie Baratte, who has known Abbot Academy—and now Phillips—for over thirty years. As an independent school Abbot Academy had been as free to change, however difficult the process, as it was to conserve all that seemed valuable in its long heritage, no matter what the tides of change outside the gates. "Abbot really hasn't disappeared," Mlle. Baratte finishes. Indeed not. An old school is made of thousands of people, and of the ideas and the works they engender. All these have shaped the present.

APPENDIX A

Constitution of Abbot Academy

Pursuant to the authority vested in us by the foregoing subscription, and in execution of the trust thereby committed to us, We, Mark Newman, Milton Badger, Samuel C. Jackson, Samuel Farrar, Amos Blanchard, Hobart Clark, and Amos Abbot, all of Andover, in the County of Essex, and Commonwealth of Massachusetts, have proceeded to frame a Constitution for the perpetual government of the Female School or Academy endowed and intended to be established by the said subscription, which Constitution is in the following words, which we hereby adopt and establish as the basis of said Academy, and as containing the fundamental rules for its regulation in all future time.

The Board of Trustees shall consist of not more than nine nor less than five members, all of whom shall be professors of religion of the Congregational or Presbyterian denomination. They shall meet once in every year, on such a day as they shall appoint, also upon special occasions when called thereto as hereafter directed; and a major part of the Trustees shall, when regularly convened, be a quorum, of which quorum a major part shall have power to transact the business of their trust. The said Board shall perpetuate its own body by filling all vacancies.

There shall be chosen annually, by ballot, a President, Clerk and Treasurer, as officers of the trust, out of their own number, who shall continue in their respective offices till their places are supplied by a new election; and upon the decease of either of them another shall be chosen in his room at the next meeting.

The President shall give his voice and vote in common with any other member; and whenever there shall be an equal division of the members on any question it shall determine on that side whereon the President shall have given his vote; and in his absence at any meeting of the Trustees another shall be appointed, who shall be vested with the same power during such absence. He shall call special meetings upon the written application of any two of the Trustees for that purpose.

The Clerk shall record all votes of the Trustees, inserting the names of those present at every meeting. He shall keep a fair record of every donation, with the name of each benefactor, and the purpose to which it is to be appropriated, if expressed. If he shall be absent at any meeting of the Trustees, another shall be appointed to serve in his room during such absence.

The Treasurer shall keep fair and regular accounts of all monies received and paid by him, and his accounts shall be annually audited by a committee of the Trustees appointed for that purpose. He shall also, if required, give bond for the faithful discharge of the duties of his office, in such sum as the Trustees shall direct, and with sufficient sureties.

The Trustees shall appoint such Principal Instructor, whether male or female, and such assistants, in and for the service of the Academy, as they shall judge will best promote its usefulness, and as its funds may permit. They shall also have power to remove any instructor or assistant when, in their judgment, the good of the school requires it.

The Principal Instructor, whether male or female, shall be a professor of the Christian religion, of exemplary piety, of well-bred manners, of a cultivated taste, of a natural aptitude for government and instruction, and of good natural and acquired abilities.

It shall be the duty of the Trustees, at least as often as once a term, either as a Board or by a Committee, to visit the Academy, and inquire into the state of the school, the conduct of the instructors, the proficiency of the students, and to suggest such means as they think proper for improving the system of female education. The Trustees shall also determine the qualifications requisite to entitle youth to an admission into this Seminary.

As the manners and improvement of the scholars are liable to be much affected by intercourse with the families in which they board, and as it is important that they should be conversant with persons of good character only, no members of the School shall be permitted to board in any family which the Trustees disapprove.

The Principal Instructor, whether male or female, shall, in the management of the School, conform to the regulations established by the Trustees, and shall have power from time to time to make such other consistent rules as shall be found necessary for the internal management of the School, which rules shall always be subject to the revisal and approbation of the Trustees.

The primary objects to be aimed at in this School shall ever be to regulate the tempers, to improve the taste, to discipline and enlarge the minds, and form the morals of the youth who may be members of it. To form the immortal mind to habits suited to an immortal being, and to instil principles of conduct and form the character for an immortal destiny, shall be subordinate to no other care. Solid acquirements shall always have precedence of those which are merely showy, and the useful of those which are merely ornamental.

There shall be taught in this Seminary Reading, Spelling, Chirography, Arithmetic, Geography, Composition, History, Geometry, Algebra, Natural Philosophy, Grammar, Rhetoric, Chemistry, Intellectual Philosophy, Astronomy, Sacred Music, and such other Sciences and Arts, and such of the languages, ancient or modern, as opportunity and ability may permit, and as the Trustees shall direct.

Trusting to the All-wise and Beneficent Disposer of events to favor this our humble attempt to advance the cause of human happiness, we humbly commit it to his patronage and blessing.

IN WITNESS WHEREOF we have hereunto set our hands, this Fourth day of July, in the year of our Lord, One thousand eight hundred and twenty-eight.

> Mark Newman
> Milton Badger
> Samuel C. Jackson
> Sam'l Farrar
> Amos Blanchard
> Hobart Clark
> Amos Abbot

APPENDIX B

Trustees of Abbot Academy

Edward Taylor 1859–1869
Warren Fales Draper 1868–1905 (Treasurer 1876–1900)
George W. Coburn 1870–1890
Rufus S. Frost 1870–1894
Col. George Ripley 1870–1908 (Clerk 1878–1900,
President 1901–1902, Treasurer 1901–1902)
Egbert Coffin Smyth 1870–1888
Rev. J. Henry Thayer 1870
Hiram W. French 1873–1879
Rev. Francis Howe Johnson 1877–1889 (Clerk 1877–1878)
Edward G. Porter 1878–1900
John Wesley Churchill 1879–1900
William H. Wilcox 1879–1882
James White 1882–1886
John Byers 1884–1889
Mortimer B. Mason 1886–1908
Arthur Stoddard Johnson 1890–1912
Henry H. Proctor 1890
Horace H. Tyer 1890–1900
Mrs. John M. Harlow 1892–1904
Henrietta Learoyd Sperry 1892–1901
John Phelps Taylor 1892–1916 (Clerk 1901–1902)
Marcus Morton 1896–1935 (President 1913–1917 and 1919–1935)
John Alden 1900–1916 (Clerk 1902–1916)
Mary Donald Churchill 1900–1930
E. Winchester Donald 1900–1904
Daniel Merriman 1900–1912 (President 1902–1912)
Samuel L. Fuller 1902–1906 (Treasurer 1903–1906)
George H. Gordon 1904–1912
Edward C. Mills 1904–1913
George Ferguson Smith 1905–1938
Burton S. Flagg 1906–1964 (Treasurer 1906–1964)
Rev. Markham Winslow Stackpole 1908–1930
George Gilbert Davis 1910–1921
Charles H. Cutler 1913–1940
Albert Fitch 1914–1920
Charles H. Oliphant 1914–1926 (Clerk 1917–1919)
Grace Carleton Dryden, '86, Alumnae Trustee 1915–1921
Edward Barton Chapin 1920–1952 (Clerk 1920–1935,
President 1935–1952)
Anna Nettleton Miles, '93, Alumnae Trustee 1921–1927
Bertha Bailey 1923–1936

APPENDIX C

Faculty of Abbot Academy, 1936–1973

Name	Degrees and Colleges	Subject	Dates of Abbot tenure
Rebekah Munroe Chickering	AB Bryn Mawr College	*English*	1898–1937
Laura Keziah Pettingell	AB; MA Smith College Ed.M. Harvard U.	Head, Classics Dept. Substitute and ass't teacher *Latin* *Problems of Democracy*	1916–1918 1922–1924 1936–1940
Bertha Morgan Gray (Mrs. Chester)	Artistic Diploma, Curry School of Expression	*Dramatic Interpretation Spoken English*	1917–1948
Octavia Whiting Mathews	AB Colby College Studied at Mt. Holyoke Studied at Madrid Centro de Estudios Históricos y Científicos	*Spanish*	1917–1940
Helen Dunford Robinson	AB Smith College	*Latin*	1918–1945
Ruth Stephens Baker	AB Smith College MA Columbia Univ.	*French* and *German*	1920–1941
Helen Dearborn Bean	AB Wellesley College Studied at U. of Oxford	*History*	1920–1939
Marie DeLa Niépce Craig (Mrs.)	Couvent du Sacré Coeur Brevet d'Institutrice	*French*	1920–1939

Alice Sweeney	AB Vassar College	*English*	1920–1922
		Acting	1935–1956
		Principal	1946–1947
		Director of	
		Studies	1938–1956
Fanny Bigelow Jencks	AB Mt. Holyoke	*Biology*	
		Sec'y to	1921–1932
		Principal	
		Registrar	1932–1936
		Acting Head	1936–1937
		of School	
Kate Friskin	Studied at Glasgow	*Pianoforte*	1922–1961
	Athenaeum and with	*Theory of*	
	Sophie Weisse and	*Music*	1948–1961
	D. F. Tovey and	*Choral Music*	1948–1961
	Tobias Matthay		
Walter Howe	BM Va. Institute of	*Choral Music*	1922–1948
	Music	*Pianoforte*	
	A.A.G.O. American	*Organ*	
	Guild of Organists	*Theory of*	
		Music	
Mary Carpenter	Graduate of the Boston	*Physical*	1925–1945
	School of Phys. Ed.	*Education*	
	B.S. Ed. Boston Univ.		
Mary Gay	Graduate Boston Museum	*History of*	1933–1953
	of Fine Arts	*Art*	
		Art	
Eunice Murray Campbell (Mrs.)	AB Tufts College	*Business*	1934–1942
	Studied at Harvard Grad.	*Principles*	
	School and Simmons		
	Col.		
Evelyn Mann Rumney	AB Russell Sage College	*English*	1934–1939
	MA Columbia Univ.		
Gertrude Tingley	Studied with Mme. Povla	*Singing*	1934–1964
	Frijsh, Percy Rector		
Barbara Humes	Sarah Lawrence College	Assistant to	1935–1950
	Katherine Gibbs School	Principal	
Gladys Brannigan	AB; MA Geo.	*Drawing*	1936-1937
	Washington U.	*Painting*	
	Graduate Nat'l Academy		
	of Design		

Mary Elaine Dodge	AB Mount Allison Univ. B.H.S. McGill Univ.	*Household Science*	1936–1956
Isabel Maxwell Hancock	AB Hollins College Studied at Univ. VA.	*Mathematics* Director of Admissions	1936–1963 1956–1963
Jeanne Vical Miller (Mrs.)	B.Ph. (Langues Vivantes) Université de France Diplôme de L'Institut de Phonétique, Paris	*French*	1936–1940
Roberta Gilmore Poland (Mrs. Burdette)	AB Swarthmore College MA Univ. Penn.	*Physics Biology General Science*	1936–1944
Winthrop Horton Richardson	AB Brown Univ. BD Andover-Newton Theological School	*Bible*	1936–1941
Virginia Paine Rogers	AB Wheaton College Studied Speech and Dramatic Technique at Marie Ware Laughton	*Spoken English*	1936–1942
Eleanor Morin Tucker	AB; MA Smith College	*Chemistry Mathematics* Director of Studies Acting Principal	1936–1969 1956–1966, 1968–1969 1966–1968
Ena Marston	AB; MA Mills College MA Radcliffe College	*English*	1937–1938
Gertrud Rath	AB Hollins College MA Texas Univ.	Assistant to Principal	1937–1945
M. Dorothy Baker	St. Mary's College Cheltenham, England Member of the Royal Society of Teachers	*English*	1938–1950, Feb. 53– June 53
Lydia Glidden Ciullo (Mrs.)	BS Jackson College	*Business Principles*	Jan. 1938– June 1939
Marjorie Hill	AB Mt. Holyoke College MA Radcliffe College	*History* Office Assistant	1938–1939

Francis Merritt	Studied w/Alexandre Jacobleff, Edwin C. Taylor, Eugene Savage, Anthony Thieme, Richard Andrew, Robert C. Vose, Charles F. Connick	*Painting* *Modelling* *Drawing*	1938–1941
Rowena Lincoln Rhodes	Grad. of Bouvé-Boston School of Phys. Ed. Studied at Conn. College for Women	*Physical* *Education*	1938–1942
Laura Huntington Smith	AB Vassar College MA Radcliffe College	*History*	1938–1943
Hilda Ruby Baynes	B.ès L. U. de Paris Diplôme de L'École de Préparation des Professeurs de Français, Sorbonne. Certificat de Phonétique, U. de Paris	*French*	1939–1949
Constance Clark	U. of Prague Summer Study, Cambridge U.	*History* Office Assistant	1939–1940
Harriet E. McKee	AB Vassar College MA Columbia U.	*Latin* *Greek* ... *History*	1939–1961
Anne Rechnitzer	Ph.D., U. of Vienna	*French* *German* *History*	1939–1945
Catherine Jane Sullivan	AB Wheaton College Grad. Study at Boston U. and Harvard Univ.	*Remedial* *Reading* Alumnae Secretary	1939–1958 1952–1973
Lucile Burdette Tuttle	AB Denison Univ. Grad. Study at Radcliffe	*English* Co-Acting Principal Director of Residence	1939–1944 1947–1948 1946 and 1947
Dorothea Wilkinson	U. of King's College Woodford School for Teachers, Southsea, England	*English*	1939–1952

Hélène M. Crooks	Baccalauréat, Sorbonne AB Vassar College AM Columbia U. Graduate Study at the Sorbonne & the Middle- bury French School	*French*	1940–1941
Brainard F. Gibbons	BS Colgate U. FD NYU BD St. Lawrence U.	*Bible*	1940–1942
Anna Elizabeth Roth	Barnard College Ph.B. Syracuse Univ. MA; Ph.D., Radcliffe College	*History*	1940–1952 and 1955–1956
Justina Ruiz	MA Madrid Central U.	*Spanish*	1940–1942
Mary Mills Hatch (Mrs. Harold Marnham)	Studied at Cal. Col. of Arts & Crafts. Atelier de Paul Bornet, Paris. École de L'Arts et Decorative, Paris. Studio of Charles Wood- bury, Boston, U. of London, England	*Painting Drawing Modelling*	1940–1943
Ruth Louise Elvedt	Bouvé-Boston School of Phys. Ed. BS Simmons College	*Physical Education*	1941–1944
Irene Nechama Fischer (Mrs. Eric)	U. of Vienna Institute of Tech., Vienna	*Mathematics*	1941–1942
Etiennette Reine- Marguerite Trouvé	B.Ès L. Sorbonne Licence ès Lettres Sorbonne Diplôme de L'École Nationale des Langues Orientales Vivantes	*French*	1941–1945
Estrella Fontanals de Baldi (Senorita Paul)	Baccalaureat, Madrid central Col for women. Madrid "Centro de Estudios Historicòs" (Spanish History, Lit- erature, Art) Graduate Study at the Sorbonne and at Columbia U.	*Spanish*	1942–1943

America De Alonso (Senora Juan)	Escuela De Education, Montevideo, S.A.	*Spanish*	1942–1943
Minna S. Calhoun (Mrs. Alexander D.)	BS; MA Northwestern U. U. of Chicago	*Mathematics*	1942–1945
Mary Dooley (Later Mary Dooley Bragg)	AB Wellesley College	*Business Principles Speedwriting, Typing*	1942–1944 1948–1949
Bernard T. Drew	AB Bates College MA; STB Boston U.	*Bible*	1942–1944
Lucretia Lawrence Hildreth	AB Mount Holyoke College	Librarian	April, 1942–1944
Vera Fisherova Beck	AB Rockford College Ph.D. Charles IV U. Prague Research Fellow, Harvard Univ.	*Spanish*	1943–1944
Louise Loring Coffin	AB Radcliffe College Grad. Study U. No. Carolina and Harvard Univ.	*Biology General Science*	1943–1957
Maud Cabot Morgan (Mrs. Patrick)	BA Barnard College Cours de Civilization, Sorbonne, Paris Art Students League, N.Y. Hans Hofmann Art School, Munich and New York	*Painting Drawing Modelling Art*	1943–1945 and 1951–1962
Edith Hedin	AB Radcliffe MA Yale Univ.	*English German*	1944–1945
Arnold M. Kenseth (The Reverend)	AB Bates College STB Harvard Divinity School	*Bible*	1944–1946
Eleanor Ninas Little	AB Univ. of Kansas City; BS in L. S. Columbia Univ.	Librarian	1944–1946
Katherine MacDonald	Bouvé-Boston School of Phys. Ed. BS Ed. Tufts College	*Physical Education*	1944–1948

Marion Russell MacPherson		*Business Principles* Executive Secretary of Alumnae Relations	1944–1947
Jean Katherine Nevius	AB Wheaton College Grad. study at Columbia	*English*	1944–1945
Catherine Padwick	BS Boston Univ. MA Middlebury College Grad. Study at Toronto Univ.	*English*	1944–1945
Germaine Arosa	Prix d'excellence de diction et Comédie, Paris; Middlebury College School of French	*French*	1945–1969
William Abbott Cheever	Boston Museum School of Fine Arts; Paige Travelling Scholarship	*Art*	1945–1951
Gwendolyn Elroy	Bouvé-Boston School of Phys. Ed.; BS. Ed. Tufts College	*Physical Education*	1945–1950
Gerda Ruth Kaatz	AB Univ. of Kansas City; MA State Univ. of Illinois; Ph.D. State Univ. of Iowa	*Spanish* Assistant to the Principal	1945–1956 1951–1957
Edith Hilliard Prescott	AB Radcliffe College; Grad. Study at U. of N.H.	*Latin*	1945–1946
Ruth Crupper Reeves (Mrs.)	AB Hollis College	Administrative Asst.	1945–1954
Marjorie Faunce Stevens (Mrs. Mervin E.)	AB Boston University	*Mathematics*	1945–1958
Elinor Litchfield Strickland	Leland Powers School Recreation Training School of Chicago	*Dramatics*	1945–1946

Pauline H. Anderson	AB Keuka College BS in L. S. N.Y. State College for Teachers, Albany	Librarian	1946–1950
Marthe Marie Baratte	Baccalauréat ès-Lettres-Latin-Langues-Philosophie, Université de Rennes, France; AB Connecticut College; MA Cornell University; Diplôme de Phonétique; La Sorbonne, Université de Paris	*French*	1946–1973
Raymond H. Coon	N.E. Conserv. of Music; Studied with Heinrich Gebhard, Boston.	*Pianoforte*	1946–1963
Edith A. Grassi	AB Tufts College MA Wellesley College	*History, Latin*	1946–1952
Mildred Althea Hatch	AB Boston Univ. Grad. Study at Boston Univ.	*Latin* Administrative Assistant	1946–1961
Oril Lucille Hunt	BS Univ. of Arizona; Grad. Study at Syracuse Univ.	*Physical Education*	1946–1947
Landelle Sam McMurry	AB; MA Vanderbilt		1946–1960
Rev. Alfred Warren Burns	AB Bowdoin College; BD Episcopal Theological School	*Bible*	1947–1948
Gladys Morley Ortstein (Mrs. Frederick W.)	Lawrence Commercial School	*Typing*	1947–1952
Katherine Peterson Wieting (Mrs. Gilbert W.)	B.R.E. Boston Univ. School of Religious Ed.; MA Boston University	*Bible*	1947–1949
Carolyn Goodwin	AB; MA Smith College	*Mathematics* Director of Studies	1948–1973 1970–1973

Emily Hale	Leland Powers School, Boston; Cornish School, Seattle; Speech Institute, London; Univ. of Wisconsin Summer School	*Dramatic Interpretation* *Spoken English*	1948–1957
Adele D. Bockstedt	AB Mt. Holyoke College; MA Columbia	*French*	1949–1954
Dorothy Y. Judd	BS William & Mary School of Physical Education; BS Ed. Tufts College	*Physical Education* and *Spanish*	1949–1973
Rev. Hans Sidon	AB; BD Univ. of Dubuque; Ph.D. Grad. School, Southern Baptist Theological Seminary	*Bible*	1949–1966
Mary Howe Baker (Mrs. Robert H.)	AB Vassar College AM Radcliffe College	Librarian	Dec., 1950–1965
Virginia Peddle	BS Bouvé-Boston School of Physical Education	*Physical Education*	1950–1954
Elizabeth Rohrbach (Mrs.)	AB Meridian College; MA Columbia Univ, Grad. study at Bread Loaf School of English	*English*	1950–1952
Barbara Madison Stanhope	AB Bates College; MA Univ. of Maine; Grad. study at Bread Loaf School of English	*English*	1950–1952
Lola Monbleau (Mrs. Charles)	Jackson College; Julius Hart School of Music, Hartford, Conn, Studied with Rhea Massicotte	*Singing*	1951–1955
Shirley J. Ritchie	BS State Teachers College, Trenton, N.J.	*Physical Education*	1951–1973
Mary L. Spurway (Mrs. Kenneth)	The Dragon School, Oxford, England; Malvern Girl's College	*Latin*	1951–1952
Barbara Ann Buckley	AB Boston Univ.	*Spanish*	1952–1953

Howard A. Coon	R.I. School of Design	*Art*	1952–1956
Marion G. DeGavre (Mrs. Paul C.)	AB New Jersey College for Women	*Latin*	1952–1970
Patience Hunkin	AB; AM Cambridge U. Docteur de l'Universite de Strasbourg.	*English* *History*	Oct. 52– Feb. 53
Eleanor Victoria Jennings	AB William Smith Coll. MA Smith College	*History*	1952–1955
Marguerite Jupp	AB; MA Radcliffe Coll.	*English*	1952–1953
Ingrid Agnette Wulff	AB London Univ. Grad. study: Zurich Univ.	*English*	1952–1954
Jean Elizabeth Johnson	AB Wisconsin Univ. MA Univ. of Hawaii	*English*	1953–1956
Elizabeth Miller Pratt	AB Smith College MA Columbia	*History* Admin. Asst.	1953–1956
Lucette Bowers	AB Wellesley College; MA in Modern Dance, Sarah Lawrence College	*Physical Ed.* (Dance)	1954–1955
Margaret R. Cassidy	AB Vassar College	*English* *Mathematics*	1954–1957
Violet F. Edmonds	AB Girton College, Cambridge Univ. Oxford Diploma in Education	*English*	1954–1955
Edith Temple Jones	AB Middlebury College Grad. study at N.Y. State College for Teachers; McGill Univ. & the Sorbonne.	*French*	1954–1967
Marjon Bertha Ornstein	AB Guilford College; MA Middlebury College Grad. School of French in France; Studies at Sorbonne; Brevet de l'Aptitude à l'Enseignement du Français hors de France.	*French*	1954–1957

Ellen Stahle (Mrs. Charles)	Piano Pedagogy w/ Dr. Nagy at Boston Univ.; Studied with Frances Mann, Julliard School	*Piano*	1954–1969
Jane D. Baker	AB Middlebury College Grad. study at Boston Univ.	*English*	1955–1958
Mary Hinckley Crane	AB Bryn Mawr College	*English* *History of Art* Principal	1955–1956 1956–1966
Gertrude Ehrhart	Studied with Isidore Luckstone. Solo appearances with Boston Symphony & Handel & Haydn Society; Joint recitals with Nicolas Slonimsky, Carol Salzedo and Eugene Goosens.	*Singing*	1955–1958 1958–1962
Ella O. Greenall	BS Boston University	*Remedial Reading* and *Language Training*	1955– Feb. 69
Franey Jensen	AB Bombay University; Grad. of the State Gymnastic Inst. Copenhagen & of the Central Gymnastic Inst., Stockholm	*Physical Education*	1955–1956
Donald Outerbridge	AB Harvard Univ.	*History of Art*	1955–1958
Louise Tarr Stockly	AB Vassar College; MA Columbia Univ.	*English*	1955–1956
Joan Adaskin	BA Western Reserve Univ.	*Mathematics*	1956–1959
Janet Bolen	BS Madison College	*Physical Education*	1956–1960
Cynthia Burns	AB Stanford University MAT Radcliffe	*English*	1956–1958
Patience Haley	AB Oberlin College	*Art*	1956–1959

Mary Boosalis Nagler	Women's College of Univ. No. Carolina; Martha Graham School of Dance; American School of Ballet	*Physical Education*	1956–1957
Jirina Anna Stacho	MA; Ph.D. Charles Univ. of Prague; Diploma of the Univ. of Grenoble; Certificat de l'Ecole supérieure de préparation et de perfectionnement des professeurs de Française à l'étranger, Sorbonne; Columbia Univ.	*History*	1956–1958
J. Pamela Tinker	BS Sheffield, England; Diploma in Administration, University of Leeds.	*Chemistry* *Biology* (Fulbright Exchange Teacher)	1956–1965 1952–1953
Ann Sanford Werner (Mrs. Paul)	AB Bryn Mawr College Grad. study at Columbia	*English* *Latin*	1956–1962
Paul Werner	BS Lafayette MA Univ. of Pennsylvania	*Mathematics*	1956–1958
Paula Betinchamps	Fulbright Exchange Teacher from Belgium École Normale Moyenne de L'État, Liège, Belgique; British Council Summer School, Brussels. Casa de la American Latina, Université Libre de Bruxelles, Universidad Menéndez Pelayo, Satander, España. Instituto di Cultura di Bruxelles, Universitá di Perugia, Italia.	*French*	1957–1958

Carolyn Butler (Mrs. J. Konrick)	AB Wellesley College	*Physical Education*	1957–1970
Janet Fraser	AB Wellesley College	*History*	1957–1959
John S. Iverson, Jr.	AB Yale University MA Univ. of No. Carolina	*History English*	1957–1958
Marion McEnery	BA Wellesley College MA Boston Univ.	*History*	1957–1961
Elizabeth Anne Quimby	AB Jackson College; Grad. Study at Chicago Conservatory	*English*	1957–1960
Sylvia Seldon	AB Univ. of Wisconsin; MA Hartford School of Religious Education	*Bible*	1957–1960
Olthje Christine von Erpecom	Studied with Mme. Paula Frijsh, Percy Rector Stephens, Isidore Luckstone	*Speech* & *Drama* Dean of Students	1957–1969 1966–1969
Grace Whitney	AB Smith College	*Language Training*	1957–1964
Hilary Andrade-Thompson	AB Honors London Univ. Certificate in Education	*English*	1958–1960
Dorothy Dains	AB Pembroke College	*Mathematics*	1958–1964
Margaret G. Howland	AB Barnard College MA Bryn Mawr College Grad. study at Radcliffe	*History History of Art* Curator, John Esther Art Gallery	1958–1963
Virginia Kroenlein McKinley (Mrs. George E.)	BS Boston Univ. AB Barnard College	*Physical Science Chemistry*	1958–1959, 1960–1963
Ann Norwood (Mrs. Richard)	AB Wellesley College	*History*	1958–1961
Suzanne Tallot (Mme. Jacques)	Licencée es Lettres University at Rennes	*French*	1958–1960
Kathleen Von Tress	AB Univ. of Pennsylvania	*English*	1958–1959

Yi-an Rosita Chang	Julliard School of Music Studied with Madame Olga Samaroff and James Friskin. Solo appearances with the Los Angeles Philharmonic and Hollywood Bowl Symphony orchestras, Concerts in Europe and the Far East	*Piano*	1959–1962
Louise Courtois	Baccalauréat es lettres Certificat d'aptitude à l'enseignement de l'anglais Sorbonne; Episcopal Training College; Edinburgh; AB Mt. Holyoke	*French*	1959–1960
Georgia Anne McIlwaine	AB Univ. of Chattanooga	*Mathematics*	1959–1960
Margot Warner	Studied with Nadia Boulanger, Hilda Roosevelt, Von-Warhlich, Marie Sundelius, Olga Averino & Fritz Lehmann	*Choral music Singing Music Theory*	1959–1969
Frances Burns (Mrs. James)	AB Trinity College A.M.T. Radcliffe	*Mathematics*	1960–1962
Gwen Ferris (Mrs. Gerald D.)	AB Smith College AM Middlebury; Sorbonne	*French*	1960–1962
Louise G. Lewis	AB Barnard, MA Columbia Univ; Grad. study at the Univ. of Montpellier, the Sorbonne; Bryn Mawr	*English*	1960–1962
Dorothy Potter (Mrs. Bruce)		Secretary Director of Residence	1960– 1962–1963
Barbara Blagdon Sisson (Mrs. John H.)	AB Vassar College MA Wellesley College	*English*	1960–1973

Blair Harvie Danzoll	AB Wheaton College	*Latin* & *Greek*	1961–1966
Anne Harriss (Mrs. Bruce Bugbee, in 1962)	AB Bennington College	*English*	1961–1973
Virginia Powel (Mrs. Har- ford, Jr.)	Harriet Sophie New- comb College	*Art*	1961–1973
Caroline Bridgman Rees	AB Smith; MA Yale	*History*	1961–1963
Judith Bratt	AB Vassar College	*Mathematics*	1962–1965
Jorunn Lita Buzzi	Studied at Sönderborg Idratshöjskden, certifi- cates from Snoghöj gymnastikhojskole, Denmark and Statens Gymnastikkskole, Norway.	*Physical Education*	1962–1963
Elizabeth George Foulke	AB Bryn Mawr MA Univ. of Pennsyl- vania	*History* Admin. Asst. Director of Studies	1962–1965 Jan. 63– June 63
Janice Fukushima	BA Radcliffe College	*English*	1962–1963
Georgiana Mathews (Mrs. John M.)	AB Wheaton College AM Middlebury College Université de Paris	*French*	1962–1963
Mary Sophia Minard	AB Smith College MALS Wesleyan Univ.	*History*	1962–1973
Erika Maria Niemann	Diploma in Math & Physics from Free Uni- versity in West Berlin, Diploma in Education from the Studien semi- nar in West Berlin, Zehlendorf	*German Physics Mathematics*	1962–1963
Carolyn C. Pike	Phys. Educ. Diplomas from Dalhousie Univ. Nova Scotia, Memorial Univ. of Newfoundland	*Physical Education*	1962–1962

Lily Siao	BS & MS. Julliard School of Music; Fulbright Grant to Paris 1961–1962.	*Piano*	1962–1965
Ruth Stevenson	AB Smith College MA Univ. of Richmond	*English*	1962–1965
Margaret Graham Way	BA Honors, University of Cambridge, England	*English*	1962–1965
Anne Lise Witten (Mrs. Oscar)	Univ. of Frankfort; The Sorbonne; Grad.	*French History*	1962–1973
Edwina Frederick (Mrs. Wayne)	BS in Education Southeast Missouri Coll; MA Columbia Univ. & Sorbonne	*French*	1963–1973
Frances Howard (Mrs. Lynwood)	BS Farmington State Col.	Dietitian House Super- intendent	1963–1970
Barbara Dorothy Keener	BA Science, BA Science Teaching, Gordon College	*Physical Education Biology*	1963–1964
Jean Mary St. Pierre	AB Wheaton College MA Columbia Univ.	*English*	1963–1973
Ruth Ford Duncan (Mrs. Ford)	BA Connecticut College	Dir. of Admissions	1964–1969
Sylvia Kuzminski	BA Merrimack College	*Mathematics*	1964–1967
Louise Shaw	BS Tufts College	*Physical Education*	1964–1967
Helen Smith	BS Central Conn. State Col MS Cornell Univ.	*Physics, Science*	1964–1967
Madge Baker	MA Vassar College	*History*	1965–1968
Jonatha Ceely (Mrs. Robert P.)	BA Vassar College; MA University of Michigan	*English*	1965–1969
Margaret Couch	BA Wheaton College	Librarian	1965–1973
Georgina M. Huck	BA Vassar College; Yale School of Grad. Studies; N.Y. Univ.; Univ. of Breslau	*German, History*	1965–1969

Carolyn Johnston	BA Radcliffe College; Tufts University	*English* Dean of Students	1965–1970 1970–1973
Carolyn Kellogg	BA Reed College	*Biology*	1965–1970
Christina A. Rubio	Studied under Marina Noreg, Birger Bartholin, Olga Preobrajenska, and Egarova	*Dance*	1965–1973
Elizabeth Sargent Roberts (Mrs.)	B. Mus. Boston Univ. College of Music; Piano with Gregory Tucker; Ensemble with Wolfe	*Piano*	1965–1973
Linda Sevey	BA Pembroke MAT Harvard	*History of Art*	1965–1967
Mrs. Harry Vickers	BS, M.I.T.	*Mathematics Chemistry*	1965–1968
Rae Anderson Horne (Mrs. Timothy)	BA Vassar College, MAT Stanford Univ.	*English*	1966–1971
Faith Howland Kaiser	BA Wellesley College; Harvard Univ. Grad. School Arts and Sciences	*Latin, Greek* Admissions	1966–1973
Mrs. Richard Merrill	U. of Guanajuato	*Spanish*	1966–1968
George Edward Andrews II	BA Trinity College; Boston University Graduate School of Theology	*Religion* (jointly appointed with P.A.)	1967–1968
Carole Buhler	Beloit College	*Spanish*	1967–1968
Ruth Harris (Mrs. Peter Hayne)	B. Ed. Keene State College; M.A.L.S. Wesleyan Univ.; State Univ. of N.Y., Buffalo	*Mathematics*	1967–1971
Marianne Branch Kehrli (Mrs. Peter)	BFA Moor College of Art; Beaux Arts, Paris; Columbia Univ. Teachers College; Smith College Grad. School	*History of Arts*	1967–1969

Wendy Snyder (MacNeil)	BA Smith College; M.A.T. Harvard Univ.; M.I.T.	*Visual Perception, Photography*	1967–1973
Meriby Sweet	BA Univ. of Maine	*Speech, Drama*	1967–1969
Hilda Whyte (Mrs. James)	BS Michigan State Univ.	*Physics*	1967–1973
Joy Renjilian Burgy (Mrs. Donald T.)	Mt. Holyoke BA, Middlebury College Graduate Work (no degree)	*Spanish*	1968–1971
Donald Gordon	BA Yale; MA Univ. Penn.	Principal	1968–1973
Marjorie Harrison	BA Conn. Coll. for Women	*Physical Education*	1968–1973
Marilyn Hoyt (Mrs. Robert)	BS Denison Univ., M.I.T.	*Chemistry*	1968–1973
Garrett Kaufman	BA Univ. of Arizona; MA Stanford Univ.	*English*	1968–1969
Catherine Seanne Kirkland	License Sorbonne; Matrise Sorbonne	*French*	1968–1973
James Frederick Lynch	BA Amherst	*Mathematics*	1968–1973
Frederick Pease, Jr.	BA Yale; BD Union Theological Sem.	*Religion*	1968–1969
Stephanie Blake Perrin (Mrs. Stephen)	Barnard; BA Boston Univ. M.A.T. Harvard	*Art History* Curator, John Esther Art Gallery	1968–1973
Audrey Bensley (Mrs. Gordon G.)	Hood, Jackson, Univ. of New Hampshire	*Ceramics*	1969–1973
Susan Clark	BA Swarthmore; MA Yale University	*Latin, Greek*	1969–1973
Brian Davidson	BA Tufts University; University of Southern California	*Speech & Drama*	1969–1971
Paul Dyer	Washington & Jefferson Univ. Indiana Univ.	*English*	1969–1970

Ronald G. Giguere	BA Assumption College; MA Trinity College; Certificat: Sorbonne; University of Massachusetts	*French*	1969–1973
Stephen Graham	BA Princeton University	*History*	1969–1972
Ulrich Hepp	University of Zurich	*French, German*	1969–1973
Susan Hosmer	BS Univ. of Vermont	*Philosophy*	1969–1972
Georges N. Krivobok	BA Swarthmore; MA Middlebury	*French*	1969–1973
Stephen Perrin	BA Columbia University	*Humanities*	1969–1973
Priscilla Peterson	B. of Music, Lawrence University	*Music* Admission	1969–1971
Peter T. Stapleton	BA Yale University; MAT Harvard University	*English;* Asst. to the Principal	1969–1973
Rowland Sturges	BA Harvard	*Music*	1969–1971
Patricia Edmonds	BA Mount Holyoke; MAT Harvard University	*English*	1970–1971
Patricia Freund	BA Smith College; MFS Yale School of Forestry	*Biology, Ecology*	1970–1972
Sherry Gershon	BA University of Missouri; Wesleyan Univ.	*History*	1970–1973
Robert Horvitz	Yale	*Arts*	1970–1971
Christine Marie Kalke	BA Wayne University; MA Columbia University	*Latin, Greek*	1970–1973
Frances N. Ladd	BA Connecticut College	*English, Speech*	1970–1973
Robert T. Laurence	BS Ohio State University	*Mathematics*	1970–1972
Michael F. McCann	BA Middlebury College	*Biology*	1970–1973
Robert R. McQuilkin	BA Princeton University; MA Columbia University	*English*	1970–1973
David S. Tower	BA Williams College	*Mathematics*	1970–1973

Adele Babcock	BA Radcliffe College	*Voice*	1971–1972
Andrew Johnston	BA Yale University	*English*	1971–1973
Nancy Price	BA Mount Holyoke College; MAT Harvard University	*English*	1971–1972
Andrew Strauss	BA Dartmouth College; JD New York University	*Mathematics*	1971–1973
Philip R. Trussel	BFA University of Texas; MFA Yale University School of Art and Architecture	*Visual Studies*	1971–1973
Keder Bayard	MS, LLD University of Haiti, MA Wesleyan University; Fairfield University	*Mathematics*	1972–1973
Patricia Corkerton	BA Skidmore College; Boston University; Middlebury College	*Spanish*	1972–1973
Barbara Hawkes	BS Tufts University; MS Northeastern University	*Biology, Ecology*	1972–1973
Donald R. Parkhurst	BD Purdue University; MAT Harvard University	*Chemistry*	1972–1973
Alexandra K. Rewis	BA Smith College; MAT Yale University	*English*	1972–1973
Theodore J. Warren, Jr.	BS Paul Quinn College; diploma, Lincoln Business College; BD Payne Seminary, Wilberforce University; Boston	*History*	1972–1973

Notes

I. Early Days, 1828–1852

1. OF TIMES, TOWN, AND FOUNDING FATHERS

1. Phebe and Philena McKeen, *Annals of Fifty Years: A History of Abbot Academy, Andover, Mass., 1829–1679* (Andover, Warren F. Draper, 1880), I, 3. (Philena, who was Phebe's sister and Abbot Academy's longest tenured principal, 1859–1892, wrote only the first and last pages.)
2. Claude M. Fuess, *An Old New England School: A History of Phillips Academy*, Andover (Boston, Houghton Mifflin, 1917), 55–56.
3. Philip J. Greven, Jr., *Four Generations: population, land, and family in colonial Andover, Massachusetts* (Ithaca, Cornell University, 1970), 222–289.
4. Joseph Kett, *The Rites of Passage: Adolescence in America, 1790 to the Present* (New York, Basic Books, 1977), 14–37.
5. Abiel Abbot, *History of Andover from Its Settlement to 1829* (Andover, Flagg and Gould, 1829), 63.
6. Fuess, *New England School*, 110.
7. Quoted in Sarah Loring Bailey, *Historical Sketches of Andover, Massachusetts* (Boston, Houghton, Mifflin, 1880), 129.
8. From Abigail Foote's diary, quoted in Thomas Woody, *A History Of Women's Education in the United States* (2 vols., Science Press, 1929; rep. Octagon Books, New York, 1966), I, 161–162.
9. See Eleanor Flexner's discussion of women's opportunities during the colonial period, in *Century of Struggle* (New York, Atheneum, 1973), 3–22.
10. Conversation with Kathryn Sklar, based on her research in progress on the genesis of "higher" education (beyond grammar school) for young women in New England.
11. "The Direction of Feminine Evolution," in *The Potential of Woman*, ed. Seymour M. Farber and Roger H. L. Wilson (New York, McGraw Hill, 1963), 258. In 1810 96 percent of all woolen cloth produced in the United States was made in private homes. By 1830 half of it was factory made; by 1840 there were 800 cotton factories in New England.
12. Quoted in a paper by Scott Paradise on the history of Andover, Massachusetts, read before the Bay State Historical League at the meeting of

the Andover Historical Society on 3 October 1931.

13. Records of Andover Town Meeting, 7 January 1787.

14. Quoted in John Demos, "The American Family in Past Time," *American Scholar*, 43, No. 3 (Summer 1974), 427.

15. See Nancy F. Cott, *The Bonds of Womanhood: 'Women's Sphere' in New England, 1780–1835* (New Haven, Yale University Press, 1977), 101–103; Kenneth Lockridge, *Literacy in Colonial New England: An Enquiry into the Social Context of Literacy in the Early Modern West* (New York, Norton, 1974), 38–43, 140–141. Andover women's illiteracy is discussed in Bailey, *Historical Sketches*, 550.

16. Anonymous poem read by Professor Calvin Stowe at the opening of Smith Hall, Abbot Academy, 1854. This piece of doggerel "made a deal of sport," said witnesses; quoted in Abbot Academy *Bulletin* (November 1930), 22. It was later discovered to have been written by Samuel Gray "Esq.," who was elected to the Abbot Board of Trustees the next year.

17. Quoted in Frederick S. Allis, *Youth from Every Quarter* (Andover, Phillips Academy, distributed by the University Press of New England), 109.

18. Reverend Justin Edwards, quoted in Bailey, *Historical Sketches*, 473.

19. Bailey, 87; Abbot, *History of Andover*, 194–195.

20. Abbot, *History of Andover*, 147.

21. Quoted in Bailey, *Historical Sketches*, 558–559.

22. Abbot, *History of Andover*, 3. The entire book is a paean to Andover's virtues and a near-whitewash of its faults.

23. Thomas Houghton, Esquire, who came to Andover in 1789. Quoted in Claude M. Fuess, *Andover: Symbol of New England* (Andover Historical Society, 1959), 207.

24. Greven, *Four Generations*, 269.

25. Quoted in Fuess, *Andover*, 272.

26. An often-used book in early female seminaries was an English text containing not a single word about the United States, reissued in this country in 1799 by a leading Hartford citizen. Its title: *A Mirror for the Female Sex: Historical Beauties for Young Ladies Intended to Lead the Female Mind to the Love and Practice of Moral Goodness*. A typical passage: "Politeness and good breeding are such requisite introductions into genteel society that its is absolutely astonishing anyone can gain admittance into it who are deficient either in the one or the other." Quoted in Kathryn Kish Sklar, *Catharine Beecher: A Study in American Domesticity* (New Haven and London, Yale University Press, 1973), 75.

27. Catharine Beecher, *Educational Reminiscences and Suggestions*, (New York, J. B. Ford, 1874), 25.

28. Unsigned article in *Journal of American Education*, 4, No. 2 (March

and April 1829), 127. Originally printed in the *Boston Advertiser*.

29. Rush's Commencement Address at the Philadelphia Young Ladies Academy given in 1787. In 1792 this academy became the nation's first incorporated girls' school.
30. Quoted in Alma Lutz, *Emma Willard* (Boston, Beacon Press, 1964), 25.
31. Ibid., 27.
32. Catharine Beecher, "Female Education," in *American Journal of Education*, 2, Nos. 4 and 5 (April and May 1827), 265. Beecher's biblical reference is to Ezekiel's vision.
33. Barbara M. Cross, in an article on Catharine Beecher in *Notable American Women*, ed. E. T. James, J. W. James, P. S. Boyer (Cambridge, Harvard University Press, 1971), I, 121.
34. Beecher, "Female Education," 221.
35. 16 November 1839, quoted in Sklar, *Beecher*, 94.
36. The editors of *American Annals of Education* 6, 137) wrote that the closing could be partly explained by the fact that "a single school of this description would not accommodate more than one fourth of those who ought to attend such an institution." Two years later, the school reopened to become the most faithfully attended high school in Boston.
37. Jane Brodie Carpenter, *Abbot and Miss Bailey, and Abbot in the Early Days* (Andover, Abbot Academy, 1959), 282–283.
38. Records of South Church, Andover, Massachusetts. The elders set up this system in 1757 to replace the "most pious" standard because the earlier criterion sowed so much ill feeling among those not chosen.
39. Kett, *Rites*, 85.
40. Most of the evidence is circumstantial. For example, Jackson did more work to carry forward the founding of Abbot than any other person. Furthermore, his wife Caroline was a forward-looking and liberal-minded person who was likely to have pushed as hard as she dared on the subject of women's education (she assumed a much more radical stance on the slavery issue than did her husband, but they worked together to salve the Parish's wounds on this subject). Most important, Phebe McKeen concluded to her satisfaction during her research into Abbot's history in 1879 that the couple had indeed been the initiators of the plan. Phebe McKeen knew Jackson personally, and had access to Abbot friends who were Jackson's colleagues and acquaintances back in 1827 and 1828. We have no direct evidence, however. Jackson is known to have kept a diary, but it is either hidden from historians or simply lost. All we have from Jackson family records are reminiscences of a great-granddaughter, Sara Knowles Jackson Smith, who wrote in 1944 that "it was chiefly through his efforts and influence that Abbot Academy was founded."
41. A helpful account of Jackson's background and education has been assembled by Eleanor Campbell in her book about the West Parish

Church, *West of the Shawsheen* (Andover, West Parish Church, 1975), 71–72, 105–110.

42. See Ann Douglas, *The Feminization of American Culture* (New York, Alfred Knopf, 1977), chapters 1 and 2.

43. The original membership in 1826 was 41 males and 82 females. During Jackson's tenure, 107 males joined the Church, while 214 females did so. Much the same ratio held at South Church, Andover's largest parish. In a single decade (1828–38), 230 females joined South Church, while only 136 males did so. (Records of South Church, Andover.) Just as in West Parish Church, however, men kept formal control of all South Parish business till well into the twentieth century. Women were not admitted as members of the South Parish, even though they were welcomed in the South Church, a corporately distinct organization.

44. See Campbell, *West of the Shawsheen*, 61.

45. Edwards A. Park, *Memorial* to Samuel C. Jackson (1879).

46. The West Parish Church records reflect the energy and legal acumen Jackson gave equally to the resolution of problems brought to him by men and those brought by women. As Parish Clerk and minister, Jackson functioned as a kind of benevolent trial judge for the disputes and charges brought by the deacons or by one parishioner against another. The scope of problems given formal hearing is somewhat narrower than in the eighteenth century, when Reverend Phillips held sway—most of those recorded in the official record comprise individual offenses against a church member's responsibility (Sabbath breaking, or "neglecting worship") but men are occasionally charged with drunkenness by one of the "brothers," and women with adultery. Only men might speak in church or bring charges or make defenses; of one woman offender it is written that "her burden was double: she was a sinner and a woman" (Campbell, *West of the Shawsheen*, 33), thus must find a brother to speak for her at the hearing. Jackson heard and decided some of these cases in consultation with the entire congregation. He was also invited to many a home to adjudicate complex civil disagreements before they came to county court, and to help draw documents of trust, some of these making him guardian of minor children or trustee. See also Campbell, *West of the Shawsheen*, 32–33, and chapter on Jackson, in *West Parish Church, Historical Sketches* (Andover, West Parish Church, 1906).

47. Characterization of Farrar by Professor Edwards Park in his address to the graduating class of 1878, quoted in McKeen, *Annals*, 11.

48. Claude Fuess says of the "Latin Commons" that they lined up "like a row of tenements," reflecting Farrar's character as a "frank utilitarian," and preserving "in their general outlines that unadorned simplicity characteristic of the packing box." Fuess, *New England School*, 229–230.

49. Sarah Stuart Robbins, *Old Andover Days: Memories of a Puritan Childhood* (Boston, Pilgrim Press, 1908), 42–43.
50. From a penciled draft of a talk probably given by Jackson at the opening of Smith Hall, 1854.
51. From Reverend Park's address to Abbot's graduating class of 1878. Quoted in McKeen, *Annals*, 11.
52. Robbins, *Old Andover Days*, 117.
53. Marion Edwards Park, in a speech to the Abbot Academy Alumnae Association and Boston Abbot Club, 15 February 1938.
54. Quoted in Leo Kanowitz, *Women and the Law, the Unfinished Revolution* (Albuquerque, University of New Mexico Press, 1969), 35. See also Douglas, *Feminization*, 51.
55. Quoted in Carpenter, *Abbot*, 157.
56. Ibid., 159.
57. Quoted in a speech by Marguerite C. Hearsey, 1954, manuscript in Abbot Archives. The reader may assume that unpublished material on Abbot, including manuscripts, letters, journals, scrapbooks, minutes and reports to the Trustees, and special files are kept in the Abbot Academy Archives, Oliver Wendell Holmes Library at Phillips Academy, unless otherwise noted.
58. In a letter written 16 March 1916, N. C. Abbott, Superintendent, Nebraska School for the Blind. After 1830 the name is often spelled with two t's.
59. Abbot, *History of Andover*, 8.
60. Trustee Minutes, 7 November 1828.
61. Trustee Minutes, 21 May 1829.

2. PIOUS PIONEERS

1. The "foregoing page" mentioned in the first line of Jackson's letter was the first Abbot Female Academy prospectus, which Jackson enclosed with his message to his sister. "The deacon" is a Mr. Solomon Holt, friend and landlord of the young Jackson and pillar of his new parish; "Phebe" is Holt's daughter.
2. The five lay Abbot Trustees were to help drive Captain James Stevens off the Board of Directors of the Andover Bank because he voted for Jackson in 1832. (Bankers, of course, were in the hot seat in 1832, while ministers occupied more neutral ground). See "A Sketch of the Early Days of the Woolen Industry in North Andover, Massachusetts," address delivered before the North Andover Historical Society, 13 February 1925.
3. Federal Writers Project for the State of Massachusetts of the Works Progress Administration, *Massachusetts* (Boston, Houghton, Mifflin, 1937), 48.

484 NOTES TO PAGES 32-34

4. McKeen, *Annals*, 18. Although there were no "graduating classes" until 1853, each of the early alumnae is designated by the year she left Abbot. Mrs. Bullard actually attended Abbot for five years: 1829, 1832, and 1834–1837.

5. Ibid., 20.

6. Ibid., 31.

7. Ibid.

8. Ibid., 19.

9. From oral reminiscences of one of M. C. Thomas' students and Bryn Mawr Trustee Emeritus, Class of 1920.

10. Letter written in 1837 by Phebe Chandler (no recipient recorded in Abbot Archives copy); and Mrs. Bullard quoted in McKeen, *Annals*, 26.

11. Phebe Chandler, 1836, quoted in *Bulletin* (November 1928), 11–12.

12. Unsigned article, "The Education of Females," *American Journal of Education*, 2 (1827), 339.

13. Alumna reminiscence quoted in McKeen, *Annals*, 32.

14. Nathan Lord, *Memorial to Samuel Gilman Brown* (New York, Trow's, 1886), 68.

15. Original manuscript of Chandler letter, 1837.

16. William J. Bacon, in Lord, *Memorial*, 32.

17. Quoted in McKeen, *Annals*, 26.

18. See Charles D. Stewart, "The Pastor of the Bees," *Atlantic Monthly* (July 1928), 92–103.

19. Alumna accounts may have exaggerated Abbot's virtues, but at least until Farwell's administration one gets the strong impression that adults gave orders and students sat up and took notice. This was the behavior expected of girls and young women in the these times; exceptions appear to have been rare.

20. Recollection of Captain John Codman, Phillips Academy Class of 1823, quoted in Fuess, *New England School*, 168.

21. Recollection of Gen. H. K. Oliver, ibid., 167–168.

22. See Kett, *Rites*, 46–47.

23. Asa Farwell to Phebe McKeen, 8 February 1879.

24. It is almost certain that the "canny Squire," as Jane Carpenter calls Farrar (see *Abbot*, 170), originated this arrangement. It was identical to the one he urged on Phillips Academy's new Teachers Seminary, founded the year after Abbot's opening, and on Phillips Academy itself when the sensitive and scholarly Osgood Johnson took over from Adams. By 1834, Johnson had decided it was too much for him, and refused to stay unless the Trustees would guarantee him $1000 a year and a house to live in. This they promptly did, but Johnson soon died anyway. Phillips Academy salaries provided a discouraging contrast to Abbot then as in more recent times: Headmaster Samuel Taylor's salary stood at $1200 from 1838 to 1885–and he received free housing in the bargain.

25. Farwell to Phebe McKeen, 8 February 1879. The most eloquent description of a principal's financial desperation can be found in Goddard's letter to the Trustees, 16 February 1831.
26. Reverend Leander Thompson, quoted in *Courant* (January 1889) 17.
27. McKeen, *Annals*, 42.
28. "Memorialists' Petition," printed by the Trustees of Abbot Academy with their reply of September 1848.
29. Recollections of Miss Hannah Kittredge, 1849, reported in *Bulletin* (November 1928), 12.
30. Elizabeth Stuart Phelps, *Chapters from a Life* (Boston, Houghton Mifflin, 1896), 62.
31. Susanna Jackson to Phebe McKeen, 1879.
32. See Trustees Minutes, 23 October 1863; McKeen, *Annals*, 61. In 1865 Farwell sold his house to the Abbot Trustees for $4,500, a tidy sum for those days.
33. Catharine Beecher, "Suggestions Respecting Improvements in Female Education" (Hartford, Packard and Butler, 1829) 61.
34. In his final Report to the Trustees, 1852. Quoted in McKeen, *Annals*, 16.
35. Woody, *History*, I, 357.
36. Quoted in McKeen, *Annals*, 16.
37. Robbins, *Old Andover Days*, 4.
38. Ibid., 4.
39. Phelps, *Chapters*, 25–26.
40. Quoted in McKeen, *Annals*, 17–18.
41. Henrietta Jackson to Margaret Woods Lawrence, 1837. Quoted in Margaret Woods Lawrence, *Light on the Dark River* (Boston, Ticknor, Reed, and Fields, 1853), 80.
42. Ibid., 44.
43. Robbins, *Old Andover Days*, 3.
44. Quoted in Carpenter, *Abbot*, 188.
45. Bailey, *Historical Sketches*, 569.
46. Ibid., 586.
47. Phelps, *Chapters*, 56.
48. There are two sets of population figures for Andover in 1850: one for population within the original boundaries, including the modern Andover and the modern North Andover (6,945), the other for population in the original South Parish alone (4900). By the mid-nineteenth century, the area of the township as originally laid out had proved too large to be manageable, and town leaders began to plan its division into Andover (the original South Parish) and North Andover (the original North Parish). The formal division took place in 1854.
49. The few early alumnae whose fathers' occupations are known list them ("farmer," storekeeper," "minister") in ways that make analysis of family wealth difficult if not impossible. An examination of tax records each fifth year from 1830 to 1850 reveals that only about one third of the

Abbot parents who lived in Andover paid "Town and County" (property) taxes at all. Of course, some of the non-taxpayers were Seminary professors or others living in buildings owned by the Trustees of Phillips Academy (Professor Austin Phelps lived in one of the most elegant houses on the Hill, yet paid only $2.67 tax in 1850); a few others were probably renting houses or farms. Still, the data tend to confirm the image of the early Abbot which its nineteenth-century admirers project: a frugal enterprise accessible to applicants from a wide range of economic circumstances. The taxes parents paid Andover in 1850 ranged from $1.85 (parent-Trustee Samuel Fuller) to $302.69 (parent John Smith). The average tax bill for nineteen parents was $54.00, the median $14.35. Three fathers paid over $163.00; all the rest paid less than $50.00. Of the last group four paid less than $5.50.

50. Henry Ward Beecher, *Norwood, or Village Life in New England*, ca. 1867, 1892. (New York, Fords, Howard, and Hulbard), 3.

51. It must be remembered that children ten to nineteen years old provided a substantial proportion of family income. A daughter in school could mean factory wages forgone as well as tuition fees paid for. According to Daniel Webster, however, a male workman in 1843 could save $12.00 a month after paying essential expenses—and would continue to do so as long as the Whigs kept the protective tariff high. (Speech in Andover, 5 October 1843, to 5,000 Essex County Whigs, see Fuess, *Andover*, 278.)

52. Quoted in McKeen, *Annals*, 164. Brown was speaking at Abbot's 50th anniversary and describing the past. A letter to the Trustees, 25 July 1836, explained his desire to leave Abbot and return fulltime to Andover Theological Seminary and gave "The wants of the Academy" (a better heating system, proper equipment for teaching physics, more books, a boarding-house, etc.) as his chief reason for resigning.

53. Ibid., 147.

54. Letter to the Misses McKeen, *Annals*, 31.

55. T. D. P. Stone, "Boarding House Regulations of the Abbot Female Seminary."

56. Mary Lyon in her paper addressed "To the Friends of Female Education," quoted in McKeen, *Annals*, 22.

57. "K" in article memorializing Emma Taylor, *Courant* (June 1887), 23. Zilpah Grant was the other "nursing mother."

58. C. Beecher, "Suggestions," 1829, 68.

59. Mary Lyon, quoted in McKeen, *Annals*, 23.

60. McKeen, *Annals*, 23.

61. Already there were numerous brother-sister pairs at Phillips and Abbot Academy. A careful comparison of names and home towns for 1846, for example, shows that roughly one sixth of Abbot girls had brothers at Phillips. Not surprisingly, a majority of the sibling pairs came from Andover. Families who had to pay board as well as tuition were much

more likely to spend their money on their sons.

62. Quoted in Sydney R. MacLean, "Mary Lyon," in *Notable American Women*, 445, from ML's letter to Zilpah Grant, 4 February 1934.

63. United States Commissioner of Education (USCOE), *Reports* for 1887–1888, 598.

64. Typed transcript of manuscript account of "Commons life," Abbot Academy Archives. See also Carpenter, *Abbot*, 226–230.

65. Julia Pierce, letter to her mother, 21 April 1840.

66. Emma Williard's appeal to the New York Legislature for funds to help support Waterford Academy (made before her final move to Troy, New York). A $2000 subsidy passed in the Senate, but was defeated in the House. Though many privately operated boys' schools received state aid, Mrs. Willard's academy was allowed only a pittance from the state Literary Fund—and even this was soon ended by the N.Y. Board of Regents. Quoted in Woody, *History*, I, 311.

67. Kett, *Rites*, 61.

68. H. W. Beecher, *Norwood*, 26.

69. Letter to Mary Dutton, 8 February 1830, quoted in Sklar, *Beecher*, 96. In Massachusetts at least, women seem to have taken this advice. Mavis Venovskis, a student of demographics and educational history, found that one in four Massachusetts women alive in 1860 had taught school at some time during her life. *Women in Education in Ante-Bellum America*, University of Wisconsin Monograph, 1975.

70. See Laura Ingalls Wilder, *Farmer Boy* (New York, Harper and Row, 1933), 1–12.

71. See Laura Ingalls Wilder, *These Happy Golden Years* (New York, Harper and Row, 1943), 1–10.

72. Letter to her mother, 21 April 1840.

73. Fuess, *New England School*, 204.

74. See Abbot Academy Catalogues, 1842–1852.

75. Letter to "the Misses Marland," 1833.

76. Abbot Archives.

77. Alumna letter, Abbot Archives; Pierce letter, Abbot Archives.

78. See also Kett, *Rites*, 102. Kett adds that boarding school also served to keep the attractions of mill work beyond reach, and generally dampened "the tendency of young people to push too quickly into active life."

79. Cyrus Hamlin, *My Life and Times* (Boston, Chicago, Pilgrim Press, 1893), 187–188. I am indebted to Professor Cyrus Hamlin of Toronto University for information about his family, and for several bibliographical suggestions.

80. From letter to MWL, 1841, quoted in Lawrence, *Light*, 169.

81. Quoted ibid., 1842, 190.

82. Quoted ibid., 192.

83. Ibid.

3. "A VERY LIBERAL SERIES OF STUDIES"

1. From a circular advertising the opening of Oberlin, 1833.
2. Quoted in Francis Wayland, *The Elements of Moral Science*, ca. 1835, 2nd ed. 1837; ed. Joseph L. Blau (Cambridge, Harvard University Press, 1963), x-xi.
3. Quoted in Fuess, *New England School*, 243.
4. Mrs. Almira Hart Lincoln was Emma Willard's sister. For years she served as Mrs. Willard's assistant principal at Troy Academy, and her texts are consciously designed for the use of young ladies.
5. Unsigned article on the "Hartford Female Seminary," *American Journal of Education*, 4 (1829), 261–265.
6. Quoted in McKeen, *Annals*, 18.
7. Quoted in Carpenter, *Abbot*, 186.
8. Quoted in Lutz, *Emma Williard*, 91.
9. Recollections of a Phillips Academy alumnus, Class of 1811. Quoted in Fuess, *New England School*, 170.
10. Charles H. Burroughs in a widely read address first given at Portsmouth, New Hampshire, and reprinted in pamphlet form, as well as in the *American Journal of Education*, 3 (1828), 53–58.
11. Almira Hart Lincoln (Phelps), *Lectures on Botany* (4th ed., Hartford, F. J. Huntington, 1835), 14.
12. From preamble to "fathers' " resolution introducing music to Fryeburg Academy, Maine, 1803. Quoted in Harriet Webster Marr, *The Old New England Academies* (New York, Comet Press Books, 1959), 223.
13. Published in 1854, quoted in Woody, *History*, I, 407–408.
14. Unsigned article, "The Education of Females," *American Journal of Education*, 2 (1827), 485.
15. "Thoughts on the Education of Females" by "H." in the *American Journal of Education*, 1 (1826), 402.
16. William Russell, *The Education of Females*, an address read at the close of the term at Abbot, 21 November 1843, printed at the Abbot Trustees' request, (Andover, Allen Morrill and Wardwell, 1843), 16.
17. Lincoln, *Botany*, 2.
18. Carpenter, *Abbot*, 276. In a letter written in 1834, a Teachers' Seminary student described an evening lecture and its aftermath: "We had our room pretty well filled & to crown the climax, some of the fellows gallivanted the ladies home."
19. Ibid., 186.
20. Lincoln, *Botany*, 15.
21. William Paley, *Natural Theology* (New York, the American Tract Society, n.d.), 34. The complexity of Paley's language is a tribute to Abbot Seniors' reading vocabulary. For example, in his chapter on "The Human Frame," Paley writes, "The nerves which supply the fore-arm, especially the inferior cubital nerves, are at the elbow conducted by a

kind of covered way between the condyles, or rather under the inner extuberances of the bone" (83).

22. Unsigned article (probably written by Woodbridge or Russell), "Method of Teaching Geography and History," *American Journal of Education*, 2 (1827), 520–521. It is also possible that the piece was written by Samuel E. Hall, whose *Lectures on School-keeping* contained similar instructions: begin with the neighborhood.

23. Unsigned article, "Suggestions to Parents," in *American Journal of Education*, 2 (1827), 548.

24. Quoted in Carpenter, *Abbot*, 189.

25. Richard Benson Sewall, *The Life of Emily Dickinson* (New York, Farrar, Straus and Giroux, 1974), I, 22.

26. Abel Flint, *Murray's Abridged English Grammar* (Hartford, Peter B. Gleason, 1818).

27. Unsigned book review in *American Journal of Education*, 2 (1827), 743.

28. In William Russell's *Address* (1843), 12.

29. Ibid.

30. Quoted in Marr, *Academies*, 187.

31. Letter to the McKeen sisters, quoted in McKeen *Annals*, 27.

32. Quoted in Marr, *Academies*, 262.

33. Ibid., 276.

34. Originally published in *Harper's New Monthly Magazine*, reprinted in *American Annals of Education*, 17 (1858), 445.

35. Elizabeth Emerson, quoted in Carpenter, *Abbot*, 187.

36. Ibid.

37. Mrs. Griggs to Phebe McKeen, 1879.

38. Quoted in *Brown Memorial*, 20–21.

39. Anonymous, *The Pastor's Daughter: a Memoir of Susan Amelia W——, Who Died January 20, 1843, Aged 19 Years* (New York, American Tract Society, n.d.), 6.

40. Ibid., 40–41, 44, 57, 83.

41. Sklar, *Beecher*, 12–13. Sklar quotes a letter written by Charles Beecher to his brother Henry Ward in 1857, to show how deeply entangled with family relationships the conversion process could be: "How can we affect our children as Father did us, if we have not the same concern for them, the same sense of their awful danger?" (231).

42. See Kett, *Rites*, 63, 68–70.

43. Letter from Jonathan French Stearns, Phillips Academy class of 1826, in Fuess, *New England School*, 150, 251.

44. McKeen, *Annals*, 34 and S. E. Jackson, *Reminiscences of Andover* (Andover, Andover Press, 1914), 10.

45. Sklar, *Beecher*, 80.

46. Unsigned article in *The Biblical Repository* (January 1840).

47. See Sklar, *Beecher*, 143. Catharine Beecher's early articles were unsigned; thus Woods in his reply referred to their author as "he."

48. See Kett, *Rites*, 68. Abbot's Trustees recognized this blurring of sectarian divisions in their alteration of the Academy constitution. They asked the Massachusetts General Court in 1838 to strike the original criterion for membership on the Board—that all "be professors of religion of the Congregational or Presbyterian denomination"—and substitute the requirement that all be "professors of religion of some Evangelical denomination." The General Court complied.

49. Sklar, *Beecher*, 27.

50. "Women and Revivalism, 1740–1840" (Barbara Easton's study of women's conversion journals, in a paper presented at the Third Berkshire Conference, June 1976) suggests a reason: considered inferior by men, feeling vaguely victimized themselves, women found that the concept of the depravity and helplessness of the sinner seeking conversion matched their experience more neatly than did men's. See also Barbara Sicherman, "American History," in *Signs* (Winter 1975), 476.

51. Unsigned article, *American Journal of Education*, 1 (1826), 401–402.

52. From *Ladies Magazine*, 1830, quoted in Douglas, *Feminization*, 57.

53. Mary Ryan, *A Woman's Awakening: Revivalist Religion in Utica, N.Y., 1800–1835*, Paper delivered at Third Berkshire Conference of Women Hitsorians, June 1976.

54. Douglas, *Feminization*, 11–12, and entire section, "Imitation and Rivalry: Pulpit Envy," 103–109.

55. See Kett, *Rites*, 84, 119.

56. Quoted in Douglas, *Feminization*, 112. Other critics worried about the "saccharine simplification of dogma" that the Sunday School movement appeared to encourage. (Ibid., 5.)

57. Quoted in Flexner, *Century*, 61.

58. JAP to her mother, 24 January 1841. See also letter from E. P. Blodgett to Phebe McKeen, 10 April 1878.

59. Francis Wayland, *Occasional Discourses*, 323. Quoted in Blau, ed., *Moral Science*, xxv.

60. Wayland, "The Dependence of Science on Religion," quoted ibid., xxviii.

61. Blau, ed., *Moral Science*, xxi.

62. Russell, Address, 7–8. See Douglas, *Feminization*, 58, for confirmation of Abbot's singularity as compared with the more superficial foci of the average female academy.

63. Quoted in Carpenter, *Abbot*, 19.

64. Farrar to the Trustees, 12 June 1851.

65. The only mention of all this in the Trustees' Minutes is made when the claim was first entered by Mrs. Johnson, 25 August 1848.

66. "Points" written in Samuel Jackson's hand, a summary of the claim and of the depositions of witnesses made (one assumes, though there is no mention of a court) to the probate judge.

67. See Fuess, *New England School*, 235.

68. "Points."
69. Testimony of Samuel Farrar, Mary Griffin, neighbor, and Mrs. George Abbott. It is interesting that Farrar, being a thoroughly interested party, should have been allowed to bear witness in favor of Madam Abbot.
70. See "Statistics on School Attendance and Number of Schools, Massachusetts, 1837–1880," in Alexander James Field, "Educational Expansion in Mid-Nineteenth Century Massachusetts: Human-Capital Formation or Structural Reinforcement?" *Harvard Educational Review* (November 1976), 527, for statistical evidence of the incorporated academies' success in holding students as compared with that of unincorporated academies.

II. Solid Acquirements

4. MID-CENTURY TRANSITIONS

1. Phelps, *Chapters*, 133.
2. Fuess, *New England School*, 308.
3. Unsigned tribute in Abbot Archives. The context suggests it is written by a contemporary teacher. The following two quotes are from the same source.
4. *Andover Advertiser*, I (23 July 1853), 2.
5. *The Experiment*, I, No. 1, 8 June 1853. The title of this "publication" was probably not original. The Putnam Free School in Newburyport also "published" an *Experiment*. Such student newsletters were widely encouraged by progressive pedagogues of the nineteenth century.
6. Ibid.
7. The figure can be accounted for in part by the preponderance of women over men in Massachusetts, but it also reflects a nationwide trend for teachers.
8. On the face of it, this removal of responsibility looks like as nice a piece of male chauvinism as one could ask for. However, the Phillips Academy Trustees had long since done the same for their Principal, Osgood Johnson, at Johnson's urgent request. Johnson insisted that he was too busy to be Phillips Academy's personally liable business manager as well as its headmaster. In the larger world of academies and seminaries, it was becoming increasingly common to separate financial responsibility from daily educational concerns. On the other hand, practical considerations also made it easier for Abbot's Old Guard to accept the Trustees' new commitment once a woman was chosen principal. Miss Hasseltine's salary of $500 was about half of what a man would receive for similar work, and in addition she had to pay her own room and board. Bradford's Abigail C. Hasseltine received $500 in 1847; Phillips'

Samuel Taylor $1200 in the same year, when Phillips Academy's Classical Department enrollment (141) was lower than Bradford's. (True, Taylor was responsible for student discipline in the English Department as well, even though he was not involved in English Department teaching or curricular planning. The combined enrollment of English and Classical departments was 303 in 1947.)

9. Annie Sawyer Downs's reminiscences of Miss Hasseltine, Abbot Archives. Two of the "three valuable teachers" were Miss Hasseltine's sisters; it was common for sisters to take teaching posts together.

10. In a letter to the McKeens, *Annals*, 47.

11. Quoted in Carpenter, *Abbot*, 186.

12. Letter to Phebe McKeen, undated.

13. *Bulletin* (April 1931), 13–14; letter to J. Carpenter from Charlotte H. Swift, '58, written in 1921; letter to Phebe McKeen from Elizabeth Emerson, '56, written in 1878.

14. Unsigned report. At this time examiners usually came from outside the school. Occasionally the Trustees Minutes note appointees to the Examining Committee, as in 1840 when all four ministers on the Board did the job (Minutes, 3 December 1840), and 1855, when the Examiners were "Professor Haven of Amherst College, Reverend George B. Jewett of Nashua, and Charles K. Dilloway of Roxbury" Minutes, 9 November 1855.

15. Peter Byers died in 1856 before Punchard School actually opened. Punchard started with two transient principals, but was by 1858 (and until 1886) in the highly competent hands of William G. Goldsmith, Harvard A.B., who had been for several years before 1858 a much respected teacher in the Phillips Academy English Department.

16. Fuess, *New England School*, 316.

17. Theodore Sizer, in his book *The Age of the Academies* (New York, Teachers College, 1964), dates the end of the age in the 1880's, when enrollment in public schools passed that of private academies. It came earlier in Massachusetts, the first state to support private secondary schools widely *and* the first to initiate public ones on a large scale. Woody, (*History*, I, 393), says that "the great day of the female seminary" ended in 1860. From 1830 to 1860 the Massachusetts General Court passed 21 acts of incorporation for female seminaries; after 1860 there were almost none. Of course, private academies flourished longer in the post-bellum South. The national figures are interesting. In 1860 there were no more than 40 genuine public high schools in the whole country. In 1870 there were 160 high schools and 1400 private academies with a total enrollment of about 18,000 students 15 and over. By 1900 the number of public high schools had grown to 6005 while the private academies increased only slightly, and the total secondary school enrollment was 1,174,520 males and 1,268,684 females.

18. Trustee Minutes, 13 October, 1853.

19. Quote from Jackson's sermon, "Religious Principle—A Source of Public Prosperity," Election Sermon delivered before the Massachusetts legislature, Governor, Lieutenant Governor, and Governor's Council following the 1842 election, 7 January 1843. It was a great honor for Jackson to have been invited to give this sermon, as well as one more indication of his stature among his contemporaries. Though he resigned from the West Parish Church partly out of discouragement over his failure to mediate the "schism" between the abolitionists and the more moderate antislavery faction in his congregation, he seems also to have made the move for positive reasons—a sense of the wider horizons and larger work awaiting him outside the West Parish. After his resignation, he moved to a house on School Street next door to both Abbot and Phillips Academy, joined the Seminary Church, and never again attended services at West Parish so far as is known, in spite of the keen regret his parishioners felt upon losing him.

20. See Patricia Albjerg Graham, *Community and Class in American Education 1865–1918* (New York, John Wiley, 1974), especially 21, 225. Graham carefully demonstrates the flaws in the myth of equal educational opportunities of which late 19th century Americans became so fond.

21. Park served from 1851 to 1900 and was president 1859–1900, Smith from 1849 to 1859 and president 1854–59.

22. Douglas, *Feminization*, 148; Reverend Williams S. Hubbell on Park's 90th birthday, E. A. Park folder.

23. Obituary in New York *Christian Advocate*, 1900. According to J. Earl Thompson, Jr., *Andover Newton Quarterly* (March 1968), 208, Park was "Andover's most original thinker and stimulating teacher" during the mid-century period. While Park was wielding his "tremendous power" (Fuess, *Andover*, 346) in New England's pulpits and the seminary classrooms, no one seems to have dared oppose him in print. After his death, his dogmatic, emotional nature was better documented. "He loved the men who agreed with him, and dropped them when they differed from him." (New York *Christian Advocate*, 1900.) Jonathan Edwards' insistence on each soul's responsibility for its own salvation became for Park at times a merciless demand. (His wife was Edwards' great grand-daughter.) Small wonder that he was in his last years "driven in upon himself, a solitary figure" (except for Philena McKeen's loyal friendship) "with much bitterness in his heart for the new Andover." (Daniels Evans in "A Giant of Yesterday," a review of Frank H. Foster's biography of Park, *Advance*, March 1937.) Park was father of Agnes Park, Abbot 1850–52 and 1856–58. (Abbot's Preparatory Department was extant in those years.) He was also a Trustee of Smith College and a Fellow of Brown University.

24. One of the wealthiest people in mid-century Andover, Smith was a man of great benevolence, active with his brother John (also an Abbot parent) in the founding of Andover's Memorial Hall (public) Library (1870) and other local institutions. At the Smith brothers factory, later Smith and Dove Co., Peter Smith was Superintendent of Works. John Smith, the firm's president, was Andover's richest citizen. So much did his workers revere John Smith that they once re-roofed his large house as a surprise for him while he was away in Scotland on one of his re-cruiting trips—an interesting gesture, considering that his annual earn-ings were about $50,000, while his workers earned an average of $409 a year (1875 figures: the average for Massachusetts linen workers was $417). See Mary S. Minard, "Immigrants from the Scottish Lowlands: Their Life in Andover, Mass.," M. A. thesis in Liberal Studies, Wes-leyan University, 1970, Wesleyan University Library. Both men were parishioners and devoted admirers of Samuel Jackson; they stayed loyal even after John Smith left the West Parish following the members' "schism" over abolition to help found the Free Christian Church in 1846, an abolitionist institution.

25. Alpheus Hardy in *Memorial* to Peter Smith, (Andover, 1881).

26. See letter of 15 June 1849, to Reverend J. L. Taylor, President of the Abbott Trustees (the handwriting is almost unreadable).

27. Sewall, *Emily Dickinson*, 447. Dickinson heard Park's sermon in 1853. Just afterward she wrote, "I never heard anything like it, and don't expect to again."

28. Jackson, *West Parish Sketches*, 29.

29. A precise accounting of the gifts for Smith Hall can be found in Mc-Keen, *Annals*, 60–62.

30. Quoted in McKeen, *Annals*, 51.

31. Phelps, *Chapters*, 134.

32. *The Weekly Picayune*, New Orleans, 30 August 1852.

33. Phelps, *Chapters*, 134. Mrs. Stowe's high-spirited children added to the gaity of the levees. An Abbot girl kept a journal in 1861 (hereafter called Student Journal, '61; the journal is unsigned as well as unpagi-nated). She wrote that she "hardly knew whether to go" to one of the Stowes' levees. "I have heard it said that Harriet and Eliza Stowe, the twins (Abbot alumnae of the class of 1855) are great hands to make fun of people. They will stand by the door and laugh at anyone they happen to see." (She did go, and had a "pleasant time" after all.)

34. McKeen, *Annals*, 51.

35. *Bulletin* article (November 1930). 25.

36. Alumna reminiscence, McKeen, *Annals*, 124.

37. In Annie Sawyer Downs's news article on Abbot's Semicentennial, *Lawrence American*, June 1879. Philena McKeen's scrapbook, pp. 38–40, Abbot Archives.

38. Joseph Kett's study of adolescence in the nineteenth century suggests

that Abbot's transformation was typical of a general trend toward structured learning environments for youth 1840–1880. See *Rites*, 111–112.

39. Minutes, 31 (sic) June 1859.

40. Alice G. Emerson to Philena McKeen, 14 January 1878. Miss Emerson arrived at Abbot in 1860.

41. Minutes, 2 March 1854.

42. *Courant* (January 1898), 42, an account of Susannah E. Jackson's reminiscences of her childhood.

43. Ellen Punchard may have tried Punchard under its first and most disorganized principal, but if he kept any records, none have survived.

44. Did Abbot undermine the support of Andover's prosperous and influential citizens for public schools, as Horace Mann accused all private schools of doing? (See Graham, *Community*, 10.) The answer is unclear. Founder Jackson seems to have worked as hard for public education as for private. Clearly Abbot's example stimulated some of the local interest in a free high school. And the small number of day scholars attracted to Abbot from 1859 to 1892 suggests that the Academy had little interest in competition with the public schools once Punchard High School was well under way and Abbot had become a full-fledged boarding school.

45. Quoted in Jean Sarah Pond, *Bradford, a New England Academy*. Sesquicentennial Edition. Revised and supplemented by Dale Mitchell (Bradford, Mass., 1954), 134.

46. From "Mrs. Professor Hitchcock's" letter to the McKeens, McKeen, *Annals*, 48.

47. Speech by Marion Edwards Park at the dinner of the Abbot Academy Alumnae Association and Boston Abbot Club, Hotel Somerset in Boston, 15 February 1938, Abbot Archives. Marion Park, the President of Bryn Mawr College from 1922 to 1942, was Edwards and Ann Maria Park's only granddaughter. Though she did not grow up in Andover, she visited often until her grandparents' death. She and her brother Edwards both found their grandfather Park terrifying, according to friends.

48. *The First Convention Ever Called to Discuss The Civil and Political Rights of Women* (Seneca Falls, New York, 1848), 6.

49. Jackson, *Reminiscences*, 27.

50. See Gerda Lerner, "The Lady and the Mill Girl," *Mid Continent American Studies Journal* (Spring, 1969, 5–15), also Sklar's discussion of the same topic in *Beecher*, 192–195.

51. Bushnell, speech quoted in Douglas, *Feminization*, 52.

52. Reverend Bushnell's book was first published in 1847. It was revised and reprinted numerous times through 1861. See also Reverend James P. Hoppin, address to Abbot Female Academy, July 1856, on "The Relations of Christ to Education" (Andover, Warren Draper, 1856).

53. In "The Cult of True Womanhood: 1820–1860," in *The American Family in Social and Historical Perspectives*, ed. Michael Gordon (New York, St. Martin's Press, 1973), 224–225.

54. Fredrika Bremer quoted in Oscar Handlin, ed., *America* (New York, Harper and Row, 1949), 221.

55. I. Löwenstern, (1866) quoted ibid, 181.

56. See Sklar, *Beecher*, 33–35, 158–159.

57. John P. Hale, speech (1858).

58. Maria J. B. Browne, *Address to the Graduating Class of 1857*, 5, 7. The *Address* was printed as a keepsake for alumnae.

59. Maria J. B. Browne described herself as "Teacher of Abstract Sciences and Belles Lettres" in the 1856–57 Catalogue, the first such designation found in Abbot documents.

60. Emma Taylor to Phebe McKeen, 3 February 1878.

61. Later Western College for Women. The "Holyoke Plan" involved a missionary commitment to education of young women from a broad spectrum of income groups. See Woody, *History*, I, 458.

62. E. A. Park in memorial to Phebe McKeen; Philena McKeen, *Sequel to Annals of Abbot Academy* (Andover, Warren F. Draper, 1897), 47.

63. Ibid.

64. Speech by Anna L. Dawes, '70, after the Alumnae Association Luncheon, 6 June 1921.

65. Quoted in Henrietta Learoyd Sperry, "Miss McKeen as a Teacher," *Courant* (June 1892), 7.

66. Katherine Roxanna Kelsey, *Abbot Academy Sketches 1892–1912* (Boston and New York, Houghton, Mifflin, 1929), 8.

67. Professor John Phelps Taylor, quoted in *Memorial to Warren Fales Draper* (Andover, Andover Press, 1905).

68. Sperry in *Courant* (June 1892), 6; see also Blanche E. Wheeler Williams, *Mary C. Wheeler* (Boston, Marshall Jones, 53–54), reminiscences of Mary C. Wheeler, '65. MCW received "an extraordinary training in logic and argument" at Abbot, writes Mrs. Williams.

69. Dawes, *Speech*, 1921.

70. Phebe McKeen's published works include numbers of magazine stories and articles written during the 1850's and '60's under the name "Jenny Bradford," and the following books:

> *Thornton Hall; or, Old Questions in Young Lives*, New York, Randolph, 1872.
>
> *Theodora: A Home Story*, New York, Randolph, 1875.
>
> *Annals of Fifty Years: A History of Abbot Academy, Andover, Mass., 1829–1879*, "by Philena McKeen and Phebe F. McKeen. With an introduction by Edwards A. Park, D.D.", Andover, Warren F. Draper, 1880.
>
> *The Little Mother and Her Christmas and Other Stories*, Boston, Lothrop, 1881.

Sketch of the Early Life of Joseph Hardy Neesima, Boston, Lothrop, 1890.

The published *Theodora* lacked one chapter that Phebe McKeen had included in her original version, a long and suspenseful account of the heroine's passage through New York City during the draft riots of 1863. The publisher feared to lose his Southern audience, which might reject the chapter's sympathetic treatment of the Negro. It is a pity, for this section is especially eloquent of Phebe McKeen's own understanding of complex interracial and ideological conflicts. Fortunately, it can still be read; the Abbot *Courant* editors obtained a manuscript copy and printed the entire chapter in their January 1898 issue.

71. Abby Wood Collins, '71, to Phebe McKeen, 28 February 1879.
72. Dawes, *Speech*, 1921.
73. See *The Congregationalist*, 8 July 1875; also alumna recollection of the joint rule of the McKeen sisters, *Bulletin* (April 1931), 17–28. *The Congregationalist*, a denominational periodical published in Boston, often carried news of Andover Hill's three educational institutions.
74. Quoted in McKeen, *Annals*, 218. The student editors of *Courant*, Abbot's twice-yearly magazine published from 1873 to 1974, referred to the McKeens as Abbot's "double star" (June 1892, 10).
75. Marion Park, *Speech*, 1938.
76. McKeen, *Sequel*, 159.
77. Alice G. Emerson letter (1878).
78. Phebe McKeen, *Theodora*, 98.
79. Ibid., 333.
80. Ibid., 136.
81. Alice G. Emerson letter.
82. Letter to "Carrie Felton," 29 December 1863, from Judiciary Hospital, D.C., Abbot Archives. Another soldier's letter (1865) is in the form of a long moral poem, probably copied by numbers of convalescents who could think of nothing original to say to their benefactors. It ends with this verse about the yarn with which the socks were knit:

> It measures too, the thread of life,
> Which may be smooth or rough;
> You are just narrowing for the heel
> While I am toeing off.

83. McKeen, *Annals*, 194–195.
84. Phebe McKeen, *Theodora*, 358.
85. Harriet Beecher Stowe, *The Chimney Corner*, by Christopher Crowfield, pseud. (Boston, Ticknor and Fields, 1868), 30.
86. Quoted in Carpenter, *Abbot*, 252.
87. Ibid., 252. It is interesting that Bradford's enrollments continued to drop during this time. Only seventy girls in all attended in 1862, sixty-eight in 1863. The faculty had been reduced to four.
88. Alumna quoted in *Courant* (June 1890), 19–21.

5. ABBOT IN THE GOLDEN AGE

1. Phebe McKeen, *Theodora*, 98.
2. See Francine duPlessix Gray, "Women Writing about Women's Art," in the *New York Times Book Review* (4 September 1977), 3, 18.
3. See the "Literary Exercises" prepared for '87's Class Supper, 8 June 1887, at French Hall (Davis Hall). This seventy-two-page manuscript account (unpaginated) is a kind of yearbook, with Class History, Poem, statistics (extremely helpful to the historian), descriptions of favorite teachers and courses.
4. See Sewall, *Dickinson*, 237.
5. The 1863 booklist for this course (and its later printed syllabi) make clear that it was a combined History and Literature course. For example, students read Hume's *History of England* Volume I, covering English history through the year 1216; Tennyson's *Idylls of the King* and *Morte d'Arthur*; and Shakespeare's *Macbeth* and *King Lear*, along with older versions of the same legends and several novels by Sir Walter Scott. Later Chaucer in the original Middle English is included. The topics covered such problems as "Number VIII: Nature, Extent, and Causes of the Change which Developed English from Anglo-Saxon."
6. Written in May 10, 187–(no year given on original letter).
7. See Abbot Female Academy Catalogue, 1852.
8. The average age of the Seniors of 1885 at graduation was twenty-two, the oldest twenty-four ("Perce Ad Majora," the manuscript class book of 1885), that of the Seniors of 1887, twenty-one ("Literary Exercises"). A spot check of birthdates for day scholars from the town of Andover suggests an average of twenty-one for Seniors of the McKeen period. See also Harvard Catalogues, 1858–1859, 1865–1866. Harvard required French for three terms out of eight, and offered French, German, and Spanish as electives in the junior and senior years. Harvard was more advanced in its modern language offerings than most colleges, thanks to the improvements introduced by George Ticknor during his tenure as Professor of French and Spanish Languages and Literatures and Professor of Belles Lettres during the years 1819 to 1835. Ticknor had studied abroad, and was determined that Harvard should be more than a glorified secondary school, in spite of the age group it served at that time and its long tradition of mechanical recitation of grammatical rules, of reciting verbatim rather than oral exchange. See David B. Tyack, *George Ticknor and the Boston Brahmins* (Cambridge, Harvard University Press, 1967), 92-94.
9. McKeen, *Annals*, 85.
10. The first native German teacher, Fraulein Adelheid Bodenmeyer, actually made some attempt at expurgation, but it was too feeble and too late. When the students' texts of *Der Neffe als Onkel* arrived, the fraulein

took a red pencil and (according to one alumna's recollections) showed each girl how to bracket the "objectionable phrases" that they "might be omitted. The result, of course, was that we learned those phrases at once. I still know a few mild curses in German. But Fraulein was a real teacher." Quoted in *Bulletin* (April 1932), 24.

11. A phalanx of costume- and scenery-makers must have had to accompany the actresses themselves in production of extravaganzas like Schiller's play *Die Huldigung der Kunste*, performed in 1891.

12. *Andover Townsman*, 13 February 1891.

13. Marjorie Housepian Dobkin, *The Making of a Feminist: Early Journals and Letters of M. Carey Thomas*, (Kent, Ohio, Kent State University Press, 1979, in press). A few boys' preparatory schools, Exeter and Round Hill among them, offered French and Spanish (Round Hill taught German and Italian also); but these were exceptions to the rule.

14. I am indebted to Stephen Whitney, teacher of French at Phillips Academy since 1936, and to Hale Sturges, Chairman of the Phillips French department, 1973–1978, for their assistance in making these comparisons over time. See also Theodore Sizer, *Secondary Schools at the Turn of the Century* (New Haven, Yale University Press, 1964), 67. In nineteenth century schools and colleges, "languages were taught to be read, not spoken."

15. Fuess, *Old New England School*, 263.

16. In 1865 four of Taylor's assistants petitioned the Trustees to strengthen the feeble mathematics course offered by the Classical Department, and after this, Phillips' mathematics gradually improved. Catalogues show that Phillips' "English Department" took mathematics more seriously. Its curriculum throughout this period was much like Abbot's except for the dearth of modern languages and the addition of Bookkeeping and Surveying. There was also much overlap in book lists, though Wayland, Smellie, Upham, Paley, and Lincoln remained English Department offerings for some time after Abbot had dropped them. However, the English Department remained the Phillips Trustees' neglected stepchild during the Taylor era in spite of its relatively large enrollment.

17. Pond, *Bradford*, 203.

18. Phebe McKeen gives a lively account of these dead bones in chapter 6 of the *Annals*, p. 79. They were not "as one of our Hibernian friends fancied, the cherished relics of the founder" but the remains of a Prussian mercenary shot by his British superiors for desertion, probably during the Revolution. The bones were acquired by a Vermont physician and medical teacher, who sold them to Abbot when he retired. The bones are now part of the Art Department's equipment at Phillips Academy.

19. Letter to Trustees, 13 November 1879.

20. Philena McKeen in *Courant* (June 1893), 3.

21. Larcom, *A New England Girlhood* (Boston, Houghton Mifflin, 1889), 200.
22. From an unsigned article in *The Ladies Wreath*, III, 1852.
23. Abby Wood Collins, '71, letter to Phebe McKeen, 28 February 1879.
24. Student Journal, 1861.
25. From three manuscript sources, all in Abbot Archives:
    Emma P. Meacham, Composition Book, fall 1873.
    Harriet Wetmore Chapell, Journal 1874–77, hereafter referred to as Chapell, Journal.
    Sarah R. Coburn, Composition Book 1859–60.
    Emma Meacham's notebook also contains two short plays, entitled "Charades."
26. *Courant* (June 1873), 8–10. Miss Twichell tendered no apologies to Edgar Allan Poe.
27. A June '91 clipping on p. 129 of McKeen Scrapbook.
28. *Courant* (November 1881), 33; (June 1892), 33.
29. Young's involvement with Abbot demonstrates the benefits of the Academy's Hilltop connections. From 1853 to 1855, at the beginning of his distinguished career in astronomical research and teaching, Young taught in the Phillips Academy English Department, which offered all science courses taught at Phillips. Doubtless one of the Trustees or another of Abbot's friends remembered him and suggested he be invited to return.
30. The *Congregationalist*, 1879, McKeen Scrapbook, p. 54.
31. From student letter, *Courant* (June 1891), 36.
32. Chapell, Journal (11 February 1874), 63; (21 May 1874), 146.
33. Catalogue of Abbot Academy, 1869–70, p. 21.
34. *Courant* (June 1890), 28. "Do you remember," an alumna asked Miss Phebe, "how we all went into Boston for a concert and some of us missed the train and came back in a great covered wagon and you tucked us all into bed—and went flitting about from one to the other with little doses of Sconiti and Bryonia?" Collins letter.
35. Phebe McKeen reported that the Abbot library had grown to 1880 volumes in 1879. She does not apologize for the small numbers of books but says instead that because the library "has been gathered under a sense of actual need, it has a goodly proportion of books in constant use." McKeen, *Annals*, 92.
36. McKeen, *Annals*, 95.
37. See letter written by Herbert D. Russell, Phillips Academy Class of 1890, to his "Mamma," 8 February 1888, Phillips Academy Archives. After describing the wag's exploit, Russell says: "The P.A. faculty are considering his expulsion." In the end he and the Abbot girl who in-

vited him were dismissed. See letter from Barbara Moore Pease, Class of 1911, to her granddaughter, Carlie Pease, Class of 1975, 6 April 1974. Mrs. Pease's mother lived in the same Smith Hall room with the girl who invited the boy.

38. H.G., A.A. '81, in the *Phillipian's* Abbot column, October 1879.
39. See Caroll Smith-Rosenberg, "The Female World of Love and Ritual: Relations between Women in Nineteenth-Century America," *Signs: Journal of Women in Culture and Society*, I, No. 1 (Autumn 1975), 3. The entire article is of interest.
40. See also ibid., 17–18.
41. The number of births for each married woman was 7.04 in 1800, 5.42 in 1850 and 3.56 in 1900.
42. Over the long run, this constitutes a sharp rise in real costs, not just a reflection of inflation. Prices were quite stable throughout the years from Abbot's founding through 1914, except for the Civil War period. There was a deflation of all commodity prices during the last two decades of the nineteenth century. Representative figures from the wholesale price index (1910–14 = 100):

    1835 — 100
    1843 — 75 (the lowest figure for the period
            1830–1914)
    1860 — 84
    1864 — 193
    1869 — 151
    1876 — 110
    1880 — 100
    1890 — 82

Much of the cost increase at Abbot is a reflection of raises in teachers' salaries. Teachers-as-colleagues were more expensive than teachers-as-assistants. According to Warren Draper's Treasurer's Accounts (1876–1901) teachers earned $400–$500 a year plus room and board, roughly comparable to the wages of highly skilled male factory hands and foremen. This was a great improvement over the $1.00-a-day of Abbot's early decades, though less than an experienced woman could earn in Boston public high schools ($1000 after 1880). Money bought more in those days, but it often bought different things; thus cost-of-living comparisons over a long time period are difficult to make. Thanks to Abbot's penury, however, we have one source that shows what Andover citizens paid for transportation at mid-century: Nathaniel Swift, Treasurer from 1852 to 1876, kept the Abbot accounts for 1857–1865 in the unused portion of a livery stable account book. It is interesting to see that in 1852, Fiske Abbott took Lady and a chaise to Lawrence and back for 75¢, and Warren Barnard paid $1.50 to use Jim along with a rented saddle for "4 ours". In 1970, when wholesale prices were on the average about eight times the 1852 level, an Andover inhabitant could take the bus to Lawrence and back for 70¢.

43. Richard Sennett, "Middle-Class Families and Urban Violence," in Gordon, *Family*, 128. See also Kett, *Rites*, 60, 143.

44. John and Virginia Demos, "Adolescence in Historical Perspective," in Gordon, *Family*, 214. See also James McLachlan, *American Boarding Schools* (New York, Charles Scribner's Sons, 1970), 93. About twice as many Abbot students came from cities (population over 50,000) during the years 1861–1890 as in the school's first thirty years, a change that was undoubtedly hastened by the boarding arrangements. However, girls from smaller towns and rural areas still predominated, outnumbering city students a little more than two to one. From 1891 to 1913 about 600 came from towns, 290 from cities; the predominance thus continues into the twentieth century. Thus "the whole hot-bed system of city life" (J. Stainback Wilson, 1860) propelled fewer students to Abbot than to more isolated boarding schools. See Kett, *Rites*, 136.

45. *Courant* (June 1887), 26. See also Sewall, *Dickinson*, 121-123. As Austen Dickinson, Emily's brother, grew older, it saddened him that towns like Amherst were being abandoned for the rush and excitement of the cities.

46. Vernon L. Parrington, *Main Currents in American Thought*, 3 vols. (New York, Harcourt Brace, 1927–30), III, 48. The attraction Westerners felt for eastern New England can also be explained by their ancestry, for 90 percent of the migrants to the Ohio valley before 1850 had come from New England.

47. Undated letter.

48. *Courant* (November 1879), 13.

49. Class of '87, "Literary Exercises."

50. The following undated summary was found in the McKeen Scrapbook, last page, part of a four-page circular on Abbot or pp. 1–4 of an early Sargent's Handbook-type publication. The date must be between 1870 and 1876 to fit tuition board figures ($276 for the English course). Yet the total number of those attending is far higher than the number counted by Jane Carpenter in 1913 (4638). The phrase "number of pupils connected with the school" probably should read "number of pupils plus number of years beyond one that each was connected with the school." The compiler apparently went through each catalogue and counted names listed from each state without regard for repetiton of names in subsequent catalogues. Because several of the earliest catalogues are missing entirely, this listing, read with the above qualifications in mind, may well be the most accurate available.

Table, taken from the annual catalogues, showing the number of pupils connected with the school since May 6th, 1829, and the States and countries from which they came.

Maine,	278	Michigan,	6
New Hampshire,	542	Illinois,	27
Vermont,	134	Missouri,	10
Massachusetts,	4427	Iowa,	6
Rhode Island,	27	Wisconsin,	6
Connecticut,	97	California,	25
New York,	122	Minnesota,	5
New Jersey,	23	Oregon,	4
Pennsylvania,	26	Indian Territory,	10
Delaware,	2	Colorado,	6
Maryland,	1	Nova Scotia,	1
District of Columbia,	7	Canada,	5
Virginia,	8	England,	5
South Carolina,	1	New Brunswick,	11
Georgia,	4	South America,	2
Florida,	14	Persia,	1
Alabama,	5	Turkey,	12
Texas,	7	Africa,	16
Tennessee,	6	China,	2
Kentucky,	1	Total,	5927
Ohio,	35		

51. Unsigned article on the goals of education, "Protest from the Rank and File," *Courant* (January 1884), 17.

52. See Graham, *Community and Class*, 37–46.

53. See U.S. Commissioner of Education, *Reports*, 1872, 798–799, "Statistics of Institutions for the Superior Instruction of Females"; ibid., 1889–90, 752–753, "Courses of Study Leading to the Degree of A.B. in 15 Colleges and Seminaries for Women."

54. Chapell, Journal (24 April 1874), 118. Fortunately for the Abbot historian, Harriet wrote what she pleased—"after all, what is the good of a true journal if it is not egotistical" (p. 135)—and illustrated her entries profusely. The six pages torn out (29–30, 129–130, and 237–238) are tantalizing (pages 237–238 apparently describe a trip to Martha's Vineyard with her fiancé, and page 239 finds her "thoroughly alarmed" with herself), but their absence little mars the whole. Harriet Chapell Newcomb brought the Journal back to Abbot in 1926 at the request of her classmates, so that the Alumnae Association might publish excerpts. While it was in Abbot's possession, someone, probably Flora L. Mason, editor of the *Journal of an Abbot Academy Girl* (Taunton, Massachusetts, Charles W. Davol, 1927), tore out, then tore in half, about a quarter of the pages. Were they thought irrelevant or offensive? Perhaps the deed was done to prepare the original Journal for

exhibition at Abbot in 1927. Fortunately, the destroyer thought better of throwing the torn pages away—except possibly for the six mentioned above—and in 1976 they were restored.

55. Ibid., (4 May 1874), 124.
56. Ibid., 102–103, 7 April 1874.
57. Ibid., 88, 23 February 1874.
58. Abbot Academy Catalogues, 1884–1887.
59. Chapell, Journal (4 January 1874), 5, 6. Andover's mud impressed many students. The *Courant* editors of 1874 found it worthy of a poem. "The Last of the Sidewalks," describing a Rip Van Winkle character who goes to sleep in the seventeenth century and wakes in the nineteenth to find all his favorite walk-ways covered with "heartless stones"— except in Andover:

> . . . when he got to Andover
>   His joy I can't repeat
> To find that *mud* two inches deep
>   There covered every street.

Courant (spring term 1874), 71
The students of all three Andover Hill institutions raised enough funds through musicales and readings to contribute substantially to the building of sidewalks. By 1880 the Andover selectmen had authorized a "ribbon of concrete" up School Street and along Main Street to serve the three campuses.

60. Chapell, Journal (19 April 1874), 112; (24 April 1874), 117; (20 February 1874), 217.
61. Ibid. (1 January 1874), 2.
62. Ibid. (1 January 1874), 2–3; (17 February 1874), 73; (6 September 1874), 194–195.
63. Ibid. (14 January 1874), 15.
64. Ibid. (4 April 1874), 100; (26 April 1874), 118.
65. Ibid. (1 January 1874), 3.
66. Ibid. (17 September 1874), 197.
67. Ibid. (22 April 1877), 247.
68. Ibid. (11 March 1877), 244.
69. Ibid. (22 April 1877), 245–246.
70. Conversation, 25 March 1976.
71. Quoted in Nancy Sahli, "Changing Patterns of Sexuality and Female Interactions in Late Nineteenth Century America." Paper given at Third Berkshire Conference of Women Historians, 11 June 1976, 8.
72. Quoted in Edith Finch, *Carey Thomas of Bryn Mawr* (New York, Harper and Bros., 1947), 47.
73. Quoted in Sahli, "Changing Patterns," 15.
74. Ibid.
75. Letter, December 1881.
76. See Woody, *History*, II, 201.   No list of Abbot rules seems to have

survived from the McKeen years, but there are continual references in *Courant* and in alumna reminiscences to their abundance and strictness. The 1874 Seniors' own rules for graduation attire may reflect their character in some measure:

> "Rules of dress for Graduation. Passed, Jan. 7, 1874. Muslin dresses to trail not more than eight inches. No lace on them. No lace handkerchiefs. Overskirts *perfectly* plain. No jewelry. No feathers. Not more than 3 buttons on gloves—color, white, or pearl or cream tint. The expense is not *limited*, but try to dress as simply and economically as possible."

77. Alumna of the 1880's, quoted in Carpenter, *Abbot*, 265.
78. Student Journal, 10 September 1861 entry.
79. Student letter, 7 October 1888, quoted in *Bulletin* (April 1932), 19; Carpenter, *Abbot*, 265. The rest of Miss McKeen's "lecture":

> She said we ought not to eat between meals at all, except just before or just after a meal. She said our moral condition and spiritual life were lowered by the pickles we ate. Said we would not be permitted to go to other rooms if we went to eat and drink. Then she said we reminded her of the Israelites in the wilderness, longing for the something and onions they had in the land of Egypt. Quite a pat illustration, only I don't long for onions. She reminds me of the headings of some of the pages in *Exodus*, viz. "Divers laws and ordinances."

80. James Fullerton Muirhead, quoted in Gordon, *Family*, 199.
81. Larcom, *Girlhood*, 166.
82. Student Journal, 1861.
83. The Trustee Minutes record that Miss Merrill's salary was set at $700 on 13 June 1888. There is no mention of any raise before this, but her compensation may have been gradually increased from $400 in 1881.
84. Alumnae quoted in Carpenter, *Abbot*, 255, and in Kelsey, *Sketches*, 38, 43.
85. "Literary Exercises," 1887.
86. Ibid.
87. Chapell, Journal (7 January 1874), 9–10.
88. Ibid., 205; sketch from same page; (17 October 1874).
89. "Nor should we forget the tents," wrote the *Courant* editors (November 1879), "and the coming of those sons of Ham, with their songs and merry laughter, who, by some magic art, converted one of those tents into a dining hall for the hungry multitude."
90. Frances Swazey Parker, A.A. '86, quoted in the *Abbot Bulletin* (April 1931), 27.
91. In its day, at least one reviewer considered *Thornton Hall* "the most graphic and telling picture of school-girl life we have ever read." "The Contributions of Abbot Academy," *Literary World*, 21 June 1879.
92. *Thornton Hall*, 267.

93. Alumna recollection, letter to Phebe McKeen, Abbot Archives, un-
    dated. Miss Wardwell taught at Abbot from 1859 to 1864.
94. *Thornton Hall*, 44, 48.
95. Ibid., 56–58.
96. Chapell, Journal (19 April 1874), 114; (4 October 1874), 202; (17 Oc-
    tober 1874), 205; (9 December 1874), 207; (9 December 1874), 208.
97. Ibid. (3 February 1874), 51; (24 April 1874), 118; (21 May 1874), 145;
    (1 August 1875), 225.
98. *Courant*, June 1879, 27.
99. Letter to Phebe McKeen, February 24, 1879,, Abbot Archives. The
    Moores soon moved from Ypsilanti and the *Commercial* to bigger
    things in Detroit, but while Alice Moore was there, she was lyrical.
    She rejoiced to Miss Phebe that her work gave her "as wide an out-
    look" as her husband, and that "he is just as much and more my lover
    than ever." (Moore was an 1874 graduate of Phillips Academy: the
    two had found time enough in Andover to fall in love, in spite of
    Abbot's rules.)
100. *Courant* (June 1873), 25.
101. Ibid. (June 1874), 73.
102. Ibid. (November 1873), 30–31.
103. Ibid., 27.
104. *Phillipian*, 13 January 1883.
105. *Courant* (January 1888), 1–2.
106. *Courant* (June 1890), 1.
107. Mary Gorton *Courant* (June 1892), 21.
108. The disappearance of the flitting scholar also explains apparently re-
    duced enrollments: 184 different students attended Abbot in 1854–55,
    but the average enrollment for each of the three separate terms was
    only 106, close to the yearly average (108) from 1875 to 1885.
109. The grade and age distribution in public high school enrollments of
    this period also shows a preponderance of students in lower grades.
    Nationally, in 1892, 49 percent of fifteen-year-olds were enrolled in
    high school, while 25 percent of seventeen-year-olds were so enrolled,
    the majority of them girls. Abbot's Junior Middle and Senior Middle
    (second and third year) classes were usually the largest; the age of
    these students was probably sixteen to nineteen until 1878–79, when a
    fifth year "Graduating Class" was set above the Senior class (though
    still called Seniors everywhere but in the catalogue, just to be con-
    fusing) to accommodate those students who wished to study music or
    art, along with the regular studies, and to spread the whole course
    over an extra year. After 1879 they were a little younger.
110. *Courant* (June 1873), 19.
111. Marion Park, *Speech*, 1938.
112. "Literary Exercises," 1887.
113. *Courant* (June 1891), 16.

114. The following entry in the Class of '86 Tree Song competition suggests that Seniors had not entirely lost their senses of humor over these solemn traditions:

> As round this stately twig we draw,
>   No joy our hearts doth move,
> For we know well the winter's spell
>   To it will fatal prove.
>
> And though perchance it 'scapes the blast,
>   It will grow scant and scanter,
> For creeping things, with teeth and wings,
>   Will eat it up instanter.

Courant (June 1868), 39.

115. *Boston Daily Advertiser*, 18 June 1890.
116. Composed by Samuel Morse Downs in 1876.
117. 4 July 1878.

6. PROGRESS OF A VICTORIAN SCHOOL

1. Chapell, Journal (11 February 1874), 61.
2. In remarks made at the Abbot Alumnae Association's Jubilee luncheon, 1921.
3. Caroline S. Rogers recalls that her mother, Lucy Amelia Abbot, disliked her stay at Abbot in the 1880's partly because she wanted to be married instead—and "they kind of frowned on that." Some of the reasons for the McKeens' anxiety about hasty decisions are perhaps demonstrated by German historian Karl T. Griesinger's observations of American courtship, published in *Lebende Bilder aus Amerika*, 1858. The following passage is quoted in Handlin, *America*, 252. Griesinger recounts the careful arrangements that accompany a German couple's engagement and marriage, then exclaims,

> How far different in America! The American is abrupt; he has no time to beat around the bush. He meets a girl in a shop, in the theater, at a ball, or in her parents' home. He needs a wife, thinks this one will do. He asks the question, she answers. The next day they are married and then proceed to inform the parents. The couple do not need to learn to know each other; that comes later.

While Theodora is thinking that the dashing Colonel Bell will do quite well as a husband, Phebe McKeen as narrator and guardian angel cannot resist warning her: "Take care, Theodora! Will he do to rest on for life?" McKeen, *Theodora*, 363.
4. See Carpenter, *Abbot*, 264.
5. McKeen, *Annals*, 216.
6. Sklar, *Beecher*, 321.

7. From Beecher, "Letters to the People on Health and Happiness," quoted ibid, 321.

8. Undated letter, Abbot Archives. A. Bancroft graduated in 1883.

9. Fuess, *New England School*, 261–262.

10. Emily Means in *McKeen Memorial*.

11. Chapell, Journal (31 May and 4 June 1874), 153–155.

12. *Phillipian*, 2 November 1878. See also ibid., 11 November 1882, when the Cads invited Abbot girls to come to another football match but "the fates otherwise decreed."

13. Philena McKeen, Letters to Bancroft, Summer 1885 (undated) and 14 September 1885 (Phillips Academy Archives). See also McKeen Letter to Irene Draper, 24 August 1888, Abbot Archives, asking that she make sure the "Misses Gilette do not rent their house to anyone who plans to put a boy in any room which looks out over our grounds, north, east or south."

14. Stearns's letters to his sister Mabel, 22 June 1890, Phillips Academy Archives.

15. Ibid., 14 June 1890.

16. *Courant* (February 1876), 13.

17. *Courant* (November 1873), 2: "Our afternoon walks are enlivened by the playful gambols of the younger and more sprightly sojourners in the classic shades of Andover. Oh Phillipians, how long will you abuse our patience? ... Are you nothing daunted by our nightly guards— the shades and shutters ... nothing by the frowning dignity of us all?"

18. Stearns to Mabel, 15 June 1890.

19. See letters of Charles Phelps Taft in Scott Hurtt Paradise, *Men of the Old School: Some Andover Biographies*, Andover, Mass., Phillips Academy (1956), 201.

20. The average in the 1880's was five brother-sister pairs a year, as far as can be told from a matching of names and home towns.

21. *Courant* (November 1876), 32; (June 1877), 22.

22. Chapell, Journal (24 May 1874), 146–147.

23. Abby W. Collins to Phebe McKeen.

24. Stearns to Mabel, 20 March 1887. In 1889 Abbot again attended the Phillips Academy "Winter Tournament," but this time "Some of the wrestling and sparring was, by previous arrangement, over before we arrived on the scene. Those not afflicted with too tender hearts thoroughly enjoyed the skill displayed in the few contests we saw." *Courant* (June 1889), 34.

25. *Phillipian*, 6 December 1879, 25 November 1882, 13 January 1883. "Frolicsome Fem-Sems" had to go to Pomps Pond in 1882–1883 because the "Cads" skating rink was closed.

26. *Harper's New Monthly Magazine*, 16, 73, quoted in Woody, *History*, I, 105.

27. Fuess, *New England School*, 254.

28. See especially Herbert D. Ward, Phillips Academy Class of 1880, *The New Senior at Andover* (Boston, Lothrop, 1891). Though Ward attended Phillips under Bancroft, the forbidding Principal of his book is generally recognized as Taylor—in spirit if not in flesh.

29. Chapell, Journal (18 January 1874), 21; (27 May 1874), 151.

30. McKeen, *Sequel*, 153. Quoted by Professor Churchill.

31. Pond, *Bradford*, 185.

32. *Congregationalist*, September 1878.

33. Oberlin was the first coeducational college; however, appearances deceive, for until 1852, fewer than a quarter of Oberlin's 369 women took the regular B.A. The rest took the "literary course," and all were scoffed at as "maids" by many of the men students, who thought them only good for housework. Oberlin's overall success encouraged Antioch to open as a coeducational college in 1852. In 1858, Iowa State became the first state university to accept women; Boston University and Cornell became co-ed in 1869 and 1874; Swarthmore was founded as a co-ed college in 1869. Men students resisted coeducation in several state colleges and universities, but it was implemented anyway as the most economical way to offer higher education to women.

34. Henry Barnard, ed., *American Pedagogy* (Hartford, Brown and Gross, 1876), 389. The Boston School Department conducted a survey of physicians in 1890 to gain the benefit of their opinions before making a decision on high school coeducation. Thirty physicians were for coeducation, seventeen against. One proponent, a Dr. Otis, agreed with the opposition that girls needed "partial rest once a month...at the menstrual epoch," but since girls work faster, he felt they could afford to relax and give the boys time to catch up with them. Albert Blodgett, M.D., argued against coeducation, because "certain functions which have lain dormant until this time are awakening into life, and arouse new and unknown sensations and emotions." This could cause "vast harm" in high schools, since they draw on such a variety of neighborhoods. United States Commissioner of Education, *Reports*, 1891–92, pp. 854–856.

35. Miss McKeen's niece, Mrs. Charles McKeen Duren, wrote the following in answer to inquiries about McKeen Family Papers from Alumnae Secretary and record-keeper Jane Carpenter: "All letters of her own she burned, i.e., what she wrote, and if there were letters of pupil friends to her they would be private. Her letters to us are personal, of course." (20 December 1910). Mrs. Duren mentioned "copious outlines for chapel talks" given by Philena McKeen, but says nothing of Phebe's letters, nor of the journal she reputedly kept. The tendency to destroy private papers which Abbot principals seem to share is an impediment for the historian; it is, however, common among women. Fortunately, trustees and friends saved some letters from Miss McKeen and others, and donated them to the school.

36. Abbot Archives. During the last half of the nineteenth century, Abbot was frequently spelled with two t's. The practice waned through the Bailey era from 1912 to 1935, but it was not until 1935 that the Trustees arranged to put Abbot's legal name in line with twentieth-century usage. By act of legislature April 4, 1935, Abbot dropped the extra *t* which the Academy had officially carried ever since the turn of the century, when the corporation's title, changed in 1879 from the original "Trustees of Abbot Female Academy of Andover" to "Trustees of the Abbot Academy" was changed again to "Trustees of the Abbott Academy." The reason for the switch to the double-*t* Abbot remains a mystery; there is no mention of it in the Trustee Minutes or in other sources. Sarah Loring Bailey in her *Historical Sketches of Andover* provides one possible explanation: many of the Andover Abbots, descended from the two related George Abbots who were among Andover's earliest settlers, began adding *t* to their family names in the 1820's and '30's. According to one genealogy, Nehemiah Abbot, Madam Sarah's husband, used an extra *t* for a while. (Abbot Archives.) Perhaps "Abbott" looked more fashionable, and the Trustees of the McKeen era, loyal to Sarah Abbot's relatives, wished to stay in step. Whatever their motives, they sowed a vast if petty confusion. From 1879 to 1935 the Academy was referred to indiscriminately as Abbot and Abbott in news columns, parent letters, even in its own official publications. It is Abbott on the 1860–78 catalogues and Abbot on the catalogues from 1878–1879 on. It is Abbott on some late McKeen era diplomas and Abbot on others, Abbott on pages 2–14 of the November 1879 *Courant* and in the Advertising section, Abbot on pages 1 and 16–40 of the same issue. The Act of 1935 finally settled this trivial matter by returning to the spelling Sarah Abbot used at the time the Academy was founded.
37. McKeen, *Annals*, 73.
38. I. J. Benjamin (1862), quoted in Handlin, *America*, 273.
39. Student Journal, 1861.
40. Lectures by George Burnap, *The Sphere and Duties of Women*, 5th ed. (Baltimore, 1854), 47.
41. *Thornton Hall*, 8–9.
42. Dobkin, *Feminist* (in press).
43. *Theodora*, 243.
44. Louisa May Alcott, *Little Women* (Boston, Little Brown, 1946), 431; originally published in 1869.
45. *Theodora*, 384.
46. Letter to Anna Dawes, 1876.
47. Chapell, Journal (28 December 1875), 227.
48. Qouted in *Courant* (January 1892), 31.
49. Chapell, Journal (3 February 1874), 49–50.
50. Quoted in McKeen, *Annals*, 221. Interestingly, Peabody himself saw

no reason why men and women should not share classrooms even while they pursued different educational goals.

51. It is difficult to trace the political attitudes that were evolving within the Abbot community during the last half of the nineteenth century. There was no local Woman Suffrage league that students or faculty might join until after 1900; in fact the entire Merrimack Valley area seems to have been dry soil for the Woman Suffrage movement, even though Massachusetts as a whole was considered the "nerve center" and "home of the Woman Movement" after the Civil War. See Lois Bannister Merk, "Massachusetts and the Woman Suffrage Movement," unpublished dissertation on file in the Schlesinger Library, Radcliffe College, Cambridge, Massachusetts. The Massachusetts Woman Suffrage Association introduced a full or partial woman suffrage act to the General Court almost every year after its founding in 1870, but the most suffrage advocates could get was the School Suffrage Act in 1879, allowing women the vote on local educational matters. After this, opposition hardened. The fate of the Municipal Suffrage Act of 1889 was typical: the House defeated it 139–90, with members from North Andover, Lawrence, Methuen, and Lowell all voting nay, and the member from Andover failing to vote at all.

Suffrage organizations themselves became riddled with disagreements over strategy: should they try for a federal amendment, or concentrate on state or municipal suffrage? Should they welcome the help of the Massachusetts WCTU members (12,000 in the 1880's to the MWSA's 400) in pushing "license suffrage," whereby women could vote only on liquor issues, or refuse to divert their energies into such narrow channels? Andover's Temperance Movement was no help at all when the MWSA introduced its local suffrage resolutions of 1882 and '83, for these were soundly defeated by the Town's male voters.

The Abbot record is ambiguous. Several leaders of the MWSA were familiar to Abbot girls: Wendell Phillips, John Greenleaf Whittier, Elizabeth Stuart Phelps, and Bronson Alcott—although there is no record during the McKeen era of any lecture that specifically urged woman suffrage. Congregationalist Abbot tended not to attract feminist students or teachers, in contrast to schools founded by the Society of Friends or other denominations that welcomed a female ministry. Andover's November Club, founded in 1889 with much help from Philena McKeen, Annie Sawyer Downs, Emily Means, and other Abbot women, had a "Social Science Department," a serious study group that held prepared monthly discussions on issues of government, law, politics, money, and banking and presented one program a year to the full membership. Agnes Park, and later teachers Rebekah Chickering and Katherine Kelsey, took turns as chairmen of the Social Science Department through 1907; indeed, most of Abbot's teachers were founding members or officers of the November Club. One of the organization's first and most memorable events was a visit by Julia Ward Howe (later made an honorary member) during which she spoke of "woman suffrage in such a winning, womanly way as to rob the movement of half its terrors" (ms. History of the November Club, 1959). The Social Science Department ceased to exist after the passage of the XIXth Amendment in 1920, for most of its members had joined the League of Woman Voters.

52. *Courant* (January 1887), 25.

53. From speech by Asa Farwell at the Semicentennial, quoted in Mc-Keen, *Annals*, 170.

54. Undated letter but almost certainly spring 1892, Abbot Archives.

55. There was one woman of Philena McKeen's traditionalist faith who did become an ordained minister. Antoinette Brown completed the theological course at Oberlin in 1850, and though she and her one female classmate were refused permission to graduate with their class, a New York state parish admitted her to its pulpit in 1853. She lasted a year, being dismissed "at her own request" in 1854. (Quoted in Barbara M. Coleman article, *Notable American Women*.) She was an exception to the overwhelming exclusion of women from the traditional Protestant ministry. It is true that a few unordained women ministers preached to frontier congregations, and that sects which had traveled farthest from the conservative Congregationalists and Presbyterians of Andover Hill occasionally ordained women during the last half of the century. Abbot alumna Mary Hannah Graves, '58, became a Unitarian minister in 1871, the year Anna Howard Shaw received her license to preach to Methodist congregations. Many women served as Elders in the Society of Friends. But A.T.S. never had a woman student, and Andover Hill's Protestants would not even acknowledge Quakers or Unitarians as fellow Christians.

56. Quoted in J. Earl Thompson, Jr., "The Andover Liberals as Theological Educators," *Andover Newton Quarterly*, (March 1968), 8, No. 4, 209. Original quote from F. H. Foster, *The Life of Edwards Amasa Park* (New York, Fleming H. Revell, 1936).

57. Philena McKeen, letter to Mary Belcher, 29 November 1890.

58. The two men had published *Review* articles which, said the Visitors, were "not in harmony with sound doctrine as expressed in" the Seminary's original Creed with its stringent conditions for personal redemption, and its injunctions against Atheists, Infidels, Jews, Papists, Mohemetans, Arians, Pelagians, Antinomians, Socinians, Sabellians, Unitarians, and Universalists. (Andover Theological Seminary professors were obliged periodically to renew the oath in public.) Following the trial, Churchill was exonerated, but Smyth's answer that the Creed "may be adjusted to a larger knowledge and life than were open to its framers" (*The Andover Case*, Boston, Stanley and Usher, 1887—a 194-page hearing transcript—pp. xii, xxii) was not good enough for the

Visitors. He was formally removed from his Chair in Ecclesiastical History. Yet ultimately the Visitors and old soldier Park lost the war: Smyth's appeal to the Massachusetts Supreme Court took so long that the sound and fury had disappeared by the time his case had been referred back to the Visitors on technical grounds; he never actually stopped teaching. It was the proud, eloquent Park who found when the time came to write his final Book that the old doctrines interested practically no one anymore: "He had nothing to say," wrote Fuess, perhaps a bit harshly (p. 346). Fuess said of Park's career, "In retrospect, Professor Park seems to those who knew him to have been far greater than anything he ever did" (p. 319). Elizabeth Stuart Phelps was kinder. "He was unquestionably a genius," she wrote of him in his old age. "There is something sad and grand about his individualism, as there is about . . . the last king of a dynasty." (Phelps, *Chapters*, 38.)

59. Phelps, *Chapters*, 60.

60. Dawes, (Class of '70), *Speech*, 1921.

61. Douglas, *Feminization*, 149. Historian Ann Douglas describes Edwards Park as both a "superb scholar" and a master of "the sentimental appeal, which he endowed with an intellectual integrity and conviction it was seldom to display again." Park brought Protestantism "one step nearer to the feminine subculture it both courted and feared," writes Douglas (ibid., 148, 151). All the evidence we have suggests that the McKeen sisters brought Abbot forward to meet him.

62. One of the two class surveys we have, recorded by the historian of '87 in the "Literary Exercises," gives us these figures on seventeen Abbot students' opinions of the McKeen strictures. Cards: "5 for [in favor of playing cards], 2 against, the rest in moderation." Theatre: "10 for, 2 against, the rest in moderation." Dancing: "8 for, the rest do not dance." Drinking: "all but 3 have signed the temperance pledge." These students' church affiliations suggest the distribution of sects at Abbot: 10 were Congregationalist, 3 Presbyterian, 2 Baptist, one "New Church," and one undeclared.

63. Letter to Mrs. Draper, 24 August 1888.

64. Dawes, *Speech*, 1921.

65. See *Courant* (June 1885), 30.

66. Emily Means, '68, in *McKeen Memorial*.

67. J. P. Taylor, *Draper Memorial*, 7.

68. Ezra Abbot to Draper, 9 January 1875, Cambridge.

69. Sklar, *Beecher*, 82.

70. Taylor, *Draper Memorial*, 7.

71. Letter, 16 March 1864.

72. The Andover Press and Bookstore closed in 1866, and Draper took the business downtown, a better site in any case for his reform activities.

73. Into his house Draper built the first bathroom in the town of Andover, and fitted it with a copper bathtub.

74. Sklar, *Beecher*, 78.
75. Ibid.
76. In *The Western World, or Travels in the United States*, (1849), I, 134–135.
77. Volume I, No. 12.
78. *Courant* (January 1890), 29.
79. Welter, in Gordon, *Family*, 226.
80. Abbot Catalogue 1873–74, p. 21.
81. K. T. Griesinger (1858) in Handlin, *America*, 262.
82. Chapell, Journal (4 January 1874), 8.
83. Ibid. (25 January 1874), 33–34.
84. Taft, in Paradise, *Men*, 202.
85. Student Journal, 1861.
86. Helen M. Copeland to Phebe and Philena McKeen, 15 April 1879, Abbot Archives. Mrs. Copeland suffered through a marriage with a "professing Christian . . . whose conscience and religious education" turned out to have been "entirely neglected." This did not trouble her at first, for "my delight was in his smile and favor, to gain which I often sacrificed my faith and duty." Finally, at age 33, mother of five children and "feeling utterly wretched and helpless, I gave up my will into His hands, crying 'Lord, save or I perish'. . . . And in that hour I was healed, body and soul!" Though her husband and children "resisted and rejected that blessed Master" for over a year, she won them to Christ at last, showing them that it was no longer enough to "live for self." Thus did the McKeens help to inspire a conversion in one who had long since left the Family.
87. See *Theodora*, 198–199.
88. James McLachlan describes the appeal of the boys' boarding schools which assumed the religious functions of the ideal nineteenth-century family (*Boarding School*, 134). Vassar College in its early advertisements made certain to refer to its students and teachers collectively as "the family."
89. Kett, *Rites*, 116.
90. E. S. Phelps Ward, quoted in Fuess, *New England School*, 319.
91. Marion Park, *Speech*, 1938.
92. Marginal notes facing p. 2 of the *Syllabus*, published by Warren Draper (Andover, 1879).
93. See Eleanor Flexner, *Century of Struggle; The Woman's Rights Movement in the United States* (New York, Atheneum, 1973), 220. Flexner's Quaker forbears were heavily involved with women's rights. Sarah Grimke in *The Equality of the Sexes and the Condition of Women* (Boston, 1838), 9–10, asserted that the Scriptures were not divine; instead, they "reflected the agricultural, patriarchal society which produced them." Such relativism appalled the Congregationalists and other Protestant conservatives of the time.

94. Clipping pasted in Church History *Syllabus*, p. 23.
95. *Courant* (December 1880), 20.
96. Ibid. (June 1890), 37; (June 1881), 26.
97. Phelps, *Chapters*, 42. It is interesting that the Seminary liberals eventually gained enough strength and support to found South End House in Boston in 1891.
98. ELA, '87, in *Courant* (June 1887), 22.
99. Letter, 22 January, 1879.
100. A characterization found repeatedly in news articles (see *Boston Advertiser and Congregationalist*) after 1875.
101. In Park, *Speech*, 1938, Marion Park told of her Aunt Agnes' gradual repudiation of the Congregationalist Phillips Academy Church; it is possible that Miss McKeen went to Episcopal services with Agnes, who was a close friend. Agnes Park's explanation, according to Marion Park: "she was tired of being told for seventy years how to be a good boy and had decided to leave the Academy Chapel." Interestingly, Both Harriet Beecher Stowe and her sister Catharine became Episcopalians toward the ends of their lives.
102. Changes in Abbot's charter reflect this shift, which continued after Miss McKeen's retirement. In 1838 the Trustees and the General Court substituted for the stricture that all Trustees be "professors of the religion of the Congregational or Presbyterian denomination" the requirement that they be *"professors of Religion of some Evangelical denomination a Majority of whom shall be Trinitarian Congregationalists."* Thus Baptists and Methodists could be included. By 1902 the wording had changed again: "At least two-thirds [of the 12 member board] shall be members of some evangelical church." Finally, in 1941, "any provision as to church membership or other qualification heretofore established" was "expressly revoked."
103. John Phelps Taylor's address to the Class of 1891.
104. *Courant* (February 1876), 36; (November 1878), 32, (November 1876), 35–36.
105. See paper given by Barbara Welter at the Third Berkshire Conference, 10 June 1976, "Defenders of the Faith: Novels of Nineteenth Century Religious Controversy"; also Douglas, *Feminization*, Chapter III, "The Domestication of Death," especially pages 200–207.
106. McKeen, *Annals*, xvi, xvii.
107. Letter, 31 August 1890.
108. *Andover Townsman*, 20 April 1898.
109. Professor Churchill in *McKeen Memorial*, 13.
110. Alumna letter, "F.S.P."; quoted in *The Abbot Bulletin* (April 1931), 26–29.
111. Darwin himself was conservative enough about women. In the section on Sexual Selection in *The Descent of Man*, he wrote: "The chief distinction in the intellectual powers of the two sexes is shown by man's

attaining to a higher eminence, in whatever he takes up, than can woman—whether requiring deep thought, reason, or imagination, or merely the use of the senses and hands. . . . We may also infer, from the law of the deviation from averages, so well illustrated by Mr. Galton in his work on 'Hereditary Genius,' that if men are capable of a decided pre-eminence over women in many subjects, the average of mental power in man must be above that of woman." And two paragraphs later, "These . . . faculties . . . will have been developed in man, partly through sexual selection,—that is, through the contest of rival males, and partly through natural selection,—that is, from success in the general struggle for life. . . . It is, indeed, fortunate that the law of equal transmission of characters in both sexes prevails with mammals; otherwise it is probable that man would have become as superior in mental endowment to woman as the peacock is in ornamental plumage to the peahen." Quoted in Ruth Hubbard, "Sexism in Science," *Radcliffe Quarterly*, 62, No. 1 (March 1976), 10.

112. *Courant* (January 1881), 16.
113. Quoted in McKeen, *Annals*, 183.
114. *Courant* (January 1881), 18.
115. Stowe, *Chimney Corner*, 108.
116. *Thornton Hall*, 261.
117. Massachusetts passed a law allowing women attorneys to practice in 1882. There were 9,015 woman physicians and surgeons in the U.S. in 1910. The number of patents taken out by women increased from 965 in the decade ending in 1865 to 21,784 in the period 1886–1894. There were fifteen professional nursing schools in 1880 with 157 graduates and thirty-five in 1890 with 471 graduates. In 1880 the total number of women employed was 14.7 percent of the female population; in 1890, 17.4 percent. Wages and salaries ranged from 40 to 80 percent of men's pay for the same work.
118. *Courant* "Editors' Drawer" (January 1875), 27.
119. *Courant* (November 1873), 39. Prudence Palfrey also contrasts sadly with Aldrich's resourceful boy urchins in *Story of a Bad Boy* and even with the Irish cook in *A Rivermouth Romance*. It was all right to be an eccentric woman if you were a foreigner.
120. Quoted in a speech by Marguerite Hearsey at the 125th Anniversary, 8 May 1954.
121. Speech reported in the *Marysville Daily Appeal*, 26 April 1878, Abbot Archives. Mary Belcher's statistics may have come from Catharine Beecher's informal survey of American women.
122. *Courant* (June 1879), 7.
123. *Courant* (January 1884), 17.
124. Quoted in Handlin, *America*, 244.
125. Marion Park, *Speech*, 1938.
126. Letter to Treasurer Nathaniel Swift, 9 March 1875.

127. MPK, '84, in *Courant* (June 1882), 21.
128. Henrietta Learoyd Sperry, in *Courant* (June 1892), 8.
129. Semicentennial speech of President Paul A. Chadbourne of Williams College (Abbot parent), quoted in McKeen, *Annals*, 224.
130. Ibid.
131. See McLachlan, *Boarding School*, 189–218, and Kett, *Rites*, 183–189. McLachlan dates this change about a decade earlier than Kett; the difference seems to be a function of McLachlan's concentration on developments in the private education for boys.
132. Kett, *Rites*, 231.
133. Ibid., 102, 111, 137, 143, 152.
134. Ibid., 138.
135. Between 1870 and 1910 the number of positions in the service sector and the professions increased fourfold from 230,000 to 1,150,000, while manufacturing jobs were two and a half times greater (2,250,000 to 6,300,000).
136. In return, the sisters wrote hundreds of encouraging, interested letters to alumnae, and welcomed them warmly back at the school. "My dear little schoolmistress" one of Phebe's letters to Julia Twichell, '79, began, and went on to bring comfort and sympathy to this young graduate much tried by her job in a district school. (Manuscript of a talk by Katherine Kelsey, 28 February 1932.)
137. Emily Means, *McKeen Memorial*.

III. Forth and Back, 1885–1912

7. EXPANSION

1. For example, Vassar admitted girls fifteen years of age and older.
2. Or, as a speech given by college president R. H. Jesse in 1896 was entitled, "What Constitutes a College and What a Secondary School?" The question was still a live one in 1896, even though the Report of the Committee of Ten, which both Jesse and Commissioner W. T. Harris helped to write, had been in circulation over two years, supposedly settling the matter. Jesse asserted that "the chief aim of the private secondary school is to get students ready for college, its subordinate aim to fit them for life," a conclusion that the Abbot faithful were doing their best to disprove. See Sizer, *Secondary Schools*, 34.
3. U.S. Commissioner of Education, *Reports*, 1889–90, II, 746.
4. Letter, July 1877, Abbot Archives. Miss McKeen's new salary was $1100, Miss Phebe's, $900. The salaries were actually somewhat larger, since both women received room and board, considered to be worth $200–300 per person. Miss Johnson's salary was later reduced to $2500,

a match of that awarded Phillips Academy's Bancroft in 1873 and still a handsome sum for a woman educator.

5. *Courant* (June 1877), 4.
6. Semicentennial program, transcript, unpaginated, Abbot Archives.
7. The charts contained in the U.S. Commissioner of Education's annual *Reports* comparing curricular offerings and facilities (libraries, observatories, etc.) at leading women's schools and colleges are excellent sources for the reader concerned with Abbot's place in the realm of secondary and higher education. Judged according to the Commissioner's criteria, Abbot's facilities in 1876 were superior to those of ninety-nine of the 147 degree-granting "colleges" on the Office of Education's list. Only twenty-five of the 147 had larger libraries. Just sixteen of all 225 colleges and seminaries had any income from endowment at all. (Median income for these endowed institutions was $900 per year. USCOE, *Reports*, 1876, 690–696.) Even after Abbot had disappeared from the list of institutions for the "higher education of women," comparison of curricular offerings (1889 *Reports*) suggests that Senior-Middle and Senior Abbot students read most of the same philosophy history and mathematics books as did upperclasswomen students at about half of the fifteen "leading colleges," including Albert Lea College in Minnesota, where Abbot's Principal-to-be, Laura Watson, was teaching in 1889. Bryn Mawr, Wellesley, Vassar, Smith, Radcliffe, and Barnard, however, were clearly offering more advanced work.
8. McKeen, letter to Trustees, 24 April 1879.
9. Ibid., 13 November 1879.
10. Quoted in Handlin, *America*, 100.
11. Abby Wood Collins letter.
12. McKeen, *Report*, 15 January 1884.
13. See McKeen Scrapbook, p. 93, *Boston Journal* article of 1885.
14. McKeen, *Sequel*, 7.
15. Quotes from letters written by alumnae in 1879 to Phebe and Philena McKeen. The letters are overwhelmingly discouraged and discouraging.
16. Letter to Miss McKeen, 10 June 1884.
17. Indeed, Miss McKeen disliked any traveling beyond her familiar haunts. "How does a body go from Andover to Burlington, and when does she get there, if no evil befalls her?" Miss McKeen asked her teacher-friend Emma Meacham in a letter written 25 April 1879. See also *McKeen Memorial*.
18. Means, in *McKeen Memorial;* McKeen, *Sequel*, 8.
19. Commencement was nostalgia itself, as can be seen on pages 26–27 of *Courant* (November 1878), "Soliloquy of an Old Scholar":

> I see the long procession
> Still passing to and fro;

The Juniors hot and restless,
The Seniors subdued and slow.

And a mist obscures my vision;
And a sigh escapes my heart.

Alas! among these numbers
I have no lot, nor part.

Luckily, merry class parties and reunions always followed this teary occasion.

20. McKeen, *Sequel*, 10.
21. Ibid., 13, 14.
22. Ibid., 14.
23. Ibid., 18.
24. Phelps, *Chapters*, 56.
25. Miss McKeen, letter to Warren and Irene Draper, July 1888.
26. *Courant* (January 1891), 4.
27. *Courant* (January 1889), 8.
28. McKeen, *Sequel*, 21.
29. Ibid., 23.
30. Ibid.
31. Ibid., 26.
32. Mr. Richardson, the architect, quoted in McKeen, *Sequel*, 31.
33. Rosamond Randall Beirne, *Let's Pick the Daisies: The History of the Bryn Mawr School, 1885–1967* (Baltimore, Maryland, 1970), 17.
34. Phelps, *Chapters*, 14.
35. Letter to the Trustees, 6 November, 1891.
36. *Courant*, editors (June 1892), 45.
37. *Bulletin* (April 1926), 17.
38. Trustees' Memorial Minute written by Bertha Bailey at Miss Watson's death, 5 December 1924.
39. *Courant* (January 1875), 27.
40. All figures on alumnae before 1871 are approximate, because records were incomplete until the Alumnae Association was organized in spite of prodigious efforts made after 1871 to learn about early alumnae.
41. When the political world began to take interest in Calvin Coolidge, a friend wrote Miss Watson asking her about him, for he had been her contemporary at St. Johnsbury Academy. She replied that she had not known him well. He was "occupied solely with his Latin and Greek, in which branches he was rather weak." Letter to Catherine Sandford, October 1920.
42. Arthur Drinkwater, Phillips Academy Class of '96, in conversation, 28 December 1976. Drinkwater knew Miss Watson through his mother, who had been her roommate at Mt. Holyoke, as well as by her reputation on Andover Hill during his four years as a student at Phillips. She came often to visit the Drinkwater family, and in that easy setting

he found her "friendly" and good humored. Mary Byers Smith, '04, reports that her brother at age sixteen was one of Miss Watson's favorite companions on her frequent geology field trips. Many of Miss Watson's woman associates recognized and admired her drive, but remember her as being rather reserved, except with close friends.

43. See Kathryn K. Sklar, "The Founding of Mount Holyoke Seminary— A Case Study in The History of Female Education in New England, 1790–1837," unpublished paper.

44. See Sizer, *Secondary Schools*, 34.

45. *Courant* (June 1879), 5, 6. Anna Dawes was a particularly colorful alumna. As a U.S. Senator's daughter and hostess she knew and reveled in state affairs during her long residence in Washington. She wrote many magazine articles, served as trustee of Smith College 1889–1896, and back at home in her native Massachusetts became a director of the state Child Labor Commission and the Massachusetts Prison Association. She was also President of the Abbot Academy Alumnae Association from 1910 to 1914.

46. The cost of Bradford's inertia is suggested by its enrollment figures around the turn of the century. The student body declined from 107 in 1898 to 48 in 1901, when Bradford announced a college preparatory course, adding it to its five-year course much as Abbot had done ten years earlier. After this, enrollments climbed again. In 1920, the College Preparatory and the "Junior College" course had equal numbers, but by 1932 the Junior College students so outnumbered College Preparatory students that Bradford applied for a Junior College charter, and Abbot took Bradford's place as New England's oldest incorporated boarding school for girls.

47. Quoted in Sizer, *Secondary Schools*, 55.

48. Quoted in David Tyack, ed., *Turning Points in American Educational History* (Waltham, Ginn-Blaisdell, 1967), 375.

49. Harvard's admissions figures for 1889 are instructive: of 352 students admitted only 97 (27 percent) had prepared at public high schools. Twenty-three of the thirty public schools from which this minority came were New England institutions.

50. National Education Association, *Report of the Committee of Ten on Secondary School Studies, with the Reports of the Conferences Arranged by the Committee* (New York, 1894), 63–64, 73–74, 90–91, 163, 175.

51. Alice Whitney in conversation with Helen Eccles, 8 April 1977.

52. Quoted from the Committee of Ten *Report*, 1893, in Sizer, *Secondary Schools*, 117.

53. Eleanor Thomson Castle, interview, 18 June 1974.

54. See Sizer, *Secondary Schools*, 45–47.

55. Report on Thanksgiving 1892 by editors in *Courant* (January 1893), 44.

56. Schedule for 1892–1893 as described in *Courant:*
    Up 6:30, breakfast 7:00
    Silent Hour 7:45–8:15 (meditation)
    8:30 to Hall for prayers
    Classes till 3:30 then walks to Indian Ridge,
      Sunset Rock with study afterwards.
    5:30 dinner.
    "half hour" meditation, then study till 9.
    Lights out at 10.
57. *Courant* (January 1898), 42.
58. Laura Watson, Report to the Trustees for 1893–94.
59. William James, *Psychology* (New York, Henry Holt, 1892)—a 478-page abridgment of the monumental *Principles of Psychology* which James himself made for college use, adding chapters on the physiology of the senses.
60. Ibid., 1, 3.
61. Ibid., 189–216.
62. Ibid., 467.
63. Private school attendance began declining in 1894 after years of steady rise in enrollments. The average school lost 10 percent of its enrollment a year from 1895 to 1898, when applications began rising again.
64. Miss McKeen had alerted the Trustees to the gravity of these problems in a letter to the Trustees, 16 June 1891: "The evil was serious and many rooms were unfit for use. The same persons are unwilling to risk their health and comfort there another season. The supply of hot water was quite insufficient. Bathing in tubs had to be given up for the most part till warm weather." Little could be done, however, to permanently remedy the situation at the time.
65. The Trustees also did their part to help Miss Watson deal with troublesome "Cads" and their relations with the Abbot students. Noting "certain matters of discipline and conduct" with which they felt Dr. Bancroft should be dealing, they appointed a Trustee committee to talk with him and Mr. Hardy of the Phillips Board. Was it just the ordinary refusal of Andover Hill's boys and girls to stay in their assigned spheres, or something special? (*Minutes*, 14 February 1894.) Arthur Drinkwater, only surviving member of the Phillips Class of 1896, remembers a decorous form of panty raid which the "Cads" made once every spring during his four years at Phillips Academy in defiance of all attempts to foil it: large numbers of "Cads" crept through the Grove or climbed the fence on a Wednesday washday and stole all the girls' clothes off the clothesline. The clothes would eventually be returned with equal stealth to odd places on the Abbot campus. This could have been the problem these dignified gentlemen were addressing. On the other hand, a fire was set in vacant Smith Hall at

about this time, and the special committee may have been a response to that.

66. See Laura Watson's reports to the Trustees, 1893–1897.
67. One result of the increase in day students was a sharp rise in the numbers of Abbot-Phillips sister-brother pairs to about a dozen a year through the 1890's.
68. Conversation, 29 April 1977.
69. McKeen, *Sequel*, 160. Perhaps because of this pressure, College Preparatory students were not recognized as graduating Seniors at Commencement time until 1899.
70. From M. B. Ripley's lecture in the Town of Andover course, 1941.
71. Kelsey, *Sketches*, 51.
72. Henrietta Learoyd, '68, later Henrietta Sperry, taught five years in the 1870's, serving as acting Principal the year the McKeen sisters went abroad. She was elected Trustee of Abbot Academy in 1892.
73. In *Education* (March 1894), quoted in Sizer, *Secondary Schools*, 153.
74. "Literary Exercises," 1887.

8. FUTURES

1. *The American Mind*, quoted in Lawrence Cremin, *The Transformation of the School: Progressivism in American Education, 1876–1957* (New York, Knopf, 1961), 90.
2. *Courant* (June 1911), 6.
3. Undated letter to "Mary." As Abbot record-keeper and historian Jane Carpenter put it in a letter to Markham Stackpole, 1 November 1922, Miss Means "was not especially careful herself about dates." This carelessness hampers writers of footnotes, if no one else.
4. Harriet Martineau, quoted in Woody, *History*, II, 8, had observed in 1836 that American women were "free to engage in only seven occupations, teaching, needlework, keeping boarders, working in cotton mills, book binding, type-setting, and housework." Woody comments that exceptions could be found to this statement, but finds it essentially valid. For fifty years after this, men preferred not to notice the women who did achieve distinction. Of 633 entries in *Appleton's Cyclopedia of American Biography* (published in 1886), nineteen describe women.
5. In 1910, 19 percent of college professors were women, 93 percent of nurses, 79 percent of librarians and one percent of lawyers and clergy.
6. Edward Sanford Martin, *The Unrest of Women* (New York, Appleton, 1913), 5; first serialized by Curtis Publishing Co. in 1912.
7. Barbara Cross, ed., *The Educated Woman in America: Selected Writings of Catharine Beecher, Margaret Fuller, and M. Carey Thomas* (New York, Teachers College Press, 1965), 38.
8. Cremin, *Transformation*, 89.

9. Beirne, *Daisies*, 26.
10. From *American Traits*, Professor Hugo Munsterberg, quoted in USCOE, *Report* (1900–01), 1299–1300.
11. Dobkin, ed., MCT, Unpublished journal, 2 January 1872, and 8 January 1871.
12. Cross, *Educated Woman*, 34. A visit to Vassar in the early 1880's when Dean-elect Thomas was collecting ideas for the organizing of Bryn Mawr only confirmed her earlier images. To her adult eye, Vassar looked like no more than a "glorified boarding school." Smith was a little sounder, having better teachers than Vassar, thought Carey Thomas. (Finch, *Carey Thomas*, 47.)
13. Quoted in Beirne, *Daisies*, 3.
14. Quoted by Dobkin in a talk given at the Third Berkshire Conference of Woman Historians, 10 June 1976.
15. E. Clarke, in "Sex in Education," USCOE, *Reports*, (1900–01), 1276–1277. See also article by M. C. Thomas, "Present Tendencies in Women's College and University Education," *Educational Review* (1908), 64–85, excerpted in Cross, *Educated Woman*, 162.
16. Quoted in Cross, *Educated Women*, 36.
17. *Godey's Lady's Book*, April 1870.
18. Helen Ekin Starrett, *After College What? For Girls* (Boston, Thomas Y. Crowell, 1896), 5–27; see also "What Becomes of College Women?" *North American Review* (1895), 546–553.
19. "Professor Moore" (no first name given), quoted in *Bulletin* (February 1960), 11.
20. See *Courant* (June 1896), 24.
21. Joseph Gilpin Pyle in "Should Women Vote?", quoted in Lois W. Banner, *Women in Modern America* (New York, Harcourt Brace Jovanovich, 1974), 89.
22. *Courant* (January 1907), 35. A Miss Bissel rang changes on the same theme at an assembly held 30 January 1904, adding this further argument:

    > Only a small proportion of women are well educated, and if the ballot were granted (to women) it would simply increase the number of ignorant voters, while the vote of the colored women in the South would double the troubles of the government. *Courant* (June 1904), 31.

23. Interview with Mary Byers Smith, '04, 15 April 1975.
24. True, Abbot alumnae benefited, as did all women, from the "feminization of teaching" that drove men from the profession as the century wore on. We have already seen how cynical were many schoolboard members' motives in hiring women teachers for the subsistence wages men refused. By midcentury a penny-pinching Massachusetts school committee was even screening women for a superintendency, explaining that "As there is neither honor nor profit connected with this

position, we see no reason why it should not be filled by a woman."
Quoted in Woody, *History*, I, 516.

25. These and other statistics in this section were derived as follows: For
the earliest period (1829–92), a random sample of 500 was drawn from
the 2741 alumnae files. For the later period (1893–1912), I and my student research assistants used a larger sample (one in three folders) for
alumnae occupations. To obtain data on husbands' occupations, we
checked every folder from 1893 to 1912, and in addition cross-checked
Phillips Academy records wherever there was a Phillips-Abbot or
A.T.S.-Abbot marriage. Where the expression "all alumnae" is used,
the information given has been obtained from a direct count from the
1913 Catalogue, not from a sample of folders. One must still be wary
of any tabulation of occupations. Social scientists have found that the
same individual is likely to describe his or her occupation differently
at different times (See Michael B. Katz, "Occupational Classification in
History," *Journal of Interdisciplinary History* [Summer 1972]). For
example, a college professor may call herself a "teacher" in one questionnaire, a "scholar" in another, a "professor" in a third. A small contractor may say he is a businessman but may also call himself an
"artisan," a "carpenter," or simply "self-employed." We have used
four occupational categories similar to those Katz employs in his 1970
study of Hamilton, Ontario, in classifying occupations according to a
simple income and social status hierarchy. Two further difficulties for
the Abbot historian are that some alumnae did not return the questionnaire, and only 227 out of a sample of 327 married alumnae filled
in the answer to the question on "husband's occupation." We tried to
get reliable figures on parent occupations in order to see whether
these showed social mobility by way of an Abbot education or through
marriage from "lower" to "higher" status, but the data here was so
incomplete that no conclusions could be drawn about Abbot Academy's capacity to confer increased status and social eligibility on potential brides. At the least, one can surmise from 1890–1913 figures
that an Abbot education did not *lower* social status for eligible women.
The overwhelming majority of fathers had to be fairly wealthy to
send daughters to Abbot after 1890. (A number of studies of private
school families suggest that family income must ordinarily be at least
ten times the tuition if the parents are to consider private school for
their children. Abundant scholarship aid can alter this picture somewhat—but not much.) And over 80 percent of Abbot alumnae married
into income and status groups similar to those comprising the parent
group for 1892–1913 as a whole.

26. 18 June 1879. At the Semicentennial celebration, Trustee-Professor
Edwards Park remarked that "it is natural for a young divine to be
attracted to a scholarly woman; 179 such cases have occurred in An-

dover since the founding of Abbot Academy." This is much lower than the 25 percent derived from a direct count. We assume from the context that Park was referring to the number of alumnae who married Andover Theological Seminary students or graduates.

27. Mary R. Kimball, '43, to Phebe McKeen, 15 March 1879.

28. Title of lecture at Abbot, 22 January 1916.

29. This is what Kate Wiggin says about Abbot in her autobiography, *My Garden of Memory* (Boston, Houghton Mifflin, 1923), 53: "I, still 'uneducated,' strange to say, having sipped momentarily at five founts of learning, was left behind for six months at Abbot Academy, Andover, Massachusetts, one of the best boarding schools for girls in New England. I was a sore trial to the Faculty for I was, in a manner of speech, a senior in Literature, a junior in French and Latin, a sophomore in Grammar, a freshman in History, and a poor risk for the preparatory department in Mathematics! It was a good atmosphere for a girl; simply and sincerely religious, refined and gracious in its social life. Punctuality, decorum, studious habits, good manners and speech, obedience to rules—these were all presupposed and they actually existed."

30. 1892 figures. By 1894 when Mrs. Brown's term ended, membership had more than doubled.

31. Numbers of these late brides, about whom the tradionalist women's magazines fretted so, may simply have been following Miss Phebe's advice to choose a husband with the greatest care. Divorce was legally difficult and socially devastating, though more frequent all the time. The divorce rate doubled in the fifteen years after 1890.

32. Abbot Alumnae files, *Before 1900* section.

33. See Abbot *Bulletin*, May 1936.

34. "Octave Thanet" took "Octave" from her Abbot Academy roommate, named Octave, and "Thanet" from a message written on a freight car. She wrote fifteen books and many stories and articles under her penname.

35. "Blythe Halliday's Voyage," in Anna Fuller, *A Bookful of Girls* (New York, G. P. Putnam & Sons, 1905), 62.

36. *Courant* (January 1897), 49.

37. George McMichael, *Journey to Obscurity: The Life of Octave Thanet* (Lincoln, University of Nebraska Press, 1965), 38.

38. Alice French to Anna Dawes, 4 July, 1868, quoted ibid., 39.

39. From E. S. Phelps, *The Silent Partner* (1871), quoted in Parrington, *Main Currents*, 62.

40. Review of article "The English Workingman," in *Lippincott's*, probably April 1879, McKeen Scrapbook, 54.

41. Alice French, *The Man of the Hour*, by Octave Thanet, pseud. (New York, Grosset & Dunlop, 1905), 437.

9. "A NEW ENGLAND ARISTOCRAT"

1. Letter to author from Dorothy Bigelow Arms, '11, 4 December 1975.
2. Interview, Mary Byers Smith, '04.
3. Ibid.
4. Miss Means could find plenty of outside support for her disdain of "useless degree-getting," as M. B. Smith terms her attitude. It is quite likely that she knew the opinions of G. Stanley Hall, the "father of modern psychology" (a designation of approval or opprobrium, depending on one's point of view) whose work was becoming as influential as that of his fellow university president and intellectual adversary, Charles W. Eliot. Hall in his widely read *Adolescence* (1904) declared that college preparation standards "as now enforced, are almost an unmitigated curse to high schools"; they have imposed a "uniformity" that is "dear to the inert mind." Because of them, schools have changed in fundamental ways. "There is no more wild, free, vigorous growth of the forest, but everything is in pots or rows like a rococo garden" (pp. 508–514). All gatherings of educators end in anxious discussion of the technicalities of college admission, protested Hall. Secondary school textbooks are written by college professors; courses and methods, and even sports and student life are "made at Harvard or Yale" (p. 520). Hall declared that the secondary school "should primarily fit for nothing, but should exploit and develop to the uttermost all the powers, for this alone is liberal education" (p. 525). All pages are of the 1916 reprinting of *Adolescence: Its Psychology, Anthropology, Sociology, Sex, Crime, Religion and Education*, 2 Vols. (New York, D. Appleton).
5. Six of the thirty first CEEB exam readers were women, including Helen Jackson, Abbot '95, B.A. Mt. Holyoke, 1900, who took part in the readings for 1901, held at Columbia University.
6. Quoted by Banner, *American Women*, 38.
7. Although there was puffery in Abbot's claim that the final two years of its Academic Course equaled the first two years of the best colleges, there was no doubt about the requirement that students entering this two-year course come with high school diploma in hand. An able student could find challenging work at the "Academy." One young woman (Mary Katherine Woods, '05) studied a year at Abbot *after* a year at Mt. Holyoke, and became a prominent journalist soon after her graduation.
8. Interview, Mary Byers Smith.
9. Trustee Minutes, 19 June 1899.
10. Interview, Alice Sweeney, '14.
11. *Courant* (January 1923), 27.
12. E. A. Means, letter to Burton S. Flagg (undated).
13. Jews "would not be admitted to the best Saratoga hotels, not even

were they the Rothschilds in person. In the land of democracy . . . I would have thought such restrictions fantastic. However, these were the facts," wrote Italian traveler Carlo Gardini in 1891, quoted in Handlin, *America*, 349.

14. M. C. Thomas, press release to the *Baltimore American*, 1890, quoted in Beirne, *Daisies*, 6.

15. Barbara Moore Pease, '11, letter (undated, 1975). A graduate of the Means years tells of a Senior who got on the train for New York and home as usual, but disembarked at New Haven to visit a young male friend for two days. Parents and Principal were frantic; once found, the young woman was suspended for spring term. However, Miss Means allowed her to graduate with her class, and won admiration for her fairness thereby, as well as gratitude from the Senior's family, to whom Emily Means had shown great compassion.

16. Recollections of Mildred Bryant Kussmaul, '13.

17. Ibid.

18. Interview, Mary Byers Smith, confirmed in Castle interview.

19. Quotations from a letter written by Delight Gage, '01, to Miss Hearsey about the Abbot Hall portrait of Miss Means, painted at last in 1954 from a photograph, since she would allow none to be painted from life.

20. M. B. Smith, *Courant* (June 1929), 12.

21. Emily Means's summer island was more than a refuge. It was a place where she could exercise her talent for design on the building of her two houses, and generally live a life uncluttered by social pressures. Local people admired her independence; they enjoyed the unusual sight of a diminutive woman rowing her guests between island and shore. Their attitude and Miss Means's sense of humor are wonderfully expressed in Mary Byers Smith's favorite Means story, passed on to her by Emily Means herself:

> Miss Means and Miss Root often used to stay together on her island in Maine. At one time they had Mr. Downs, the music teacher, visiting them. It was a very cold day, and they had given him a shawl and left him standing with the shawl on the point. A few days later, two fishermen spoke to her. "Miss Means," they said, "we were out on our boat the other day and we saw something strange that you had put over there on the point. We rowed ourselves up a little closer and a little closer, and we was saying, 'She's got her a scarecrow on the island.' Finally we got up close to the point and we saw what it was and we says to ourselves, 'Them women has made themselves a *man!*'"

22. M. B. Smith, *Courant* (June 1929), 12, 13.

23. Interview, A. C. Sweeney.

24. Interviews with Mary Byers Smith, '04, Mildred Bryant Kussmaul, '13, and Constance Parker Chipman, '06. On the other hand, younger alum-

nae remember her vividly as a patient, competent assistant principal. She seems to have become a more effective math teacher with age. (Letter from Cynthia James Tharaud, '32, among other sources.)

25. Jane Carpenter in *Annals of the Alumnae Association*, quoted in Carpenter, *Abbot*, 309.

26. Constance Chipman, interviewed by B. Floe and Margot Kent, '75.

27. Flagg reported in the 5 June 1931 Treasurer's report (p. 4) that "the enclosed letter was recently discovered inside of the chimney in the basement of Draper Homestead":

> Andover, Mass.,
> November 29, 1899
>
> My Dear Nephew,
>   If anything should happen to me whereby I should not be able to give information you will find the Academy account books and other valuable papers down cellar in the back side of the brick closet by the furnace. Take a hook or big nail and stick it into one of the nail holes in the board next to the bottom one on the east side (outside) of the closet and pull towards the south. The board will slide and you will see an iron handle. Pull on that and you will find the papers.
>
> Yours
>
> W. F. Draper (Signed)

Draper was nothing if not thorough.

28. The Trustee Minutes contain Draper's carefully penned offer for this gift, (Minutes, 3 December 1902) as well as this characteristic dedication of one of the Drapers' many smaller gifts:

> Recognizing the Divine goodness and mercy that have followed us all the days of our life, and desiring to give some expression of our gratitude to the Lord for all his benefits, we have decided to celebrate the 54th anniversary of our marriage on this 24th day of May 1902, by a gift to Abbot Academy of $1000 for the founding of a Library Fund. . . . (June 24, 1902)
>
> Warren F. Draper
> Irene P. Draper

The Drapers donated over $80,000 to Abbot during WFD's lifetime. "Abbot Academy was his child," the Trustees wrote of Draper on his death (Minutes, 8 March 1905); "by [his] will he made her his heir," leaving $41,880 worth of printing equipment and hundreds of back copies of *Biblioteca Sacra*, unwanted by most of the world by the time Irene Draper died in 1916.

29. Quoted in *Courant* (June 1907), 8–19.

30. Taylor, Letter to E. A. Means, 21 June 1906.

31. See Trustees Minutes, 1901–04.

32. Not a simple result of the trial, but a symptom—as was the trial's

outcome—of the movement away from precise adherence to the old Congregationalist doctrines and toward the "Social Gospel," the active implementation of Christian principles through social service.

33. Paraphrased by Hall in *Adolescence*, 574. Hall records the opinions of twelve male physicians on the special health needs of young women and the abuse of health by college women to support and complement Thornton's view, and of one woman, Dr. Mary P. Jacobi, who disagrees, saying, "there is nothing in the nature of menstruation to imply the necessity or even the desirability of rest for a woman whose menstruation is really normal" (p. 586). He then proceeds to refute Jacobi by citing studies of "irregularity" among high school and college women, and pointing out that even these results are skewed in favor of the casual view of menstruation, since few college students will "increase the prejudice" against women's higher education by confessing weakness on a questionnaire (p. 589). Hall himself thought that girls should be instructed on menstruation by *married* instructresses in "a certain mystic and religious tone which should pervade all and make everything sacred" (p. 640). The ideal boarding school for girls from thirteen to twenty should schedule "monthly sabbaths of rest" at "this time of sensitiveness and perturbation" (p. 639).

34. Kett, *Rites*, 174–175.

35. Sara Burstall, citing the NEA inquiry of 1904, quoted in Tyack, *Turning Points*, 395–396.

36. The most vivid account of this incident was communicated to the writer by Barbara Moore Pease, '11, who was "Becca's" roommate.

37. In 1908, for example, no C.P. Seniors appeared in *The Tempest*, nor did any take part in *Twelfth Night* in 1911. One of the nine C.P. Seniors was a servant in the 1907 play; fourteen of the sixteen Academic Seniors made up the rest of the cast.

38. Frances Cutler Knickerbocker, '05, in *Bulletin* (February 1960), 10.

39. *Courant* (February 1905), 33–36.

40. Ibid., 7.

41. Interview, Helen Abbott Allen Anderson, '32.

42. Phillips Academy Trustee Minutes, 30 April 1900 and 14 May 1900.

43. Interview, Constance Chipman.

44. Interview, Ruth Newcomb, '10.

45. We are indebted to Barbara Brown Hogan, '40, for preserving her aunt's scrapbooks and lending them to us.

46. See letter from Father, 18 March 1907, Brown Scrapbook.

47. Letter to Mrs. Brown from Emily Means, 10 April 1909, Brown Scrapbook.

48. Written next to a theatre program offering "the Best in Vaudeville."

49. Here is most of the rest of the "slush."
        Darling,

As I sat here all alone trying to study, I could not make my mind stay on my book. It was always upstairs and wondering dear what you were doing, and when a little tap came at the window, my heart flew up in my mouth for I knew dearest by some little feeling way down in my heart that it was from you.

50. The Phillips Academy Catalogues for 1906–1908 list no J. W. Scott, nor is his name on any of the alumni lists. R. T. Tree, however, was a Scientific Course student in 1906–07, who graduated in 1910. Tree lived at a popular boarding house, "Mrs. Tree's" (perhaps one run by a relative—Tree himself came from Ithaca, N.Y.) and it is possible that J. W. Scott was boarder in the same house even though not a member of the Academy or the Theological Seminary. It also may be that Scott's name is missing from the lists because his stay at Phillips Academy was so short lived (for reasons that may already be evident).

51. June Wermers in conversation, 8 December 1976. She knew Miss Brown as teacher and dean during her four years as a student in Lawrence High School.

52. *Courant* (January 1912), 21.

53. Woody, *History*, II, 202.

54. From the Report to the Trustees of their Nominating Committee, John Alden, Burton Flagg, Donald Merriam, and Markham Stackpole.

55. Reverend John Calvin Goddard, Secretary, Maria H. Hotchkiss School Association, letter to M. Stackpole, 29 June 1911.

56. Mrs. Clara Martin Poynter, letter to M. Stackpole.

57. B. Bailey, letter to M. Stackpole, 18 September 1911.

IV. Against the Tide, 1912–1954

1. Joseph K. Hast, *A Social Interpretation of Education* (New York, 1929), quoted in Kett, *Rites*, 237.

2. Dewey, *Democracy and Education* (1916) and *The School and Society* (1899), quoted in Cremin, *Transformation*, 118, 124.

3. See U.S. Census figures from *Historical Statistics*, Series E, 135–166, 183–186, Consumer Price Index figures.

4. Sara Burstall, 1908, quoted in Tyack, *Turning Points*, 394.

5. See Paula S. Fass, *The Damned and the Beautiful: American Youth in the 1920's* (New York, Oxford University Press, 1977), 25.

6. Observations of Dr. Joseph Rice, 1892, quoted in Tyack, *Turning Points*, 315.

7. Interview, Mary Byers Smith.

8. Interview, E. T. Castle.

9. Observations of Peter A. Demens, a turn-of-the-century Russian visitor, and Giuseppe Giacosa (1908), quoted in Handlin, *America*, 335, 397.

10. THE LADIES STAND FAST

1. Kelsey, *Sketches*, 113.
2. B. Bailey, letter to Mr. Stackpole, 18 September 1911.
3. Evelyn M. Walmsley to Mr. Stackpole, Wellesley, Massachusetts, 31 August 1911.
4. As Marion Park put it (*Speech*, 1938), "Miss Bailey was the kind of person who . . . is perhaps most useful in the work of the world, because she took no time in establishing or underlaying her own position or her own contribution. All her time was put into the work itself."
5. Walmsley to Stackpole and Nominating Committee, 1912.
6. Interview, Mildred Bryant Kussmaul, also testimonial after Miss Bailey's death made in *Courant* (December 1935), 22, by Charlotte Morris Perot, '15. Miss Bailey "probed my soul . . . I was an open book to her—but she read that book with understanding and love."
7. B. Bailey, Chapel talk, 7 January 1917.
8. Ripley, lecture, 1941. See also letter of advice from outgoing Student Council president Eleanor Harryman to 1934–35 president Cecile Van Peursem: "Above all, don't try to keep anything from Miss Bailey. She'll find out anyway and it doesn't do any good."
9. Finch, *Carey Thomas*, 47–48.
10. Report to the Trustees, 22 February 1922, signed by Nellie M. Mason, Chairman, Alice C. Sweeney, Ruth E. Marceau, Ruth S. Baker, Dorothy Hopkins.
11. The Trustees' Minutes record an I.Q. ranking of new students for the fall of '26 as follows:

    Exceptionally High: 1
                  High: 29
                Normal: 33
                   Low: 16

    The faculty also administered placement tests for specific subjects, such as French, German, Math, and English grammar. In 1927 some entering students scored "almost zero" on the latter two. Bertha Bailey to the Trustees, October 1927.
12. B. Bailey to Markham Stackpole, 22 June 1911, introducing herself to the Abbot Trustees.
13. Undated speech, Abbot Archives.
14. Christmas sermon, 13 December 1914.
15. Kett, *Rites*, 196, 210.
16. Chapel talk, 27 January 1918.
17. Summary by Carpenter, *Abbot*, 18.
18. Quoted from the Pledge, Patriotic League.
19. *Courant* (June 1920), 28, 29.
20. Quoted in Abbot *Bulletin* (April 1932), 16.
21. The exact date and occasion for this speech are unidentified. The con-

text suggests it was given before some professional educators' association in winter or spring 1918.

22. Historian Lois Banner in *Women*, 137, demonstrates how broadly shared was this sense that "men (through their disastrous wars) were threatening to destroy the social order," and the women of the world must become the builders and the peacemakers.

23. Chapel talk on "Leadership," 27 January 1918 (Exodus 3:1–12, 4:1–12).

24. Fass, *The Damned*, 23.

25. B. Bailey, speech, "After Victory—What?" (undated).

26. A typical menu: Toasted and buttered English Muffins, cocoa, dark bread and butter, celery, cheese and baked apples. *Bulletin* (April 1926), 3.

27. The order in which this sermon (undated like many of Bertha Bailey's talks) appears in the files suggests that it was made *before* the XIX Amendment granting women suffrage was passed. It is the only evidence that Miss Bailey was Abbot's first suffragist principal.

28. Martin, *Unrest*, 26.   Some women of conservative Andover finally came around to founding a Suffrage League in 1913, following much polite debate. They rallied, they paraded (though quietly) through 1916, by which time most local leagues had combined with the National Association, the General Federation of Women's Clubs (a last hold-out), and numerous male Progressives and Wilsonian Democrats to push the XIX Amendment through Congress and the states.

29. Vida Scudder and Dorothy Dunbar Bromley, quoted in William H. Chafe, *The American Woman, 1920–1970* (New York, Oxford University Press, 1972), 92–93.

30. Memorial Minute, in *Trustee Minutes*, 23 October 1922.

31. In 1890 there were 10 divorces for each 100 marriage licenses issued; in 1924, 42.

32. Lewis Terman study, 1938.

33. Quoted in Banner, *Women*, 145. See also Christina Simmons, "Sexual Options of the New Woman: the New Sexuality of the 20's," paper given at the Third Berkshire Conference of Women Historians, Bryn Mawr College, 11 June 1976. Ms. Simmons describes the reification of psychoanalysis as a prime source of authority in intellectual discourse, the widespread use of Freudian terms, and the influence of newly reported investigations in the fields of biology and anthropology on the social expectations and behavior of educated Americans. Judge Ben Lindsey's *Companionate Marriage* (1927) was serialized for the masses in *Redbook* magazine. Far from being an energy-draining activity, as it was perceived to be in Victorian times, sexual expression was seen as increasing physical and psychic power. As Margaret Sanger put it in her widely read *Happiness in Marriage* (1926), "to be strongly sexed means that the life force can suffuse and radiate through the body and soul. It means radiant energy and force in every field of endeavor." Quoted in Simmons manuscript, p. 3.

34. See Fass, *The Damned*, 120–121, and chapter 6 in its entirety, "Sexual Mores in the World of Youth."

35. Many alumnae (a few still simmering) have described this practice. The most graphic account comes from Alexina Wilkins Talmadge, '22, whose aunt, wanting to send a bit of home food to her faraway niece, made her a whole box of beaten biscuits, a Southern specialty for an Alabama girl who missed Southern food. "I was called into the office and Miss Bailey said 'Now you have this package and we'll let you look at it to write and thank whoever sent it to you, but you can't have the food.' And I said, 'Well thank you very much. I hope the maids enjoy eating it.' . . . I don't know where I found the nerve to say that." (Interviewed by Beverly Floe, 19 June 1977.)

36. Interview, Frances Flagg Sanborn, 6 November 1976, and with teacher, 4 February, 1975.

37. *Courant* (January 1931), 56.

38. Interview, Constance Chipman.

39. Interview, M. B. Smith.

40. Letter to author, 16 April 1976.

41. Letter to author, 29 April 1976.

42. Published in 1907 and quoted in Cremin, *Transformation*, 109.

43. All quotes from talk on "Manners," undated, about 1923.

44. Letter to author from Cynthia James Tharaud, '32, 8 January 1976.

45. Alumna letter to Jane Carpenter, *Bulletin* (April 1932), 25.

46. *Courant* (January 1921), 33–34.

47. Fass, *The Damned*, 25.

48. Quoted in Carpenter, *Abbot*, 5.

49. Interview, Helen Allen (Henry) Anderson, '32.

50. Interview, Alan Blackmer, Phillips Academy English Department 1925–1968, Dean of Faculty 1955–1968; and letter to the author, John Barss, Phillips Academy Physics Department 1923–65, Chairman 1948–65.

51. Bertha Bailey reported proudly in a letter to anxious parents, 28 October 1927, that there would be no danger to Abbot students from the 1927 polio epidemic, in spite of four cases having developed at Phillips, because "There is ordinarily no communication between the students of the two schools. We will take further measures to prevent contacts between them."

52. The age of menarche had decreased about 4 months each decade since the 1850's when Abbot first began providing day-and-night supervision for girls and young women.

53. Quoted in Kett, *Rites*, 224. Puffer's book was published in 1912 and introduced by G. Stanley Hall.

54. Alfred E. Stearns, in *The Challenge of Youth* (Boston, W. A. Wilde, 1923), 159.

55. *Educational Review*, February 1914, quoted in Woody, *History*, I, 513. Male public school teachers were equally concerned for their image and their profession. "A boy needs forceful, manly control," read the

1904 report of the New York Male Teachers Association in justifying its proposal that all boys over ten be taught by men. In vain. Pressured by women's rights and Progressive lobbyists, New York equalized salaries for men and women teachers in 1920, and men nearly ceased applying to the New York system in protest or resentment.

56. See Claude M. Fuess's schoolboy novel, *The Andover Way* (Boston, Lothrop, Lee & Shepard, 1926), a marvelous story of virility gained.

57. Stearns, *Challenge*, 28.

58. Ibid., 128.

59. Ibid., 132.

60. Stearns, letter to Hopkins, 23 February 1931, Phillips Archives; also interview, Philip K. Allen, P.A. '29.

61. Among other sources, interview, George Sanborn, 6 November 1976. These games had been going on for some time before Phillips Academy teacher Sanborn began courting Frances Flagg, '26, during calling hours. Ruth Newcomb, '10, well remembers the high demand for the calling-parlor's only "bathtub," a window seat where you could sit right next to your caller until the chaperone noticed and shooed you into separate chairs.

62. *Courant* (February 1932), 3.

63. Interview with E. Barton Chapin, Jr., P.A. '36, 20 December 1976.

64. Phelps, *Chapters*, 25.

65. In 1924–1925, students came from 19 different states, China, Japan, Korea, and British Honduras. The New England states and New York continued to be most heavily represented.

66. Interview, Abby Castle Kemper, '31, 8 November 1976. Mrs. Alexina Wilkins Talmadge, '22, originally of Selma, Alabama, confirms the welcome afforded to the few deep South students who came to Abbot in her time.

67. According to Jane Sullivan, '31, Miss Bailey forbade admission to Lawrence day scholars for two years after a series of disturbances which Abbot girls created on the electric cars that ran south from Lawrence.

68. At the Trustees' meeting of 3 October 1930, Miss Bailey reported that the new "Hebrew student . . . seems happy and well-liked."

69. Helen Epler, '24, in *Bulletin* (April 1930), 15.

70. A few one-year C.P. alumnae dispute the welcome. Jane Sullivan, '31, remembers these students being considered "poison" at worst to the close, established school community. "At best you were just there," says Miss Sullivan. "The faculty were glad to have us because of the money," but they certainly didn't put themselves out for the one-year girls, whose main purpose was college preparation. (Interview, 19 February 1977.) A minority of faculty feared that one year was simply not enough for students to gain what Abbot had to offer, or to accustom themselves to the school's routine.

71. See especially E. B. Von Weber interview.

72. Miss Chickering became, if anything, more absent-minded with time. The Class of '29 elected her Secretary of the Navy in its Yearbook, because "she's so often in a fog." A famous tale of this era describes her walking past the Draper laundry chute on the way to Chapel, books in one hand, laundry in the other. Supposedly, she stopped, deposited her books in the laundry chute, and carried her laundry bag to the Chapel. This seems far-fetched, but several alumnae swear it's true, and one remembers seeing her in Chapel that day, holding her laundry bag in her lap. Interview, E. B. Von Weber.

73. In *Adolescence*, 562, 561, 589, 533, and 610, the chapter entitled "The Education of Girls." Hall's book was reprinted three times in its complete and abridged versions before its author's death in 1924. Kett (*Rites*, 228, 235), points out that Hall was most influential among parents and teachers, having founded the "child study" movement in the 1880's, and lectured to countless lay audiences, including the National Congress of Mothers in 1897, where he gave the major address. Psychologists like James, Dewey, and Thorndike grew skeptical of Hall, and largely ignored him.

74. Harriet Murdock Andersson, '17, letter to author, January 1976.

75. Undated speech cited above, note 13. See also *American Quarterly*, December 1975, special issue, "Victorian Culture in America," for an excellent general reference.

76. It was typical of Abbot faculty to hold off the use of an innovation like "intelligence" testing until it had been proven in other schools. Experimental "Progressive" schools—Dalton was one—and adventurous traditional shops such as the Bryn Mawr School had been testing students since the first decade of the century. By 1918 there were over 100 different standardized achievement tests available and several versions of mental ability tests. Americans' enthusiasm for the quantitative led to abuses almost immediately. For example, with the World War Army classification tests in mind, President George Cutten of Colgate stated in 1922 that only 15 percent of American youth had IQ's high enough to profit from college education.

77. Abbot played host to librarians' organizations for at least two conferences; as one of the most extensive libraries to be found in any girls' school, it was an appropriate and much appreciated site for meetings. By the mid-twenties the Abbot Library contained 6000 volumes, and Miss Hopkins' reputation had enlarged as well. She was President of the New England School Library Association for several years during her fourteen-year stay at Abbot, and in some demand as a lecturer on the educational uses of book, periodical, and painting collections. She left Abbot in 1934 to organize a teaching library at St. Paul's School, Concord, New Hampshire.

78. Miss Bailey's concern with behavior as the proof of learning suggests

she may have read the writings of psychologist Edward L. Thorndike as well as those of William James.

79. *Courant* (March 1918), 38.

80. Lucy Drummond, quoted in Carpenter, *Abbot*, 125.

81. Quotes from Kemper interview. Further data from brief talks with members of Classes of 1925, '26, and '27 at their 50th reunions. One 1928 graduate who went on to agricultural school says that Abbot prepared her well in chemistry and geology.

82. See Principal's Report, 1912–15.

83. Undated clipping in Bailey era scrapbook, unpaginated.

84. *Courant* (January 1922), 35.

85. Interview, Abby Kemper, '31.

86. Kathryn Whittemore Knight, '33, letter to "Dear Abbot Friends," 8 April 1949, Alumnae files.

87. *Bulletin* (April 1924), 6.

88. See Cremin, *Transformation*, 189.

89. *Bulletin* (April 1931), 9.

90. *Courant* (June 1929), 19.

91. From Rebekah Chickering's student examination folder.

92. Kett, *Rites*, 236.

93. *Courant* (January 1922), 37, 38.

94. Interview, Mary Carpenter Dake, teacher from 1925 to 1945.

95. A small residue of nineteenth-century strictures on women's physical activity remained through the Bailey era. Miss Bailey only permitted riding after assuring herself that Mr. Cross at the Salem Street Riding Academy "took the greatest care in the selection of horses and grooms." (Principal's Report, 1912–15, p. 13). Most track events short of shot putting and javelin throwing were part of the array of physical activities, but high and broad jumping must be practiced only in moderation, and "contests in high or broad jumping are not permitted," Miss Bailey assured the Trustees in 1915 (Principal's Report for 1912–15, p. 8). Dancing was always encouraged—single-sex dancing, that is.

96. See Cremin, *Transformation*, 184.

97. *Courant* (January 1922), 33.

98. Jean Pond, in *Bradford* (2nd edition) disputes this, contending that Bradford began a Cum Laude Chapter under Marion Coates, whose tenure ended in 1927. Conversation with a Bradford archivist in December 1976 suggests that the seeming conflict hangs on a question of definition. Bradford held its first Cum Laude Chapter meeting as an "honor society" early in 1926 before that society was officially registered with the national organization. Abbot's Cum Laude Chapter was chartered on 10 May 1926.

99. Conversation, spring 1969, with a girl wishing to enter an elective for which 55 upperclassmen had applied.

100. See Kemper interview, 8 November 1976.

101. Two members of 50-year class reunion, 1976.

102. New Year's sermon, 1934.

103. *Courant* (December 1935), 35, 31. The respect she commanded among co-religionists outside of Abbot is suggested by her frequent talks to South Church women's groups and, most dramatically, by an invitation in the spring of 1931 from the Presbyterian Board of Foreign Missions to join a Commission to travel to the Orient and study and report on Christian education there. She never did take the trip, being too much involved with Abbot.

104. This and the following quotations are from B.B.'s handwritten notes for her Theism course, 1925–26.

105. Miss Bailey kept all the students' answers to this problem folded in her Theism syllabus.

106. See interview with A. C. Kemper, who did not feel this way but knew students who did, and for the following incident, conversation with alumna, Class of 1932, 2 May 1976.

107. Letter to "Dear Abbot Friends," note 86 above.

108. *Courant* (December 1935), 23.

109. See also Ripley, lecture, 1941.

110. Class Book, 1913, characterization of the Student Council.

111. Among other sources, interview with Frances Flagg Sanborn, '26, 6 November 1976, and a letter from Jane Baldwin to the author, 1975. Mrs. Sanborn says that Student Government at its best was strong. Jane Sullivan, '31, remembers Miss Bailey "playing favorites" sometimes, however. One episode in particular continues now and then to haunt Jane Baldwin '22: "During my senior year when I was president of Student Government, one of the younger girls, cute and attractive with great big, soft brown eyes, broke a rule which came under the category of a report to Miss Bailey. When I asked Miss Bailey what should be done about the child's invitation to the P.A. prom the following week, Miss Bailey said, 'I leave that entirely up to you, Jane.' I don't know whether that was for character building for me or just 'passing the buck.' After much agony I told the child she could not attend the prom. She was shattered and so was I, but eventually she married that P.A. boy in spite of missing the prom and so my *entire* life was not ruined."

112. Edie Damon, '32, to Polly Bullard, '24. Every year from 1922 on, each President wrote a lengthy set of suggestions and instructions for the succeeding one.

113. See Mary Carpenter Dake interview (among other sources), and *Courant* (December 1935), 35: Rockwell testimonial quoting Miss Bailey's letter to a girl whose mother had died.

114. There are but a few references in available sources to "Miss Morse," whom Burton Flagg termed Miss Bailey's "intimate life friend" (Treasurer's Report to Trustees, 2 June 1938.) She died soon after Bertha

Bailey came to Abbot. Before this final separation, the two women had been close companions, often sharing an apartment.

115. There was, as far as can be discerned, only one other person besides Miss Bailey who knew about this student's condition. Though this ex-teacher prefers to remain anonymous, she provided a first-hand account of Miss Bailey's calm and sympathetic handling of the girl and her parents.

116. *Courant* (June 1920), 40. The taxicab story was told me by Mrs. Helen Barss, who was serving as Assistant to Principal Marion Coates of Bradford at the time (1921). Mrs. Barss was in the taxicab.

117. E. Boutwell Von Weber interview. This role as organizer for others' ideas was one Miss Bailey had played for years. W. T. Chase, who knew her work at Taconic, described her in a letter to Flagg (29 August 1911), as "the balance wheel" of that school, rather than the initiator.

118. Burton Flagg, speaking before the Alumnae Association and Boston Abbot Club, 8 February 1936.

119. See Carpenter, *Abbot*, 104. The Infirmary building fund was anonymously begun by Professor Taylor's great friend Melville Day, one of Phillips Academy's major benefactors, who made a $5000 gift with the condition that the building be named for Taylor's wife, Antoinette Hall Taylor. The building was completed in the spring of 1914.

11. HIGH AND LOW

1. Elizabeth Davis, quoted in *Bulletin* (November 1924), 10.

2. Figures from U.S. Office of Education, *Biennial Survey of Education, 1932–1934*, *Bulletin* No. 2 (1935), 19.

3. Miss Hopkins encouraged faculty and students to leave behind nine-teenth-century prejudices against the reading of fiction and magazines. Miss Watson's librarian, the gifted Mabel Bosher, '94, had greatly helped Abbot over this hump by enlarging the lending library of "good fiction" originally begun by the students in 1892. Still *Courant* editors felt they must warn every girl in 1894 to "guard especially against the sensational novel. It directs attention from studies [and] indulges a taste for excitement" (January 1894, 22) and then shuddered in 1897 to think that "never has magazine literature been more alluring than it is today" (January 1897, 34). But when Miss Bosher made newspaper subscriptions a regular library responsibility, even these conservative youngsters could allow that "the daily newspaper is conceded to be a teacher of morals," besides giving worthy religious, political, and philosophical news (June 1894, 32).

4. Flora Mason, '89, Fund Chairman, *Bulletin* (November 1924), 13.

5. "Those who will make women of power," added the Alumna Loyalty Pledge (April 1924, p. 1).
6. A full account of Abbot's Centennial celebration can be found in Jane Carpenter's *Abbot and Miss Bailey* and in the *Bulletin* of November 1929.
7. It is true that Markham Stackpole had been associated with Phillips from 1907 to 1922 as school minister, but this was not the role in which he addressed the assembly.
8. *Bulletin* (November 1929), 29.
9. Ibid., 16.
10. The Trustees entered the new assets in their books as "the Centennial Fund for Teaching." The word "Endowment" reappeared in 1929 when the Trustees determined to continue the loyalty drive in an attempt to build endowment after the Centennial was over.
11. Sixty percent of the total alumnae body contributed. This total included all nongraduates as well as recipients of the Abbot diploma. The holdouts tended to be older alumnae who had left the school after a year or so.
12. See letters to Miss Bailey from Dr. Jane Greeley, '84 ,and Marcia Eastman, among others, quoted in Reports prepared for the Trustees meeting, 5 December 1929.
13. This was book value: the market value was considerably greater in June 1929.
14. Letter to Miss Bailey, quoted in Reports submitted at Trustees' meeting, 5 December 1929.
15. Quoted in Carpenter, *Abbot*, 131.
16. Page 189 of the first volume of Trustees' records. This was the reconvened December Board meeting. The Executive Committee meeting of 5 December 1929 could not be officially convened either, since only Miss Bailey and those indefatigable gentlemen Flagg and Stackpole were present.
17. A brief market recovery was just around the corner: by May 1930 a few Harvard experts were assuring a grateful nation that the worst was over. Not till late summer of 1930 was it clear how serious the situation was.
18. Treasurer's Report (6 March 1930), 8, 10.
19. Executive Committee Minutes, 6 March 1930.
20. Ibid.
21. *Bulletin* (November 1930), 32.
22. Jane Carpenter's dedication to Burton S. Flagg, *The Bailey Years*.
23. Treasurer's Report, 1 June 1934.
24. Treasurer's Reports, June 1931 and 1932. By 1932 the market value of several Abbot securities had fallen to one fifth of their book value.
25. Biennial Survey (1932–1933), 19.

26. Interview, 14 March 1977, with Louis Finger, Andover Savings Bank President 1958–1963. Flagg was still quite young when he accomplished this in 1917. It is impossible to detail all the extra duties Flagg took on, but one example is suggestive: whenever a secretary at Merrimack Mutual became engaged, Flagg took her aside and taught her how to draw up a family budget.

27. See especially Burton Flagg's article, "Serving Two Masters," originally an address to the Mutual Convention in Savannah, Georgia, published in *Mutual Insurance Bulletin* (November and December 1934), 5–9.

28. Research on Flagg is confounded by the conflicting views one hears from townspeople. It is not so hard to learn what he *did*: of the eight citizens contacted, each from a different segment of the Community, both his friends and his critics agree on this, and likewise agree on the practical importance to Abbot of his business and town connections. The effect on Abbot of the *image* he presented is far harder to calculate. Humility is in order.

29. The only clue to this invitation is the copy of an undated letter Flagg wrote—refusing election—to Frederick Harlan Page, President of the Andover Theological Seminary (later Andover-Newton Theological School) from 1928 through the 1940's. There is no record in the Andover-Newton Trustees' minutes of invitations to prospective Board members tendered and refused, only of invitations accepted. Thus the exact date of Flagg's honor cannot be known.

30. Anne Flagg was also an accomplished, generous person, though her influence was much more quietly exercised than was her husband's. She was a Trustee of Danvers Mental Hospital, active in the November Club, and in South Church where she was both deaconess for many years and president of several Church societies. The hostess and the house at 22 School Street were considered worthy to provide hospitality for five headmasters who came to celebrate Phillips' Sesquicentennial.

31. Trustee Minutes, 30 June 1940.

32. This move caused not a little comment in the town: a man of Flagg's stature and comparative wealth becoming a $2.00 taxpayer? The Abbot Trustees' rejoinder: "he deserves it." (Louis Finger interview.) Flagg's frugality was legend. When on business in Boston or New York, he could rarely bring himself to take a taxi, no matter how inconvenient the subway. He made croquet wickets for his children out of the hoops of his mother's worn-out skirts. After his death in 1971, friends who helped clean out his house found an entire storage room filled with nested cardboard cartons, scraps of string, and carefully folded paper bags. This very conservatism in personal spending was (in part) what gave him the wherewithal to be so generous to others—such ac-

tions as supporting deserving young men in college, providing mainte-
nance jobs to Kennebunkport neighbors during the worst of the
Depression even when they didn't need doing. Louis Finger, interview;
Frances Flagg Sanborn, letter to the author, 1 August 1977.

33. I am indebted to Barton and Melville Chapin for many of their recollections about Flagg's appearance and manner. In almost every case
their memories have been confirmed by other observers also, including
Adeline M. Wright, William Doherty, and Louis Finger.

34. Interview with Mary Carpenter Dake.

35. See interview with Eleanor Tucker, July 1975, and with Frances Flagg
Sanborn, '26, 6 November 1976.

36. *Bulletin* (May 1936), 7.

37. Treasurer's Report, 3 December 1931.

38. ΟΙ ΕΦΙΚΝΟΥΜΕΝΟΙ (*The Achievers*), Worcester Academy *Bulletin*, ca. 1937, p. 90. See also interview with William Doherty, 1 March
1977. Doherty says that Phillips Headmaster Alfred Stearns and Andover High School Principal Nate Hamblin were also part of the
group.

39. Interview, 1 March 1977. Doherty's information dates in part from his
thirty-nine-year tenure as School Committee member beginning in
1935. One of Doherty's teacher-friends had the job of quietly informing new teachers of this "requirement." Confirmed by Frederick S.
Allis, Andover School Committee member 1956–59, and in part by
Adeline M. Wright, elementary school teacher in Andover 1937–1976.
The year before being permanently hired (shortly after Flagg resigned
from the School Committee), Mrs. Wright was approached by Superintendent Henry Sanborn, who asked, "By the way, where do you go
to church?" The answer was "South Church." His rejoinder: "Well,
that's fine then." She had heard talk of the old Smart & Flagg requirement, but said that in her day it no longer obtained. Pressures on
Andover teachers were far kinder than those brought to bear in Lawrence, where Catholic Church membership was one prerequisite for
all teacher candidates and a $2000 payment to three School Committee
members was the other, according to two Andover School Committee
members, and five teachers who applied for jobs in both systems between 1930 and 1952.

40. William Doherty, 1 March 1977, and Louis Finger, 14 March 1977,
the day before his sudden death. Doherty was more friendly with
rival insurance brokers than with Flagg, and soon to become involved
in the insurance business himself. Finger, Flagg's long-time friend and
colleague, served as full-time Vice President and Treasurer of the
Savings Bank 1934–1958 and was President after Flagg's resignation in
1958 (until 1963). Philip K. Allen, Trustee of Abbot 1948–1973, says
of this "patriarch of the town" and the tales both likely and unlikely:

"I'd heard the stories told by those who envied his enormous success. I just put them on the back burner."

41. Irene R. Draper, quoted in 50th Anniversary Tribute to Burton S. Flagg, p. 30.

42. Treasurer's Report, 6 March 1936. Flagg reported to the Trustees that Miss Helen Robinson, Latin teacher, was "recovering steadily," but would be absent at least six weeks. "In view of her mental and physical condition, I took occasion, as Treasurer to assure her that . . . there would be no discounting of her compensation while she was away from school in attendance upon recovery, with the hope that she would secure full relaxation and added strength. I trust the Trustees will approve of this action." At this point, how could the Trustees refuse? It is interesting that Flagg took this kind of job onto himself with no evident effort to consult either the Executive Committee or Esther Comegys, then Acting Principal of the school. Apparently, his colleagues were glad to have him do it.

43. Margaret Van Voorhis, 14 December 1947.

44. Interview, Melville Chapin.

45. Treasurer's Report, 5 December 1929.

46. Ibid., 4 March 1938.

47. Conversation with F. F. Sanborn, 31 January 1977. There are many other evidences of Flagg's attitude, including his memorial of Lauren Dearborn to the Trustees on 27 January 1921 as a "master workman," of Michael Scannell to the faculty on 2 March 1933 as a "noble and beautiful spirit."

48. Treasurer's Report, 6 June 1930.

49. I am grateful to Wayne A. Frederick and Professor Roger F. Murray for advice in judging the character of Flagg's investments. Though small, the endowment helped to keep tuition from rising even higher than it did in the mid-twenties: Flagg calculated that Abbot's costs per pupil were three times as great in 1926 as they were in Miss Means's day, but tuition only doubled (from $600 to $1200) for boarders. Day student tuition went from $100 to $300; both tuitions rose again, to $1400 and $350, the following year. It is interesting that in the year that Flagg made his analysis (1926), national public school costs per pupil averaged $102.05, and that the increase in Abbot costs so far outdistanced the cost of living, even when schools' needs are made a primary criterion for "living" expenses. See above, Chapter 9; also consumer price index figures, *Historical Statistics*, Series E, 135–186. Abbot's endowment at this time was larger than that of many boys' schools of similar size, including Pomfret, Taft, Deerfield, St. Marks, and Hotchkiss.

50. "50th Anniversary Tribute to Burton S. Flagg," compiled for a celebration which took place in 1956, p. 30.

51. Treasurer's Report, 6 June 1930.

52. April 1924, p. 9. Jane Sullivan, '31, who later became Alumnae Secre-

tary, says that Abbot's annuity plan was one of the first among all secondary schools in the nation.

53. Ibid., 28 May 1940. It is possible that Flagg spread Abbot's deposits around to avoid any appearance of collusion with the Andover Savings Bank. Some deliberate division of deposits was necessary after the establishment of Federal Deposit Insurance in 1933, but Flagg followed the practice for years before FDIC began insuring deposits up to $5000. By 1934 the Andover Savings Bank held $46,000 of Abbot's total $178,000 of savings bank deposits (26 percent). The amount did not afterward increase, even though the percentage did (to 40 percent in 1937, for example) as Flagg renewed his search of the securities market for bargains.

54. See Treasurer's Report, 6 December 1934.

55. Flagg cautiously bought and sold securities throughout the Depression, always looking for a sound bargain. In spring 1931, for example, he sold a $3000 Pennsylvania Light and Power bond and bought a $3000 Pennsylvania Power and Light bond, "an even exchange for a stronger bond" (Treasurer's Report, 5 June 1931), though few but Flagg could know the difference. For the most part, however, the 1929–30 portfolio was sound enough to be worth hanging on to. Of the 35 bonds Abbot held in 1930, only 7 had been replaced by 1932, and only 4 more by 1934. Abbot's 16 stock holdings did not change at all between 1930 and 1932; in the next two years only 3 purchases and one sale of stock were made.

56. Treasurer's Reports and Frances Flagg Sanborn, conversation of 31 January 1977. A "staunch Republican," Flagg had plenty of company. In 1928 almost every Abbot student "voted" for Republican, Protestant Hoover over Democrat, Catholic Al Smith (*Bulletin*, November 1932, 14, 15), doubtless a mirror of their parents' political leanings, and supported Hoover again in 1932. See also interview with Alexina Wilkins Talmadge, '22 19 June 1977, by Beverly Floe.

57. Public school teachers had also made gains: the average U.S. teacher made approximately $1500 per year in 1926, whereas in 1915 it had been $543 ($328 in the South for white teachers, about $160 for blacks). Inflation had canceled out about half of the increase, however. Rural teachers fared worst (their high school salary average was nearly $1000 lower than that of urban teachers); the Abbot Trustees did not use them as a basis of comparison.

58. Treasurer's Report (5 December 1940), 6.

59. In "Serving Two Masters," article in the *Mutual Insurance Bulletin* (November-December 1934), 8.

60. See Treasurer's Reports, 2 March 1934, 27 May 1935; and Flagg, ibid., 6–9.

61. Treasurer's Report, 7 December 1933.

62. Principal's Reports to Trustees, 10 November 1930, 5 June 1931.

63. See Treasurer's Reports, 5 December 1935, 3 December 1936.

64. Treasurer's Report, 3 March 1933.
65. Among other tuition reductions, the Trustees established three regional tuition grants ($400 each) especially for the daughters of alumnae, or for candidates recruited by alumnae, to encourage alumnae efforts. Alumnae continued to give to the Alumnae Fund throughout the Depression. (There were 69 *new* donors in 1933.) Since half of the Fund supported the Emergency Tuition Fund (the other half went to the alumnae office and *Bulletin*), some alumnae were in effect paying for others' daughters to attend Abbot.
66. See alumnae records for 1932–35. Of the 80 percent of alumnae who answered the alumnae office's questionnaire item on parent's occupation, 18 percent had fathers who were physicians or lawyers; 20 percent were involved in relatively small and essential local businesses (such as "apple growing"). Twenty-four percent were working for or running large national concerns or were bankers and brokers and presumably vulnerable in ways the above were not. Seventeen percent were unclassifiable (e.g. "manufacturer"). See also survey made by Tamblyn and Brown in 1937–38, *Report* to Trustees, p. 32. This professional fundraising firm concluded that Abbot had few if any chances to draw on "outstanding wealth."
67. Treasurer's Report, 3 March 1933.
68. USCOE, *Bulletins*, 1934–1936.
69. *Bulletin* (November 1933), 22.
70. The competition worsened as the decade progressed. Gone were the days when nearly every C.P. Senior could be certain of admission to her college of first choice. (See Principal's Report, October 1926.) Miss Bailey described to the Trustees how difficult it was to help the one-year C.P. Specials of 1935 gain admission. Several of them waited all summer before finally being accepted. "It does not seem to me either necessary or desirable to go through such a period of strain in order to be 'educated,'" she wrote. (Principal's Report, 4 October 1935). At the same time, hard-pressed small colleges were compounding the schools' enrollment problems by "raiding the secondary schools" for 17-year-olds able to do their freshman year work, as Boston's Porter Sargent wrote Flagg. (Letter, 6 January 1933. Sargent was "School Advisor" for many parents seeking private school placement for their children.) Their success is borne out in U.S. Office of Education figures on postgraduate pupils in private schools. There were 6665 in 1928 and only 2458 in 1933.
71. USCOE, *Bulletins*, 1930–1934. Constance Chipman, in her Report to the Trustees, 5 October 1934, wrote that "the crowded high schools, and premature social life fostered there," were among her most persuasive arguments in her drive for new enrollees among alumnae families and acquaintances.

72. Jane Sullivan, interview with Ruth Newcomb; and interview with Abby Kemper.
73. Student Government records, 1933, 1934.
74. Field Secretary's Report to the Trustees, 4 December 1934.
75. Treasurer's Report, 1 June 1934.
76. Ibid., 1 March 1934.
77. Quoted in *Courant* (June 1932), 46.
78. Letter, 8 January 1976, from Cynthia James Tharaud, '32.
79. In Report to Trustees, 5 December 1935.
80. Undated speech given to the Wellesley alumnae, "Preparing the Undergraduate." The context suggests 1934.
81. Mary Crane, Abbot Principal 1955–1966, in conversation 29 April 1977.
82. Eleanor Wells, '36, *Courant* (December 1935), 2.
83. Ibid., 9.
84. "Our Miss Bailey" by Frances Swazey Parker, '86, *Bulletin* (May 1935), 11.
85. Principal's Report, 5 December 1935.
86. Kemper, interview.
87. Chipman, interview.

12. SINGULAR WOMEN

1. In conversation, December 1976. All further references to Marguerite Hearsey's statements not otherwise attributed come either from conversations held with the author or from written responses to the author's questions made between March 1975 and December 1977.
2. Alumnae and faculty recollections.
3. See especially Christmas sermon, 1950, and prayers on VE Day, 1945, Abbot Archives. Many alumnae speak of how moving they found MCH's prayers, and mourn the fact that so few of them have been preserved.
4. Letter from Mary Gorton Darling, '86, to Burton Flagg, 23 April 1936. The letter described the despondent gatherings of her classmates in the winter of 1936 and the elation they all felt at MCH's appointment. Mary Darling lived near Hollins and knew her work there. She told Flagg she wished her husband had not sunk all his pre-cash "gold into N.Y., N.H. & Hartford stocks and U.S. Steal [sic]" and thus prevented the Darlings from making a whopping contribution to Abbot.
5. M. C. Dake, interview, and letter, 27 March 1977; news release April 1935 and recommendations collected by Radcliffe College from Sophie Hart, Professor of English Composition, Wellesley, and Professors Robert J. Manner and Karl Young, Yale University.
6. Alumnae and faculty recollections.

7. Melville Chapin, Alice C. Sweeney, and M. C. Hearsey, in conversation or interview, or both.

8. At least three of those leading lights of Andover who were well aware of Bertha Bailey hardly remember MCH at all. Interviews with Louis Finger and William Doherty, among others.

9. Alumnae and faculty recollections. The dates of Miss Sweeney's service on the faculty: September 1921–June 1922, substituted for Rebekah Chickering; September 1922–December 1922, substituted for Martha H. Howey. September 1935–June 1956, member of English Department, Chairman 1938–56. Director of Studies, 1938–56. Acting Principal, 1946–47.

10. Letters to parents from ACS 12 February 1948 and 25 February 1943.

11. Miss Hearsey became a director of the Headmistresses Association just two years after arriving at Abbot; she was later nominated for President, but declined. She became director of the NAPSG in 1940, and was President for two years during the War. A colleague from a Maryland school remembers the awe in which she was held by the other heads. "She was the intellectual—she was too busy with her committee work to have a drink with us. But such a *nice* person!" MCH was also a member of the committee that edited the College Entrance Examination Handbook after 1944. She gave a Commencement address or two each year, and was a member of the NAPSG School and College Conference Committee.

12. Interviews, Alan Blackmer, Louis Finger; conversation, John M. Kemper (1970), among others.

13. Alumnae and faculty recollections.

14. Interview, Alan Blackmer.

15. Alice C. Sweeney, *A Brief Account of the Years When Miss Hearsey was Principal of Abbot Academy and Selections from her Speeches* (privately published, 1957), 36.

16. Interview, M. Chapin.

17. Interview, C. Chipman. Miss Hearsey affectionately puts it this way: "He grew more leisurely in his visits to the school as he grew older—he was full of anecdotes. His love for the school and his knowledge of every detail of it inside and out [were] phenomenal."

18. Letter from MCH, 9 February 1950.

19. Faculty, alumnae, and Trustee recollections. Interview, Melville Chapin, Barton Chapin, Jr. Miss Hearsey served on the Executive Committee, the Committee on Educational Policy, and the Committee for Planning of the Future.

20. Interview, M. Chapin.

21. Quoted in Principal's Report, 8 April 1949.

22. Katherine Stirling Dow, '55. Her recollection is one of many similar ones offered by alumnae of the Hearsey years' religion program. From

all accounts, the reverends Winthrop Richardson and Graham Baldwin were equally successful.

23. Twenty-seven of the thirty-six 1936 Seniors were CP students; seven others went on to professional schools and just one finished her education with Abbot in the time-honored Academic Course manner. Subsequent years show the same pattern.

24. Private schools in general gained 12.5 percent in enrollment over 1936–37, and Abbot's gain was just about proportionate. Miss Hearsey reported the school at "maximum capacity" with all available cottages in use in the fall of '37 (Report to Trustees, 16 October 1937), though, as will be seen, the Principal's idea of "maximum capacity" changed according to the number of good applicants available. The rise failed to continue for 1938–39 after the national economic relapse, but Abbot held its own, losing just four students for that year and staying at 160 for the following two years. Enrollment began to rise again in 1940–41. By comparison, a survey of girls' schools reported by Flagg in successive December Treasurer's Reports from 1937 to 1939 noted that the percentage of schools with full or near-full attendance fell from 68 in 1937 to 53 in 1939.

25. Hale Sturges, Chairman of the Phillips Academy French department, points out that it is difficult to make precise comparison of texts used in the nineteenth century and those read today, because so many of the earlier, more complex texts were not read as literature but laboriously decoded line by line, much as Latin or Greek texts tend to be.

26. Principal's Reports, 10 June 1937 and 2 December 1937.

27. Faculty recollections.

28. Martha Hale Shackford, 9 November 1934, in recommendation of MCH.

29. *Bulletin* (October 1938), 8.

30. Faculty recollections.

31. Sweeney, *Brief Account*, 16–17.

32. Alumnae recollections, and for the most positive comments of all, Student Council President letters sent to MCH in honor of her retirement, spring 1955.

33. Two Student Council secretaries' accounts of typical Student Council meetings: January 11, 1938–"Instances of flirting with clerks . . . were mentioned. Miss Carpenter will speak with her corridor." October 21, 1942–"Pett called a meeting to say that Gym suits must be worn for tennis; more speed in getting to chapel in morning; no sweaters in the diningroom; no suits or reversibles to Vespers, also no suits to lectures. Table manners, running in corridors and confusion in Tiffin room brought up."

34. Principal's Report, 2 March 1934.

35. Opening Chapel speech, 30 September 1937.

36. Faculty recollections.
37. *Circle* (1939), 74.
38. Recollections of a Homestead resident, Class of '47, and of a later alumna, '62.
39. Alumnae recollections.
40. *Circle* (1940), 57.
41. "Abbot in *Our* Day." Account written in the winter of 1976.
42. Alumnae and faculty recollections. "You are always running," Miss Sweeney observed to Beverly Brooks. "There's no other way I can do everything I want to do," was the reply.
43. Undated memo from MCH (probably late 1940's) which describes her own and her teachers' largely futile attempts to help an unstable student during the school year, and the girl's resort to summer psychotherapy. MCH wonders in print whether Abbot's resources are adequate to such students' needs, but there is no discernible action to create new ones. See also Principal's Report, 8 December 1953.
44. Tribute written for Flagg's 80th birthday.
45. Virginia Woolf, *A Room of One's Own* (New York, Harcourt, Brace, 1929), 91.
46. For this and the foregoing quote, MCH in Opening Chapel services, 26 September 1940 and 24 September 1952. Many other Chapel talks reiterate the theme.
47. Beverly Brooks Floe, '41; Carol Hardin Kimball, '53 (who arrived at the very end of this "little golden age"); Mary Howard Nutting, '40; Genevieve Young, '48 (Alumna Trustee).
48. This is not to say that all schools involved in the Eight Year Study abandoned *their* traditions. Winsor School took rich advantage of the stimulation offered by the requisite visits to far-flung laboratory schools, the faculty work to devise alternative curricula, and the emphasis on projects and field trips, without sacrifice of its emphasis on basic academic excellence. (Valeria Knapp, interview, and recollections of a member of the Headmistresses Association who observed the results of the Eight Year Study.)
49. Interview, A. C. Sweeney.
50. Cremin, *Transformation*, 184–185.
51. Principal's Report, 16 April 1948.
52. See Barbara Moore Pease, '12, to her granddaughter, 6 May 1974, and other alumnae recollections.
53. Trustee Minutes, 7 March 1905, following Draper's death.
54. See Principal's Report, 10 June 1937. "Pure Bulfinch!" exclaimed Larson on his first visit to the Abbot Chapel.
55. Trustees' Proposal to Harkness, May 1938; typed carbon in Abbot Archives.
56. See also *Courant* (June 1938), 5, 6, for an optimistic student view of these radical building plans.

57. Harkness did make some small donations to Lady Margaret Hall College in Oxford University (1930) and to Barnard and Sarah Lawrence Colleges (1939), but his only other gifts to secondary schools were made to boys' prep schools. The bulk of his money went to Exeter, Yale, and Harvard.

58. In one article, (*Bulletin*, May 1941) 3, Miss Hearsey quoted A. E. Housman to the Dear Old Girls to invoke the Abbot of their time:
That is the land of lost content
I see it shining plain,
The happy highways where I went
And cannot come again.

59. Report to Trustees from Tamblyn and Brown, 8 December 1938.

60. Quoted by Flagg in Treasurer's Report to Trustees, 8 December 1938.

61. Letter to Flagg reported to Trustees 7 December 1939.

62. Charles Cutler, Trustee, to Miss Hearsey, 18 March 1939; also Alumnae Office staff recollections.

63. Fund Office personnel decided, as they mailed off the 8 percent payments year after year of Mrs. Emily Abbey Gill's long life, that she was not so eccentric after all.

64. Treasurer's Report 2 June 1938, 2–3.

65. Engineer's Report, quoted in Treasurer's Report, 28 May 1941.

66. This was manifestly an excellent buy in the money market, but it should be noted that all money was fairly cheap in 1941. Loans averaged 2–3 percent interest.

67. Principal's Report, 7 December 1940.

68. See Principal's Report, 28 May 1942.

69. Interest in the Current Events elective and in foreign affairs debates was reported at an all-time low in June 1938. Principal's Report, June 1938; also *Courant*, 1937–39.

70. Principal's Report, 8 December 1938.

71. *Circle*, 1940, accounts of QED discussions, 61; *Courant* articles; *Bulletin*, October 1939, description of student's "desperate desire to be of service." p. 9. In 1940–41 Miss Hearsey and several faculty worked to raise money for Chinese Relief, and Fidelio sang for Chinese Hospitals on the radio.

72. *Bulletin* (May 1940), 4.

73. Letter to "Dear Madam," Abbot Academy, Andover, Massachusetts, from Mrs. June Peel, formerly of City of Bath Girls School, 20 January 1976.

74. Letter from alumna, Class of '41, confirmed by other alumnae recollections.

75. A year later, Reverend Winthrop Richardson went to California and enlisted in the Navy.

76. Faculty and alumnae recollections.

77. Alumna reminiscence, dated October 1977.

78. Alumnae recollections. The only printed record of this incident is a brief *Courant* reference to the students' fund-raising campaign, and the 1941 *Circle* characterization of *"Courant's* courageous editor" B. Brooks. B. B. Floe recalls few of her own activities, but classmates remember them vividly.
79. *Bulletin* (October 1942), 3.
80. Ibid.
81. Principal's Reports, 3 April 1941 (description of NAPSG meetings), and 7 October 1942. See also MCH Opening Chapel Speech, September 1942:

   > Art and music and philosophy and literature, Latin and Greek and even history . . . have been suspended in the colleges for men. They will have to be sustained largely by women. . . . Here, in this peaceful spot . . . you are fighting to preserve and pass on what civilization holds dear.

82. Dewey, quoted by Cremin, *Transformation,* 220; see also 218–219.
83. Cremin, *Transformation,* 155.
84. Recollections of alumnae, Class of '41. For students' continuing sense of the seriousness of these years, see Student Council Presidents' letters to MCH and all *Courants,* 1941–1946.
85. Presidents' letters to MCH. Four fifths of all students had summer jobs during the war years.
86. *Christian Science Monitor,* 21 August 1943.
87. In one year of the War, the Smith College appointment bureau got requests for 720 teachers—and could fill only twenty of them.
88. The one exception to the trend was the year 1942–43. Unfortunately, no precise accounting of the ratio between applicants and places is available; one must rely on general statements made in the Principal's and Treasurer's Reports to the Trustees. Too, one must remember in assessing these matters that most girls' boarding schools of the 1940's tried to have all applications for the following school year completed by mid-December; thus a school full of prospective students in March was not such an accomplishment then as it is in the 1970's.
89. Lower, at least, than Abbot's most direct competitors: Shipley, Dana Hall, Ethel Walker, Miss Porter's at Farmington, Miss Hall's and Concord. Northfield School's tuition in 1948 was $1050; Putney School's was $1400.
90. Miss Hearsey reported in May 1943 that several scholarship students' families would need no scholarship help the following year.
91. The author's general reservations about "intelligence" tests have various sources, but one must be especially careful with the differing results obtained when different test forms are used for different years, as they were in the case of the American Council Psychological Examinations administered in 1938 and 1940. (The "new form" was in use

in 1940). See also Miss Hearsey's reservations as expressed in her Principal's Report, 10 December 1954.

92. Principal's Report, 5 October 1944.

93. Principal's Report, 10 June 1946.

94. The Trustees discussed what impact this might have on Abbot, but "no conclusion was reached." Executive Committee Minutes, 18 January 1946.

95. World Federalists who doubled as *Courant* editors spread their views on the magazine's editorial pages in 1947–48, and a small group published a mimeo rag called *Peace A Paper* in 1948–49.

96. Principal's Report, 17 May 1945.

97. Alice Sweeney opposed the idea of a Parents' Day because it smacked of "selling the school," a process which she considers a travesty of good education. (Interview).

98. Alumnae recollections, 1941, 1948.

99. Principal's Report, 5 March 1943, and p. 3 of 2 March 1944, on the Headmistresses Association and NAPSG subcommittee and plenary meetings. The Brearley School, the Winsor School, the Bryn Mawr School (all of them day schools), the Friends academies, and Northfield under Abbot alumna Mira Wilson (Northfield Principal from 1929 to 1952) were among the few girls' schools to admit blacks. Faculty at Putney and other outspoken progressive schools scorned most private schools' racism.

100. Fuess in letter to Winslow Ames, 21 January 1944.

101. Since the Japanese student lost all access to her parents' funds, Abbot kept her on at full scholarship, and two of her classmates—with their parents—found money to support her freshman year at Barnard College. The Youngs were introduced to Abbot by Mrs. Minna Calhoun, Abbot mathematics teacher, whose husband was held in a Japanese internment camp in the Philippines throughout the war. Their original family name was Yun, but their father had dropped it when he left China.

102. Letter, September 17, 1976.

103. After the war, Oxford gratefully returned Abbot's hospitality and that of other schools which had taken dons' children by inviting the principal of each host school to a special summer session held at Oxford in 1947, all expenses paid. Miss Hearsey could not go, but Eleanor Tucker represented Abbot in her stead.

104. Principal's Report, 2 December 1943; also 2 March 1944, and 17 May 1945. This was in clear contrast to the Bailey era, when with a few exceptions, the administration and Trustees simply awarded whatever monies were necessary to fill the school.

105. Andrea Warburg (Kaufman), '40.

106. Beth Chandler Warren, '55, interview, 6 March 1977. The lecturer

was apparently Estelle M. Osborne, an instructor at New York University when she came to Abbot in 1948–49.

107. Principal's Report, 8 April 1949.

108. Reported ibid. The one young man who did come to visit for an evening was carefully seated at the Emma Willard faculty table for dinner.

109. See especially Principal's Report (7 December 1944), 2.

110. An example from MCH's commencement address to Williston Academy:

> A southern friend of mine tells a story of a young colored girl who was working for her and who, she discovered, had never been to school. She persuaded her to go, and made the necessary arrangements. A short time later she met the girl and asked her how things were going—how she liked school. "Well, ma'am, not too good. The teacher she say 2 and 2 am for, but La, Miss Kate, what am dat to me?"
>
> The contrast between the attitude expressed in that remark with the attitude of this audience of young people needs no elaboration. There is no need to impress upon a group like this the value of learning. There is no danger of such indifference on your part . . .
> (Manuscript in MCH's handwriting, Abbot Archives, undated.)

111. Alice Sweeney, 23 May 1977, in conversation.

V. The More Things Change, 1945–1963

13. TEACHERS AND STUDENTS AND HOW THEY GREW

1. Miss Hearsey admired Mildred Thompson, Dean of Vassar College, and listened with care to her address to the Headmistresses Association on the U.S. Army's experience with language teaching in 1945. The account of prewar and wartime French at both Abbot and Phillips Academies derives from conversations with Beverly Floe, '41, Barbara Brown Hogan, '40, and Stephen Whitney, Phillips Academy French teacher, 1936–77 (Chairman, 1969–73).

2. Phillips teacher recollection.

3. T. S. Matthews, *Great Tom: Notes Toward the Definition of T. S. Eliot* (New York, Harper and Row, 1974), 150.

4. Interviews, Alan and Josephine Blackmer, alumnae and teacher recollections, and Matthews, 148, 149. Emily Hale's Andover years may have been an especially suspenseful time in her life, because Eliot's wife Vivienne finally died in 1947, and it was eight years before TSE surprised almost everyone by marrying his secretary at age sixty-eight.

Only then did Emily Hale's "platonic affair" with him end. (See ibid., 148–151.)

5. Matthews says it is not known whether Eliot actually altered those poems and verse-plays which he showed to her in manuscript following their discussions of them; but one Andover friend whom she had known since her young womanhood in Chestnut Hill and who visited with her at least once a week during her Andover years is certain that the versions he showed her were often early drafts, and that he did incorporate many of her suggestions. Her letters from him, once opened, may tell.

6. Matthews says Emily Hale retired "unwilling" from Abbot at age 65 (ibid., 150). An Andover friend vaguely remembers some tiff with Mary Crane, MCH's successor, but M. Crane remembers no such thing. Miss Hale's life had changed the year before, when Eliot married his secretary: "Thus ended Emily's precarious happiness," says Matthews (ibid.). We do not know how Eliot's remarriage affected her Abbot career.

7. Ibid., 142. Aunt Agatha functions as wise, nurturing aunt to Harry, the principal character, and as years-ago lover to Harry's father. Eliot seems to have incorporated some of his own central qualities in each man. (Harry was "Eliot's mouthpiece," says Matthews, p. 127.) Was Emily Hale+Aunt Agatha all these things to Eliot?

8. Interview, '56 alumna.

9. Interview, Mlle. Arosa.

10. May Sarton, *The Small Room* (New York, W. W. Norton, 1961), 203–204; interview, Beth Warren, '55.

11. See also Beth Warren, '55, for a student's perception of the same phenomenon.

12. Marie Baratte, in conversation, December 1976.

13. Alumnae recollections, 1938–48.

14. Eleanor Tucker, interview. Miss Tucker's chemistry lab under the Chapel in Abbot Hall was one of the few places in the school where Howe's covert practicing could be heard.

15. Letter, E. M. Thomas to SML, 18 March 1975.

16. This and subsequent quotes from E. M. Thomas, interview, 5 December 1976.

17. This did not mean listening in on calls (though alumnae are sure that one teacher did so) but receiving the call and ascertaining whether a male voice went with a Phillips beau or a brother at college before transferring the call to the Abbot student.

18. Ellen Eaton to Philena McKeen, 30 January 1879.

19. Interview, E. M. Thomas. Genevieve Young, '48, who loved Abbot, also remembers her own and her friends' perception of the faculty as "remote beings"—but accepted this as natural.

20. Alumnae recollections, including about half the discontented alumnae queried on this point. When asked how she used her free time, one early sixties student responded as follows:

> I ate. I gained twenty pounds a year. It was disgusting. Lots of times I felt there was nothing to do but eat. We would get a gallon of ice cream from down town and a bottle of chocolate sauce and just gorge ourselves on Saturday afternoon. I had a real need to do things with my hands, but there was nothing to do. The art studio was closed on weekends. There were no crafts, no photography. So we ate instead. I also went on walks. I took all the approved walks and a lot of unapproved ones as well. Our Senior year, we'd sign out for a two-hour walk and go swim in Pomps Pond in our underwear. That was great fun.

21. Letter to the author, 7 January 1976. A '64 graduate "tried out all the churches in Andover" to relieve Sunday boredom. "That Christian Science business kind of scared me because they really tried to convert me," she says.

22. Letters found in a file box in a secret compartment after Sherman House was closed in June 1977: dated June '63, June '51, June '58, undated (order and cast of characters suggest about 1953), and June '58. Because one young teacher who arrived in 1958 and lived in Sherman House confirms the co-ed roof parties of her earliest years at Abbot, the references in the letters to these affairs seem credible. For twenty-six years, Sherman House residents followed the injunction of those 1950–51 students who spent three hours carving out the space under the floor boards: "DON'T TELL ANYONE." One finally did tell the author in winter '76 when she heard the news that Sherman would be closed, and the letters came to the Archives in 1977, some water-soaked, some mouse-eaten, but all readable. The author found a shiny new marijuana pipe in the hidden compartment after a Sherman student had moved the letters for safe-keeping in June 1977, and for all she knows, it's still there.

"Hatchet" is Miss Mildred Hatch, Latin teacher and (most importantly here) Director of Residence during the 1950's.

23. Principal's Report, 9 December 1949. In 1958, Mary Crane, Miss Hearsey's successor, wrote of the "child-centered families of the mid-twentieth century", and the difficulties their self-centered offspring caused Abbot. Principal's Report, 5 February 1958.

24. Sylvia Thayer, '54. Sylvia was president of the Student Council in the year that the council decided to examine the basic question, "If all rules were abolished, what would be necessary to acheive a good community life?" They went at the problem hammer and tongs, with Miss Hearsey sitting in now and then, and finally decided on a set of standards for behavior fairly consistent with Abbot's traditional rules. On these, they and the faculty eventually built a new, slightly different

student handbook and rule system, and a continuing plan for the counseling of ninth and tenth graders by Student Council members.

25. The '55 graduate is Katherine Stirling Dow; the older alumna is Dorothy Bigelow Arms, '11, (letter to the author, spring 1976).

26. Conversation with the parent of the girl (the parent was Abbot '23); Alice Sweeney, interview. One Catholic girl, on the other hand, told Miss Sweeney that she particularly enjoyed Bible class. "Dr. Sidon thinks just the way I do," she said.

27. See *Courant* (May 1948), 7. This is the first recorded protest. The hymn was sung through 1973, in spite of protests, few of them serious.

28. E. M. Thomas; alumnae of '54, '64.

29. The years 1952, 1956, 1959, 1962.

30. Interview, B. C. Warren; Autobiographies for class of 1961; interview, E. Tucker.

31. June '64; undated.

32. Teachers and alumnae recollections.

33. A. C. Sweeney, recollections.

34. A. C. Sweeney; M. C. Hearsey; student government records, 1936–1955.

35. Sweeney, *Brief Account*, 36.

36. See Student Council Minutes, 1 October 1944.

37. M. C. Hearsey, A. C. Sweeney, student government records.

38. Manuscript of speech to the faculty, MCH; September 1948.

39. Sweeney, *Brief Account*, 30.

40. Alumnae and faculty recollections.

41. Alan Blackmer also "thought a lot of the native French teachers." Interview.

42. Interviews, G. Arosa, B. C. Warren.

43. Alumna, '56.

44. Alumnae and teacher recollections.

45. Alumnae recollections.

46. Student Council president of 1945–46, in letter to her successor.

47. B. C. Warren, '55; Genevieve Young, '48.

48. Joan Van Ness List, '41.

49. Conversation, alumna of '56; alumna letter to Germaine Arosa. See also letter from V. ("Teddy") Edmonds to Mary Crane, 11 October 1961.

50. Alumnae recollections.

51. EMT, letter to SML, and interview.

52. The application rate would easily survive a tuition hike to $2000 the following year.

53. Germaine Arosa; A. C. Sweeney; Sylvia Thayer, '54; M. C. Hearsey; student government records, 1946–1954.

54. 2 March 1949, Abbot Archives; also quoted in Sweeney, *Brief Account*, 55.

55. MCH, parent recollections. See also parent letters to MCH, 19 June 1950, thanking her for the growth Abbot had fostered in her daughter, but adding, "Frankly, I think that some of the restrictions are too rigid." MCH wrote back: "I am eager to know just what you had in mind" (June 22, 1950). MCH worried now and then "that the rumor about our being very strict might become a deterrent in enrollment" (Principal's Report, December 9, 1949).

56. Letter, Joan Van Ness List.

57. Letter from student, summer, 1949, quoted in Principal's Report, 6 October 1949.

58. Talk to Boston Abbot Club, 2 March 1949. See also letter from MCH to parent, 22 June 1959.

59. Sweeney, *Brief Account*, 40; interview, Helen Allen (Henry) Anderson.

60. See especially Miss Hearsey's poem for the school, "These have I loved . . .", *Bulletin* (May 1955), 2, 3.

61. Teachers and alumnae recollections.

62. Pamela Daly Vose, *The Masters School: A Retrospective Portrait, 1877–1977* (The Masters School, 1977); conversations with Valeria Knapp, Director of Winsor School 1951–63; Virginia Dean of St. Paul's School; and other school administrators active in the 1950's.

63. Teachers and Trustee recollections.

64. Mary Crane had no graduate degree, but she had studied at the Sorbonne and at the Fogg Museum in Cambridge.

65. Trustees' recollections.

66. Interview, Helen Allen (Henry) Anderson.

67. Paul Werner, letter to MC 31 July 1956, and Ann Werner to MC, 19 May 1956. In another Werner letter (undated, probably fall 1956) Ann Werner assures Mrs. Crane that she had decided to have their mail delivered to Ripley house so that her husband "has no occasion to make himself conspicuous if people still object to men on campus."

68. As one alumna has put it, "They would let you write to boys at other schools—you couldn't get pregnant through the mails—but not P.A. because it was too close." According to alumnae ('54, '55), all letters postmarked "Andover" had to be opened by faculty members and read in their presence.

69. Principal's Report, 3 June 1957; letter to SML, August 1977.

70. Principal's Report, 2 October 1958.

71. Abbot Academy Handbook for students and their parents, 1964–65, pp. 27, 18.

72. Alumnae and faculty recollections: manuscript copies of M.H. Crane's Chapel talks, Abbot Archives. These are extraordinary in their warmth and their use of imaginative metaphors for faith. In general they communicate Christian values as well, perhaps, as anyone could to an audience laced with skeptics.

73. Undated exchange in folder full of Abbot teachers' defense of classics,

including long excerpt from college Latin teachers defending their subject. Phillips Academy Archives.

74. See especially Ann Werner, undated letter to Mary Crane.

75. Louisa Lehmann Birch, letter to author, 17 March 1976.

76. *Bulletin* (October 1964), 4.

77. Mary H. Crane, interview 8 March 1976. Several of her friends and teachers confirm both her assessments of the Trustees' wishes and her accomplishment of them.

78. Ibid.

79. See MCH, report to the Trustees on long-range planning, 2 June 1947.

80. Principal's Report, 1 June 1948.

81. Sweeney, *Brief Account*, 30; interviews, MCH, G. Arosa.

82. Principal's Reports, 2 March 1944, 25 May 1944.

83. G. Arosa. Mlle Arosa says that she and her colleagues often discussed the problem of overwork and privacy, but seldom or never mentioned it to MCH.

84. Faculty and alumnae recollections. Mary Crane says that the only assured family time that she and her daughters had together all week was Sunday afternoon, for an hour of tea and cinnamon toast.

85. See Principal's Report, 13 November 1956.

86. Teachers' and Trustees' recollections.

87. Barbara Brown Hogan and many others.

88. Teacher's recollection.

89. Alumnae and teachers' recollections.

90. Mary Crane often conveyed her frustration over the multiple demands on her time, in Principal Reports and *Bulletin* notes. See a typical example in *Bulletin* (May 1964), 4.

91. Teachers' recollections.

92. Student, parent, and grandparent letters from Dean's files.

93. Interview, Carolyn Goodwin.

94. Principal's Reports 5 February 1958, 7 March 1960, 2 June 1960, 7 November 1963. After a while, the Board's resistance to Mrs. Crane's suggestions and requests begins to seem remarkable to the outside reader of Abbot records. Two recent Abbot Trustees and long-time Abbot friends are convinced that this resistance centered in Robert Hunneman, Board President from 1952 to 1965.

95. Interview, Crane era teacher, 14 June 1977.

96. The Abbot tenure figures for teachers during the Hearsey years are the more striking given the inevitable volatility of the teacher supply during World War II. Two factors in the rapid national turnover after the mid-fifties were the high demand for teachers and the near universality of the TIAA annuity program, Social Security, and state-mandated pension programs, which meant that by 1960 a teacher could shift from school to school without loss of pension funds. Interestingly, experienced teachers continued to leave the profession alto-

gether in times of both high employment and scarce jobs, at the beginning of a trend that would continue at least through 1976.

Percent teaching with twenty or more years experience:
1961   27.6%
1966   21.4%
1971   18.3%
1976   14.1%

97. Jean Dietel Bennett (Mrs. John), AA 1963–1973. Audrey Nye Bensley (Mrs. Gordon), AA 1965, PA 1973– . Anne Harriss Bugbee (Mrs. Bruce), AA 1959, PA 1973– . Edwina Frederick (Mrs. Wayne), AA 1962–1973. Faith Howland (Kaiser), AA 1966–1973. Carolyn Lumsden Johnston (Mrs. Malcolm), AA 1965, PA 1973– . Mary Sophia Minard, AA 1961, PA 1973– . Virginia Powel (Mrs. Harford), AA 1959, PA 1973– . Christina Alonso Rubio, (Mrs. Angel), AA 1965, PA 1973– . Jean Mary St. Pierre, AA 1963, PA 1973– . Barbara Blagdon Sisson (Mrs. John), AA 1964–1973. Anne Lise Witten (Mrs. Oscar), AA 1962, PA 1973–76.

14. HISTORY IN THE MAKING

1. Quoted in Principal's Report, 2 June 1952. Conant made his speech in April 1952.
2. Ayer School Survey, quoted in fall Principal's Reports from 1948 to 1951.
3. Principal's Report, 3 December 1948.
4. Ibid., 6 June 1949.
5. James B. Conant, *Education and Liberty: The Role of Schools in a Modern Democracy* (Cambridge, Harvard University Press, 1953), 78.
6. Ibid., 137, 138.
7. Arthur Bestor, *Educational Wastelands; the retreat from learning in our public schools* (Chicago, University of Illinois Press, 1953); also Albert Lynd, *Quackery in the Public Schools* (Boston, Atlantic Monthly Press, Little Brown, 1953). The average state department of education had two people in 1860.
8. Conant, *Education and Liberty*, 62.
9. Speech to the first faculty meeting, 13 September 1947, manuscript.
10. Quoted in Principal's Report, 6 December 1951. These resolves are all the more admirable considering that it was the Republican leadership of Congress that had initiated the loyalty investigations after the war— and Abbot's constituency, like that of most independent schools, remained overwhelmingly Republican.
11. Ibid., 8 December 1953.

12. Ibid., 7 October 1954.
13. Ibid., 8 December 1953.
14. See ibid., 6 June 1949. The nearly universal rumor at the time was that the two chief organizers of the Putney strike were Communists. However, not one of several Putney teachers consulted who were taking one side or another can say with certainty that this was the case, nor can the daughter of the then-Director or the parent-consultant called in to help mediate the dispute. The organizers' methods, which would have been familiar enough in a large textile mill, were a shock to long-time teachers in this small, informal, school community. Since the principal figures are now dead, we will probably never know —even if it mattered.
15. Ibid., 7 October 1954, 11 April 1952, 10 December 1954.
16. Twenty-five percent in most women's colleges in the early 1950's.
17. Teachers' recollections; interview, A. C. Sweeney.
18. Dean's files; alumnae and parent recollections.
19. Interview, A. C. Sweeney; Principal's Report, 16 April 1953.
20. In June of the year before the first wave of war babies began applying to secondary schools, Miss Hearsey reported to the Trustees that Abbot was "overflowing"; a long waiting list of able candidates had impelled the school to write over 100 families that further applications could not be considered. (Principal's Report, 7 June 1954.)
21. Conant, *Education and Liberty*, 29–54.
22. Flagg's little sermons to Miss Bailey and the Trustees on this subject (3 December 1931) are interesting. He doubtless made sure Miss Hearsey heard his ideas as well. He believed firmly that the small school was of most benefit to the individual student. See also Seymour B. Sarason, *The Culture of the School and the Problem of Change* (Boston, Allyn and Bacon, 1971), 94–103. Sarason reports research begun in the early 1960's which confirms what Abbot parents seemed to know without resort to social science: that all students are more positively involved in the out-of-class life of a small school community than in a large school, and that the beneficial effect on a student's total performance is particularly significant for "marginal" students.
23. Parent and alumnae recollections.
24. Interviews and conversations with representative local citizens, including three public school teachers. One of the latter says about Abbot admissions in the late thirties and mid-sixties, "The dumbest kid could get in if her parents were the right social class."
25. Alumna recollection (graduate of 1955).
26. One fourth to one third of the student body each year was composed of alumnae relatives. When the admissions office asked new enrollees why they had come to Abbot in the fall of 1949 and 1950, eighty-three answered that friends or relatives had told them of Abbot, nineteen had been urged to apply by college admissions officers or school guidance counselors, six day students said, "I live in Andover," seven

boarders mentioned Phillips Academy connections, and just eight had responded to advertisements or picked up catalogues in school placement agencies.

27. Interviews and conversations with local citizens. Principal's Report, 7 November 1963: "Community relations . . . are still minimal," writes Mrs. Crane. Tamblyn and Brown in their 1966–67 Report to the Trustees, wrote that community leaders found Abbot Academy rather removed from the town, as contrasted with Phillips Academy. For example, Miriam Putnam, Andover's Head Librarian at Memorial Hall Library for twenty-five years, has said that Abbot was glad to help out in any emergency (such as Hungarian Relief in 1956) but that the steady, close relations of earlier years had essentially disappeared by 1950. "Phillips was much more involved," she says.

28. Interview, Caroline Stevens Rogers.

29. Other hardworking Trustees can be found in this full account of the Board as it stood in the Spring of '57 when the Trustees were just beginning to gear up to a new level of involvement in Abbot affairs. The short biographical sketches make clear how much besides Abbot the Trustees had in common. From *Bulletin* (May 1957), 2–3:

The Board of Trustees of Abbot Academy consists of seventeen members, nine men and eight women; it meets four times a year. Now serving on the Board are the following:

• ROBERT I. HUNNEMAN of Boston and Brookline, President of Board. A graduate of Noble and Greenough School, Mr. Hunneman holds an A.B. from Harvard and LL.B. from Harvard Law School. He is a partner in the law firm of Palmer, Dodge, Gardner & Bradford of Boston. He is a trustee of Radcliffe College, and Treasurer and Trustee of Noble and Greenough School.

• J. RADFORD ABBOT of Andover. A graduate of Phillips Academy, Mr. Abbot has an A.B. from Harvard and a M.Arch. from the Harvard School of Architecture. He is an architect.

• JANE BALDWIN '22 of New York City. Since 1930, Miss Baldwin has been a trust administrator of the Irving Trust Co. She is a former alumnae trustee.

• MRS. HERBERT CARTER (Pauline Humeston '27) of Englewood, N. J., alumnae trustee. She has an A.B. degree from Wellesley. She has two sons and a daughter.

• MARGARET CLAPP, president of Wellesley College. She holds an A.B. degree from Wellesley and a Ph.D. in history from Columbia. Her biography, *Forgotten First Citizen: John Bigelow*, was awarded the Pulitzer Prize for biography in 1948.

• MRS. ALEXANDER CRANE, principal. A graduate of the Winsor School, she studied at the Sorbonne for one year as the recipient of the Nora Saltonstall Scholarship. She received an A.B. degree from Bryn Mawr, *cum laude*. She has four daughters.

- BURTON S. FLAGG of Andover, treasurer of Abbot since 1906. A graduate of Worcester Academy, he has an A.B. dgeree from Brown. He has been president of the Merrimack Mutual Fire Insurance Company since 1923, and president of the Andover Savings Bank. In addition, he holds office in many civic, financial, religious and fraternal organizations. Three daughters and two granddaughters attended Abbot.
- MRS. LENERT W. HENRY (Helen Allen '32) of Hingham, Mass. She has an A.B. degree from Smith. A former alumnae trustee, she was chairman of the Gymnasium Fund Drive. She has three sons.
- MRS. WILBUR K. JORDAN of Cambridge, Mass. Mrs. Jordan received an A.B. degree from Vassar and an M.A. from Radcliffe. Her husband is the president of Radcliffe.
- REV. SIDNEY LOVETT, chaplain of Yale University since 1932. A graduate of Browne and Nichols, he received an A.B. degree from Yale. He holds two honorary degrees, an A.M. from Yale and a Doctor of Divinity from Dartmouth. He has long been active in welfare work. His wife is Esther *Parker* Lovett, 1908.
- E. BENJAMIN REDFIELD, JR. of Swampscott, Mass. He is a special agent of Northwestern Mutual Life Insurance Co. He is director of many business and civic organizations. He was chairman of the Parents' Committee of the Abbot Gymnasium Fund, and is now chairman of the Abbot Development Fund. His daughter, Deborah, graduated from Abbot in 1950.
- MRS. HORATIO ROGERS of North Andover, Mass. A graduate of Winsor, Mrs. Rogers received an A.B. degree from Bryn Mawr. She served overseas with the Children's Bureau of the American Red Cross in World War I.
- GEORGE F. SAWYER, of Andover. He is a graduate of Phillips Andover, and has an A.B. degree from Yale and an M.B.A. from Harvard. He is vice-president of the First National Bank of Boston. His daughter, Elizabeth, attended Abbot.
- DONALD B. SMITH of Wellesley Hills, Mass. He is a graduate of Mt. Allison University and holds a Ph.D. from Harvard Graduate School of Arts and Sciences. He is an economic consultant. His daughter, Cynthia, graduated from Abbot in 1945.
- STODDARD M. STEVENS, JR. of Short Hills, N. J. He holds an A.B. degree from Cornell and an LL.B. from Columbia. He is a partner in the law firm of Sullivan and Cromwell in New York City. His daughter, Marion, graduated from Abbot in 1944.
- MRS. H. GUYFORD STEVER (Louise Risley '37) of Belmont, Mass., alumnae trustee. She holds an A.B. degree from Smith and an M.S. from Simmons College of Social Work. She has two sons and two daughters.

- GARDNER SUTTON, comptroller and clerk of Board. A graduate of Noble and Greenough, he holds an A.B. degree from Harvard. His wife, Elizabeth *Southworth* Sutton, 1930, and his two sisters are Abbot alumnae.

30. The planning began in earnest shortly after VE Day, and never really stopped until Miss Hearsey's retirement in 1955. MCH had hoped to pick up the Draper Hall project where it had been left off in 1941, but most of the Trustees found roof revision less than compelling, and this plan was finally dropped. It is intriguing to watch the Chapel's "maximum seating capacity" expanding through the fifties. In 1947 the absolute limit was 200, but need had found a way to squeeze in new benches and molify the fire department when by 1955, 225 looked like the magic number.

31. It did not appear suddenly. Barton Chapin's board had been inquiring of other schools about their salary scales since 1940. In 1942 the Principal's salary was raised, along with that of several others, but Miss Hearsey was still receiving substantially less than Miss Bailey did in 1930. The Trustees asked Miss Hearsey to investigate the possibility of a published salary scale in 1944. She presented a detailed report (4 October 1945), and they accepted in principle the salary scale idea (then $1400 to "at least $3000"), but inflation played such havoc with materials and maintenance costs from 1946 to 1948 that the salary problem was deferred.

32. Miss Hearsey told the Trustees in the Principal's Report, 17 May 1945, that "salaries a good deal higher than our present ones have been offered some of our teachers," this presumably to woo them away from Abbot. And the shortage of teachers would continue for almost twenty years.

33. This figure includes "living," as nearly as Flagg could calculate it. Complete salary figures were not kept on file between 1936 and 1966. As early as 1943 Miss Hearsey expressed her concern about the growing differential between women's compensation inside and outside of teaching, noting that many government jobs gave a young woman just out of college $2400, twice the cash salary she would then have received at Abbot. That same year the Headmistresses Association appointed a Professional Standards Committee to keep member schools in close touch with the situation. (Principal's Report, 2 December 1943. See also ibid., 9 December 1949 and 10 December 1954.) In all but starting salaries for inexperienced teachers, Abbot lagged well behind the salary scale recommended in the fall of 1954 by the Salary Study Committee of the Headmistresses Association ($3000 plus living for a ten-year teacher and $4000–4700 plus living for a retirement-age teacher).

34. Undated Treasurer's memorandum. Its position in the files suggests that it was written in either March '49 or March '50.

35. The Trustees had instituted Abbot's own retirement fund in 1937, one year after fixing the retirement age at sixty-five. They built it up

slowly by applying one percent of the payroll to it each year, an entirely too modest sum which they raised to a less modest 3 percent in 1940. This internal fund allowed the Trustees and Treasurer to continue to use "special legislation . . . to cover individual situations," in Flagg's words. Its "wisdom [is] clear," Flagg wrote on Katherine Kelsey's death. "No system of ordinary accumulated pension payments could have been so adequate" for Miss Kelsey. (Treasurer's Report, 7 December 1939. See also ibid., 9 April 1937.) No other retirees received such liberal grants as Katherine Kelsey and Flora Mason, however; those who left the school before retirement got none at all, no matter how long they had worked for Abbot, until the school joined TIAA. In his usual fair-minded way, Flagg allowed his sense of duty to overcome his personal opinion and launched the initial investigation into the TIAA plans and procedures. He first laid them before the Trustees in 1940. (Treasurer's Report, 5 December 1940.)

36. It was bringing Marie Craig through her long old age that finally decided the Trustees on a change. She retired at seventy in 1938; she required a special bonus of $15 a month in 1940, an "emergency grant" in 1944, help to pay the premium on her life insurance, the interest on her loans, the rent for her rooming house, etc. through 1945. (Treasurer's Reports, 5 December 1940 and 18 January 1945.)

37. Beverly Brooks Floe '41. Because BBF did not have this teacher in class, her friends gave her the job of telling Miss Hearsey about her, which she did, feeling "terribly uncomfortable" over the sad errand. A. Kubler-Merrill, '56, and a Crane-era teacher describe two others of the Crane period as well. See also Principal's Report 7 March 1960, in which Mary Crane describes the older teachers' need for funds to supplement their pensions, since TIAA and Social Security came so late in their careers.

38. Miss Hearsey suggested that such a plan be created (Principal's Reports, 2 October 1947 and 8 April 1949) but in vain. Periodically the Trustees considered it and tabled it.

39. Interviews with Trustees. One long-time faculty member describes a Mrs. B. who was "a smarty—she invested well. She had something on which to live and the school didn't have to help her and it didn't."

40.

	INCOME			FIXED COSTS		OPERATING EXPENSES	FINAL BALANCE
	Tuitions	Investment	Other (mostly alumnae gifts)	Depreciation + $500 Summer faculty grant	Retirement and Pensions		
1939	$195,049	18,409	1,622	3,569	632	192,565	+ 18,315
1948	265,925	21,352	3,557	6,531	14,073	280,200	− 9,969

41. Principal's Reports, 1 May 1945, 2 June 1947, 2 October 1947, 5 June 1950, 13 April 1951, 4 October 1951, 11 April 1952.

42. MCH in letter to fathers of recent graduates, 23 July 1951. See also Principal's Report, 12 April 1954.

43. Principal's Report, 11 April 1952.

44. Abbot never did get the hoped-for $300,000, but the gymnasium was fully paid for (total cost, $223,632) and the remaining $10,000 that was eventually raised (spring 1956 figures) went to its maintenance fund.

45. According to the accounting in a February 1962 *Bulletin* (pp. 4-6) based on 2100 alumnae's replies to a questionnaire, (60 percent of the total), 27 percent from the classes before 1930 had always been single compared with 23 percent from the after-1930 alumnae. The younger group included many college-age women who were probably planning to marry.

46. "Bits from the Treasurer's Desk," *Bulletin* (February 1955), 8-9.

47. Surveys, 1950-51, 1955-56, 1960-61, from Dean's Office files, Abbot Archives. The range of IQ scores is interesting: for Seniors, 77-166 in 1951, 84-175 in 1961. Contrary to what one might expect, the lowest scores were not made by foreign students.

48. Miss Hearsey, speaking in 1939 on "Women of Tomorrow," became the first Abbot Principal we know of to support careers for mothers: "It has been conclusively proved that there is nothing incompatible between women's work and marriage and motherhood." But the old Abbot values still held firm. "Far more important (she went on) is her impact upon tomorrow's world as a stabilizing, humanizing force."

49. Principal's Reports and odd packets of letters record the extraordinary numbers of faculty leaves taken to care for ill relatives throughout the twentieth century, tapering off only after the federal Old Age Assistance program was created in 1935. Teachers might suddenly have to leave Abbot for a week, or for a year. Once large numbers of Abbot women were living in apartments outside the dormitories, the aged mothers, sisters, and aunts came to join them in Andover.

50. Della D. Cyrus in "Why Mothers Fail," *Atlantic Monthly* (March 1947), 59. Cyrus wrote a reasonably sophisticated version of an issue much less subtly argued in the pulp magazines and on the women's pages. See also Erik H. Erikson, *Childhood and Society* (New York, W. W. Norton, 2nd edition, 1963), 288-298.

51. Cyrus, "Why Mothers Fail," 58.

52. E. S. Martin in *The Unrest of Women*, 9.

53. Betty Friedan, *The Feminine Mystique* (New York, 1963), 70, 74.

54. Interestingly, a survey of alumnae records for the Class of 1955 shows that forty-two of the seventy-three members of the class did eventually take paid jobs. Of these, sixteen have worked five years or more in jobs that suggest clear commitment to a career. Several others answered

the 1974 questionnaire by saying "to work full time beginning 1975." (These figures are rough, because about 10 percent of the folders are incomplete.)

55. Friedan, *Mystique*, 73.
56. See also ibid., 296–297.
57. Teachers' recollections.
58. See William Manchester, *The Glory and the Dream* (Boston, Little Brown, 1973), 477–81, and Gael Greene, *Sex and the College Girl* (New York, Dell Publishing, 1964). The Greene book is perhaps the most reliable accounting of a subject endlessly discussed in popular books and articles.
59. Greene, *Sex*, 34.
60. Brooks School in North Andover appears far more often than does Phillips Academy in Principal's Reports and *Cynosure* accounts of co-ed plays and clubs during the fifties and early sixties. Brooks boys became the first to take male leads away from Abbot drama buffs in 1964, a move that stimulated much private regret among the newly limited actresses.
61. From time to time Miss Hearsey had invited lecturers or psychologists to talk about sex and hygiene, and to speak privately with any interested student. Graduates of '41 felt she was doing this "as a matter of duty" rather than from any sustained conviction on the matter. A Mrs. Phillips was more successful in 1947, but only returned one year after that.
62. Alumnae of 1956, 1960, 1962, and 1972, and three teachers, 1959–1973.
63. Two alumnae of 1962.

VI. The Final Decade, 1963–1973

1. Morris Dickstein, *The Gates of Eden: American Culture in the Sixties* (New York, Basic Books, 1977), chapters 1 and 2.

15. THE TRUSTEES DECIDE

1. CEEB scores demonstrate an upward trend in tested academic ability of applicants:
(Range 200–800)

Median Score of Scholastic Aptitude Test of Abbot Girls Taken in the Spring of 11th Year

	Verbal	Math
Class of 1951	433	438
Class of 1956	503	515
Class of 1961	533	548

2. From Re-Evaluation Report, written by Valeria Addams Knapp (Winsor School), E. Phillips Wilson (Phillips Exeter Academy), and Alnah James Johnson (Chairman, Dana Hall).

3. Recollections of two alumnae, class of 1962.

4. Alumna, '62, recollection.

5. Alumnae and teachers' recollections.

6. "There's too much to do," she wrote alumnae in the May 1962 *Bulletin* (p. 4), a refrain echoed in many a Principal's Report as well—though usually she couched the observation as a challenge rather than a lament.

7. Alumnae recollections. Among Abbot Seniors, the private women's colleges were slowly giving way in popularity to a range of coeducational and public institutions; in 1935, 75 percent of the Seniors attended the traditional four-year women's colleges, most of these (21 of 29) going to Smith, Vassar, or Wellesley. In 1950 exactly half of all Seniors went to the traditional colleges. In 1962 fewer than one third of the Seniors went on to these colleges, with just half of the subgroup attending Smith, Vassar, or Wellesley. That year students applied to 67 different colleges and universities, including junior colleges.

8. *Cynosure*, 14 April 1961.

9. Ibid., 21 January 1963.

10. Parent of 1959 graduate, in conversation. See also Principal's Report, 5 February 1958, for Student Council complaint over the same issue.

11. *Cynosure*, 3 June 1961, 1 December 1961.

12. Ibid., 1 June 1962.

13. Ibid., 5 May 1962.

14. *Sargent's Handbook of Private Schools*, 44th ed. (Boston, Porter Sargent, 1963), 103.

15. Trustee Minutes, 7 February 1963.

16. Trustee Minutes, 25 April 1963.

17. Cresap, McCormick and Paget, Abbot Academy, "A Study of Organization and Administration" (January, 1964), pp. III–6, III–7, III–12, IV–6, IV–7.

18. Interviews, Allen and Finger. Finger remembered that Flagg was particularly saddened by having to resign from the Abbot Board because it was the very last responsibility he had held onto as he gradually retired from his extraordinarily active life of public service.

19. Cresap Report, p. III–8.

20. Teacher recollections.

21. Two teachers' assessment of the problem.

22. Membership in the three subcommittees was as follows:
Administrative Policies Committee

Mrs. Wilbur K. Jordan, Chairman
Mr. Grenville Benedict (Dean of Students, Phillips Academy)
Mrs. Abby Castle Kemper (Abbot, '31, wife of John M. Kemper, Phillips Headmaster)
Miss Alice Sweeney

Buildings and Ground Committee
Mrs. Horatio Rogers, Chairman
Mr. Radford Abbot
Mr. Philip K. Allen
Mr. Gardner Sutton (Ass't. Treasurer)

Planning and Development Committee
Mr. Robert Hunneman, Chairman
Mrs. Helen Allen Henry
Mr. Benjamin Redfield

23. Mrs. Crane had been recommending increases to the Trustees for years, but never forcefully enough, she fears. She regrets she did not "take more of a lead in requiring the Trustees" to raise salaries. (MC, interview.)

24. The largest jump was taken in the two years after Mary Crane left. Exact percentages of increases:

highest salary	45.5
median salary	33.3
low salary	38.9

25. The Independent School Talent Search Program was begun in 1963 and soon attracted foundation support; its resources were greatly amplified after 1965, when the federal Office of Economic Opportunity agreed to fund up to four students at full tuition for each full scholarship Abbot (and other independent schools) provided for candidates chosen by ISTS.

26. Muthoni found a special welcome at Virginia Powel's home, where she went often to get help with her English writing from Harford Powel, Ginny's husband and an English teacher on leave from Phillips Academy because of illness. When she left Abbot she gave Harford Powel a watercolor painting she had made from memory of her village home in Kenya (she had not been able to return for two years), along with the poem entitled "My Last Day in Kenya."

27. See Principal's Reports, 25 May 1944, and 2 December 1943. Some of Abbot's scholarship and recruiting effort was geared to attract students from different sections of the country. Following are data on geographical distribution of girls entering in September 1962, when Abbot accepted 30 percent of its applicants:

California	2	New York	4
Connecticut	11	North Carolina	1
Maine	4	Ohio	1
Massachusetts:		Pennsylvania	5
Boarders	18	Rhode Island	2
Day	11	Virginia	1
Michigan	1		
Mississippi	1	*Foreign Countries:*	
Montana	2	England	1
New Hampshire	6	The Netherlands	2
New Jersey	3	The Philippines	1

The Principal and Trustees felt that Abbot should be still more diverse; they wished to attract black students (there had been none since 1956) and more foreign students. Mary Crane and the Administrative Policies Committee made this happen.

28. Report of Committee to Study Financial Needs, chaired by Gardner Sutton, 1964.
29. Jean Bennett and Germaine Arosa served two terms together; Carolyn Kellogg Salon, Carolyn Goodwin, Dorothy Judd, and Jean Bennett were a typical 1965–67 roster.
30. Principal's Report, 7 November 1963.
31. Teachers' recollections, especially Virginia Powel, interview.
32. Teachers' recollections. "Some housemothers were extremely stupid," says one teacher, who had carried corridor supervision herself and knew how complex the job could be. "We were [she goes on to acknowledge] super-critical of them, sometimes unreasonably so."
33. Letter, 22 August 1977.
34. Alumnae recollections.
35. Sherman House letter, undated.
36. Sherman House letter, 29 May 1964.
37. Letter to the author, Winter 1976.
38. See Principal's Report, 5 February 1963.
39. Cresap Report, p. IV–17.
40. Principal's Report, 7 March 1960.
41. Mrs. Crane in interview.
42. See Cresap Report, pp. IV–16 and IV–17; also Principal's Report, 28 May 1963, with "observations," MC's special report on school needs attached.
43. Information from author's attendance at trustees' meetings, Putney School, Putney, Vermont, from 1958 to 1970, as well as from Mrs. Crane's Principal's Reports to the Trustees (especially 22 April 1965, a summary of past recruiting problems), including news from the Headmistresses Association and the NAPSG.
44. Alumnae and faculty recollections. Miss Hatch is remembered as a demanding teacher and an eminently fair Director of Residence. A

typical comment: "Miss Hatch was a favorite person, an angel! For her to hold that job and be able to keep her sense of humor and fairness was really extraordinary" (alumna, '62).

45. Alumnae and faculty recollections.

46. Account from alumnae, Trustees' and teachers' recollections. See also Executive Committee Minutes, 18 January 1966, and Principal's Report, 27 January 1966.

47. Observations confirmed by numerous faculty recollections.

48. Report of Tamblyn and Brown, 1966–67, and admissions records. The quality of applicants held up fairly well. The median for Abbot girls' scores on CAAT's (Comprehensive Academic Aptitude Test, a kind of group IQ test) ran at the 66th percentile for the Class of 1967, still above the independent school median of the 63.7 percentile but not so impressive as in 1961.

49. Interview, P. K. Allen; see also Executive Committee Minutes, 19 July 1965, when the Trustees considered transferring the Admissions Director to a job in the Alumnae Office.

50. Interviews of three Trustees; quotation from P. K. Allen.

51. Interviews of two Trustees.

52. Mary Crane, "The Objectives of Abbot Academy," February 1965.

53. Trustees' recollections. One of the three Trustees who made this observation feels Mary Crane may not really have had a chance because "she had the Board Chairman against her from the beginning." A fourth Trustee thought she was "very good," even though she "hadn't a great deal of influence with the girls," and was "surprised" when she was asked to resign.

54. Alumna recollection, townsperson recollection.

55. Principal's Report, 31 May 1964.

56. Mrs. Crane served on several of the NEACSS Accreditation (or "Evaluation") committees, visiting other schools as the NEACSS had visited Abbot to evaluate their programs and their status as member schools in good standing.

57. A sample of such news from 1961–63:

Reports in the section "What Schools are Doing": of Asian and Russian language courses and "problem-oriented" social science courses.

A report of mathematics courses guided by the SMSG (the University-Secondary School teacher-staffed School Mathematics Study Group) May 1962, January 1963.

Reports of major fund drives in many schools.

A report of an advanced biology course partially taught at a local medical school.

Reports of institution of humanities courses in several schools.

Reports of school-sponsored field work and travel projects, including the Abbot NAIS-sponsored tour of Greece co-led by Mary Crane during the spring vacation of 1962. (Cost: $695.00)

58. *Bulletin* (May 1963), 4. See also ibid. (February 1963), 2, and Mary Crane, "The Objectives of Abbot Academy," February 1965.
59. Mary Crane, interview, and Principal's Report, 5 November 1964. See also Principal's Report, 20 October 1962.
60. Trustee Minutes, 3 November 1966.

16. "MAKE NO LITTLE PLANS"

1. M. H. Crane interview.
2. Interviews, E. M. Tucker and P. K. Allen.
3. Trustee recollection, teachers' recollections.
4. According to V. Powel, the dark room built next to the fourth-floor Draper art studios during that exciting "experimental and often frenzied first year" (*Cynosure*, 31 May 1968) had to be moved after students twice left water running in and over sinks and down three stories onto Eleanor Tucker's desk. Enough was enough.
5. Interview, Eleanor Tucker; alumnae recollections.
6. Interviews, Jean Bennett, Carolyn Goodwin. Germaine Arosa remembers students rather suddenly finding that they could make sense of writers like George Sand, whose peculiar sexual foci had seemed inaccessible before.
7. Recollections of alumnae, faculty, and townspeople. Philip Allen, Mr. Andover Republican himself, had invited Thomas, whose granddaughter was in the graduating class.
8. *Cynosure*, 13 October 1967.
9. Alumnae recollections of students of classes of '49, '54, '57, '59, '63, '68. The '59 graduate shared her friends' feelings even though she felt certain that "Abbot was one of the best girls' schools available." See also occasional remarks in publications from about 1935 to 1963. An example: *The Page*, (16 January 1948), a student mimeo rag, described Abbot French students' experience at a French movie shown on the Hill. It was so fast-moving that "even the French students at P.A. didn't understand it." Another: *Cynosure* (June 1966), projecting the P.A. prom weekend schedule, told how escorts would take their dates "up to the great adult world of the P.A. Prom."
10. Mary Crane interview.
11. Summary of discussions on planning the physical plant, 1967.
12. Speech at the annual meeting of the Abbot Alumnae Association, 13 May 1967. Excerpted in *Bulletin* (May 1967), 3. Allen threw another smoke screen before *Cynosure* reporters just after Donald Gordon had been hired, telling them (by their account) that, "the firm hand of a man was preferred over that of a woman because of the current difficulty in raising money for such programs as the Building Funds." *Cynosure*, 10 November 1967.

13. Interview, J. K. Dow. Dow was a member of the Search Committee, along with H. Henry, F. Jordan, and A. Kemper.
14. See Elizabeth B. Hall, "The Vanishing Headmistress," in *The Independent School Bulletin* (October 1966), 39–41, and Cary Potter, "Some Further Observations on the Vanishing Headmistress," ibid., 42–43. Hall describes the cultural and ideological roots of the problem, Potter the practical dimension. In two of the years (1964 and 1965) during which the NAIS solicited names of potential administrators from member schools, a list of 145 promising people included only fourteen women. The disparity could be partly explained by the small size of most girls' schools and the tendency of public schools to reserve many administrative jobs for men.
15. Interviews, Allen and Dow.
16. Interview, P. K. Allen.
17. Alumni records, Philips Academy Archives; Donald Gordon in conversation and in talks to the Abbot faculty.
18. Donald Gordon and Peter Stapleton, "The Amateur Sandwich," manuscript, 75 pages (partially unpaginated), and "Toward a Human Headmaster," *Independent School Bulletin* (December 1970), 22–24. Gordon acknowledges that "The Amateur Sandwich" "is almost a period piece now," being a "plainly irreverent effort" to describe the multiple demands on the school head during a time of rapid change, from which society has retreated part way in the late seventies. (Letter to Beverly Floe, 6 November 1975, and interview with the author, summer 1975.)
19. "Sandwich," chapter 4, p. 1.
20. *Cynosure*, 10 November 1967.
21. *Cynosure*, 31 May 1968.
22. Principal's Report, June 1967, and faculty recollections. Several faculty members say that Miss Tucker was "absolutely exhausted" by the spring of 1968. Gordon LeMayer had taken over some of the duties of the Director of Studies for 1967–68, but "Tuck" still bore a terrific load. By 1969 three people were doing the jobs she managed alone for one of her two years as Acting Principal.
23. *Cynosure*, 31 May 1968.
24. Donald Gordon in his Installation address, November 1968.
25. *Cynosure*, 13 December 1968.
26. Nancy Steele in *Cynosure*, 3 October 1968.
27. And let the traditional dodges cease: no more would parents come to Abbot to pick up daughters of a Saturday and drop them in Boston for a day of shopping and fun, as a few had done before to bring them out of reach of the omnipresent Abbot chaperone. Alumna recollection, Class of 1968, and interview of alumna, Class of 1970, by Mary Jean Hu.
28. *Cynosure*, 14 November 1968.
29. Teachers' recollections. Of the latter argument, one teacher who was

on the spot in 1966–67 says, "We really did talk about that, really did," as though no sane person would believe her.

30. Teachers' recollections.
31. Two teachers' recollections; secretary's recollections.
32. Interview, G. Arosa, and teacher recollection of Arosa's position.
33. Gordon in conversation, recollections of one Trustee and several teachers.
34. An Arts building was first formally proposed to the Trustees in April 1965, following an extensive faculty-trustee study of building needs.
35. Miss Porter's ($3.8 million), Ethel Walker ($5.3 million), Northfield-Mt. Hermon ($12.6 million), and several other farther-flung competitors, such as Foxcroft ($3.9 million) and Andrews School ($11 million) all had higher endowments than Abbot in 1968–69, when Abbot's was $2,291,000. Emma Willard, Westover, and the Masters School stood as $2.3 million, $1.7 million, and $2.4 million, respectively. All figures represent market value, a volatile index in these years. (Figures from *Voluntary Support of Education*, 1968–69 issue. Porter Sargent's *Handbook of Private Schools* for the same year records slightly different amounts.)
36. It is worth quoting the observer mentioned in the last chapter, a cautious man, a professional fund-raiser, and an Abbot friend, who has this to say about Abbot's fund-raising efforts before 1968: "I've come to the conclusion that Abbot was what it was because men always controlled the finances as trustees, treasurers, and business managers. They held the lid on but never got very excited about raising money to improve the status of women, whether students or teachers."
37. From $75,856 to $74,805 in combined alumnae-friend donations. A minor economic recession during the 1968–69 school year may have accounted for the slowdown.
38. Conversation, Carolyn Goodwin. Without endorsing his every move or the speed with which he made them, Miss Goodwin says she can understand Gordon's reasoning.
39. Interviews, J. K. Dow, Philip Allen, Donald Gordon, Helen (Henry) Anderson, and Alice Sweeney.
40. The year 1964–65 was right after the Trustees began trying earnestly to respond to the Cresap consultants' opinion that salaries must go higher. Meanwhile, the cost-price index had risen by 12 percent between 1964 and 1969. Some of the salaries were for new positions, some simply much higher (Gordon's was 40 percent larger than Miss Tucker's had been; a married man with two children, he would be earning by his third year at Abbot about twice the salary and benefits that she seemed to require). Total administrative salaries in 1967–68 were $21,600 (with secretarial salaries, $33,100); in 1969–70, $53,000 (secretarial, $47,000). The average teacher's salary went from $5751.72 to

$6656.25 in the same two years. Men's salaries for 1969–70 were $550 higher than the average for longer tenured women, but by 1972, salaries for male and female teachers were, on the average, just about equal, with the men's slightly lower. Administrative salaries would take another jump in 1970–71 to $75,700. "What would Mr. Flagg have thought?" one alumna has asked, knowing the answer. Flagg inveighed against the tendency of schools to pile on administrators (in one of his last "Comments of the Treasurer," 4 June 1962), and finished by quoting an admired college professor: "Someone should rise up and say, 'We teach'!"

41. Alumna recollection.

42. Alumnae recollections.

43. Abbot's town meeting did not spring from nowhere. Friends' schools had quietly run school affairs by student-faculty consensus for decades, and town meetings had been under discussion in some established independent schools for several years. The Cambridge School, of Weston, where Philip Allen had taught for two happy years as a young man, instituted a town meeting in 1967 which was much like Abbot's later version. Allen and his wife Betty had met periodically since 1966 with Abbot student government officers, lending encouragement to their bid for more recognition and responsibility. Abbot's new school government was conservative compared with arrangements invented by some of the "free schools" that included all academic matters as well as social ones under town meeting jurisdiction, and made the majority decision final.

44. Interview, Gordon, summer 1975, and *Andover Bulletin*, Phillips Academy (November 1963), 4, 5.

45. The first town meeting vote required shirts or dresses for Sunday dinner, and "left up to the teacher's discretion whether or not informal clothes should be allowed in the classroom"; but these qualifications were soon dropped. Actually, the famous "tie shoes" had gone out in the spring of 1969. Gordon was asking Student Council members why they objected, and one girl described the process by which girls' feet were tested each fall, then retested in the spring, telling him that her feet won an A— for her first fall test, but had deteriorated to a B+ by spring after a year of tie shoes. According to a teacher who was also there, "Don just exploded at that point. So much for tie shoes."

46. Rev. James Rae Whyte, quoted by F. A. Allis, in *Youth From Every Quarter* (Andover, 1978), pp. 660.

47. Like almost all town meeting committees, this one consisted of volunteers; if there were more volunteers than could be accommodated, the town meeting officers selected the committee, often staffing working subcommittees with the surplus.

48. A two-thirds quorum rule prevented votes being controlled by aggres-

sive minorities but the rule was later changed to allow a vote in the meeting that followed, after minutes had been published and fair warning of issues to be decided had been given.

49. *Cynosure*, 7 November 1969.
50. Teachers' recollections. See also the Acting Principal's Report to the Trustees, 18 February 1968, concerning teachers who "do very little work for the school outside of the classroom."
51. Interview, Gordon.
52. Abbot *Forum* (Fall 1969), 13. See also Stapleton's article, "Make It Yourself Exams for Do It Yourself English," *English Journal*, Vol. 62 #2, February, 1973, 275–277.
53. Abbot *Forum* (Fall 1968), 15.
54. Interview, alumna.
55. Gordon, "If Not Now, When?" *Andover Bulletin* (November 1969), 2.
56. Conversation, Marion Finbury, confirmed by alumnae recollections.
57. Conversation, Finbury and Gordon.
58. Conversation, Finbury. An average of one Senior a year from 1966 to 1969 went from Abbot to Radcliffe, slightly more than the average for 1950–66.
59. Interview, Gordon.
60. Abbot *Forum* (December 1971), 6.
61. Observations of many teachers and of four parents; alumnae recollections.
62. *The Choate News*, 25 January 1969, quoted in Alan R. Blackmer, *An Inquiry into Student Unrest in Independent Secondary Schools* (Boston, National Association of Independent Schools, 1970), 20.
63. Address given at M.I.T., 4 March 1969.
64. *Report of the Faculty Steering Committee*, Volume I (Phillips Academy, Andover, 15 December 1966), 4.
65. 7 November 1969.
66. Title of chapter taken from the 24 March 1970 *Look* article by "Thomas Doland" (pseudonym), in Marc Liberle and Tom Seligman, editors, *The High School Revolutionaries*, (New York, Random House, 1970). According to Richard Sheahan, the *Look* issue hit the newsstands the day the New Abbot Fund opened at the Yale Club in New York City. "It was awful," he says. A Trustee who was sympathetic to Gordon's efforts remembers being "appalled. Only a trash magazine such as *Look* would have published it without verifying it."
67. Ibid., 188, 184, 183.
68. Ibid., 184.
69. Letter to the author, Jane Baldwin.
70. Interviews, Allen and Dow.
71. *Cynosure*, 12 December 1969.
72. Allis, *Youth*, 663–665; Phillips teacher recollections.
73. Recollections of four students and six teachers.

74. Alumni records, Phillips Academy Archives.

75. In a single winter month (February 1973), for example, Gordon traveled to three different conferences (he was on The Independent School Association of Massachusetts Board of Directors) and spent four days in South Dakota seeing that all was well with the six Abbot girls there.

76. Gordon, letter to Stapleton, 6 January 1969.

77. "Sandwich," chapter 3.

78. Ibid., chapter 6.

79. Ibid. The Principal's files from the Gordon years are filled with letters that begin with such phrases as "This has been a wild period, and I am embarrassed to be delayed" (letter to teacher, 7 May 1969); "June is ripping . . . and I suddenly remembered that we had never gotten together to discuss your contract" (letter to teacher, 31 [sic] June 1970); "I feel badly about our delay (letter to teacher, 5 May 1969); "I still love you—never fear—but the pile on my desk *does* get in the way" (letter to teacher, 2 October 1972).

80. Interview, Gordon.

81. Speech presented at "Old Scholars Day," the first day of Abbot's fiftieth anniversary celebration, 10 June 1879, quoted in McKeen, *Annals*, 173.

82. Alumnae recollections; quotes from 1972 and 1970 graduates.

83. *Circle* (1970), 3. Charles Dickens' opening passage from *A Tale of Two Cities* provided the Class of 1970 with the epigraph, and their metaphor for the year.

84. Letters from alumnae, Classes of 1970 and 1971.

85. Carolyn Johnston finds it amusing that these magical eyes should have so utterly failed her one working Saturday, when one independent character named Tara Sartorius carried the lumber for an enormous water bed frame past her open office door piece by piece, hammered it together up on the third floor of Draper, and filled the mattress with 100 gallons of water, all without a trace of suspicion from the Dean's Office.

86. One consequence of Abbot's enlarged constituency was the smaller proportion of alumnae relatives that attended in the seventies: an average of about 10 percent instead of the steady 15–18 percent of the fifties and early sixties. According to Faith Howland Kaiser, another group all but ceased to apply: the daughters of Latin American diplomats and businessmen. The "new Abbot" was apparently too liberal for their parents' tastes.

87. Many day scholars throughout Abbot's history felt they "had the best of both worlds," but others complained bitterly about Abbot's niggardly accommodations for them and its refusal to invite them to such special occasions as the Christmas Dinner, etc. "We were treated like dirt," says a '31 alumna. The low point came when Bertha Bailey refused "for about two years" [say two alumnae] in the mid-twenties

to admit any day scholars from Lawrence at all, following several incidents of day-girl misbehavior on the Lawrence-Andover bus.

88. See Minutes, Investment Committee Meeting, 27 February and 12 May 1970; Minutes, Trustees' Meeting 5 June 1970.

89. Recollections, Gordon.

90. "Forum Mail Bag," *Forum* (March 1970), 10.

91. See, for example, the proposal for a Human Relations Center, Trustee Minutes, 28 January 1972, and Executive Committee minutes, 19 April 1972 and 17 May 1972.

92. The first year of the exchange, the order was in reverse; but the Abbot girls felt the Dakota girls would feel more at home at Abbot if they knew a few Abbot students before they arrived, so the 1972–73 program worked as described.

93. Several of the Abbot girls shared their Rosebud experiences with others in poetry:

THE OCEAN

Flat
rolling flat
reaches out to draw me to those
    hills
those hills brown, dusty and
    low . . .
this wind
that plays ring-around-the-rosie
    with the reeds

That same wind sends prairie
    weeds
    racing across the bare, dusty
    lawns
blowing the dresses of the little
    Indian girls
playing hopscotch
in the streets
Yesterday

that wind brought the ice and snow
    knives
    to slice the house
    rattling the window panes.

It powers the long, low barges
    loaded with clouds
    that sail across the bright blue
    sea
    each day

and sends the high pitched voices
    of children
that are churning the settled sands
    of my mind

loosening the silt
that had gathered there.

Mary Clements

94. Recollections, faculty.
95. Carolyn Goodwin, "Observations on Indian Exchange after One Week," 3 January 1972; teacher reports and Dakota students' evaluations of the program, Abbot Archives; and *Cynosure*, 9 January 1972. A teacher had commented of one, "I fear she was not overenthused by medieval history," but the Indian girls said they admired Abbot's classes and liked the way Abbot students "were not afraid to speak their minds" in class. One of the shyest girls found Abbot girls "very nice, a lot nicer than the girls in St. Francis," even though she never did smile.
96. Interviews, Beth Warren, and Carolyn Johnston, and conversation, black alumnae of 1973 and 1974.

17. ENDINGS AND BEGINNINGS

1. *Phillipian*, 17 March 1883.
2. See letter to Mary Lyon, quoted in full in Phebe McKeen, *Annals*, 23–25.
3. *H. C. Journal* (16 May 1874), 138.
4. *Phillipian*, 27 May 1882.
5. *Courant* (January 1913), 29–30.
6. Speech to Boston Abbot Club.
7. Blackmer, *Student Unrest*, 47.
8. *Phillipian*, 3 March 1975; headline quoted from interview with Donald Gordon.
9. *Newsweek* (27 January 1968), 68.
10. *Time* (26 September 1969), 43.
11. *Saturday Review* (17 May 1969), 81.
12. George Gilder, "On Rediscovering the Difference," in *National Review*, (3 August 1973), 832–833. Excerpted from Gilder's *Sexual Suicide* (New York, Quadrangle Press, 1973).
13. Virginia Knapp, interview. See also the interesting volume of letters on coeducation vs. single-sex schooling collected and published by the NAPSG, *Sharing*, ed. Constance B. Pratt (n.p., 1974).
14. Ronny Winchel, Diane Fenner, and Philip Shaver, "Impact of Coeducation on 'Fear of Success' Imagery Expressed by Male and Female

High School Students," manuscript, 1974, later published in the *Journal of Educational Psychology* (October 1974), it summarizes the research on this matter from 1953 through 1974 and adds the authors' findings. Forty-one percent of females in a coeducational high school responded negatively to the projective cue, "After mid-year exams are over, Ann finds herself at the top of her first-year class in medical school"; that is, they finished the story with a grim ending of some kind, or an assurance that "Ann" had cheated on her exams and was therefore not really at the top of her class at all. Just 16 percent of females in an all-girls' high school of comparable constituency came to such negative conclusions. The effect of elementary school attendance was most striking: only one of twenty-six girls who had attended non-coed elementary schools showed "fear of success," whether they were attending a coed or a non-coed high school. Horner's findings indicate that such anxiety becomes more common in college, especially in coeducational colleges. Increasingly precise use of Horner's measures of "motive to avoid success" suggests that subjects' answers reflect not what they feel but what they think women feel or ought to feel. See Eleanor E. Maccoby and Carol N. Jacklin, *The Psychology of Sex Differences* (Stanford, Calif., Stanford University Press, 1975), 140–163. The reader must come to her or his own conclusions as to the difference between the two.

15. Among other sources, Helen S. Astin, *The Woman Doctorate in America* (New York, Russell Sage, 1969), and Mary J. Oates, Susan Williamson, "American Higher Education and the Career Choices of Women, 1900–1970," paper delivered at the Berkshire Conference, June 1975. Some of these findings probably reflect the informal opportunities open to the girls and women from upper socioeconomic groups who make up the majority of the students in all-girls' private schools and women's colleges. A few studies cited by the authors are controlled for social class, however. In these the beneficial effect of the single-sex institution still obtains, though not so dramatically.

16. Floyd Allport (1929), quoted in Banner, *American Women*, 150–151.

17. Quoted in Jean S. Harris, "Let's Hear It for Coeducation, Folks," *Independent School Bulletin* (December 1973), 6.

18. Quotation from M. C. Thomas, "Should the Higher Education of Women Differ from that of Men?" (1901), in Cross, ed., *Educated Woman*, p. 154. Thomas' argument became practical as well as idealistic as she neared the end of her long tenure as President of Bryn Mawr. She became convinced that the financial resources of the nation would be made fully available to women only if women and men attended the same schools and colleges, both public and private.

19. S. Hyde, "The Case for Coeducation," memorandum to the Phillips Trustees, September 1970.

20. Phillips Faculty Meeting Minutes, 16 April 1967.

21. S. Hyde, memorandum to Phillips-Abbot Coordinating Committee, 26 May 1971.

22. Jean Bennett, interview. Phillips Dean of Students J. R. Richards does not remember this incident. He recalls only his general admiration for the Abbot sex education course: "She was doing a whale of a job," he says.

23. Phillips Faculty Meeting Minutes, 21 April 1970.

24. Phillips Trustee Minutes, 23–24 April 1970.

25. Teachers' and Trustees' recollections.

26. Interview, E. Barton Chapin. See also Kemper's partly humorous letter to Robert Hunneman, President of Abbot's Board, *Bulletin*, February 1955, on the occasion of the fund-raising for the Abbot gymnasium, in which Kemper lists all his Abbot connections and declares his respect for the school and Miss Hearsey, then goes on to describe an Abbot principal's special burden: "as if all those girls were not a sufficient handful, she must struggle with the incredibly difficult problem for a headmistress, of having all my boys for such close neighbors! They, not to mention men generally, are little help when one strives to inculcate in young ladies some semblance of learning at this all too readily divertible age."

27. Interview, Barton and Melville Chapin.

28. S. Hyde, "Case for Coeducation."

29. Ibid.

30. Phillips Trustee Minutes, October 30–31, 1970.

31. Carolyn Johnston, memorandum to "the Big 8, re Boy-Girl Relations," 16 November 1970.

32. Julia Owen, "The Case for Coeducation: A Study of the Phillips-Abbot Academy Merger," p. 25; teachers' recollections.

33. *Cynosure*, 5 October 1971.

34. Hyde, memorandum of March 1969: "Some Questions about the School Program."

35. Recollections of alumnae, 1970–73, and of Carolyn Johnston.

36. Alumnae and alumni recollections.

37. Undated. The location in the box suggests 1969–70 or 1970–71.

38. Interview, alumna Class of 1973.

39. Alumnae recollections. See also a sample protest, *Cynosure*, 5 October 1971: "Abbot students aren't apathetic towards sports. No! . . . They HATE it . . . (at least they hate competitive and organized sports.)"

40. Charlie Finch, Jr., *Cynosure*, 6 June 1969. Many Abbot alumnae have powerful memories of the difference in tone. A typical graduate (Class of 1970) does not remember her classes very well, except Joy Burgy's "superb" Spanish class, but as a whole, "Abbot was bliss, it really was," she says. "It was kind of *in* to be cynical at P.A., but we loved our school. All my best friends are still the ones I made at Abbot."

41. Allis, *Youth from Every Quarter*, 666, 668–669.

42. Phillips teachers' recollections; see also Hyde, memorandum of March 1969: "Some Questions about the School Program," on the "unproductive conflict of opposing attitudes" among Phillips faculty.
43. Pieters, "Some Ideas opposed to Coeducation at Andover," 12 March 1971.
44. Phillips Trustee Minutes, 30 April–1 May 1971.
45. The favorite epithet–pet name for Philip K. Allen of certain Phillips Trustees.
46. Report of the July 1971 meetings of the Abbot-Phillips Coordinaton Committee, p. 5.
47. Kemper in memorandum to the Phillips Academy Trustees, 25 August 1971.
48. Phillips Trustee Minutes, 29–30 October 1971.
49. Hyde in conversation, 13 May 1978.
50. S. J. Gilbert, "Life on the Farm," *Cynosure*, October 1971.
51. Faculty recollections. Allis says that it was difficult to find out exactly what this course was really like because the teacher wouldn't allow Phillips teachers to visit her class when the two departments were trying to make joint plans. (Letter to author, 28 June 1978).
52. Conversations with D. Gordon, P. Stapleton, and R. Sheahan.
53. Alumnae recollections. See also statistics compiled by Sally S. Warner from the questionnaire of 8 December 1971 given to all Abbot students enrolled in coordinated classes in both schools. Thirty-nine students responded, and although there were many criticisms and suggestions (e.g., "P.A. should not be allowed to manipulate A.A. A.A. should not bow to P.A.'s every whim" [two respondents]), there was also clear, overwhelmingly positive expression of benefits gained.
54. Letter, D. A. Gordon to T. R. Sizer, 16 June 1972.
55. Ibid.
56. T. R. Sizer, "Speculations on Andover, I," memorandum to the Trustees (12–13 July 1972), 4.
57. Sizer, "Speculations, II: The Issue of Coeducation," memorandum to the Trustees (11 September 1972), 6–8.
58. Report of July 1971 meetings of the Abbot-Phillips Coordination Committee, 5.
59. T. R. Sizer in conversation.
60. See F. A. Peterson, report to the Phillips and Abbot Faculties on analysis of the September 1972 administration of QUESTA I to new students at Abbot and Phillips, 18 January 1973. (Abbot Archives.) See also Priscilla Peterson, "Report from Boston University Summer School" to Donald Gordon, 17 September 1969, on the average SSAT scores of accepted and rejected candidates for 1966–67 through 1969–70. The average SSAT "total" scores of admittees (63rd percentile in 1963) began climbing in 1969 (71st percentile) and continued to rise through 1972–73; no records now exist for the 1970–73 period, but

F. Howland remembers the 72–73 average as being about the 80th percentile. Abbot was regaining the position it had held in the 1940's and the 1957–64 period. Carolyn Goodwin recalls that in the late 1930's and 1940's, when she taught at a "feeder school" for private preparatory schools, the most able girls were always steered toward Abbot, the top boys toward Exeter, and the near-top boys toward Phillips. See statistics of Abbot Seniors' college acceptances, 1965–73, in Dean's File, Archives. See also Report of Office of Research and Evaluation, "Fall Term Grades 1972–73," which breaks down grades by individual course and by sex. High honor grades went more to boys than to girls, but male-female averages are almost identical. Of course, the few Abbot students who were not academically inclined tended to avoid coordinated courses altogether when they had a choice. In a national measure of academic ability, five 1973 Abbot Seniors were National Merit finalists (4 percent); nineteen were "commended" (15 percent), and two black students won special achievement awards. One of the finalists was named a Presidential Scholar, though she refused to go with the other 120 Presidential Scholars to the ceremonies at Nixon's White House. Five percent of Phillips Seniors the same year were finalists.

61. "Speculations, II," 8.
62. Interviews, J. K. Dow and Chapin. Quotations are from Dow.
63. Donors who had given or pledged money to the New Abbot Fund on the assumption that half the total would be used for the Arts building were told that their money would be gratefully added to the general fund to cover operating costs and add to endowment, and (at Jane Baldwin's suggestion) were asked if they would prefer to rescind their donations. Just one donor did so, recalling a $10,000 contribution.
64. According to Faith Howland, 50 percent is about average for girls' boarding schools and coed boarding schools outside of the most highly endowed three (Andover, Exeter, and St. Paul's), whose tuitions are relatively low. This suggests the unusual attractive powers of Abbot from 1969 to 1971.
65. Letter to John M. Kemper from Brooks Potter, of Choate, Hall and Stewart (Phillips Academy attorneys), 22 October 1970. Potter pointed out that Phillips' original Charter of 1780 is legally a "pre-Dartmouth Charter," established before the Dartmouth College vs. Woodward case of 1819, and therefore, "cannot be altered or amended by the legislature without the consent of the corporation." The Phillips Trustees had to be certain to frame the "merger" legislation in such a way that the risk of losing this "special status" was minimized, Potter wrote.
66. Letter, Mary Howard Nutting to Philip K. Allen, 5 August 1972.
67. Letter, Beverly Brooks Floe to Philip K. Allen, 12 August 1972. Record by Gordon's secretary, Molly A. Chamberlain, of the July 17th meeting of T. Sizer and D. Gordon.

68. Gordon, notes on report to students, 13 September 1972.
69. Letter, Gordon to Mary H. Nutting, 14 August 1972.
70. Memoranda to Trustees, 11 and 15 September 1972.
71. Interview, Dow.
72. Letter, Guerin Todd to Mrs. Helen Blague Giles, 18 September 1972.
73. Lacking a tuition increase, Abbot's deficit promised to move from a budgeted $28,200 in 1972–73 to $281,500 in 1976–77 (five-year projection developed for the Trustees by Griggs and Dow).
74. Gordon, memorandum to Abbot Trustees, 11 September 1972.
75. Letter to Mary H. Nutting.
76. Allis, *Youth from Every Quarter*, 679.
77. Resolution of the Abbot Trustees, 22 September 1972.
78. Minutes of Phillips Trustee meeting, 23 September 1972. Melville Chapin, an attorney, confirms that the final arrangement made between Phillips and Abbot was not legally a merger, but an "Agreement of Association" made under Chapter 180 of the statutes of the Commonwealth of Massachusetts. It was effected by a decree of the Supreme Judicial Court.
79. Letter to the author.
80. Gordon and Sizer took responsibility for this. See "Agenda re T.S. and D.G., A.A./P.A. Operations '72–73," 9 October 1972, typed by Gordon's secretary.
81. Manuscript notes of speech to both boards of Trustees, undated.
82. Sizer, "Speculations, II," 19. On 15 September 1972 the Phillips Board voted nearly all of the proposals Sizer made in this document, and the Abbot Board agreed to the same terms within the following two weeks.
83. Notes on Group 3 discussion and Abbot Town Meeting. Report to the Faculty Appointment Working Party and the Residential Planning Working Party.
84. Letter to Gordon, 17 October 1972.
85. Interview, F. Howland; confidential memorandum to Gordon, 17 October 1972, on "procedural difficulties at this stage of the game."
86. There was one further reason for the disparity between the numbers of Abbot and Phillips teachers released. Phillips' custom was to hire most young, inexperienced teachers on a one-year non-renewable contract as "teaching fellows." Thus eight or ten recent college graduates came and left each year as a matter of course—and they were not counted in the number let go in 1973.
87. Roemer McPhee in *Cynosure*, 20 April 1973.
88. *Cynosure*, 20 April 1973.
89. QUESTA II of 1972, a questionnaire given to boarding school students all over the country, showed that Abbot students were the *only* ones of those questioned who endorsed their school's counseling system by a majority of responses. (Records in Dean's office, Phillips Academy).

90. See R. Griggs memorandum to Trustees, "Legal and Moral Obligations of Abbot Academy for Non-academic Staff," 12 January 1973, and Trustee Minutes, 15 February 1973.

91. Donald Gordon writes that the first person to suggest the idea of an Abbot Academy foundation or "association" to him was his wife Josie. (Letter to author, 25 June 1978). He passed it on to the Abbot Board—several of whose members, he realizes, may well have thought along similar lines before this.

92. Abbot Academy Constitution. Interestingly, the Phillips Academy's Constitution contains almost identical language in its description of the Headmaster's duties. The similarity is probably not coincidental: it is likely that Abbot's original Trustees read Phillips Academy's constitution before writing their own. It is of more-than-symbolical importance, because the charter of the Abbot Academy Association grants the Phillips Headmaster a veto over its major decisions.

93. Early residents of Abbot Cluster, male or female alike, insist that it was "absolutely the best Cluster in the School." One male student who never knew Abbot as a separate school feels that he was nevertheless enrolled.

94. Interviews by B. Floe and author, and conversations with alumnae classes of 1926, 1931, 1938, and 1942.

95. Interviews by P. Marvit and L. Kennedy of former Abbot students from Abbot Class of 1973 and Phillips Academy Class of 1976. See also *Cynosure*, 20 April 1973: "Every day brings a new shower of facts that destroy the option of closing our eyes to next year."

96. Interviews, five alumnae. Bethiah Crane Acceta, '62, thinks this process had begun during her last years at Abbot.

97. Interview, alumna, Class of 1973.

98. In November 1976 Stephen Perrin spoke his feelings—still strong—in a poem of remembrance.

> Yes, I do remember Abbot:
> that's the school
> that burned
> —or was consumed (same thing)
> down to the ground,
> nothing left
> but a few aging women
> kicking among the bricks
> for traces
> of the girls they'd lost—
> oh, and teachers,
> again not many,
> the taste of ashes
> in their throat.

99. Interview by Louise Kennedy.

100. Eight-five adults are listed in the Catalogue for 1972–73, eight as "administration," fifty-seven as faculty and resident advisers.
101. D. Gordon conversation, May 1978.
102. Alumnae recollections; Allen, interview.
103. Teachers' recollections.
104. Gordon conversation, May 1978, and in letter to Hubert Fortmiller, 28 March 1978.
105. Conversation, spring 1976.
106. Conversations, Abbot staff members and faculty, 1975–78, as well as personal recollections. Typical remarks: "I'd never encountered anything like that extraordinary friendliness in the faculty—not before or since" (teacher in her 40's). And Marie Bonde at the retirement party given in Draper Hall for her and Jes Bonde, 1976, to which Marguerite Hearsey, Mary Crane, and many Abbot faculty and staff came: "This is the most elite party I've been to since Abbot days." In contrast (and at an extreme) two former Abbot kitchen workers complained of being "peasants" under the new regime (fall 1975).
107. Interview, P. K. Allen.
108. Because end-of-term chores intervened, the show was not repeated. Bruce Bugbee made a video tape, which makes it easy to recapture. After all, the Follies had not been written primarily for Phillips Academy.
109. Interview by Louise Kennedy.

Index

The index following is not definitive. Minor references have been excluded; certain names and titles are omitted because they are listed elsewhere: all trustees and all teachers from 1936 to 1973 not mentioned in the text, for example, are listed with their dates of service in Appendices B and C; and titles of books and periodicals mentioned only in footnotes are not indexed. Individuals mentioned in endnotes who have provided or confirmed information are not listed in the index unless they are also mentioned in the text. (Names of virtually all these contributors can be found in the acknowledgements.) Numbers of pages with illustrations are set in italic. The following abbreviations are used: Abbot Academy, AA; Phillips Academy, PA; Andover Theological Seminary, ATS. Dates immediately following names of alumnae refer to the year their classes graduated from Abbot Academy.

Peabody, Elizabeth, 10
Pease, Carlie, '74, granddaughter of
Barbara Moore Pease, 500n37
Pease, Mrs. Charles B. F. See Cole,
Mary Jessie
Pease, Mrs. Maurice Henry. See
Moore, Barbara
Pedagogy, 48–58, 227–229. See also
Teaching
Pendleton, Ellen Fitz, Trustee, and
President of Wellesley College,
203; chaired a symposium on
Art and Life," 244
Pensions: none, annual grants in-
stead, 252; Faculty Retirement
Plan (1946) mandatory, 330–331,
353, 445, 562n35, 563n36. See
also Salaries
Perrin, Stephanie Blake (Mrs.
Stephen), Curator, John-Esther
Art Gallery, PA Instructor in
Art, 401
Perrin, Stephen (Steve), Instructor
in Humanities, 382–383, 384–385,
440, 442, 448; poem of remem-
brance, 583n98
Pestalozzi, Johann Heinrich, 55
Peterson, Frederick Almond (PA
'34), PA Instructor in English,
first dean of coed Summer School,
413
Peterson, Priscilla, Instructor in
Music, admissions, 396, 580n60
Phelps, Mrs. Austin. See Stuart,
Elizabeth
Phelps, Rev. Professor Austin, father
of Elizabeth Stuart Phelps, 485n49
Phelps, Elizabeth Stuart, 1858 (Mrs.
Herbert Dickinson Ward), 35, 39,
223; student at "Nunnery," 40,
69; novels about heaven, 139;
speaker at Abbot, 511n51; on Rev.
Edwards A. Park, 512n58
Phelps, Mary Gray (changed name
to Elizabeth Stuart Phelps). See
Phelps, Elizabeth Stuart
Philadelphia Young Ladies Acade-
my, first incorporated girls' school
(1792), 481n29
Phillipian, 115

Phillips, Rev. George, progenitor of
Samuel Phillips, Jr., 24
Phillips, Madam Phebe Foxcroft,
wife of Samuel Phillips, Jr.: influence on education in Andover
and first founding gift ($5000) to
ATS, 12; prompted admiration of
lawyer, Samuel Farrar, 21; friendship with Madam Abbot, 24
Phillips, Samuel, Jr. ("Judge"):
founder of Phillips Academy, Andover, 6, 7; on education and religion, 11; left trust for education
of female instructors for public
schools, 11–12; intended to join
wife in founding an academy for
girls in North Parish, 21; family
connections with Madam Sarah
Abbot, 156, 410; rose from the
grave, 449
Phillips, Wendell, abolitionist, speak-
at Abbot, 511n51
Phillips-Abbot couples, 367. See also
Coordinate education
Phillips-Abbot Madrigal Society, 366
Phillips Academy (Andover, Mass.):
founding (1778), 6; first incorporated boarding school U. S. A.,
6; Trustees in common between
PA and AA, 17, 20, 362, 410, 418;
"Latin Commons," 20, 482n48;
dormitory construction and bathrooms, 152; donated English hall
clock to AA, 158; curriculum, 164;
drama and singing groups with
Abbot Academy, Fidelio and PA,
223, 339; $6,000,000 building pro-
gram, salaries raised, scholarship
program expanded in 1960's, 362;
PA–Abbot Madrigal Society, 366;
"inferiority" of Abbot to PA,
367, 570n9; radical activity and
fantasies, 390; holds power to
make decisions on merger, 413–
416; stereotypes of students at PA
and AA, 419–421; participation in
athletics with, 447; Faculty Follies
make fun of, 448–449. See also
Allen, Philip K.; Coordinate education; Gordon, Donald A.

Library of Congress Cataloging in Publication Data

Lloyd, Susan McIntosh, 1935–
    A singular school : Abbot Academy, 1828–1973.

    Includes bibliographical references and index.
    1. Abbot Academy, Andover, Mass.—History.
I. Title.
LD7251.A52L55   373.744'5   78-31700
ISBN 0-87451-161-5 (University Press)